iOS App Development for Non-Programmers
Book 3: Mastering Xcode 7 and Swift

Kevin J McNeish

iOS App Development for Non-Programmers
Book 3: Mastering Xcode 7 and Swift

Author

Kevin J McNeish

Technical Editor

Greg Lee

Photography

Sharlene M McNeish

Copy Editor

Mia A. Huff

1716 Union Mills Rd.

Troy, VA 22974

434-979-2417

http://iOSAppsForNonProgrammers.com

ISBN 978-0-9882327-8-5

Contents

Dedicated to Steve Jobs

The night it was announced Steve Jobs had passed away, by coincidence my wife and I already had tickets to San Francisco for early the next morning because I was scheduled to speak at a Silicon Valley Code Camp.

After arriving in San Francisco, we drove to Cupertino to make some sense of the loss of a great visionary. The flags at Apple were flying at half-mast and many others had gathered to honor him with candles, flowers, posters, and apples.

We first drove to the home where Steve created the first Apple computer and then on to the last place he called home in Palo Alto where many others gathered to pay respects and where his silver Mercedes (famously without license plates) still sat in front of his house.

It was there I purposed to write this book series and do for *iOS* app development what Steve had done for users of iOS devices—make app development accessible to the masses of non-programmers, teaching them to create apps that surprise and amaze their users.

Foreword

This is the fourth edition of the third book in a series designed to teach non-programmers to create *iOS* apps. Many books designed for beginning iOS app developers assume *way* too much. This book series intends to rectify that by assuming you know *nothing* about programming.

The information in this book is critical to being productive in the new **Xcode 7** environment. It will save you countless of app development hours because it teaches you to leverage the full power of Xcode.

Each chapter and set of step-by-step instructions has been reviewed by people like yourself—with little or no experience in creating apps.

Once you master Xcode, you will be able to move on to learning the core technologies necessary for creating great apps. This includes designing a great user experience as well as learning how to make use of the many tools available in Apple's Software Developer Kit. All these topics are covered in other books in our *iOS App Development for Non-Programmers* series with you, the non-programmer, in mind.

So buckle up, and let's get started.

Introduction

Have you ever taken a peek inside the cabin of a commercial or military aircraft? There are more buttons, switches, lights, and gauges than you can imagine a use for.

Xcode can be a bit like that.

In this book you will learn all about the different features of Xcode and how to use them to your advantage in creating apps that surprise and amaze your users.

What Makes This Book Special?

What sets this particular book apart from others is the features it contains. The original text for this book started out as a word processing document, and then we spent *many* hours converting and formatting it specifically for an exceptional experience.

Movies

Throughout this book are links to movies that demonstrate the more difficult concepts as well as concepts that are easier learned through a visual aid! Just go to the link in your web browser to watch the instruction in high quality video and narrative!

Glossary

This book contains over 100 entries in the glossary that help you recall the meaning of the new terms you encounter as you learn the ins and outs of Xcode.

This Book Has a Forum!

To get answers to your questions and engage with others like yourself, check out our forum: http://iOSAppsForNonProgrammers.com/forum

Chapter 1: The Basics

Welcome! This is the part of the book where you learn how to get yourself and your computer set up for app development, get your hands on the code samples that come with this book, and learn some of the basics of Apple's Xcode software development tool.

Sections in This Chapter

1. *Getting Set Up*
2. *Downloading the Sample Code*
3. *Xcode Version 7*
4. *Xcode—the Big Picture*
5. *Understanding Workspaces*
6. *Opening an Existing Project*

7. *Creating a New Project*

8. *Running the New Project*

9. *Summary*

Getting Set Up

Before going further in this book, you need to accomplish four primary tasks:

1. Get an Intel-based Mac computer you can build iOS Apps on (any Mac built after 2006).
2. You must have OS X El Capitan or OS X Yosemite installed on your Mac.
3. Register as an Apple developer (free): http://developer.apple.com/programs/register/
4. Download and install Xcode (free): https://developer.apple.com/xcode/downloads/

Downloading the Sample Code

We have spent a lot of time putting together relevant samples for you. Follow these steps to download and install this book's sample code on your Mac:

8. In the browser on your Mac, go to this link:

http://www.iOSAppsForNonProgrammers.com/SamplesXC9.html

9. When you get to the download page, click the **Download Sample Code** link (Figure 1.1).

*Figure 1.1 Click the **Download Sample Code** link.*

10. If Safari is your default web browser, when you click the link, you will see a blue progress indicator in the upper-right corner of the browser (Figure 1.2).

Figure 1.2 The download progress indicator

11. When the blue progress bar completely fills, and then disappears, the download is complete. To view the downloaded file, click the Show downloads button in the upper-right corner of Safari (Figure 1.3).

Figure 1.3 Click the Show downloads button.

This displays the Downloads popup. Click the small magnifying glass on the right (Figure 1.4).

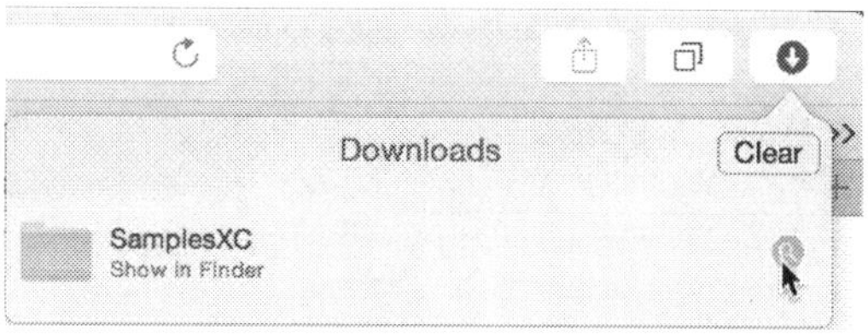

Figure 1.4 Click the magnifying glass to see the samples.

12. This displays the downloaded **SamplesXC** folder in the Finder (Figure 1.5).

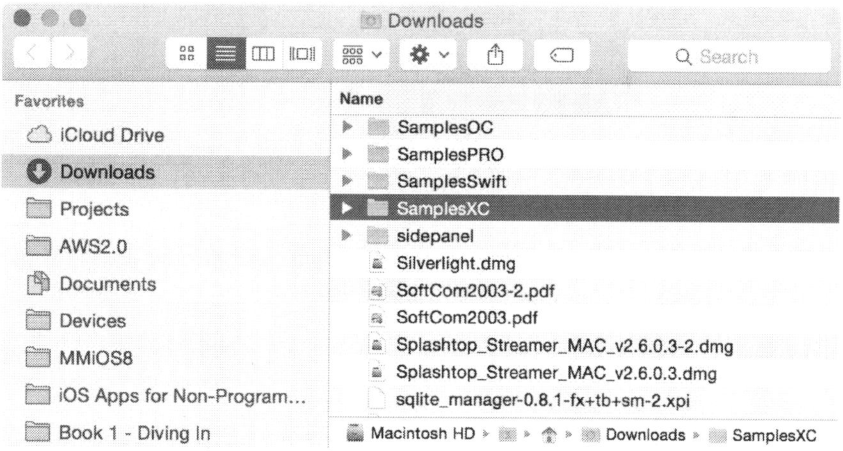

*Figure 1.5 The downloaded **SampleXC** folder*

13. Let's make a copy of this folder and save it in the **Documents** folder (you can choose a different destination folder if you prefer).

14. With the **SamplesXC** folder still selected, press the **Command** key (the key to the left of the spacebar), and while holding the key down, press the **C** key (in other words, press **Command+C**). This makes a copy of the folder in memory.

15. Next, on the left side of the Finder window, click the **Documents** folder as shown in Figure 1.6, and then press the **Command+V** keys to add a copy of the **SamplesXC** folder into the **Documents** folder.

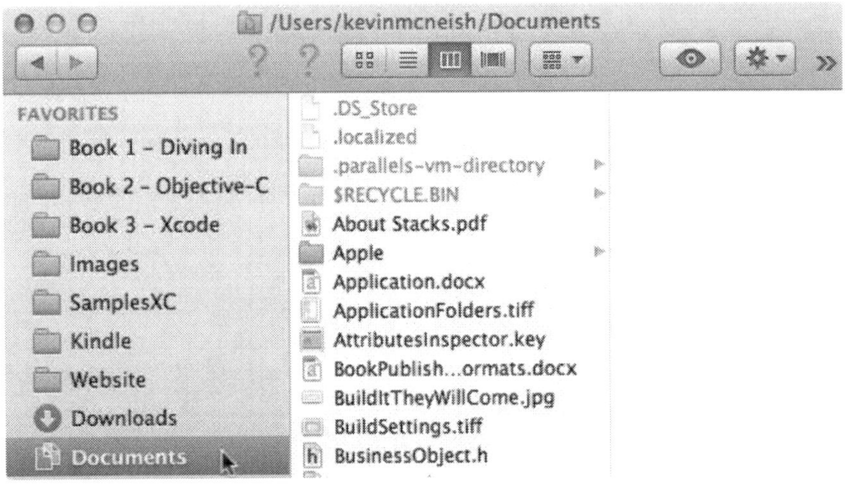

*Figure 1.6 Select the **Documents** folder.*

16. Double-click the **SamplesXC** folder in the right-hand panel of the Finder window and you will see a list of sample project folders.

Throughout this book, there are exercises where you change the code in the sample projects. If you ever need to get a fresh start, you can copy projects from the **Downloads** folder to the **Documents/SamplesXC** folder.

Xcode Version 7

I used Xcode version 7.1 when writing this book. If you are using an older version of Xcode, I highly recommend upgrading to version 7 so you can follow along more easily. I also used OS X Yosemite, so if you are using a different version of OS X, your screens will have a slightly different appearance, but the content will be the same.

To find out which version of Xcode you're using, from the Xcode menu, select **Xcode > About Xcode**. This displays the About Xcode dialog (Figure 1.7) that shows the version of Xcode you are currently running.

Figure 1.7 The About Xcode dialog tells you which version of Xcode you're running.

Xcode—the Big Picture

Let's take a high-level look in this chapter at the different areas of the Xcode user interface to familiarize you with the big picture.

The Xcode window is divided into five main areas as shown in Figure 1.8.

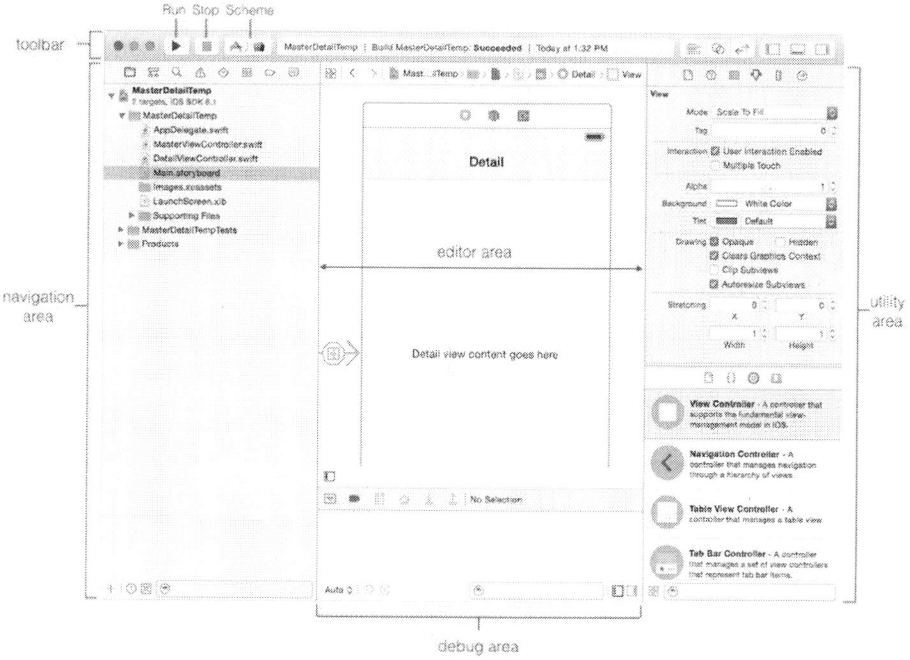

Figure 1.8 The main areas of the Xcode window

- The **Run**, **Stop** button and **Scheme** controls on the left side of the toolbar at the top of the Xcode window let you run your project in the Simulator or on a device.

In the center of the toolbar, the ***activity viewer*** keeps you posted on the progress of tasks that Xcode performs.

The toolbar buttons on the right allow you to toggle the display of editors and views.

- The navigation area on the left contains eight navigation tools that allow you to navigate your project files, symbols, search results, issues, breakpoints, and more. The eight icons at the top of the Navigation Area allow you to select the different navigation tools.

- The editor area in the center of the window is one of the most important areas in Xcode. It's where you spend the majority of your time whether it's designing your user interface or writing code.

  It's the only area in Xcode that can't be hidden. This area is home to the *Interface Builder* Editor and its Document Outline, Code Editor, Project Editor, and Entity Data Model Editor.

- The Debug area at the bottom center contains tools that help you debug your apps and contains the Variables view and the Console.

- The utility area on the right contains the Inspector pane (on top) which includes six different inspector tools that help you to create your user interface and to provide quick help when you need it. The six icons at the top of the Utility Area allow you to select the different inspector tools.

- The Utility Area also contains the Library Pane, which includes four separate libraries of *UI* objects, code snippets, media, and file templates. The four icons at the top of the Library pane allow you to select the different libraries.

All of these areas and the tools they contain are covered in detail in upcoming chapters.

Understanding Workspaces

We will cover workspaces later in this book series, but for now you just need to know that a ***workspace*** is an Xcode container that can contain multiple projects.

Up to this point, with the simple demo projects that you have been working with in earlier books in this series, there has been no need for a workspace because there has only been one project, which contained everything.

When you create more complex apps that span multiple projects, it makes sense to take advantage of this Xcode feature to group related projects together.

Opening an Existing Project

There are a number of ways to open an existing project. When you first launch Xcode, you will see the Welcome to Xcode window (Figure 1.9), unless:

Figure 1.9 The Welcome to Xcode window

1. You have unchecked the **Show this window when Xcode launches** check box in the Welcome window.

2. A project was still open the last time you quit Xcode. In this case, the next time you open Xcode, it automatically opens the project without showing the Welcome to Xcode window.

If you want to display the Welcome to Xcode window, just select **Window > Welcome to Xcode** from the menu.

If you don't see the project that you want in the list, you can click the **Open another project...** button. This launches the Open dialog (Figure 1.10) in which you can navigate to the location where the project resides on your computer. You can then select the .xcodeproj file and click the **Open** button (don't do this now).

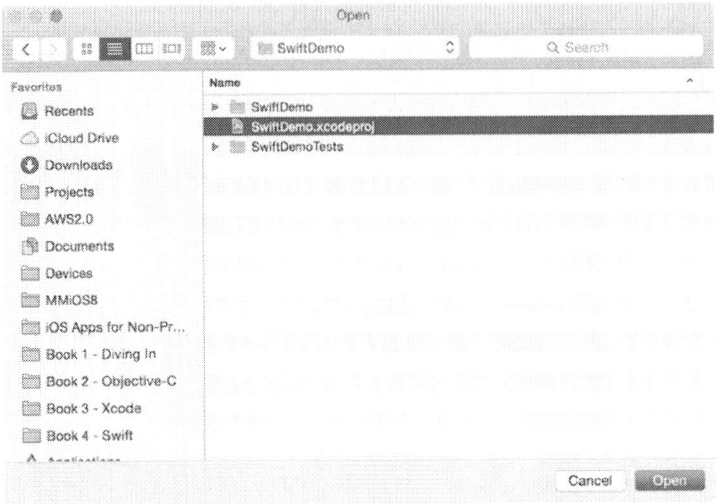

Figure 1.10 The Open dialog allows you to open an existing Xcode project.

You can also open a project using the Mac OS X Finder application. To launch Finder, go to the dock (usually located at the bottom of your Mac window) and select the happy-face icon.

In Finder, just navigate to the folder on your Mac that contains the project and double-click the project's .xcodeproj file.

Opening Multiple Projects

You can have multiple Xcode windows open with each containing different projects. To open additional Xcode windows, select **File** > **Open...** from the menu (or press **Command+O**), and then select the project to be opened.

You can move between multiple Xcode windows from the Xcode **Window** menu (Figure 1.11). The project that you currently have open is shown with a check mark next to it.

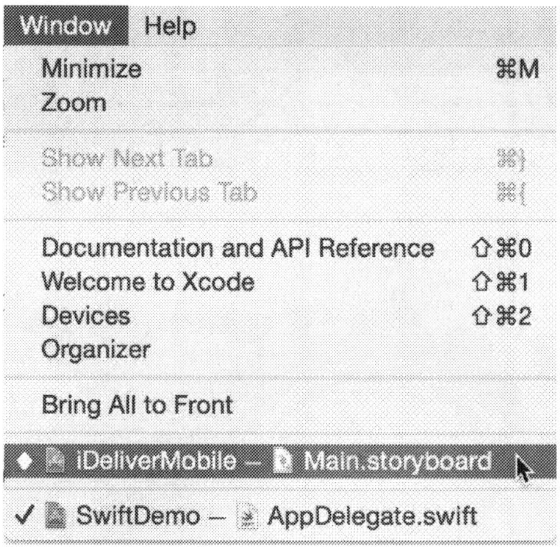

*Figure 1.11 Navigate to another Xcode window using the **Window** menu.*

To go to a different project, just select it from the **Window** menu. If you find having multiple Xcode windows open to be confusing, I recommend closing one project before opening another.

Creating a New Project

To help you get a hands-on look at Xcode, let's create an Xcode project! Along the way, I will provide detailed information on each step to provide a broader understanding of creating a project in Xcode.

1. If you haven't already done so, open Xcode. If a project is already open in Xcode, close the project by selecting **File > Close Project** from the Xcode menu.

2. If the Welcome to Xcode window appears, click **Create a new Xcode project**. Otherwise, select **File > New > Project...** from the menu. This launches the New Project dialog (Figure 1.12).

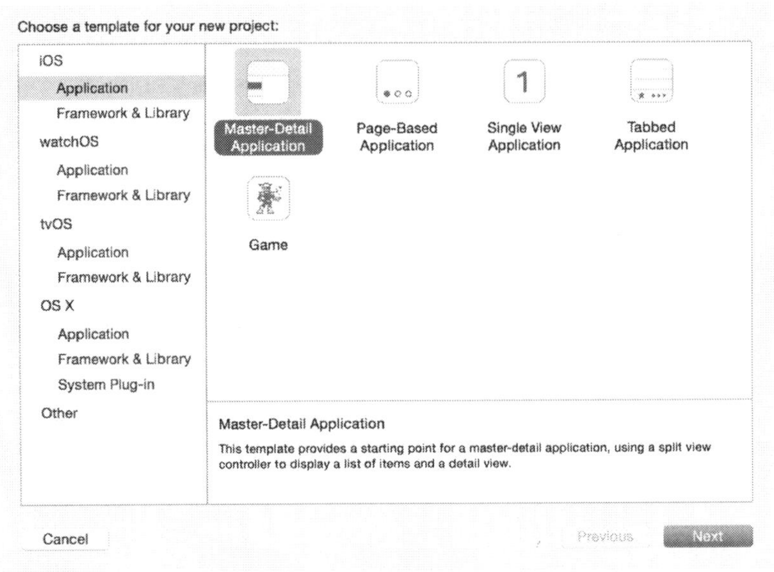

Figure 1.12 The New File dialog

3. Since you can create many types of applications using Xcode, the panel on the left side of the dialog has options for all applications types. Since you are creating iOS apps, you should always select one of the sub-items under **iOS** when creating a new project.

4. When you select the **Applications** sub-item under **iOS**, the right panel lists the project templates shown in Figure 1.12.

   Table 1.1 provides a brief explanation of each of these templates.

   Each template gives you a slightly different starting project that gives you a head start in the right direction for the specific type of ***app*** that you intend to create.

Table 1.1 Project templates

Template	Description
Master-Detail Application	Provides a starting point for an application where the initial view contains a master list. When the user selects an item from this list, it displays another view that contains details for the selected item. The built-in **Contacts** app is a good example

	of this.
Page-Based Application	Provides a starting point for a page-based application. As indicated by it's icon, the main view peels back to show an associated view beneath it. The built-in iOS **Maps** app is a good example of this.
Single View Application	Provides a starting point for an application with a single view. An app with just one view is very rare, but this is an "as easy as it gets" project template great for simple demos.
Tabbed Application	Provides a starting point for an application that has a tab bar. The built-in iOS **Clock** app is a good example of a tabbed application.
Game	Provides a starting point for a game.

Ultimately, after you create your project, you can change it to be just like any one of the other project templates.

5. Select the **Master-Detail Application** project template and click the **Next** button. This displays the second step of the New Project dialog (Figure 1.13).

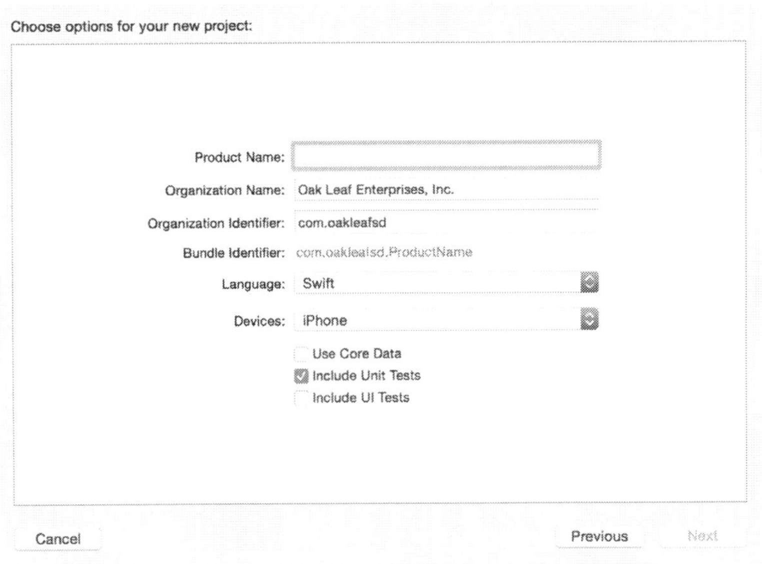

Figure 1.13 The second step of the New Project dialog

6. In the **Product Name** box, enter **MasterDetailDemo**. This specifies the name of your app and the name of the project. Although you can enter spaces in the product name, I prefer not to because Xcode also names some of the classes based on the product name and converts any spaces to underscores, which gets ugly.

   Xcode remembers what you enter for all the options on this dialog except **Product Name** (which makes sense, since you don't want to create two products with the same name). The next time you create a new project, the values you entered the last time for the other fields are automatically displayed—including the type of project template that you selected.

7. In the **Organization Name** box, enter your company name, or just your name if you don't have a company.

8. The **Organization Identifier** is part of the information used to uniquely identify your product. One of the best ways to make this identifier unique is to use your company's *URL* in the format **com.yourcompany**. For example, my company identifier is **com.oakleafsd**. If you don't have a company name, you can use **edu.self**.

9. After entering the **Product Name** and **Organization Identifier**, notice that these two pieces of information are joined together

(***concatenated*** in programming jargon) to create the bundle identifier (Figure 1.14)

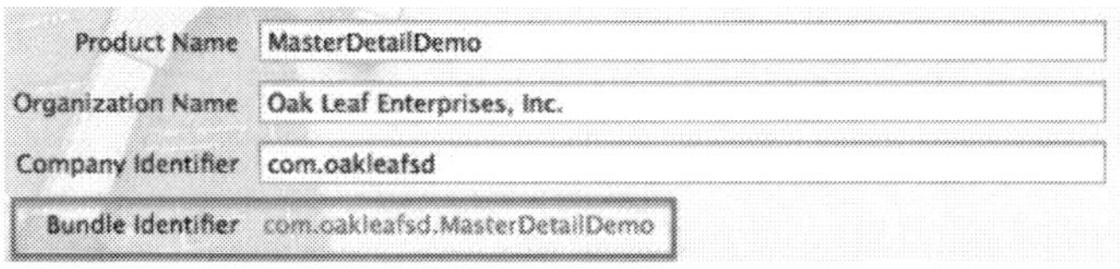

Figure 1.14 The bundle identifier includes the ***Organization Identifier*** *and* ***Product Name****.*

The ***bundle identifier*** is Apple's way of uniquely identifying your app. You can change this default bundle identifier after creating your project (as discussed later in this chapter). The term ***application bundle*** is used to refer to your app file because it contains your executable as well as any resources bundled with it. More on that later.

10. The Language selection box lets you select either **Swift**, or **Objective-C**. Choose Swift, since this is Apple's newest (and best) language for creating apps.
11. The **Devices** selection box offers three options:
    - **iPad** – Creates an app that only runs on the iPad
    - **iPhone** – Creates an app that only runs on the iPhone
    - **Universal** – Creates an app that runs on both the iPhone and the iPad

    If it makes sense for your app, you should create a universal app that runs on both the iPhone and iPad. Doing so greatly expands your audience, and typically, when a user owns both an iPhone and an iPad, they much prefer running the iPad version of the app whenever possible because of the extra screen real estate. Regardless of what you enter for **Device Family**, you can change your mind later.

    For this sample project, select **Universal**.
12. The **Use Core Data** option appears if you select either the **Master-Detail Application** or **Single View** template. This option is intended for apps that store *data* on the user's device. However, even if you do want your app to store data on a user's device, *don't select this option*. The

architecture of the code added to your project when this option is selected is *not* a best practice. Uncheck this option for the demo project.

13. The bottom check boxes specify whether you want to add unit and/or UI tests to your project. Check **Include Unit Tests** and uncheck **Include UI Tests**.

14. Click **Next** to accept these settings and to display the next screen of the dialog, which prompts you for the location in which to save your new project (Figure 1.15).

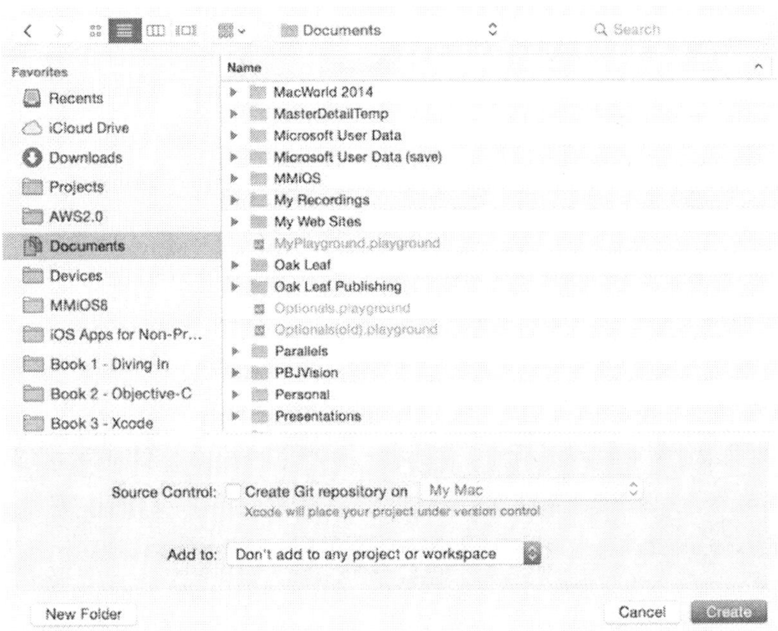

Figure 1.15 Select a folder in which to save your project in

You can use the **Favorites** folders on the left side of the dialog to choose a location in which to save your project. You can save the new project anywhere you want, but if you would like some direction on where to save it, select the Documents folder on the left side of the dialog as shown in Figure 1.15.

15. Before continuing, notice the Create local git repository on check box at the bottom of the dialog.

    This option specifies whether you want version control for your project (you do). You will learn more about version control later in the book, but for now, just know version control allows you to keep track of individual changes to your project and even revert back to a particular version of the project. When you have multiple developers working on a project, version control also helps to prevent conflicts that arise when two developers try to edit the same file. Select the **Create a local git repository on** check box.

Leave the list box on the right set to **My Mac**.

16. Click the **Create** button to store your new project in the **Documents** folder. After a few seconds, you can see your new project displayed in Xcode's Project Navigator (Figure 1.16).

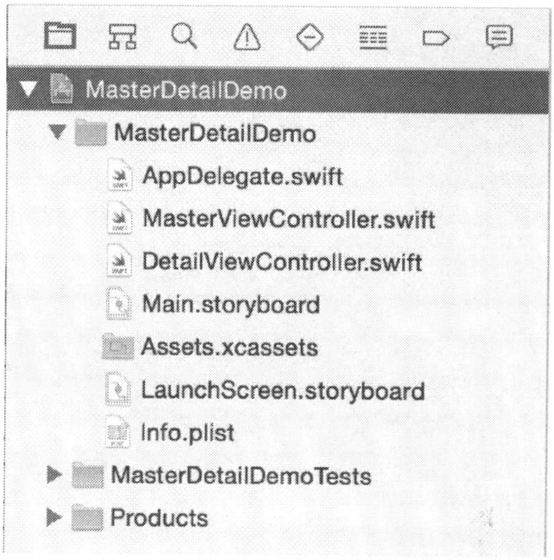

*Figure 1.16 The new **MasterDetailDemo** project*

Running the New Project

As you have already seen in earlier books in this series, on the left side of the Xcode toolbar are the **Run** and **Stop** buttons, which allow you to run your app either in the iOS Simulator or on an actual device and then stop it when you have finished.

To the immediate right of the **Stop** button is the **Scheme** selection control. This is a two-part button that does something different when you click on the right or left. For now, click on the right side of the control and you should see the options listed in Figure 1.17. This specifies where you want your app to run when you press the **Run** button.

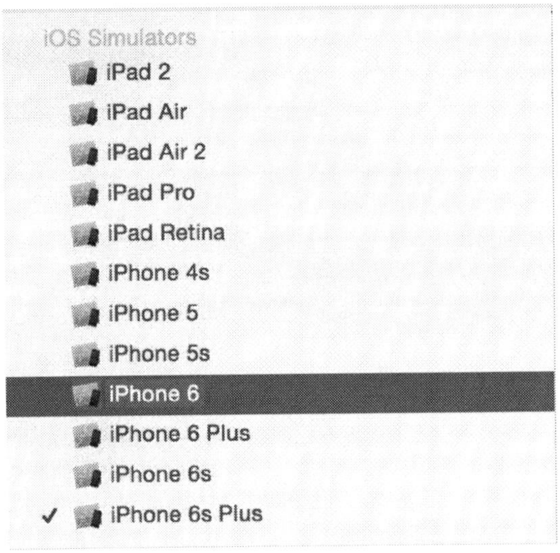

*Figure 1.17 The **Schemes** options*

When you first create a new project, the scheme is set to the value that you last selected. You can select the iPhone or iPad Simulators to see how your app looks in each. However, to run the app on an iOS device, you must pay the annual fee to be part of the iOS Developer Program. You will learn more about schemes later in this book in *Chapter 14: Working With the Project Editor*.

Now let's run the project.

1. First, make sure that **iPhone 6** is selected in the **Scheme** control.
2. Click the **Run** button to build the project and run it in the iOS Simulator.
3. If all goes well, a **Build Succeeded** image appears briefly in the Xcode window (Figure 1.18).

Figure 1.18 The build succeeded!

Afterward, the activity viewer indicates the app is running in the Simulator (Figure 1.19).

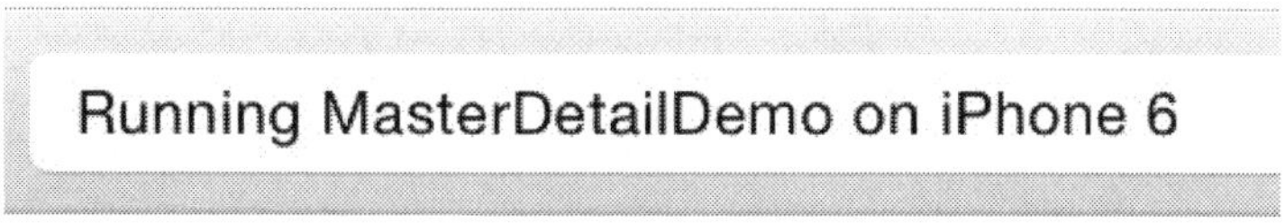

Figure 1.19 The activity viewer indicates the app is running in the Simulator.

If Xcode encounters any problems when trying to build your project, a **Build Failed** image appears briefly in the Xcode window (Figure 1.20).

Figure 1.20 The build failed!

In addition, if the build was unsuccessful, the activity viewer displays **Failed** as well as the number of errors in the project (Figure 1.21).

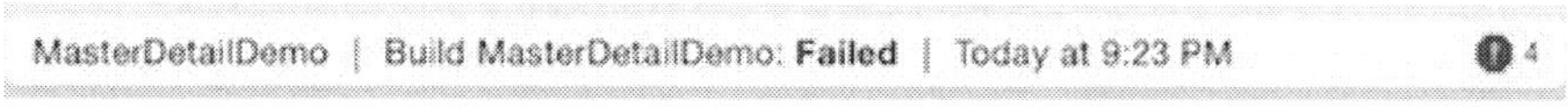

Figure 1.21 The activity viewer indicates a problem with the build.

If the build succeeds, Xcode's **Stop** button turns from gray to black, indicating that the app is running in the iOS Simulator (Figure 1.22).

*Figure 1.22 The **Stop** button turns black when the app is running in the Simulator.*

After several seconds, you should be switched automatically to the iPhone Simulator (Figure 1.23).

Figure 1.23 The ***MasterDetailDemo*** *app in the Simulator*

We will explore this **MasterDetailDemo** app in depth later on, but feel free to play around with it now by clicking the plus (+) and **Edit** buttons. After adding items to the master list, you can select an item in the list and see it in the detail *view*.

4. Now let's go back to Xcode. The iOS Simulator and Xcode are two different Mac OS X applications. Therefore, to go back and forth between Xcode and the iOS Simulator, you can either click on the Xcode window if it's visible (it should be) or press **Command+Tab**, just as you would to go between any other Mac OS X applications.

5. When you're back in Xcode, click the **Stop** button. This stops the app from running in the iOS Simulator.

6. Now let's see how the app looks in the iPad Simulator. Select the **iPad Air** option from the **Schemes** control and click the **Run** button. After several seconds, the app appears in the iPad Simulator (Figure 1.24).

*Figure 1.24 The **MasterDetailDemo** app in the iPad Simulator*

Notice that, when the app is running on the iPad, it changes to use the split *view controller* commonly used in built-in iPad apps. We will take a closer look at the iOS Simulator in the next chapter, but for now, feel free to play with the app by clicking on the **Master** button, adding and editing items, and so on.

7. Now go back to Xcode and press the **Stop** button to stop the app from running in the Simulator.

Summary

Here is an overview of what you have learned in this chapter.

- The **Run, Stop,** and **Scheme** controls in the toolbar at the top of the Xcode window let you run your project in the Simulator or on a device.

- In the center of the toolbar, the activity viewer keeps you posted on the progress of tasks that Xcode performs.

- The buttons on the right side of the toolbar allow you to toggle the display of editors and views.
- The Navigation area on the left side of the Xcode window contains eight navigation tools that allow you to navigate your project files, symbols, search results, issues, breakpoints, and more. The eight icons at the top of the Navigation area allow you to select the different navigation tools.
- The Editor area in the center of the window is one of the most important areas in Xcode. It's where you spend the majority of your time whether it's designing your user interface or writing code.
- It's the only area in Xcode that can't be hidden. This area is home to the Interface Builder Editor, Code Editor, Project Editor, and Entity Data Model Editor.
- The Debug area at the bottom center contains tools that help you debug your apps and contains the Variables view and the Console.
- The Utility Area on the right contains the Inspector pane (on top) including six different inspector tools that help you to create your user interface and to provide quick help when you need it. The six icons at the top of the Utility Area allow you to select the different inspector tools.
- The Utility Area also contains the Library Pane, which includes four separate libraries of UI objects, code snippets, media, and file templates. The four icons at the top of the Library pane allow you to select the different libraries.
- You can have multiple Xcode windows open with each containing different projects.
- Since you can create iOS, Apple Watch, Apple TV and Mac OS X desktop applications using Xcode, the panel on the left side of the New Project dialog has options for both types of applications. Since you are creating iOS apps, you should always select one of the sub-items under **iOS** when creating a new project.

- When creating a new project, each template gives you a slightly different starting project that gives you a head start in the right direction for the specific type of app that you intend to create.

- The *bundle identifier* is used to uniquely identify your app.

- The iOS Simulator and Xcode are two different Mac OS X applications. To go back and forth between Xcode and the iOS Simulator, you can either click on the Xcode window if it's visible or press **Command+Tab**, just as you would to go between any other Mac OS X applications.

Chapter 2: Working With the Simulator

In this chapter, we will start you off with one of the more fun and impressive features of Xcode—the iPhone and iPad Simulator. We have created a sample app for you that fully demonstrates the *amazing* features of the Simulator.

Sections in This Chapter

1. *The SimulatorDemo Project*
2. *Installing Apps on the Simulator*
3. *Uninstalling Apps From the Simulator*
4. *Performing Touch Gestures*
5. *Choosing a Simulator Device*
6. *Rotating and Shaking the Simulator*
7. *Simulating Home, Lock, and a Memory Warning*
8. *Toggling the In-Call Status Bar*

9. *Simulating a Hardware Keyboard*

10. *Simulating External Displays*

11. *Setting the User Location*

12. *Optimizing Your App With Color Debugging*

13. *Saving Screen Shots*

14. *Using the Printer Simulator*

15. *Summary*

16. *Step by Step Movie 2.1*

The iOS Simulator does a great job of simulating the iPhone and iPad experience. It's great that you don't have to connect a physical iOS device to your computer to test your app. Before continuing, I'd like to be clear that you *should* eventually test your apps on a real device for two key reasons:

1. The iOS Simulator is forgiving. If you don't have all of the files bundled with your app, the Simulator can find them anyway. But, if you try to run your app on a real device, it may crash.
2. The Simulator has a lot more horsepower than an actual device: it has the full benefit of your development machine's processing power and memory. You must run your app on a device to check its true performance.

The SimulatorDemo Project

With that caution in mind, let's take a closer look at some of the features of the iOS Simulator. To get the best feel for the Simulator, you will use the **SimulatorDemo** project. This project gives you information about all the Chief Executive Officers of Apple over the years and also includes a map to help demonstrate some of the mapping capabilities built into the Simulator.

1. Open the **SimulatorDemo** project located in the folder you have stored this book's sample code in.
2. In the Project Navigator, drill down into the **SimulatorDemo** > **UI** node. Notice the **Main.storyboard** file shown in Figure 2.1.

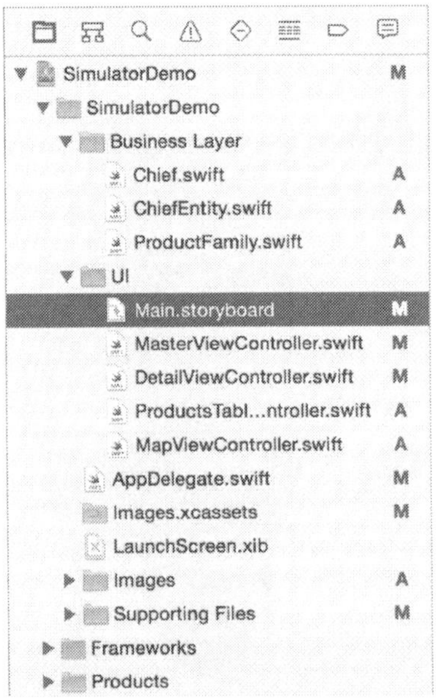

*Figure 2.1 The **Main.storyboard** file*

3. Select the **Main.storyboard** file to display the storyboard in the Interface Builder editor in the center of the Xcode window.

4. From the Xcode menu, select **Editor** > **Canvas** > **Zoom** > **50%**. This zooms out the canvas so you can see all *scenes* in the storyboard (Figure 2.2).

Figure 2.2 The universal storyboard

This is a universal storyboard that allows you to lay out both iPhone and iPad user interfaces. In previous versions of Xcode you needed two storyboards—one for the iPhone and one for the iPad. Once you get the hang of it, the universal storyboard is much easier to work with. You no longer need to keep two storyboards in sync with each other!

Let's see how the project looks at run time.

5. At the top left of the Xcode window, make sure the **Scheme** is set to run in the iPhone Simulator. If it's not, just click the right side of the **Scheme** control, and then select **iPhone 6** (Figure 2.3).

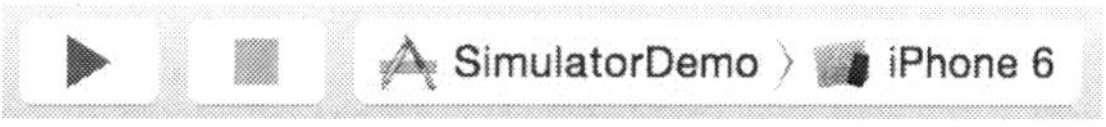

Figure 2.3 Select iPhone 6

6. Click the **Run** button to run the app in the iPhone Simulator. After several seconds, you should see the list of Apple chiefs (Figure 2.4).

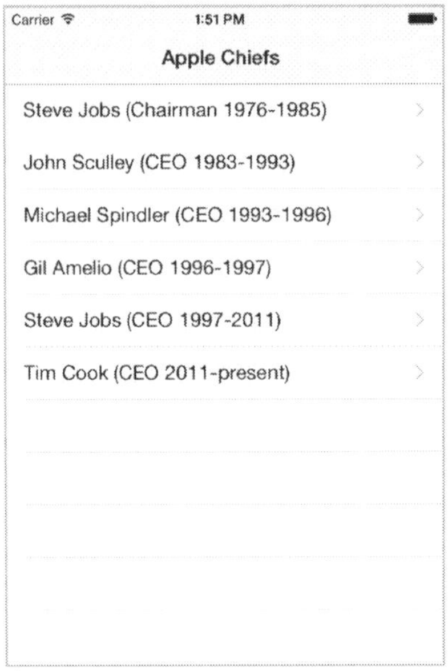

Figure 2.4 The list of Apple chiefs

7. Select the first item in the list, and you will see the detail screen as in Figure 2.5.

Figure 2.5 The iPhone detail scene

8. Now let's see how the app looks on the iPad. Go back to XCode and press the **Stop** button.

9. In the Scheme control, select any of the iPad simulators, such as **iPad Air**.

10. Click the **Run** button. When the app appears in the Simulator you automatically see the detail view with a layout designed specifically for the iPad that takes advantage of its larger size.

11. Click the **Chiefs** button at the top-left corner of the scene. This displays a list of chiefs you can choose from (Figure 2.6).

    In *Chapter 8: Laying Out the User Interface*, you will learn how to design a universal storyboard like this that provides a different UI for iPhone and iPad.

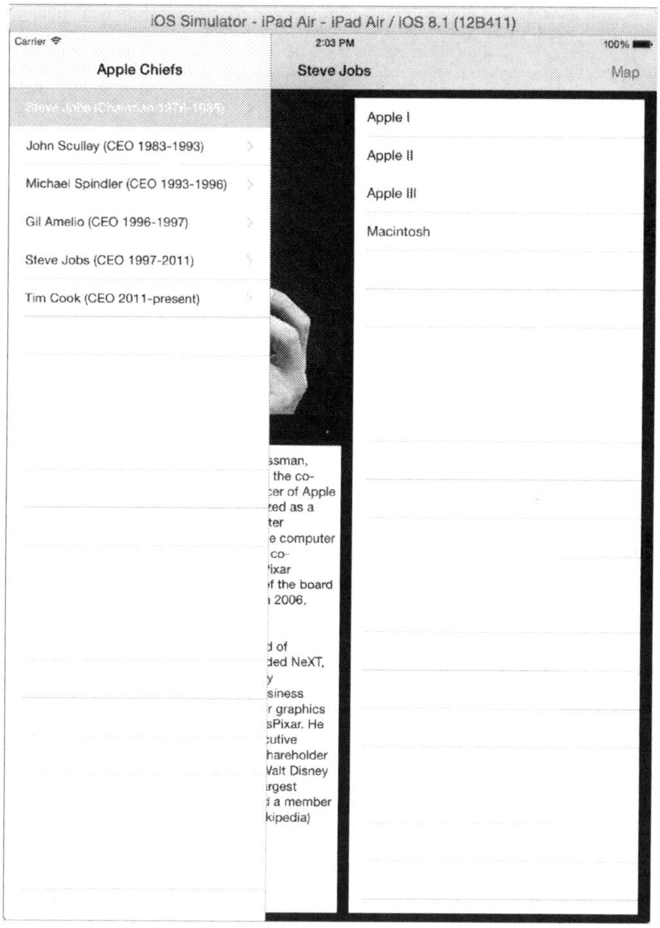

*Figure 2.6 The **SimulatorDemo** app running on the iPad*

Installing Apps on the Simulator

When you run your app in the Simulator for the first time, Xcode automatically installs the app in the Simulator for you. Since the Simulator is not a real device separate from your development computer, Xcode is actually copying files to a specific location on your computer.

All Simulator files are stored within the directory beginning with:

User/<user name>/Library/Developer/CoreSimulator/ Devices

Each folder in this directory (Figure 2.7) represents a different device available in the Simulator's **Hardware > Device** menu. You can easily determine which device you most recently used by checking the **Date Modified** attribute.

*Figure 2.7 The **Devices** directory*

To get to the files for a specific app, drill down into one of the **Devices** folders to the following subfolder:

<device>/data/Containers/Data/Application

The **Application** folder contains a subfolder for each app you have run in Simulator for that device. Each folder is named with a universally unique identifier (UUID) as in Figure 2.8. Again, to determine the app most recently run, check the **Data Modified** attribute.

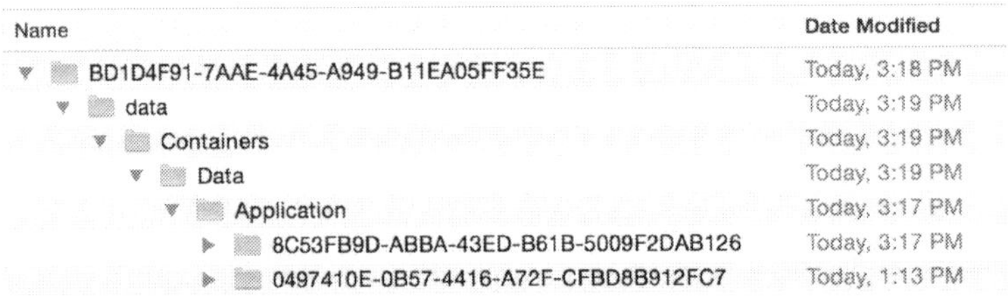

*Figure 2.8 **Application** folders*

Each app gets its own **Documents** folder in which it can read and write files. You will learn more about the **sqlite** files shown in Figure 2.9 in *Chapter 12: Working with Core Data*. The **Library** folder contains a **Preferences** subfolder in which user preferences are stored. The **tmp** folder is used by your app to store temporary files.

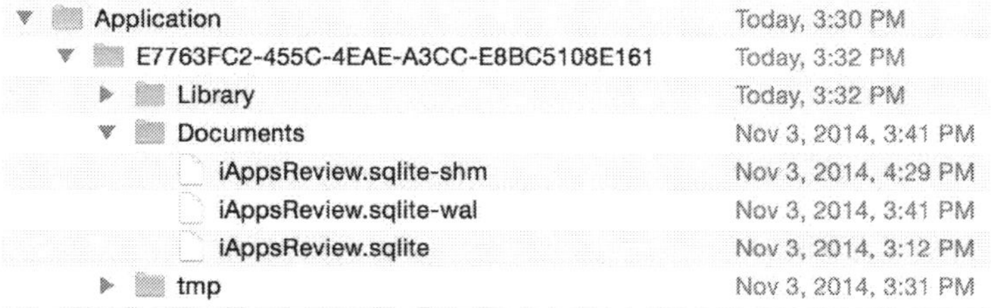

Figure 2.9 App subfolders

Core Data. The **Library** folder contains a **Preferences** subfolder in which user preferences are stored. The **tmp** folder is used by your app to store temporary files.

Navigating to the Simulator Files

By default, the root **Library** folder (**User/<user name>/ Library**) is hidden in Mac OS X, so to navigate to the iPhone Simulator files:

1. Go to the Finder application on your Mac.
2. Hold the **Option** key down, and then click on the **Go** menu.

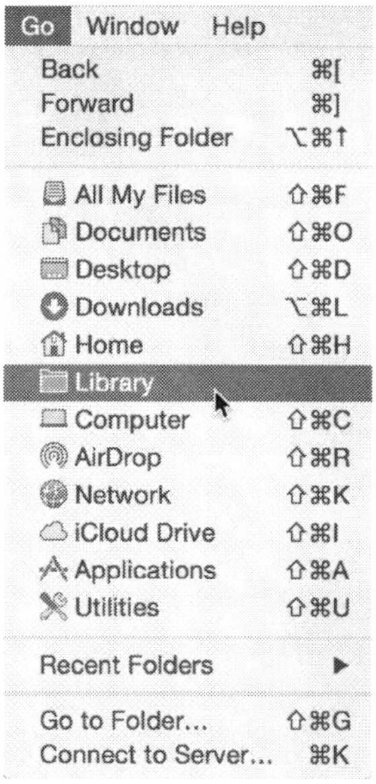

*Figure 2.10 Select the **Library** menu option.*

3. Holding the **option** key adds the **Library** folder in the menu (Figure 2.10). Selecting **Library** from the menu opens a Finder window with the **Library** folder selected. You can then drill down into the **Library** folder to find the Simulator files you want.

Usually, the main reason you want to locate an app's Simulator files is to examine the app's database file. The **mmBusinessObject.swift** class file included in this book's sample code, reads and writes to the app database. I have added a **print()** statement to this class that displays the location of the app's **Documents** folder in the Console the first time you access the database at run time (Figure 2.11). This makes it easy for you to locate the database file.

*Figure 2.11 The full **Documents** path in the Console.*

App Icons

The first time your app is run in the Simulator, an app icon is added to the Simulator home screen. To see the app icon for the **SimulatorDemo** app as shown in Figure 2.12 (along with icons for any other apps that you have run in the Simulator), just click the Simulator's Home button (the large round button at the bottom), or, if there is no Home button, select **Hardware > Home** from the Simulator menu.

Figure 2.12 The SimulatorDemo app icon

If you don't supply icon images for your app by adding them to your project, your app icon will just be a white icon containing light gray grid lines (not impressive).

When building apps for others, I recommend you at least get a basic placeholder icon in place. Customers are always delighted to see a company or app-specific icon in the Simulator.

Apple has very specific requirements for the size of app icons. This is discussed in greater detail in *Chapter 14: Working With the Project Editor*.

In addition to running your app from Xcode, you can also run the app directly in the Simulator. If the app is already running, click the **Stop** button in Xcode. Next, **Alt+Tab** back to the Simulator and click on your app icon. The Simulator launches the app for you—just like a real device.

Uninstalling Apps From the Simulator

To uninstall an app from the Simulator, hold the mouse down on an app icon until it starts to shake. The Simulator displays a small black **X** in the upper-left corner of each icon as shown on the left in Figure 2.13.

When you click the **X**, the Simulator displays a confirmation dialog as shown on the right in Figure 2.13. Just click **Delete** to remove the app from the Simulator. When you are finished deleting an app, select **Hardware** > **Home** from the Simulator menu to exit edit mode.

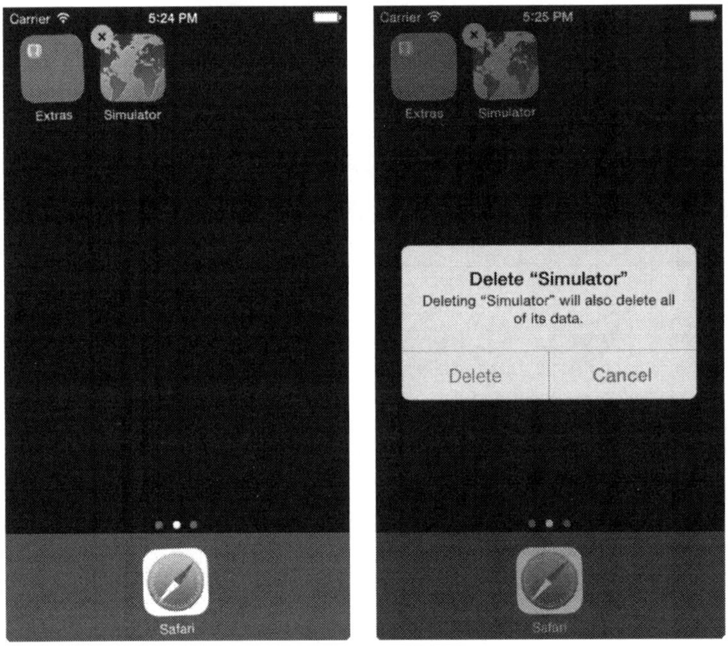

Figure 2.13 Click and hold the mouse down on an app icon to put the Hone screen in edit mode.

Removing an app from the Simulator completely deletes the subfolder for that app from the **Simulator** folder. The next time you run the app in the Simulator, a new subfolder is created for the app.

If you want to completely remove all the apps that you have added to the Simulator and reset the environment to factory settings, select **iOS Simulator** > **Reset Content and Settings** from the Simulator menu.

Performing Touch Gestures

Since your development machine doesn't have a touch screen, you can't touch the surface of the Simulator as you can with a real device. So, the Simulator allows you to perform touch gestures by means of your mouse in combination with other keystrokes. **Table 2.1** shows the mouse action and keystrokes to perform each gesture.

Table 2.1 *Simulator key strokes*

Gesture	Mouse and/or Keyboard Combination
Tap	Click the mouse.
Double-tap	Double-click the mouse.
Touch and Hold	Click and hold the mouse.
Swipe	1. Click and hold the mouse button where you want to start the swipe. 2. Move the pointer in the direction that you want to swipe, and then release the mouse.
Flick	1. Click and hold the mouse button where you want to start the flick. 2. Move the pointer in the direction that you want to flick and release the mouse button.
Drag	1. Click and hold the mouse button where you want to start the drag. 2. Move the pointer in the direction that you want to drag.

Pinch	1. If zooming out, hold your mouse pointer near the middle of the screen. If zooming in, hold your mouse pointer near the outer corner of the screen. 2. Hold the Option key down (this displays two circles on the Simulator that represent two fingers). The closer you are to the middle of the screen, the closer the two circles should be placed. 3. If you want to move the circles at the same time with the same distance between them, hold down the Shift key and move your mouse pointer. 4. If zooming in, click the mouse pointer and drag it toward the edge of the screen. If zooming out, click the mouse pointer and drag it toward the center of the screen. 5. If you want to continue to zoom in or out, keep holding the Option key, and then click and drag.
Rotate	1. Place the pointer on the location where you want to rotate. 2. Hold down the Option key to add two fingers. 3. Move your mouse pointer to bring the two fingers closer together or further apart. 4. To move the center of the pinch target, hold down the Shift key and move your mouse pointer. 5. Hold down the mouse button and move your mouse pointer with a circular motion.

Two-finger drag	1. Place the pointer on the location where you want to perform the two-finger drag. 2. Hold down the Option key to add two fingers. 3. Use your mouse pointer to move the circles representing two fingers to the start position. 4. To move the center of the pinch target, hold down the Shift key and move your mouse pointer. 5. Hold down the Shift key and mouse button, moving the mouse pointer in the direction you want to drag, then release the Shift key and mouse button.

Choosing a Simulator Device

As you have already learned, you can choose the device on which to run your app in the Simulator by selecting it from the **Scheme** control in the Xcode toolbar. The iOS Simulator also allows you to choose the following devices from its **Hardware** > **Device** menu:

- iPad 2
- iPad Air
- iPad Air 2
- iPad Air Pro
- iPad Retina
- iPhone 4s
- iPhone 5
- iPhone 5s
- iPhone 6
- iPhone 6 Plus
- iPhone 6s
- iPhone 6s Plus

Note that if you select a different Simulator device when your app is running, it will kick you out of your app!

Since these options are still included in Xcode, you can use them to test new rumored iPhone and iPad sizes before they are officially supported in the Simulator!

Rotating and Shaking the Simulator

After you have designed the user interface for your app, you can test how it looks in different orientations by rotating the device in the Simulator. Let's give it a try.

1. If it's not already open, open the **SimulatorDemo** project in Xcode and select one of the iPhone Simulators in the Scheme control.
2. From the Simulator's **Hardware** menu, select **Rotate Left** to rotate the Simulator to landscape mode.
3. Select **Rotate Left** again. This places the iPhone in upside-down-portrait orientation (Figure 2.14).

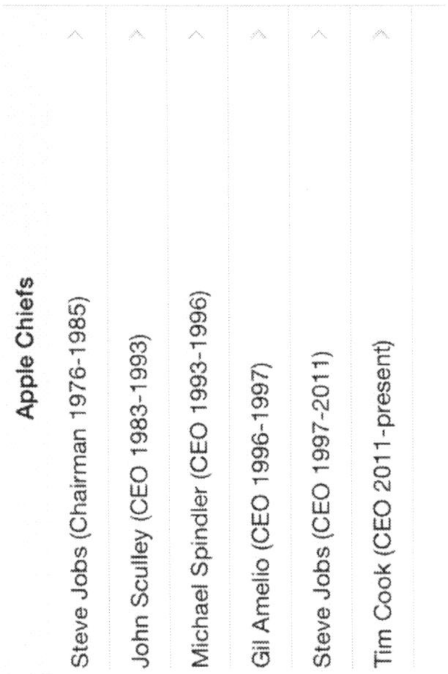

Figure 2.14 Upside-down portrait orientation

According to Apple's UI standards, your app should *not* support this orientation. If it does, it will get rejected when you submit it to the Apple store.

Why isn't this orientation supported? Because you don't want your user holding the phone upside down. When a call comes in it places their mouth on the speaker and ear on the microphone—not an easy way to talk on the phone!

4. Now go the opposite direction by selecting **Hardware** > **Rotate Right** from the menu twice to return to regular portrait mode.
5. Select an Apple chief from the list. This navigates to the next view, providing details regarding tenure, vital statistics, and a short biography (Figure 2.5).
6. Click the **Key Products During Tenure** row to see the **Products** view. This is a simple *table view* that lists the key products created during the selected chief's tenure. If you rotate the device right and left, you can see the table width adjusts according to the width of the screen. If you select **Steve Jobs (CEO 1997-2001)**, the list of products doesn't fit on the screen, but you can scroll down to see all the products.

Slowing Down Animations

Here's a cool trick to get the Simulator to rotate in slow motion:

1. In the Simulator **Debug** menu, select **Toggle Slow Animations in Frontmost App**, and then rotate the Simulator to see the effect.
2. To turn off slow motion, just select **Toggle Slow Animations in Frontmost App** again.

This is actually a very useful feature if you need to slow down the ***animations*** in your app to figure out what's gone wrong if an animation isn't working correctly.

Shaking the Simulator

In built-in iOS apps, the shake gesture can be used to go to the next song in iTunes or to undo typing. Fortunately, the iOS Simulator allows you to initiate a shake gesture so that you can test your shake handling code.

1. Run the **SimulatorDemo** app in the Simulator and click on any of the Apple chiefs to navigate to the detail view.
2. From the iOS Simulator's **Hardware** menu, select **Shake Gesture**. This displays an alert as shown in Figure 2.15.

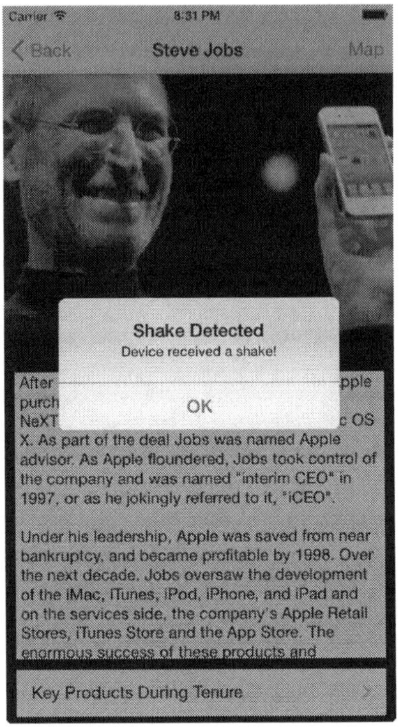

Figure 2.15 You can initiate a shake gesture in the iOS Simulator.

Obviously this alert is only for testing purposes so that you can make sure the shake was handled properly by your app. If you want a quick peek at the code that responds to the shake event in the **SimulatorDemo** app, go to Xcode, select the **DetailViewController.m** file and check out the **motionEnded:withEvent** method.

Simulating Home, Lock, and Memory Warning

The **Hardware** menu has a **Home** option that closes any app that is currently open and goes back to the Home screen as shown on the left side of Figure 2.16. You can also do the same thing by pressing the large Home button at the bottom of the Simulator.

*Figure 2.16 The Simulator's **Home** and **Lock** options*

The **Hardware > Lock** menu option doesn't close your app, but it does lock the Simulator, as shown in the image on the right side of Figure 2.16. If you click the slider and move it to the right, you unlock the Simulator so that your app opens back up again. This feature allows you to test any code in your app that runs when the iPhone goes to sleep or wakes up.

Simulating a Memory Warning

iOS devices have limited memory, so it's important that you respond when your app is alerted that memory is getting low. The Simulator allows you to check your app's response to a memory warning. To see this in action:

1. Run the **SimulatorDemo** app and click on any of the Apple chiefs to navigate to the detail view.
2. From the iOS Simulator's **Hardware** menu, select **Simulate Memory Warning** to display an alert as shown in Figure 2.17.

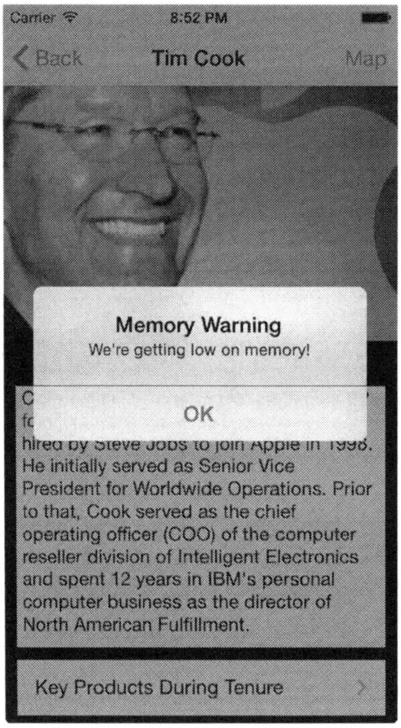

Figure 2.17 Generating a memory warning

Here is the code located in the **DetailViewController.m** file in the **didReceiveMemoryWarning** method that displays this alert:

```
override func didReceiveMemoryWarning() {
   super.didReceiveMemoryWarning()

   let alertController = UIAlertController(
   title: "Memory Warning",
   message: "We're getting low on memory!",
   preferredStyle: .Alert)

    let OKAction = UIAlertAction(
        title: "OK",
        style: .Default) { (action) in
            // ...
        }
    alertController.addAction(OKAction)

    self.presentViewController(alertController,
        animated: true) {
```

```
            // ...
        }
}
```

This method is automatically called when the app receives a memory warning from iOS. You can place code in this method that frees up resources and their associated memory.

Toggling the In-Call Status Bar

When someone accesses your app during a phone call or FaceTime call, a green bar appears at the top of the iPhone screen (Figure 2.18).

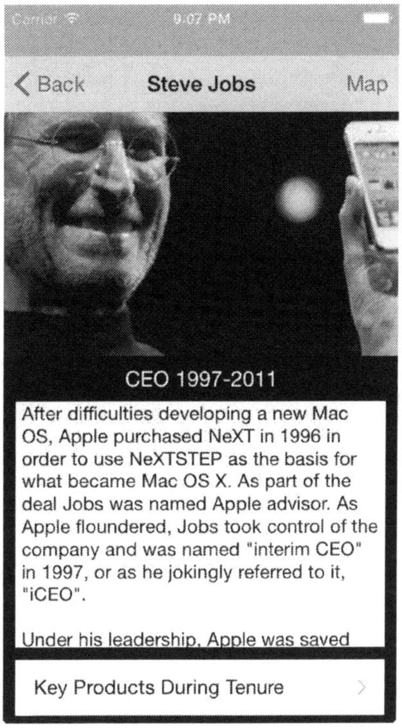

Figure 2.18 The In-Call Status Bar

You can simulate this by selecting **Hardware > Toggle In-Call Status Bar** from the Simulator menu. The in-call status bar is slightly larger than the regular status bar when the phone is in portrait orientation, but is the same size in landscape orientation. Toggling the in-call status bar on and off allows you to make sure that your app resizes properly when the in-call status bar is displayed.

Simulating a Hardware Keyboard

Normally, when an input control receives focus in your app, the iOS keyboard is automatically displayed on the device as shown in the image on the left in Figure 2.19.

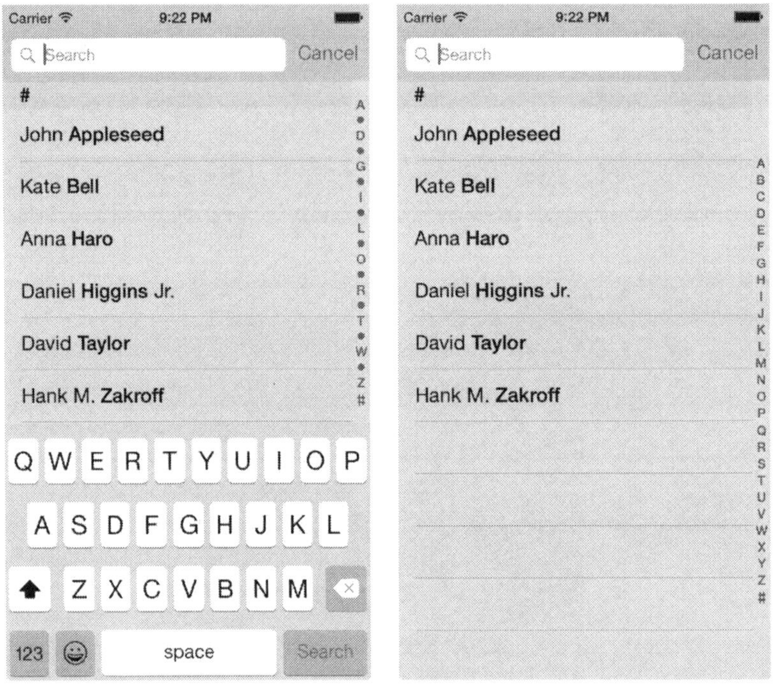

Figure 2.19 The software keyboard is hidden (right) when simulating the hardware keyboard on the right.

However, if you use a keyboard dock or a wireless keyboard on the iPad, the software keyboard doesn't appear on screen. You can simulate this if you select **Hardware** > **Simulate Hardware Keyboard** from the Simulator menu. Choosing this option hides the software keyboard, but you can use the keyboard on your Mac to enter information instead.

Simulating External Displays

Most iOS devices support the ability to display content on a TV by means of an audiovisual cable. The iOS Simulator **Hardware** > **TV Out** menu provides options for testing the output of your app on several screen resolutions:

- 640 x 480
- 720 x 480
- 1024 x 768
- 1280 x 720 (720p)
- 1920 x 1080 (1080p)

Apps do not automatically display content on an external device unless you are mirroring the iOS display using AirPlay. To display information on an external monitor, you must write code that specifically sends output to an external monitor.

To see this code in action:

1. Open the **SimulatorDemo** app in Xcode. Make sure the **Scheme** is set to run in one of the iPhone Simulators (this takes up less space on your screen than the iPad Simulator). Click **Run** to run the app in the Simulator
2. From the Simulator menu, select **Hardware** > **TV Out** > **1024 x 768** (you can choose a lower resolution if the window is too big for your screen). When you choose one of these **TV Out** resolutions, a rectangular window is displayed with a black background.
3. In the iPhone Simulator, select any Apple chief to navigate to the detail view.
4. Click the **Map** button on the right side of the navigation bar. The first time that you view this map in the Simulator, you are asked if it's OK for the app to use your current location. Go ahead and click **OK** because it's not really getting your actual location since the app is running in the Simulator.

   The iPhone Simulator zooms in on a pin dropped on Apple headquarters in Cupertino, CA. In the **External Display** screen, the pin is displayed in the same location but zoomed out a bit further (Figure 2.20). This is a good use of the external monitor. It shows the larger context of the iPhone map pin's location.

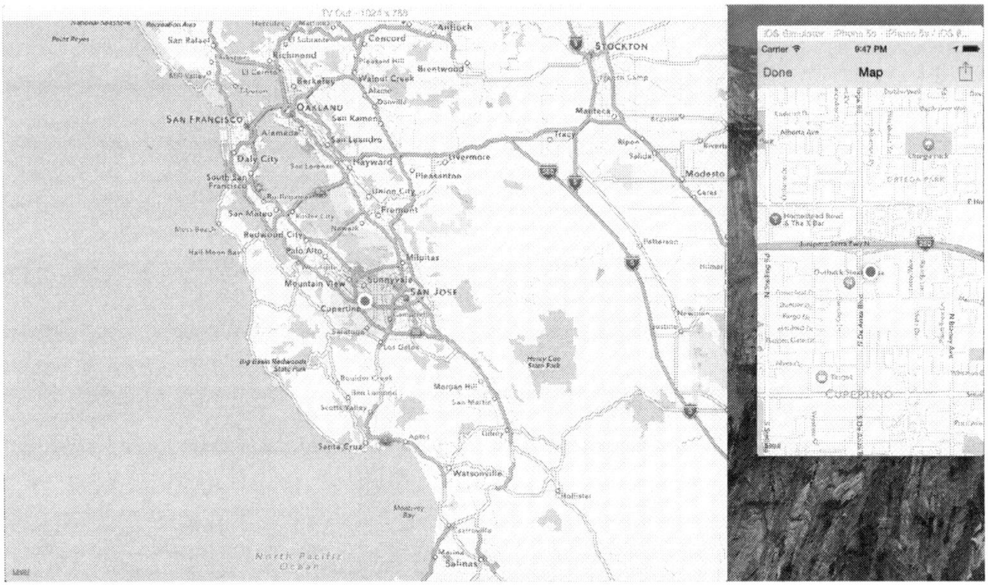

Figure 2.20 You can test the TV output of your app.

5. Now let's have a bit of fun with the TV Out option. Although the Simulator has the default location set to Apple headquarters in Cupertino, you can change the location. From the Simulator menu, select the **Debug > Location > Custom Location...** option. This launches the Custom Location dialog (Figure 2.21).

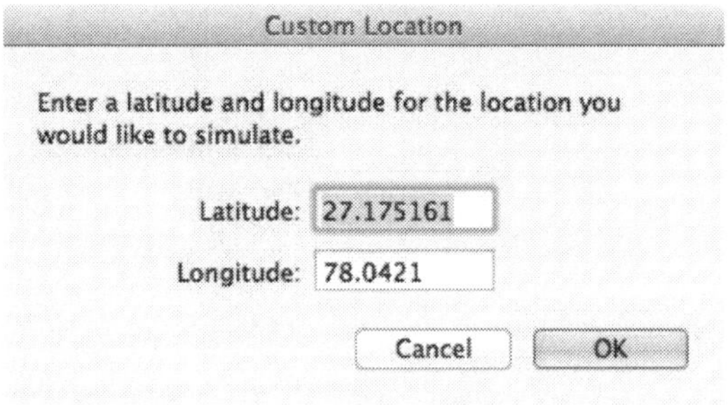

Figure 2.21 You can change the user location of the Simulator to any coordinates.

6. In the Latitude box, enter **27.175161**, and in the Longitude box, enter **78.0421**, and then press OK. This causes the Simulator and the TV Out window to change location on the map. As you can see, these are the coordinates of the Taj Majal in Agra, India. (How much fun is this?) If you're having some fun with this, here are a few more locations to try:

   - Eiffel Tower: **Latitude**: 48.857988, **Longitude**: 2.295091

- Hilton Hawaiian Village Hotel: **Latitude**: 21.283873, **Longitude**: -157.836

- Great Wall of China: **Latitude**: 40.354317, **Longitude**: 116.0064

7. To close the TV Out window, go to the Simulator's menu, and then select **Hardware** > **TV Out** > **Disabled**, which shuts down the app in the Simulator.

The next section discusses other options for setting the "current location" in the Simulator.

Setting the User Location

In addition to setting a custom location's latitude and longitude, the Simulator offers the following choices:

- **None** – Removes the pin showing the user's current location from the map.

- **Apple** – Apple headquarters' coordinates (1 Infinite Loop, Cupertino, CA)

- **City Bicycle Ride** – Simulation of a bike ride in Cupertino

- **City Run** – Simulation of a city run in Cupertino

- **Freeway Drive** – Simulation of a freeway drive in Cupertino

The **Custom Location** and **Apple** options both show a fixed point on the map. All of the other options show a moving point.

Optimizing Your App With Color Debugging

The Simulator's **Debug** menu has the following options that you can use to optimize your app for the absolute fastest performance. Here is Apple's description of each:

- **Color Blended Layers** - Shows blended view layers. Multiple view layers that are drawn on top of each other with blending enabled are highlighted in red. Reducing the amount of red in your app when this option is selected can dramatically improve your app's performance. Blended view layers are often the cause for slow table scrolling.

- **Color Copied Images** - Shows images that are copied by Core Animation in blue.

- **Color Misaligned Images** - Places a magenta overlay over images where the source pixels are not aligned to the destination pixels.

- **Color Offscreen-Rendered** - Places a yellow overlay over content that is rendered offscreen.

When you select one or more of these options, the iOS Simulator color-codes the UI elements that can be optimized for better performance. For example, in Figure 2.22, the **Color Blended Layers** option has been chosen.

*Figure 2.22 The **Color Blended Layers** option*

The objects shown in red can potentially be optimized for display by changing their *attributes* such as **opaque** and **backgroundcolor**.

Saving Screen Shots

At times you need to take screen shots, or capture an image of the screen in the Simulator. You may want to do this when submitting your app to the App Store, since Apple requires you to submit screen shots along with your app.

To take a snapshot of a screen in the Simulator, just select **File > Save Screen Shot** from the Simulator menu, or press **Command+S**.

The screen image is saved to your Mac's **Desktop** folder. The image is stored as a PNG file and the file name contains the date and time of the screen shot.

Using the Printer Simulator

Apple has additional hardware and I/O (input/output) tools that used to be bundled in the Xcode installer, that you can download separately. These include:

1. Bluetooth Explorer
2. HomeKit Accessory Simulator
3. IO Registry Explorer
4. Printer Simulator

The Printer Simulator allows you to test your app's AirPrint capabilities. AirPrint technology allows your app to print to an AirPrint-enabled printer. Currently, all major printer vendors support AirPrint, so chances are good that your users have an AirPrint-enabled printer.

So let's download the package that includes the Print Simulator and give it a try.

1. Navigate to the following link in Safari on your Mac development machine:

   https://developer.apple.com/downloads

2. In the list on the right, look for **Hardware IO Tools for Xcode** 7. Click its plus (+) button and click on the link on the right to download the installer.

3. Go to the Downloads folder and double-click the **Hardware_IO_Tools_for_Xcode_7.dmg** file to launch the Hardware IO Tools installer (Figure 2.23).

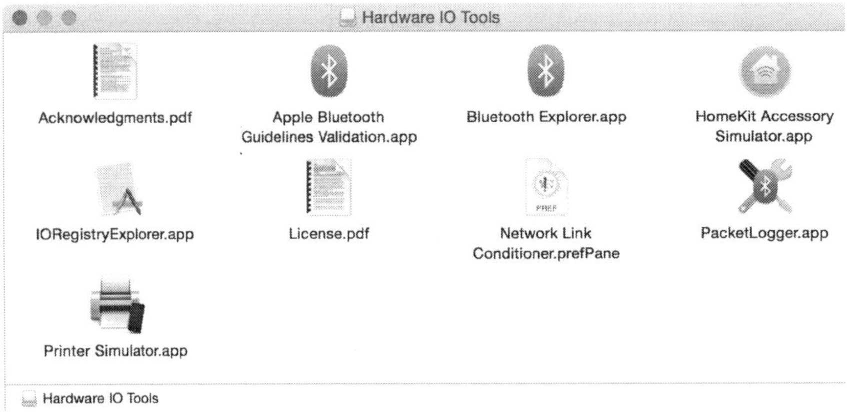

Figure 2.23 The Hardware IO Tools Installer

4. Double click **Printer Simulator.app** to run the Print Simulator. If a warning dialog is displayed, click **Open** to display the Printer Simulator (Figure 2.24).

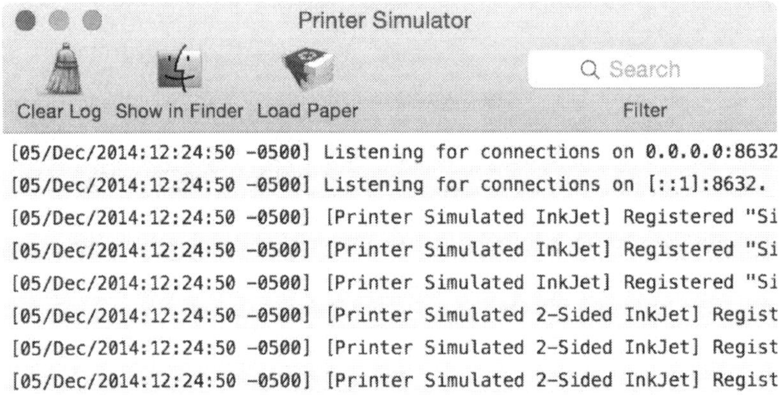

Figure 2.24 The Printer Simulator

5. Click the **Load Paper** button to see the Load Paper dialog (Figure 2.25). This dialog allows you to change the paper size for each simulated printer. You can make changes in this dialog and click OK. Otherwise, click **Cancel** to close the dialog.

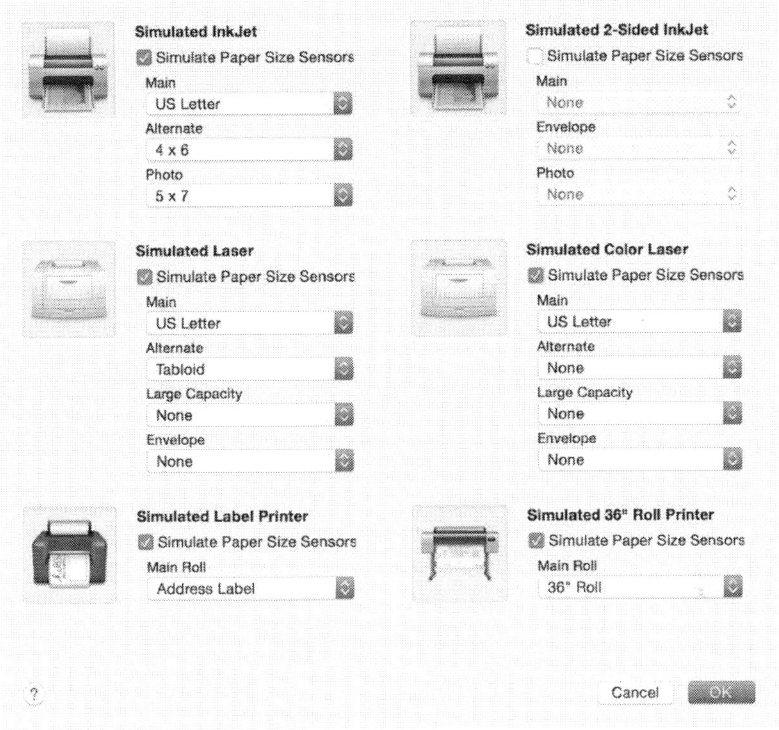

Figure 2.25 The Printer Simulator's Load Paper dialog

Now you're ready to test the Printer Simulator from the **SimulatorDemo** app.

1. Open the **SimulatorDemo** project in Xcode.
2. Select any of the Simulator devices in the Scheme control and then click the **Run** button.
3. Select any Apple chief from the list in the first view.
4. Click the **Map** button on the upper right of the navigation bar to display the map view.
5. Click the action button at the top right of the Map navigation bar to display the Printer Options panel (Figure 2.26). This panel allows you to select a printer and number of copies.

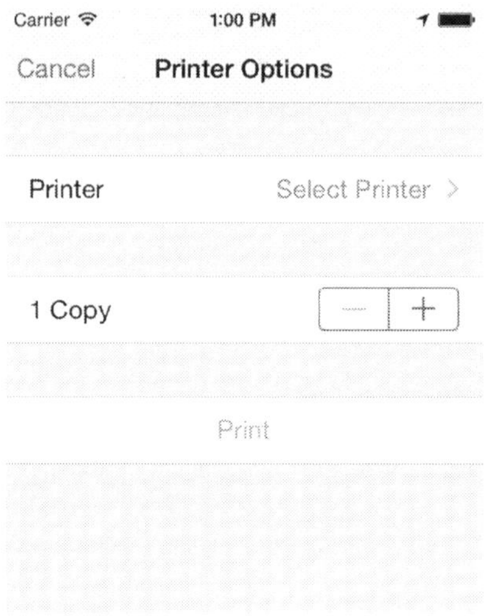

Figure 2.26 The Printer Options panel

6. Click the **Printer** row at the top of the panel to slide the Printer panel into place so you can select a printer (Figure 2.27). If you have any AirPrint-enabled printers on your network, these are also added to the list of printers (the first row shows my EPSON WF-3540 printer).

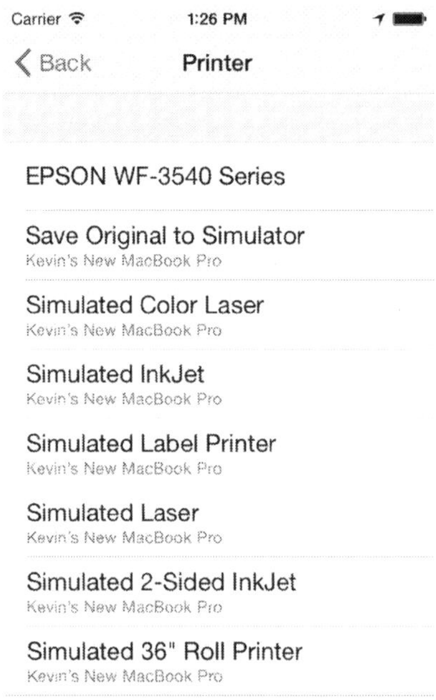

Figure 2.27 The Printer panel

7. For now, select the **Simulated Color Laser** option. This takes you back to the Printer Options panel, where an extra **Double-sided** option is now

available. This option is available when you select **Simulated Color Laser**, **Simulated Laser**, and **Simulated 2-Sided Inkjet**.

8. Click the **Print** button. A panel appears that displays a **Preparing page 1 of 1...** message in its center.

Afterward, a PDF of the map appears on your computer as shown in Figure 2.28.

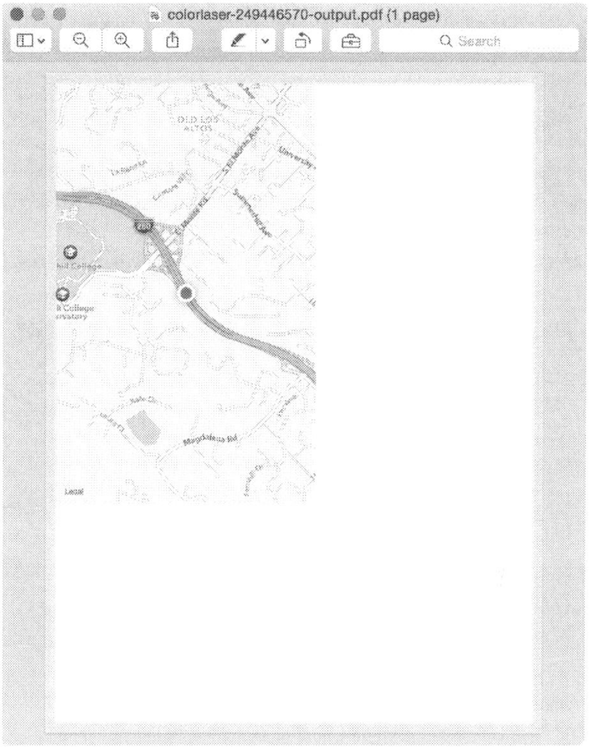

Figure 2.28 The map PDF

Pretty nice! While selecting a printer and printing output, the Printer Simulator dialog displays all commands that the Printer Simulator is executing.

To see the code that makes all of the print magic happen, go to the **MapViewController.swift** class and check out the **printMapView** method.

Summary

Here are the highlights of what you learned in this chapter.

- You *must* eventually test your apps on a real device for two key reasons:

  1. The iOS Simulator is forgiving. If you don't have all of the files bundled with your app, the Simulator can find them anyway. But if you try to run your app on a real device, it may crash.
  2. The Simulator has a lot more horsepower than an actual device; it has the full benefit of your development machine's processing power and memory. You need to run your app on a device to check its true performance.

- You can find the Simulator's app files in the following folder on your Mac:

  User/<username>/Library/Developer/CoreSimulator/Devices/ <device>/data/Containers/Data/Application

- You can uninstall an app from the Simulator just as you do on a real device.

- You can choose the device on which to run your app in the Simulator by selecting it from the Scheme control in the Xcode toolbar.

- You can test how your app looks in different orientations in the Simulator by rotating the device.

- The iOS Simulator allows you to initiate a shake gesture so that you can test your shake handling code.

- The Simulator allows you to check your app's response to a memory warning.

- The Simulator allows you to simulate the iPhone's in-call status bar.

- The Simulator allows you to simulate a hardware keyboard.

- The Simulator provides options for testing the TV output of your app on several screen resolutions.

- In addition to setting a custom location's latitude and longitude, the Simulator offers the following choices:

  1. Apple Stores
  2. Apple
  3. City Bicycle Ride
  4. City Run
  5. Freeway Drive

- The Simulator allows you to test printing wirelessly from an iOS device using AirPrint technology.

- The Simulator's has the following options that you can use to optimize your app for the absolute fastest performance:

  1. Color Blended Layers
  2. Color Copied Images
  3. Color Misaligned Images
  4. Color Offscreen-Rendered

- To take a snapshot of a screen in the Simulator, just select **File** > **Save Screen Shot** from the Simulator menu, or press **Command+S**.

- The Simulator allows you to test printing wirelessly from an iOS device using AirPrint technology.

Step-By-Step Movie 2.1

This movie takes you step-by-step through the process of installing and uninstalling apps from the Simulator.

http://www.iosappsfornonprogrammers.com/B3M21.9.html

Chapter 3: Command Central—the Xcode Toolbar

The Xcode toolbar provides quick access to many of the common tasks you perform while creating apps, as well as much of the core functionality of Xcode. In this chapter, you will learn important information on using the toolbar to select schemes, editors, and views that will make you more productive in Xcode.

Sections in This Chapter

7. *The Organizer Window*

8. *The Documentation Viewer*

9. *Summary*

Showing and Hiding the Toolbar

The Xcode toolbar is displayed at the top of the Xcode window by default as shown in Figure 3.1.

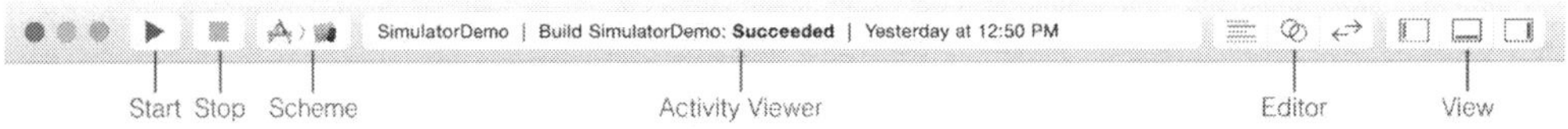

Figure 3.1 The Xcode toolbar

If you want to hide the toolbar, select **View** > **Hide Toolbar** from the Xcode menu. To display it again, select **View** > **Show Toolbar** from the menu.

Run, Stop, and Schemes

As you have already seen, on the left side of the toolbar are the **Run** and **Stop** buttons, which allow you to run your app either in the iOS Simulator or on an actual device and then stop it when you have finished.

To the immediate right of the **Stop** button is the **Scheme** selection control. This is a two-part button that does something different when you click on the right or left. For now, click on the right side of the control and you should see the options shown in Figure 3.2. These options specify where you want your app to run when you press the **Run** button.

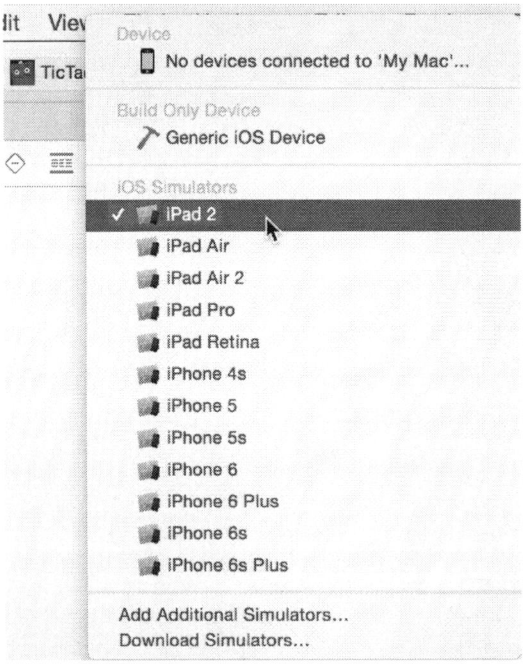

Figure 3.2 The Schemes selection control

You can select the iPhone or iPad Simulators to see how your app looks in each. However, to run the app on an iOS device, you must pay an annual fee to be part of the iOS Developer Program. You will learn about schemes later in *Chapter 14: Working With the Project Editor*.

Working With Editors

The Editor toolbar button group (Figure 3.3) contains three buttons that affect the Editor region located in the center of the Xcode window:

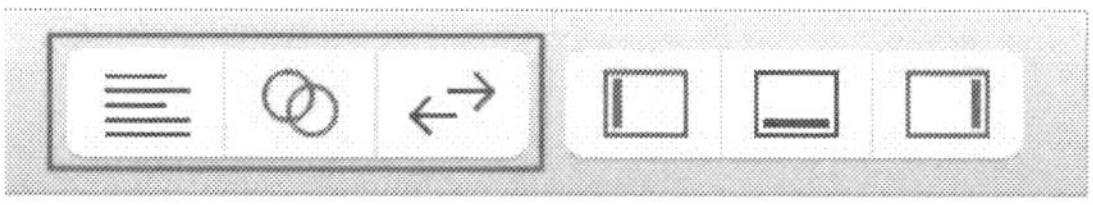

Figure 3.3 Editor toolbar buttons

- Standard Editor
- Assistant Editor
- Version Editor

Only one of these buttons can be selected at a time. If you press one button, the other button that was selected automatically pops up.

Standard Editor

The left Editor button displays the Standard Editor. This editor mode displays a single pane in the center of the Xcode window. For example, Figure 3.4 shows a storyboard file displayed in the Standard Editor.

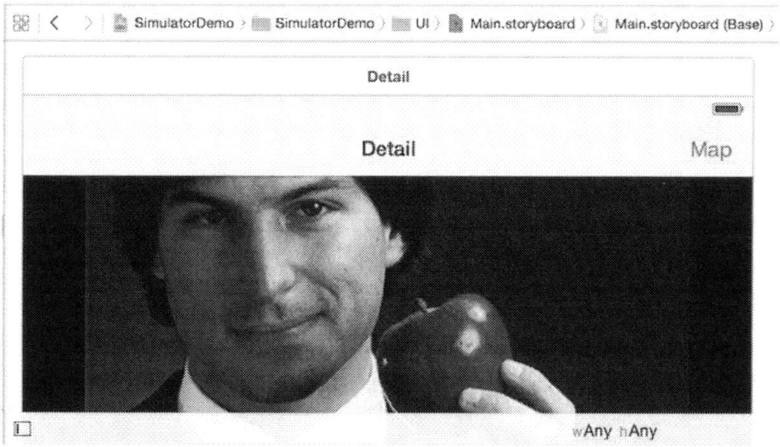

Figure 3.4 The Standard Editor

If the Assistant or Version Editor is open, clicking this button closes those editors, leaving the single editing panel open in the center of the Xcode window.

Assistant Editor

Selecting the center Editor button in Figure 3.3 displays the Assistant Editor. When you click this button, it examines the file currently open in the Standard Editor and opens a second window containing a related file. For example, if you have a storyboard scene selected, it opens the associated view controller file (Figure 3.5).

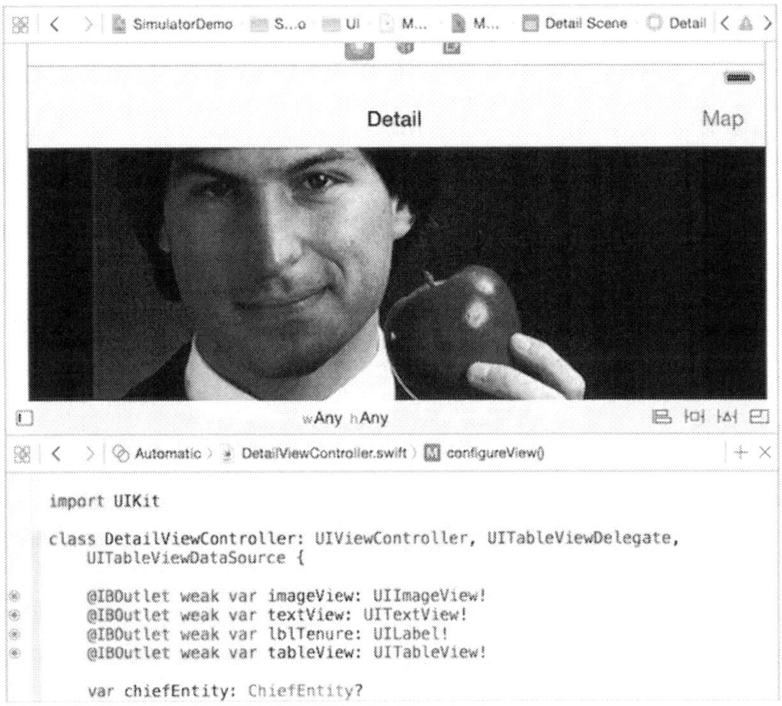

Figure 3.5 The Assistant Editor displayed on the bottom

The Assistant Editor can be displayed either on the bottom, as in Figure 3.5, or on the right, as in Figure 3.6.

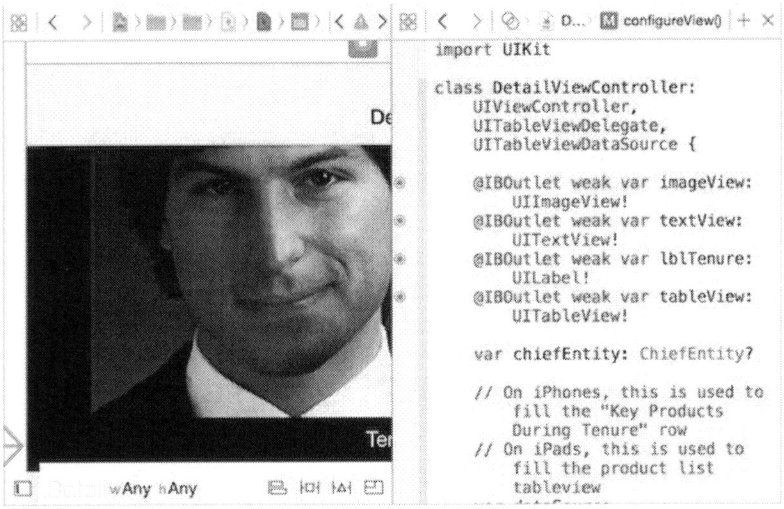

Figure 3.6 The Assistant Editor displayed on the right

To change how the Assistant Editor is displayed, from the Xcode menu select **View > Assistant Editor**, and you will see the options shown in Figure 3.7.

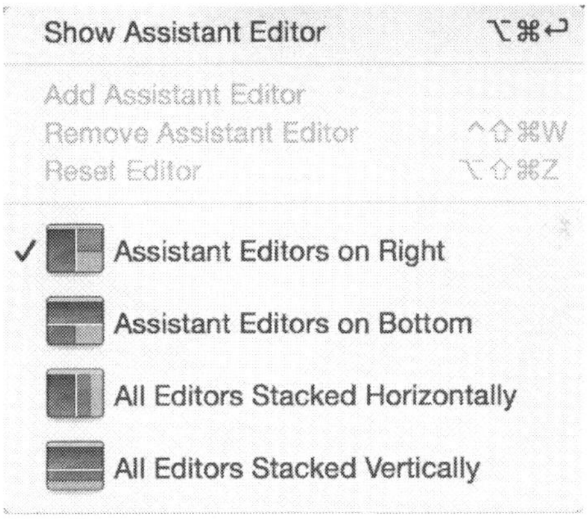

Figure 3.7 Assistant Editor Viewing Options

The bottom four options let you move the Assistant Editor to the right, bottom, or stacked horizontally or vertically. You can add/remove Assistant Editors using the **Add Assistant Editor** and **Remove Assistant Editor** options. The **Reset Editor** option removes all Assistant Editors except the first Assistant Editor that you opened.

The Assistant Editor can get out of sync. In Figure 3.8, the **Detail** scene is selected in the editing panel. The **DetailViewController.swift** file should be displayed, but **MasterViewController.swift** is displayed instead.

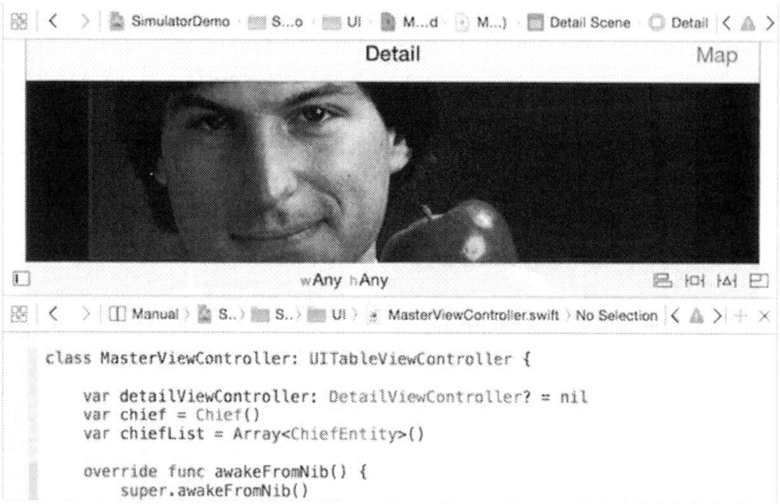

Figure 3.8 The Assistant Editor is displaying the wrong associated file.

If you look closely at the top of the Assistant Editor, you can see a jump bar (Figure 3.9).

*Figure 3.9 The jump bar is set to **Manual.***

Each segment in the jump bar is a button. Notice the **Manual** button on the left. This indicates the Assistant Editor will not automatically change its contents based on the file currently selected in the Standard Editor. To change this, click the **Manual** button in the jump bar, select **Automatic**, and then select the associated file (in this case, **DetailViewController.swift**) as in Figure 3.10.

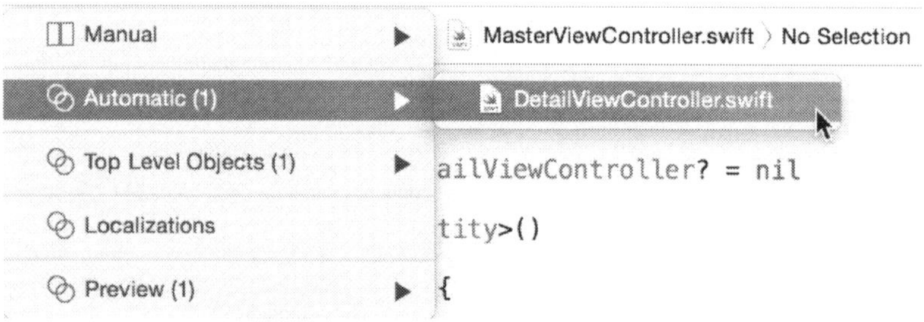

*Figure 3.10 Setting the Assistant Editor to **Automatic**.*

Doing this changes the jump bar button from **Manual** to **Automatic** (Figure 3.11).

Figure 3.11 The jump bar is set to Automatic.

After setting the jump bar to **Automatic**, the Assistant Editor is in sync, automatically selecting the correct counterpart for the file selected in the Standard Editor.

At times, you may want to view two different sections of a large code file at the same time (rather than scrolling up and down to view them). You can easily open the same code file in the Assistant Editor by selecting **Navigate > Open in Assistant Editor** from the Xcode menu. When you do this, you can see two views of the same source code file and can scroll independently to a different section of the code file in each.

Version Editor

The Version Editor allows you to see multiple versions of your project files side by side to see what has changed and when it was changed. This is useful when you want to look back in time to see how something used to work as well as to find out why it's not working now!

When you click the **Version Editor** button in the Xcode toolbar (the button on the far right in the **Editor** button group), it displays the current file version on the left and the older file version on the right (Figure 3.12).

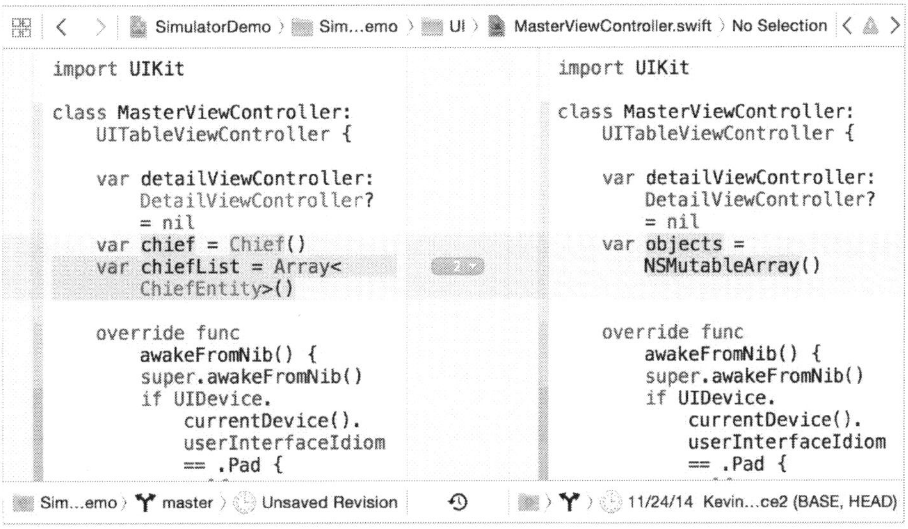

Figure 3.12 The Version Editor.

Between the two views is a dropdown that allows you to discard changes. In the center of the toolbar at the bottom of the Version Editor is a clock icon. If you click this button it displays a slider in the center of the two panels, which you can use to look back in time at different versions of your file to compare them. If you use the Mac OS X Time Capsule to back up your Mac, this is a familiar user interface.

Working With the Tab Bar

Another great feature of Xcode is the tab bar (Figure 3.13). In the same way that you can have multiple tabs in Safari, you can have multiple Xcode tabs that allow you to switch quickly between multiple files in the same or different editors.

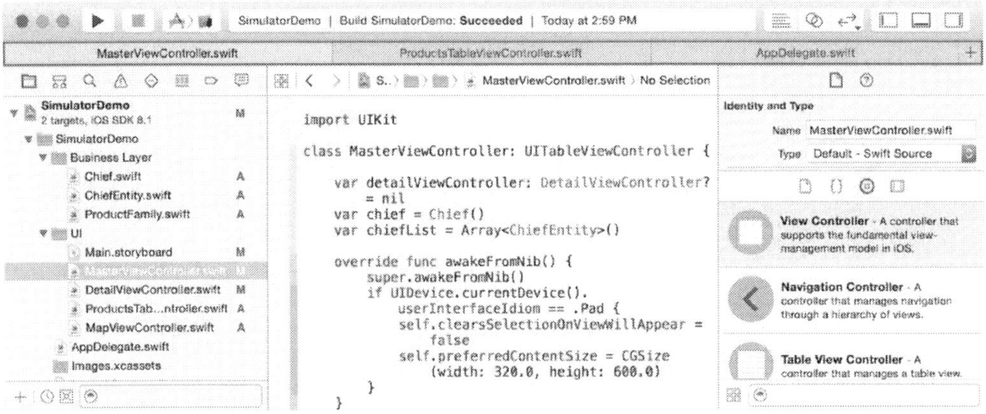

Figure 3.13 The Xcode tab bar.

To enable the tab bar, from the Xcode menu select **View** > **Show Tab Bar**. To hide the tab bar, select **View** > **Hide Tab Bar**. When you show the tab bar, it increases the height of the Xcode toolbar and displays the tab bar the full width of the Xcode window. Whichever editor you had open becomes the first tab as shown with the **MasterViewController.swift** tab in Figure 3.13.

Opening, Closing and Ordering Tab Bars

You can add a new tab to the toolbar by either clicking the plus (+) button on the far right of the toolbar or by selecting **File** > **New** > **Tab** from the Xcode menu. Creating a new tab in this way adds a new tab to the tab bar that contains the same file that you had open in the previously selected tab. Because you probably don't want two tabs that display the same file, after creating a new tab, you can go to the Project Navigator and select a different file to be displayed in that tab.

To remove a tab, hover your mouse pointer over the tab, and then click the small "x" that appears on the left (Figure 3.14). You can also close a tab by selecting **File > Close Tab** from the Xcode menu.

Figure 3.14 Closing a tab.

You can move a tab to a different position in the tab bar by clicking and dragging it to a new location.

Xcode remembers the tabs that you have open, so when you close Xcode and open it again, it restores your tabs just as they were.

Naming Tab Bars

By default, the name displayed on the tab is the same name as the file that it contains. If you want to use a tab for a specific purpose, you can give the tab a permanent name. When you do this, regardless of which file is open in the tab, the tab name stays the same. To create a permanent name, double-click the tab and enter the name. The tab will keep that name until you close it.

Opening Files With the Navigation Chooser

Xcode has another interesting option for opening files in a tab bar or in a new window. If you select **Navigate > Open in...** from the Xcode menu or **Option+Shift+Click** a file in the Project Navigator, it displays the navigation chooser dialog shown in Figure 3.15.

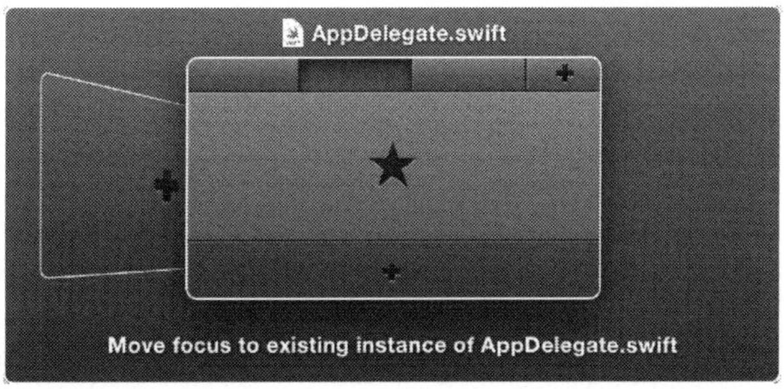

Figure 3.15 The navigation chooser dialog lets you pick where to open a file.

The rectangle in the middle of the dialog is a representation of the Xcode window that you currently have open. At the top of the rectangle is a representation of the number of tabs that you have open (in this case, three). The tab that you currently have selected in Xcode is represented as a teal blue rectangle with a star in the center. If you have any Assistant Editors or other Xcode windows open, these are also displayed in the navigation chooser.

As you select different tabs in this dialog, helpful text is displayed above and below the rectangle. In Figure 3.15, the text above the rectangle indicates **AppDelegate.swift** is the file currently open in the tab. Below the rectangle, the text tells you that clicking this tab will **Move focus to existing instance of AppDelegate.swift**. Selecting other tabs in this rectangle results in a display of helpful text that tells you which file you are replacing if you choose that particular tab to load your selected file. If you want to display the file in a new tab, just click the plus (+) button at the top-right of the rectangle.

If you want to open the file in a new Xcode window:

1. Click the rectangle on the far left in the popup. This slides the main rectangle out of the way and moves the other rectangle in place.

2. Click the plus sign in the middle of the rectangle. This opens the selected file in a new Xcode window.

You can also use the navigation chooser to set focus to another window or tab. To do this, select **Navigate > Move Focus to Editor...** from the Xcode menu, which displays the navigation chooser. Select a window or tab and Xcode sets focus to it.

If you aren't impressed with the navigation chooser, feel free to skip it and use the menu options instead!

File Navigation Preferences

In Xcode's Preferences dialog, several options under **Navigation** settings (Figure 3.16) allow you to change Xcode's behavior when opening or selecting files. To open the Preferences dialog, select **Xcode > Preferences...** from the menu.

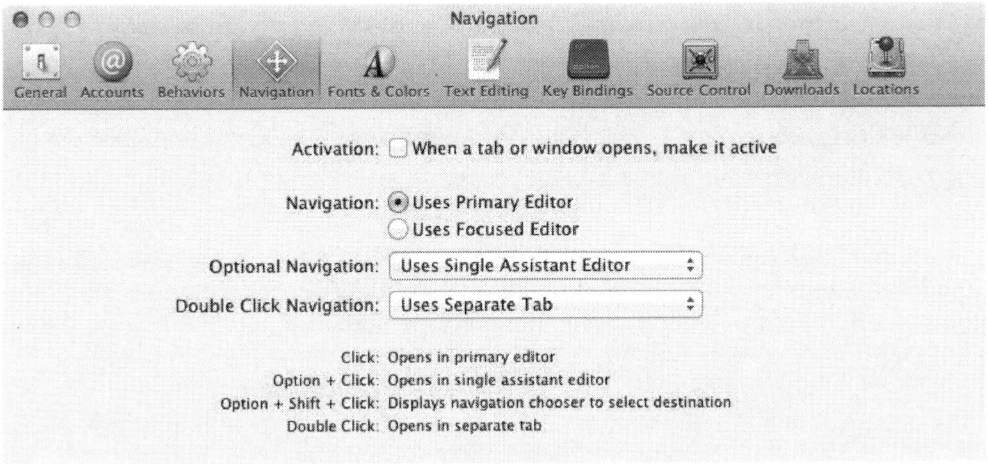

Figure 3.16 File Navigation preferences.

The following sections describe each setting in detail.

Activation

By default, this option is selected, so when a new tab or window opens, it gets focus, or becomes active. If you don't want the new tab or window to become active, uncheck this option.

Navigation

This setting specifies what happens when you either click a file in the Project Navigator or choose to open a file another way. The options are:

- **Uses Primary Editor** (default) – The file is opened in the primary editor pane (not in the Assistant Editor).

- **Uses Focused Editor** – The file is opened in whichever editor panel currently has focus (either the Primary or Assistant Editor).

Optional Navigation

This setting specifies what happens when you **Option+Click** a file in the Project Navigator. The choices are:

- **Uses Single Assistant Editor** (default) – If the Primary Editor pane has focus, the file is opened in the Assistant Editor pane. If the Assistant Editor pane has focus, the file is opened in the Primary Editor pane.

- **Uses Separate Assistant Editor** – The file is opened in a new Assistant Editor pane.
- **Uses Separate Tab** – The file is opened in a new tab. If it's already open in another tab, then that tab receives focus.
- **Uses Separate Window** – The file is opened in a new window. If it's already open in another window, then that window receives focus.

Double-Click Navigation

This setting specifies what happens when you double-click a file in the Project Navigator. The choices are:

- **Uses Separate Tab** – The file is opened in a new tab. If it's already open in another tab, then that tab receives focus.
- **Uses Separate Window** (default) – The file is opened in a new window. If it's already open in another window, then that window receives focus.
- **Same as Click** – The same action as specified for a single click is performed.

At the bottom of the Preferences dialog, the options that you have selected are summarized based on the mouse buttons and keys used to select the file.

Personally, I don't like the default double-click behavior that opens a file in a separate Xcode window, so I change the setting on my machine to **Uses Separate Tab**. That said, if you are working with a large monitor, you may want to open a file in a separate window so you can use your screen real estate to view multiple windows at the same time.

Changing Views

The **View** toolbar button group (Figure 3.17) contains three buttons that toggle (show/hide) the display of three main viewing areas in Xcode. One or more buttons can be selected at the same time.

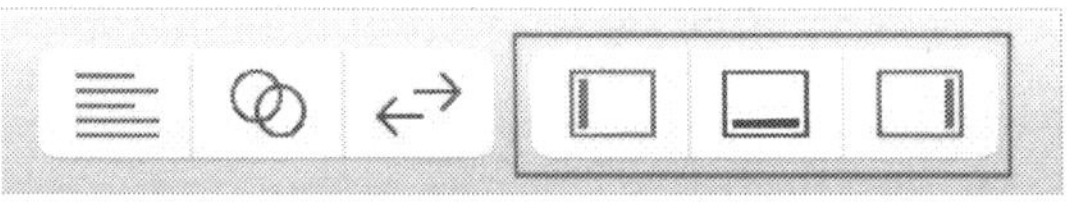

Figure 3.17 Change views with the View toolbar buttons.

From left to right, these buttons toggle the display of the following areas:

- Navigator View
- Debug Area View
- Utilities View

Navigator View

The left View button in Figure 3.17 toggles the display of the Navigator view displayed on the left side of the Xcode window (Figure 3.18).

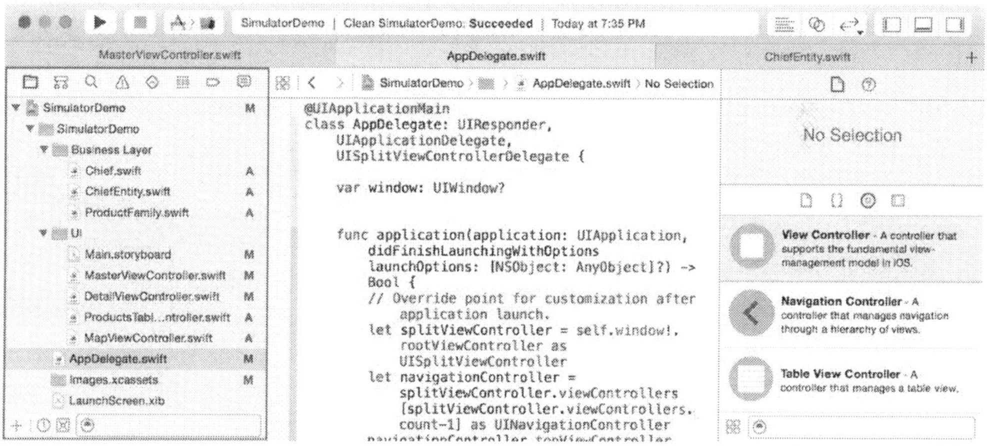

Figure 3.18 The Navigator view.

The Navigator view contains eight navigation tools:

- **Project Navigator** - Allows you to manage the files associated with your project.
- **Symbol Navigator** - Provides an overview of your project's symbols (classes, protocols, enums, etc.).
- **Find Navigator** - Allows you to search for (and optionally replace) text in your project files.
- **Issue Navigator** – Displays *compiler* errors and warnings.
- **Test Navigator** - Allows you to run tests on your project's code.
- **Debug Navigator** - Displays *call stack* of your app at run time.

- **Breakpoint Navigator** – Manages your app's *breakpoints*.
- **Report Navigator** - Displays the reports Xcode automatically generates for building, archiving, and source control tasks.

Each navigator can be selected by clicking the corresponding button in the toolbar at the top of the Navigator panel. All navigator tools are covered in detail in *Chapter 4: The Navigators*.

Debug Area View

Let's move on to the center button in the **View** toolbar button group (Figure 3.17). This button toggles the display of the Debug Area view (Figure 3.19), which is located at the bottom center of the Xcode window.

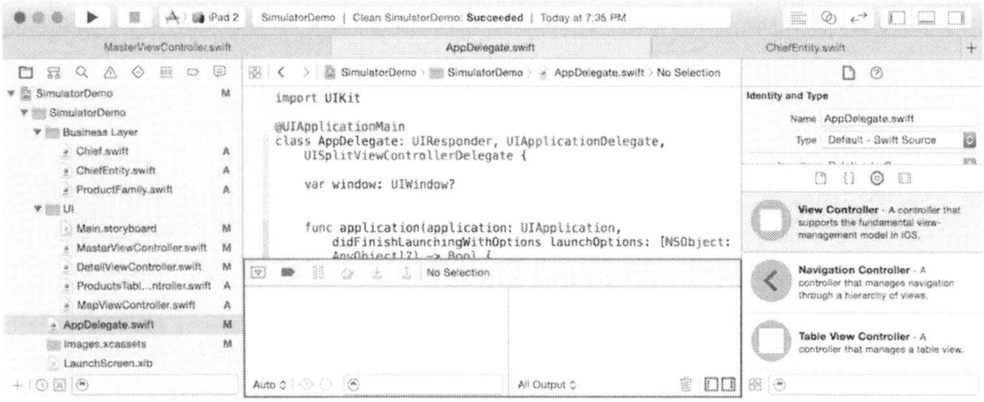

Figure 3.19 The Debug Area view button.

The Variables View (shown on the left) comes alive when you run your app and hit a breakpoint. It allows you to quickly see the values of variables. The Console on the right lets you view program output such as the output of **print()** commands and debugger output.

There are three buttons on the bottom right of the Debug Area view (Figure 3.19).

These buttons allow you to:

- Clear the Console (left button),
- Show/hide the Variables View (center button), and
- Show/hide the Console (right button).

At the top left of the Debug Area view are toolbar buttons (Figure 3.20).

Figure 3.20 The Debug Area toolbar buttons.

The button on the far left with the down arrow hides the Debug area. The other toolbar buttons allow you to toggle breakpoints and step through your app in the debugger.

Utilities View

Now let's move to the right button in Xcode's View toolbar button group (Figure 3.17). This button toggles the display of the Utilities view on the right side of the Xcode window (Figure 3.21).

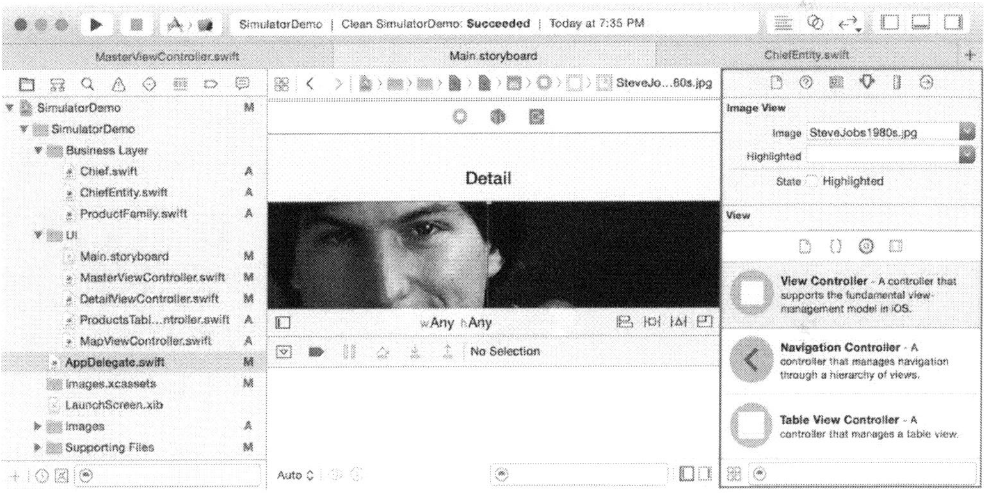

Figure 3.21 The Utilities view.

The Utilities view includes the Inspector pane at the top, and the Library pane at the bottom (Figure 3.22). You most often use the Inspector and Library panes when designing your app's user interface.

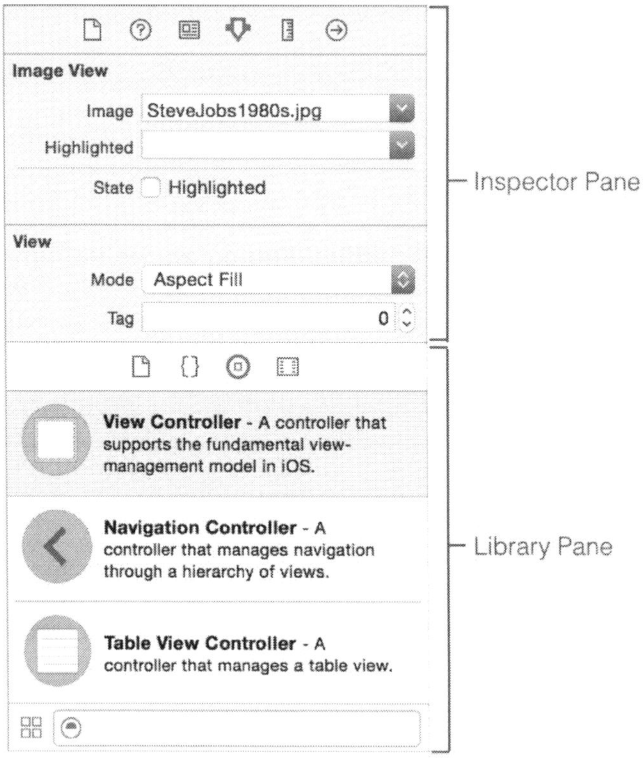

Figure 3.22 The Inspector and Library panes.

You can vary the size of the Library and Inspector panes by clicking and dragging the top of the Library pane's toolbar.

The Inspector Pane

The Inspector pane, located at the top of the Utilities view, contains six different inspector tools:

- **File Inspector** - Provides detailed information regarding the file currently selected in the Project Navigator.

- **Quick Help Inspector** - Provides quick, abbreviated information on the *object* that you currently have selected in the editor pane.

- **Identity Inspector** - Allows you to view and set identifying information on the currently selected UI object including its class.

- **Attributes Inspector** - Allows you to view and edit the attributes of the currently select UI object. The attributes vary greatly depending on the type of object selected.

- **Size Inspector** - Allows you to specify the position and size of UI objects, including how the size and position change as the orientation or size of the view changes.

- **Connections Inspector** - Allows you to view and edit connections to the currently selected UI object.

Note that some of the inspectors are only visible if you have a UI object selected in the editor.

Each inspector can be selected by clicking the corresponding button in the toolbar at the top of the Inspector panel (Figure 3.22).

Each inspector tool is covered in detail in *Chapter 5: The Inspectors.*

The Library Pane

The Library pane, located at the bottom of the Utilities View, contains four different libraries:

- **File Template Library** - Allows you to add new files to your project.

- **Code Snippet Library** - Allows you to add common pieces of code to your project in order to avoid typing the same code over and over again.

- **Object Library** - Contains a list of UI objects that you can drag and drop on the design surface when laying out your user interface.

- **Media Library** - Contains a list of media (such as images) that you have added to your project.

At the bottom left of the Library pane (Figure 3.23) is a button that toggles between showing items as icons with associated descriptions and icons with no description.

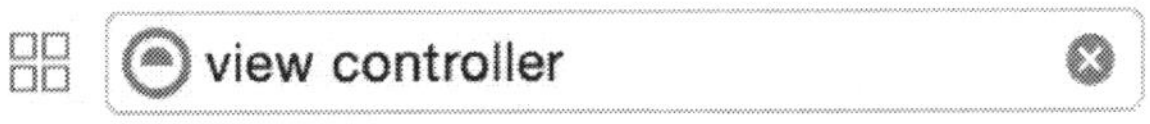

Figure 3.23 The library icon button and filter.

A filter control to the right of this button allows you to enter search text and displays all items that contain the specified filter text. For example, if the Object Library is displayed and you enter the filter text shown in Figure 3.23, only UI objects that contain the phrase “view controller” will be displayed in the library.

In the Template Library and Code Snippet Library, the filter acts on the item descriptions rather than the name of the item itself. In the Object Library, the filter acts on the name of the item, not its description. Note that the filter text doesn’t automatically get cleared when changing to a different library, so make sure you clear it when moving to another library pane.

Each library is covered in detail in *Chapter 6: The Libraries*.

The Documentation Viewer

The Documentation Viewer (Figure 3.24) allows you to search and read Apple’s documentation for the Cocoa Touch Framework. To launch the Documentation Viewer, select **Window > Documentation and API Reference**.

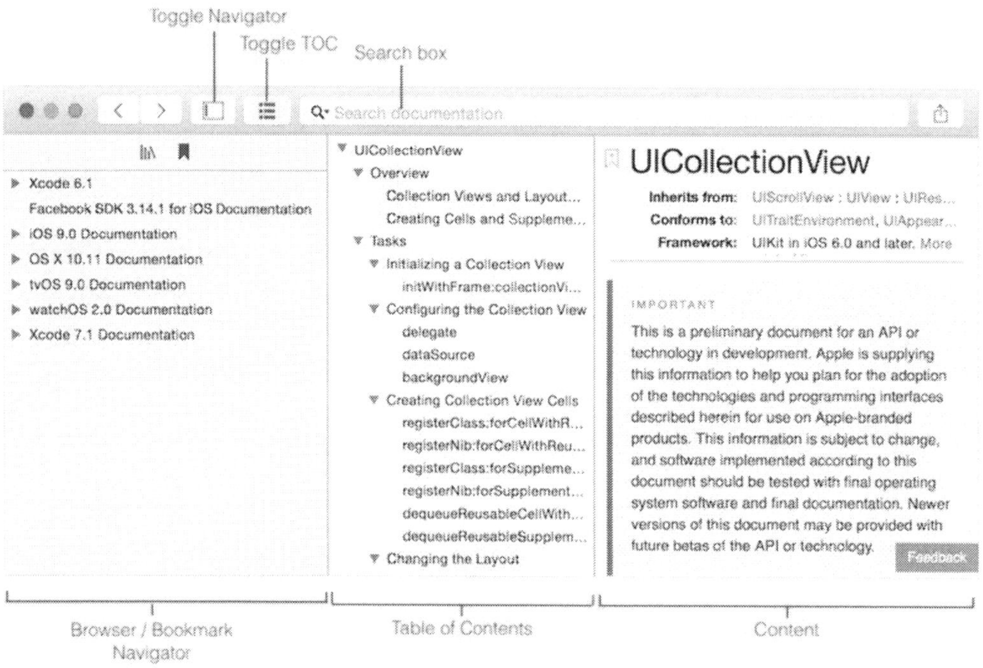

Figure 3.24 The Documentation Viewer.

At the top of the Documentation Viewer is a search bar. When you enter a search phrase and press **Enter**, a list of search results is displayed. Search results are displayed under the following categories:

- **Top Hit** - This is the help topic that most closely matches your search criteria.
- **API Reference** - Results in this category include formal class reference documentation that lists classes (and their members), protocols, categories, and so on. This documentation tends to be brief and to the point, so it's helpful for more experienced developers and can be a tough read for the uninitiated.
- **SDK Guides** - Results in this category lead you to system guides that provide a broader picture of the technologies on you are seeking help on. If you are new to a particular subject, system guides can be a great way to grasp the main concept. Then you can go back to the reference documentation for more details.
- **Tools Guides** - You will get results in this category if you search for information on any of Xcode's tools such as the Explorers, Inspectors, or Libraries. These topics provide a broad picture of how to make use of these tools but often don't include much detail.
- **Sample Code** - If you're fortunate, the topic you are searching has associated sample code. Sometimes looking at someone else's code can be a great help in understanding how to write code yourself. However, be forewarned that these samples can be somewhat "dated," and *can contain code that is deprecated or no longer the approach recommended by Apple*!

If you select a result under the **Sample Code** category, the content pane displays details about the sample code (Figure 3.25).

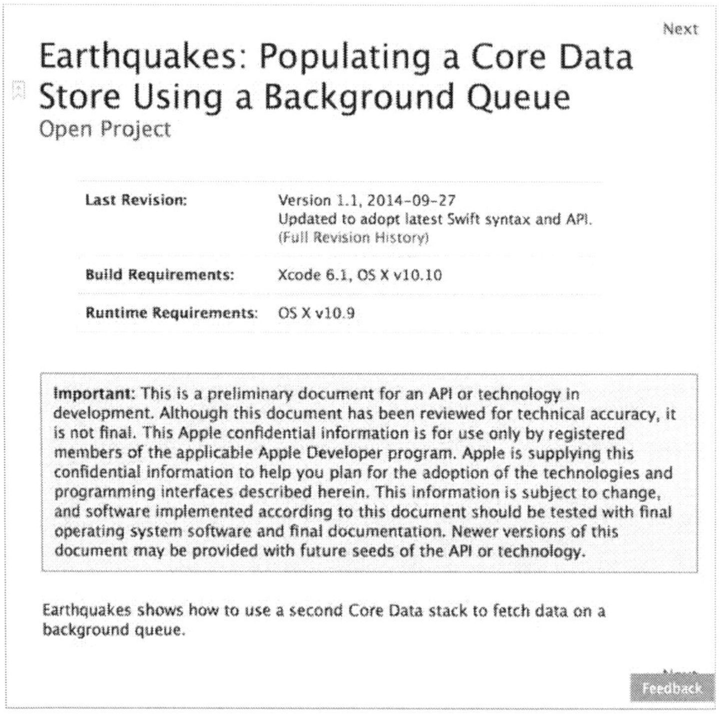

Figure 3.25 Sample Code Details.

Before viewing the sample code, take a close look at the **Last Revision** section. Consider this the "how fresh is this code" date. Apple changes the iOS ***SDK*** (software development kit) frequently, so make sure you are looking at a code sample that is relatively new and contains the most up-to-date techniques.

To view the sample code, just click the **Open Project** link at the top of the panel and it automatically opens the code sample in Xcode.

Documentation Bookmarks

If you want to find a particular page of documentation again, you can bookmark it. To do this, just right-click the content pane and select **Add Bookmark**.

You can view the bookmarks you have created in the left pane of the Documentation Viewer Figure 3.24.

To delete a bookmark, select the bookmark in the panel on the left and press the **delete** key.

Table of Contents

The second panel from the left in the Documentation Viewer contains a table of contents that allows you to easily navigate to all the topics in the currently open document. Just make sure the Table of Contents button at the top of the panel is selected (Figure 3.24).

All in all, the Documentation organizer can be a useful tool in conjunction with Google searches to supplement where Apple's code samples may lack.

The Devices Window

The Devices Window (Figure 3.26) allows you to manage the physical iOS devices you use for testing your iOS apps as well as the Simulators.

Figure 3.26 The Devices window.

The Devices window allows you to examine device logs, installed apps, and also allows you to take screen shots from the selected device.

The Organizer Window

To launch the Organizer Window, select **Window > Organizer** from the Xcode menu. The Organizer window (Figure 3.27) contains two section. You select each section by clicking the corresponding button at the top of the Organizer window:

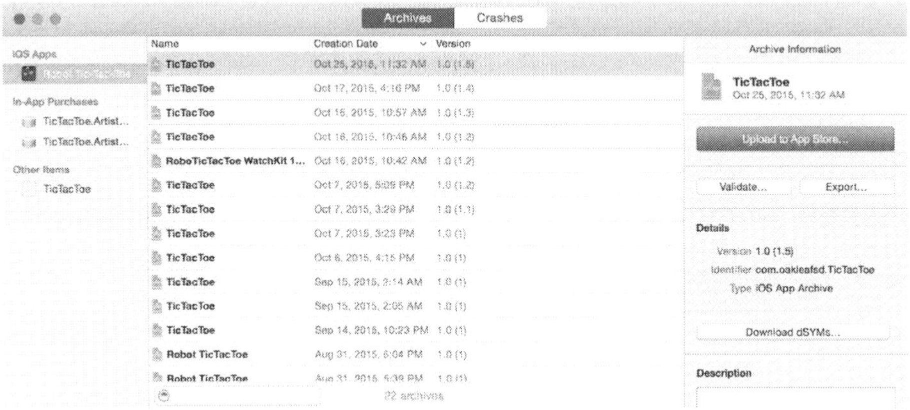

Figure 3.27 The Organizer window

- **Archives** – Helps you to manage your project archives, which are created when you distribute your project. You will learn more about this organizer later in this series when learning to get your apps ready for the App Store.

- **Crashes** - Allows you to view detailed information about crashes that have occurred in your app.

The Projects Window

To launch the Projects Window, select **Window** > **Projects** from the Xcode menu. The Projects window (Figure 3.28) helps you manage your projects and their associated data. It allows you to manage the snapshots (project state saved at different points in time) of your project.

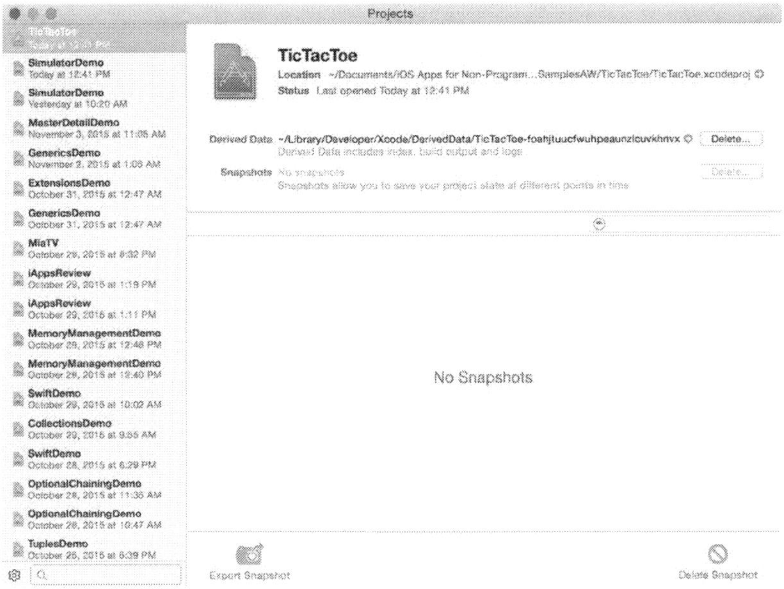

Figure 3.28 The Projects window

Summary

- The Xcode toolbar provides easy access to some of the functions you perform most often.
- You can show/hide the toolbar by selecting **View > Show Toolbar** and **View > Hide Toolbar** from the menu.
- The **Schemes** control allows you to select where you want your app to run—in the iOS Simulator, iPad Simulator, or on an attached iOS device.
- The **Editors** toolbar button group has three buttons that affect the Editor region located in the center of the Xcode window:
  - **Standard Editor** - Displays a single editing pane in the center of the Xcode window.
  - **Assistant Editor** - Allows you to edit a file related to the file open in the Standard Editor.
  - **Version Editor** - Allows you to see multiple versions of your project files side by side to see what has changed and when it was changed.

- The Xcode tab bar allows you to switch quickly between multiple files in the same or different editors.
- In Xcode's Preferences dialog, there are several preferences that allow you to change Xcode's behavior when opening or selecting files.
- The **View** toolbar button group toggles the display of the following areas:
    - Navigator View
    - Debug Area View
    - Utilities View
- The Navigator view contains eight different navigation tools:
    - **Project Navigator** - Allows you to manage the files associated with your project.
    - **Symbol Navigator** - Provides an easy way to view the symbols (classes, protocols, functions, structs, enumerations) in your project.
    - **Find Navigator** - Allows you to search for (and optionally replace) text in your project files.
    - **Issue Navigator** - Provides details regarding compiler errors and warnings.
    - **Test Navigator** - Allows you to run tests on your project's code.
    - **Debug Navigator** - Allows you to see the *call stack* of your app at run time
    - **Breakpoint Navigator** - Allows you to manage your app's breakpoints.
    - **Report Navigator** - Allows you to view the reports that Xcode automatically generates for building, archiving, and source control tasks.
- The Debug Area view contains the Variables view and the Console.

- The Utilities view contains the Inspector pane and the Library pane.
- The Inspector pane contains six different inspector tools:
    - **File Inspector** - Provides detailed information regarding the file currently selected in the Project Navigator.
    - **Quick Help Inspector** - Provides quick, abbreviated information on the object that you currently have selected in the editor pane.
    - **Identity Inspector** - Allows you to view and set identifying information on the currently selected UI object, including its class.
    - **Attributes Inspector** - Allows you to view and edit the attributes of the currently select UI object. The attributes vary greatly depending on the type of object selected.
    - **Size Inspector** - Allows you to specify the position and size of UI objects, including how the size and position change as the orientation or size of the view changes.
    - **Connections Inspector** - Allows you to view and edit connections to the currently selected UI object.
- The Library pane, located at the bottom of the Utilities View, contains four different libraries:
    - **File Template Library** - Allows you to add new files to your project.
    - **Code Snippet Library** - Allows you to add common pieces of code to your project in order to avoid typing the same code over and over again.
    - **Object Library** - Contains a list of UI objects that you can drag and drop on the design surface when laying out your user interface.
    - **Media Library** - Contains a list of media (such as images) that you have added to your project.

- The Documentation Viewer provides fast access to you to search for and read Apple's iOS documentation.
- The Devices Window allows you to manage the physical iOS devices you use for testing your iOS apps as well as the Simulators.
- The Organizer Window contains two section:
    - **Archives** – Helps you to manage your project archives, which are created when you distribute your project. You will learn more about this organizer later in this series when learning to get your apps ready for the App Store.
    - **Crashes** - Allows you to view detailed information about crashes that have occurred in your app.

The Projects Window helps you manage your projects and their associated data. It allows you to manage the snapshots (project state saved at different points in time) of your project.

Chapter 4: The Navigators

In the previous chapter, you were given a high-level overview of Xcode's Navigator tools. In this chapter, we'll take a closer look at each and learn best practices for making the most of these tools in your daily app development.

Sections in This Chapter

1. *The Project Navigator*
2. *The Symbol Navigator*
3. *The Find Navigator*
4. *The Issue Navigator*
5. *The Test Navigator*
6. *The Debug Navigator*
7. *The Breakpoint Navigator*

8. The Report Navigator

9. Summary

Here is a list of the navigator tools in the Navigator pane on the left side of the Xcode window along with the keystrokes you can use to select each navigator:

- Project Navigator (Command+1)
- Symbol Navigator (Command+2)
- Find Navigator (Command+3)
- Issue Navigator (Command+4)
- Test Navigator (Command+5)
- Debug Navigator (Command+6)
- Breakpoint Navigator (Command+7)
- Report Navigator (Command+8)

You can also select each navigator by clicking the corresponding button in the toolbar at the top of the Navigator panel (Figure 4.1).

Figure 4.1 The Navigators toolbar.

The following sections discuss each navigator in detail.

The Project Navigator

The first button on the left of the Navigator toolbar selects the Project Navigator (Figure 4.2), the navigator you will use most often.

The Project Navigator lists all files associated with your project, including source code files, storyboards for laying out the user interface, settings files, images, and frameworks. This is the place where you can add new files, delete files, and select files to be edited.

Figure 4.2 The Project Navigator.

If the Navigator view is not visible, you can display it by selecting **View** > **Navigators** > **Show Navigator** from the Xcode menu.

The first item listed in the Project Navigator in Figure 4.2 represents the project itself. The folders nested below the project in the Project Navigator are called ***groups***. A group is a means for organizing related files together. When you create a new project, several groups are already added to your project.

- The root folder, or group, is named the same as your project and is the second item listed in the Project Navigator. It contains your project's main source code and UI files.

- The **Supporting Files** group contains project settings files.

- The **<ProjectName>Tests** folder contains classes that you can use to test the code in your project.

- The **Frameworks** group lists the Cocoa Touch frameworks referenced in your project. By default, a few of the basic frameworks are automatically added to your project. As you use other features of the Cocoa Touch Frameworks, you can add other frameworks to your project.

- The **Products** group contains your app file. This file *is* your app. More on that later. It also contains a .xctest file that executes when you run the app tests you have created for your project.

Here are some important points to note about the Project Navigator:

- Groups don't directly correspond to folders on your hard drive but are a logical grouping of related items.

- You can act on multiple files at one time by selecting all the files that you want to affect. To select multiple files, hold the **Command** key down as you click. To select a range of files, click the first file that you want to select, hold the **Shift** key down, and then click the last file that you want to select.

- You can create a new group by right-clicking the node under which you want the new group to be located and then selecting **New Group** from the shortcut menu. Afterward, enter the name of your new group in the Project Navigator.

- To create a new group from existing project items, select the items in the Project Navigator, right-click, and then select **New Group from Selection**.

- You can drag and drop to move items from one group to another and to reorder items within a group.

- You can drag and drop items from one Xcode project window to another.

- You can sort items in a folder either alphabetically or by type. To do this, right-click the group and then select either **Sort by Name** to sort alphabetically or **Sort by Type** to sort by the type of file.

- The small letters to the far right of the Project Navigator (shown in Figure 4.2) are used for source code control purposes. You will learn more about source code control later in this book series.

- It's easy to miss, but at the bottom of the Project Navigator is a small toolbar that provides some handy functionality (Figure 4.3).

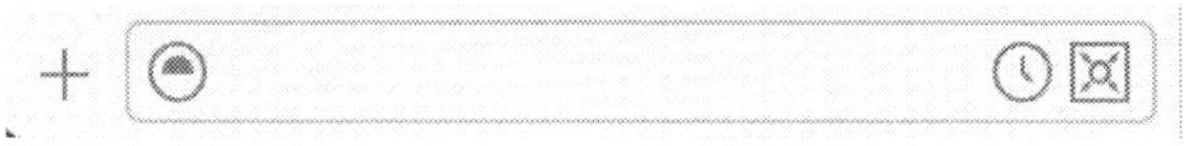

Figure 4.3 The Navigator toolbar.

Here is a description of each control from left to right:

- **Add a new file** – Clicking the plus (+) button displays a popup menu that allows you to add a new file or existing file(s) to the currently selected group.

- **Show files with matching name** – When you enter a filter string in this search box, only the files containing the characters that you entered are displayed in the Project Navigator.

- **Show only recent files** – Hides older files in your project.

- **Show only files with source-control status** – Only shows files that have the small source code letter to the far right.

Buttons in this toolbar that are toggled on are blue, and buttons that are toggled off are black.

Note: If your project files are suddenly "missing," you may have accidentally selected one of these toolbar buttons or entered filter text. To get your files back, either click the button again or click the clear button in the search box.

Adding New Files to the Project

You can add a new file to the project several ways:

- Type **Command+N.**

- From the Xcode menu, select **File > New > File....**
- Right-click a group in the Project Navigator and then select **New File...** from the shortcut menu.
- Click the plus (+) button in the toolbar at the bottom of the Project Navigator and select **New File...** from the popup menu.

New files are added to the project directly below the item currently selected in the Project Navigator. Regardless of how you initiate adding a new file, the New File dialog appears (Figure 4.4).

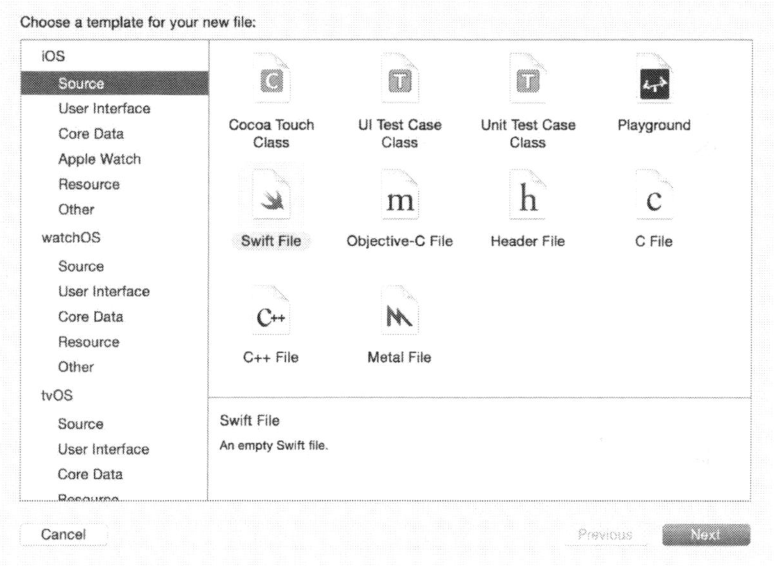

Figure 4.4 The New File dialog.

On the left side of the dialog is a panel divided into four categories—**iOS**, **watchOS**, **tvOS**, and **OS X**. Make sure you select subcategories below the **iOS** category when building iOS apps.

When you select a category in the panel on the left, the panel on the right displays the file templates associated with that category. For example, in Figure 4.4, the **Source** category is selected in the panel on the left, and the following file templates are displayed on the right:

- Cocoa Touch Class
- UI Test Case Class

- Unit Test Case Class
- Test Case Class
- Playground
- Swift File
- Objective-C File
- Header File
- C File
- C++ File
- Metal File

After selecting a file template, you click the **Next** button and an option panel appears prompting you for additional information based on the file template you have selected.

After filling out the options panel and clicking **Next**, you are prompted for a location in which to save the file. The default location is the project's root folder, but you can alternately choose to create a new folder to store the new file in.

Adding Existing Files

At times, rather than creating new files, you may want to add existing files to your project. You can add an existing file to the project in several different ways:

- Type **Option+Command+A.**
- From the Xcode menu, select **File** > **Add Files to "Your Project Name"....**
- Right-click a group in the Project Navigator and select **Add Files to "Your Project Name"...** from the shortcut menu.
- Click the plus (+) button in the Project Navigator toolbar and select **Add Files to "Your Project Name"...** from the shortcut menu.

All these options launch the Add File dialog (Figure 4.5). You use the controls at the top and left side of the dialog to navigate to the folder that contains the file(s) you want to add to the project.

Figure 4.5 The Add File dialog.

You can select a single file or multiple files to be added to the project. You can even select a folder and all its content and any subfolders will be added to the project.

- If the **Copy items if needed** option is selected, Xcode makes a copy of the item that you are adding to the project and stores it in the folder that you specify (if it's not already below the project's file structure). If this option is not selected, Xcode adds a reference to the file but does not make a copy of it.

- The **Added Folders** option allows you to specify how Xcode should handle folders that are added to the project. If **Create groups** is selected, when a folder is added to the project, a logical group is created for the folder in the Project Navigator, (not a *physical* folder). If **Create folder references** is selected, a physical folder is created below the project root folder when a folder is added to the project.

- The **Add to targets** option specifies that you want Xcode to add the selected files to the proper project build phase based on the kind of file(s) you are adding. For more information, check out the section **The Build Phases Pane** in *Chapter 14: Working With the Project Editor*.

When you are ready to add the file(s) to the project, just click the **Add** button and they will be added to the project and appear in the Project Navigator.

Deleting Files

If you no longer want a file in a project, you can delete it by right-clicking the file in the Project Navigator and selecting **Delete** from the shortcut menu (or you can just select the file and press the **Delete** button). When you do this, the Delete File dialog appears (Figure 4.6).

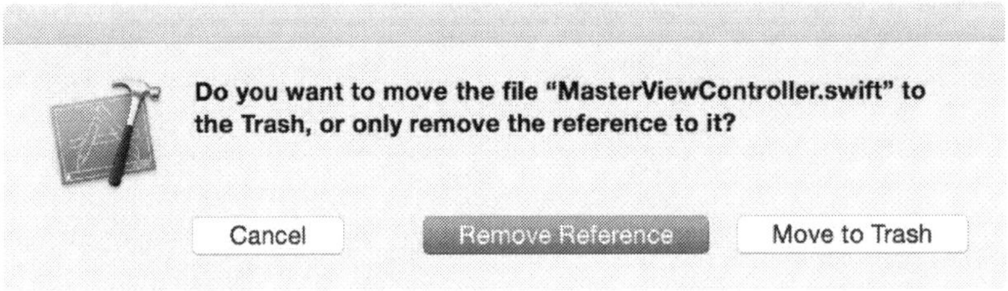

Figure 4.6 The Delete File dialog.

If you select **Cancel**, the file is not deleted. If you select **Remove Reference**, the file is removed from the project but not physically deleted from your computer. If you select **Move to Trash**, (you guessed it) the file is moved to the Trash.

The Symbol Navigator

The Symbol Navigator (Figure 4.7) provides an easy way to view the symbols (classes, protocols, functions, structs, enumerations, and so on) in your project. I like to use the Symbol Navigator to quickly view all the classes in a project and their hierarchy.

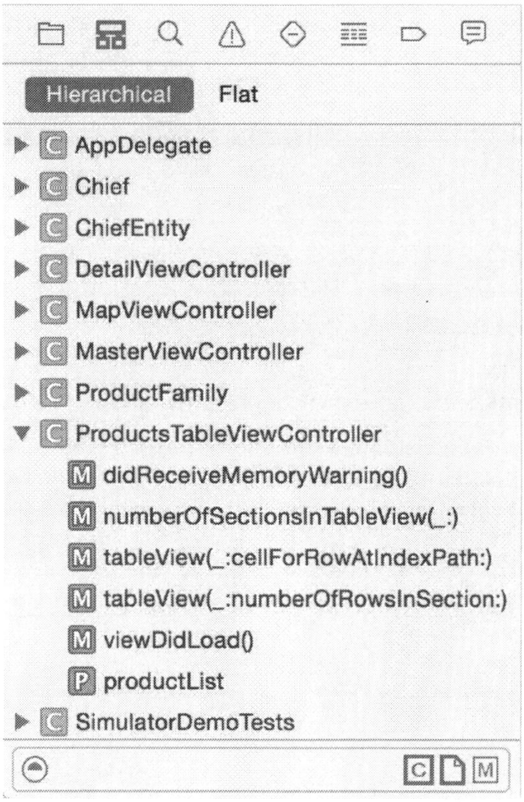

Figure 4.7 The Symbol Navigator.

You can view the Symbol Navigator by clicking the second button from the left in the Navigator toolbar or by pressing **Command+2**. You can also display the Symbol Navigator by selecting a symbol in a code file and then selecting **Navigate > Reveal in Symbol Navigator** from the Xcode menu.

By default, all the classes declared in your project are displayed in the Symbol Navigator in alphabetical order. At the top of the Symbol Navigator, you can select to display either a **Hierarchical** view of the classes, where *subclasses* are nested below *superclasses*, or a **Flat** view, where all classes are displayed in a list with no indication of class hierarchy (you won't see a difference in projects that have no subclass code files).

If you select a symbol in the Symbol Navigator list, it displays the associated code file in the Code Editor. If you expand a class node, it displays the class members, including methods, properties, and variables. If you select a class member, it jumps to the member declaration in the Code Editor.

At the bottom of the Symbol Navigator is a toolbar that allows you to restrict which symbols are displayed.

Here is a description of each control in the Symbol Navigator toolbar from left to right:

- The search box on the left side of the Symbol Navigator toolbar allows you to enter a filter string. Only the items containing the characters that you enter are displayed in the Symbol Navigator.
- **Show only class and protocol symbols (hide other global symbol types)** – Hides all symbols except classes and protocols. This is on by default.
- **Show only project-defined symbols** – Shows only the symbols defined in your project. This is on by default.
- **Show only containers (hide members)** – Hides the class properties, and methods, only showing the class itself. This filter is off by default.

Buttons that are toggled on are blue, and buttons toggled off are black.

The Find Navigator

The Find Navigator (Figure 4.8) allows you to search for (and optionally replace) text in your project files.

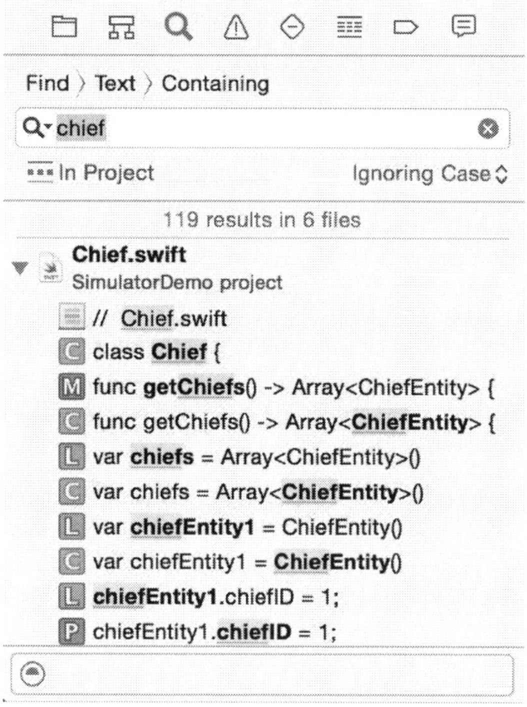

Figure 4.8 The Find Navigator.

You can view the Find Navigator either by clicking the third button from the left in the Navigator toolbar or by pressing **Command+3**.

The Find Navigator works in conjunction with Xcode's Find Bar (Figure 4.9).

Figure 4.9 Xcode's Find Bar.

The Find Bar is used to search for (and optionally replace) text in the code file that is currently open in the Code Editor. You can display the Find Bar by pressing **Command+F**. The Find Navigator goes further by allowing you to search all files in your project for text.

The Find Navigator and Find Bar are synchronized to work together. If you enter text in the Find Navigator search box, the text is automatically displayed in the Find Bar search box and vice versa.

When you press **Enter**, all files in your project are searched for the specified text string, and results are shown in the area below the search controls (Figure 4.8).

The total number of occurrences found is listed in the Find Navigator. Figure 4.8 shows 119 results in 6 files. The results are listed with each source code file as a root node and the occurrence of each string in that file below it. If you select a result in the list, that file is displayed in the Code Editor with the search text highlighted. You can narrow the find results further by entering text in the control at the bottom of the Find Navigator.

If you select **Replace** from the option control at the top left of the Find Navigator, it adds a **Replace** box and **Preview**, **Replace**, and **Replace All** buttons (Figure 4.10).

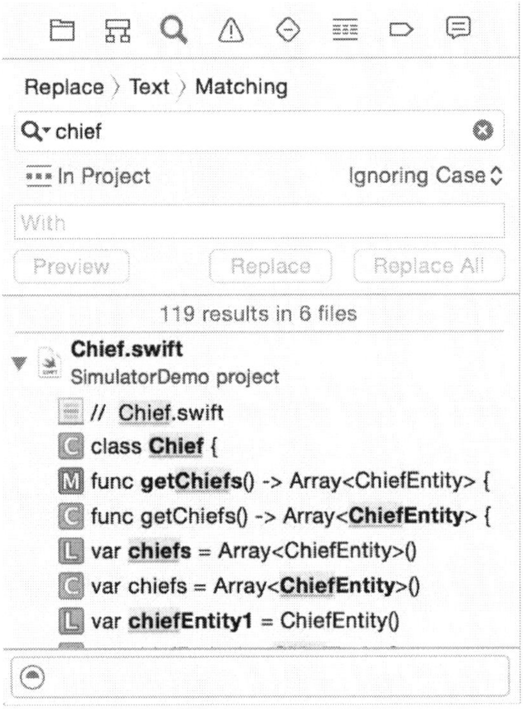

Figure 4.10 The Find Navigator's Replace option.

If you enter text in the **Replace** box and then click the **Preview** button, a preview window appears (Figure 4.11). On the left side is a list containing occurrences of the search text. Each occurrence has a check box that you can check/uncheck to specify which occurrences you want replaced with the new text.

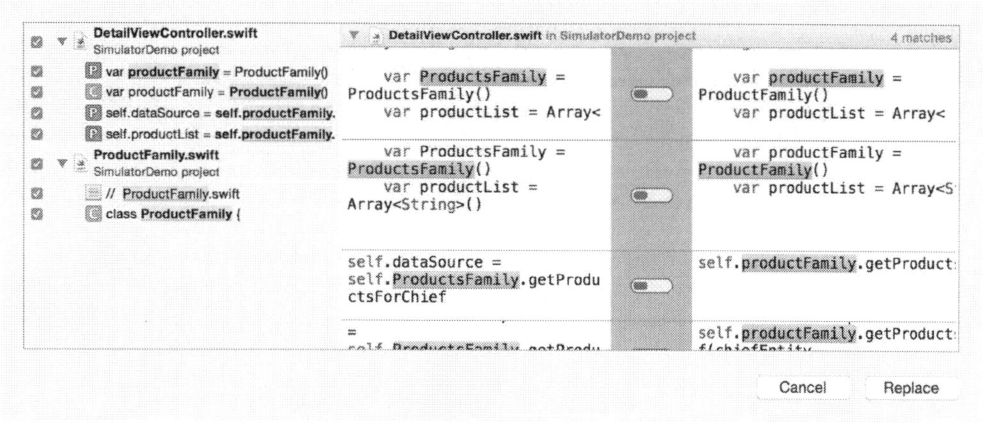

Figure 4.11 The Find Navigator Preview.

The preview dialog contains a panel that displays:

- How the code will look if you make the change (the code file on the left).
- What the current code looks like (the code file on the right).

A center area between the two code files contains a switch for each occurrence of the search string. The switches are synced with the check boxes in the list on the left and allow you to specify which occurrences you want replaced. When you have selected all the occurrences that you want replaced with the new text, click the **Replace** button.

Instead of using the Find Navigator's Preview window, you can select individual occurrences in the Find Navigator's results list (Figure 4.10) and then click the **Replace** button to change an individual occurrence. You can also click the **Replace All** button to replace all occurrences of the searched text with the specified replacement text.

The first time you replace text in your project, Xcode asks if you want to enable automatic snapshots (Figure 4.12). Automatic snapshots is an Xcode feature that automatically saves a copy of your project before you make a significant change, so you can easily roll back if you decide not to make the change after all.

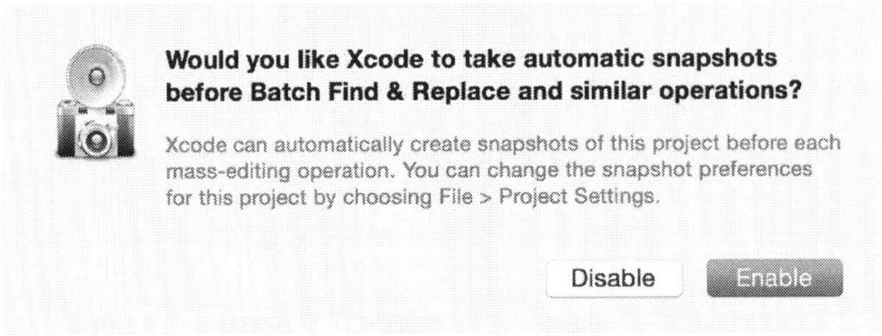

Figure 4.12 Xcode asks to enable automatic snapshots.

Xcode's **Find** menu offers a variety of options that make it easy to find the text that you are looking for in your projects or in the currently selected file.

The Issue Navigator

The Issue Navigator (Figure 4.13) displays details of compiler errors and warnings.

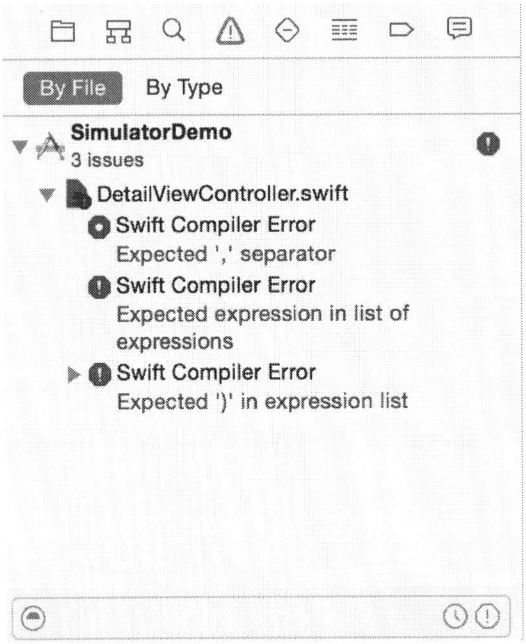

Figure 4.13 The Issue Navigator.

To view the Issue Navigator, either press the fourth button from the left in the Navigator toolbar (the button with the exclamation mark) or press **Command+4**. You can also display the Issue Navigator by clicking on an error or warning in the activity viewer in the center of the Xcode toolbar.

To view the source code associated with a particular issue, just click the warning or error in the Issue Navigator list. At the bottom of the Issue Navigator is a small toolbar that lets you filter issues in the list.

Here is a description of each control in the toolbar from left to right:

- The search box on the left side of the Issue Navigator toolbar allows you to see only the issues containing the characters that you enter.
- **Show only issues from the latest build** – Hides issues that were found after the last project build. This filter is off by default.
- **Show only errors** – Hides all warnings. This filter is off by default.

Note: If you prefer to not see errors and warnings as you type code, you can turn this behavior off in Xcode's preferences. To do this, select **Xcode > Preferences** from the menu, and then select the **General** tab. At the very top of the dialog, uncheck the **Show live issues** option

The Test Navigator

The Test Navigator (Figure 4.14) allows you to view and run the tests you have created for your project.

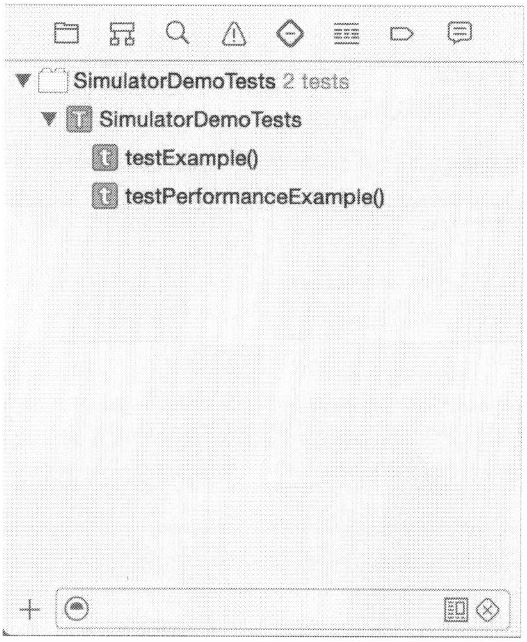

Figure 4.14 The Test Navigator.

To view the Test Navigator, you can press the fifth button from the left in the Navigator toolbar or press **Command +5**.

The Debug Navigator

When your app is running, the Debug Navigator (Figure 4.15) allows you to see the ***call stack*** of your app.

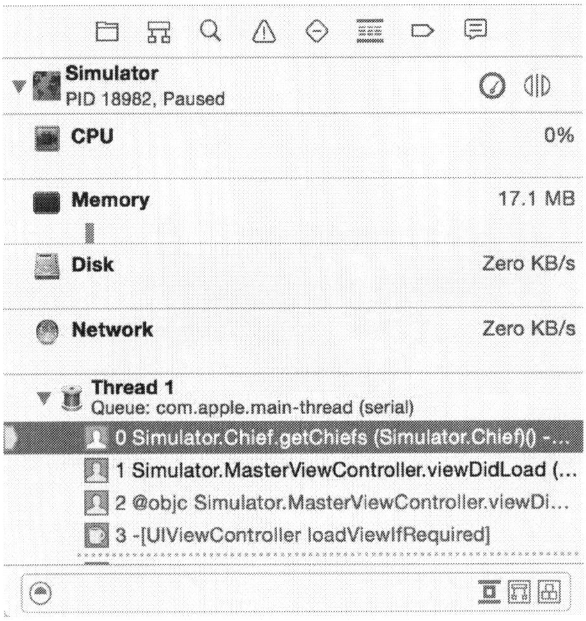

Figure 4.15 The Debug Navigator.

The call stack is a "breadcrumb trail" of how execution arrived at the current line of code (this line of code called that line of code which called this other line of code and so on). At times when you are debugging your app, this is a critical piece of information.

To view the Debug Navigator, press the sixth button from the left in the Navigator toolbar or press **Command+6**. The Debug Navigator is automatically displayed when you hit a breakpoint while running your app. At run time, when your app is stopped at a breakpoint, you can also display the Debug Navigator by selecting **Navigate > Reveal in Debug Navigator** from the Xcode menu.

In Figure 4.15, execution is stopped in the Chief object's **getChiefs** method. As you look down the list in the Debug Navigator, you can see previous methods in the call stack that caused execution to arrive at the **getChiefs** method. The blue icon with the white person icon indicates code found in your project. The purple icon with the cup indicates Cocoa Touch Framework methods and functions.

If you click an item representing code found in your project, it displays the line of code that caused execution to jump to the next item up in the list.

At the bottom of the Debug Navigator is a toolbar (Figure 4.15) containing controls that change the level of information displayed in the list.

Here is a description of each control in the Debug Navigator toolbar from left to right:

- The search box on the left side of the Debug Navigator toolbar allows you to see only the threads containing the characters that you enter.
- **Show only stack frames with debug symbols and between libraries** – Hides threads that may not be relevant to your code. This option is on by default.
- **Show only crashed threads and threads with debug symbols** – Choosing this option helps focus your debugging efforts by hiding calls that are far removed from your code. This is off by default.
- **Show only running blocks when in Queues view** – This option is off by default.

Memory and CPU Gauges

The Debug Navigator displays gauges that indicate **CPU** and **Memory** usage. If you click one of these gauges, Xcode displays a full report including a preliminary diagnosis of any problems (Figure 4.16). You can click the **Profile in Instruments** button to launch Instruments for a more detailed analysis.

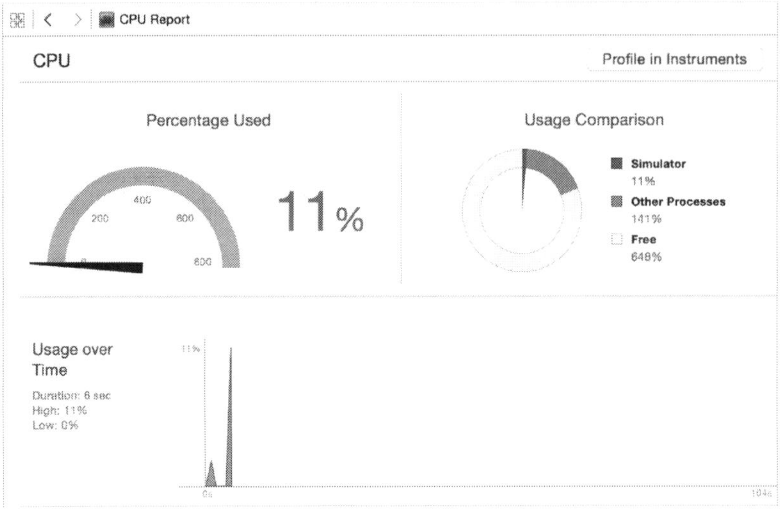

Figure 4.16 The Memory and CPU Usage report.

The Breakpoint Navigator

The Breakpoint Navigator (Figure 4.17) allows you to manage your app's breakpoints. You typically use the Breakpoint Navigator when you want to perform an action on all breakpoints in an app. You can view the Breakpoint Navigator by clicking the seventh button from the left in the Navigator toolbar or by pressing **Command+7**.

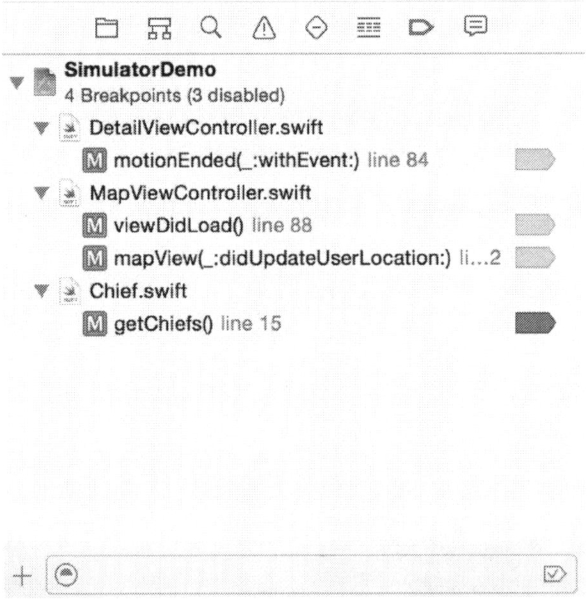

Figure 4.17 The Breakpoint Navigator.

The Breakpoint Navigator lists each source code file with its respective breakpoints nested below it. If you select a particular breakpoint in the list, the associated code file displayed in the Code Editor with the selected breakpoint in view.

You can use the Breakpoint Navigator to add, edit, or delete individual breakpoints. To do this, right-click a breakpoint and select an option from the shortcut menu.

If you want to act on all breakpoints in the list, right- click the project item at the top of the list and all actions in the shortcut menu are applied to all breakpoints.

At the bottom of the Breakpoint Navigator is a small toolbar that lets you add or filter breakpoints in the list.

Here is a description of each control in the Debug Navigator toolbar from left to right:

- **Create a breakpoint** – The plus (+) sign allows you to add a new breakpoint.
- The search box on the right of the Breakpoint Navigator toolbar allows you to see only the breakpoints containing the characters that you enter.
- **Show only enabled breakpoints** – This option hides all breakpoints that are disabled.

The Report Navigator

The Report Navigator (Figure 4.18) displays the reports that Xcode automatically generates for building, archiving, and source control tasks. You can view the Report Navigator by clicking the eighth button from the left (which is also the last button on the right) or by pressing **Command+8**.

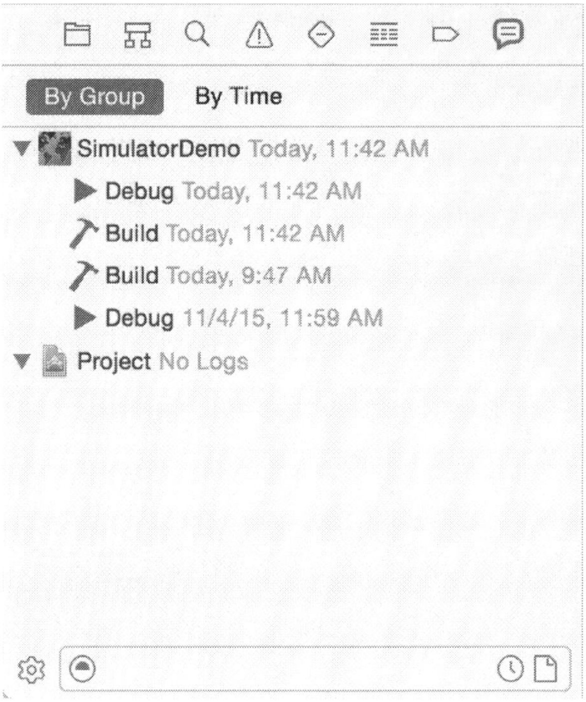

Figure 4.18 The Report Navigator.

Five types of logs can be viewed from the Report Navigator:

- **Build** – Generated when you build your project
- **Debug** – Generated when you run or debug your app
- **Source Control** – Generated when you perform a task associated with source control
- **Archive** – Generated when you archive your app, which is part of the process that prepares your app to be shared with others
- **Test** - Generated when you run unit tests on your app.

At the bottom of the Report Navigator are filter controls that allow you either to show only recent reports, local reports, or to show only reports containing the text that you enter.

Summary

- The Project Navigator is the navigator you use far more than any other. It lists all files associated with your project including source code files, storyboards for laying out the user interface, settings files, images, and frameworks.
- The Symbol Navigator provides an easy way to view the symbols (classes, protocols, functions, structs, enumerations, and so on) in your project.
- You can use the Symbol Navigator to quickly view all the classes in a project and their hierarchy.
- The Find Navigator allows you to search for (and optionally replace) text in your project files.
- The Find Navigator works in conjunction with Xcode's Find Bar.
- The Issue Navigator allows you to view details of compiler errors and warnings.
- The Test Navigator allows you to manage and run unit tests you have created for your app.
- When your app is running, the Debug Navigator allows you to see the call stack of your app.
- The *call stack* is a "breadcrumb trail" of how execution arrived at the current line of code (this line of code called that line of code which called this other line of code and so on).
- The Debug Navigator contains gauges showing CPU and memory usage.
- The Breakpoint Navigator allows you to manage your app's breakpoints. You typically use the Breakpoint Navigator when you want to perform an action on all breakpoints in an app.
- The Report Navigator allows you to view the logs that Xcode automatically generates for building, archiving, testing, and source control tasks.

Chapter 5: The Inspectors

In Chapter 3, you were given a high-level overview of Xcode's Inspector tools. In this chapter, we'll take a closer look at each and learn best practices for making the most of these tools in your daily app development.

Sections in This Chapter

Here is a list of the inspector tools found at the top of the Utilities view on the right side of the Xcode window along with the keystrokes you can use to select each inspector:

- File Inspector (Option+Command+1)
- Quick Help Inspector (Option+Command+2)
- Identity Inspector (Option+Command+3)
- Attributes Inspector (Option+Command+4)
- Size Inspector (Option+Command+5)
- Connections Inspector (Option+Command+6)

You can also select each inspector by clicking the corresponding button in the toolbar at the top of the Inspector panel (Figure 5.1). You must have a UI file such as a storyboard selected to see all six buttons.

Figure 5.1 The Inspector toolbar.

The following sections discuss each inspector in detail.

The File Inspector

The File Inspector (Figure 5.2) provides information such as name, file type, location, version, localization, and source control for the file currently selected in the Project Navigator. I often use the File Inspector to find out where a particular project or file is located. You can view the File Inspector by clicking the first button on the left in the Inspector pane.

Figure 5.2 The File Inspector.

Identity and Type

The **Identity and Type** section of the File Inspector displays the name, type, and location of the selected file.

- **Name** – Contains the name of the selected project file.
- **Type** - Specifies the type of file selected. You rarely need to change this value.
- **Location** - This list box allows you to view and change the location of each file. The choices are:
    - **Absolute Path** - This is a good choice for files that are in a directory on a network shared by multiple developers. However, if you choose this option and then move the file at a later date, Xcode will not be able to find it. If this happens, you can click the small folder icon to the

right of this setting and select the file in its new location.

  - **Relative to Group** - This is the default option, and for good reason. With the file location set to this value, you can move the project to another directory, and the reference to the file will not be broken. The path of the file is set relative to the group in which it is contained.

  - **Relative to Project** - This option is similar to the default **Relative to Group** setting, except the file's path is relative to the root project folder.

  - **Relative to Developer Directory** - The file path is relative to the folder where Xcode is installed.

  - **Relative to Build Products** - The file path is relative to the folder in which Xcode saves the project's build products such as the application bundle.

  - **Relative to SDK** - The file path is relative to the folder in which the iOS SDK is stored. All Cocoa Touch frameworks in your project have their location set to this value.

- **Full Path** - The full path to the selected file is displayed here. If you click the small circular arrow to the right of this setting, it launches a Finder window that opens to the folder containing the selected file.

Interface Builder Document

This section is only visible when a UI file such as a storyboard is selected.

- **Opens in** - This setting indicates the oldest version of Interface Builder that can open the UI document. For new projects in Xcode 7, this setting defaults to Xcode 7. This setting is important to development teams where some developers are using older versions of Xcode.

- **Builds for** - This setting specifies the version of iOS you are targeting for your app. By default, Xcode targets the latest version of iOS. However, if your app does not use the features in the latest version of iOS, you can change this setting to target an older iOS version. This allows your app to have a broader audience since not all users update to the latest version of iOS as soon as it is released.

- **View as** - This feature allows you to view your UI in different versions of iOS. The current options are **iOS 7.0 and Later**, and **iOS 6.1 and Earlier**.

- **Use Autolayout** - This setting specifies whether you want to use Xcode's Auto Layout feature. It's selected by default when you create a new UI file such as a storyboard. Selecting this setting locks you into deploying your app for iOS 6 or newer since this feature is not supported in older versions of iOS. For more information, check out *Chapter 8: Laying Out the User Interface.*

- **Use Size Classes** - This setting allows a storyboard to work with all available screen sizes on any iOS device. For more information, check out *Chapter 8: Laying Out the User Interface.*

- **Global Tint** - This option allows you to specify a tint color for your primary user interface elements such as navigation bar titles and buttons as well as toolbar buttons. The default is blue.

Localization

This section lists the different languages for which the selected file is *localized.*

Target Membership

This section specifies the target(s) in which the file is included. For more information, see *Chapter 14: Working With the Project Editor* in the section **Understanding Products and Targets**.

Source Control

This section provides information regarding source control status of the selected file. You will learn more about source control later in this book series.

The Quick Help Inspector

The Quick Help Inspector (Figure 5.3) is a handy tool when you are first learning iOS app development.

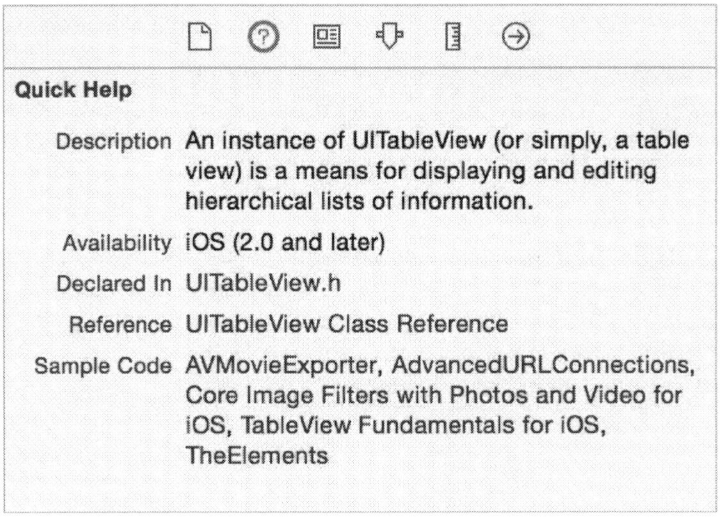

Figure 5.3 The Quick Help Inspector.

It provides concise documentation for the object that you currently have selected in the editor pane. This can be a UI control or even a keyword in a source code file. You can view the Quick Help Inspector by clicking the second button from the left in the Inspector toolbar.

Another nice feature is the **Sample Code** section at the bottom of the pane where you can see sample code for the object that you have selected.

- **Description** - Provides a brief description of the selected object.
- **Availability** - Specifies the versions of iOS in which the selected object is available.
- **Declared In** - Specifies the **class header file** in which the class of which the object is an *instance* has been declared.
- **Reference** - Provides a link to the class reference documentation. If you click the link, the reference documentation is displayed in Xcode's Organizer window.
- **Guides** - Provides links to any programming guides that contain information about the selected object. If you click the link, the programming guide is displayed in Xcode's Organizer window.

- **Samples** - Provides links to any code samples that demonstrate how the selected object can be used. If you click the link, the sample documentation is displayed in the Documentation Viewer.

The Identity Inspector

The Identity Inspector (Figure 5.4) is most often used to view and set the class of an object.

Figure 5.4 The Identity Inspector.

This inspector is only active when you select a UI object in the Xcode design surface. You can view the Identity Inspector by clicking the third button from the left in the Inspector toolbar.

The different sections of the Identity Inspector are outlined below. You will most often use the **Custom Class** section of this inspector, but the other sections have some interesting features.

- **Custom Class** - Displays the **Class** and **Module** of the selected UI object. There are times when you may want to change this class as you will see later in this book series.

- **Identity** - The **Restoration ID** setting is part of the "state preservation and restoration" feature that will be covered later on in this book series.

- **User Defined Runtime Attributes** - These attributes are intended for use with your custom classes. It allows you to specify a property and an initial value that gets set at run time when the UI is first loaded. This saves you from writing a few lines of code, but I think it's best to write code so it's obvious to other developers how initial values get set in your project.

- **Document** - This section has settings that allow you to more easily identify the selected UI object.

    - **Label** - Provides a way for you to specify a friendly name for a UI object that makes it easier to identify in the Document Outline view.

    - **Object ID** - A unique ID assigned by Xcode that you can't change or access from code (I'm not sure why it's even visible).

    - **Lock** - This setting allows you to lock or unlock an individual control. The default value is **Inherited - (Nothing)**, which indicates that the object inherits its setting from the UI document (such as the storyboard). The possible values are **Nothing**, **All Properties**, **Localizable Properties**, and **Non-localizable Properties**.

Figure 5.5 shows how a locked text field (the one on the bottom) looks when you select it in the design surface. The resizing handles on the sides of the text field are grayed out.

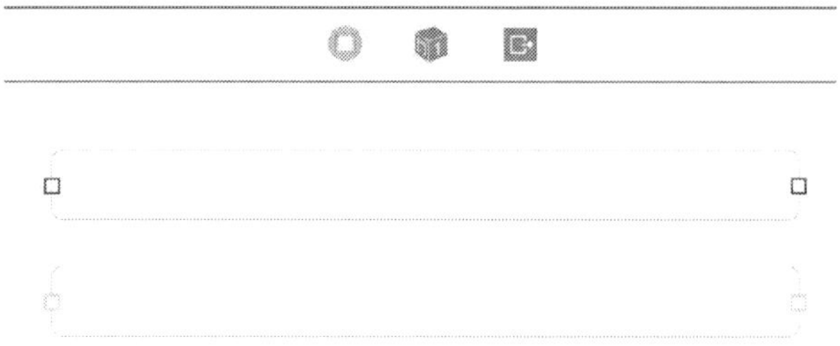

Figure 5.5 The bottom text field is locked.

- **Notes** - The controls in this section allow you to enter a note associated with a particular UI object.

  You can set the note's justification, font color, background color, font size, spacing, hyphenation, and so on. You must type the text of the note first and then select the text in order to apply these different text attributes.

The Attributes Inspector

The Attributes Inspector (Figure 5.6) is available when you select a UI object in the Xcode design surface. You use the Attributes Inspector frequently when laying out your app's user interface. You can view the Attributes Inspector by clicking the fourth button from the left in the Inspector toolbar.

The three main sections displayed in the Attributes Inspector differ depending on the UI control selected in the design surface.

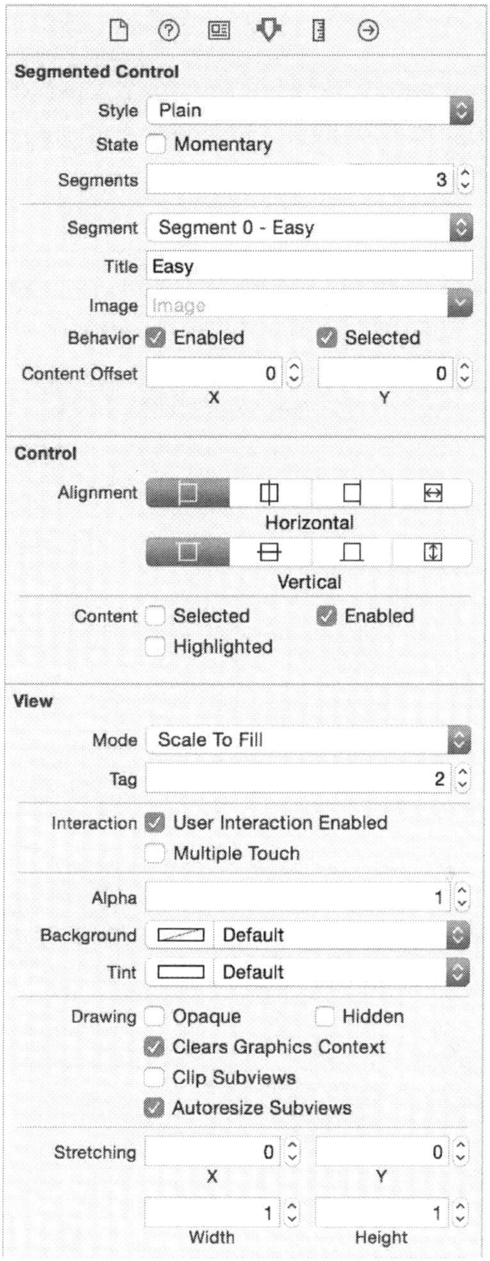

Figure 5.6 The Attributes Inspector.

UI Object-Specific Section

The very first section in the Attributes Inspector changes depending on the type of UI object that you have selected. In Figure 5.6, you can tell that a segmented control has been selected because the first section says **Segmented Control**.

Control Section

The **Control** section only appears when you have selected a UI control that has internal content that can be aligned (such as buttons, text boxes, and switches).

The **Enabled** setting allows you to specify if a control is enabled for touch events. You may want to disable controls that you don't want the user to access until another action has been performed. All UI objects that are based on **UIControl** have **Selected** and **Highlighted** properties, which do something different (or nothing at all) with different controls.

View Section

The **View** section allows you to define how a UI object looks and how the user interacts with it.

- The **Mode** setting typically isn't important unless you are working with a control such as an image view that has content of varying sizes. Unless the image that you are displaying is the exact same size as the image view (highly unlikely), you should choose one of the following **Mode** settings to suit your needs.

Figure 5.7 Scale to Fill, Aspect Fit, and Aspect Fill modes (from left to right).

  - **Scale To Fill** scales an image's width and height to fill the image view *frame*. The image on the left in Figure 5.7 (as seen in the **SpringsStrutsDemo** project) is set to **Scale To Fill**, so you see the entire original image.

  - **Aspect Fit** scales an image while keeping its aspect ratio (the ratio between height and width) until the largest dimension of the image (height or width) is equal to the height or width of the image view. This leaves empty space either above and below or right and left of the image. The original image in the center of Figure 5.7 has a greater width, so there is extra space above and below it.

- o **Aspect Fill** scales an image while keeping its aspect ratio until the smallest dimension (height or width) is equal to the height or width of the image view. This causes part of the image to be trimmed off. The image on the right in Figure 5.7 has a smaller height, so the left and right of the image are trimmed off.
- o **Redraw** is an advanced feature that allows you to customize how your content scales.
- o The **Center**, **Top**, **Bottom**, **Left**, **Right**, **Top Left**, **Top Right**, **Bottom Left**, and **Bottom Right** settings all pin the image to the specified area of the image view. Any part of the image that doesn't fit is cropped off.

- The **Tag** setting is a useful way to assign an integer identifier to a UI object so you can reference it from code in the view controller without having to create a property. You can use the **viewWithTag:** method of the **UIView** class to get a reference to the control at run time. For example, if you set a UI object's **Tag** to **3**, you can get a reference to that object at run time using this code:

```
let textField = self.viewWithTag(3)
    as UITextField
```

- **User Interaction Enabled** is a bit different from the **Enabled** setting under the **Control** section. Unchecking **User Interaction Enabled** doesn't affect the appearance of the UI object (as can the **Enabled** setting), it simply prevents a user from interacting with the control.
- **Multiple Touch** specifies whether your UI object responds to a single touch (a single finger touching the object) or multiple touches. The default is "single touch," but you can change this setting if you want to create some custom code to handle multiple touches.

- The **Alpha** and **Background** color settings go hand in hand. The **Alpha** setting specifies the transparency of a color, where **0** is transparent and **1** is opaque. In Figure 5.8, the view on the left has its background color set to orange and its **Alpha** to **1** (opaque). The view on the right also has its background color set to orange, but the **Alpha** value is set to **.5**, making it semi-transparent.

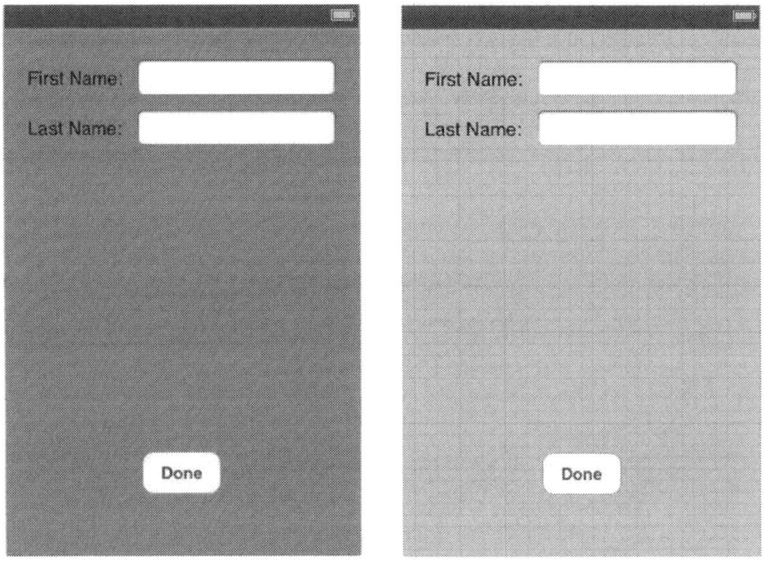

*Figure 5.8 The **Alpha** setting specifies a color's transparency.*

- **Tint** specifies the color of key user interface elements such as navigation buttons and toolbar buttons. The default is blue.

- **Drawing** is the next section in the Attributes Inspector. It contains the following settings:

  - **Opaque** – When selected, it specifies that nothing behind the UI object is visible. Selecting this option improves performance at run time because it indicates there is no content in the underlying view that needs to be displayed. The **Alpha** setting, discussed earlier, works with this setting to make sure the entire control is opaque.

  - **Hidden** – When selected, it completely hides the UI object at run time. You can use this setting to selectively show and hide controls.

  - **Clears Graphics Context** – This check box is checked by default and should rarely be unchecked. If it is unchecked, the area covered by the UI object is drawn in transparent black before the control itself is drawn—usually an unnecessary step.

  - **Clip Subviews** – When this setting is on (it's on by default), any views contained within the selected object are clipped, or cropped to fit within the bounds of the parent object. This is a setting that you don't need to worry about very often.

  - **Autoresize Subviews** – When this setting is on (it's on by default), any views contained within the selected object are resized when the object is resized.

- **Stretching** is the final section in the Attributes Inspector. The **X**, **Y**, **Width**, and **Height** settings allow you to specify which portion of the control should be stretched when the UI object is resized. This is an advanced setting that you don't normally need to change.

That covers the basics of the Attributes Inspector. You will be learning more about it in *Chapter 8: Laying Out the User Interface*.

The Size Inspector

The Size Inspector (Figure 5.9) is available when you select a UI object in the Xcode design surface. It allows you to specify the position and size of UI objects, including how the size and position change as the orientation or size of the view changes. You can view the Size Inspector by clicking the fifth button from the left in the Inspector toolbar. You will learn about these settings later, but first, you will learn about the UI layout options.

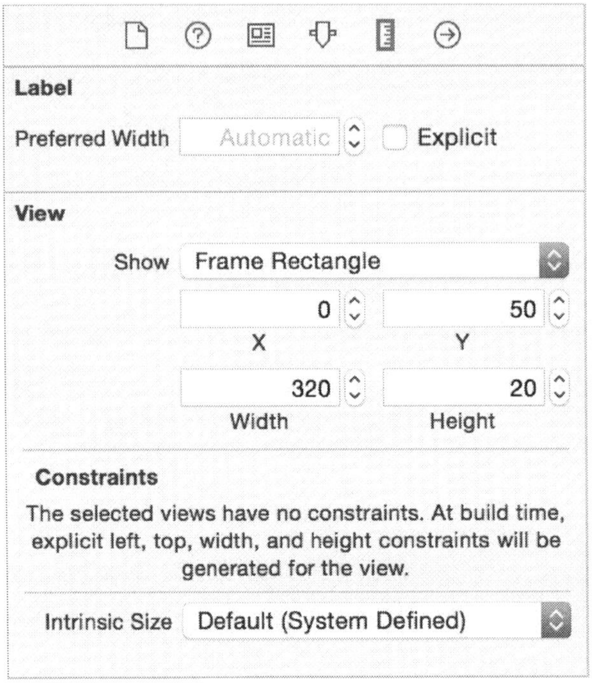

Figure 5.9 The Size Inspector.

The size and position settings of your UI control are important for two reasons:

1. To adapt to the changing size of the parent view when the user rotates the iOS device.

2. To adapt to the size of different iOS devices such as the iPhone 4, iPhone 5, iPhone 6, iPhone 6 Plus, iPad, the iPad mini, and whatever new device size Apple produces in the future.

User-Interface Layout Options

There are two ways you can specify the size and position of UI controls in your views. The two choices are:

1. Springs and Struts

2. Auto Layout

The Size Inspector looks and behaves very differently depending on which one of these options you choose.

Earlier in this chapter, under the section **The File Inspector**, you were introduced to the **Use Auto Layout** setting. If this check box is unselected, the storyboard uses the older springs and struts technology for laying out the user interface. If it's selected, the storyboard uses the newer Auto Layout approach.

We'll be diving into both of these options in *Chapter 8: Laying Out the User Interface*, but let's take a quick look.

Springs and Struts

The classic springs and struts approach to laying out your UI works well for very simple user interfaces.

As shown in the **Autosizing** section of the Size Inspector in the bottom-left corner of Figure 5.10, the inner square represents the UI control that is currently selected in the design surface. The outer square represents the view that contains the UI control. The "I" bars between these two squares are known as "struts." You can select struts to pin the UI control to one or more sides of the parent view.

The arrows inside the inner rectangle are known as "springs." You can select these arrows to specify if you want the control's width and height to resize as the parent view changes size.

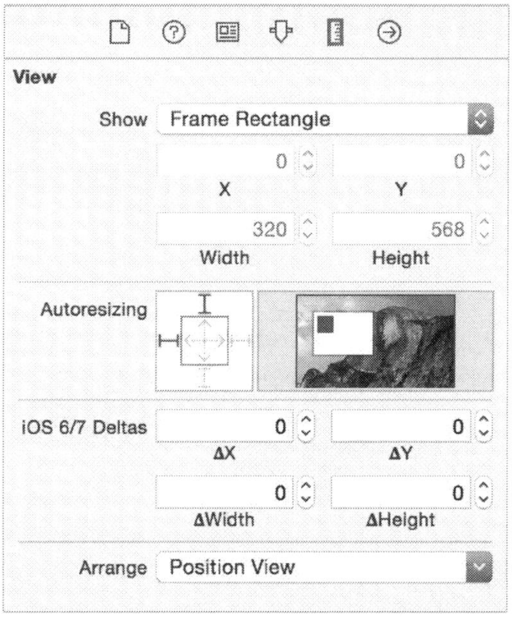

Figure 5.10 The springs and struts layout controls.

The springs and struts approach works fine for very simple user interfaces that mostly include table views.

The downside of springs and struts is that it is pretty limited in what it can do. You need to write code to size and position controls in cases that are not easily handled by the Size Inspector. If you use springs and struts, you can't use Xcode's newer Size classes that make it easy to create a user interface for your app that looks great on all iOS devices.

Auto Layout

In contrast with the hard-coded nature of springs and struts, the newer Auto Layout feature is a *descriptive* layout system.

Auto Layout supports far more complex UI layouts, so you rarely need to write code to ensure your UI positions and resizes properly as the size of the screen changes. It is a *complete* replacement for the classic springs and struts.

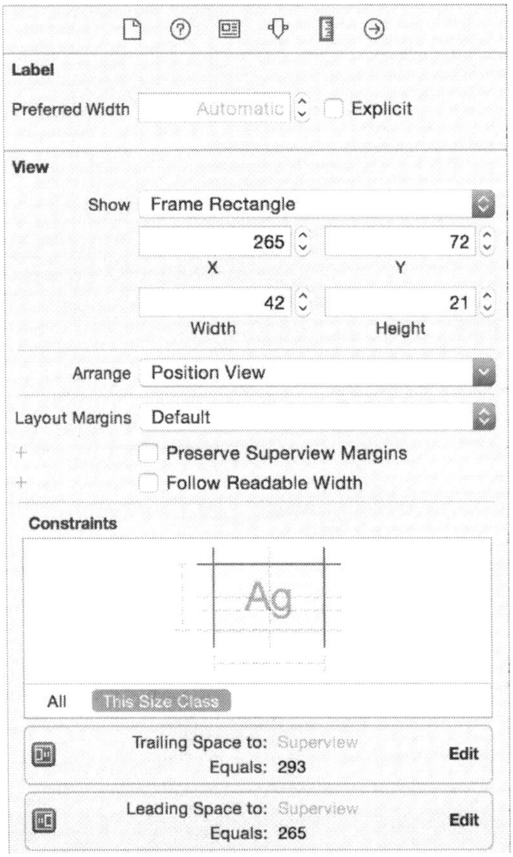

Figure 5.11 Auto Layout settings in the Size Inspector

As shown in Figure 5.11, *with* Auto Layout, you use constraints to specify the alignment, centering, spacing, width, and height of a UI control. When you have Auto Layout turned on, you will see the **Content Hugging Priority**, **Content Compression Resistance Priority** and **Constraints** sections in the Size Inspector. You will learn how to use all these settings in *Chapter 8: Laying Out the User Interface.*

The Connections Inspector

The Connections Inspector (Figure 5.12) is available when you select a UI object in the Xcode design surface. It shows you all the connections to and from the selected object and allows you to connect UI controls to code in the associated view controller. You can view the Connections Inspector by clicking the button on the far right in the Inspector toolbar.

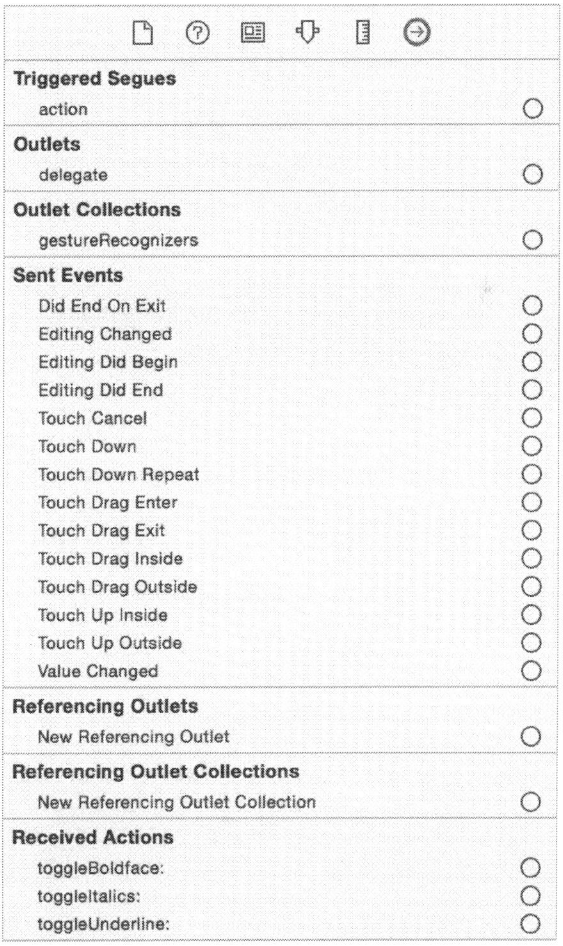

Figure 5.12 The Connections Inspector.

The main sections in the Connections Inspector are:

- Triggered Segues
- Outlets
- Outlet Collections
- Sent Events
- Referencing Outlets
- Referencing Outlet Collections
- Received Actions

Figure 5.12 shows all the available sections when a text field is selected in the design surface. Depending on the type of UI object selected in the design surface, you may see fewer sections.

Triggered Segues

The **Triggered Segues** section allows you to view and manage *segue* connections between the selected object and another scene.

As you learned in *Book 1: Diving Into iOS*, one of the signature features of iOS is the way transitions are made from one scene to another. Typically, when the user touches a UI object, the current view is moved out of the way using animations such as sliding, curling, and dissolving. A segue allows you to define the control that fires that transition, the type of transition, and the scene that is moved into place and becomes the current view.

When you create a segue by **Control+Dragging** from a UI control to another scene on the storyboard, the segue shows up in this section. For example, Figure 5.13 shows a triggered segue for a table view cell selected in the design surface. This segue is **push** and connects the row to a **Table View Controller**.

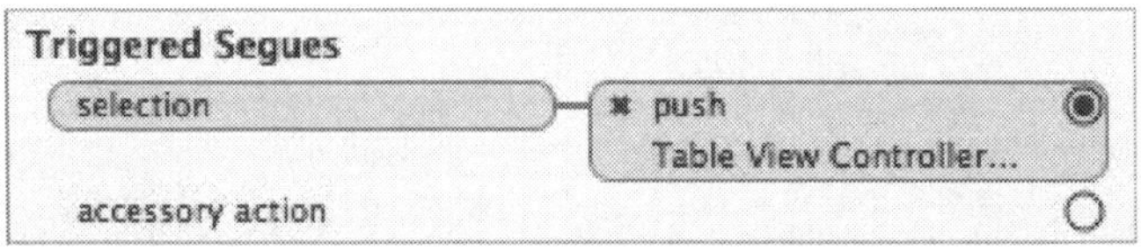

Figure 5.13 A triggered segue in the Connections Inspector.

If you hover your mouse pointer over the rounded rectangle on the right side of Figure 5.13, it highlights the associated view controller in the storyboard.

You can delete the segue by clicking the small **x** in the **push** rectangle on the right. Although you *can* create a segue by **Click+Dragging** from the connection well (the small circle) on the right to a scene on the storyboard, it's much easier to just **Click+Drag** from the control itself in the design surface.

Outlets and Outlet Collections

An ***outlet*** is a special property that holds a reference to a user-interface object.

The **Outlets** section of the Connections Inspector contains one or more built-in outlets for the user- interface control that is currently selected in the design surface. For example, if you select a Table View object, the **Outlets** section contains **dataSource** and **delegate** outlets. If you select a navigation bar in the design surface, you will see the built-in outlet properties shown in Figure 5.14.

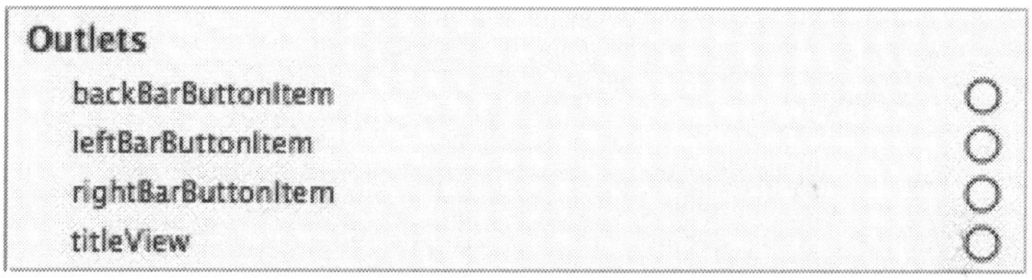

Figure 5.14 Navigation Bar outlets.

To connect a UI object to an outlet, just **Click+Drag** from the outlet connection well to the outlet. There are some outlets you can't connect in this way. For example, the **leftBarButtonItem** and **rightBarButtonItem** outlets of the navigation bar can only be connected by dragging and dropping a **Bar Button Item** on the left or right side of the navigation bar.

The **Outlet Collections** section of the Connections Inspector only appears if you have selected a user- interface object that the user can tap, pinch, swipe, or interact with by using one of the standard iOS gestures. When you have a user-interface object selected, a **gestureRecognizers** outlet collection is displayed in this section.

You will learn more about connecting outlets in *Chapter 9: Creating Connections.*

Sent Events

Sent Events is the next section in the Connections Inspector. To understand the settings in this section, you first need to learn the basics of events in iOS.

In the same way that objects have properties and methods, they can also have ***events***. In this context, an event is an action that occurs in a control that is usually initiated by the user. For example, there are events related to a user touching a control (Touch Down, Touch Up Inside), changing its value (Value Changed), as well as other editing-related events (Editing Did Begin, Editing Did End).

When an event occurs on an object, it can *send* a notification *message* to one or more *target* objects (thus the term *sent events*). You can use the Connections Inspector to register a *target* object as well as an ***action*** to be performed by that object. Typically, your view controller is the target object, and a method on the view controller, an *action method*, is designated as the action to be performed.

For example, in the conceptual image shown in Figure 5.15, the button on the left is the event *sender*. It has a **Touch Up Inside** event. The View Controller on the right is registered as a *target* for this event, and the **getFahrenheit** method is specified as the action. At run time, when a **Touch Up Inside** event occurs on the button (triggered by a user lifting their finger off the button), the button calls the **getFahrenheit** method on the view controller target object.

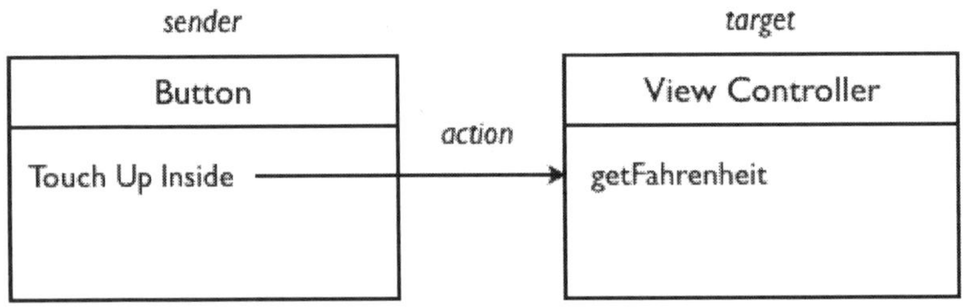

Figure 5.15 ***Button*** *is the sender,* ***View Controller*** *is the target, and* ***getFahrenheit*** *is the action.*

You are going to learn much more about events in *Chapter 9: Creating Connections.*

Referencing Outlets and Referencing Outlet Collections

The **Referencing Outlets** and **Referencing Outlet Collections** sections of the Connections Inspector are similar to the **Outlet** and **Outlet Collections** sections discussed earlier except that the “referencing” sections are used to create and connect your own custom outlets rather than built-in outlets.

By default, when you add a UI object to a scene at design time, there is no way to reference it from the associated view controller code file because a property is not automatically created to reference it. This approach makes your view controller lighter (take up less space in memory) because properties are not unnecessarily added for UI objects that you never reference from the code file.

However, when you do need to reference a UI object from the associated view controller code file, you need to create an outlet.

Xcode also allows you to reference more than one UI object from a single outlet by means of outlet collections.

Both outlets and outlet collections are covered in detail in *Chapter 9: Creating Connections.*

Received Actions

The **Received Actions** section of the Connections Inspector contains a list of built-in actions that can be executed by the selected UI object. Only a few UI objects have received actions (text fields, text views, and web views). Figure 5.16 shows the **Received Actions** for a text field object.

*Figure 5.16 A text view object’s **Received Actions**.*

To connect a UI object to a received action, just click in the connection well and drag down to the UI control. In Figure 5.17, a connection is being made between the text view’s **selectAll** received action and the **Select All** button.

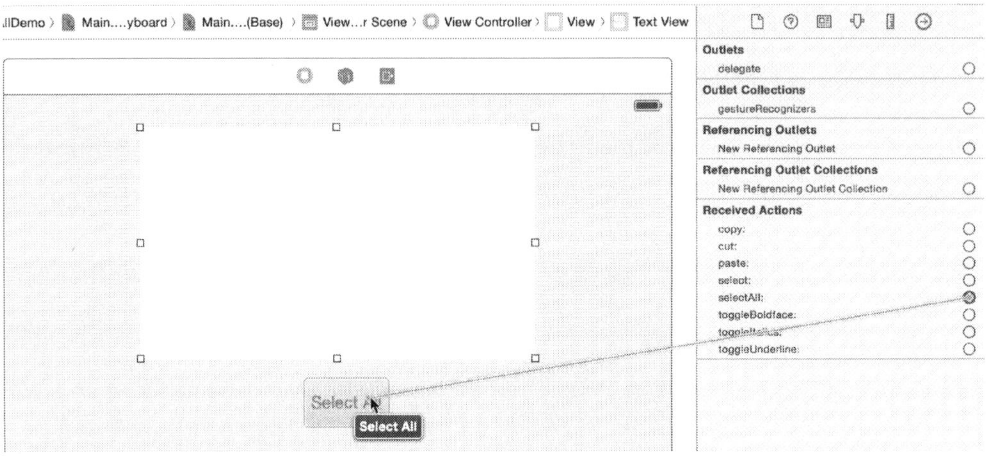

Figure 5.17 Connecting a received action to a UI object

When you let go of your mouse, a popup menu appears allowing you to select the object event that triggers the action. In Figure 5.18, the **Touch Up Inside** event of the button is selected.

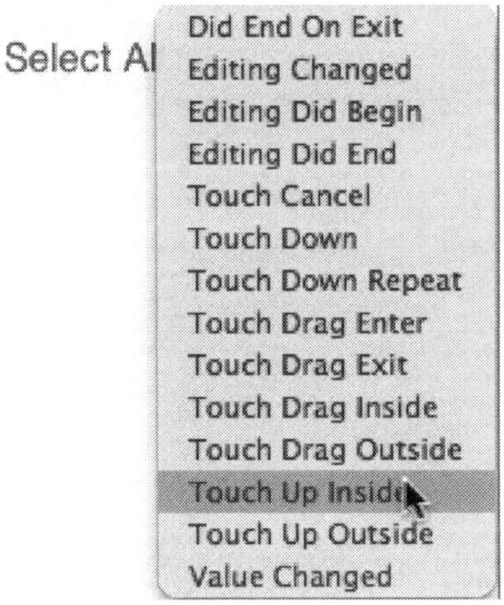

Figure 5.18 Select an event to trigger the action.

With this connection between the text view's **selectAll** received action and the button's **Touch Up Inside** event, when the user taps and lifts their finger off the button at run time, the text view's **selectAll** action is executed and all the text in the text view is selected.

You will learn much more about connecting controls to events in *Chapter 9: Creating Connections.*

Summary

- The File Inspector provides information such as name, file type, location, version, localization, and source control for the file currently selected in the Project Navigator.

- The Quick Help Inspector provides concise documentation for the object that you currently have selected in the editor pane. This can be a UI control or even a keyword in a source code file.

- The Identity Inspector is most often used to view and set the class of an object.

- You use the Attributes Inspector frequently when laying out your app's user interface. It's only visible when you have a UI control selected in the design surface. It allows you to view and set a variety of attributes of the selected object.

- The Size Inspector allows you to specify the position and size of UI objects, including how the size and position change as the orientation or size of the screen changes.

- There are two ways you can specify the size and position of UI controls in your views. The two choices are:

    1. Springs and Struts - This approach is good for very simple user interfaces and works with all versions of iOS. The downside is that you need to write code to size and position controls in cases that are not easily handled by the Size Inspector.

    2. Auto Layout - The newer Auto Layout is a *descriptive* layout system. It supports far more complex UI layouts, so you rarely need to write code reposition and resize UI controls.

- The Connections Inspector shows you all of the connections to and from the selected object and allows you to connect UI controls to code in the associated view controller.

- An *outlet* is a special property that holds a reference to a UI object.

- In the same way that objects have properties and methods, they can also have a set of *events*. In this context, an event is an action that occurs in a control, and is usually initiated by the user.

Chapter 6: The Libraries

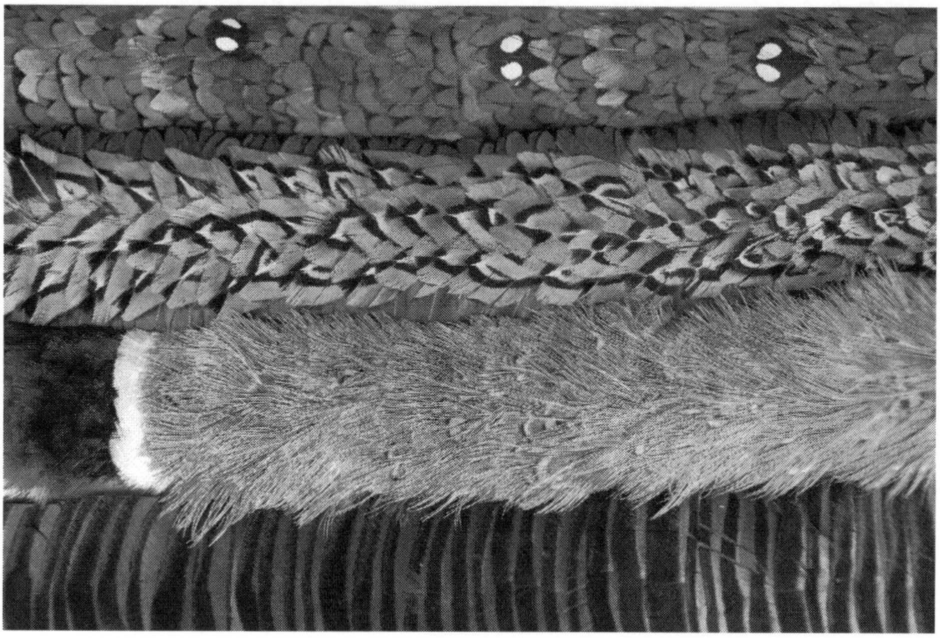

As we have worked our way around the Xcode tool set, we will now take a look at the Library tools. Here you will find extremely useful information that shows you how to increase your productivity with code snippets as well as detailed information on the user-interface objects found in the Object Library.

Sections in This Chapter

1. *Getting to Know Your Libraries*
2. *The File Template Library*
3. *The Code Snippet Library*
4. *The Object Library*
5. *The Media Library*
6. *Summary*

Getting to Know Your Libraries

If you have skipped some of the other chapters to get to "the good stuff," I don't recommend skipping this one. In particular, I recommend looking closely at the Code Snippet Library as well as the Object Library because they contain information that will provide a great boost to your app development.

The Library pane, located at the bottom of the Utilities View on the right side of the Xcode window, contains four different libraries:

- File Template Library
- Code Snippet Library
- Object Library
- Media Library

I haven't listed the keystrokes you can use to display each library, because they involve a ridiculous 4-key combination (for example, **Control+Option+Command +1**). It's much easier to just click the corresponding button in the Library toolbar (Figure 6.1).

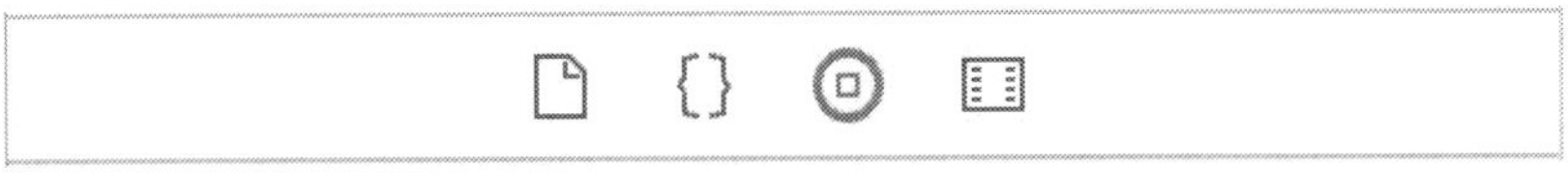

Figure 6.1 The Library Toolbar.

At the bottom left of all library panes is a button that toggles between showing items either as an icon with an associated description or as icons with no description (Figure 6.2).

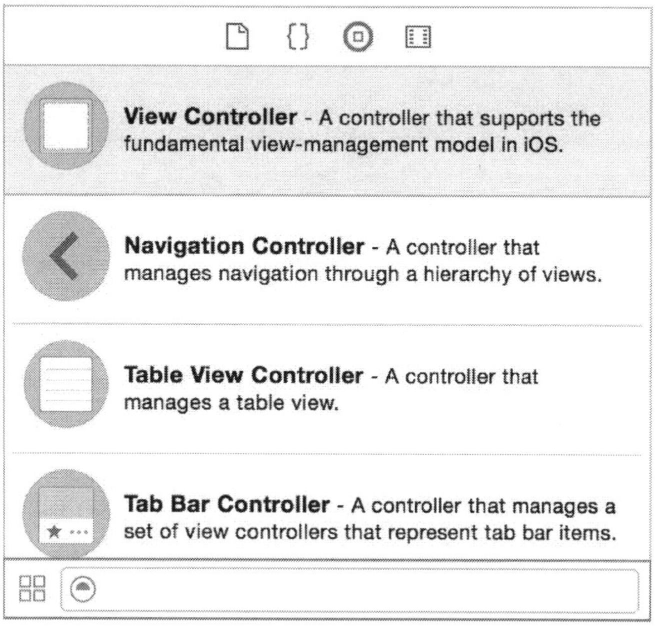

Figure 6.2 The Library Icon/List toggle buttons & search bar.

The filter control at the bottom of all library panes (Figure 6.2) hides all items that do not have the specified filter text. In the File Template Library and Code Snippet Library, the filter acts on the item name and descriptions. In the Object Library, the filter acts on the name of the item, not its description. Note that the filter control doesn't clear when changing to a different library (although it should), so make sure you clear it when moving to another library pane.

The File Template Library

The File Template Library (Figure 6.3) allows you to add new files to your project. I don't recommend using it, so if you want to skip this section, feel free! If you want to know more, read on.

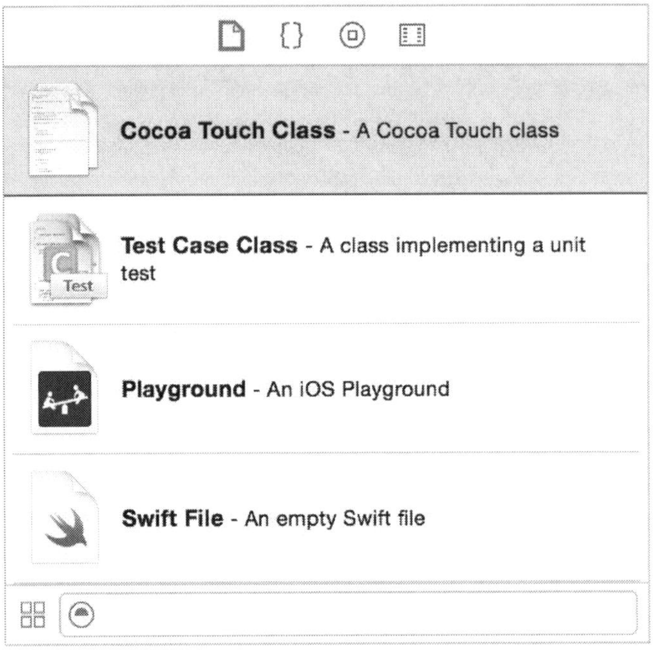

Figure 6.3 The File Template Library.

You can view the File Template Library either by clicking the first button on the left in the Library pane or by selecting **View** > **Utilities** > **Show File Template Library** from the Xcode menu.

To add a new file to your project using the File Template Library, drag a file template from the library and drop it in the Project Navigator.

It's an odd tool because it does everything that the New File dialog does and *less*! Here's what's wrong:

1. It's missing a few of the templates that are available in the New File dialog.

2. After you drop a template in the Project Navigator, it doesn't display an options dialog that allows you to configure the file that is added to the project (it only displays a Save As dialog).

3. The templates are listed by category (mirroring the order in the New File dialog), but there is no indication of where the categories begin and end.

I recommend using the New File dialog instead.

The Code Snippet Library

The Code Snippet Library (Figure 6.4) allows you to easily add commonly used code to your project. This helps speed your app development because you avoid typing the same code over and over again. It's also useful tool for adding shortcuts to Swift programming constructs for which there are no built-in Code Completion shortcuts such as enumerations, extensions, and protocols.

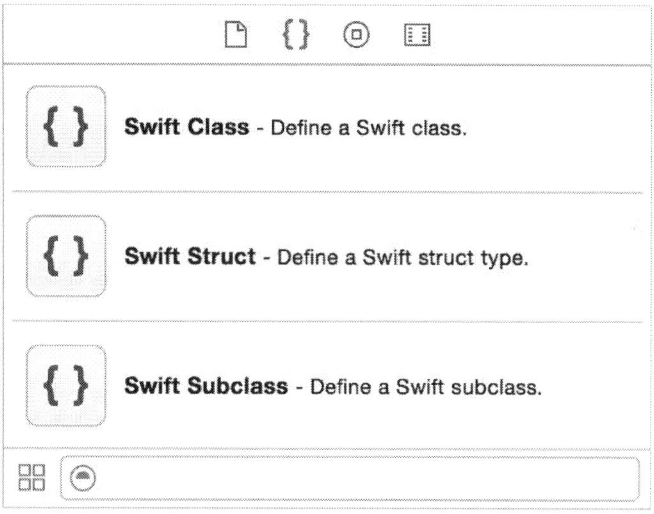

Figure 6.4 The Code Snippet Library

Currently, there are only three built-in code snippets that are Swift-specific. All the other snippets are written in Objective-C. Fortunately, you can create your own Swift code snippets as you'll see in just a bit.

You can view the Code Snippet Library either by clicking the second button from the left in the Library pane or by selecting **View > Utilities > Show Code Snippet Library** from the Xcode menu.

You can use code snippets in two ways:

1. In the Code Editor, type the associated code snippet shortcut (more on that in a moment), then press **Tab** or **Enter**, and Xcode will automatically insert the code snippet.

2. Drag a code snippet from the Code Snippet Library, and then drop it in a source code file.

In previous versions of Xcode, if you didn't know the shortcut for a particular code snippet, you could just click the snippet in the Code Snippet Library to display the help popup, and then click the **Edit** button. This is no longer an option unless you are looking at your own custom code snippets.

It's easy to use the second option and drag and drop a code snippet. Just drag an item from the Code Snippet Library and drop it into your code file (Figure 6.5).

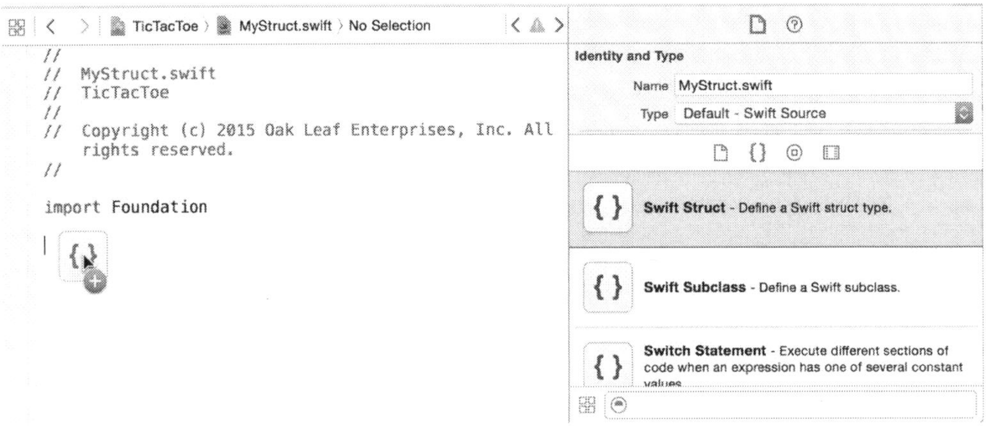

Figure 6.5 Dragging a code snippet into the Code Editor.

Creating Your Own Code Snippets

One of the best features of code snippets is that you can create your own custom snippets. To do this, just highlight a section of code in a code file and drag it into the Code Snippet Library.

The following steps show how to do this using Swift class extensions as an example:

1. Open the **LibraryDemo** project by selecting **File > Open...** from the Xcode menu. In the Open dialog, navigate to the folder where you have stored this book's sample code and drill down into the **LibraryDemo** folder. Select the **LibraryDemo. xcodeproj** file, and then click the **Open** button.

2. Now you need to locate the code that you want to add as a snippet. In the Project Navigator panel, drill down into the **LibraryDemo** node, and then select the **StringExtensioin.swift** file. Near the top of the code file, you can see the following class extension declaration:

```
extension String {
}
```

3. Next, select all the lines of the class extension code. To do this, just click to the left of the **extension** declaration, hold down the mouse button, and drag down over the closing curly brace. Then, drag the code to the Code Snippet Library (Figure 6.6).

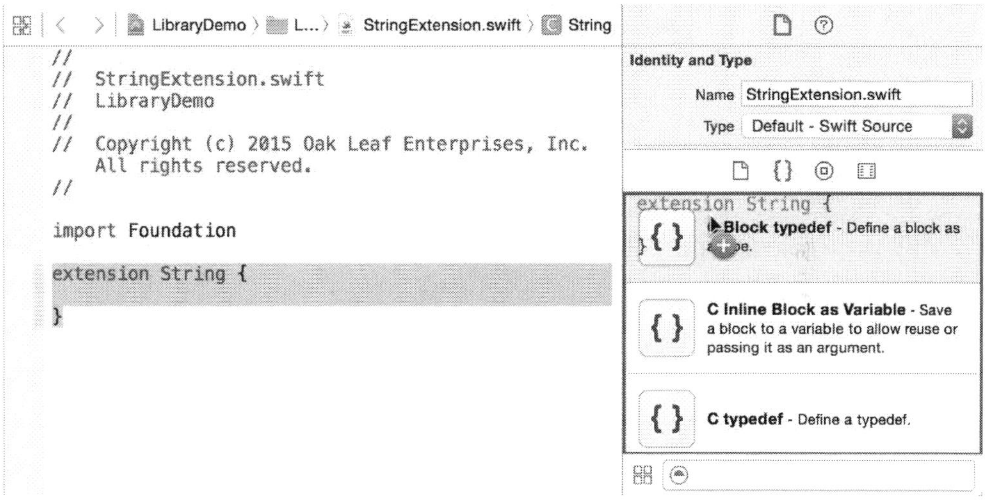

Figure 6.6 Dragging code into the Code Snippet Library.

4. Release the mouse button to add the code to the Code Snippet Library. This displays the Code Snippet popup (Figure 6.7).

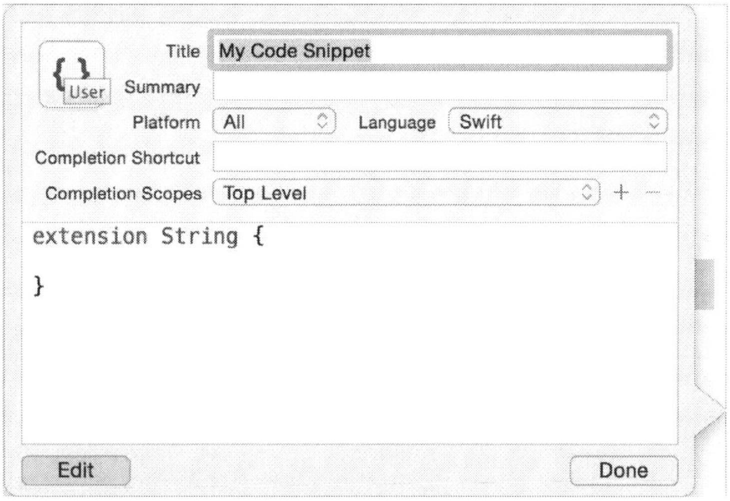

Figure 6.7 The Code Snippet popup.

Here is a description of the fields in the popup (don't change them yet; you will do that in the next step):

- **Title** - The title given to the code snippet in the Code Snippet Library list
- **Summary** - The description given to the code snippet in the Code Snippet Library list
- **Platform** - The choices are **All**, **iOS**, **OS X**, **tvOS**, and **watchOS**. When creating a generic code snippet (such as the class extension that you are about to create), you can specify **All**.
- **Language** - When you are writing in Swift, you should pick **Swift** from the many languages in this list box.
- **Completion Shortcut** - The character string used as a shortcut to display the code snippet popup help in the editor. You should choose something short, intuitive, and easy to remember.
- **Completion Scopes** - This setting determines when the snippet appears in Xcode's *Code Completion* list. This is an important setting because it may not make sense for your code snippet to appear at all times. The plus (+) and minus (-) buttons allow you to add/remove multiple completion scopes.

Here are the options that specify when the code snippet appears in the Code Completion list:

- **All** - The code snippet always appears in the Code Completion list.
- **Class Implementation** - When you are in a source code file and your cursor is between the opening and closing curly braces but outside a method
- **Code Expression** - When you are between a set of curly braces
- **Function or Method** - When you are inside a function or method
- **String or Comment** - When you are inside a string declaration
- **Top Level** - When you are inside a code file but outside any class declaration.

At the bottom of the popup is a code window where you can edit your code snippet. You can add placeholders that allow you to fill in the blanks when you use it. All you have to do is enter the following token in your code snippet in the position where you want the placeholder to be:

<#TokenName#>

Whatever you enter for **TokenName** gets displayed as a prompt for what to enter, so you should provide short, meaningful token names.

5. Now it's time to fill in the Code Snippet popup and create a class extension code snippet. Enter the following values for each field:

   - **Title**: Swift Class Extension
   - **Summary**: Declares a Swift class extension
   - **Platform**: All
   - **Language**: Swift
   - **Completion Shortcut**: ext
   - **Completion Scopes**: **Top Level** is set by default.
   - In the code snippet box at the bottom of the popup, replace **String** with the following token:

     ```
     extension <#class name#> {

     }
     ```

6. When you've finished, the Code Snippet popup should look like Figure 6.8.

7. Click the **Done** button to close the popup and save the new code snippet.

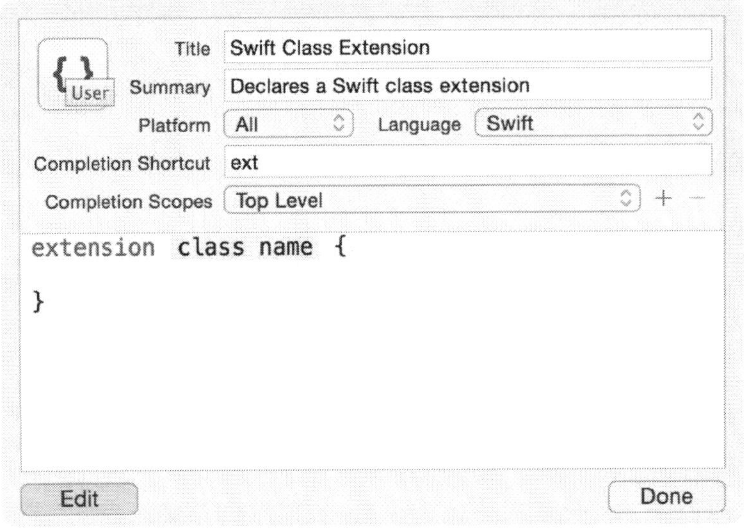

Figure 6.8 The completed Code Snippet popup.

Now you're ready to try out the new code snippet by creating an extension of the **NSManagedObjectContext** class:

1. Right-click the **StringExtension.swift** file in the Project Navigator and select **New File** from the popup menu. On the left side of the New File dialog under **iOS**, select **Source**. On the right side of the dialog, select **Swift File** and then click **Next**.

2. In the Save File dialog, change the name of the file to **NSManagedObjectContextExtension.swift** and then click **Create**

3. At the top of the code file, add the following import statement:

```
import Foundation
import CoreData
```

4. Below the new **import** statement, type the **ext** code completion shortcut and the Swift Class Extension code snippet should appear in the completion list (Figure 6.9).

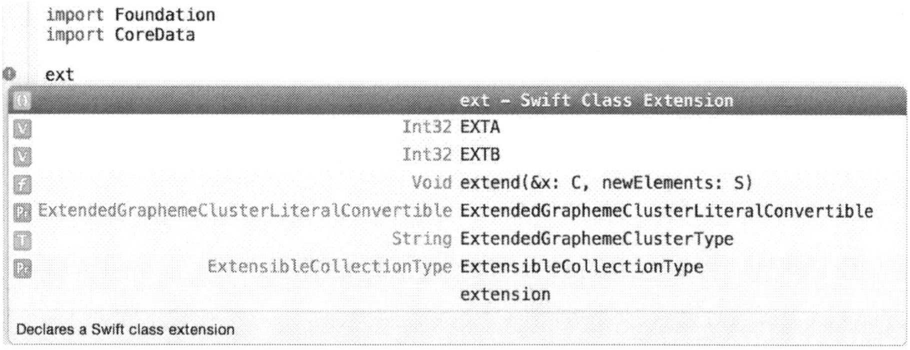

Figure 6.9 Using the new Class Extension code snippet.

5. Press **Tab** to add the code snippet. Notice that the highlight is on the placeholder token that you created and it is prompting you to enter the class name (Figure 6.10). You will see error icons because the code is not completed yet.

```
import Foundation
import CoreData

extension class name {

}
```

Figure 6.10 The newly entered code snippet.

6. Type **NSManagedObjectContext** to replace the token. The error icons will go away, and your code is now complete as shown in Figure 6.11!

```
import Foundation
import CoreData

extension NSManagedObjectContext {

}
```

Figure 6.11 The completed code snippet.

If you want to delete one of your custom code snippets, just select it in the Code Snippet Library, press the **Delete** key, and then press the **Delete** button in the confirmation dialog.

Now that you know how to create your own custom snippets, whenever you find yourself entering the same code repeatedly, create a code snippet instead and save yourself time and energy!

Code Completion Preferences

Xcode has several preference settings that affect the behavior of code completion. To view these, select **Xcode > Preferences** from the menu, and then select the **Text Editing** button at the top of the dialog. Here is a list of the settings and a description of each:

- **Suggest completions while typing** – When this setting is on (the default), code completion automatically pops up while you are typing in a code file. If you turn this off, code completion does not automatically pop up, but you can manually bring up the code completion popup—either by pressing the **Escape** key, by pressing the **Option+Space** keys, or by selecting **Editor > Show Completions** from the Xcode menu.

- **Use Escape key to show completion suggestions** – When this setting is on (the default), you can press **Escape** to bring up a list of code completions. If you turn this option off, pressing **Escape** dismisses accessory views in the editor, but you can still use **Option+Escape** to manually bring up code completion.

- **Automatically insert closing braces ("}")** – When this setting is on (the default), if you enter an open curly brace (to indicate the beginning of a method) and then press **return**, a closing curly brace is automatically added for you. If you turn this option off, you must manually enter the the closing curly brace.

- **Enable type-over completions** – When this option is turned on (the default), the editor adds a closing character that you can type over (kind of a "ghost" character). This helps prevent duplicate closing characters in cases where you type the opening and closing character in quick succession.

- **Automatically balance brackets in Objective-C method calls** – This setting is Objective-C specific. When this setting is on (the default), if you type a right square bracket "]" to end a method call but forget to enter a left square bracket "[" at the beginning of a method call, Xcode automatically adds the opening square bracket for you. If you turn this option off, you need to manually enter the opening square bracket.

The Object Library

The Object Library (Figure 6.12) contains a list of UI objects that you can drag and drop onto the design surface when laying out your app's user interface (you can also double-click an object to add it to a scene). You can view the Object Library by clicking the third button from the left in the Library pane or by selecting **View** > **Utilities** > **Show Object Library** from the Xcode menu.

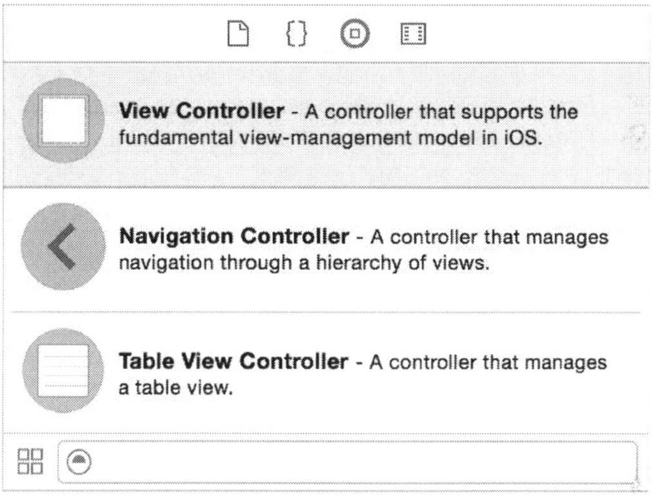

Figure 6.12 The Object Library

Chapter 7: The User-Interface Controls discusses all the controls found in the Object Library.

The Media Library

The Media Library (Figure 6.13) contains a list of media that you have added to your project. It's a watered-down version of the Media Library for Mac OS X app development. You can view the Media Library either by clicking the button on the right in the Library pane or by selecting **View** > **Utilities** > **Show Media Library** from the Xcode menu.

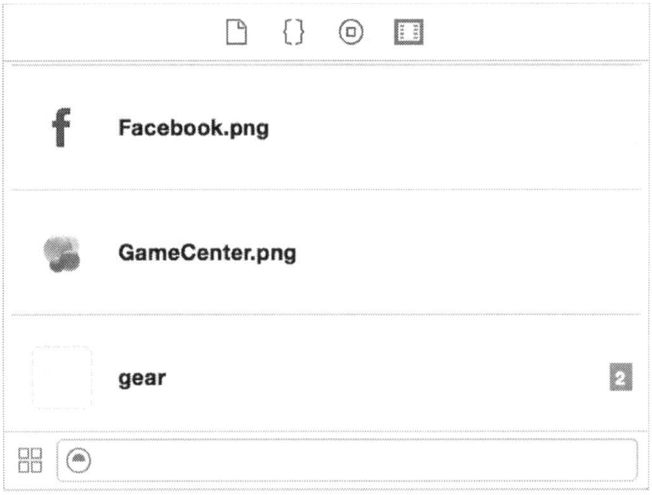

Figure 6.13 The Media Library

When you add an image file to your project in the Project Navigator, the file also automatically appears in the Media Library. You can drag an image from the Media Library and drop it on your user interface, for example, on an image view. This comes in handy because the Media Library shows you a small thumbnail of the image.

Summary

- The File Template Library allows you to add new files to your project. It's an odd tool because it does everything that the New File dialog does and *less*! It's better to use the New File dialog instead.

- The Code Snippet Library allows you to easily add commonly used code to your project. This helps speed up your app development because you avoid typing the same code over and over again.

- The Object Library contains a list of UI objects that you can drag and drop onto the design surface when laying out your app's user interface.

- The Media Library contains a list of media that you have added to your project. It's a watered-down version of the Media Library for Mac OS X app development.

Chapter 7: The User-Interface Controls

This is a critical chapter for understanding all of the user-interface objects that Apple has to offer. You will learn the basic function of each UI object, its most commonly used attributes, and see a live example of its use in one of this books many sample projects.

Sections in This Chapter

1. *The View Controllers*
2. *Custom Controls With Object*
3. *Basic Controls*
4. *The Keyboards*
5. *Table Views and Collection Views*
6. *Miscellaneous Views*

7. *Gesture Recognizers*
8. *Navigation, Tab, Search, and Toolbars*
9. *AVKit Player View Controller*
10. *Blur Effects*
11. *Summary*
12. *Step-By-Step Movie 7.1*
13. *Step By Step Movie 7.2*

The View Controllers

In this section, you will learn more about the different view controllers you can use in your apps.

View Controller

As you have already learned, every scene on a storyboard has an associated view controller (Figure 7.1) that is used to manage the view as well as any navigation bar or toolbars associated with the scene. When you are creating a scene that does not contain a table view, you typically drag a **View Controller** object onto the storyboard to create the scene. Afterward, you can drop other controls to design the user interface for the scene.

Figure 7.1 A view controller.

In this chapter's sample code, the **iDeliverMobile** project's **Location** scene is comprised of a view controller and a map view object.

Table View Controller

When you want to create a scene that contains a table view, you should start out by dropping a **Table View Controller** (Figure 7.2) on the storyboard.

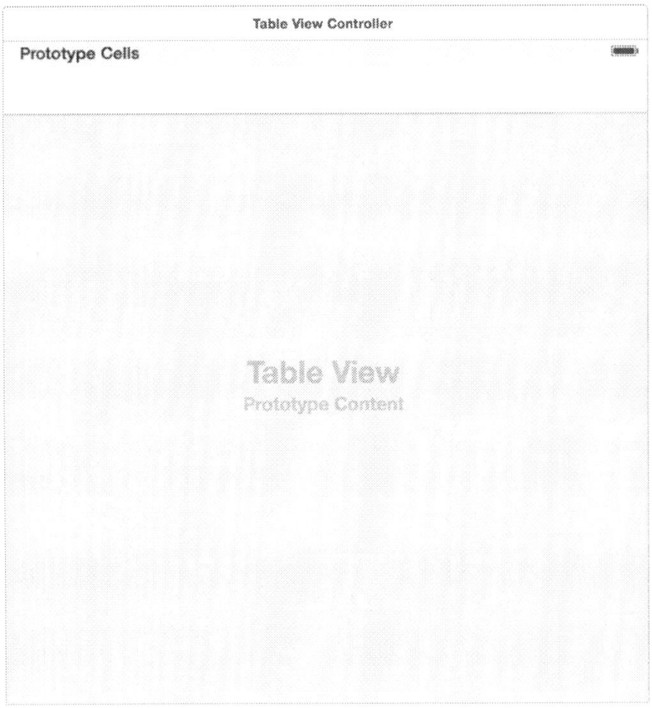

Figure 7.2 A table view controller.

The **table view controller** is a specialized subclass of the view controller that manages a table view and usually cts as the table view's data source and delegate. It is also used to toggle the table view's editing mode so you can delete or reorder items in the table view. In the **iDeliverMobile** project, all scenes containing table views are based on the Table View Controller.

Collection View Controller

The **Collection View Controller** is a specialized subclass of the view controller that manages an associated collection view.

The collection view provides an easy way to display a *collection* of items. The appearance of the collection view is highly configurable, so unlike the table view, it can be hard to tell if an app is using a collection view or not. For example, the iPad Clock app uses a collection view to display a set of clocks along the top of the app window (Figure 7.3). A collection view is also used to display the pictures in the app shown in Figure 7.4. You can see the collection view at work in this book's **CollectionViewDemo** project.

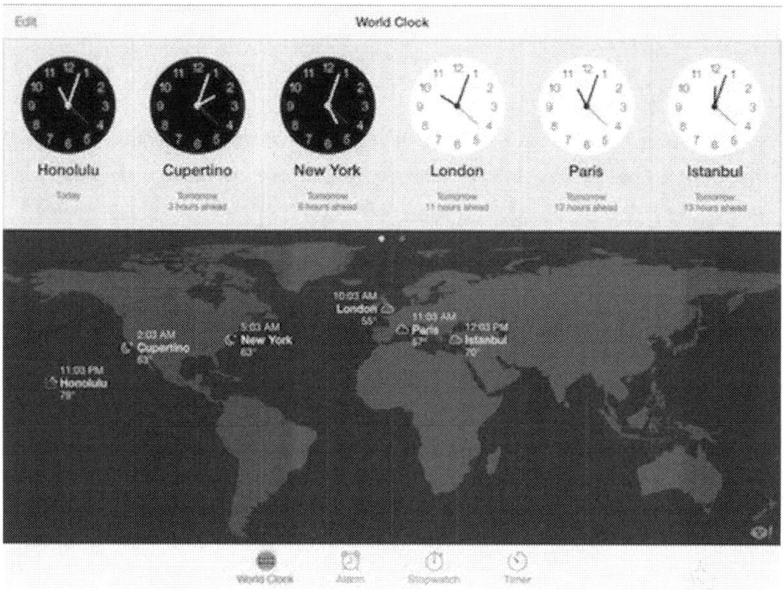

Figure 7.3 A collection view in the iPad Clock app.

Figure 7.4 A collection view displaying pictures.

Behind the scenes, a collection view controller is very similar to a table view controller. It acts as both a data source and a delegate for a collection view, and the code that you write to fill and manage the collection view with items is almost identical to the code you use to fill and manage a table view.

Navigation Controller

The **Navigation Controller** (Figure 7.5) is used to manage a set of view controllers. In most apps that contain multiple scenes, a navigation controller is the initial scene and is used to control navigation between the other scenes on the storyboard.

Figure 7.5 A navigation controller.

A navigation controller has a navigation bar that can contain a title and buttons that can be used to navigate, edit, to share content, and for your own custom purposes.

Tab Bar Controller

The **Tab Bar Controller** (Figure 7.6) is similar to a navigation controller in that it is used to manage a set of view controllers. However, the view controllers in a tab bar controller are each displayed as a tab bar item.

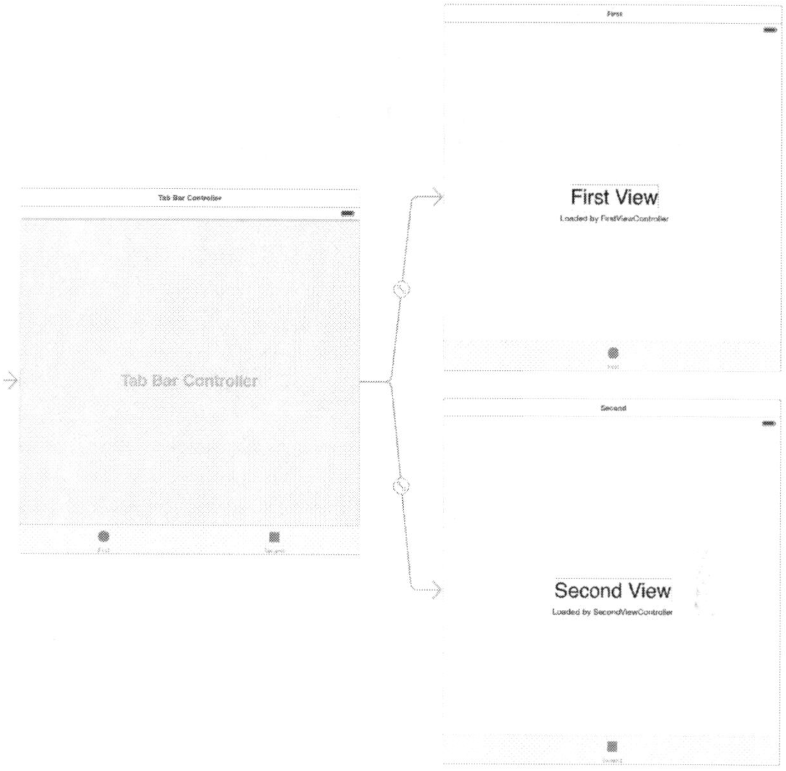

Figure 7.6 A Tab Bar Controller.

Figure 7.6 shows you what the storyboard looks like when you create a new app using the Tabbed Application project template.

To add additional tabs to the tab bar controller:

1. Drop a controller (view controller, table view controller, etc.) on the storyboard.

2. **Control+Drag** from the Tab Bar Controller to the new controller.

3. Release your mouse to display the segue popup and, under **Relationship Segue**, select **view controllers** (Figure 7.7). This adds a new tab to the tab bar controller.

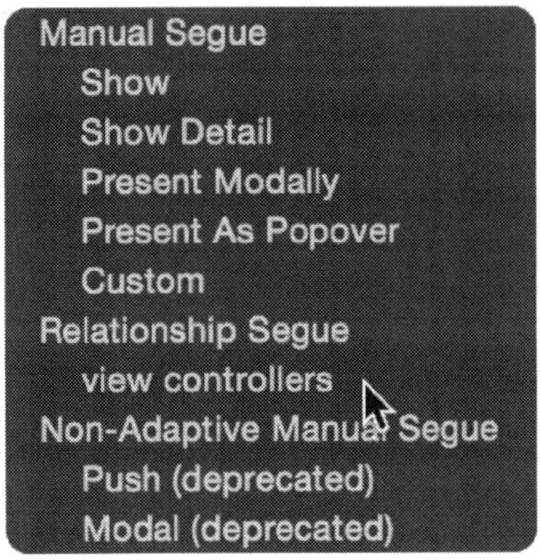

*Figure 7.7 Select **view controllers** in the segue popup.*

You can't edit the image and title of a tab bar item directly in the tab bar controller. You need to edit the tab bar at the bottom of each view controller instead.

Page View Controller

The **Page View Controller** (Figure 7.8) also manages a set of view controllers. It uses either a horizontal page curl transition, like turning the pages in a book, or a vertical page curl, like turning the pages in a calendar.

Figure 7.8 The page view controller.

The **PageViewControllerDemo** project in this book's sample code provides a live example of the page view controller in action.

As with the table view controller and collection view controller, the page view controller acts as both a data source and delegate for the pages.

SceneKit View

The **Scene Kit View** is used to display a 3D scene. If you are building a game app using the Scene Kit, this is usually the view you will use as the basis for the game.

Figure 7.9 shows the default app that is created when you choose the **Game** project template in Xcode. You can see this default app in this book's sample code **GLKitViewControllerDemo** project.

Figure 7.9 A Scene Kit view.

Custom Controls With Object

The **Object** template provides a way for you to add an object to a scene that is not listed in the Object Library. This is useful in cases where you have built your own custom classes that you want to drag and drop into a scene. Adding an object to the scene in this way causes the object to be automatically *instantiated* at run time when the scene is loaded.

Follow these steps to see an example of how to use the **Object** template:

1. Open the **ObjectTemplateDemo** project by selecting **File > Open...** from the Xcode menu. In the Open dialog, navigate to the folder where you have stored this book's sample code and drill down into the **ObjectTemplateDemo** folder. Select the **ObjectTemplate.xcodeproj** file, and then click the **Open** button.

2. Select **Main.storyboard** in the Project Navigator.

3. If the Document Outline is not visible, select **Editor | Show Document Outline** from the menu, or click the rounded rectangle arrow button at the bottom left of the Interface Builder region (Figure 7.10).

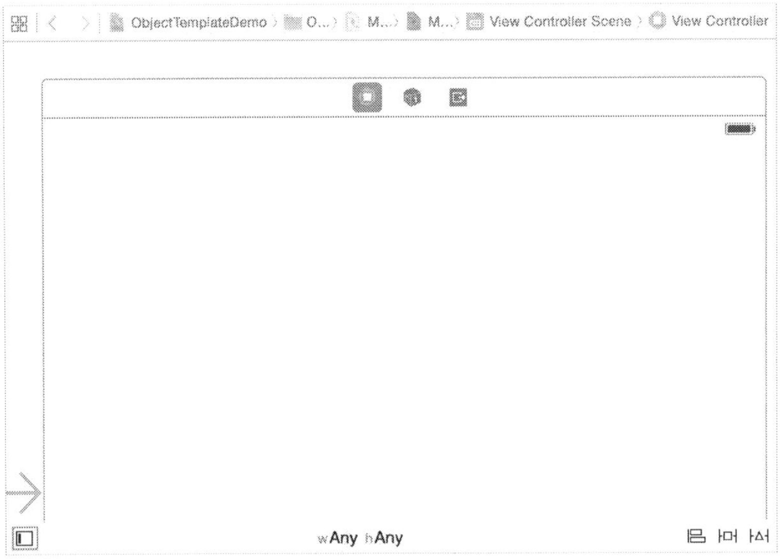

Figure 7.10 Click the rectangle button to display the Document Outline panel.

   We used the Document Outline extensively in the previous books in this series, but if you are new to the Document Outline, you just need to know that it provides a hierarchical view of all UI objects on the currently selected scene.

4. Drag the **Object** item from the Object Library and drop it into the scene in the Document Outline (Figure 7.11). Note that you have to drop the

Object at the top level of the scene hierarchy rather than below a nested user-interface object.

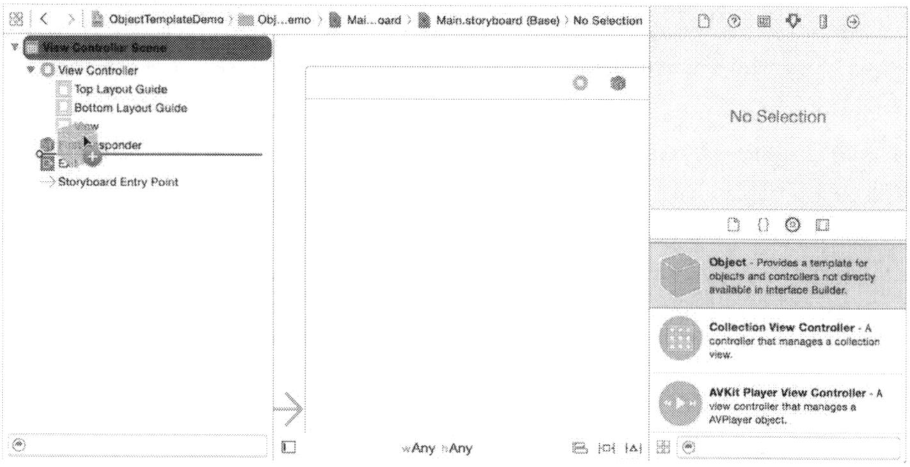

*Figure 7.11 Drop the **Object** in the Document Outline.*

5. With the **Object** still selected, go to the Identity Inspector and change the **Class** to the custom **Calculator** class as shown in Figure 7.12. Doing this also changes the description of the object to **Calculator** in the Document Outline.

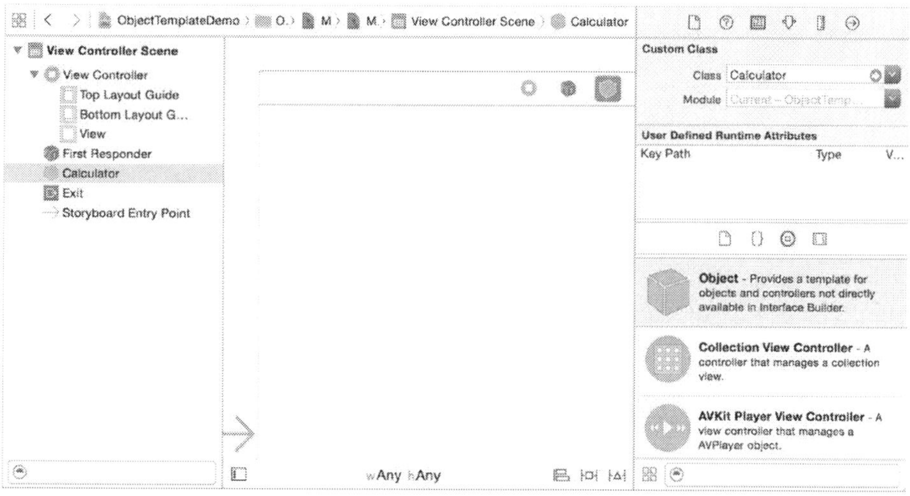

*Figure 7.12 Set the object's **Class** to **Calculator**.*

6. Now you need to create a **calculator** property from which you can reference the **Calculator** object.

To do this, first click the **Assistant Editor** button in the **Editor** button group at the top of the Xcode window. This displays the **ViewController.swift** file in the Assistant Editor.

7. Next, hold the **Control** key down, click the **Calculator** object in the Document Outline and drag down to the **ViewController.swift** file just above the **viewDidLoad** method until you see the **Insert Outlet or Outlet Collection** popup.

8. Release the mouse button and you will see the Outlet popup. Set the **Name** of the property to **calculator**, and then click **Connect** (Figure 7.13). This adds a new **calculator** property to the header file.

*Figure 7.13 Create a new **calculator** property.*

Basic Controls

In this section, you will learn more about some of the more basic, commonly used UI controls.

Label

The **Label** object (Figure 7.14) is a simple control that allows you to display variable length text.

Figure 7.14 Labels are simple and used often!

Figure 7.15 shows the attributes you set most often on a label—**Text**, **Color**, **Font**, and **Alignment**. You can also create a multi-line label by setting the **Lines** attribute.

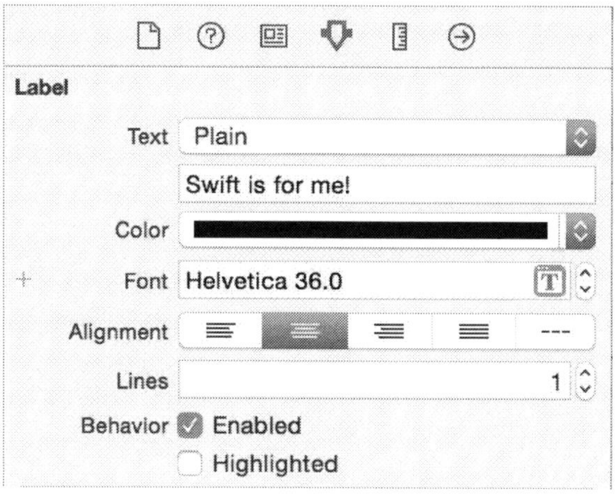

Figure 7.15 Common attributes of the Label.

Notice the list box at the very top of the attributes list. The two choices are **Plain** (the default) and **Attributed**. If you select **Attributed**, the Attributes Inspector lists many more options for customizing the label text (Figure 7.16) including the ability to bold, italicize, or underline a subset of label characters.

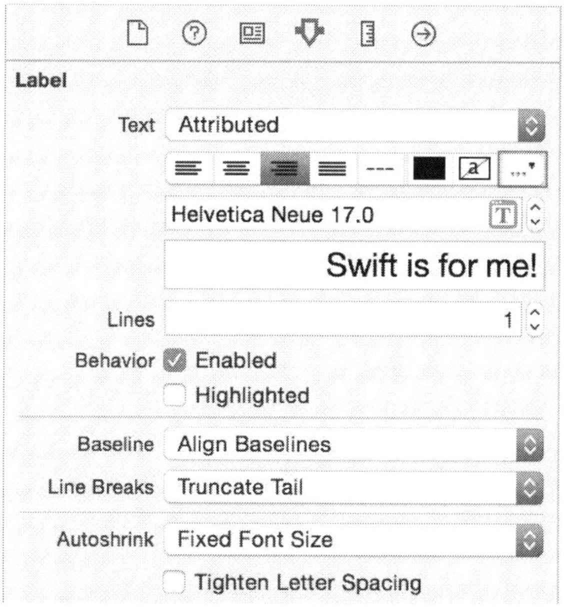

*Figure 7.16 You get extra formatting options when a label's **Text** is set to **Attributed**.*

To see all of the available attributes, click the down arrow button highlighted in red in Figure 7.16.

The **AutoShrink** option applies whether a label's **Text** is set to **Plain** or **Attributed**. There are three options that apply when a label's text does not fit in the physical space allotted for the label:

- **Fixed Font Size** - Three dots are displayed at the end of the label to indicate there is more text.
- **Minimum Font Scale** - You can specify the percentage by which the font should shrink to try to accommodate the full text.
- **Minimum Font Size** - You can specify the minimum font size to which the label should be set to try to accommodate the full text.

If you select the **Tighten Letter Spacing** checkbox, the spacing between letters is adjusted to fit the string in the label's physical space.

For more information on automatically adjusting to font sizes, check out *Chapter 15: Mastering Dynamic Type*.

Button

The **Button** is a commonly used control in iOS user interfaces. When a user taps the button at run time, it can send a message to a target object to perform a task in response to the user's interaction.

In addition to the default **System** setting shown for the **Post** button in Figure 7.17, you can set the **Type** attribute of the **Button** to change its appearance to one of several built-in styles shown from left to right:

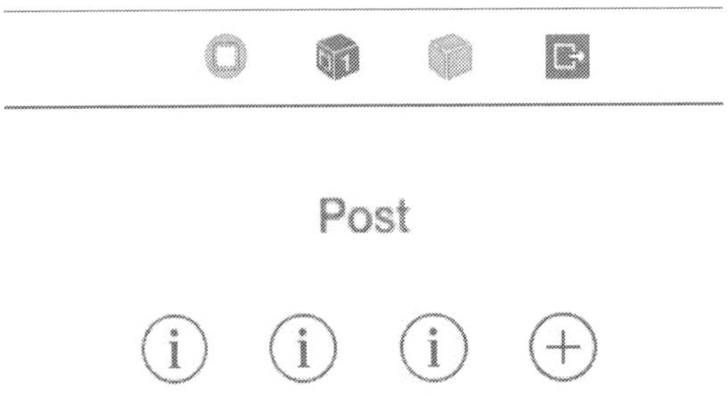

*Figure 7.17 The result of the button **Type** settings.*

- Detail Disclosure
- Info Light
- Info Dark
- Add Contact

As you can see, the first three styles look exactly the same in iOS 9.

There is also a **Custom** option that allows you to create your own unique buttons.

The **Button** has four different states:

- **Default** - The button at rest
- **Highlighted** - Occurs when the user taps the button or slides their finger over the button.
- **Focused** - Occurs when the button has focus.
- **Selected** - Normally not used for the **Button**, but for other buttons such as the segmented control.
- **Disabled** - Occurs when the button's **enabled** is **false**.

You can set a different **Title**, **Text Color**, **Shadow Color**, **Image**, and **Background Image** for each state. This provides a great deal of customization so you can provide visual cues to your users for each button state.

As with the **Label**, you can set the button's **Title** to **Plain** (the default), or **Attributed** for additional customization of the **Title**.

Segmented Control

The **Segmented Control** (Figure 7.18) contains two or more segments, each of which acts as a button. Each segment can display either text or an image.

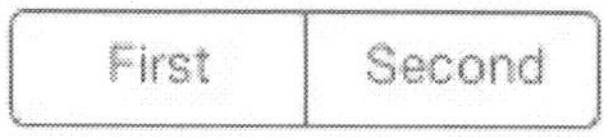

Figure 7.18 The segmented control.

The **Segmented Control** has three **Style** options to choose from, but they all look the same.

By default, when a segment is selected, the previously selected segment becomes unselected (this style is also known as "radio buttons" because it mimics the old-style car radios where pressing in one station preset number popped out the previously selected button).

If you select the **Momentary** check box near the top of the Attributes Inspector, then when the user selects a segment at run time, it momentarily highlights and then goes back to a normal state.

You can see the segmented control in action in the Map Options scene of the **iDeliverMobile** app in this book's sample code (Figure 7.19).

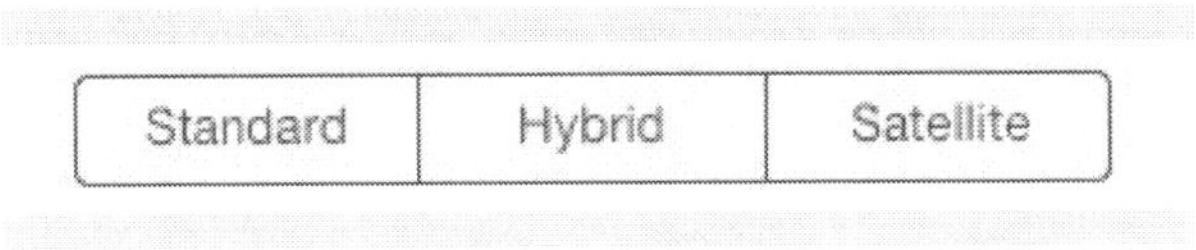

Figure 7.19 The Map Options segmented control.

Text Field

The **Text Field** is a commonly used control that allows the user to enter a short, single line of text. One of the most commonly used text fields is the search box in the iOS Safari app shown in Figure 7.20.

Figure 7.20 The search box in the Safari app is a text field.

The value entered in a text field can be retrieved from its **text** property. For example:

```
let message = self.textField.text
```

The most commonly used text field attributes are listed at the top of the Attributes Inspector (Figure 7.21). As with other text-based controls like **Label**, you can set the **Text** attribute to **Plain** or **Attributed** as well as set the **Font**, font **Color**, and **Alignment**. Text fields have two additional alignment settings—Fully Justified and Natural (left or right-aligned depending on the writing direction).

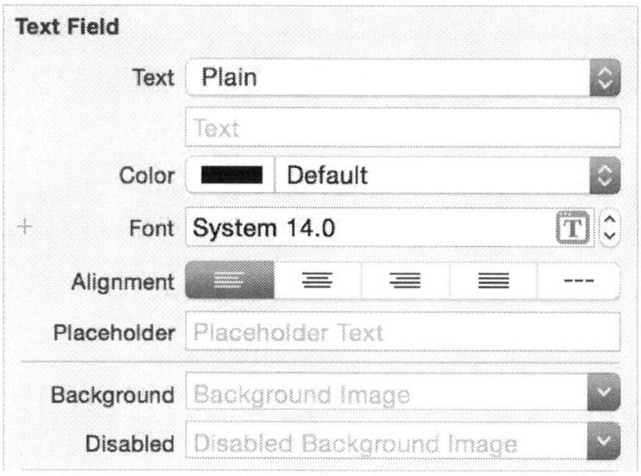

Figure 7.21 Commonly used text field attributes.

The **Placeholder** setting lets you specify light gray text that is displayed in the text field when it's empty. In Figure 7.21, the **Text**, **Placeholder**, **Background**, and **Disabled** attributes all contain placeholder text.

Text fields can optionally display a Clear button (the circular **X** button shown on the right of the text field in Figure 7.20). The clear button allows the user to clear all text from the text field. The **Clear Button** attribute (Figure 7.22) lets you to specify when the clear button appears:

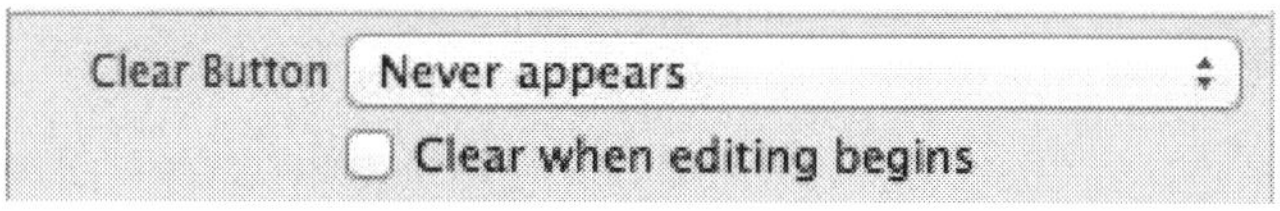

*Figure 7.22 The **Clear Button** text field attribute.*

- Never appears
- Appears while editing
- Appears unless editing
- Is always visible

When the related **Clear when editing begins** setting is selected, as soon as the text field receives focus, the text in the control is automatically cleared.

One of my favorite features of the iOS text box is that it automatically reduces the font size when the text it contains becomes too long. The **Min Font Size** attribute (Figure 7.23) allows you to specify the minimum font size to which you want the text to shrink. Make sure you set the **Min Font Size** to a smaller value than the regular font size of the text field.

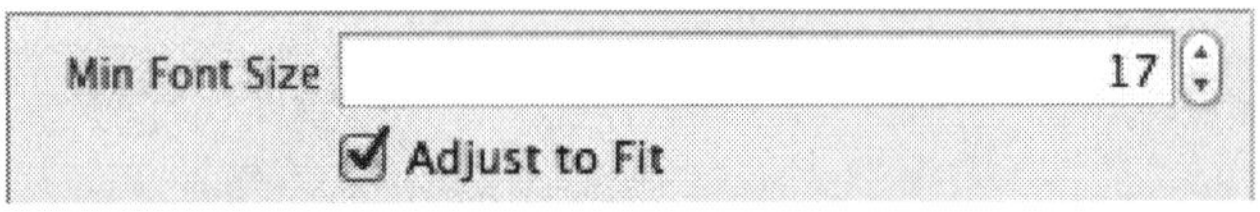

*Figure 7.23 The **Min Font Size** attribute of the text field.*

Figure 7.24 shows another set of attributes that deserves a closer look.

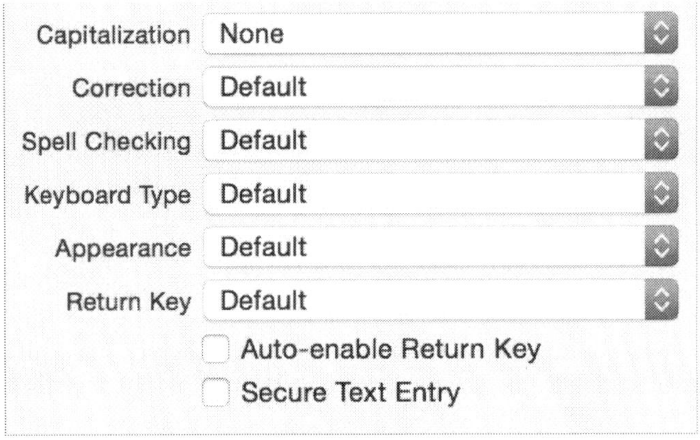

Figure 7.24 Additional text field attributes.

Capitalization

This attribute lets you specify automatic capitalization of the text entered by the user. The options are:

- **None** (the default) - No capitalization is performed.

- **Words** - The first letter of each word is automatically capitalized. This is a good choice when entering names or addresses.

- **Sentences** - The first letter of each sentence is automatically capitalized. This is a good option when entering longer text that potentially contains multiple sentences. You will rarely use this option for a text field because it is intended for short text input.

- **All Characters** - All letters in the text are automatically capitalized. This is useful in places where the text entered by the user should be in all capital letters, for example, in medical apps where the patient's last name is often capitalized.

Correction

If this attribute is selected on a text field, iOS autocorrection kicks in when the user begins typing. Autocorrection offers to complete words or presents alternatives for misspelled worlds. Use this setting with care. One of my pet peeves is text fields that have autocorrection turned on but shouldn't—such as names and addresses.

Keyboard Type

This is an attribute that you should definitely pay attention to in your apps. It allows you to specify which iOS keyboard is displayed when the user enters text in the text field. Since there are a few user-interface controls that allow the user to enter information by means of a keyboard, there is a section devoted specifically to keyboards after this section.

Appearance

The **Appearance** attribute is used to change the keyboard's color from **Default** to **Dark** or **Light**.

Return Key

This attribute specifies the text that appears in the keyboard's **Return** key. If you are using a keyboard that has a **Return** key (such as the standard or email keyboards), this attribute specifies the text of the return key. Figure 7.25 shows the **Return** key set to **Go**.

Figure 7.25 The Return key set to ***Go.***

The other options are:

- Go
- Google
- Join
- Next
- Route
- Search
- Send
- Yahoo
- Done
- Emergency Call

Auto-enable Return Key

When this option is turned on, the **Return** key in the keyboard is not enabled unless the user enters at least one character in the text field.

Secure Text Entry

When this option is turned on, it indicates the contents of the text field are secure. So, as the user types, each key is displayed briefly, and then replaced with a bold circle as shown in Figure 7.26.

*Figure 7.26 A text field with the **Secure** option turned on.*

The Slider

The **Slider** control (Figure 7.27) allows the user to select a value within a range by sliding a circular shape known as a *thumb* along a track.

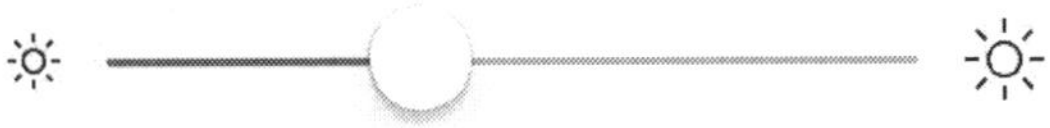

Figure 7.27 The Slider control

The most commonly used attributes for the Slider control are shown in Figure 7.28. The **Minimum** and **Maximum** attributes allow you to specify the value represented by the slider's thumb in the far left position (**Minimum**) and the far right position (**Maximum**).

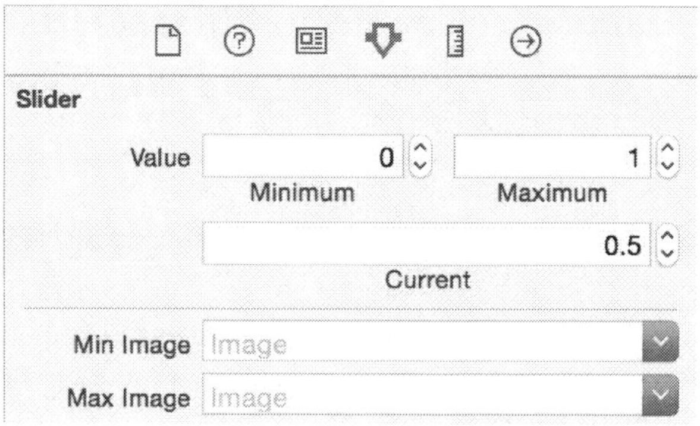

Figure 7.28 Commonly used Slider attributes.

The value of a slider control can be retrieved from its **value** property. For example:

```
let sliderValue: Float = self.slider.value
```

As shown in Figure 7.27, which is a screen shot of the Settings app's **Brightness** slider, you can specify an associated **Min Image** and **Max Image** that provide a visual cue to the user regarding what the minimum and maximum values represent.

The Switch

The **Switch** control (Figure 7.29) allows a user to toggle a value ON and OFF.

Figure 7.29 The Switch control in ON and OFF positions.

The switch control's **State** attribute allows you to specify whether the control is initially in the On or Off state. Usually, the switch is tied to a setting stored on the device, so you set the switch's state *programmatically* by means of its **On** property. For example:

```
self.swtAlert.on = alertValue
```

You can change the color of the button in the On position to something other than green by setting the **On Tint** attribute of the switch. You can change the color of the "thumb" (the white circle) by setting the **Thumb Tint**.

You can also change the switch control to display something other than the default by setting the switch's **On Image** and **Off Image** attributes.

The Activity Indicator View

The **Activity Indicator View** (highlighted in red in Figure 7.30) provides feedback to the user when a process is running in your app. It lets them know the app is doing something.

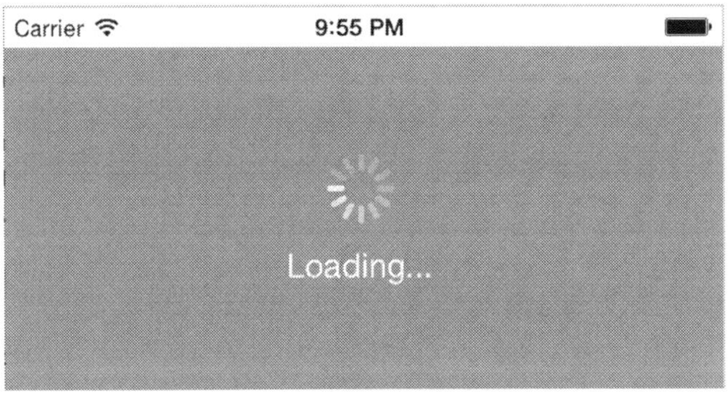

Figure 7.30 The Activity Indicator

Typically, you use an activity indicator when a process of an unknown length is executing. A good example of this are processes that retrieve data from the Internet. Many factors affect how long it takes to get information from the web (signal strength, the speed of the site from which you are getting the information, and so on).

Figure 7.31 shows the most commonly used attributes for the activity indicator view.

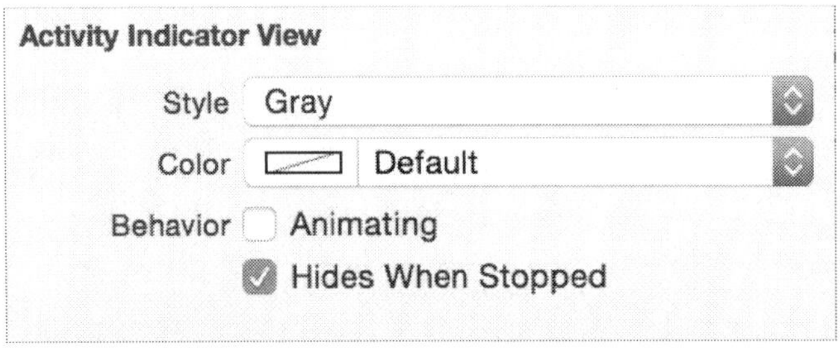

Figure 7.31 Activity Indicator View attributes

The **Style** attribute has three options that change the appearance of the activity indicator view:

- Large White
- White
- Gray

Obviously, the **Large White** setting creates a large, white activity indicator view. The **White** and **Gray** options create a smaller activity indicator view in white or gray.

If these colors don't suit your needs, you can override the color of the activity indicator view in the **Color** attribute.

The **Behavior** attribute has an **Animating** check box that, when selected, causes the activity view indicator to animate as soon as the view it's contained in is loaded. When the **Hides When Stopped** option is selected, the activity view indicator becomes invisible when it stops animating. You typically want this check box selected.

You can also tell an activity indicator view to begin animating by calling its **startAnimating** method, and tell it to stop animating by calling its **stopAnimating** method.

You can see the activity view indicator at work in the **WebViewDemo** project found in this book's sample code. As shown in Figure 7.32, the main view in this app contains a text field for entering the address of a website, a web view to display a web page, and an activity indicator view to let the user know when the app is navigating to the specified website.

*Figure 7.32 The **WebViewDemo** project demonstrates the use of the activity indicator view.*

When the app first loads, it automatically navigates to www.apple.com. Afterward, you can enter a web address in the text field and press **Return** to navigate to the website you entered. When you do this:

1. The **urlEntered:** method is executed, which in turn calls the **goToURL:** method, which calls the **startAnimating** method of the activity indicator view:

   ```
   self.activityIndicator.startAnimating()
   ```

2. When the website navigation completes, the **webViewDidFinishLoad:** method is called. It contains the following message, which is sent to the activity indicator view:

   ```
   self.activityIndicator.stopAnimating()
   ```

   This stops the activity indicator view from animating.

For the **webViewDidFinishLoad:** method to fire, the view controller needs to implement the UIWebViewDelegate protocol:

```
class ViewController: UIViewController, UIWebViewDelegate
```

Also, you must connect the web view's **delegate** property to the view controller. To do this, Control+Click the web view, drag up to the view controller icon in the scene dock, and select **delegate** from the popup.

The Progress View

The **Progress View** (Figure 7.33) is another control that allows you to indicate to the user that a process is running. In contrast with the activity indicator view, which is used for processes with an unknown duration, the progress view shows the progress of a task over a period of time or a number of steps.

Figure 7.33 The Progress View control.

Figure 7.34 shows the attributes most commonly used when setting up a progress view.

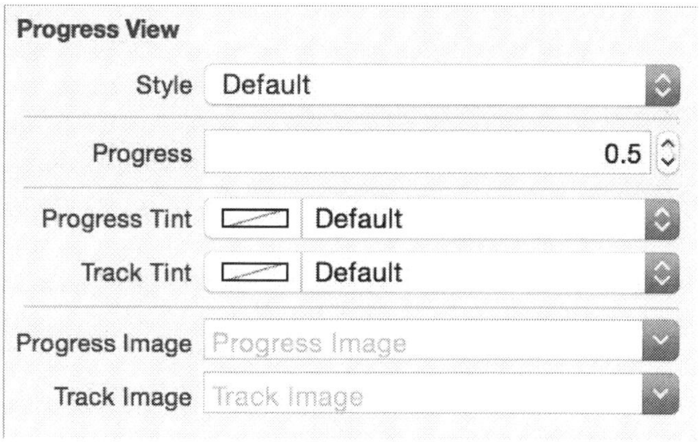

Figure 7.34 Progress Bar attributes.

The **Style** attribute has two options:

- **Default** - Displays a blue progress bar on a gray track.
- **Bar** - Displays a gray progress bar on a transparent track.

The **Progress Tint** and **Track Tint** option allows you to set the progress bar and track to any color you want.

The **Progress** attribute allows you to specify the initial progress when the progress bar is first displayed. Typically, you don't set this in the Attributes Inspector but from code within the view controller by setting the progress bar's **progress** property.

The value of the **progress** property can be a floating point number between 0.0 and 1.0. When you set the **progress** property, the progress bar displays the corresponding progress. So, if the **progress** property is 0, no progress is shown. If it's set to .5, then the progress bar is displayed at the halfway point as shown in Figure 7.33. If it's set to 1.0, then the progress bar is completely filled.

The **ProgressViewDemo** project, included with this book's sample code, provides a live example of the progress bar at work. As shown in Figure 7.35, the main view in this app has five switches. The progress bar shows the percentage of switches that are turned ON.

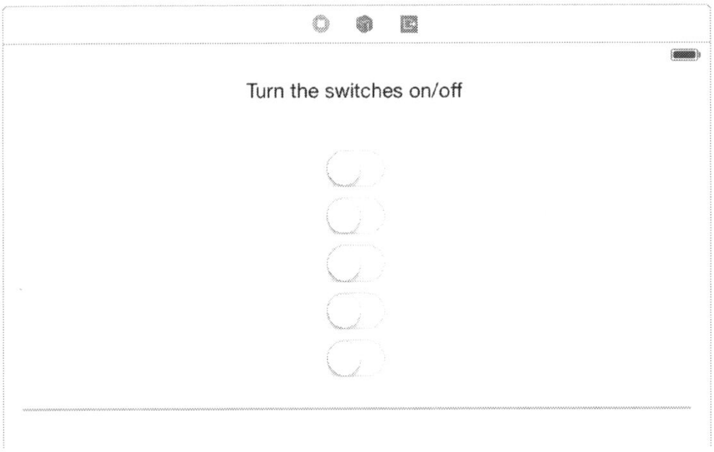

*Figure 7.35 The **ProgressViewDemo** project.*

The code in the **switchChanged:** method checks the number of switches turned ON and the following line of code sets the progress bar's **progress** property:

```
self.progressView.progress = count * 0.2
```

Since there are five switches, the total count of switches that are turned on is multiplied by .2 to come up with the corresponding percentage of switches that are ON.

The Page Control

The **Page Control** (Figure 7.36) is a commonly used control on iOS devices, including the Home screen on the iPhone and iPad. It displays one dot for each page in the app and allows you to navigate sequentially between pages by swiping the page or by tapping to the right or left of the currently highlighted dot.

Figure 7.36 The Page Control.

Figure 7.37 shows the most commonly used page control attributes.

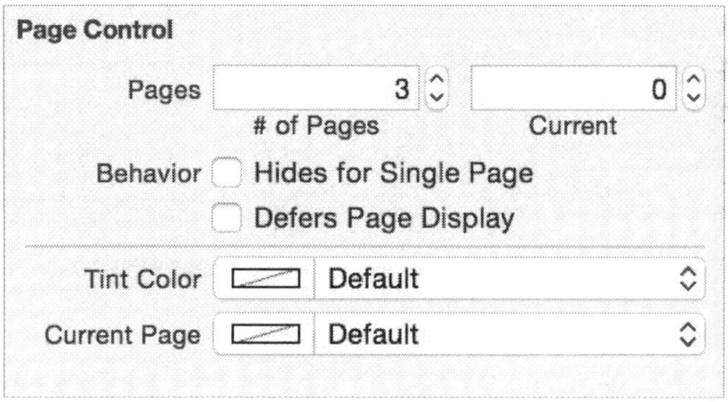

Figure 7.37 Common attributes of the page control.

The **Pages** attribute specifies how many pages are managed by the page control. One dot is displayed in the page control for each page. The **Current** attribute specifies the currently selected page. Although you can set these attributes in the Attributes Inspector, it's far more common to set these in code as you will see later in this section.

When the **Hides for Single Page** option is selected, the page control is hidden if there is only one page being managed by the control. If the **Defers Page Display** option is unchecked (the default), as soon as the user selects a new page, the current page (the white dot) is updated immediately. If you check this option, the current page is not updated in the page control until it calls its own **updateCurrentPage** method.

To see a live example of the page control at work, check out the **PageControlDemo** project in this book's sample code. This project is a simplified version of Apple's PageControl sample that provides a clearer understanding of how the page control works.

Select the **.storyboard** file in the Project Navigator to see the two scenes on the storyboard (Figure 7.38).

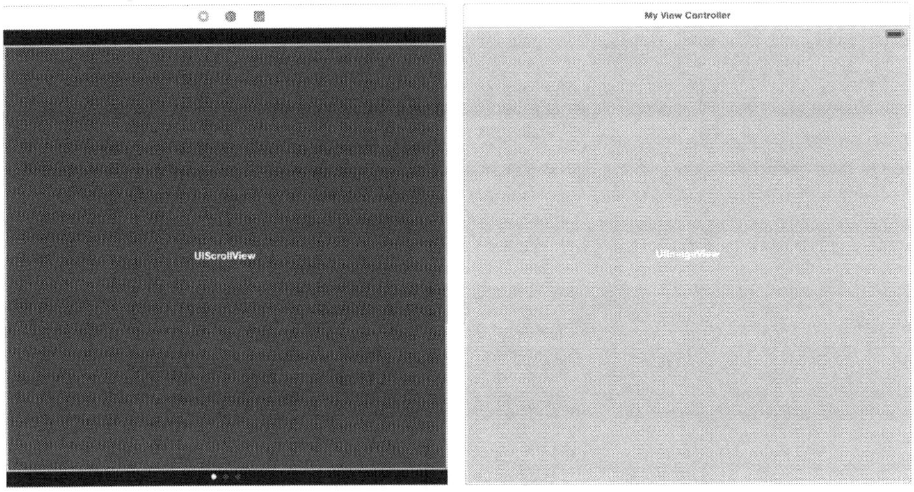

*Figure 7.38 The **PageControlDemo** project.*

The initial scene on the left side of the storyboard has a page control at the bottom with a scroll view above it.

(You will learn more about the scroll view later in this chapter.) You need a scroll view to work in conjunction with the page control so the user can scroll between different pages.

The scene on the right contains an image view control that displays the images in the app. Notice there is no segue between the scenes. Apple hasn't come up with a way for you to create a segue for the page control, so you need to write code to do this instead. At run time, one instance of the view controller on the right is created for each page in the app. These instances are loaded inside the scroll view in the scene on the left as the user navigates between pages.

Select the **ViewController.swift** file to see important code the **viewDidAppear:** method. The code in this method first creates an array of image names that will be displayed in the app. Next, a null object is created for each page in the app (one for each image) and stored in the

viewControllers array. It's more efficient to only create view controllers when you need them rather than creating them all up front.

Near the bottom of the method, the page control's **numberOfPages** is set to the number of images to be displayed, and its **currentPage** property is set to zero:

```
self.pageControl.numberOfPages = pageCount
self.pageControl.currentPage = 0
```

Finally, the **loadScrollViewWithPage:** method is called to create and load the first and second pages in the app.

You will learn more about the other methods in this view controller in the upcoming section **Scroll View**.

The Stepper Control

The **Stepper Control** (Figure 7.39) allows the user to increment or decrement an integer value. Clicking the left side of the control decrements the current value, and clicking the right side of the control increments the current value.

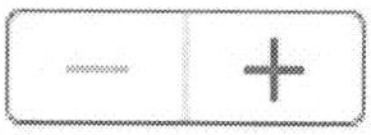

Figure 7.39 The Stepper Control.

A stepper control doesn't display the value that's being incremented / decremented, so you typically display the value in an associated label or text field.

Figure 7.40 shows the stepper control's most commonly used attributes.

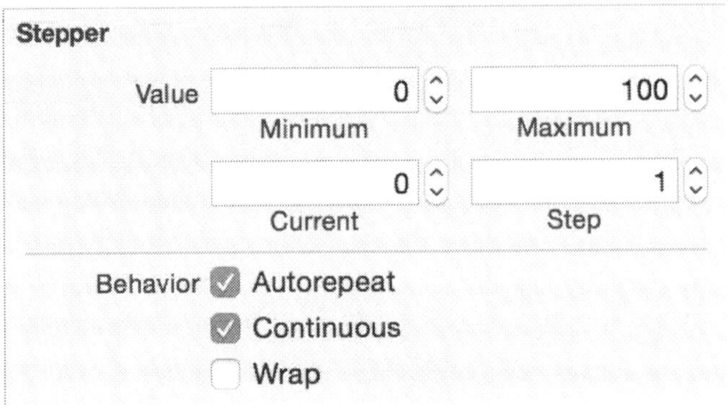

Figure 7.40 The Stepper control.

- **Minimum** - Specifies the minimum allowed value in the control.
- **Maximum** - Specifies the maximum allowed value in the control.
- **Current** - Indicates the current value of the stepper control and is normally not set in the Attributes Inspector.
- **Step** - Specifies how much to increment or decrement the current value when the user clicks the minus button or the plus button.
- **Autorepeat** - When this option is selected (the default), the user can hold down the stepper buttons and the stepper repeatedly changes the current value. The longer the user holds down the button, the faster the value is changed.
- **Continuous** - When this option is selected (the default), a change event is immediately sent each time the value changes. If it's not selected, the change event is sent only after the user has finished interacting with the control.
- **Wrap** - If this option is selected, when the stepper is at the maximum value and the plus sign is tapped, the value wraps around to the minimum (and vice versa for the minimum value). If this option is not selected (the default), the stepper doesn't go above the maximum or below the minimum.

For a live example of the stepper in action, check out the **StepperControlDemo** project in this book's sample code. If you open this project and select the storyboard, you will see the controls shown in Figure 7.41 at the top of the main scene.

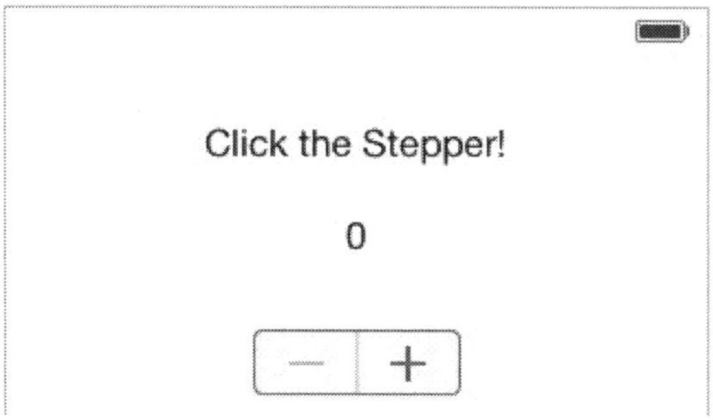

*Figure 7.41 The stepper control in the **StepperControlDemo** project.*

The stepper control is connected to the **valueChanged:** method in the **ViewController.swift** file. This method is automatically executed when the user changes the value in the stepper control. It contains the following code:

```
self.lblValue.text =
   String(format:"%.0f", self.stepper.value)
```

This code gets the current value from the stepper control's **value** property, converts it to a string using the **format:** method of the **String** class, and stores it in the **text** property of the associated label. In the method call to **format:**, the *format specifier* is **%.of**, which converts the value to a string with no decimal places.

The Keyboards

As promised, this section discusses the different iOS keyboards available to you. Each subsection is a keyboard option you can choose under the **Keyboard** attribute for the **Text Field** and **Text View** controls.

ASCII Capable Keyboard

This is the standard iOS keyboard that contains letters of the alphabet, a **Shift** key, and a **Delete** key (Figure 7.42).

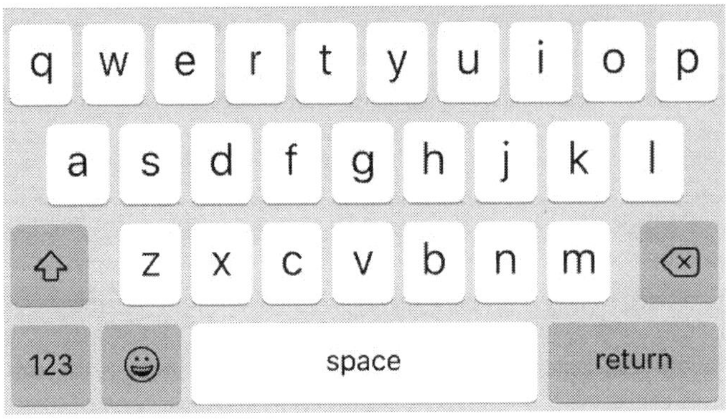

Figure 7.42 The ASCII Capable keyboard.

You should choose this option if the information entered mostly contains characters, like a name or an address.

There is a key in the bottom-left corner that takes you to the numbers and punctuation keyboard (Figure 7.43).

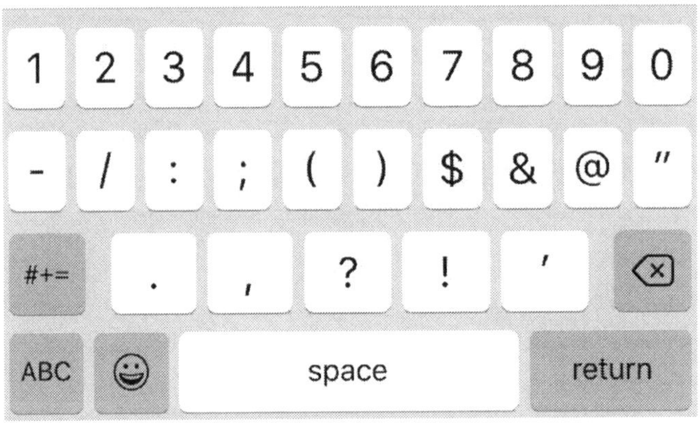

Figure 7.43 The Numbers and Punctuation keyboard.

Numbers and Punctuation Keyboard

If you set this option for the **Keyboard** attribute, it displays the numbers and punctuation keyboard (Figure 7.43). If you click the **ABC** button in the bottom-left corner, it takes you to the **ASCII Capable** keyboard (Figure 7.42).

You should choose the **Numbers and Punctuation** keyboard if the information being entered by the user is predominantly numbers or punctuation.

If you click the #+= button near the bottom-left corner of the keyboard, it displays a keyboard containing symbols and punctuation (Figure 7.44).

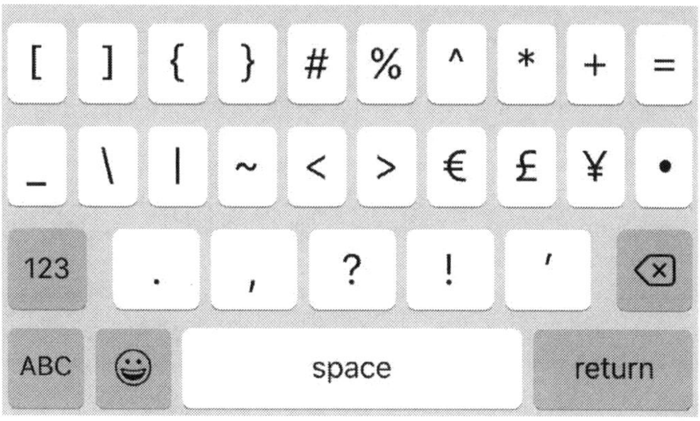

Figure 7.44 The Symbols and Punctuation keyboard.

URL Keyboard

This option displays a keyboard that is optimized for entering URLs (Uniform Resource Locators) such as a website address. As shown in Figure 7.45, the spacebar is replaced by period, forward slash, and .com keys.

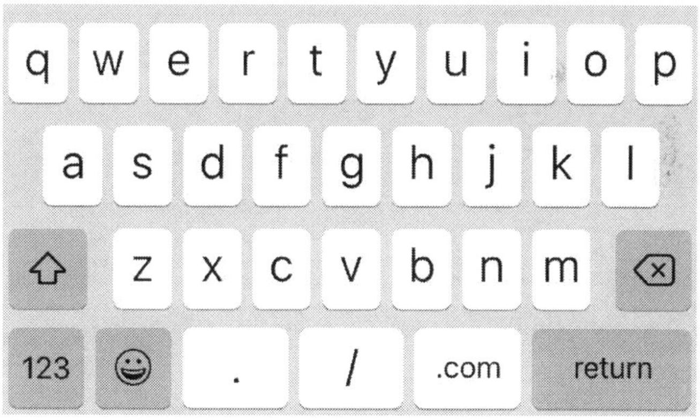

Figure 7.45 The URL keyboard.

If you click and hold the **.com** button, you can select the domains **.us**, **.org**, **.edu**, **.net**, and **.com** from a popup.

If you click the **123** button in the bottom-left corner of the keyboard, you will see the keyboard shown in Figure 7.46 where the usual special characters are replaced with characters more often found in URLs. If you click the smile emoji button you are taken to the emoji keyboard.

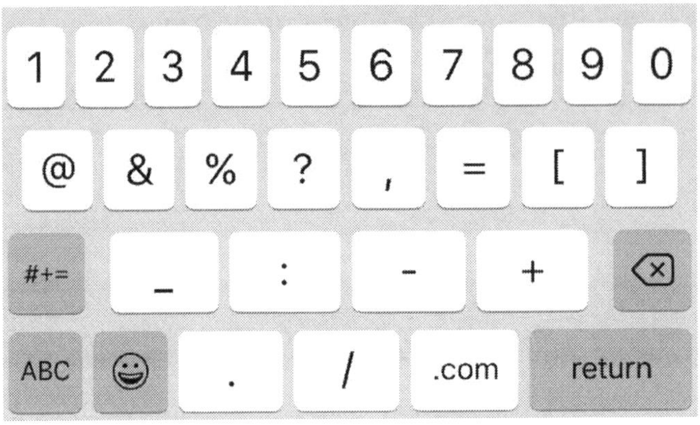

Figure 7.46 The URL Number keyboard.

Number Pad

When you select this option, it displays a numbers-only keyboard as shown in Figure 7.47. This keyboard is a good choice for allowing the user to enter integers such as age, U.S. ZIP codes, or PINs.

Figure 7.47 The Number Pad keyboard.

Phone Pad

This setting is obviously intended for entering phone numbers. As you can see in Figure 7.48, this keyboard is similar to the Number Pad but adds a +∗# key in the bottom-left corner which displays a keyboard with these additional keys as well as **pause** and **wait** buttons.

Figure 7.48 The Phone Pad keyboard.

Name Phone Pad

This option displays a keyboard that switches between a slightly modified version of the standard keyboard (Figure 7.49) for entering names, and a slightly modified Phone Pad keyboard (Figure 7.50) for entering phone numbers.

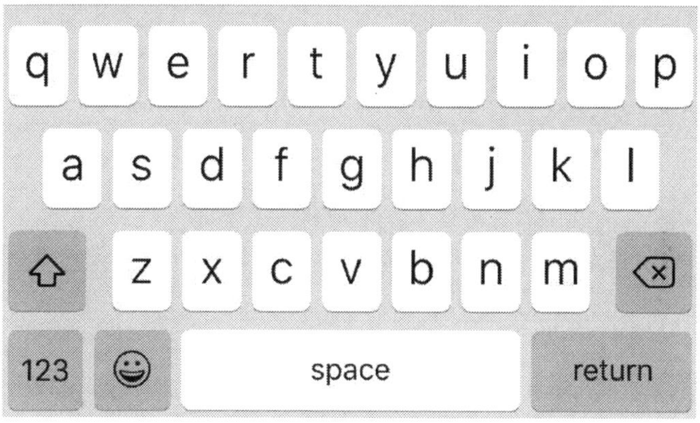

Figure 7.49 The Name Phone Pad keyboard.

Figure 7.50 The modified Phone Pad.

Email Address Keyboard

This option displays a keyboard optimized for entering email addresses. As shown in Figure 7.51, the space bar's width is reduced to make room for @, emoji, and period keys.

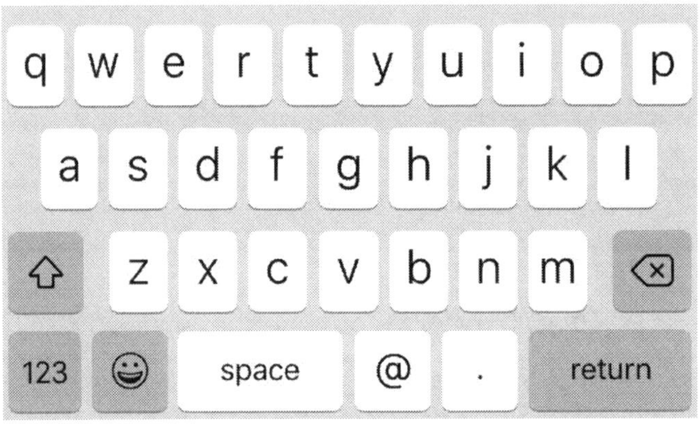

Figure 7.51 The Email Address keyboard.

If you tap the **123** button in the bottom-left corner of the keyboard, it displays the keyboard shown in Figure 7.52 where there are number keys as well as common email symbol keys.

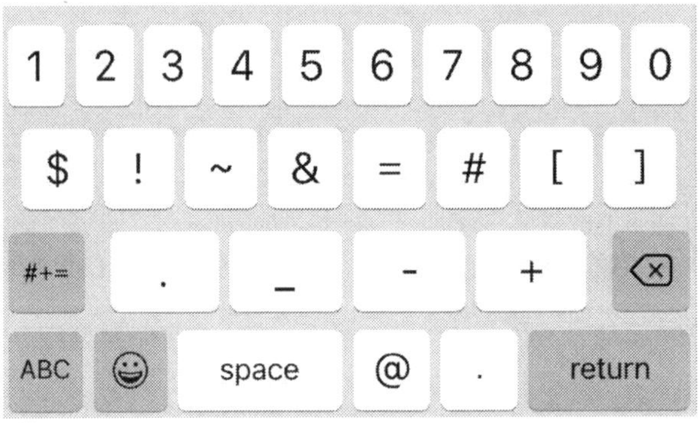

Figure 7.52 The Email Numeric keyboard.

Decimal Pad

When you select this option, it displays a keyboard with numbers and a decimal point button in the lower-left corner (Figure 7.53). Obviously, this is a good choice for entering numbers that contain a decimal point.

Figure 7.53 The Decimal Pad keyboard.

Twitter

This keyboard provides easy access to the @ and # keys commonly used when creating a Tweet as shown in the bottom-right corner of Figure 7.54.

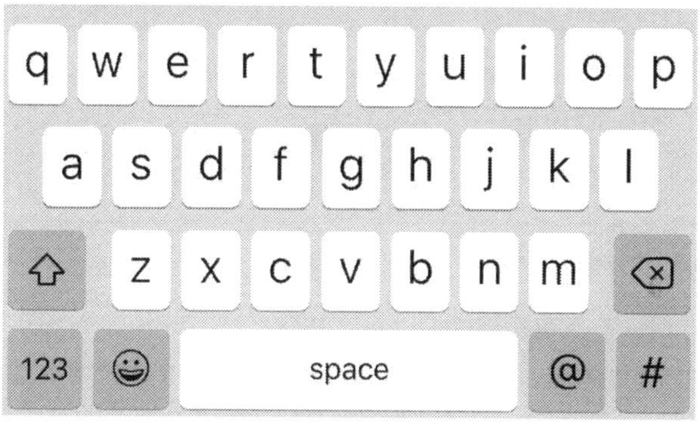

Figure 7.54 The Twitter keyboard.

Web Search

The Web Search keyboard (Figure 7.55) is optimized for web search *and* URL entry, just like the unified address bar in Safari. It features the space and . keys prominently and replaces the **return** key with a **Go** key. If you tap the **123** key in the bottom-left corner, the Numbers and Punctuation keyboard (Figure 7.43) with an additional emoji key is displayed.

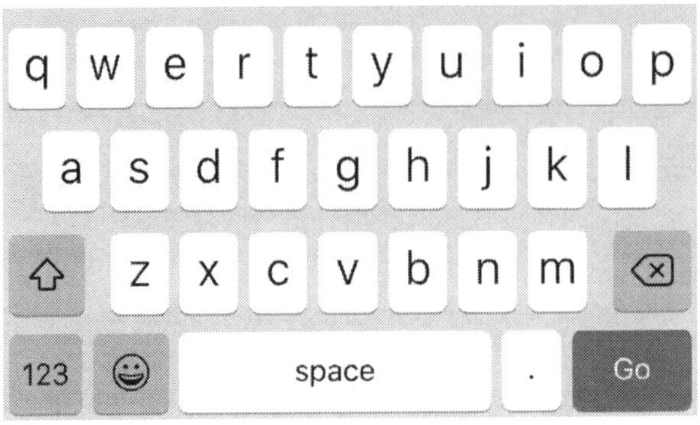

Figure 7.55 The Web Search keyboard.

Hiding the Keyboard

When a text field or text view control has focus, the keyboard is automatically displayed. You don't need to write any code to make this happen. When the user is finished with the keyboard, tapping the keyboard's **Return** button or touching anywhere on the view background should hide the keyboard. However, this doesn't happen automatically—you need to write code to hide the keyboard.

Hiding the Keyboard When the User Taps Return

Let's use the **HideKeyboardDemo** project that is part of this book's sample code to demonstrate how to hide the keyboard when the user taps the **Return** button.

1. Open the **HideKeyboardDemo** project located in the folder where you have stored this book's sample code.

2. In the Project Navigator, select the **Main.Storyboard** file to see the scene shown in Figure 7.56.

*Figure 7.56 The **HideKeyboardDemo** scene.*

At the top of the scene is a text field where the user can enter an email address. When they're finished entering the email address, they can tap the **Verify** button, which checks if the email address is valid.

3. Click the **Run** button in Xcode to run the app. When the app appears in the Simulator, click on the text field to enter an email address and the keyboard pops up (Figure 7.57). However, now the **Verify** button is hidden by the keyboard, and there is no way to tap it.

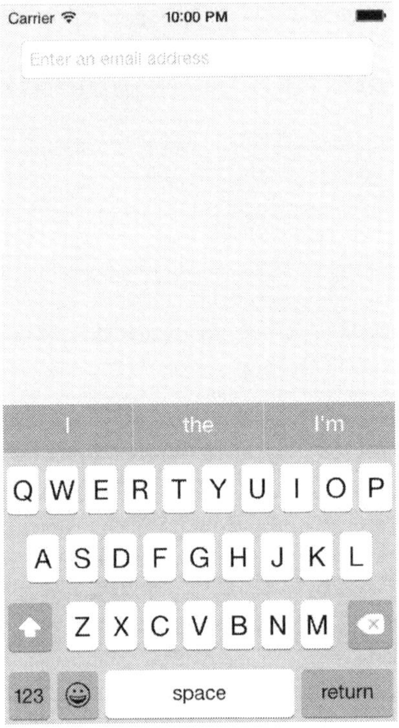

*Figure 7.57 The keyboard is covering the **Verify** button.*

4. Go back to Xcode, click the **Stop** button, and we will fix this problem by creating a method that fires when the user taps the **Return** key.

5. Select the **Main.storyboard** file in the Project Navigator, and then click the Assistant Editor button in the Xcode toolbar. This should display the **ViewController.swift** code file in the Assistant Editor.

6. Next, click the text field in the storyboard to select it, and then go to the Connections Inspector (click the button on the far right in the Inspector toolbar). In the **Sent Events** section, click the connection well to the right of the **Did End on Exit** event and drag down into the **ViewController.swift** file. When the **Insert Action** popup appears (Figure 7.58), let go of your mouse button.

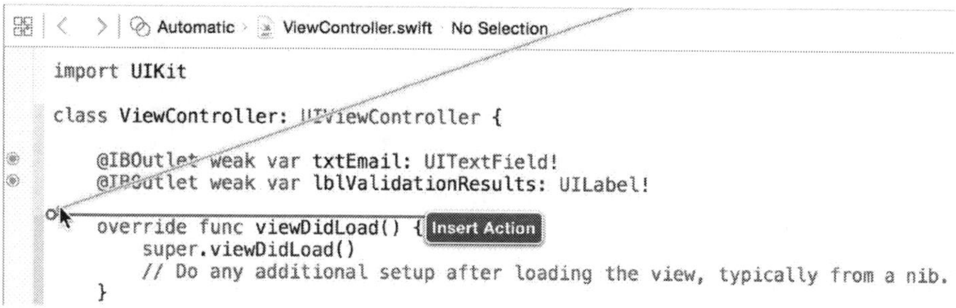

Figure 7.58 Create an action method.

7. In the Create Connection popup's **Name** text box, enter **hideKeyboard** and click the **Connect** button. This creates a new method declaration in the **ViewController.swift** code file:

```
class ViewController: UIViewController {
    @IBOutlet weak var txtEmail: UITextField!
    @IBOutlet weak var lblValidationResults:
UILabel!

@IBAction func hideKeyboard(sender: AnyObject){
}
```

8. Next, add the following code in the **hideKeyboard:** method:

```
@IBAction func hideKeyboard(sender: AnyObject){
      self.view.endEditing(true)
}
```

This method calls the **endEditing:** method to the view, which causes the keyboard to be released.

If you have multiple text fields on a scene, you can hook all of them up to this single method.

9. To see this in action, click the **Run** button in Xcode. When the app appears in the Simulator, click in the text field and enter an email address. Click the **Return** key on the keyboard, and the keyboard should slide back into the bottom of the screen.

You can now click the **Verify** button to see if the email address you entered is valid. When you click this button, the **verifyEmail:** method is called in the view controller, which in turn calls the **isEmailValid** method on the **Email** class to test its validity. This method contains real code you can use to validate email addresses in your own apps.

10. Go back to Xcode and click the **Stop** button.

Hiding the Keyboard When the Background is Touched

Let's use the same project to show how to hide the keyboard when the view background is touched.

1. In the Project Navigator, select **Main.storyboard**, and click in the gray area of the scene to select the view.

2. Go to the Connections Inspector (click the last button on the right in the Inspectors toolbar). As you can see in Figure 7.59, there aren't any events listed from which you can create connections.

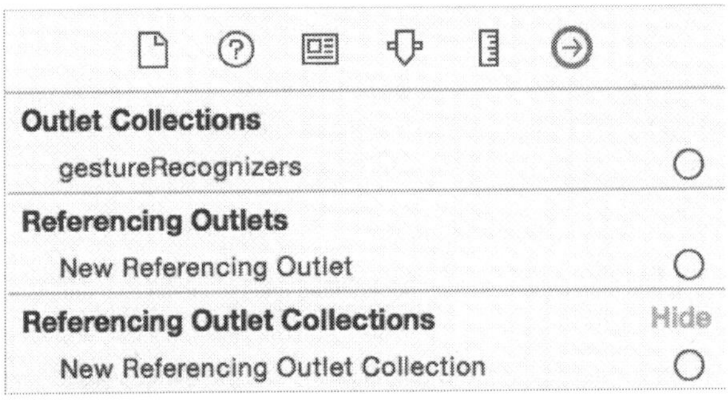

Figure 7.59 A view in the Connections Inspector.

3. This is where a gesture recognizer comes to the rescue! Go to the Object Library in the bottom-right corner of the Xcode window, drag a **Tap Gesture Recognizer** and drop it on the gray area of the view. This adds the gesture recognizer to the dock at the top of the scene (Figure 7.60).

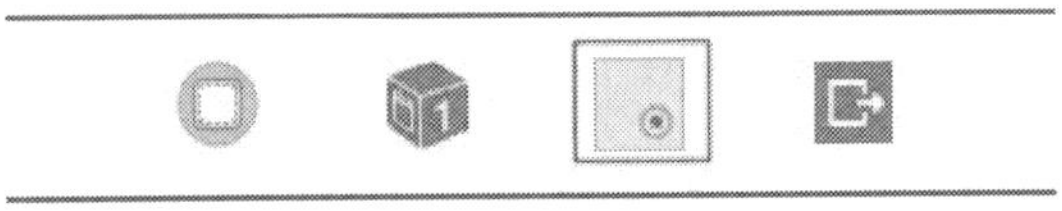

Figure 7.60 The gesture recognizer in the scene dock.

4. Click on the tap gesture recognizer in the scene dock to select it, and then go back to the Connections Inspector.

5. If the Assistant Editor is not currently visible, go to the Xcode toolbar at the top of the screen and click the center button in the **Editor** button group. This should display the **ViewController.swift** file in the Assistant Editor.

6. Under the **Sent Actions** section, click the connection well to the right of the **selector** action, drag down into the **ViewController.swift** file, and hover over the **hideKeyboard:** method. When you see the **Connect Action** popup, release the mouse button to connect the action to this method.

7. To test this, click the **Run** button in Xcode. When the app appears in the Simulator, click in the text field to bring up the keyboard. Afterward, click anywhere in the gray area of the view, and the keyboard should automatically slide back into the bottom of the view!

Table Views and Collection Views

This section covers both table views and collection views—the two user-interface controls used to display large amounts of data.

The Table View and Table View Cell

Table views and *table view cells* were covered extensively in *Book 1: Diving Into iOS* and will be covered even more thoroughly in *Chapter 13: Managing Lists of Data With Table Views*, but I'll provide a quick overview in this section.

Figure 7.61 shows a scene containing a table view that is part of the **iDeliverMobile** project found in this book's sample code.

Table views are the control most commonly used to display lists of data. A table view can have one or more sections (the table view in Figure 7.61 has two sections) and each section can have one or more table view cells.

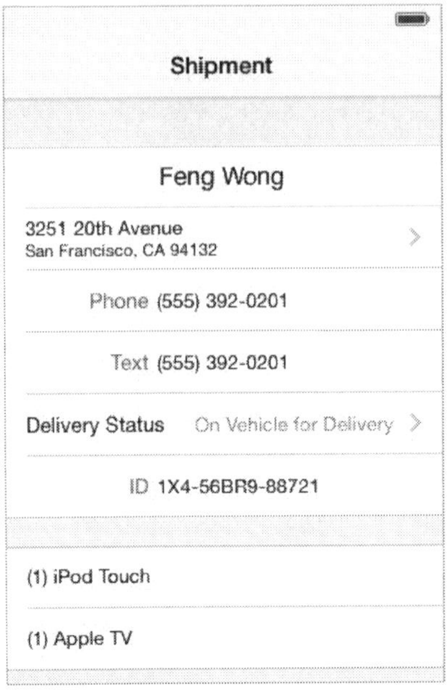

Figure 7.61 A grouped table view.

Figure 7.62 shows the table view's most commonly used attributes.

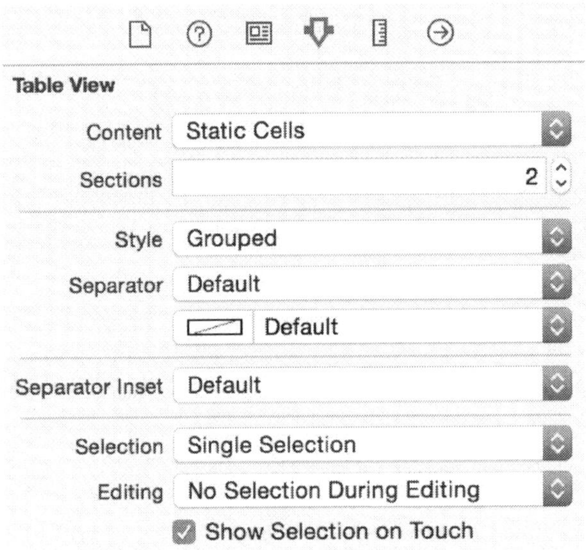

Figure 7.62 Table view common attributes.

- **Content** - The choices for this attribute are:
  - **Static Cells** - Select this option when the content of the cells is static (or unchanging), and you will set the text of the cells at design time.

- **Dynamic Prototypes** - Select this option when the content of the cells is dynamic and will be derived from data at run time.

- **Sections** - Specifies the number of sections in the table view. If the number of sections is known in advance and doesn't change, you can set it here. If it's dynamic and can change, you will set this attribute in code within the view controller.

- **Style** - The choices for this attribute are:

    - **Grouped** - This displays the *table view section* as shown in Figure 7.61.

    - **Plain** - This displays the table view so it fills the screen as shown in the iTunes app in Figure 7.63.

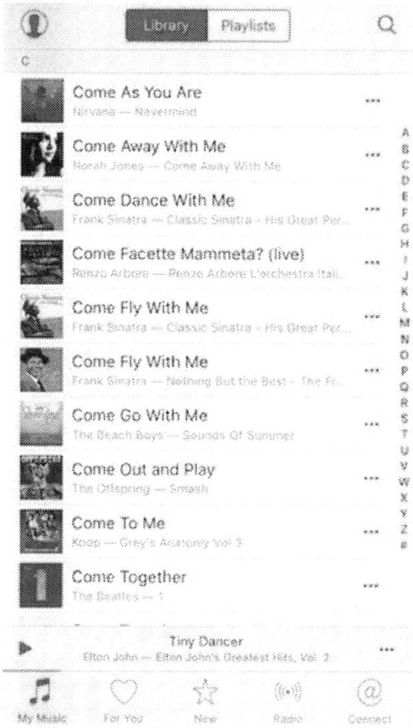

*Figure 7.63 The table view **Style** set to **Plain**.*

- **Separator** - The options for this attribute are:

    - **None** - No separator is displayed between the cells of the table view.

    - **Single Line** - Displays a single thin line between each cell.

- **Single Line Etched** - Displays an etched line between each cell (the default).

  The color selector in this section allows you to specify a color for the separator lines.

- **Separator Insets** - The options for this attribute are:
  - **Default** - By default, the separators are inset from the left edge of the table view.
  - **Custom** - When you choose this option, two spinner controls appear allowing you to specify the number of points the separators are inset from the left and right edges of the table view.
- **Selection** - The options for this attribute are:
  - **No Selection** - Prevents the user from selecting any cells in the table view. Select this option for read-only lists.
  - **Single Selection** - Only one cell can be selected at a time (the default).
  - **Multiple Selection** - Allows the user to select multiple cells in the table view.
- **Editing** - This attribute allows you to specify how many cells a user can select when the table view is in edit mode:
  - **No Selection During Editing** (default)
  - **Single Selection During Editing**
  - **Multiple Selections During Editing**

Collection Views and Collection View Cells

Collection views were discussed briefly earlier in this chapter, but we will discuss them more thoroughly in this section. Again, you can see the collection view at work in this book's **CollectionViewDemo** sample project. Figure 7.64 shows the collection view's key components.

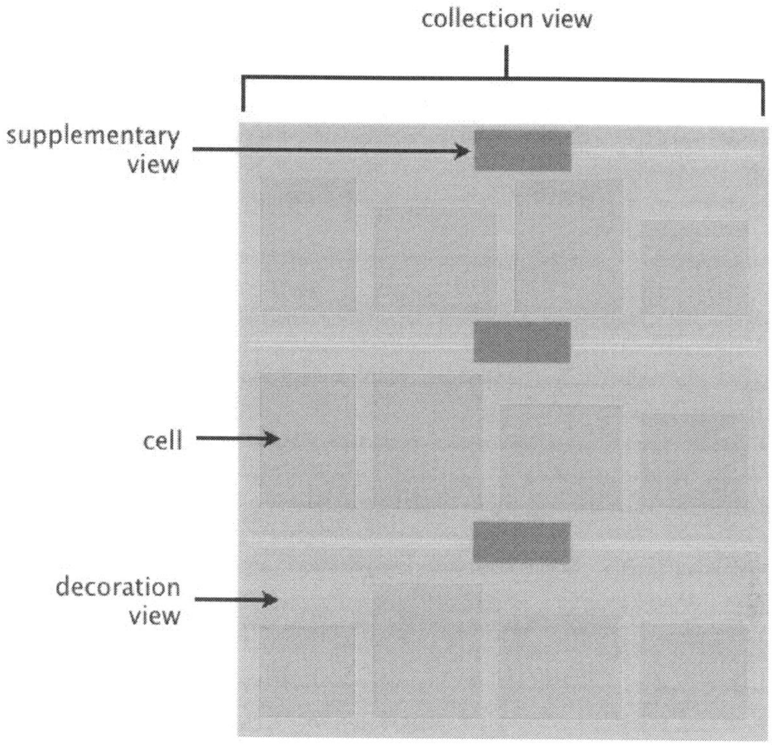

Figure 7.64 The key components of a collection view.

- **Cell** - Each item in the collection view is a cell. At design time, you drop a collection view cell on a collection view and then you configure the cell. For example, you can add an image view inside the cell for displaying pictures. If all cells in your collection view have the same appearance (most do), you can create one cell at design time that is used as a template for all cells at run time.

- **Supplementary views** - You can add supplementary header and footer views to the collection view. Typically, you do this to provide descriptive information about the items in each section.

- **Decoration views** - Provides a visual adornment for a collection view that is not tied to data. It's usually used to create a custom background for the collection view. Note that you cannot use a decoration view with Apple's default Flow Layout, which you will learn about in just a bit.

- **Layout object** - Controls the visual presentation of the collection view's content including size and positioning of cells.

Figure 7.65 shows the collection view's most commonly used attributes.

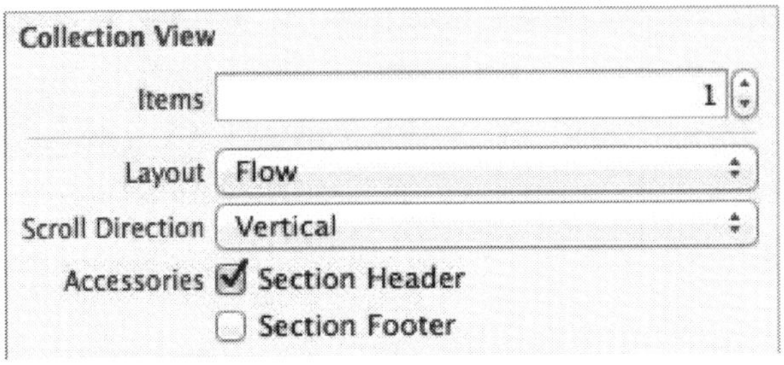

Figure 7.65 Common attributes of the collection view.

- **Items** - Indicates the number of items in the collection view. Typically, this attribute is not set at design time, but is set in code within the associated view controller based on a variable number of items to be displayed.

- **Layout** - This specifies the class that is used for the layout object. If this attribute is set to **Flow** (the default), the collection view uses Apple's Flow Layout class, which arranges cells in a line, fitting as many cells in a line as possible. It automatically flows cells to the next line as needed.

  If this attribute is set to **Custom**, it displays a combo box where you can enter the name of your custom layout class.

- **Scroll Direction** - This attribute only appears if the **Layout** attribute is set to **Flow**. You can select a scroll direction of **Vertical** (up and down) or **Horizontal** (left and right).

- The **Accessories** section only appears when the **Layout** attribute is set to **Flow**. It allows you to specify if you want a **Section Header** or **Section Footer**. If you select one of these options, an area is created in the collection view where you can add user-interface controls. Typically, you add a label to the header or footer as shown in Figure 7.66 and you set the text of the label from within the view controller at run time.

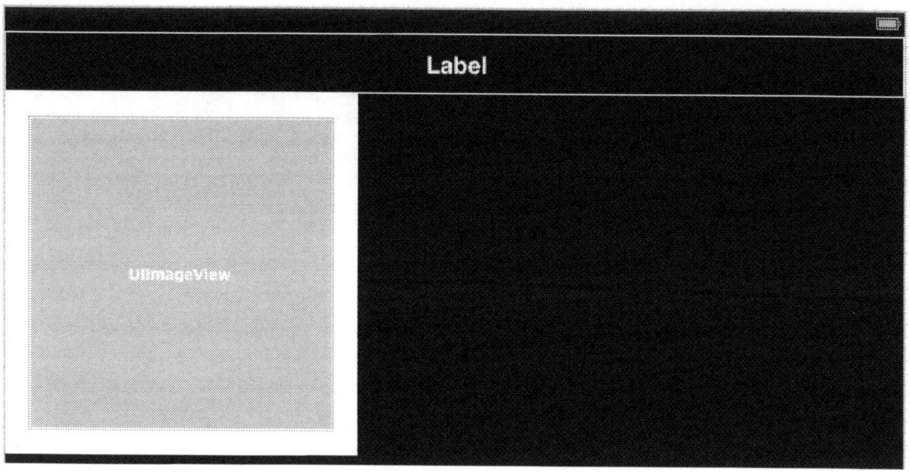

Figure 7.66 A section header at the top of a collection view.

If you are using your own custom layout rather than the default Flow Layout, you can drag a **Collection Reusable View** object from the Object Library and drop it on your collection view to create headers and footers.

Miscellaneous Views

In this section, we will cover a variety of views that allow you to display images, multiple lines of text, web pages, maps, and so on.

Image View

Many iOS apps use an **Image View** (shown in Figure 7.67) to display images, which the user can view and interact with.

Figure 7.67 An image view control at design time.

Figure 7.68 shows the images view's most commonly used attributes.

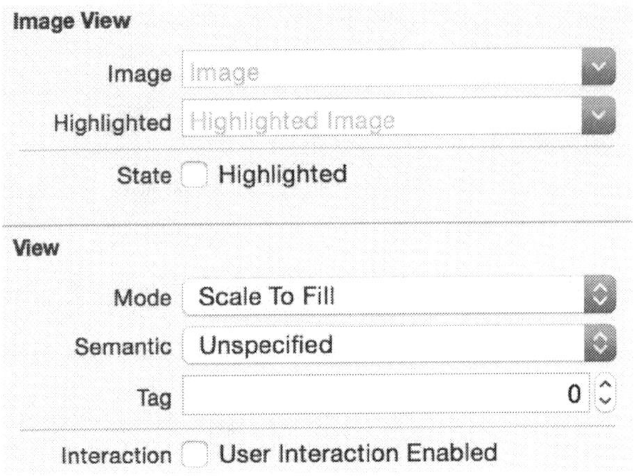

Figure 7.68 Common attributes of the image view.

- **Image** - Specifies the image to be displayed when the image view is in its normal state. From this combo box, you can select any image file that has been added to your project.

- **Highlighted** - Specifies the image to be displayed when the image view is in its highlighted state.

- **State** - If this check box is not selected (the default), the image view is in its normal state. If this check box is selected, it's in its highlighted state.

- **Mode** - This attribute allows you to specify how the appearance of images should be changed to fit into the image view. All of these options were covered earlier in *Chapter 5: The Inspectors* under the section The Attributes Inspector.

- **Semantic** - Specifies if the view should be flipped when switching between layouts.

- **Interaction** - If you want the user to be able to interact with the image view, you need to select the **User Interaction Enabled** option.

Highlighting an Image View

How does an image view get to be in a highlighted state? Oddly enough, touching or tapping the image doesn't automatically put it into this state, although that's typically what you see in apps such as the built-in Photos app. You have to take a few extra steps to make this happen:

1. Specify an **Image** and an alternate **Highlighted Image** so the user sees a change when they tap the image view.

2. Select the **User Interaction Enabled** option.

3. Write code that responds to the user tapping the image view and sets the image view's **highlighted** property to true.

Only when you do these three things does the user see the highlighted image at run time.

The **ImageViewDemo** project provides an example of how to do this. If you open the project and select the main storyboard in the Project Navigator, you will see an image view at the top of the scene that contains a picture of a young Steve Jobs. If you click on the image view and go to the Attributes Inspector, you will see the settings shown in Figure 7.69.

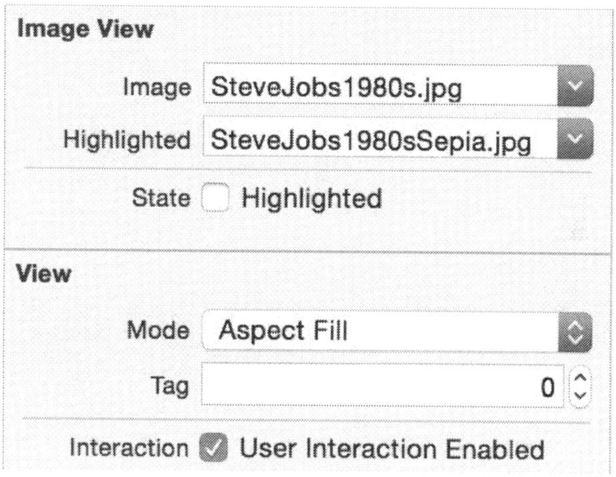

*Figure 7.69 The **ImageViewDemo** attribute settings.*

The **Image** attribute is set to a regular color image shown at the top of Figure 7.70. The **Highlighted Image** is set to a sepia version of the image shown at the bottom of Figure 7.70. Also, notice the **User Interaction Enabled** check box is selected.

Figure 7.70 The regular and highlighted images.

At run time, the user sees the color version of the image, but when they tap the image view, they will see it change to the sepia image. Go ahead and run the project to give it a try.

Go back to Xcode and select the **ViewController.swift** implementation file, you will see the following method that is run when the image view is tapped at run time:

```
@IBAction func topImagePressed(sender:
  UILongPressGestureRecognizer) {
  switch sender.state {
   case UIGestureRecognizerState.Began:
      self.topImageView.highlighted = true
   case UIGestureRecognizerState.Ended:
      self.topImageView.highlighted = false
   default:
      break
  }
}
```

This code sets the state of the image view to **highlighted** when the user taps the image view, and then sets **highlighted** to false when the user lifts their finger. You will learn more about how to connect up this method to an image view later in this chapter under the section **Gesture Recognizers**.

Displaying Multiple Animated Images

One of the more fun features of the image view is its ability to display multiple animated images. I'm sure you noticed the image view at the bottom of the scene (Figure 7.71) when you opened up the **ImageViewDemo** project.

Figure 7.71 Steamboat Willie at the helm!

Run the **ImageViewDemo** project, tap the image view at the bottom of the screen and enjoy the animation! So how do we get this magic to happen?

First of all, I took several screen shots of the Steamboat Willie cartoon and added these to the project, four of which are shown in Figure 7.72.

Figure 7.72 Several images included in ***ImageViewDemo.***

Next, I added code to load these up into the image view. To see this, go to the Project Navigator and click on the **ViewController.swift** file. You will see the following code in the **viewDidLoad** method:

```
self.bottomImageView.animationImages =
[UIImage(named:"SBW1.png")!,
    UIImage(named:"SBW2.png")!,
    UIImage(named:"SBW1.png")!,
    UIImage(named:"SBW2.png")!,
    UIImage(named:"SBW1.png")!,
    UIImage(named:"SBW2.png")!,
    UIImage(named:"SBW3.png")!,
    UIImage(named:"SBW4.png")!,
    UIImage(named:"SBW5.png")!,
    UIImage(named:"SBW1.png")!,
    UIImage(named:"SBW2.png")!,
    UIImage(named:"SBW1.png")!,
    UIImage(named:"SBW2.png")!]
self.bottomImageView.animationDuration = 3.0
self.bottomImageView.animationRepeatCount = 5
```

This code creates an array of the images (some images are added multiple times to create a better effect) and stores the array in the **animationImages** property. Afterward, the **animationDuration** is set to **3.00**. This tells the image view to display the full sequence of images over a 3 second period. The **animationRepeatCount** property is set to **5**, which tells the image view to repeat the animation five times.

Rather than start the animation immediately, I wanted the animation to start and stop when the user tapped the bottom image. So, I added code to the view controller's **bottomImageTapped:** method, which (as I'm sure you can guess) fires when the user taps the bottom image. Here's the code:

```
@IBAction func bottomImageTapped(sender:
AnyObject) {
  if self.bottomImageView.isAnimating()
  {
    self.bottomImageView.stopAnimating()
   }
   else
   {
    self.bottomImageView.startAnimating()
   }
}
```

This code first checks the image view's **isAnimating** property to see if it's already animating the images. If it is, a **stopAnimating** message is sent to the image view. If it's *not*, a **startAnimating** message is sent to the image view. Again, you will learn more about connecting up this method to the image view later in this chapter.

If you have image files that end in a number and want to display them sequentially (unlike the mix of images used in this sample), you can do this instead:

```
self.bottomImageView.image =
  UIImage.animatedImageNamed("SBW", duration: 3.0)
```

This code calls the **animatedImageNamed** method of the **UIImage** class which returns an animated image. The result is stored in the image view's **image** property rather than its **animationImages** property. With this approach, you can set the animation duration, but not the repeat count. This works well for animations that start right away and run continuously. Start the animation by storing the animated image to the **image** property and stop the animation by setting the **image** property to **nil**.

The Text View

The **Text View** (Figure 7.73) allows users to enter multiple lines of text. You can change the font, color, and alignment of text in a text view.

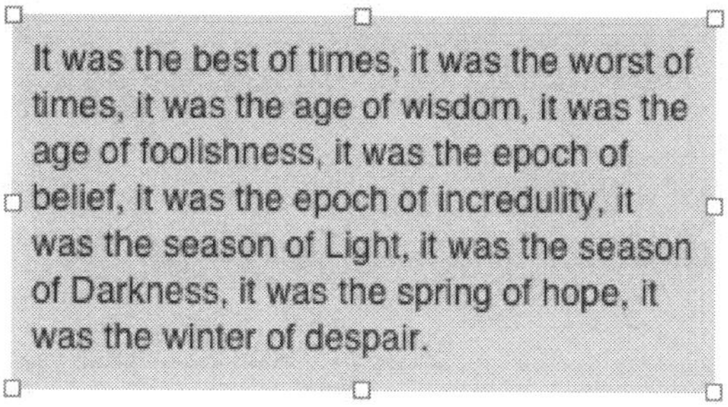

Figure 7.73 The Text View control.

The text field and text view controls are similar— both allow the user to enter text. You should use the text field in situations where there is a small amount of text to be entered (names, email addresses, postal codes, phone numbers, etc.) and use the text view for longer text entry.

As shown in Figure 7.74, the text view also has many of the same attributes as the text field. For example, you can set the **Text** attribute to **Plain** or

Attributed, and you can set the **Color**, **Font**, and **Alignment** of the text. They also share the **Capitalization**, **Correction**, **Keyboard**, **Appearance**, **Return Key**, **Auto-enable Return Key**, and **Secure** attributes. Check out the section ***Text Field*** earlier in this chapter for details on these attributes.

*Figure 7.74 Common **Text View** attributes.*

Inserting New Lines

If you are entering default text in the text view's **Text** attribute in the Attributes Inspector, just type **Option +Return**, and a new line is added to the text for you (this is a little known Xcode trick).

To add a new line in code, you can include a **\n** character in a string. For example:

```
self.textView.text = "1 Infinite Loop\nCupertino, CA"
```

This code stores a text string containing a **\n** character to the **text** property of a text view. This results in two lines of text being displayed in the text view at run time as shown in Figure 7.75.

Figure 7.75 Multiple lines of text in a text view.

Detecting Special Information in a Text View

The **Detection** section of the text view attributes contains options that are unique to the text view. You can specify that you want the text view to automatically detect the following information (these options only work if the **Editable** attribute is *unselected*):

- **Links** - When this option is selected, web addresses and email addresses are automatically hyperlinked. Tapping a web address at run time launches the Safari browser and navigates to the address. Tapping an email address opens up the Mail app and creates an email to the specified email address (this does not work on the Simulator because the Simulator doesn't have the Mail app).

- **Addresses** - When this option is selected, physical addresses are automatically hyperlinked, and tapping them at run time takes you to that address in the Maps app.

- **Phone Numbers** - When this option is selected, phone numbers are automatically hyperlinked, and tapping them pops up a dialog that asks if you would like to call the specified number. Again, this doesn't work in the Simulator because it doesn't have the ability to make phone calls.

- **Events** - When this option is selected, dates and times are automatically hyperlinked, and tapping them brings up the popup dialog shown in Figure 7.76, which offers some interesting options such as **Create Event** or **Show in Calendar**.

Figure 7.76 This dialog appears when you tap a date or time in a text view.

Web View

The **Web View** shown in Figure 7.77 (the toolbars at the top and bottom of the screen are not part of the web view) allows users to view web content within your app as well as other content such as spreadsheets, slides, word processing documents, and PDF files.

Figure 7.77 The Web View control.

Figure 7.78 shows the most commonly used properties of the web view control.

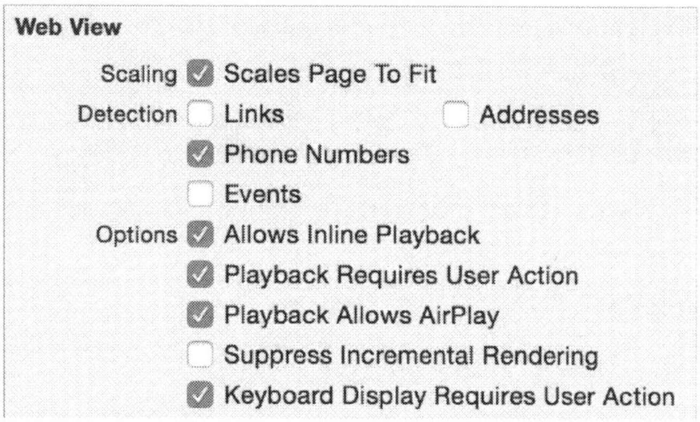

Figure 7.78 Commonly used Web View attributes.

- **Scales Page to Fit** - When this option is selected, the web page is automatically scaled to fit within the web view. Typically, you want this option selected.

- **Detection** - Just as with the text view control, you can specify that you want the web view to identify and add hyperlinks to **Links**, **Addresses**, **Phone Numbers**, and **Events**.

- **Allows Inline Playback** - Specifies if HTML5 videos display inline or use the native full-screen controller. Note that for the video to play inline, the **video** element in the HTML document must include the **webkit-playsinline** attribute.

- **Playback Requires User Action** - Specifies if HTML5 videos play automatically or requires user interaction to start playing. For automatic playback, make sure the **<audio>** or **<video>** element you want to play has its **autoplay** attribute set.

- **Playback Allows AirPlay** - Specifies if AirPlay is allowed from the web view.

- **Suppress Incremental Rendering** - Specifies if the web view suppresses content rendering until the content is fully loaded.

- **Keyboard Display Requires User Interaction** - Specifies if web content can programmatically display the keyboard.

You can see a live example of the web view at work in the **WebViewDemo** project that is part of this book's sample code.

Loading Web Content

You use the web view's **gotoURL:** method to load web content. In the **WebViewDemo** project's **ViewController. swift** file, you can see the following code in the **viewDidLoad** method:

```
self.gotoURL("http://www.apple.com")
```

This code calls the **gotoURL:** method on the view controller, passing the Apple website as an argument. The **gotoURL:** method contains the following code:

```
func gotoURL(url: String) {
  self.activityIndicator.startAnimating()
  if let url = NSURL(string: url) {
      let urlRequest = NSURLRequest(URL: url)
      self.webView.loadRequest(urlRequest)
  }
}
```

The first line of code tells the activity indicator to start animating. The next two lines of code create an **NSURL** object from the web address string, and then create an **NSURLRequest** object from the **NSURL** object. You need to do this because you can't pass a string to a web view control. It only accepts an **NSURLRequest** object (although it *would* be nice if Apple would change the web view so you *could* pass in a string).

Finally, the last line of code calls the **loadRequest:** method on the web view, passing the newly created **NSURLRequest** object.

Since the **startAnimating** method was called on the activity indicator, its **stopAnimating** method should be called when the web page has finished loading. How do we know when this occurs? When a web view finishes loading a web page, it calls the **webViewDidFinishLoad:** method on the object that has been registered as its delegate. Typically, this is the associated view controller. You can see this method in the **ViewController.swift** file:

```
func webViewDidFinishLoad(webView: UIWebView) {
```

```
    self.activityIndicator.stopAnimating()
    self.setButtonsEnabled()
}
```

The first line of code in this method is the important one in this example. It calls the **stopAnimating** method on the activity indicator. We will examine the second line of code in the next section.

Figure 7.79 shows the order of events when loading web content in a web view:

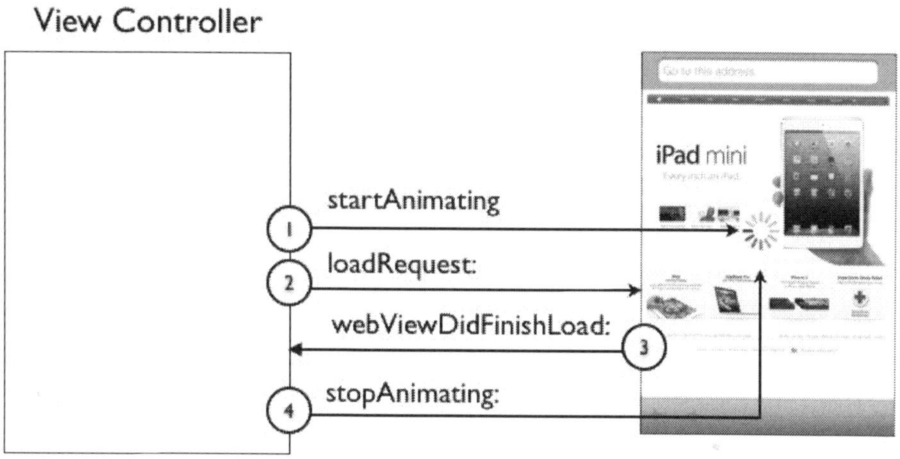

Figure 7.79 Loading web content in a web view.

1. The view controller calls the **startAnimating** method on the activity indicator.
2. The view controller calls the **loadRequest:** method on the web view.
3. When the web view has finished loading the web content, it calls the **webViewDidFinishLoad:** method of the view controller.
4. The **webViewDidFinishLoad:** method calls the **stopAnimating:** method on the activity indicator.

How does the web view know that the view controller has a **webViewDidFinishLoad:** method? Because the view controller implements the **UIWebViewDelegate** protocol:

```
class ViewController: UIViewController,UIWebViewDelegate {
```

You need to add this protocol declaration to your view controller so the web view can call back to the view controller in this way.

You also need to specify that the view controller is a delegate for the web view. To do this, **Control+Click** the web view in the storyboard, drag up to the **View Controller** object in the *scene dock*, and release the mouse button. This displays an **Outlets** popup (Figure 7.80) in which you can select the **delegate** option.

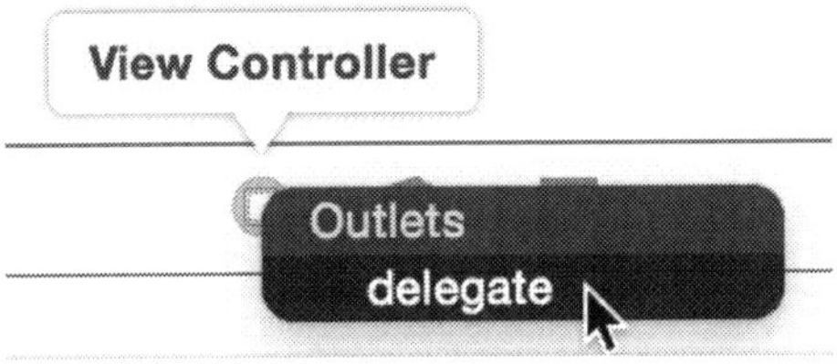

Figure 7.80 Setting the view controller as the web view's delegate.

Backward, Forward, Reload, Stop Loading

The web view control has several methods you can call to control its behavior.

- **goBack** - Loads the previous location in the web view's back-forward list (the list of content loaded in the web view during the current session).

- **goForward** - Loads the next location in the back-forward list.

- **reload** - Reloads the current page.

- **stopLoading** - Stops the web view from loading the current content.

The **WebViewDemo** project's main scene has a toolbar located below the web view that contains custom **Back** and **Forward** buttons (these buttons are not provided by Apple, so you have to build your own) that are separated by a **Fixed Space Bar Button Item** (Figure 7.81).

*Figure 7.81 The **Back** and **Forward** buttons*

When you first load the web view, there is no previous or next content, so these buttons should be disabled.

As discussed in the previous section, when web content has finished loading, the **webViewDidFinishLoad:** method is called in the view controller. This method makes a call to the **setButtonsEnabled** method, which contains the following code:

```
func setButtonsEnabled() {
  if (self.webView.canGoBack) {
   self.backButton.enabled = true;
   } else {
     self.backButton.enabled = false;
  }
  if (self.webView.canGoForward) {
    self.forwardButton.enabled = true;
  }
   else {
    self.forwardButton.enabled = false;
  }
}
```

This code checks the **canGoBack** and **canGoForward** properties of the web view and enables or disables the buttons based on the value of these properties. If **canGoBack** is true, the back button is enabled, otherwise it's disabled. If the **canGoForward** property is true, the forward button is enabled, otherwise it's disabled.

When the user clicks the **Back** button, the **goBack:** method is executed, which calls the **goBack** method on the web view:

```
@IBAction func goBack(sender: AnyObject) {
  self.webView.goBack()
}
```

When the user taps the **Forward** button, the **goForward:** method is executed, which sends a **goForward** message to the web view:

```
@IBAction func goForward(sender: AnyObject) {
  self.webView.goForward()
}
```

Loading Other Content

In addition to web content, the web view control can also load the following document types:

- Excel (.xls)
- Keynote (.key.zip)
- Numbers (.numbers.zip)
- Pages (.pages.zip)
- PDF (.pdf)
- Powerpoint (.ppt)
- Word (.doc)
- Rich Text Format (.rtf)
- Rich Text Format Directory (.rtfd.zip)
- Keynote '09 (.key)
- Numbers '09 (.numbers)
- Pages '09 (.pages)

Apple's documentation indicates that Excel, Powerpoint, and Word documents must be saved using Microsoft Office 07 or newer formats. Keynote, Numbers, and Pages documents must be created with iWork '06 or iWork '08 and must be ZIP compressed. Rich Text Format Directory (.rtfd) documents must also be ZIP compressed.

First, you need to add the file you want loaded into the web view to your project. Next, you need to write code that loads the file in the web view. The following code demonstrates how to load a PDF file into the web view:

```
let path = NSBundle.mainBundle().pathForResource(
    "Book1.pdf", ofType: nil)!
let url = NSURL(fileURLWithPath: path)!
let urlRequest = NSURLRequest(URL: url)
self.webView.loadRequest(urlRequest)
```

The first line of code gets the path to the file you want to load. The second line of code creates an **NSURL** object, and the third line creates an **NSURLRequest** object. The last line of code loads the document into the web view.

Map View

The **Map View** control (Figure 7.82) allows you to embed a map interface in your app.

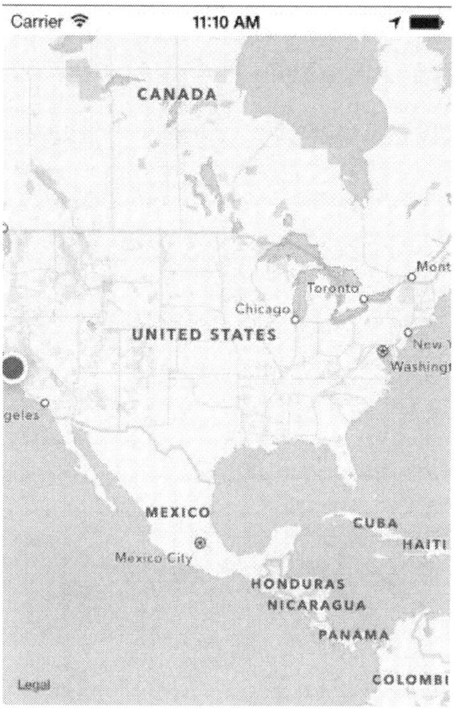

Figure 7.82 The map view control.

It's important to note that for your app to use the map view control at run time, you must include the **MapKit** framework in your project. For more information on adding frameworks to your project, check out *Chapter 14: Working With the Project Editor.*

With the map view you can:

- Display the user's current location
- Zoom in on specified coordinates
- Add annotations (in the form of pins) to the map

Figure 7.83 shows the map view's most commonly used attributes.

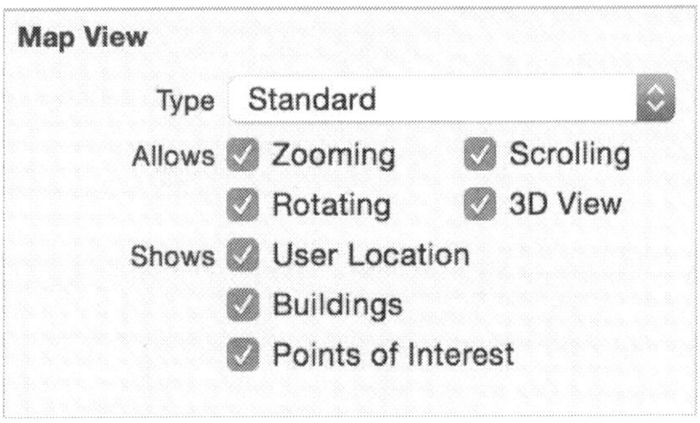

Figure 7.83 Common Map View attributes.

- **Type** - This attribute specifies the type of map to be displayed. The options are:
  - **Standard** - Displays a standard map as shown in Figure 7.82.
  - **Satellite** - Displays a map as an image taken from a satellite without displaying cities or roads.
  - **Hybrid** - Displays a combination of the satellite and standard maps including cities and roads as shown in Figure 7.84.

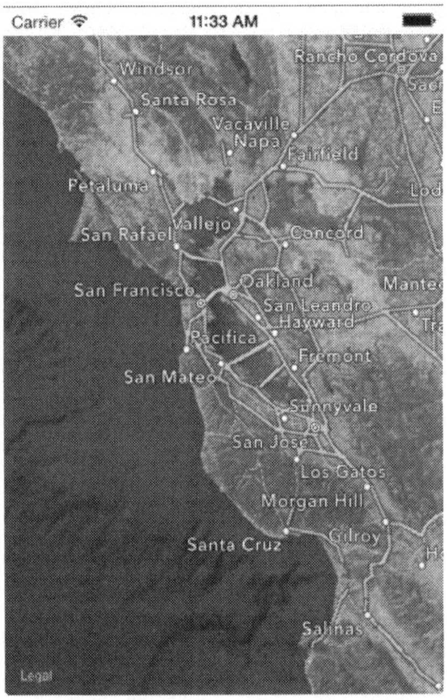

Figure 7.84 The map view in Hybrid mode.

- **Zooming** - When this option is selected, the user can use a pinch gesture to zoom in and out of the map.
- **Scrolling** - When this option is selected, the user can scroll around to different locations on the map.
- **Rotating** - When this option is selected and a camera is associated with the map, the user can rotate the map around its center point. If this option is *not* selected, the map is always oriented so true north is at the top of the map.
- **3D View** - When this option is selected, the user can view the map in 3D mode where the plane of the map can be tilted. If this option is *not* selected, the map is always displayed flat as if the user is looking straight down onto it.
- **Shows User Location** - When this option is selected, the map automatically shows the user's current location when it first loads up.

  When running in the Simulator, the map shows Apple headquarters at 1 Infinite Loop, Cupertino, CA as the user's current location. You can change this default location by selecting an alternate option in the Simulator's **Debug** > **Location** menu. The **Custom Location** menu option allows you to specify the location by longitude and latitude.
- **Shows Buildings** - When this option is selected and the camera has a pitch angle greater than zero, the map extrudes buildings so they extend above the map plane, creating a 3D effect.
- **Shows Points of Interest** - When this option is selected, the map displays information for restaurants, schools, and other points of interest.

Zooming in Programmatically

One of the most common questions for new users of the map view is "How do I zoom in automatically so the user doesn't have to manually zoom?"

Let's walk through the process step by step using the **iDeliverMobile** project as an example. In *Book 1: Diving Into iOS,* you created a scene that contained a map view control, and you added the **MapKit** framework to the project.

This scene displayed the user's location but didn't automatically zoom in. Let's fix that.

1. Open the **iDeliverMobile** project located in the folder where you have stored this book's sample code.

2. In the Project Navigator, select the **Main.storyboard** file. Scroll the storyboard so you can see the **Location** scene shown in Figure 7.85.

*Figure 7.85 The iDeliverMobile **Location** scene.*

3. In the scene dock at the top of the **Location** scene, click the icon on the left to select the view controller. Select the Identity Inspector (the third button from the left in the Inspector toolbar) and you will see the view controller **Class** is set to **ViewController**.

4. Now let's add a property to the view controller that references the map view control. This allows you to access the map view from within the view controller.

   First, you need to display the Assistant Editor. To do this, go to the toolbar at the top of the Xcode window and select the center button in the **Editor** button group. This should now show the **ViewController.swift** file in the Assistant Editor.

Next, **Control+Click** on the map view and drag down to the **ViewController.swift** file below the **class** declaration. When the **Insert Outlet or Collection** popup appears (Figure 7.86), let go of your mouse button to display the **Connection** popup. In this popup, set the **Name** to **mapView** and then click the **Connect** button. This adds a new outlet property declaration to the view controller:

```
class ViewController: UIViewController {
@IBOutlet weak var mapView: MKMapView!
```

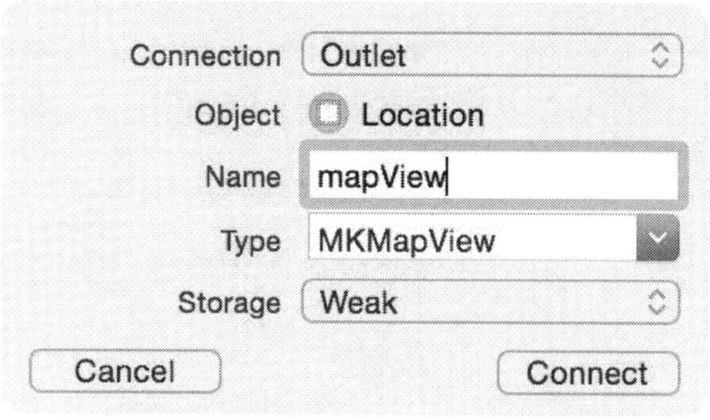

*Figure 7.86 Create a **mapView** outlet.*

5. Since you haven't imported the **MapKit** framework yet, you are going to see an error next to the new property. Add the following **import** statement to the top of the **ViewController.swift** file to get rid of the compiler error:

```
import UIKit
import CoreLocation
import MapKit
```

6. Next, you must adopt the **MKMapViewDelegate** protocol on the **ViewController**. This allows the map view to use the view controller as a delegate, and call methods that it needs on the view controller.

   To do this, add the protocol declaration highlighted in the following code:

```
class ViewController: UIViewController,
MKMapViewDelegate
{
@IBOutlet weak var mapView: MKMapView!
```

7. Now that the **ViewController** is configured to be a delegate for the map view control, let's create the delegate connection between the map view and the view controller.

   First, let's close the Assistant Editor. To do this, go to the toolbar at the top of the Xcode window and click the button on the left in the **Editor** button group.

   Next, go to the Project Navigator and select the **Storyboard** file. Afterward, **Control+Click** on the map view in the **Location** scene and drag up to the **View Controller** icon in the scene dock (Figure 7.87).

   When you release your mouse, an **Outlets** popup appears. Click on **delegate**, and this sets the view controller as the delegate of the map view.

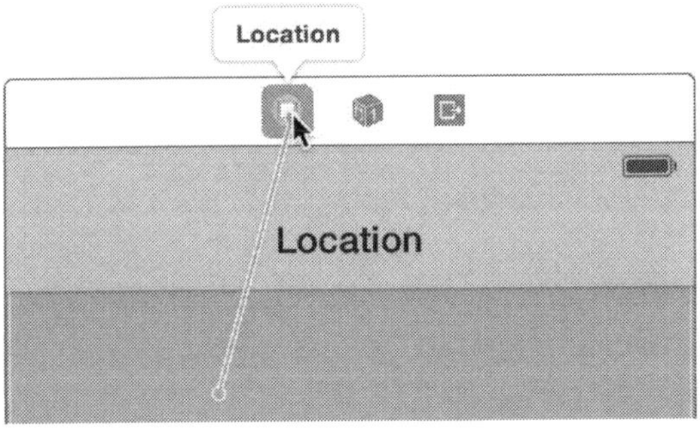

Figure 7.87 Setting up the map view delegate.

8. Now it's time to add code to the view controller that zooms in on the user's location. There are three main steps involved:

   - Create a location object specifying the latitude and longitude of the user's location.
   - Create a region object specifying the latitude, longitude, and size of the map region to be displayed in the map view.
   - Tell the map view to display the map region.

   To add this code, go to the Project Navigator and select the **ViewController.swift** file. Add the following highlighted method towards the top of the file just below the **viewDidLoad** method:

```
func mapView(mapView: MKMapView!,
didUpdateUserLocation userLocation:
```

```
MKUserLocation!) {
    // Declare a location object
let location = CLLocationCoordinate2D(latitude:
userLocation.coordinate.latitude, longitude:
userLocation.coordinate.longitude)
    // Create a region object
    let region =
    MKCoordinateRegionMakeWithDistance(location,
    2000, 2000)
    let adjustedRegion =
     self.mapView.regionThatFits(region)
    // Adjust the map view's region
    self.mapView.setRegion(adjustedRegion,
     animated: true)
}
```

The map view automatically calls this method when the user's location is updated. Since the map view's **Shows User Location** is selected, at startup when the user's location is first determined, the map view calls this **mapView:didUpdateUserLocation:** method.

The first line of code declares a location object and set its **latitude** and **longitude** properties to the latitude and longitude of the user's location, which is passed to this method in the **userLocation** *parameter*.

The next few lines of code create a **region** object using the **MKCoordinateRegionMakeWithDistance** function. This code uses the **location** object to set the coordinates of the region, and the values **2000, 2000**, which specify the size of the region in meters. If you want to zoom in further, enter smaller numbers (because you are telling the map to zoom in on a smaller area). If you want to zoom out, enter larger numbers.

The last line of code calls the **setRegion:** method on the map view, passing in the region object with the specified location and area.

9. To see how this works, click the **Run** button in Xcode. When the app appears in the Simulator, select the first item in the **Deliveries** list, and then select the address in the **Shipment** list. This displays the user's current location and zooms in as shown in (Figure 7.88).

10. Go back to Xcode and click the **Stop** button to stop the app from running in the Simulator.

Figure 7.88 The map view zooms in!

Switching Between Standard, Satellite, & Hybrid

You often want to give your users the ability to switch between standard, satellite, and hybrid map types. To show you how to do this, let's use the **iDeliverMobile** app again as an example. It has a Map Options scene that contains **Standard**, **Satellite**, and **Hybrid** buttons that we can activate for this purpose.

1. First, let's create a view controller for the Map Options scene. Go to the Project Navigator, right- click the **ViewController.swift** file, and select **New File...** from the shortcut menu.

2. On the left side of the New File dialog, select **Source** under the **iOS** section, select the **Cocoa Touch Class** template on the right, and then click **Next**.

3. In the next step of the New File dialog, select **UITableViewController** in the **Subclass of** combo box, and enter **MapOptionsViewController** as the **Class**, and then click **Next**.

4. In the **Save** dialog, click **Create**. This adds the new **MapOptionsViewController.swift** file to the Project Navigator.

5. Since the cells of the Map Options table view are static, we don't need the methods in the new table view controller that dynamically build the table view. So, in the Project Navigator, select the **MapOptionsViewController.swift** file and delete these two methods:

```
override func
   numberOfSectionsInTableView(tableView:
   UITableView) -> Int {
    // #warning Potentially incomplete method.
    // Return the number of sections.
    return 0
}

   override func tableView(tableView: UITableView,
   numberOfRowsInSection section: Int) -> Int {
    // #warning Incomplete method
    // Return the number of rows in the section.
    return 0
}
```

While you're at it, you can also delete the other methods that are commented out from the view controller since you won't be needing them.

Now you need to associate the new view controller with the Map Options scene.

1. In the Project Navigator, select the **Main.storyboard** file.

2. In the storyboard, scroll to the **Map Options** scene and click the status bar at the top of the scene to select the view controller.

3. Go to the Identity Inspector (click the third button from the left in the Inspector toolbar) and set the **Class** to **MapOptionsViewController**.

In the next steps, you will create an outlet and an action method for the segmented control (the control that contains the three map options buttons).

1. Display the Assistant Editor by clicking the center button in the Xcode toolbar's **Editor** button group. This should display the

MapOptionsViewController. swift file. If it doesn't, select this file in the Assistant Editor's jump bar.

2. **Control+Click** the segmented control and then drag your mouse to the **MapOptionsViewController.swift** file just below the **class** declaration. When the **Insert Outlet, Action, or Outlet Collection** popup appears, release the mouse button. In the Connection popup, set the **Name** to **segMapType** and then click the **Connect** button. This creates a new outlet property:

```
class MapOptionsViewController:UITableViewController {
 @IBOutlet weak var segMapType: UISegmentedControl!
```

3. Go back to the storyboard, and with the segmented control still selected, go to the Connections Inspector by clicking the button on the far right in the Inspector toolbar.

   Under the **Sent Events** section, click the connection well to the right of the **Value Changed** event and drag to the **MapOptionsViewController.swift** file below the **segMapType** property declaration. When you see the **Insert Action** popup, release your mouse button.

   In the **Connection** popup, set the action method **Name** to **mapTypeChanged,** set the **Type** to **UISegmentedControl** (Figure 7.89), and then click the **Connect** button.

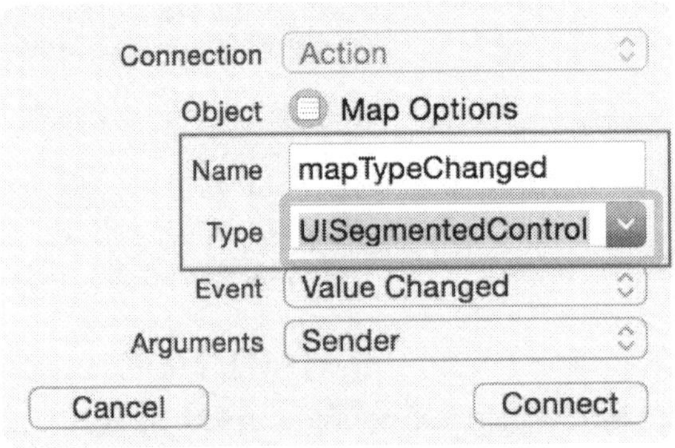

*Figure 7.89 Set the **Name** and **Type**.*

This adds a new **mapTypeChanged:** action method to the code file method to the code file:

```
class MapOptionsViewController:
UITableViewController {
 @IBOutlet weak var segMapType:
   UISegmentedControl!
@IBAction func mapTypeChanged(sender:
 UISegmentedControl) {
}
```

4. Before implementing this method, you need to add a property to this code file that will contain a reference to the map view in the Location scene. First, in the MapOptionsViewController.swift file, you need to import the MapKit header file:

```
import UIKit
import MapKit
```

5. Then, add the following property declaration:

```
class MapOptionsViewController:
UITableViewController {
var mapView: MKMapView!
```

6. You no longer need the Assistant Editor, so go to the toolbar at the top of the Xcode window and click the left button in the Editor button group.

7. Now add the following code to the mapTypeChanged: method:

```
@IBAction func mapTypeChanged(sender:
UISegmentedControl) {
switch sender.selectedSegmentIndex {
   case 0:
// Standard
   self.mapView.mapType = MKMapType.Standard
   case 1:
   // Satellite
   self.mapView.mapType =
     MKMapType.Satellite
case 2:
// Hybrid
    self.mapView.mapType = MKMapType.Hybrid
  default:
```

```
    break
    }
}
```

This method is called automatically when the user selects a button in the segmented control. It checks the segmented control's **selectedSegmentIndex** property to see which button was selected and then sets the **mapType** property of the map view accordingly.

8. Now add the following code to the viewDidLoad method so when the view first loads, the correct button in the segmented control is selected:

```
override func viewDidLoad() {
    super.viewDidLoad()
switch self.mapView.mapType {
 case MKMapType.Standard:
    self.segMapType.selectedSegmentIndex = 0
 case MKMapType.Satellite:
    self.segMapType.selectedSegmentIndex = 1
 case MKMapType.Hybrid:
    self.segMapType.selectedSegmentIndex = 2
 default:
break
    }
}
```

As the final step, now you need to add code to the **ViewController.swift** file so it stores a reference to the map view in the **MapOptionsViewController** when it segues to the Map Options scene.

1. Since you need to reference the segue between the Location and Map Options scenes in code, you need to set its **Identifier** in the storyboard. To do this, select the **Main.Storyboard** file in the Project Navigator.

2. Next, click on the segue between the **Location** and the Navigation Controller scene (*not* the Map Options scene), then go to the Attributes Inspector (click the fourth button from the left in the Inspector toolbar), and set the **Identifier** to **MapOptionsSegue** (Figure 7.90).

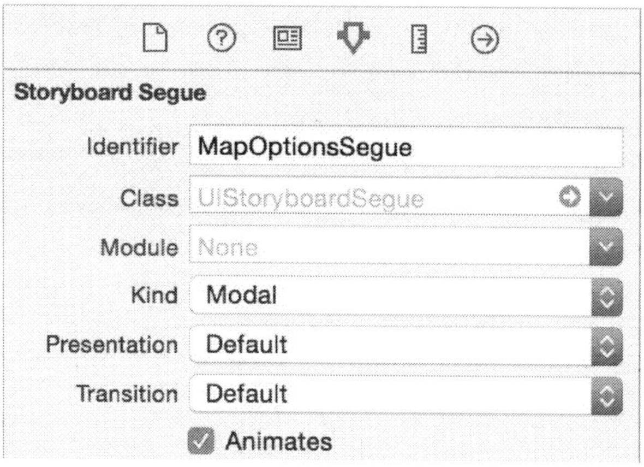

*Figure 7.90 Set the segue **Identifier** to **MapOptionsSegue**.*

3. Next, select the **ViewController.swift** file in the Project Navigator and add the following new method below the **viewDidLoad** method:

```
override func prepareForSegue(segue:
UIStoryboardSegue, sender: AnyObject?) {
 if segue.identifier == "MapOptionsSegue" {

// Get a reference to nav controller
   let navController =
     segue.destinationViewController as!
     UINavigationController
   // Get a reference to Map Options controller
   let controller =
     navController.viewControllers[0] as!
     MapOptionsViewController
   // Store a reference to the map view on
   // the Map Options controller
   controller.mapView = self.mapView
   }
}
```

This method is automatically executed when the app navigates from the Location scene to the Navigation Controller scene. The first line of code checks if the segue is the **MapOptionsSegue**. It's best to check this even if your view controller only has one segue since you may add other segues in the future.

The next line gets a reference to the Navigation Controller from the **destinationViewController** property of the segue. The following line then gets a reference to the Map Options view controller from the Navigation Controller's **viewControllers** property. The last line of code then stores a reference to the map view in the **mapView** property of the **MapOptionsViewController**.

As it stands right now, the **Done** button at the top of the Map Options scene isn't connected up so we have no way to dismiss the view. Let's fix that now.

1. In the Project Navigator, select the **Main.storyboard** file, and then at the top of the **Map Options** scene, click on the **Done** button to select it.

2. Display the Assistant Editor by clicking the center button in the Editor button group at the top of the Xcode window. This should display the **MapOptionsViewController.swift** file.

3. Go to the Connections Inspector by clicking the button on the far right in the Inspector toolbar.

4. Under the **Sent Actions** section, click in the connection well to the right of the **selector** action and drag your mouse down into the **MapOptionsViewController.swift** file, just above the closing curly brace. When you see the **Insert Action** popup, let go of your mouse button.

5. In the Connection popup, enter **done** for the action method **Name** and then click the **Connect** button.

6. You no longer need the Assistant Editor, so you can close it by clicking the button on the left in the Editor button group at the top of the Xcode window.

7. Now let's implement the **done:** method. In the Project Navigator, select the **MapOptionsViewController.swift** file. Scroll to the bottom of the code file and add the following code inside the **done:** method:

```
@IBAction func done(sender: AnyObject) {
  self.dismissViewControllerAnimated(true,
   completion: nil)
}
```

This code calls the **dismissViewControllerAnimated:** method on the view, which dismisses the Map Options view.

To see how this works at run time, click the **Run** button in Xcode, and when the app appears, navigate to the **Map Options** scene. Select a different type button in the segmented control and then click the **Done** button to return to the **Location** scene. You should see the map change to the newly selected type.

We'll be learning even more about the map view control later in this series when we discuss creating annotations and using overlays.

Scroll View

The **Scroll View** provides a way to display content that is larger than the size of the viewing area of an iOS device.

The table view is a specialized subclass of scroll view that only allows vertical scrolling as shown on the left side of Figure 7.91. The collection view, which we discussed earlier in this chapter, is also a specialized subclass of the scroll view that can scroll vertically or horizontally as shown on the right side of Figure 7.91. A scroll view is also used in the **PageControlDemo** project in conjunction with the page control.

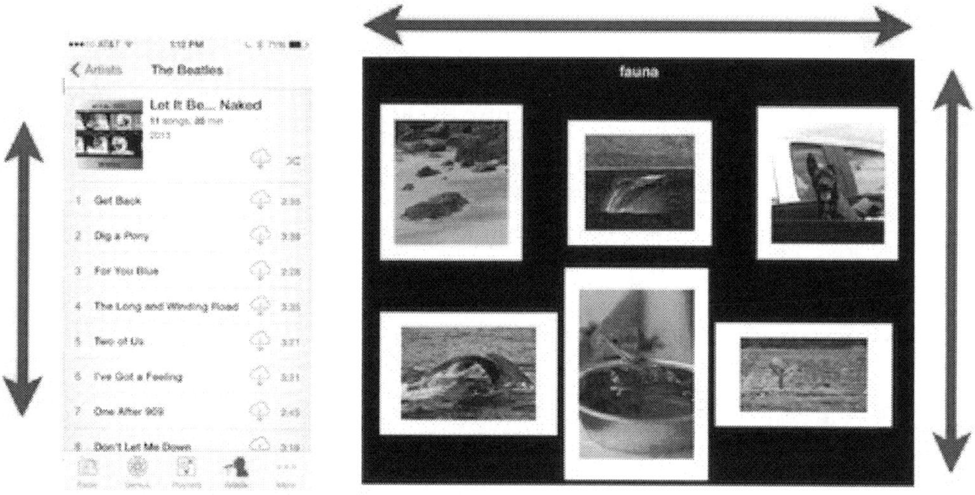

Figure 7.91 Table views and collection views are subclasses of the scroll view.

Why Doesn't My Scroll View Scroll?

This is a very common question for those first using the scroll view. Figure 7.92 shows a conceptual view of how a scroll view works. The scroll view has its own height and width (usually the height and width of the full screen), but the content you want to display is larger than the area of the scroll view.

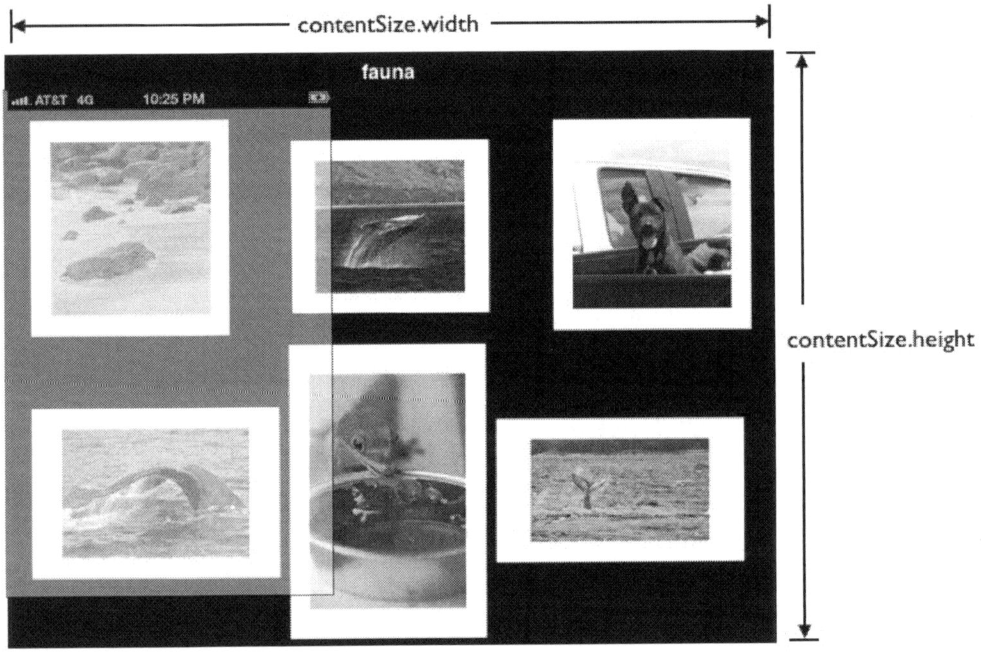

Figure 7.92 You need to tell the scroll view the size of the content you want to display.

By default, the scroll view doesn't display scroll bars. You must first set the scroll view's **contentSize** property to specify the size of your content so the scroll view knows whether to display the vertical or horizontal scroll bars (or both). Only after setting the **contentSize** property will the scroll bars appear and will you be able to scroll the content. For example:

```
self.scrollView.contentSize = CGSizeMake(width, height)
```

This code sets the scroll view's **contentSize** to the values specified in the **width** and **height** variables. If the specified width is greater than the width of the scroll view, horizontal scroll bars will appear. If the specified height is greater than the height of the scroll view, then vertical scroll bars will appear.

Date Picker

The **Date Picker** allows a user to select dates and times. Figure 7.93 shows the four main date picker styles (from top left and clockwise):

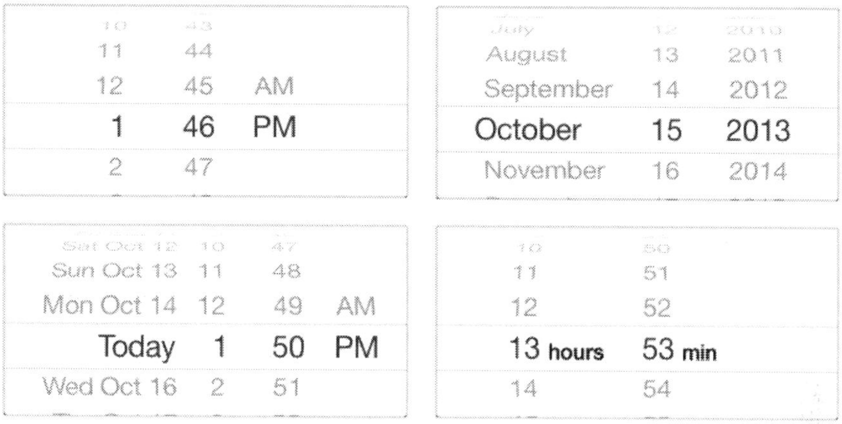

Figure 7.93 The four date picker styles.

- Time
- Date
- Count Down Timer
- Date and Time

In addition to the **Mode** attribute, Figure 7.94 shows the most commonly used attributes of the date picker:

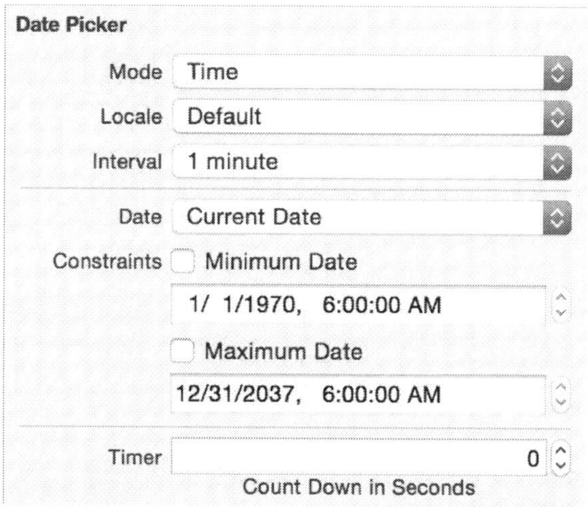

Figure 7.94 Date Picker common attributes.

- **Locale** - Specifies the locale used to format the date and time based on a geographic area. You should typically leave this set to **Default** because doing so tells the date picker to use the locale in the iOS device's Preferences.

- **Interval** - This setting is used when the date picker is displaying time information. It specifies the interval that is displayed in the minutes section of the date picker. The default is 1 minute, but you can set it to other selections such as 2 minutes, 5 minutes, 10 minutes, and so on.

- **Date** - This setting is used when the date picker displays date information. It allows you to specify the initial date and time displayed in the date picker. It's far more typical to set this value in code rather than in the Attributes Inspector.

  For example, the following code sets the date picker to the current date and time using the **NSDate** class:

  ```
  self.datePicker.date = NSDate()
  ```

- **Constraints** - These settings allow you to specify a minimum and maximum date.

- **Timer** - The **Count Down in Seconds** setting specifies the number of seconds from which the timer starts counting down when in **Count Down Timer** mode. The maximum value is 86,399 seconds (23 hours and 59 seconds).

  As of this writing, this setting doesn't work properly. If you enter a number of seconds, it displays the equivalent number of minutes in the date picker (for example, 120 seconds displays 2 minutes), but when you run your app in the Simulator, it doesn't change the starting value. Fortunately, you can set this attribute in code. For example, if you use this code in the **viewDidLoad** method of your view controller:

  ```
  self.datePicker.countDownDuration = 300
  ```

  It sets the start time to 5 minutes (300 minutes / 60 seconds per minute = 5 minutes).

Count Down Timer Mode

The **Count Down Timer** mode of the date picker can be deceptive. The date picker does not contain a timer that you can use to count down, so you will most likely only use the date picker to let the user specify the number of hours and minutes from which to count down—just as it's used in the built-in iOS Clock app.

To implement a timer, you can use an **NSTimer** object in conjunction with the date picker. To show you how this works, a **DatePickerTimerDemo** project has been included in this book's sample code. Let's check it out.

1. In Xcode, open the **DatePickerTimerDemo** project in this book's sample code.

2. In the Project Navigator, select the **Main.Storyboard** file and you will see the scene shown in Figure 7.95.

*Figure 7.95 The **DateTimePickerDemo** main scene.*

At the top of the scene is a date picker set to **Count Down Timer** mode in which the user can select the starting count down time, and at the bottom of the scene are **Start** and **Pause** buttons that start and pause the timer.

3. Let's see how this works at run time. Click Xcode's **Run** button, and when the app appears in the Simulator, accept the default time or select a different time in the date picker and then tap the **Start** button. When you do this, the date picker is hidden, the timer is displayed in a label, the green **Start** button turns into a red **Cancel** button, and the **Pause** button is enabled (Figure 7.96). The timer label is on the scene at design time but it is located behind the date picker and its **Hidden** attribute is selected.

   If you tap the **Pause** button, the timer pauses and the button text changes to **Resume**. If you tap the **Cancel** button, the timer is cancelled, the time label is hidden, the red **Cancel** button changes to a green **Start** button and the **Pause** button is disabled.

Figure 7.96 The timer is counting down!

4. Now go back to Xcode, click the **Stop** button, and let's see how the **NSTimer** class is used together with the picker view to create this app.

5. Select the **ViewController.swift** file in the Project Navigator and check out the code in the **startTimer** method. When the user taps the **Start** button, the **startCancel:** method is executed, which in turn calls the **startTimer** method:

```
@IBAction func startCancel(sender: AnyObject)
   {
      if self.isTimerStarted {
        self.cancelTimer()
      }
      else {
        // Get the # of seconds from the
        // date picker, calc minutes / seconds
        self.duration =
           self.datePicker.countDownDuration
        self.minutes = Int(floor(duration/60))
        self.seconds = Int(round(Double(duration)
         - Double(minutes) * 60))
        self.startTimer()
  }
}
```

The first line of code in the **else** statement gets the **countDownDuration** value from the date picker and stores it in a **duration** property. The value is stored as the total number of seconds. The next line of code uses the **floor** function to get the number of minutes and then uses the **round** function to derive the number of seconds. Each value is stored in a property. Next, the **startTimer** method is called:

```
func startTimer() {
   // Save the start time in the timer label
   self.updateLabel()
   // Hide the date picker, show the time
   self.datePicker.hidden = true
   self.lblTime.hidden = false
   // Change green Start button to red Cancel
   self.btnStartCancel.setTitle("Cancel",
     forState: UIControlState.Normal)
   self.btnStartCancel.setTitleColor(
        UIColor.redColor(),
        forState: UIControlState.Normal)
   // Enable the pause button
   self.btnPauseResume.enabled = true
```

```
    self.isTimerPaused = false
    // Start the timer
    self.timer =
     NSTimer.scheduledTimerWithTimeInterval(1.0,
       target: self, selector: "countDown",
       userInfo: nil, repeats: true)
    self.isTimerStarted = true
}
```

In the first line of code, the **updateLabel** method is called, which takes the start time in minutes and seconds and displays it in the timer label. After that, the date picker is hidden, the timer label is displayed, the green Start button is changed to a red Cancel button, and the pause/resume button is enabled.

The second-to-last line of code creates a timer from the **NSTimer** class and tells the timer to fire with an interval of **1.0** seconds. The **selector:** argument specifies that the **countDown** method is to be called each time the timer fires. The **countDown** method contains the following code:

```
func countDown() {
    if self.seconds >= 1 {
      self.seconds--
    }
    else {
      self.minutes--
      self.seconds = 59
    }
    self.updateLabel()
    if self.minutes == 0 && self.seconds == 0 {
      self.timerFinished()
    }
}
```

This code decrements the seconds if the number of seconds is greater than or equal to one, otherwise, it decrements the number of minutes and resets the seconds timer to 59. Next, it calls **updateLabel** to update the label with the current time. Finally, if the minutes and seconds are zero, the **timerFinished** method is called:

```
func timerFinished() {
```

```
     self.cancelTimer()
    // Play a sound to indicate timer is finished
    let soundURL =
     NSBundle.mainBundle().URLForResource("Trill",
     withExtension: "wav")
     self.avSound = AVAudioPlayer(contentsOfURL:
       soundURL, error: nil)
     self.avSound.play()
     let alertController =
       UIAlertController(title: "",
       message: "Timer Done",
       preferredStyle: .Alert)
     let OKAction = UIAlertAction(title: "OK",
       style: .Default) { (action) in
  // ...
     }
     alertController.addAction(OKAction)
     self.presentViewController(alertController,
       animated: true) {
       // ...
    }
  }
```

This code first calls **cancelTimer**, which calls the **invalidate** method on the timer to stop it. The next section of code uses the **AVAudioPlayer** class to play a sound to alert the user the timer has finished. The last section of code displays an alert containing the message **Timer Done**.

I recommend checking out the other methods in this project, including the **pauseResume:** method that changes the **Pause** / **Resume** button's text based on whether the timer is paused is not.

Setting the Date Picker Text Color

Although the date picker doesn't have a textColor attribute, it's actually very easy to change its text color. As shown in the view controller's **viewDidLoad** method, you use the date picker's setValue method which uses Key-Value-Coding (KVC) to set attribute values:

```
self.datePicker.setValue(UIColor.whiteColor(),
    forKey: "textColor")
```

Picker View

The **Picker View** (Figure 7.97) is a close cousin to the date picker. It has a similar look and feel but can contain far more than just dates or time. Since there aren't many attributes you set through the Attributes Inspector, it's best to learn about the picker view by looking at an app.

You may remember the **CollectionsDemo** sample project from *Book 4: Learn to Code in Swift,* which made use of the picker view control. That same project is also included with this book, so let's open it up and take another look.

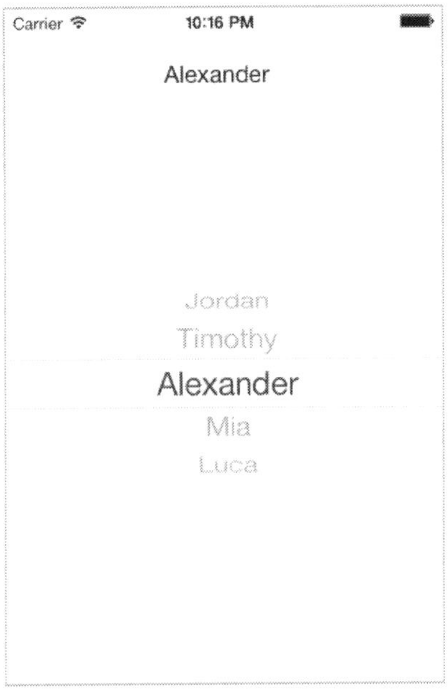

*Figure 7.97 The **CollectionsDemo** app at run time.*

1. In Xcode, open the **CollectionsDemo** project in this book's sample code.
2. In the Project Navigator, select the **Main.storyboard** file. You will see a scene that contains a label and a picker view listing cities in California.
3. Click the **Run** button, and you will see that even though the picker view displays a list of California cities at design time, it displays a list of names at run time (Figure 7.97). If you select a name in the list, it displays the name in the label at the top of the scene.
4. Let's take a look at the view controller for a quick refresher.

Select the **ViewController.swift** file in the Project Navigator. The **UIPickerViewDelegate** and the **UIPickerViewDatasource** protocols have been adopted by the view controller:

```
class ViewController: UIViewController,
    UIPickerViewDelegate, UIPickerViewDataSource
```

The **UIPickerViewDataSource** protocol has methods that determine the number of components (columns) in the picker view as well as the number of items in each component. For example, the following method specifies one component in the picker view:

```
func numberOfComponentsInPickerView(pickerView:
    UIPickerView) -> Int {
    return 1
}
```

The following method returns the number of items in the **names** array, which is used to fill the picker view:

```
func pickerView(pickerView: UIPickerView,
   numberOfRowsInComponent component: Int) -> Int
   {
       return names.count
}
```

The **UIPickerViewDelegate** protocol provides methods that specify the contents of the picker view as well as a method that can be called when the user selects an item from the picker view.

For example, the following method is called once for each item in the picker view. Given the row number passed in the **row** parameter, it returns the corresponding name from the **names** array.

```
func pickerView(pickerView: UIPickerView,
   titleForRow row: Int, forComponent component:
   Int) -> String! {
    return names[row]
}
```

When the user selects an item in the picker, the **pickerView:didSelectRow:inComponent:** method is executed:

```
func pickerView(pickerView: UIPickerView,
    didSelectRow row: Int,
    inComponent component: Int) {
     self.lblDemo.text = names[row]
}
```

This method gets a name from the **names** array based on the **row** number passed to the method and stores the name in the label's **text** property.

Ad BannerView

The **Ad BannerView** provides a view in which banner advertisements can be displayed to your users. Often, developers offer their apps for free and use banner ads as a source of revenue instead. When you include an Ad BannerView in your app, you are essentially providing an empty billboard that Apple fills with advertising content. You (and Apple) earn revenue when the user interacts with the banner ad.

Before you can include iAds in your app, you have to join Apple's iAd Network (https://developer.apple.com/iad/).

You will learn more about implementing iAds in your apps later on in this book series.

Container View

The **Container View** (Figure 7.98) allows you to break up a complex user interface into multiple parts. This is an advanced technique that we will detail later in this series. For now, just know that you can add a container view to a scene and resize it to take up a portion of the view.

When you do this, a view controller is added for the container view along with a segue that embeds the view controller as a child inside the parent view.

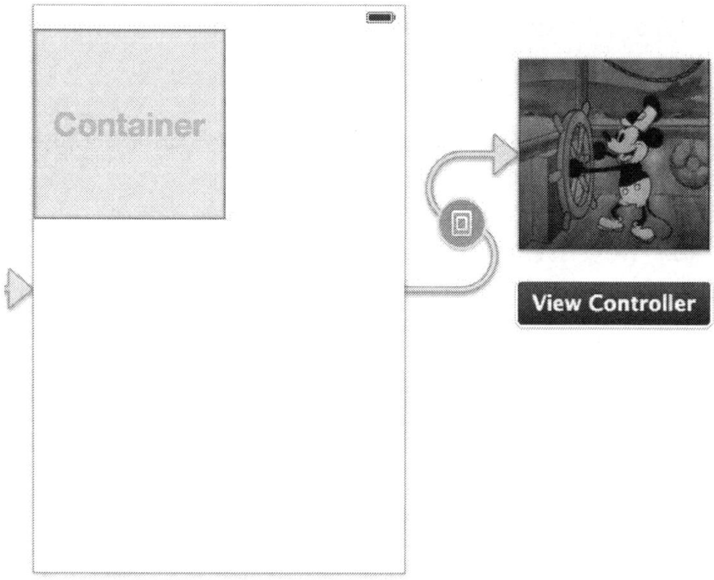

Figure 7.98 The Container View.

A **View** object is displayed in the design surface that matches the size of the container view (as shown on the upper right of Figure 7.98). You can drop user-interface controls and configure them on this subview just as you can with the main view.

Gesture Recognizers

The gesture recognizer classes make it easy for you to capture and respond to a variety of gestures from your users. Here is a list of the iOS gesture recognizers:

- **Tap Gesture Recognizer** - Recognizes single or double taps as well as taps with multiple touches.
- **Pinch Gesture Recognizer** - Recognizes pinch gestures, where the user places two fingers on the touch surface and moves them towards or away from each other.
- **Rotation Gesture Recognizer** - Recognizes rotation gestures, where the user places two fingers on the touch surface and rotates them.
- **Swipe Gesture Recognizer** - Recognizes swipe gestures, where the user moves their finger quickly across the touch surface. You can specify whether you want to detect **Left**, **Right**, **Up**, or **Down** swipe motions.

- **Pan Gesture Recognizer** - Recognizes pan gestures, where the user drags their finger on the device.

- **Screen Edge Pan Gesture Recognizer** - Recognizes pan gestures that start near the edge of the screen.

- **Long Press Gesture Recognizer** - Recognizes long press gestures, where the user touches and leaves their finger on the device for a longer period of time.

You can add multiple gesture recognizers to a view to capture a variety of user gestures.

The Tap Gesture Recognizer

You have already seen gesture recognizers at work in the **ImageViewDemo** project. Let's take a closer look.

1. In Xcode, open the **ImageViewDemo** project in this book's sample code.

2. In the Project Navigator, select the **Main.storyboard** file to see the scene in Figure 7.99. Notice in the scene dock at the top of the scene there are two gesture recognizers highlighted in red.

Figure 7.99 Gesture recognizers in the scene dock.

3. Hover your mouse pointer over the gesture recognizer on the left. A popup appears letting you know it is a **Tap Gesture Recognizer**.

4. Click on the tap gesture recognizer and then go to the Attribute Inspector (the fourth button from the left in the Inspector toolbar). At the top of the Attributes Inspector, you will see the **Taps** and **Touches** attributes (Figure 7.100).

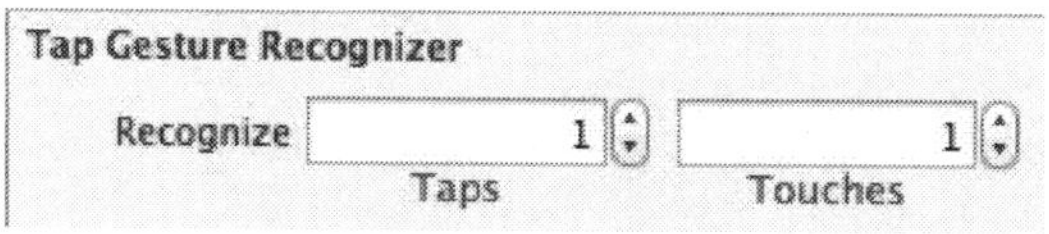

Figure 7.100 Tap Gesture Recognizer attributes.

- **Taps** - This attribute specifies the number of taps you want it to recognize (1 for a single tap, 2 for a double tap, and so on).

- **Touches** - This specifies the number of fingers required for the tap gesture to be recognized.

5. When you add a gesture recognizer to a scene, you can have it check for gestures in the entire view or within a particular user-interface control. In the **ImageViewDemo** scene, the tap gesture recognizer is only checking for taps in the image view at the bottom of the scene.

   To see this, go to the Connections Inspector (the last button on the right in the Inspector toolbar). If you hover your mouse pointer over the **gestureRecognizers** connection at the bottom of the inspector, the image view at the bottom of the scene is highlighted, indicating it is the associated user-interface control Figure 7.101.

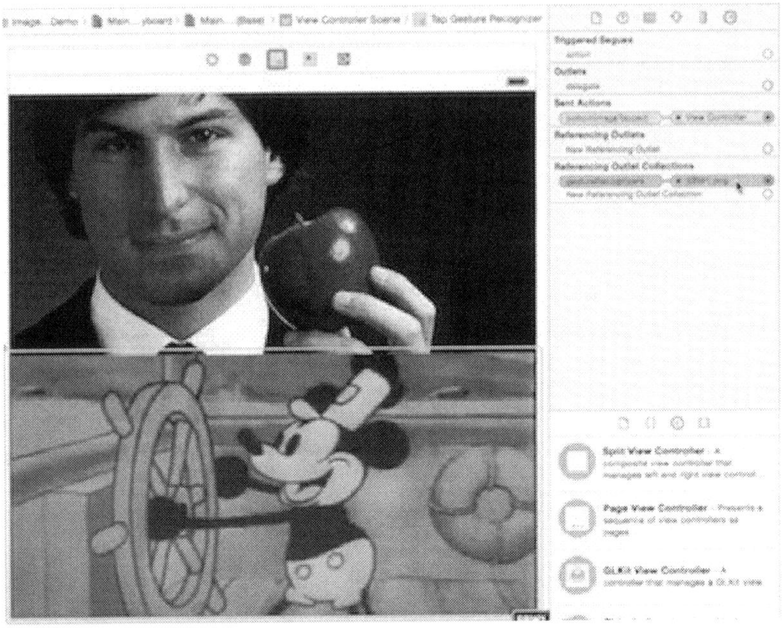

Figure 7.101 The bottom image view is highlighted.

6. Look a little further up in the Connections Inspector under the **Sent Actions** section. This tells you that when a tap gesture is recognized at run time, the **bottomImageTapped:** method of the view controller is executed.

7. To see this method, go to the Project Navigator, select the **ViewController.swift** file and scroll to the bottom of the code file:

```
@IBAction func bottomImageTapped(sender:
AnyObject) {
 if self.bottomImageView.isAnimating()
 {
    self.bottomImageView.stopAnimating()
}
else
 {
    self.bottomImageView.startAnimating()
 }
}
```

This code checks if the bottom image view is animating. If it is, it tells the image view to stop animating. If it's not, it tells the image view to start animating. This toggles the animation on and off when the user taps the image view at run time.

The Long Press Gesture Recognizer

Now let's take a closer look at the long press gesture recognizer associated with the image view at the top of the scene.

1. In the **ImageViewDemo** project, go to the Project Navigator and select the **Main.storyboard** file again. Go to the scene dock and click on the **Long Press Gesture Recognizer** on the right (Figure 7.102).

Figure 7.102 Select the Long Press Gesture Recognizer.

2. Now go to the Attributes Inspector (the fourth button from the left in the Inspectors toolbar), and you will see the attributes shown in Figure 7.103.

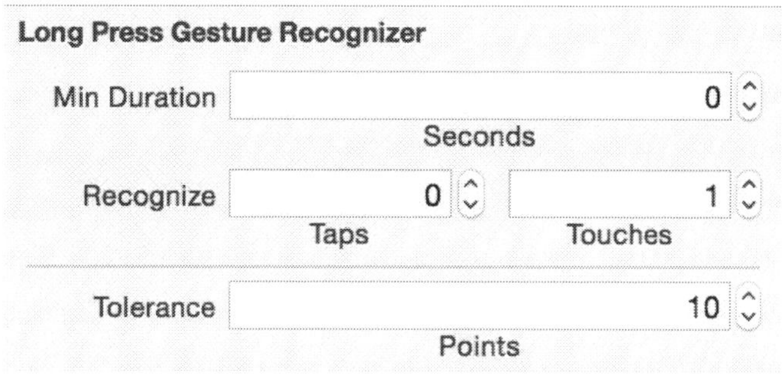

Figure 7.103 Long Press Gesture Recognizer attributes

- **Min Duration** - The minimum time (in seconds) the user must press his or her fingers on the touch surface for the gesture to be recognized. In this case, I have set the value to zero because I want the gesture recognized immediately.

- **Recognize > Taps** - The number of taps required for the gesture to be recognized.

- **Recognize > Touches** - The number of fingers required for the touch gesture to be recognized.

- **Tolerance** - The number of points the finger(s) on the view can move before the gesture fails.

3. Now let's take a look at the long press gesture recognizer's connections. With the gesture recognizer still selected, go to the Connections Inspector (the last button on the right in the Inspectors toolbar). There you can see that the gesture recognizer is connected to the top image view, and when the gesture is recognized, the **topImagePressed:** method is executed. Let's take a look at this method.

4. Select the **ViewController.swift** file in the Project Navigator to see the **topImagePressed:** method:

```
@IBAction func topImagePressed(sender:
   UILongPressGestureRecognizer) {
      switch sender.state {
         case UIGestureRecognizerState.Began:
            self.topImageView.highlighted = true
         case UIGestureRecognizerState.Ended:
            self.topImageView.highlighted = false
         default:
        break
   }
}
```

This method gets called when the state of the gesture changes. Notice this method has a **sender** parameter of the type **UILongPressGestureRecognizer**. This code checks the **state** property of the gesture recognizer.

If the gesture state is **Began**, the user has just started pressing on the image view, and the code sets the image view's **highlighted** property to **true**, which displays the sepia-toned image. If the gesture has **Ended**, that means the user has lifted their finger from the touch surface, and the code sets the image view's **highlighted** property to **false**, which displays the original full color image.

Navigation, Tab, Search, and Toolbars

In this section, you are going to learn about navigation bars, search bars, toolbars, tab bars, and the items that they contain.

Navigation Bar

You have already seen quite a bit of the **Navigation Bar**. In *Book 1: Diving Into iOS*, you saw how a navigation bar is automatically added to the top of a scene that is associated with a navigation controller as well as any other scene to which that scene segues.

The **Navigation Bar** is included in the Object Library, allowing you to manually drop it on a scene and build your own navigation. Rather than doing this, I recommend dropping a navigation controller on the storyboard and using the associated navigation bar and its built-in functionality instead.

You can't select a navigation bar that is associated with a navigation controller by clicking on it in the design surface. Instead, you need to select it in the Document Outline pane as shown in Figure 7.104.

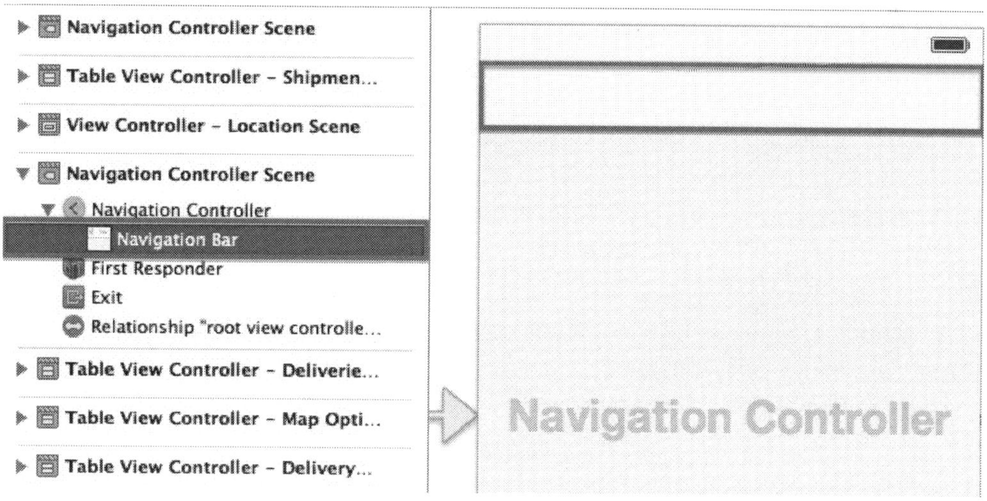

Figure 7.104 The navigation bar.

When you select a navigation bar, you will see the attributes shown in Figure 7.105 at the top of the Attributes Inspector.

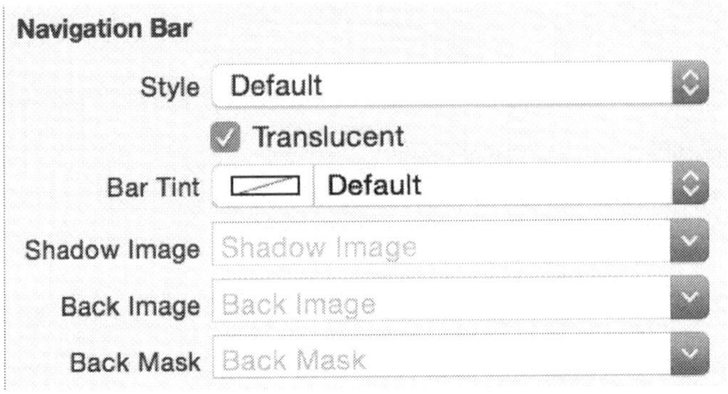

Figure 7.105 Common navigation bar attributes.

The **Style** attribute lists the following options:

- **Default** - Uses the default style normally associated with a given view. In iOS 9, this is translucent.
- **Black** - Sets the navigation bar to a solid black color.
- **Black Translucent (Deprecated)** - This option is deprecated, so don't choose it.

The **Translucent** attribute specifies if the navigation bar is translucent (it is by default).

The **Bar Tint** attribute allows you to change the color of the navigation bar to something completely different.

If you want to add a drop shadow to your navigation bar, you can create a custom Background Image and use the Shadow Image attribute to create the drop shadow.

Navigation Item

A **Navigation Item** specifies the information displayed in a navigation bar when the user navigates to a particular scene. The **Navigation Item** is included in the Object Library so you can manually drop it on a scene, but, typically, navigation items are automatically added to a scene when you adding items to a navigation controller.

By itself, a navigation bar is empty. You need a navigation item to add content to the navigation bar. To help you understand this, let's open the **iDeliverMobile** project and take a closer look at its navigation objects.

1. In the Project Navigator, select the **Main.storyboard** file. Scroll the storyboard so you can see the **Navigation Controller** and **Deliveries** scene as shown in Figure 7.106.

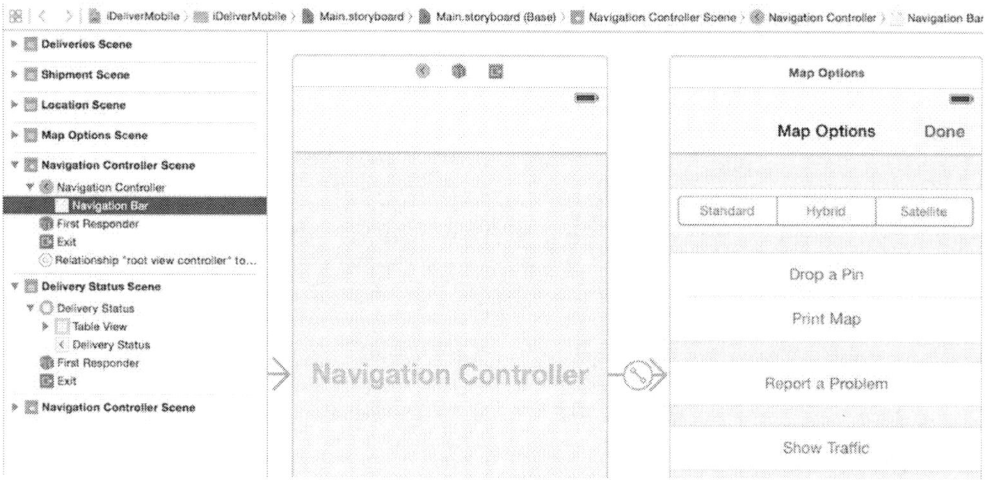

Figure 7.106 Navigation Controller & Deliveries scene.

2. Notice that the **Navigation Controller** scene contains an empty navigation bar. If you look closely in the **Document Outline** pane, you can see the **Navigation Bar** is selected.

3. If you take a closer look at the Document Outline pane, you can see the other scenes don't contain a navigation bar, but contain a navigation item instead as highlighted in Figure 7.107. So, there is one navigation bar located in the navigation controller and one navigation item in each scene.

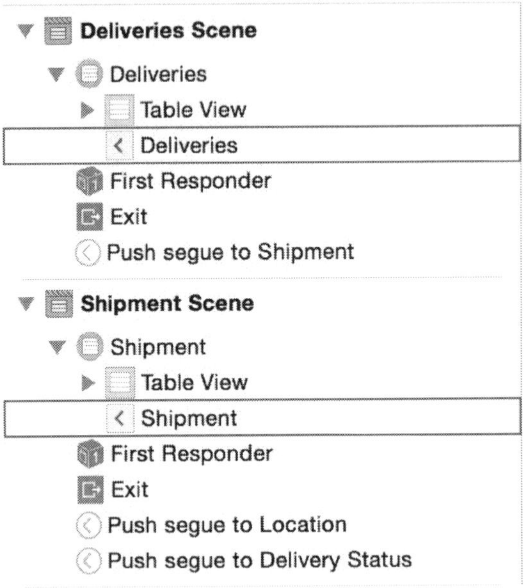

Figure 7.107 Navigation items.

4. In the Document Outline under the **Deliveries Scene** section, select the **Navigation Item** as shown in Figure 7.108. This highlights the navigation item in the **Deliveries** scene.

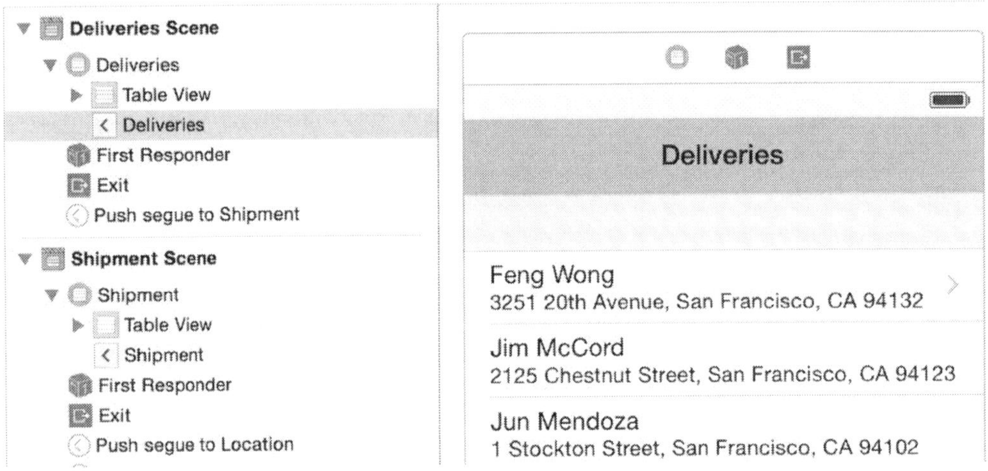

*Figure 7.108 The **Deliveries** scene's navigation item.*

5. Go to the Attributes Inspector and you can see the attributes shown in Figure 7.109. As you can see, the navigation item specifies information that is displayed in the navigation bar for this scene.

Figure 7.109 Navigation Item attributes.

- **Title** - This attribute is pretty obvious. It specifies the text that appears in the center of the navigation bar when the user navigates to this scene.

- **Prompt** - This attribute comes in handy if you want to display additional information in the navigation bar. If you specify **Prompt** text, it's displayed in the navigation bar above the title, and the navigation bar height is increased accordingly (Figure 7.110).

Figure 7.110 Navigation bar Prompt text.

- **Back Button** - This attribute specifies the text to be displayed in the back button when you navigate from this scene to the next scene and it becomes the "back" item.

  By default, a navigation bar's back button contains the title of the previous scene's navigation bar. If you want to change this to something else, you can set this attribute.

  For example, in the scenes shown in Figure 7.111, when the user navigates from the **Shipment** scene to the **Location** scene, the **Location** scene's back button would contain the text **Shipment**. However, because the **Shipment** scene's navigation item has the **Back Button** attribute set to **Back**, the **Location** scene's back button will contain the text **Back** instead.

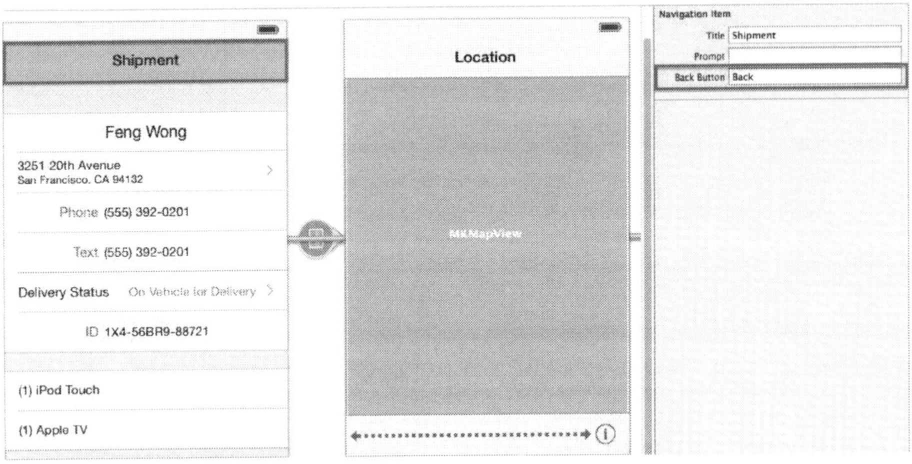

Figure 7.111 Setting the back button text.

Tab Bar

A **Tab Bar** provides tabs that allow you to switch between multiple views in your app. A tab bar is best used in apps that have different modes. For example, Figure 7.112 shows the tab bar at the bottom of the iOS Clock app, which has four distinct modes—**World Clock**, **Alarm**, **Stopwatch**, and **Timer**. When the user taps one of the bars, they are taken to a completely different mode with its own functionality and settings.

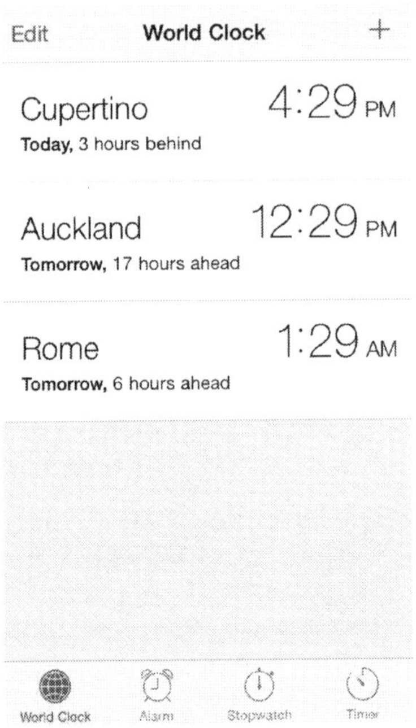

Figure 7.112 The tab bar at the bottom of the Clock app.

We discussed the tab bar controller earlier in this chapter, and we'll be diving in deeper on the tab bar when we discuss app navigation.

Tab Bar Item

The **Tab Bar Item** represents a single bar in a tab bar. The tab bar item is in the Object Library, so you can manually drag it onto a scene, but, typically, tab bar items are automatically added to a scene for you when you create a relationship segue between a tab bar controller and another view controller as described earlier in this chapter. Figure 7.113 shows the commonly used attributes for the tab bar item.

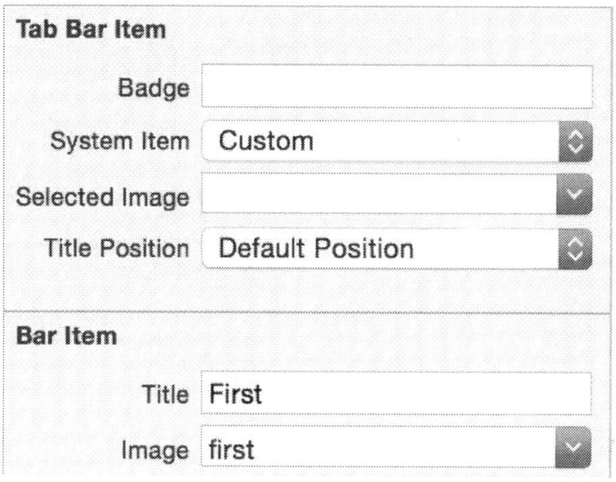

Figure 7.113 Tab Bar Item attributes.

- **Badge** - Specifies text to be displayed in the upper-right corner of the tab bar item inside a red oval as shown in Figure 7.114.

Figure 7.114 A tab bar item badge.

- **System Item** - By default, this attribute is set to Custom, which allows you to specify your own text or image to be displayed in the button. The other options provide standard iOS tab options you can use in your own apps. Figure 7.115 shows the first set of options you can choose from.

*Figure 7.115 The tab bar item **More, Favorites, Featured, Top Rated, Recents,** and **Contacts** identifiers.*

Figure 7.116 shows the second set of options you can choose from.

*Figure 7.116 The **History, Bookmarks, Search, Downloads, Most Recent,** and **Most Viewed** identifiers.*

- **Selected Image** - Specifies the image to be displayed when the tab bar item is selected.
- **Title Position** - When set to the default (**Default Position**), the title appears centered under the image. If you select the **Custom Offset** option, you can specify a **Horizontal** or **Vertical** offset.
- **Title** - This attribute allows you to enter your own custom text for a tab bar item. If you set this attribute, the tab bar item's **Identifier** attribute is automatically set to **Custom**.
- **Selected Image** - This attribute allows you to specify an image to be displayed in the tab bar item. If you set this attribute, the tab bar item's **Identifier** is automatically set to **Custom**. You can have a custom **Title** or a custom **Image**, but you can't have both on the same tab bar item.

Search Bar

The **Search Bar** (Figure 7.117) is a rounded rectangle with a small magnifying glass in the center, which the user can enter search text. When the user taps the search bar, it displays a keyboard that includes a **Search** key.

Figure 7.117 The search bar.

One of the most common places to use a search bar is with a table view. In situations where there may be hundreds of items in a table view, it's best to add a search bar that allows users to more easily find items they are looking for. Some of the built-in apps such as Contacts and Music contain search bars that do just that.

For extensive coverage of using search bars with table views, check out *Chapter 13: Managing Lists of Data* in the section **Adding a Search Bar to a Table View**.

Toolbar

The **Toolbar** (Figure 7.118) is displayed at the bottom of the screen and usually contains buttons that allow the user to perform common tasks. You were first introduced to the toolbar in *Book 1: Diving Into iOS* when you added a toolbar to the Location scene that contained a button to launch the Map Options scene.

*Figure 7.118 A toolbar containing a single **Item** button.*

When you first drop a toolbar at the bottom of a scene, it contains a single **Item** button (Figure 7.118). This is a bar button item which is described in the next section. If you select the toolbar, you will see the attributes shown in Figure 7.119 in the Attributes Inspector.

These are the same **Style**, **Translucent**, and **Tint** attributes the navigation bar has (see the section **Navigation Bar** earlier in this chapter for details). Typically, if you have a navigation bar and toolbar in the same app, you set their **Style** and/or **Tint** attributes to the same values.

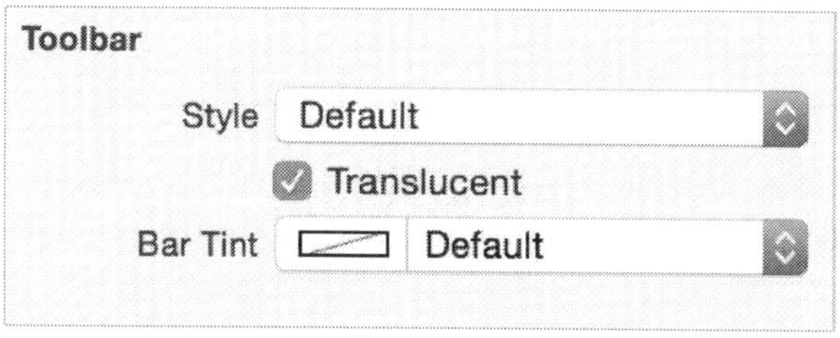

Figure 7.119 Common Toolbar attributes.

Bar Button Item

A **Bar Button Item** (Figure 7.118) can be added to either a navigation bar or a toolbar. Typically, you add buttons that provide users with quick access to commonly used functions. Figure 7.120 shows the full list of attributes for the bar button item.

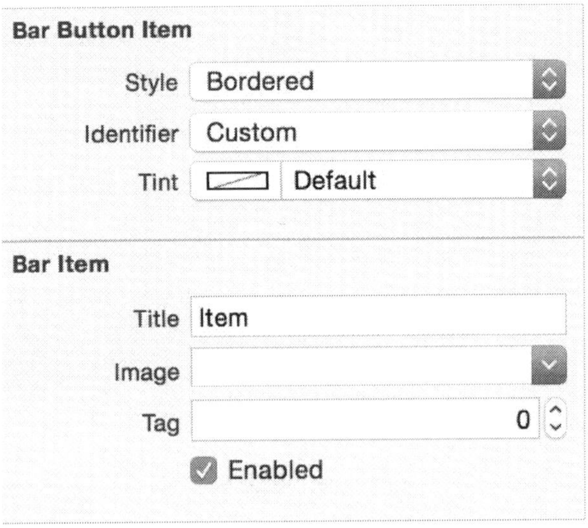

Figure 7.120 Common Bar Button Item attributes.

- **Style** - You can set this attribute to **Plain**, **Bordered** (the default), or **Done**. Figure 7.121 shows how each style looks (in iOS 9, there is no difference between the Plain and Bordered style.)

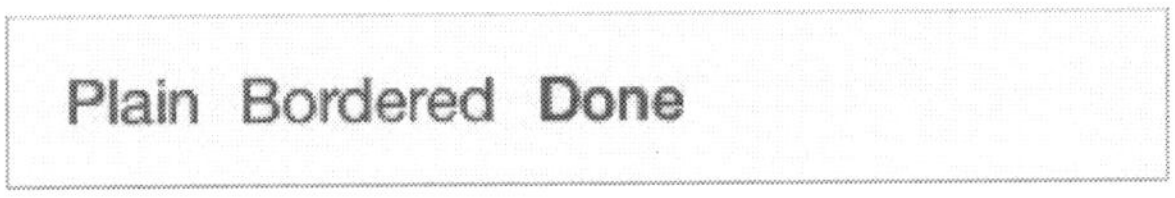

Figure 7.121 Bar button item styles.

- **Identifier** - By default, this attribute is set to **Custom**, which allows you to specify your own text or image to be displayed in the button. The other options are divided into several sections. The first section contains these options:
    - **Flexible Space** - Turns the button into a flexible space button, which is described in the next section.
    - **Fixed Space** - Turns the button into a fixed space button, which is also described in the next section.

The next set of options contains the identifiers shown in Figure 7.122. The **Add** option displays a plus sign on the button. All other options display text in the button. The **Done** and **Save** buttons' text is bolded, which indicates the button's **Style** is set to **Done**.

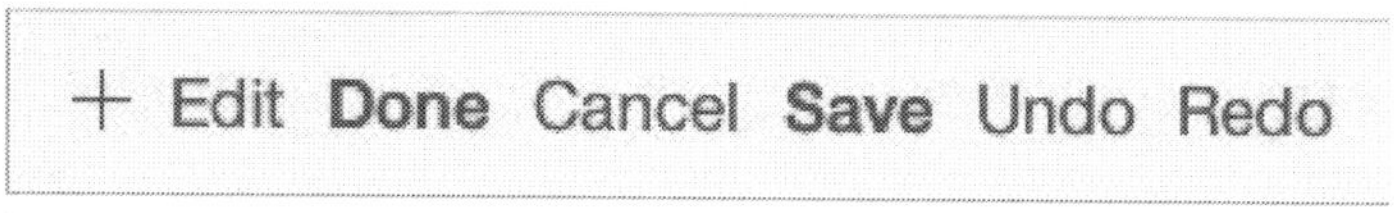

Figure 7.122 ***Add****,* ***Edit****,* ***Done****,* ***Cancel****,* ***Save****,* ***Undo****, &* ***Redo****.*

The next set of options displays a different built-in image on the button (Figure 7.123).

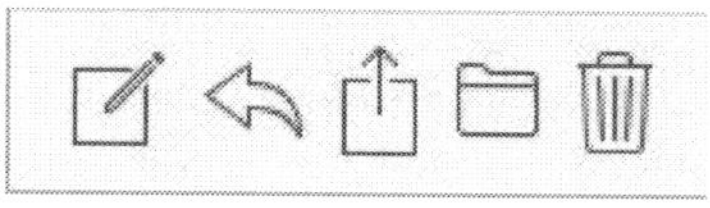

Figure 7.123 ***Compose****,* ***Reply****,* ***Action****,* ***Organize****, &* ***Trash****.*

The next options also display a different built-in image on the button (Figure 7.124).

Figure 7.124 ***Bookmarks****,* ***Search****,* ***Refresh****, &* ***Stop.***

The next three sections contain options that display the built-in images shown in Figure 7.125. As of this writing, the **Page Curl** option doesn't work—the image simply doesn't appear on the button.

Figure 7.125 ***Camera****,* ***Play****,* ***Pause****,* ***Rewind*** *&* ***Fast Forward****.*

- **Title** - This attribute lets you to specify custom text for a button. If you set this attribute, the button's **Identifier** attribute is automatically set to **Custom**.

- **Image** - This attribute lets you specify an image to be displayed in the button. Again, if you set this attribute, the button's **Identifier** is automatically set to **Custom**. You can have a custom **Title** or a custom **Image**, but you can't have both on the same button.

Fixed Space Bar Button Item

The **Fixed Space Bar Button Item** is really just a bar button item that has its **Identifier** attribute set to **Fixed Width.** It allows you to add fixed width spacing in your app's toolbars. Why do you need to do this? By default, the buttons in a toolbar are justified to the left as shown in Figure 7.118.

If you want to insert a fixed amount of space between the edge of the toolbar or between buttons, you can add a fixed space bar button item to the toolbar and adjust its width by clicking and dragging one of its sides (Figure 7.126).

Figure 7.126 A fixed space bar button item.

Flexible Space Bar Button Item

The **Flexible Space Bar Button Item** is just a bar button item that has its **Identifier** set to **Flexible Width.** It allows you to add a flexible amount of space to your toolbars.

It's flexible because it automatically adjusts in size to take up the available empty space in a toolbar. For example, if you place one on the left side of a toolbar, all the buttons are justified to the right. If you place one on the left and one on the right of a toolbar, it centers the buttons as shown in Figure 7.127.

Figure 7.127 Flexible space bar button items.

AVKit Player View Controller

The AVKit Player View Controller (Figure 7.128) provides a user interface and player to play media stored on the local device or from a URL.

Let's check out the **AVKitDemo** project included in this book's sample code that shows how to use the AVKit Player View Controller in an app.

1. Open the **AVKitDemo** project in Xcode.

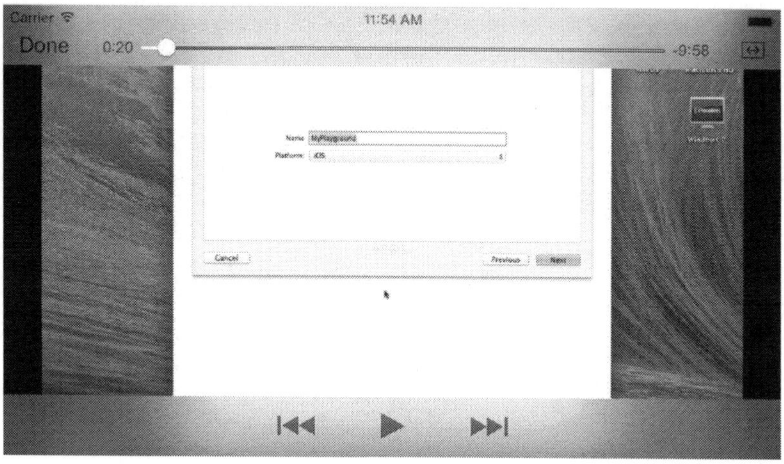

Figure 7.128 The AVKit Player View Controller.

2. Select the **Main.storyboard** file in the Project Navigator to see the scenes shown in Figure 7.129. The scene on the left contains a single **Play Video** button that, when tapped, navigates to the AV Player View Controller scene.

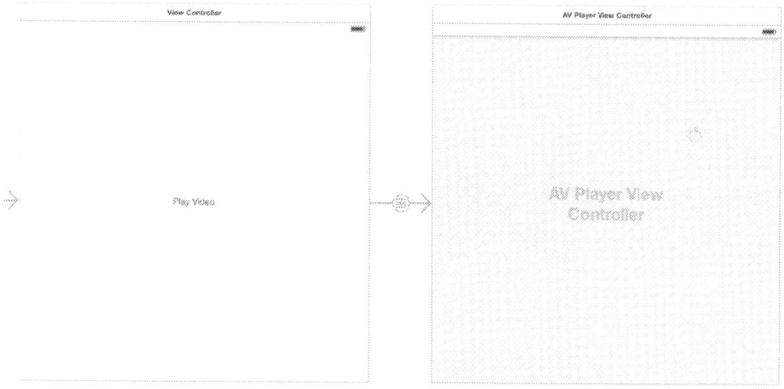

*Figure 1.29 The scenes in the **AVKitDemo** storyboard.*

3. Select the **ViewController.swift** file in the Project Navigator. This is the view controller for the initial storyboard scene. Check out the **prepareForSegue:** method:

```
override func prepareForSegue(segue:
   UIStoryboardSegue,
    sender: AnyObject?) {
      let avc = segue.destinationViewController as!
        AVPlayerViewController
        let url = NSURL(string:
```

```
            "http://www.iOSAppsForNonProgrammers.com/
               media/book4/Movie4.1.mp4")
        avc.player = AVPlayer(URL: url)
    }
```

The first line of code in this method gets a reference to the **AVPlayerViewController** from the segue's **destinationViewController** property. Next, it creates an NSURL object from the url of a video on the web (one of the movies from *Book 4: Learn to Code in Swift*. The last line of code creates an **AVPlayer** object, passing the url of the movie to be played, and stores the object in the **AVPlayerViewController's player** property.

4. Click Xcode's **Run** button. When the app appears in the iOS Simulator, click the **Play Video** button. This displays the **AVKit Player** scene, which loads the video. You can now use the **AVKit Player** controls to watch the video.

Blur Effects

Apple uses the blur effect throughout the iOS user interface in places such as Notification Center (Figure 7.130) and Control Center.

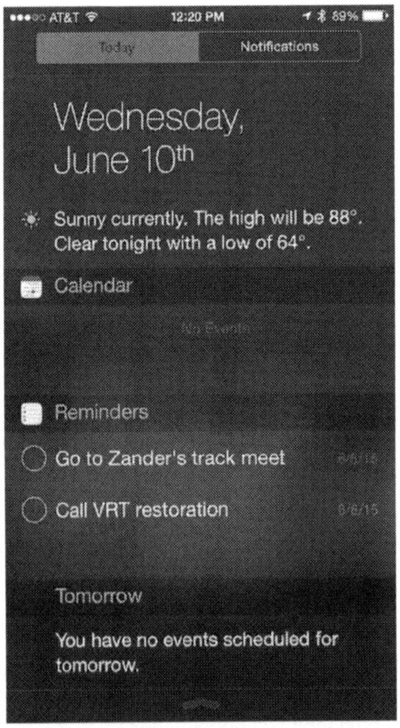

Figure 7.130 The blur effect in Notification Center.

In addition to the blur effect, notice that some of the text in Figure 7.130 such as **No Events** and the dates takes on the color of the blurred image. This effect is known as *vibrancy*.

Apple includes effect classes in Xcode (Figure 7.131) that make it easy to add blur and vibrancy effects to your apps. You can drop these on a scene and they will automatically create a blur effect on the user interface controls that are behind them. If you don't need the vibrancy effect, you can just use the **Visual Effect View with Blur** control.

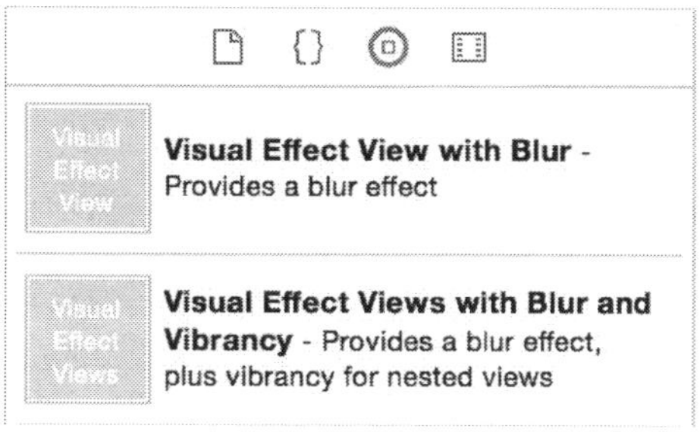

Figure 7.131 The blur effect views.

Let's check out a live example of these effects.

1. Open the **BlurDemo** project included with this book's sample code.
2. Select the **Main.storyboard** file in the Project Navigator to see the scene shown in Figure 7.132.

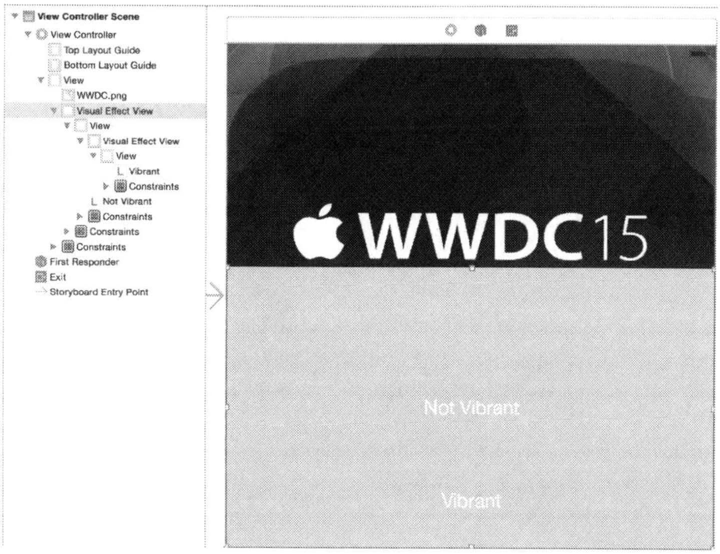

Figure 7.132 The Visual Effects with Blur and Vibrancy control at design time.

This scene contains an image view that is partially covered by a **Visual Effects with Blur and Vibrancy** control. As you can see by looking in the Document Outline panel, when you drop a Blur and Vibrancy control on a scene, it contains two **Visual Effect Views**. That's because there are two effects—blur and vibrancy.

The vibrancy Visual Effect View is nested below the blur Visual Effect View. I have added a **Not Vibrant** label to the blur Visual Effect View and a **Vibrant** label to the vibrancy Visual Effects View so you can see the difference at run time.

3. Click Xcode's **Run** button. When the app appears in the Simulator, you can see the bottom portion of the image is blurred (Figure 7.133). The **Not Vibrant** label appears just as it does at design time and the **Vibrant** label takes on the color theme of the blurred background.

4. Go back to Xcode and click the **Stop** button.

Figure 7.133 The Blur and Vibrancy effects at run time.

The Visual Effects with Blur controls have a Blur Style setting that can be set to one of three values:

- Extra Light
- Light (the default)
- Dark

Figure 7.134 shows how these settings look at run time.

Figure 7.134 The Extra Light, Light, and Dark Blur Styles (from left to right).

Summary

Here is an overview of the key points covered in this chapter on the user interface controls:

The View Controllers

- Every scene on a storyboard has an associated **View Controller** that is used to manage the view as well as any associated navigation bar or toolbars.

- The **Table View Controller** is a specialized subclass of the view controller that manages a table view and usually acts as the table view's data source and delegate. It is also used to toggle the table view's editing mode, so you can delete or reorder items in the table view.

- The **Collection View Controller** is a specialized subclass of the view controller that manages an associated collection view.

- The **Collection View** provides an easy way to display a collection of items. The appearance of the collection view is highly configurable, so, unlike the table view, it can be hard to tell if an app is using a collection view or not.

- The **Navigation Controller** is used to manage a set of view controllers. In most apps that contain multiple scenes, a navigation controller is the initial scene and is used to control navigation between the other scenes on the storyboard.

- The **Tab Bar Controller** is similar to a navigation controller in that it is used to manage a set of view controllers. However, the view controllers in a tab bar controller are each displayed as a tab bar item.

- The **Page View Controller** also manages a set of view controllers. It uses either a horizontal page curl transition, like turning the pages in a book, or a vertical page curl, like turning the pages in a calendar.

- The **SceneKit View** is used to display a 3D scene. If you are building a game app using the Scene Kit, this is usually the view you will use as the basis for the game.

Custom Controls with Object

- The **Object** template provides a way for you to add an object to a scene that is not listed in the Object Library. This is useful in cases where you have built your own custom classes that you want to drag and drop into a scene.

Basic Controls

- The **Label** object is a simple control that allows you to display variable length text.

- The **Button** is a commonly used button in iOS user interfaces. When a user taps the button at run time, it can send a message to a target object to perform a task in response to the user's interaction.

- The **Segmented Control** contains two or more segments, each of which acts as a button. Each segment can display either text or an image.

- The **Text Field** is a commonly used control that allows the user to enter a short, single line of text.

- The **Slider** control allows the user to select a value within a range by sliding a circular shape known as a *thumb* along a track.

- The **Switch** control allows a user to toggle a value ON and OFF.

- The **Activity Indicator View** provides feedback to the user when a process is running in your app. It lets the user know the app is doing something. Typically, you use an activity indicator when a process of an unknown length is executing.

- The **Progress View** is another control that allows you to indicate to the user that a process is running. In contrast with the activity indicator view, which is used for processes with an unknown duration, the progress view can show the progress of a task over a period of time or a number of steps.

- The **Page Control** is a commonly used control on iOS devices, and is seen in the Home screen on the iPhone and iPad. It displays one dot for each page in the app and allows you to navigate sequentially between pages by swiping the page or by tapping to the right or left of the currently highlighted dot.

- The **Stepper Control** allows the user to increment or decrement an integer value. Clicking the left side of the control decrements the current value, and clicking the right side of the control increments the current value.

Keyboards

- The text field and text view controls can use one of the following keyboards:
    - ASCII Capable Keyboard
    - Numbers and Punctuation Keyboard
    - URL Keyboard
    - Number Pad
    - Phone Pad
    - Name Phone Pad Keyboard
    - Email Address Keyboard
    - Decimal Pad
    - Twitter
    - Web Search
- When a text field or text view control has focus, the keyboard is automatically displayed—you don't need to write any code to make this happen. When the user is finished with the keyboard, tapping the keyboard's **Return** button or touching anywhere on the view background should hide the keyboard. However, this doesn't happen automatically—you need to write some code to hide the keyboard.

Table Views and Collection Views

- **Table Views** are the control most commonly used to display lists of data. A table view can have one or more sections and each section can have one or more table view cells.

- **Collection Views** are comprised of the following main components:
    - **Cell** - Each item in the collection view is a cell. At design time, you drop a collection view cell on a collection view and then you configure the cell. For example, you can add an image view inside the cell for displaying pictures. If all cells in your collection view have the same appearance (most do), you can create one cell at design time that is used as a template for all cells at run time.
    - **Supplementary views** - You can add supplementary header and footer views to the collection view. Typically, you do this to provide descriptive information about the items in each section.
    - **Decoration views** - Provides a visual adornment for a collection view that is not tied to data. It's usually used to create a custom background for the collection view. Note that you cannot use a decoration view with Apple's default Flow Layout.
    - **Layout object** - Controls the visual presentation of the collection view's content including size and positioning of cells.

Miscellaneous Views

- Many iOS apps use an **Image View** to display images, which the user can view and interact with.
- The **Text View** allows your users to enter multiple lines of text. You can change the font, color, and alignment of text in a text view.
- The **Web View** allows your users to view web content within your app as well as other content such as spreadsheets, slides, word processing documents, and PDF files.
- The **Map View** control allows you to embed a map interface in your app. It's important to note that with iOS 5.1 or earlier, the Map Kit framework uses the Google Mobile Maps service for map data. Newer versions of iOS use the Apple Maps technology.
- The **Scroll View** provides a way to display content that is larger than the size of the viewing area of an iOS device.

- The **Date Picker** allows a user to select dates and times. The four main date picker styles are:
  - Time
  - Date
  - Date and Time
  - Count Down Timer
- The **Picker View** is a close cousin to the date picker. It has a similar look and feel, but can contain far more than just dates or time.
- The **Ad BannerView** provides a view in which banner advertisements can be displayed to your users. Often, developers offer their apps for free and use banner ads as a source of revenue instead. When you include an Ad BannerView in your app, you are essentially providing an empty billboard that Apple fills with advertising content. You (and Apple) earn revenue when the user interacts with the banner ad.
- The **Container View** provides a way to break up a complex user interface into multiple independent parts. You can add a container view to a scene and resize it to take up a subsection of the view.

Gesture Recognizers

- The **Gesture Recognizer** classes make it easy for you to capture and respond to a variety of gestures from your users. Here is a list of the iOS gesture recognizers:
  - **Tap Gesture Recognizer** - Recognizes single or double taps as well as taps with multiple touches.
  - **Pinch Gesture Recognizer** - Recognizes pinch gestures, where the user places two fingers on the touch surface and moves them towards or away from each other.
  - **Rotation Gesture Recognizer** - Recognizes rotation gestures, where the user places two fingers on the touch surface and rotates them.

- **Swipe Gesture Recognizer** - Recognizes swipe gestures, where the user moves their finger quickly across the touch surface. You can specify whether you want to detect **Left**, **Right**, **Up**, or **Down** swipe motions.

- **Pan Gesture Recognizer** - Recognizes a pan gesture, where the user drags their finger on the design surface.

- **Screen Edge Pan Gesture Recognizer** - Recognizes pan gestures that start near the edge of the screen.

- **Long Press Gesture Recognizer** - Recognizes long press gestures, where the user touches and leaves their finger on the touch surface for a longer period of time.

Navigation, Tab, Search, and Toolbars

- A **Navigation Bar** is associated with a navigation controller and is located at the top of the screen. It can contain a title and buttons that can be used to navigate, edit, share content, and for your own custom purposes.

- A **Navigation Item** specifies the information displayed in a navigation bar when the user navigates to a particular scene.

- A **Tab Bar** provides tabs that allow you to switch between multiple views in your app. A tab bar is best used in apps that have different modes.

- The **Tab Bar Item** represents a single bar in a tab bar.

- The **Search Bar** displays a rounded rectangle with a small magnifying glass on the left in which the user can enter search text. When the user taps the search bar, it displays a keyboard that includes a **Search** key.

- The **Toolbar** is displayed at the bottom of the screen and usually contains buttons that allow the user to perform common tasks.

- A **Bar Button Item** can be added to either a navigation bar or a toolbar. Typically, you add buttons that provide users with quick access to commonly used functions.

- The **Fixed Space Bar Button Item** is really just a bar button item that has its **Identifier** attribute set to **Fixed Width**. It allows you to add fixed width spacing in your app's toolbars.

- The **Flexible Space Bar Button Item** is just a bar button item that has its **Identifier** set to **Flexible Width**. It allows you to add a flexible amount of space to your toolbars.

AVKit Player View Controller

The AVKit Player View Controller provides a user interface and player to play media stored on the local device or from a URL.

Blur Effects

- Apple uses the blur effect throughout the iOS user interface in places such as Notification Center and Control Center.

- Some of the text in Notification Center such as No Events and the dates takes on the color of the blurred image. This effect is known as *vibrancy*.

- Apple includes effect classes in Xcode that make it easy to add blur and vibrancy effects to your apps. You can drop these on a scene and they will automatically create a blur effect on the user interface controls that are behind them. If you don't need the vibrancy effect, you can just use the **Visual Effect View with Blur** control.

Step-By-Step Movie 7.1

This movie takes you step-by-step through the process of writing code that zooms in the the user's current location.

http://www.iosappsfornonprogrammers.com/B3M71.9.html

Step-By-Step Movie 7.2

This movie takes you step-by-step through the process of adding functionality that switches between map modes.

http://www.iosappsfornonprogrammers.com/B3M72.9.html

Chapter 8: Laying Out the User Interface

With the wide variety of iOS device sizes and orientations, it's extremely important that you make sure your app looks great in all environments. Fortunately, Apple's Auto Layout continues to improve with each new version of Xcode, and this chapter shows you how to take full advantage of this technology.

Sections in This Chapter

8. *Examining Auto-Generated Constraints*

9. *Moving and Resizing Controls*

10. *Creating Custom Constraints*

11. *Resolving Constraint Conflicts*

12. *Content Hugging Priority*

13. *Content Compression Resistance Priority*

14. *Creating Constraints in Code*

15. *Working with the Stack View*

16. *Summary*

User-Interface Layout Options

As you already learned in *Chapter 5: The Inspectors* under the section The Size Inspector, there are two ways you can specify the size and position of UI controls in your views:

1. Springs and Struts

2. Auto Layout

You may remember that a storyboard's **Use Auto Layout** setting found in the File Inspector (Figure 8.1) determines which user-interface layout option you are using. If this check box is unselected (it is for storyboards created using Xcode 4.4 or older), the storyboard uses springs and struts for laying out the user interface. If it's selected (it is for storyboards created using Xcode 4.5 or newer), the storyboard uses the new Auto Layout approach.

The associated **Use Size Classes** setting allows a storyboard to work with all available screen sizes on any iOS device.

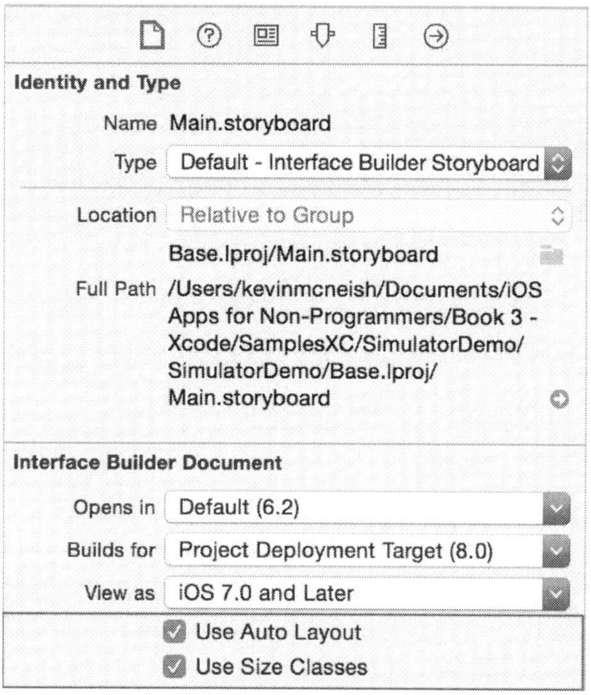

*Figure 8.1 The **Auto Layout** and **Size Classes** settings.*

Springs and Struts

The classic springs and struts approach to laying out your user interface works well for simple user interfaces. However, for more complex user interfaces, you need to write code to size and position controls when using springs and struts.

Now that Apple has provided a truly usable version of Auto Layout, I no longer recommend that you use the older springs and struts technology.

Auto Layout

In contrast with the hard-coded nature of springs and struts, the new Auto Layout feature is a *descriptive* layout system. It supports far more complex user-interface layouts, so you rarely need to write code to ensure your user-interface positions and resizes properly as the size of the parent view changes.

The main building block used in Auto Layout is called a *constraint*. A constraint describes rules for the layout of user-interface objects. For example, you can create a constraint that specifies the width of an element or the spacing between multiple elements.

Xcode includes the following capabilities:

- Constraints are only added to a scene when you specify that they should be added.
- You can quickly and easily add constraints using menu options and by using Control+Drag.
- You can update constraints and frames of UI elements separately.
- When creating dynamic views that are generated at run time, you can specify placeholder constraints.
- Xcode can automatically generate constraints for you as well as resolve issues with conflicting or ambiguous constraints.

If you are moving an app to a newer iOS version and you need to redesign the user interface to adapt to its look and feel, I recommend you remove all constraints from the scene first, reposition and resize the controls, and then have Xcode add new constraints back in for you.

As you will learn when we cover creating multi-lingual applications later in this series, Auto Layout also makes internationalization much easier.

Adapting to Size & Orientation Changes

When laying out your user interface, you want to make sure it looks good:

- On all iPhone device sizes.
- On the iPad if you are building a universal application.
- In landscape and portrait orientations.

You can use the Simulator and the Storyboard toggle switch to view your scenes in these different sizes and orientations, or you can use the iOS Previewer.

Xcode's iOS Previewer

The iOS Previewer does a decent job of displaying your scenes as they appear in the Simulator or an iOS device.

However, in more complex user interfaces there is still a difference, so I recommend checking your UI in the Simulator. Let's see how the iOS Previewer works.

1. In Xcode, open the **AutoLayoutDemo** project found in this book's sample code.
2. In the Project Navigator, select the **Main.Storyboard** file. You should see the scene shown in Figure 8.2.
3. Launch the Assistant Editor by clicking the center button in the Editor button group at the top of the Xcode window or by selecting **View > Assistant Editor > Show Assistant Editor** from the menu.

*Figure 8.2 The scene in the **AutoLayoutDemo** project.*

4. It's easiest to view two scenes side by side, so from the Xcode menu, select **View > Assistant Editor > Assistant Editors on Right**.

5. To display the currently selected scene in the iOS Previewer, in the Assistant Editor's Jump bar, click the **Automatic** or **Manual** button and select **Preview > <Storyboard Name> (Preview)**.

6. Click the + button at the bottom-left corner and select **iPhone 4 inch** to add a second preview of the iPhone. Click on the bottom of the new preview to rotate to landscape orientation (Figure 8.3).

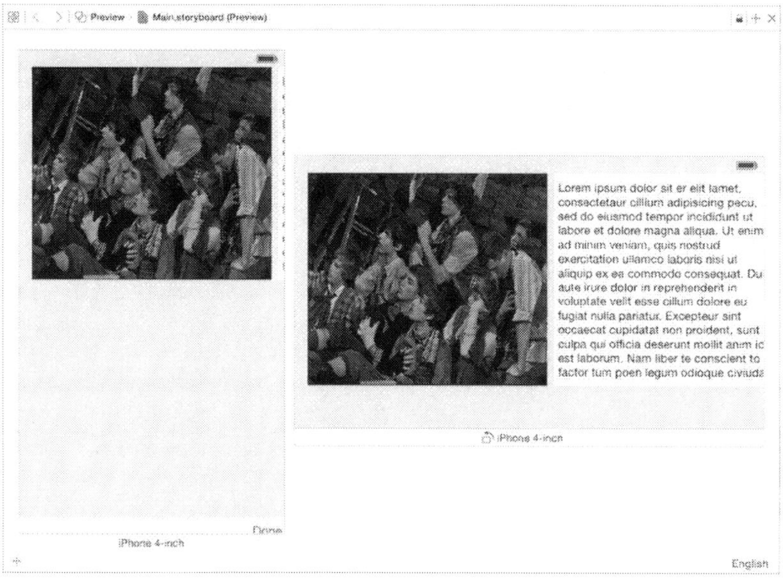

Figure 8.3 The iOS Previewer

Understanding Constraints

With Auto Layout, you create *constraints* that specify how you want controls positioned and resized. You can specify the relative size and position of a control with respect to the view that contains it or with respect to other controls in the view.

You can also use constraints to specify geometric properties of a control such as height and width. From these constraints, Auto Layout calculates the appropriate position and size of your controls at run time when the view first loads and when the size of the view changes, such as when the user changes the device orientation. Let's see firsthand how this works.

Adding Constraints to a Scene

We could manually add Auto Layout constraints for each control in the scene so they resize and reposition to fill the extra screen real estate. However, Xcode offers an option to automatically add the constraints it thinks are best to the scene. Let's try that first.

1. In the **AutoLayoutDemo** project, click the dock at the top of the scene to select it.

2. In the bottom-right corner of the Interface Builder panel is the Auto Layout menu (Figure 8.4). (It looks like a toolbar, but since Apple calls it a menu, I'll go with that.) Here is a brief description of each button:

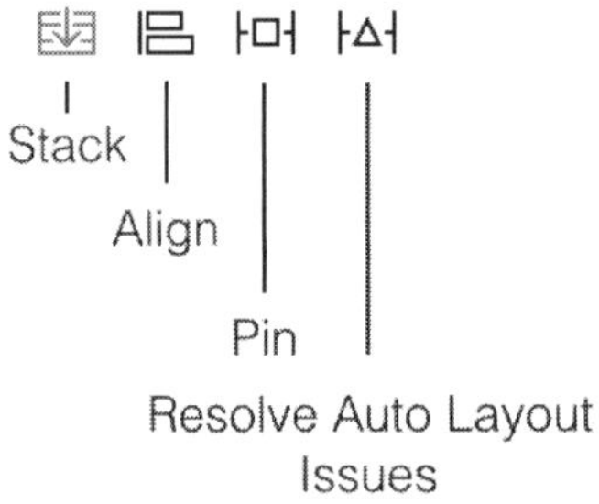

Figure 8.4 The Auto Layout menu.

- **Stack** - Stacks the selected controls horizontally or vertically within a stack view.
- **Align** - Lets you align the edges and centers of controls. Most options in this button can only be chosen if you have multiple controls selected in the design surface.
- **Pin** - Allows you to specify the height, width, and relative spacing between user-interface controls.
- **Resolve Auto Layout Issues** - Allows you to update, add, reset, and clear constraints.

3. Click the **Resolve Auto Layout Issues** button and select **Reset to Suggested Constraints** from the popup menu (Figure 8.5).

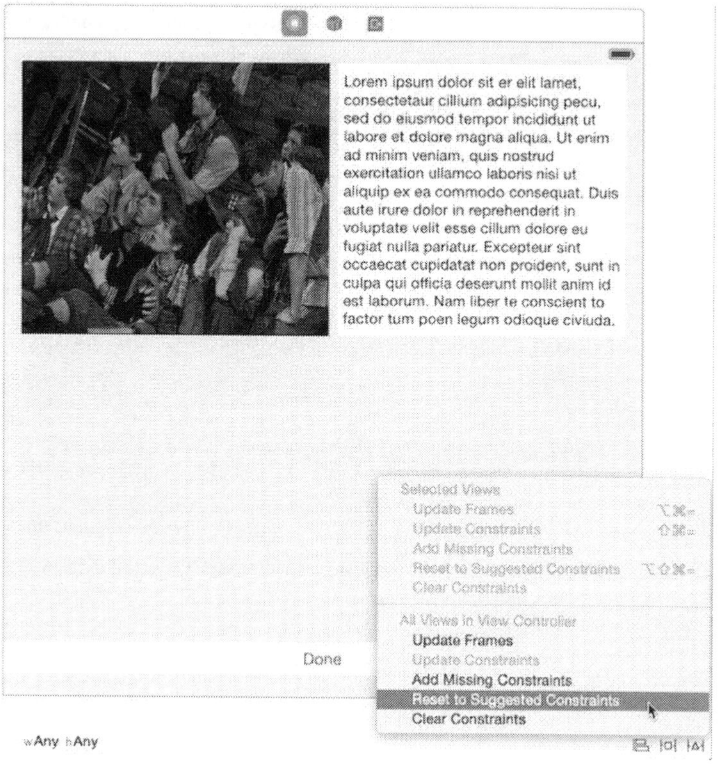

*Figure 8.5 Select **Reset to Suggest Constraints.***

4. Let's see how the new constraints affect the scene. If the Assistant Editor is off, turn it on and you will see the scene previews shown in Figure 8.6.

Figure 8.6 The scene with suggested constraints.

Notice in the portrait preview, the **Done** button now gets repositioned and resized appropriately at the bottom of the scene. This is more like what a user would expect to happen. The image view and text view are now both visible at the top of the scene, but the image view is much thinner than the text view.

Things look a bit better in landscape orientation. The **Done** button is no longer positioned off the screen, and the image view and text view are sized equally to take advantage of the additional horizontal space. It's an improvement over having no constraints, but we definitely need to tweak them a bit.

Examining Auto-Generated Constraints

Before making any adjustments, let's take a look at the constraints that Xcode automatically generated for us to achieve this resizing and repositioning behavior.

1. In the storyboard, click on the **Done** button to select it. When you do this, notice the blue `I`-bars below and to the right of the **Done** button as well as the vertical line down the left and right sides of the scene. These are visual representations of Auto Layout constraints. When you select a user-interface element, Xcode displays the constraints that apply to the selected control in the design surface.

2. Let's get a more detailed look at these four constraints. Go to the Size Inspector (select the second button from the right in the Inspector toolbar), and you will see the four constraints shown in Figure 8.7.

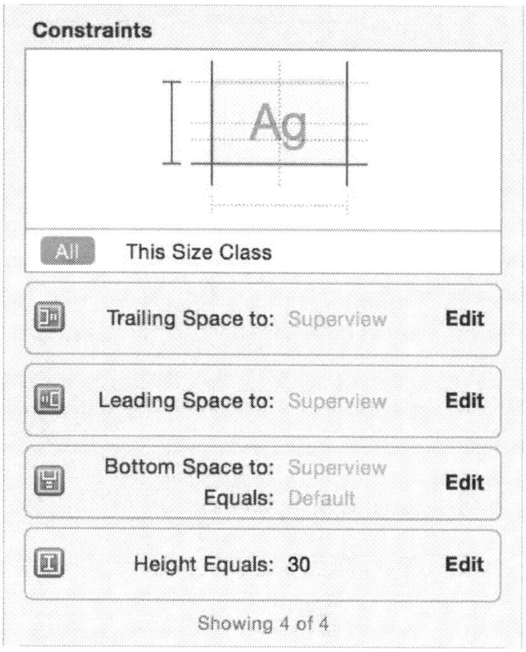

*Figure 8.7 The **Done** button's constraints.*

Here is a brief description of each constraint:

- **Trailing Space to: Superview** - In the English language, *trailing space* indicates the space between the right side of the view and the right side of the UI control. In right-to-left languages such as Hebrew and Arabic, it indicates the space between the left side of the view and the left side of the control.

- **Leading Space to: Superview** - In the English language, *leading space* indicates the space between the left side of the view and the left side of the UI control. In right-to-left languages it indicates the space between the right side of the view and the right side of the control.

- **Bottom Space to: Superview Equals: Default** - This constraint specifies that the space between the bottom of the button and the superview is the default space recommended for UI objects. This constraint was added to the view because the button was dropped on the view when the bottom-alignment guide line appeared.

- **Height Equals: 30** - Specifies that the height of the button is 30 points.

3. Hover your mouse pointer over the **Bottom Space** constraint in the Size Inspector. The associated constraint is highlighted in the design surface (Figure 8.8). This provides visual confirmation that you are looking at the correct constraint.

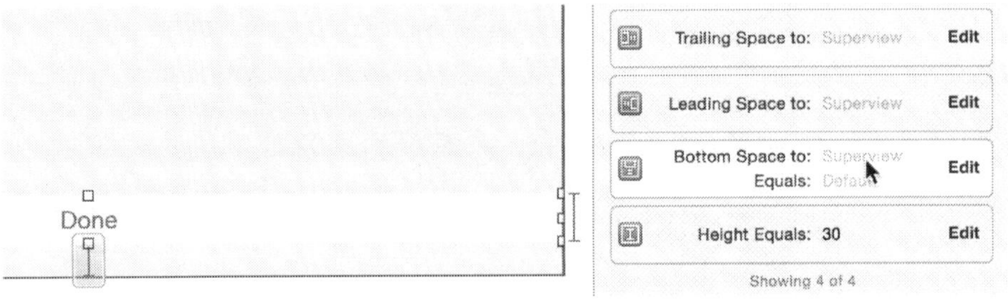

Figure 8.8 The constraint is highlighted in the storyboard.

4. Now go to the Document Outline pane, and you can see constraints are also listed there (Figure 8.9). Constraints that are specific to one particular control are listed below that control (such as the **Button** and **Image View**). All other constraints are listed under the general **Constraints** node.

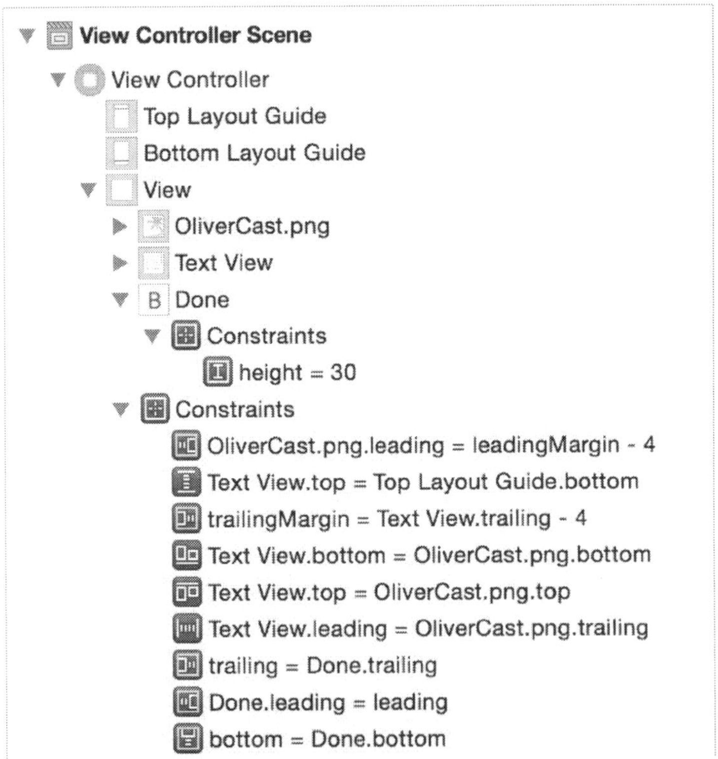

Figure 8.9 Constraints in the Document Outline pane.

Selecting a constraint in the Document Outline pane highlights the corresponding constraint and associated control(s) in the design surface.

5. Select the **bottom = Done.bottom** constraint. Go to the Attributes Inspector (click the third button from the right in the Inspector toolbar). You will see the constraint attributes shown in Figure 8.10.

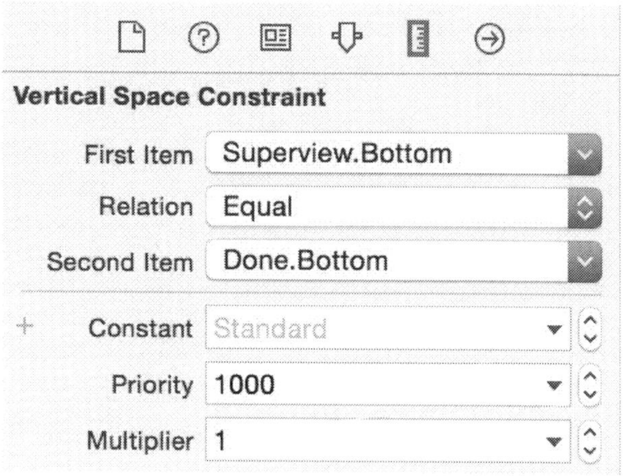

Figure 8.10 Vertical Space Constraint attributes.

In the top section, you can see the vertical spacing is a relationship between two objects. The **First Item** being the bottom of the superview, the **Second Item** the bottom of the Done button.

Apple has designed the constraint attributes to reflect a linear equation:

```
FirstItem.Attribute = (SecondItem.Attribute
* Multiplier) + Constant
```

Given the settings in Figure 8.10, the Superview's Bottom is equal to the Done button's bottom plus the Standard space.

In the **Relation** combo box, you can also specify a **Less Than or Equal** or **Greater Than or Equal** relationship between the attributes.

The **Constant** attribute can be set to:

- A number of points
- **Use Standard Value** - Specifies the "standard" space between controls as indicated by the guide lines in the design surface.

- **Use Canvas Value** - You can select this option if you have manually moved a user interface control on the canvas.

The **Priority** attribute specifies the priority of this constraint in relation to other constraints. This value can be anywhere between 1 and 1000, where 1000 indicates the constraint is required. Anything less than 1000 indicates the constraint is optional. At run time, Auto Layout compares conflicting constraints. The constraint with the higher priority is applied, and the constraint with the lower priority is not applied.

The constraint shown in Figure 8.10 could be read as "Require the vertical space between the bottom of the button and the bottom of the view to be the standard spacing for iOS apps."

6. Click on the **Done** button again to select it, and then go to the Size Inspector (second button from the right in the Inspector toolbar). Hover your mouse pointer over the **Leading Space** constraint. This highlights the constraint on the left side of the scene, which spans the scene's full height (Figure 8.11).

This constraint is more generically called **Done.leading = leading** in the Document Outline pane, and more specifically called a **Leading Space** constraint in the Size Inspector.

Figure 8.11 The leading space constraint is highlighted.

7. To see the leading-space constraint's attributes, double-click the constraint in the Size Inspector. This unselects the button, selects the constraint in the design surface, and displays the attributes shown in in the Attributes Inspector.

8. Click the down arrow on the right side of the **First Item** attribute to see additional options (Figure 8.12).

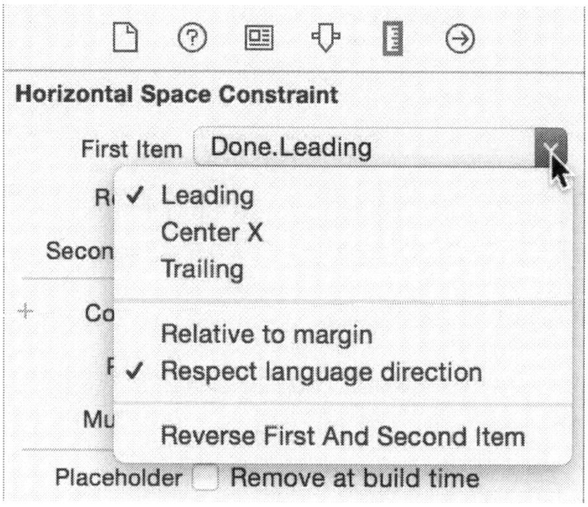

Figure 8.12 Additional constraint options.

At the top of the popup, you can set the constraint to apply to **Leading**, **Center X**, or **Trailing** space.

In the center of the popup you can specify the spacing is **Relative to margin**, specifying the spacing is to the margin of the container rather than its edge. If you uncheck **Respect Language Direction**, it changes the spacing from **Leading** and **Trailing** to **Left** and **Right**. You can choose this option if you don't want the spacing to change when the language changes.

The **Reverse First and Second Item** option switches the controls in the **First Item** and **Second Item** boxes, which also reverses the constraint's linear equation in a mathematically equivalent way.

9. Select the image view in the design surface and check out its constraints as shown in Figure 8.13.

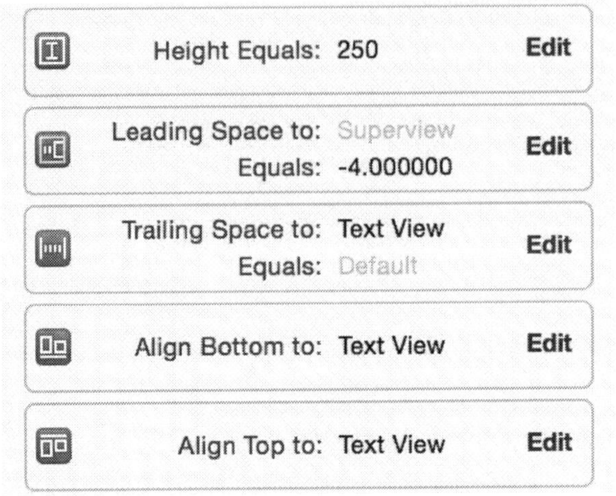

Figure 8.13 Image view constraints.

The **Height** constraint is set to 250 points, so the image view maintains its height regardless of screen size or device orientation.

The **Leading Space** constraint is set to a Constant value of 04.000000 because it is relative to the margin, rather than the edge of the view.

The **Trailing Space** constraint is relative to the **Text View** control with a **Default** spacing between them.

The **Align Bottom** and **Align Top** constraints align the bottom and top of the image view with the text view.

10. Finally, select the text view control, and you will see the constraints shown in Figure 8.14.

Figure 8.14 The text view constraints.

Most of these constraints are similar to the constraints for the image view. However, there is an additional **Top Space** constraint that specifies the space between the top of the text view and the top edge of the view. This only needs to be specified for the text view since the image view has a constraint that specifies the top of the image view is the same as the top of the text view.

I recommend hovering your mouse pointer over the various constraints in the Size Inspector to familiarize yourself with the associated constraints that get highlighted in the design surface.

Moving and Resizing Controls

After Xcode generates constraints for your scene (or if you create the constraints yourself), if you reposition or resize a UI control, you will create a conflict with the existing constraints. For example, if I move the Done button to the bottom of the scene, notice an orange dotted line marks the spot where the button used to be as shown in Figure 8.15.

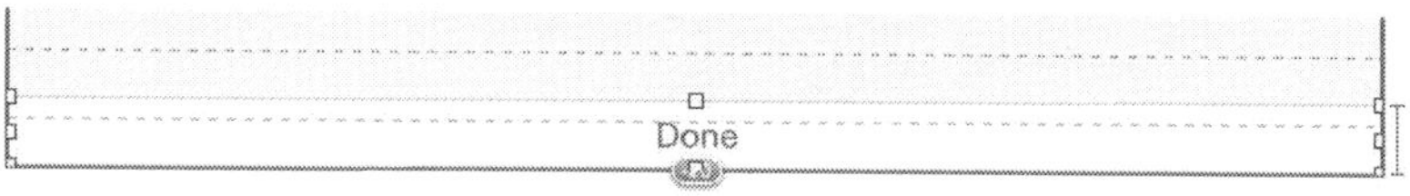

Figure 8.15 Manually moving or resizing a control creates a conflict with existing constraints.

This also creates a compiler warning. You can view details about this warning in the Document Outline. In Figure 8.16; there is an orange, circular alert at the top- right of the Document Outline.

Figure 8.16 The warning icon in the Document Outline.

If you click on this orange warning icon, the Document Outline pane slides to the left and is replaced by the Constraint Error pane shown in Figure 8.17.

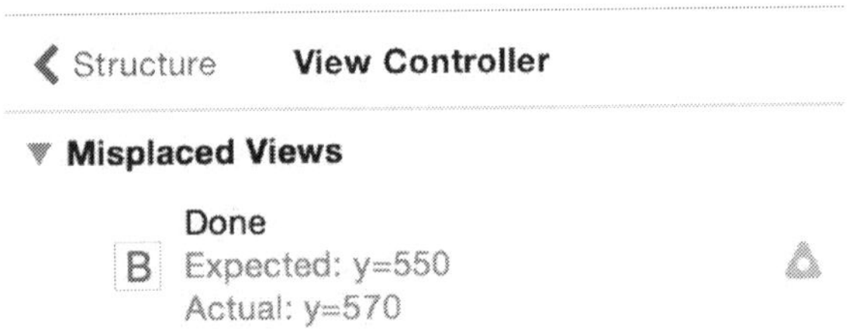

Figure 8.17 The Constraint Error pane.

The message tells us that the constraint error concerns the **Done** button and the problem is that the **y** coordinate should be at **550** points based on the original constraint, but the button is physically sitting at **570** points. If you click the warning icon in this panel, it pops up the list of options shown in Figure 8.18.

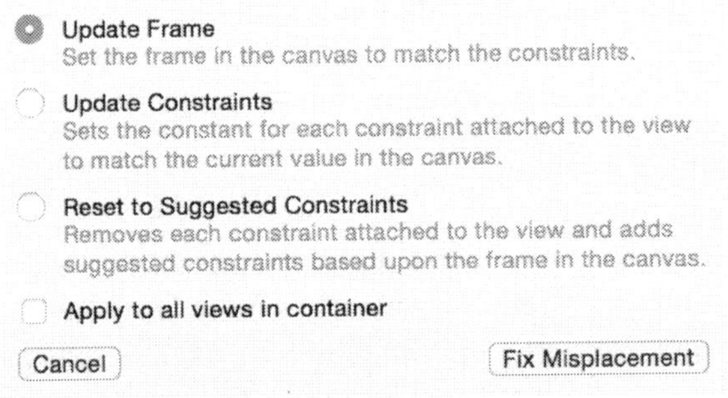

Figure 8.18 The Fix Constraint options.

Here is a description of each option:

- **Update Frame** - Moves the UI control to match the position specified in the constraint (in this case, back where it was before we moved it).
- **Update Constraints** - Updates the constraints to match the new position of the UI control. If I want to leave the control where it is, I can choose this option.
- **Reset to Suggested Constraints** - This option removes all existing constraints and adds new constraints back in to match the position of the control.

The **Apply to all views in container** specifies the option you choose should apply to all user-interface elements in the container.

Creating Custom Constraints

Since Xcode doesn't do a complete job of determining default constraints for your scenes, you need to add your own custom constraints.

For example, as shown in Figure 8.6, when the main scene in the **AutoLayoutDemo** project is displayed in portrait orientation, the text view takes up most of the available space. What if you wanted the image view and text view to take up an equal amount of space in landscape orientation? Let's give it a try.

1. **Control+Click** on the image view and drag over to the text view so it's highlighted in blue (Figure 8.19).

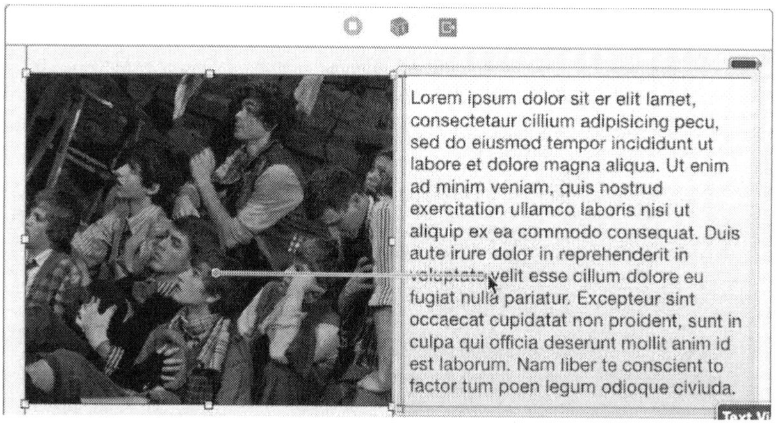

Figure 8.19 ***Control+Drag*** *from image view to text view.*

2. Release the mouse button to display the Constraint popup and select the **Equal Widths** option (Figure 8.20).

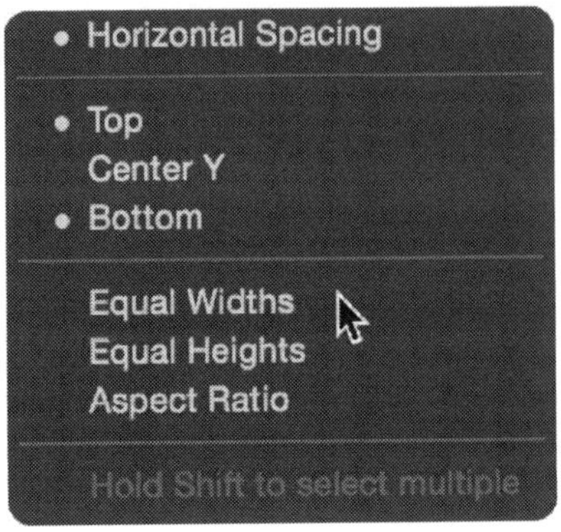

*Figure 8.20 The **Equal Widths** in the constraints popup.*

3. When you do this, you will see red lines and rounded rectangles containing numbers that indicate constraint errors (Figure 8.21).

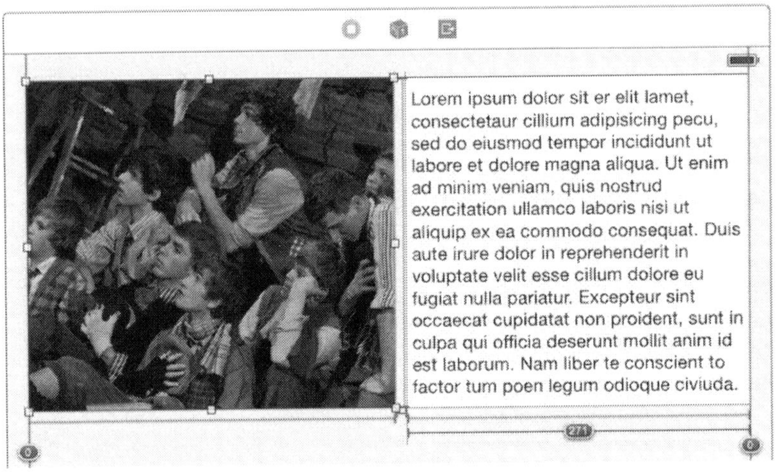

Figure 8.21 Constraint errors in the design surface.

4. Click the red icon in the upper-right corner of the Document Outline to display the Constraint Error panel (Figure 8.22).

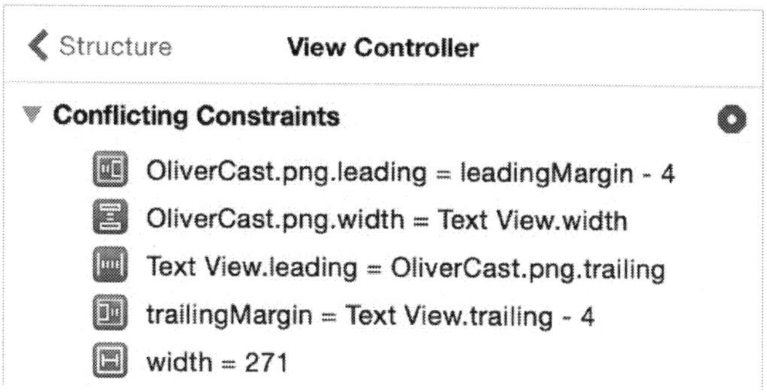

Figure 8.22 The constraint error panel.

At the top of the panel is a list of **Conflicting Constraints**. Click the red circle at the top right of the window to display a popup that lets you delete constraints to resolve the conflict (Figure 8.23). The problem is the **Width (271)** constraint. We have specified the image view and text view are the same width, but the hard-coded width of the text view doesn't make this possible. To delete the constraint, select the check box to the left of the constraint and click **Delete Constraints**.

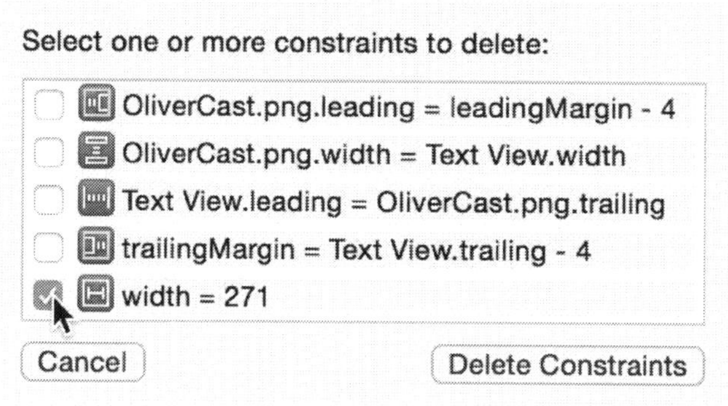

*Figure 8.23 Delete the **Width** constraint.*

5. This completely resolves the errors, but still leaves two warnings (Figure 8.24).

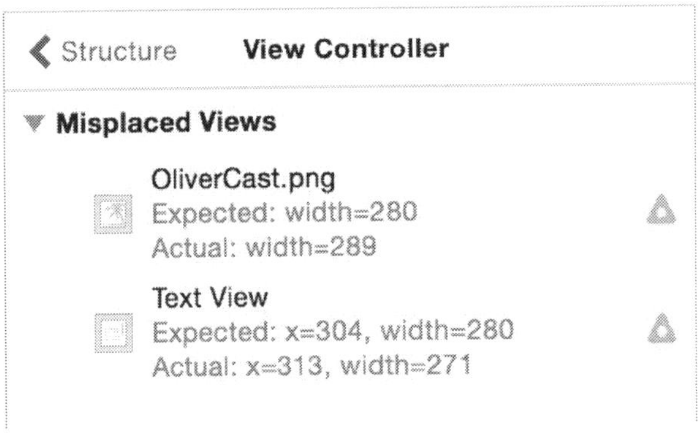

Figure 8.24 The constraint warnings.

These warnings are telling us that the image view and text view are expected to be 280 points wide, but the image view's **Actual** width is **289** and the text view's **Actual** width is **271**.

6. To fix these warnings, click on the yellow icon to the right of each warning and select **Fix Misplacement**. This adjusts the width of the image view and text view to 280 points.

7. Look in the iOS Previewer in the Assistant Editor and you can see this is a vast improvement on the layout of the user interface in both portrait and landscape orientations (Figure 8.25).

Figure 8.25 The scene looks good in portrait and landscape orientation.

8. There is another way to add the Equal Widths constraint. You can select both the image view and text view in the design surface, then click the **Pin** button in the bottom-right corner of the Storyboard editor. In the Pin popup, you can select the **Equal Widths** option and then click **Add 1 Constraint** (Figure 8.26).

*Figure 8.26 Setting **Equal Widths** in the **Pin** constrains popup.*

9. As mentioned earlier, the iOS Previewer doesn't always display scenes with 100 percent accuracy, so I recommend running the app in the Simulator and checking out both portrait and landscape orientations to make sure everything is working well.

Resolving Constraint Conflicts

At times, Auto Layout warnings are displayed in the Console when you run your app in the Simulator or an iOS Device (Figure 8.27).

```
2013-10-24 23:13:15.862 AutoLayoutDemo[3048:70b] Unable to simultaneously
satisfy constraints.
	Probably at least one of the constraints in the following list is one you
don't want. Try this: (1) look at each constraint and try to figure out which
you don't expect; (2) find the code that added the unwanted constraint or
constraints and fix it. (Note: If you're seeing
NSAutoresizingMaskLayoutConstraints that you don't understand, refer to the
documentation for the UIView property
translatesAutoresizingMaskIntoConstraints)
(
    "<NSLayoutConstraint:0x8b8a500 H:[UIImageView:0x8b8a310(136)]>",
    "<NSLayoutConstraint:0xa83a5f0 H:[UILabel:0x8b891e0]-(NSSpace(20))-|
(Names: '|':UIView:0x8b89030 )>",
    "<NSLayoutConstraint:0xa83a640 H:|-(NSSpace(20))-[UILabel:0x8b891e0]
(Names: '|':UIView:0x8b89030 )>",
    "<NSLayoutConstraint:0xa83a6d0 UIImageView:0x8b8a310.leading == UILabel:
0x8b891e0.leading>",
    "<NSLayoutConstraint:0xa83a760 UITextView:0xa265a00.width == UIImageView:
0x8b8a310.width>",
    "<NSLayoutConstraint:0xa83a790 UITextView:0xa265a00.trailing == UILabel:
0x8b891e0.trailing>",
    "<NSLayoutConstraint:0xa83a7c0 H:[UIImageView:0x8b8a310]-(NSSpace(8))-
[UITextView:0xa265a00]>",
    "<NSAutoresizingMaskLayoutConstraint:0x8a2eb20 h=--& v=--& V:[UIView:
0x8b89030(480)]>"
)

Will attempt to recover by breaking constraint
<NSLayoutConstraint:0x8b8a500 H:[UIImageView:0x8b8a310(136)]>

All Output
```

Figure 8.27 Constraint conflicts displayed in the Console

Even though the final result of the resizing and positioning of controls was correct, the Auto Layout system may find conflicts in the constraints.

The message at the top of Figure 8.27 says: "Unable to simultaneously satisfy constraints." The next paragraph states, "Probably at least one of the constraints in the following list is one you don't want." Further down, it lists the group of constraints in which there is a conflict, and near the bottom it tells you which constraint it broke to try and recover from the conflict.

This is a great feature of Auto Layout. Even though there are conflicting constraints, it does its best to come up with a best guess for a solution by breaking one of the conflicting constraints.

Looking through the list of constraints should give you a pretty good idea where the conflict lies. The constraints are displayed in the syntax of Apple's Visual Format Language. Here is some of the basic syntax of this language (for more information, check out the topic *Visual Format Language* in the Apple documentation):

- A control is represented between square brackets.

- A connection between controls and views is represented by a single hyphen or two hyphens with a number in between representing the space between the objects in points.
- The superview or parent view is represented by a single vertical line.

For example, look at the second half of the first constraint:

```
H:[UIImageView:0x8b8a310(136)]
```

- The **H** indicates this constraint applies to a horizontal orientation.
- The **UIImageView** between square brackets indicates this constraint applies to a text view.
- The **(136)** indicates the value associated with the constraint.

From this information you can derive that this is the image view's width constraint. As you look through the other constraints, it's pretty easy to see the problem. The relevant constraints dictate that:

- The image view must be 136 points wide.
- The image view width and text view width must be the same.
- There must be 8 points between the image view and text view.

When the device is in portrait orientation, all of these constraints can be satisfied. However, when the device is rotated to landscape orientation and the view becomes wider, not all of these constraints can be satisfied. For that reason, the Auto Layout system decided to break the image view's width constraint:

```
Will attempt to recover by breaking constraint
<NSLayoutConstraint:0x8b8a500
H:[UIImageView:0x8b8a310(136)]>
```

Even if you agree with the decision made by the Auto Layout system, you should still fix the conflict so your constraints are simplified and efficient.

Content Hugging Priority

You may have noticed the **Content Hugging Priority** settings in the Size Inspector (Figure 8.28).

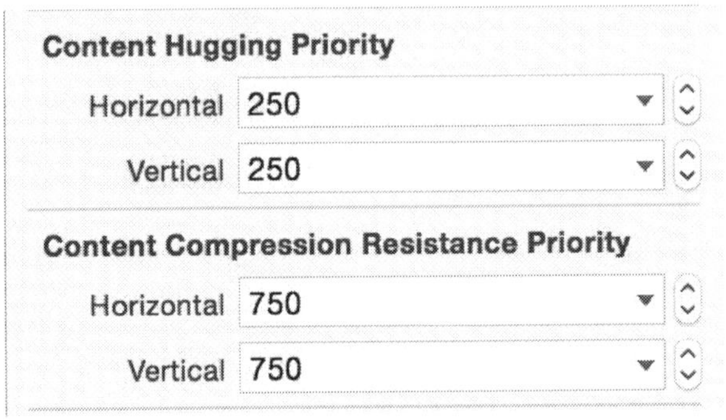

Figure 8.28 ***Content Hugging*** *and* ***Content Compression Resistance Priority*** *settings.*

These settings specify how tightly the edges of a control (both horizontal and vertical) hug its content. The higher the priority, the less likely the element will resize.

Content Compression Resistance Priority

There are also **Content Compression Resistance Priority** settings in the Size Inspector (Figure 8.28).

These settings specify how likely a control's content is to be compressed (both horizontally and vertically). The higher the priority, the less likely the content of the control will be clipped.

Creating Constraints in Code

The absolute easiest way to create constraints is by using Interface Builder. However, in some complex user interfaces, you may not be able to specify some more difficult constraints using IB. For these situations, Apple has provided the ability to create constraints in code.

We'll cover this topic more thoroughly when we come across more complex user interfaces later in this book series, but for now, Interface Builder will be able to handle the vast majority of your constraints.

For more information on creating constraints in code, check out the topic *Auto Layout Guide* in the Apple documentation.

Working with the Stack View

Apple has recently introduced a new Stack View, which makes certain auto layout tasks much easier. Let's see how it works.

1. Open the **StackViewDemo** project, which is located in the folder where you have stored this book's sample code.
2. Select **Main.storyboard** in the Project Navigator, and you will see the scene shown in Figure 8.29. At the bottom of the scene are five buttons, one for each of the five senses.

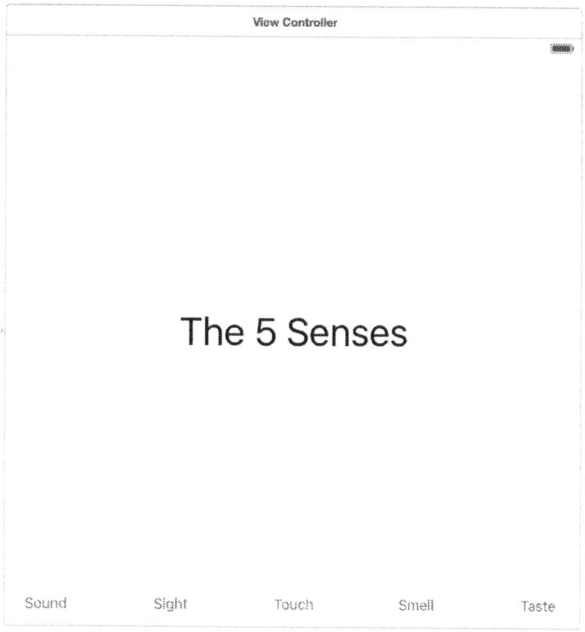

Figure 8.29 The StackViewDemo scene

3. Let's run the project so see how the scene looks in the Simulator. At the top left of the Xcode window, set the right side of the Scheme control to **iPhone 6**.
4. Click Xcode's **Run** button. When the app appears in the Simulator, you should see the screen shown in Figure 8.30. As you can see, the five labels at the bottom of the screen are not positioned or spaced properly. Click Xcode's **Stop** button and let's see how we can use a Stack View to fix this.

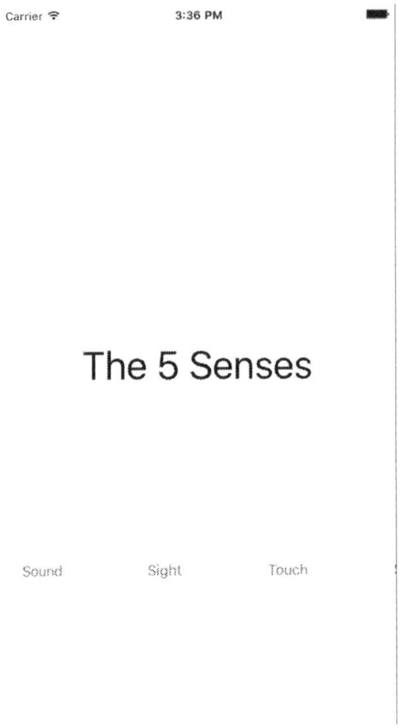

Figure 8.30 The StackViewDemo scene at run time

5. Go to the storyboard, hold down the **Shift** key, and click on each of the labels until they are all selected. Next, go to the bottom-right corner of the Storyboard editor and click the **Stack** button (Figure 8.31). This adds all of the labels to the Stack View and positions the stack view on the left side of the scene.

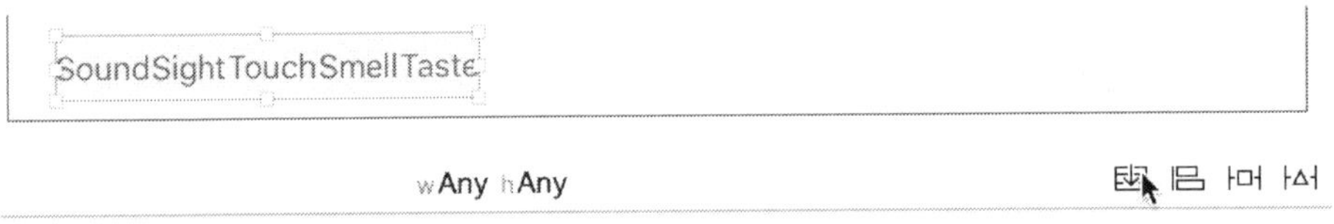

Figure 8.31 Add labels to the Stack View.

When you add UI controls to a Stack View, any existing constraints are removed from the controls.

6. Look in the Document Outline to see all labels are contained within the Stack View (Figure 8.32).

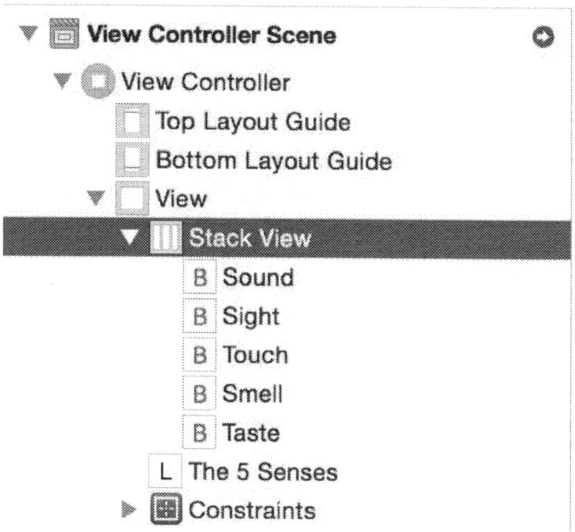

Figure 8.32 Labels within the Stack View

7. Now we need to add constraints to the Stack View so it spans the width of the scene. To do this, make sure the Stack View is selected in the Document Outline. Next, at the bottom-right corner of the Storyboard editor, click the **Pin** button. Uncheck the **Constrain to margins** check box (Figure 8.33), and set the following spacing:

   Left = 20, Right = 20, Bottom = 8

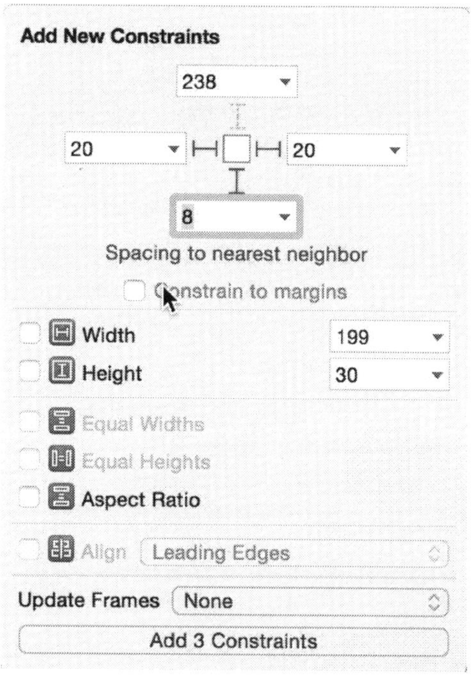

Figure 8.33 Add three constraints to the Stack View

Make sure all three I-bars are selected, then click the **Add 3 Constraints** button.

This resizes and repositions the Stack View. However, notice four buttons are pushed to the right side of the Stack View and the Sound label is expanded to take up the remaining space (Figure 8.34). Let's fix this.

Figure 8.34 Stack View resized and repositioned

Before going further, with the Stack View still selected, go to the Attributes Inspector, to see its attributes as shown in Figure 8.35.

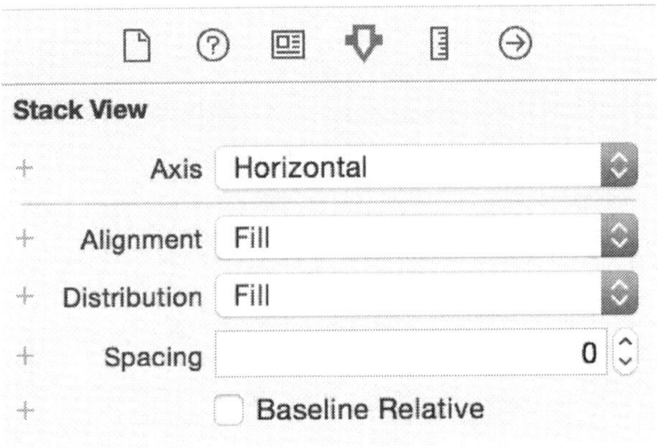

Figure 8.35 Stack View attributes

Here is a description of each attribute:

- **Axis** - Specifies if the controls contained in the Stack View are stacked horizontally or vertically.

- **Alignment** - Specifies how a Stack View lays out its contained controls perpendicular to its axis. Horizontal Stack Views have the **Alignment** options shown in Figure 8.36.

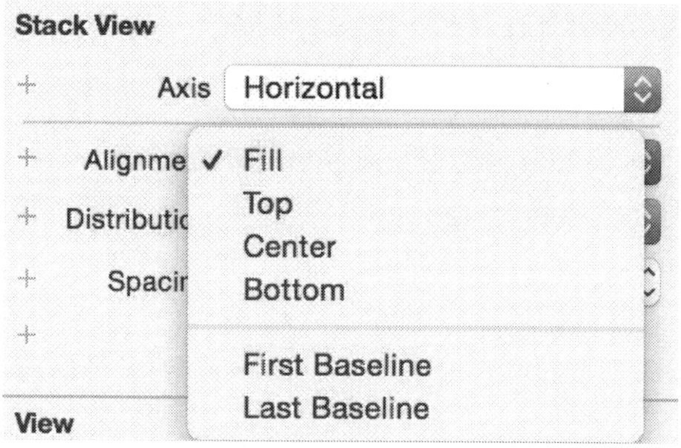

*Figure 8.36 Horizontal Stack View **Alignment** settings*

Vertical Stack Views have the **Alignment** options shown in Figure 8.37.

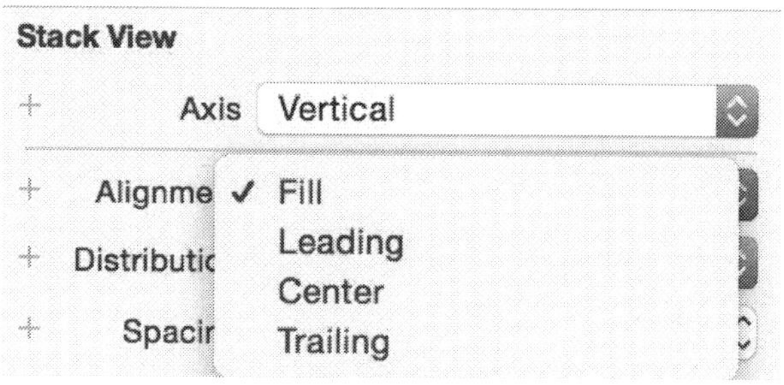

*Figure 8.37 Vertical Stack View **Alignment** settings*

- **Distribution** - Specifies how a Stack View lays out its contained control along its axis. Figure 8.38 shows the Distribution option settings.

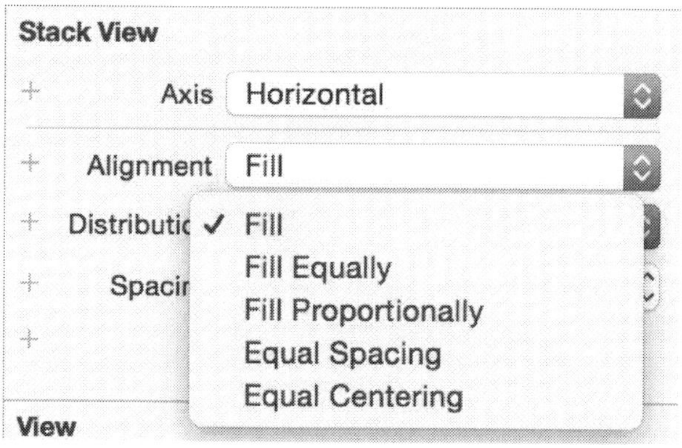

*Figure 8.38 Stack View **Distribution** settings*

- **Spacing** - Specifies the spacing between items contained in the Stack View.

1. Now let's fix the spacing of the buttons within the Stack View. To do this, change the **Distribution** option to **Fill Equally**. This changes the size of all buttons so they have equal widths. You can see this if you select each button in the Stack View as shown in Figure 8.39.

Figure 8.39 ***Distribution*** *set to* ***Fill Equally***

2. Reselect the Stack View in the Document Outline and change the **Distribution** attribute to **Fill Proportionally**. If you select each contained button you can see this resizes the buttons proportionally according to their intrinsic content size, filling the full width of the Stack View (Figure 8.40). You can see this even more clearly if you change one of the button's titles to a single letter.

Figure 8.40 ***Distribution*** *set to* ***Fill Proportionally***

3. Figure 8.41 shows the effect of setting the **Distribution** attribute to **Equal Spacing**. This adds the same spacing between each button.

Figure 8.41 ***Distribution*** *set to* ***Equal Spacing***

4. Figure 8.42 shows the effect of setting the **Distribution** attribute to **Equal Centering**. This positions the buttons so they have an equal center-to-center spacing, while maintaining the **Spacing** attribute's distance between the buttons.

Figure 8.42 ***Distribution*** *set to* ***Equal Centering***

5. At this point, there are a few layout warnings. To see these, click the orange circle containing a white arrow in the upper-right corner of the Document Outline. This displays the warnings (Figure 8.43).

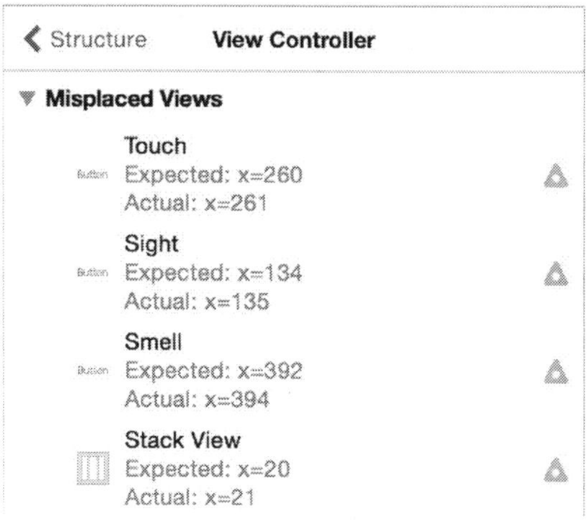

Figure 8.43 Auto Layout warnings

6. Right-click the orange triangles and with **Update frames** selected in the popup, click the **Fix Misplacement** button.

7. Click Xcode's **Run** button to see how the app looks at run time. As shown in Figure 8.44, the buttons are aligned nicely at the bottom of the scene.

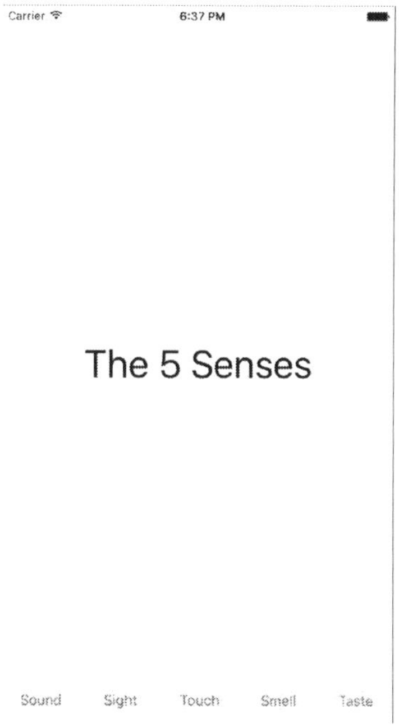

Figure 8.44 The completed scene at run time

The Stack View makes this type of layout far easier than in previous versions of Xcode!

Summary

- There are two ways you can specify the size and position of UI controls in your views:

  1. Springs and Struts

  2. Auto Layout

- The classic springs and struts approach to laying out your user interface works well for simple user interfaces. However, for more complex user interfaces, you need to write code to size and position controls when using springs and struts.

- In contrast with the hard-coded nature of springs and struts, the new Auto Layout feature is a *descriptive* layout system. It supports far more complex user-interface layouts, so you rarely need to write code to ensure your user interface positions and resizes properly as the size of the parent view changes.

- The main building block used in Auto Layout is called a *constraint.* A constraint describes rules for the layout of user-interface objects. For example, you can create a constraint that specifies the width of an element or the spacing between multiple elements.

- The iOS Previewer does a decent job of displaying your scenes as they appear in the Simulator or an iOS device. However in more complex user interfaces there is still a difference, so I recommend checking your UI in the Simulator.

- With Auto Layout, you create *constraints* that specify how you want controls positioned and resized. You can specify the relative size and position of a control with respect to the view that contains it or with respect to other controls in the view

- You can also use constraints to specify geometric properties of a control such as height and width. From these constraints, Auto Layout calculates the appropriate position and size of your controls at run time when the view first loads and when the size of the view changes, such as when the user changes the device orientation.

- Xcode offers an option to automatically add the constraints it thinks are best to the scene
- Whenever possible, you should use the guide lines in Interface Builder to place your controls so Auto Layout can use the default spacing settings.
- Apple has designed the constraint attributes to reflect a linear equation:

```
FirstItem.Attribute = (SecondItem.Attribute
* Multiplier) + Constant
```

- In the Size Inspector's **Relation** combo box, you can also specify a **Less Than or Equal** or **Greater Than or Equal** relationship between the attributes.
- The **Constant** attribute can be set to:
  - A number of points
  - **Use Standard Value** - Specifies the "standard" space between controls as indicated by the guide lines in the design surface.
  - **Use Canvas Value** - You can select this option if you have manually moved a user interface control on the canvas.
- The **Priority** attribute specifies the priority of this constraint in relation to other constraints. This value can be anywhere between 1 and 1000, where 1000 indicates the constraint is required. Anything less than 1000 indicates the constraint is optional. At run time, Auto Layout compares conflicting constraints. The constraint with the higher priority is applied, and the constraint with the lower priority is not applied.
- In English, *leading space* indicates the space between the left side of the view and the left side of the UI control. In right-to-left languages such as Hebrew and Arabic, it indicates the space between the right side of the view and the right side of the control.

- After Xcode generates constraints for your scene (or if you create the constraints yourself), if you reposition or resize a UI control, you will create a conflict with the existing constraints.
- You can view details about auto layout warnings in the Document Outline.
- Xcode offers the following options to fix problems with constraints:
  - **Update Frame** - Moves the UI control to match the position specified in the constraint (in this case, back where it was before we moved it).
  - **Update Constraints** - Updates the constraints to match the new position of the UI control. If I want to leave the control where it is, I can choose this option.
  - **Reset to Suggested Constraints** - This option removes all existing constraints and adds new constraints back to match the position of the control.
- Since Xcode doesn't do a complete job of determining default constraints for your scenes, you need to add your own custom constraints.
- The Auto Layout system checks for conflicting constraints and displays debugging information for any conflicts in Xcode's Console.
- Even if there are conflicting constraints, Auto Layout does its best to come up with a best guess for a solution by breaking one of the conflicting constraints.
- The constraint conflict information displayed in the Console uses the syntax of Apple's Visual Format Language.
- Here is some of the basic syntax of Apple's Visual Format language (for more information, check out the topic *Visual Format Language* in the Apple documentation):
  - A control is represented between square brackets.

   - A connection between controls and views is represented by a single hyphen or two hyphens with a number in between representing the space between the objects in points.
   - The superview or parent view is represented by a single vertical line.

- Even if you agree with the decision made by the Auto Layout system to break a conflicting constraint, you should still fix the conflict so your constraints are simplified and efficient.

- As you lay out your own user interfaces in Xcode using Auto Layout, you should look very carefully for conflicting constraints and fix them.

- The **Content Hugging Priority** settings specify how tightly the edges of a control (both horizontal and vertical) hug its content. The higher the priority, the less likely the element will resize.

- The **Content Compression Resistance Priority** settings specify how likely a control's content is to be compressed (both horizontally and vertically). The higher the priority, the less likely the content of the control will be clipped.

- In some complex user interfaces, you may not be able to specify some more difficult constraints using IB. For these situations, Apple has provided the ability to create constraints in code.

- Apple has introduced a new Stack View, that makes horizontal and vertical alignment auto layout tasks much easier.

Chapter 9: Creating Connections

Creating connections is one of the most common tasks you perform when creating iOS apps, so it's important you have a solid grasp of how they work and how to troubleshoot them when something goes wrong.

Sections in This Chapter

Connections in Depth

In *Chapter 5: The Inspectors*, you learned the basics of connecting user-interface objects to properties and methods in view controllers. This chapter takes a deeper dive into the subject as it discusses events and outlets in greater detail.

Working With Events

To review what you have already learned about events, in the same way that objects have different properties and methods, they can also have a set of *events*. In this context, an event is an action that occurs in a control and is usually initiated by the user tapping, touching, pinching, or otherwise interacting with the control.

When an event occurs on an object, it can send a notification message to one or more target objects. For example, in the conceptual image shown in Figure 9.1, the button on the left is the event sender. It has a **Touch Up Inside** event. The View Controller on the right side of the image is registered as a target for this event, and the **getFahrenheit** method is specified as the action method.

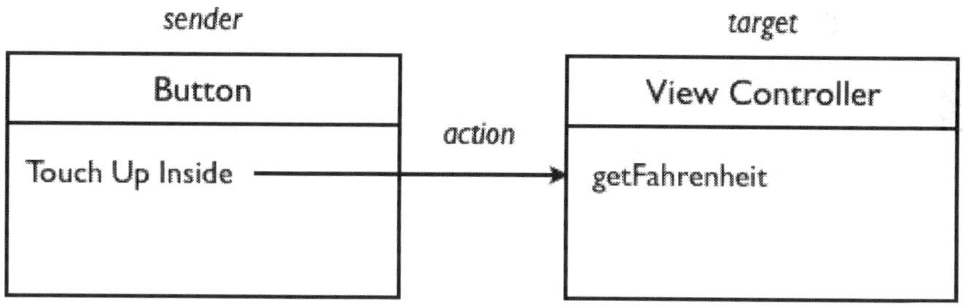

*Figure 9.1 The **View Controller** is the target and **getFahrenheit** is the action for the **Touch Up Inside** event.*

Action methods must have one of three specific *signatures*:

```
@IBAction func methodName()
@IBAction func methodName(sender: AnyObject)
@IBAction func methodName(sender: AnyObject,
   forEvent: UIEvent)
```

We will discuss these method signatures in detail in just a bit. For now, just take note of the **IBAction** attribute. **IBAction** stands for *Interface Builder*

Action and it signifies to Xcode that this method can be linked to user-interface objects.

Events Step by Step

Follow the steps in this section to see how events work in iOS apps.

1. In Xcode, open the **ConnectionsDemo** project found in this book's sample code.

2. In the Project Navigator, select the **Main.Storyboard** file, and you will see the scene shown in Figure 9.2.

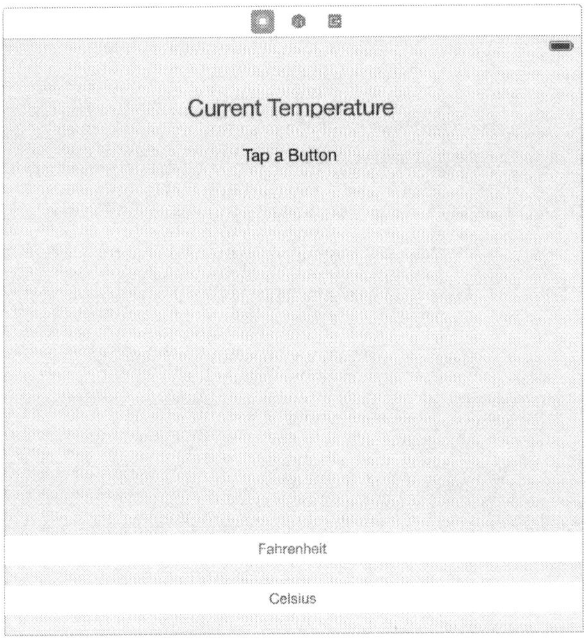

Figure 9.2 The ***ConnectionsDemo*** *main scene.*

This is a very simple scene containing two labels and two buttons. The **Current Temperature** label at the top of the view is only there to describe the contents of the scene. The **Tap a Button** label prompts the user to tap a button to display the current temperature.

We won't retrieve the current temperature from the web because it is beyond the scope of this simple app (although we will be getting data from the web later in this book series). For now, the app will use a static 41 degrees Fahrenheit and 5 degrees Celsius so as not to distract from the topic of connections.

In the next steps, you will create an action method in the view controller that fires when the **Fahrenheit** button's **Touch Up Inside** event occurs. The target method will store the Fahrenheit temperature in the label. You will also create an action method for the **Celsius** button that displays the temperature in degrees Celsius.

3. Before creating the target methods, click the **Tap a Button** label in the design surface, and then go to the Connections Inspector (the last button on the right in the Inspectors toolbar). I want you to see there are no events listed for the label (Figure 9.3). There are no events because users do not interact with labels.

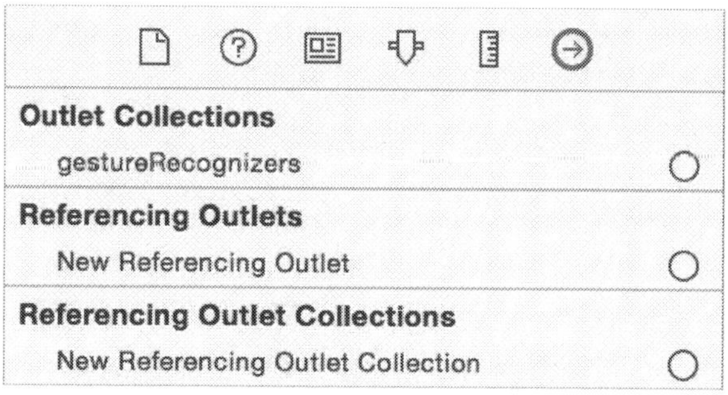

Figure 9.3 Labels do not have events.

4. Select the **Fahrenheit** button near the bottom of the scene and then look at the Connections Inspector. Notice there are many events associated with a button object (Figure 9.4).

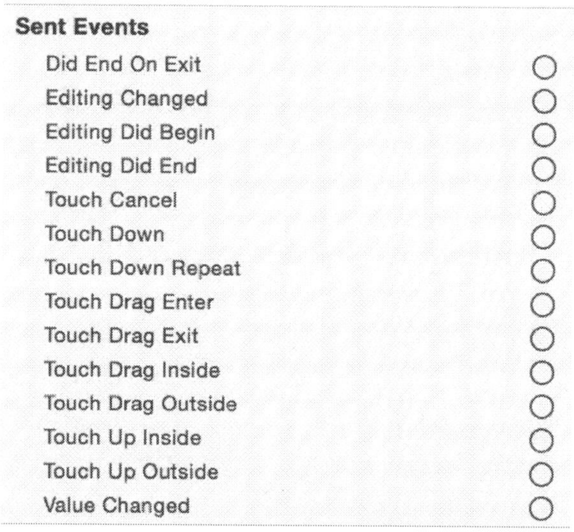

Figure 9.4 The list of button events.

The event used most often with buttons is **Touch Up Inside**. This makes sense when you think about the way most iOS apps work. When you touch a button, nothing happens until you lift your finger off the button. That's why you usually want to use a button's **Touch Up Inside** event.

5. Let's connect a target object and action method to the **Fahrenheit** button's **Touch Up Inside** event to show you how it works. You will make the view controller the target and create a new action method on the view controller.

   To do this, first turn on the Assistant Editor by selecting the middle button in the **Editor** button group at the top of the Xcode window. This should display the **ViewController.swift** file in the Assistant Editor. If it doesn't, you can select the file in the Assistant Editor's jump bar.

6. If it's not already selected, click the **Fahrenheit** button to select it. Next, go to the Connections Inspector and click the connection well to the right of the **Touch Up Inside** event. Drag your mouse pointer down to the **ViewController.swift** file, placing the pointer in the empty line below the **class ViewController** declaration (Figure 9.5).

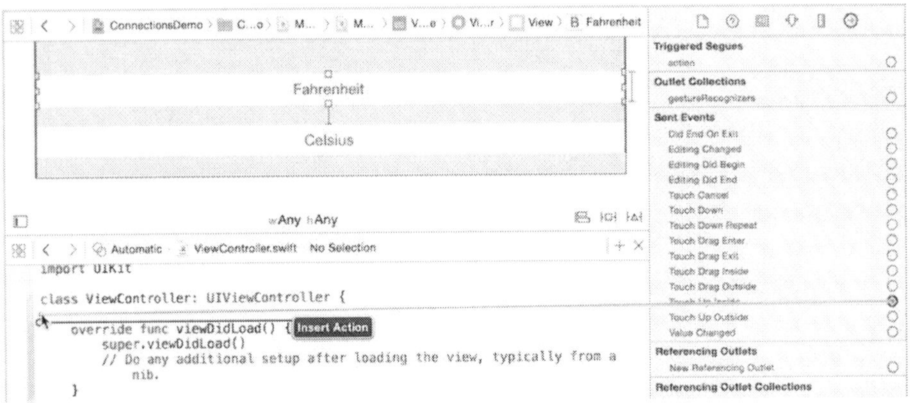

Figure 9.5 Creating an action method.

7. Let go of the mouse button. When you do this, it displays the Insert Action popup to the left of the Code Editor.

   You use the Insert Action popup (Figure 9.6) to create a new action method in the target. In this case, the target is the view controller.

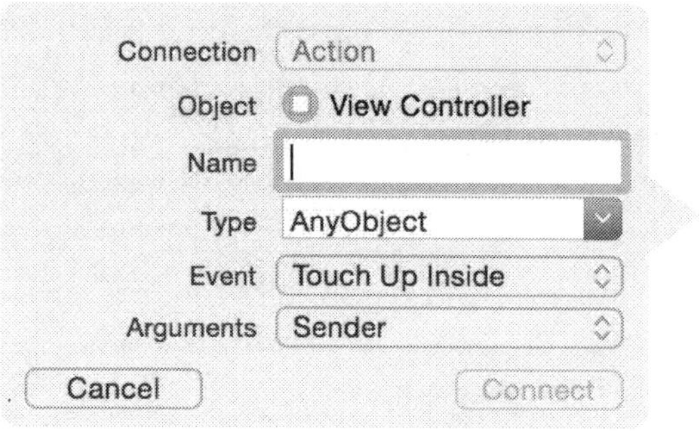

Figure 9.6 The Insert Action popup.

Here is a description of the fields in the Insert Action popup (don't change any of them yet; you will do that in the next step):

- **Connection** - This read-only field specifies that you are creating an **Action** method.
- **Object** - This read-only field specifies the target object, which, in this case, is the **View Controller**.
- **Name** - Specifies the name you want to give to the new action method.
- **Type** - If you specify in **Arguments (**further down in the popup) that you want the new action method to accept a **Sender** parameter, this combo box lets you specify the type of the parameter. It offers three choices:
    - **AnyObject** - A generic parameter type
    - **UIButton** - The type of the sender object. This option changes based on the type of the object that you are creating a connection from in the Connections Inspector.
    - You can manually type in any class name that you want. Normally, you won't do this.

  If the code you are going to write in the action method needs to examine the sender object, choose the second option (**Type**). This makes it easy to examine the object since it's set to the type of the sender. Otherwise, you should select **None** in the **Arguments** setting (described below), and Xcode will ignore this setting.

- **Event** - Specifies the event you are connecting the code to. It defaults to the method that you selected in the Connections Inspector (in this case, **Touch Up Inside**), but you can change it here if you selected the wrong event.

- **Arguments** - Specifies the arguments that are passed to the new action method. The options are:

  - **None** - Creates an action method that has no parameters. Choose this option if you don't need to know anything about the sender object or information about the event. Here is an example of an action method created with this option:

    ```
    @IBAction func methodName()
    ```

  - **Sender** - Creates a sender method that accepts a single parameter of the type specified in the **Type** field. Choose this option if you need information from the sender object. Here is an example of an action method created with this option:

    ```
    @IBAction func methodName(sender: UIButton)
    ```

  - **Sender and Event** - Creates a sender method that accepts a sender parameter and an event parameter. Choose this option when you need to know more about the event. The event parameter contains additional information such as a timestamp indicating when the event occurred as well as information about the user's touches.

    ```
    @IBAction func methodName(sender:
         AnyObject, forEvent: UIEvent)
    ```

    You rarely need the extra event information, so you seldom use this option.

8. Now you're ready to fill in the Insert Action popup. In the **Name** field, enter **getFahrenheit**. In the **Arguments** combo box, select **None** because you don't need any information from the sender object or details of the event.

9. Click the **Connect** button to insert the new action method. This adds a new action method declaration for **getFahrenheit** in the **ViewController.swift** file:

```
class ViewController: UIViewController {
   @IBAction func getFahrenheit() {
   }
```

Notice the circle in the gutter to the left of the new action method (Figure 9.7). This is a *connection indicator*.

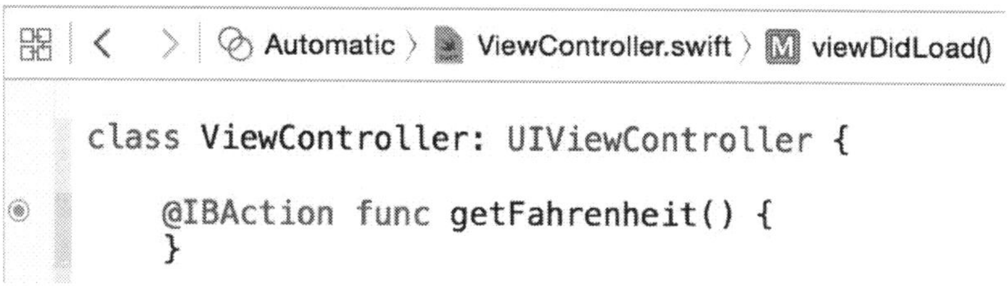

Figure 9.7 The connection indicator.

When the connection indicator has a dark gray center, the action method is connected to a UI object. When you hover your mouse pointer over the connection indicator, Xcode highlights the UI object that is connected to the action method (Figure 9.8).

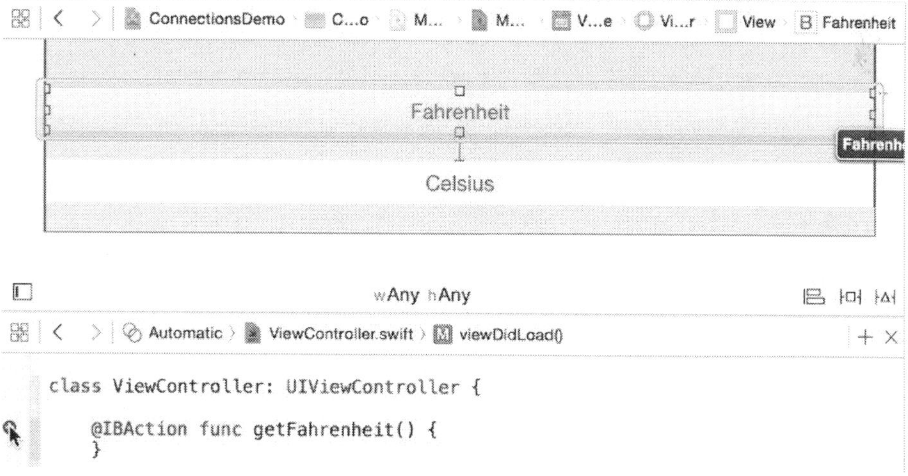

Figure 9.8 Xcode gives a visual cue indicating which UI object is connected to an action method.

Also, check out the Connections Inspector. Notice the **Touch Up Inside** connection well now has a dark gray center (Figure 9.9). It also contains text indicating the target (**View Controller**) and action method (**getFahrenheit**).

Figure 9.9 The connection well indicates the target and action method for the event.

10. Now let's create an action method for the **Celsius** button. Select the **Celsius** button in the design surface and then go to the Connections Inspector. Click the **Touch Up Inside** connection well and drag down into the **ViewController.h** code file again, this time dragging your mouse pointer below the existing **getFahrenheit** method (Figure 9.10).

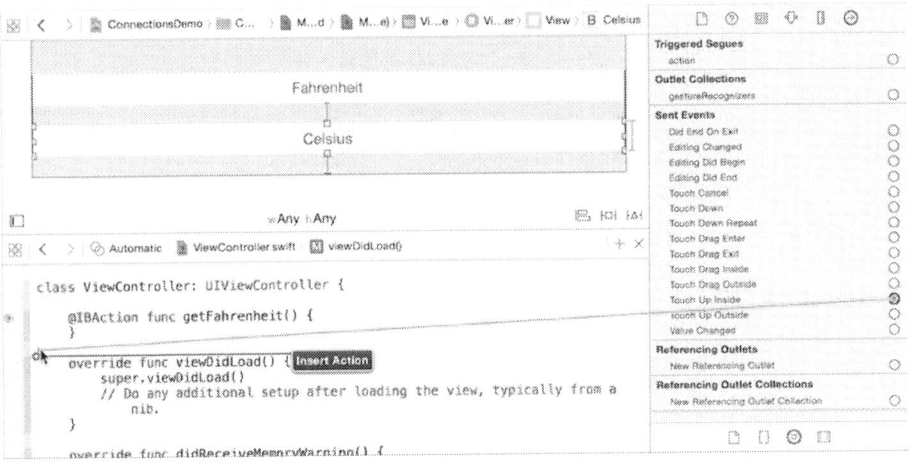

Figure 9.10 Creating the Celsius button's action method.

11. Let go of the mouse button to display the **Insert Action** popup. In the **Name** field, enter **getCelsius**, and in the **Arguments** combo box, select **None**.

12. Click the **Connect** button to add the following action method declaration to the **ViewController.swift** file:

```
@IBAction func getCelsius() {
}
```

You are going to add code to these methods that stores the current temperatures in Fahrenheit and Celsius into the **Text** property of the label.

However, before you can access the label from the code file, you must create an outlet property that references the label.

Understanding Outlets

As you have already learned, when you first add a UI object to a scene at design time, there is no way to reference it from the associated view controller code file because a property is not automatically created to reference it. When you need to reference a UI object from the associated view controller code file, you need to create an outlet.

Follow these steps to see how the Connections Inspector can easily create an outlet for you:

1. In the Project Navigator, select the **Main.storyboard** file and then click the **Tap a Button** label at the top of the scene.
2. If it's not already visible, go to the Connections Inspector (the first button on the right in the Inspectors toolbar). Click in the connection well for the **New Referencing Outlet** and then drag down into the **ViewController.swift** file just above the **getFahrenheit** method (Figure 9.11).

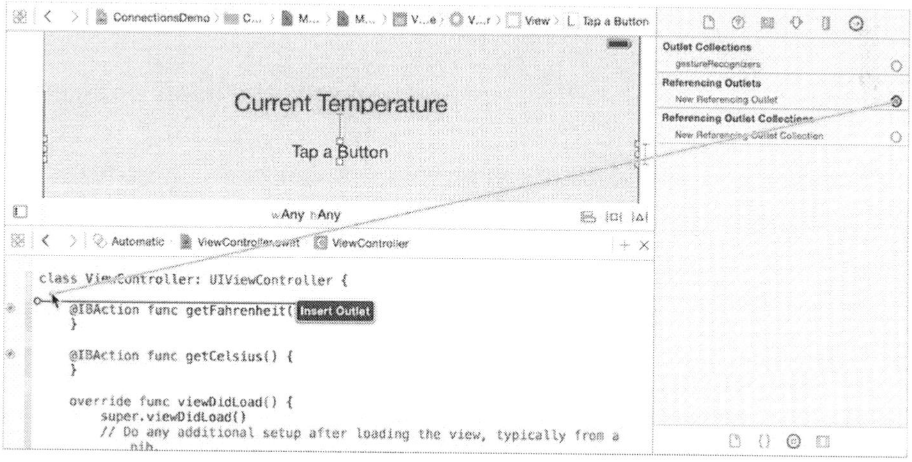

Figure 9.11 Creating a new outlet for the label.

3. Let go of the mouse button in order to display the Insert Outlet popup (Figure 9.12).

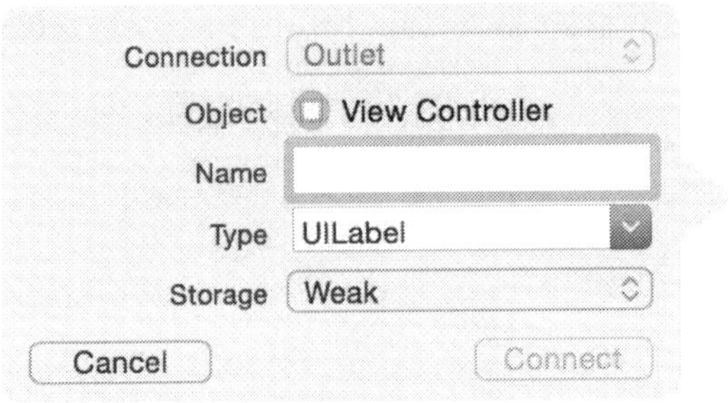

Figure 9.12 The Insert Outlet popup.

The Insert Outlet popup allows you to create a new outlet in the view controller file. Here is a description of the fields in the popup (don't change any of them yet—you will do that in the next step):

- **Connection** - This read-only field specifies that you are creating an **Outlet**.
- **Object** - This read-only field specifies that you are adding the outlet to the **View Controller**.
- **Name** - Specifies the name that you want to give the new outlet.
- **Type** - Specifies the type of the outlet property. It defaults to the type of the currently selected UI object. You can change it to a different type, but there is normally no good reason to do so.
- **Storage** - This combo box allows you to specify whether the property should have a **Weak** or **Strong** relationship to the UI object. For outlet properties, you should choose **Weak** because the view automatically retains the object for you (for more information, check out *Book 4: Learn to Code in Swift, Chapter 19: Object Lifetime & Memory Management*).

4. Now you're ready to create the outlet. You just need to set the **Name** field to **lblTemperature** and click the **Connect** button. This creates a new outlet property that connects to the label as shown in Figure 9.13.

```
class ViewController: UIViewController {
    @IBOutlet weak var lblTemperature: UILabel!
```

Figure 9.13 The new label outlet property.

Notice that the new outlet also has a connection indicator in the gutter to the left. If you hover your mouse pointer over the connection indicator, the associated label is highlighted in the design surface.

The property declaration includes the **IBOutlet** attribute. **IBOutlet** stands for *Interface Builder Outlet* and it signifies to Xcode that this property can be linked to user-interface objects.

5. Now it's time to add code to the empty action methods you created in the previous section. First, let's turn off the Assistant Editor. Go to the Xcode toolbar and click the button on the left in the **Editor** button group. Next, in the Project Navigator, select the **ViewController.swift** file.

6. Next, scroll down in the **ViewController.swift** file to the **getFahrenheit** and **getCelsius** methods. Add the following code to these methods:

```
@IBAction func getFahrenheit() {
    self.lblTemperature.text = "41 Fahrenheit"
}
@IBAction func getCelsius() {
    self.lblTemperature.text = "5 Celsius"
}
```

As mentioned earlier, this method simply hard-codes the current temperature rather than retrieving the actual temperature from the web.

7. Now click the **Run** button in Xcode. When the app appears in the Simulator, click the **Celsius** button, and you should see the text of the label change to **5 Celsius** (Figure 9.14).

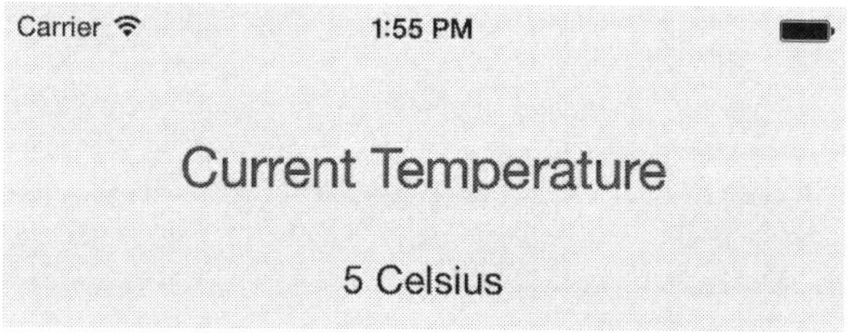

Figure 9.14 Action methods and outlets.

As expected, when the **Celsius** button is pressed, it calls the **getCelsius** method on the view controller target. The **getCelsius** action method stores a value to the label by using the outlet property.

Click the **Fahrenheit** button so the **getFahrenheit** method is called on the view controller. The **getFahrenheit** action method stores the temperature in Fahrenheit to the label by using the outlet property.

Working With Outlet Collections

An outlet collection works exactly like a regular outlet except that the outlet property is a collection that can contain many elements rather than a reference to a single UI object.

You can use outlet collections when you need to write generic code that operates on multiple UI controls. For example, in the **ConnectionsDemo** project, if you want to change all labels to a different color based on whether the **Fahrenheit** or **Celsius** button is selected, you can create an outlet collection to reference them.

Follow these steps to see how to create and use an outlet collection:

1. Select the **Main.storyboard** file in the Project Navigator.
2. Click the **Show Assistant Editor** button (the center button in the **Editor** toolbar at the top of the Xcode window) to display the Assistant Editor.
3. Click the **Current Temperature** label in the design surface to select it.
4. In the Connections Inspector, click on the **New Referencing Outlet Collection** connection well and then drag down into the **ViewController.swift** file, just above the existing **lblTemperature** outlet as shown in Figure 9.15.

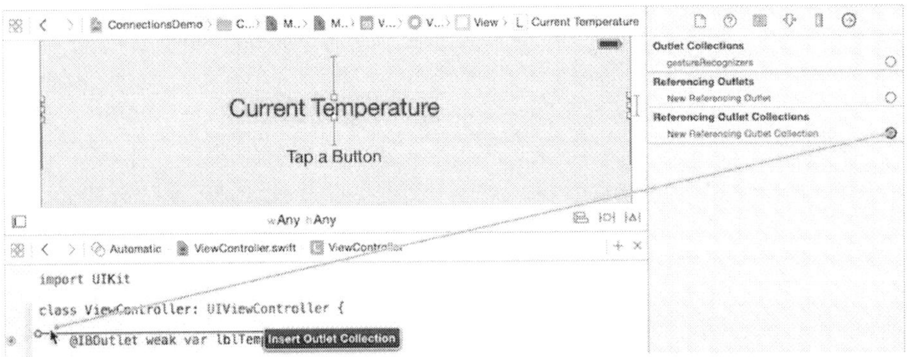

Figure 9.15 Creating an outlet collection.

5. Let go of the mouse button to display the **Insert Outlet Collection** popup (Figure 9.16). This is similar to the regular Insert Outlet popup except that it creates a collection property.

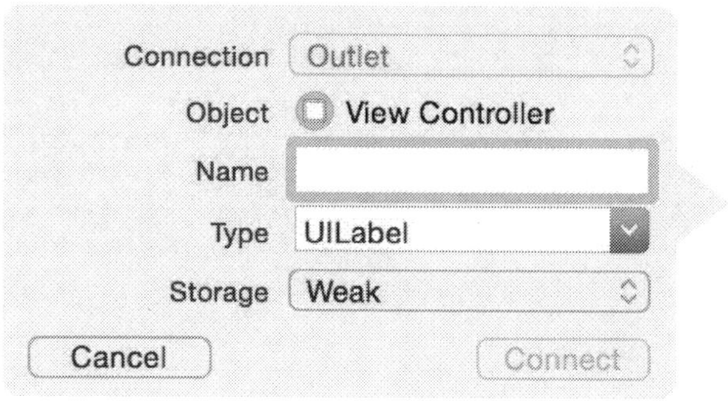

Figure 9.16 The Insert Outlet Collection popup.

The Insert Outlet Collection popup contains the following fields:

- **Connection** - This read-only field specifies that you are creating an **Outlet Collection.**
- **Object** - This read-only field specifies that you are adding the outlet collection to the **View Controller**.
- **Name** - Specifies the name that you want to give the new outlet collection.
- **Type** - Specifies the type of the outlet collection property. Defaults to the type of the currently selected UI object. Although you can change this to a different type, there is normally no good reason to do so.

6. In the **Name** field, enter **lblCollection**. Accept the default **Type** of **UILabel** and then click the **Connect** button to create a new outlet collection property:

```
@IBOutlet var lblCollection: [UILabel]!
```

As you can see, the **lblCollection** property is an array of **UILabel** objects.

7. Now let's connect the other label to this same outlet collection. To do this, click the **Tap a Button** label in the design surface. Next, go to the Connections Inspector and click the **New Referencing Outlet Collection** connection well (even though we're not creating a new outlet

collection). Drag down into the **ViewController.swift** file and hover over the existing **lblCollection** outlet collection property until the entire line turns blue and the **Connect Outlet Collection** popup appears (Figure 9.17).

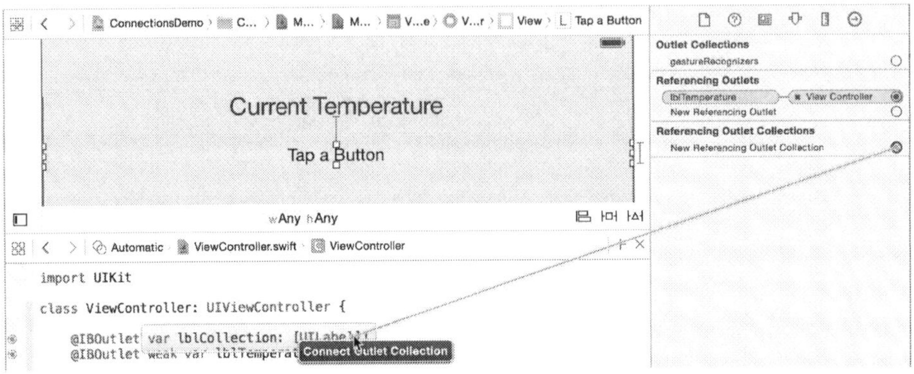

Figure 9.17 Connect the label to the outlet collection.

8. Release the mouse button to create the connection to the outlet collection. In the Connections Inspector, you should see a new item under **Referencing Outlet Collections** showing the connection to the **lblCollection** on the View Controller (Figure 9.18).

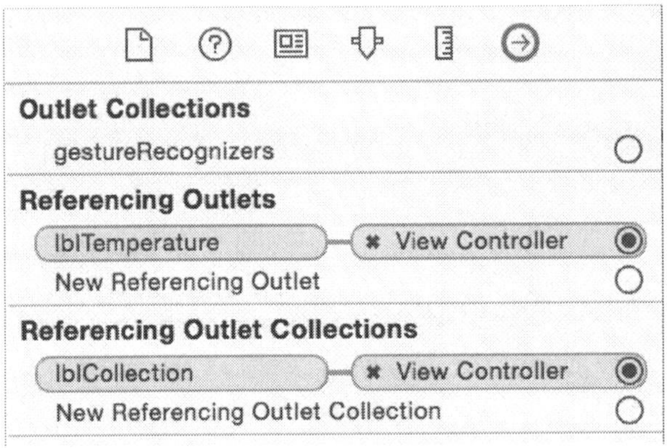

Figure 9.18 The new connection to the outlet collection.

Hover your mouse pointer over the outlet collection property in the view controller. This displays a popup next to all collection items (Figure 9.19).

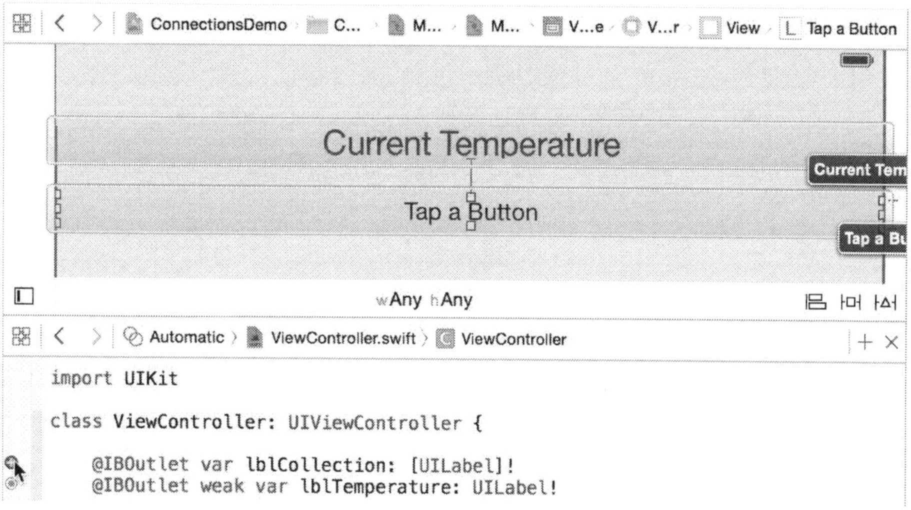

Figure 9.19 Hover your mouse over the outlet collection.

Now that the outlet collection has been created and both labels are connected to it, you can write code that uses the outlet collection to set the color of the labels. You will add a new method that sets the color of the labels. You can then call this new method from the existing **getFahrenheit** and **getCelsius** methods.

1. First, hide the Assistant Editor. To do this, select the **Show Standard Editor** (left button) in the **Editor** toolbar button group at the top of the Xcode window.

2. Next, select the **ViewController.swift** file in the Project Navigator to open it in the code editor.

3. Scroll to the bottom of the **ViewController.swift** file and add the following **setLabelColor:** method right before the closing curly brace:

```
func setLabelColor(color: UIColor) {
    for label in self.lblCollection {
        label.textColor = color
    }
}
}
```

This code uses the **lblCollection** outlet collection to cycle through all labels and set them to the color specified in the **color** parameter.

4. Next, add the following code to **getFahrenheit** and **getCelsius** that calls the new **setLabelColor:** method:

```
@IBAction func getFahrenheit() {
      self.lblTemperature.text = "41 Fahrenheit"
      self.setLabelColor(UIColor.redColor())
}

@IBAction func getCelsius() {
      self.lblTemperature.text = "5 Celsius"
      self.setLabelColor(UIColor.blueColor())
}
```

5. To test the new code, click Xcode's **Run** button and when the app appears in the Simulator, click the **Fahrenheit** button to see the labels turn red (Figure 9.20). Then click the **Celsius** button to see the labels turn blue.

Figure 9.20 The outlet collection is used to set the color of both labels.

Outlet Collection With Different Types of Objects

At times, you may want to create a collection of different object types and write generic code that works with these objects. To create a collection that works with different controls, when you first create the outlet collection, in the **Insert Collection Outlet** popup (Figure 9.16), set the **Type** to **UIControl** (or you can choose another type that suits the kind of objects in the collection). This allows any subclass of **UIControl** to be part of the collection.

Here is an example of this type of collection:

```
@IBOutlet var controlCollection: [UIControl]!
```

When you write generic code to affect all objects in this type of collection, you can reference the objects using the **UIControl** type. For example, the following method disables all controls in the **controlCollection**:

```
func disableControls() {
    for control in self.controlCollection {
    control.enabled = false
    }
}
```

This code takes advantage of polymorphism as described in *Book 2: Learn to Code in Swift* in *Chapter 15: Inheritance & Polymorphism*.

Troubleshooting Connections

A common problem that you will encounter in your app development cycle is lost connections. You may accidentally delete a connection, or you may remove a UI object or add a new one back to the view and forget to connect it to the outlet. In any case, the resulting symptom is that the object is no longer affected by the code that you write to manipulate it.

To show an example of this, follow these steps that first break but then restore a connection:

1. If it's not already open, in Xcode, open the **ConnectionsDemo** project.

2. In the Project Navigator, select the **Main.storyboard** file to display it in the design surface.

3. Near the top of the scene, click the **Tap a Button** label and then go to the Connections Inspector. Under the **Referencing Outlets** section, click the small **x** in the **lblTemperature** outlet as shown in Figure 9.21.

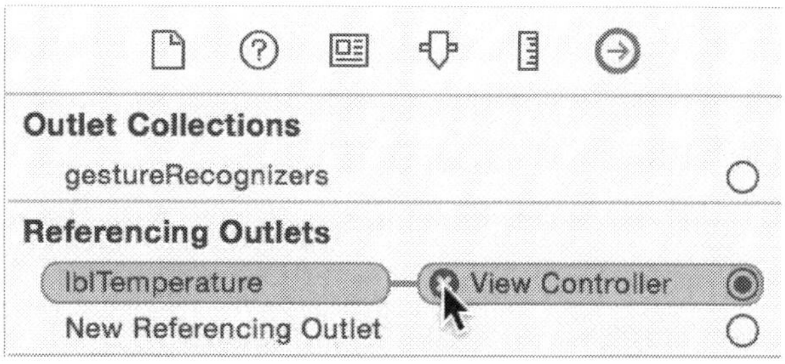

Figure 9.21 Deleting the outlet connection.

Doing this removes the connection between the label and the outlet property. It also removes the outlet from the Connections Inspector.

You can also see that the connection indicator (highlighted in red in Figure 9.22) for the **lblTemperature** outlet is now empty, indicating there is no connection to the outlet.

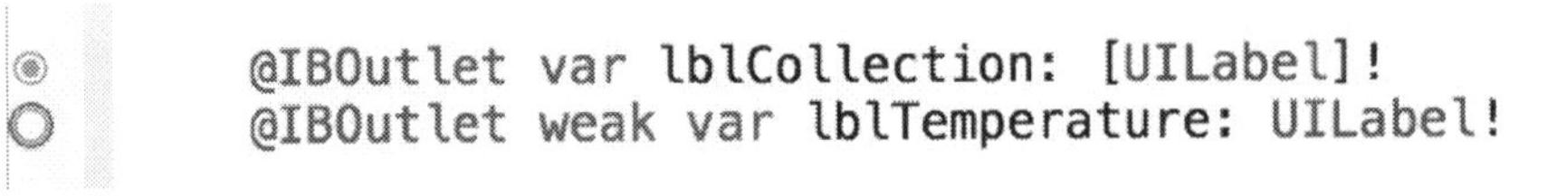

Figure 9.22 The deleted outlet connection.

Whenever you see an empty connection indicator like this, it should raise a red flag that something is wrong!

4. Click the **Run** button in Xcode to run the app in the Simulator. When you click the **Fahrenheit** button, you will see the error shown in Figure 9.23.

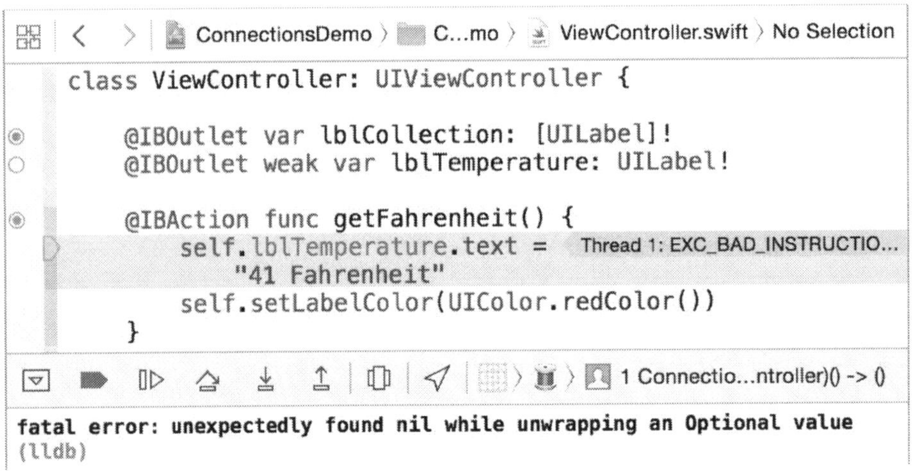

Figure 9.23 The broken connection error.

The error in the Console says: **Unexpectedly found nil while unwrapping an Optional value**. Take another look at the label outlet property:

```
@IBOutlet weak var lblTemperature: UILabel!
```

The exclamation mark at the end of the property declaration explicitly unwraps the reference to the label object. However, since the connection is broken, there is no reference and thus the error.

5. You can fix the connection in one of two ways. The first way is to click the **Tap a Button** label in the design surface, and then in the Connections Inspector, click the **New Referencing Outlet** connection well and drag down to the existing **lblTemperature** property outlet (Figure 9.24).

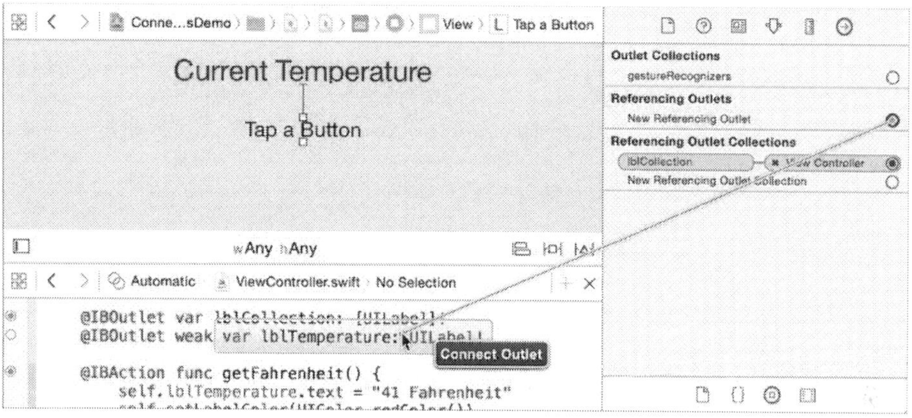

Figure 9.24 Reconnecting the outlet using the Connections Inspector.

The second option allows you to reconnect the outlet without using the Connections Inspector. All you have to do is to hover your mouse pointer over the empty connection indicator for the **lblTemperature** outlet and then drag to the **Select a Button** label (Figure 9.25).

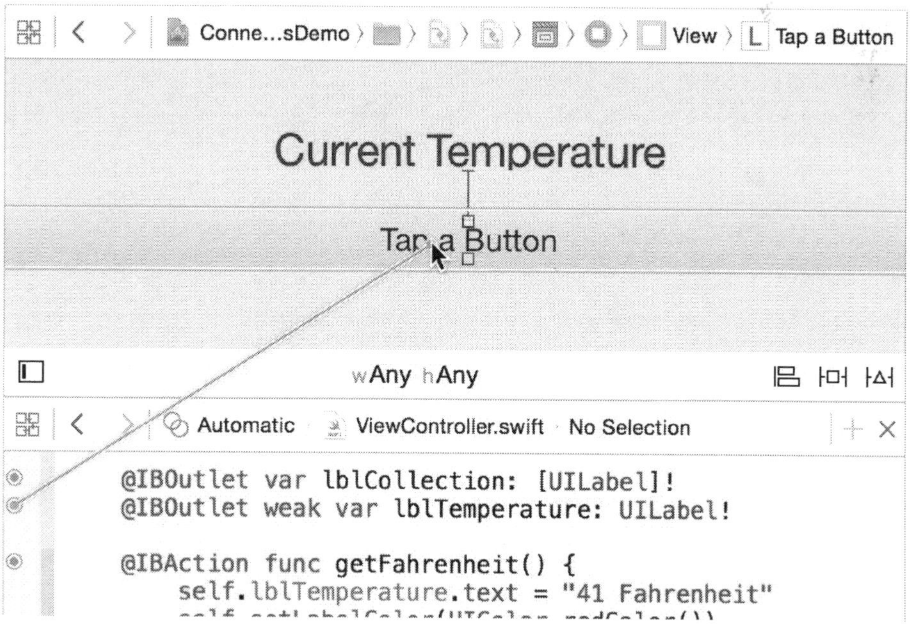

Figure 9.25 Reconnecting the outlet directly.

Choose one of these two methods now to reconnect the label to the outlet.

6. Click Xcode's **Run** button to run the app in the Simulator again. When you press the **Fahrenheit** and **Celsius** buttons, the temperature should appear in the label again. Problem fixed!

Summary

- In the same way that objects have different properties and methods, they can also have a set of *events*. In this context, an event is an action that occurs in a control and is usually initiated by the user tapping, touching, pinching, swiping, or otherwise interacting with the control.
- When an event occurs on an object, it can send a notification message to one or more target objects.
- Action methods must have one of three specific signatures:

```
@IBAction func methodName()
@IBAction func methodName(sender:
AnyObject)
@IBAction func methodName(sender: AnyObject,
   forEvent: UIEvent)
```

- The **IBAction** attribute stands for *Interface Builder Action*, and it signifies to Xcode that a method can be linked to user-interface objects.
- The **IBAction** attribute is equivalent to **void**, which is appropriate because action methods do not return a value.
- Labels do not have events because users do not interact with labels.
- The event used most often with buttons is **Touch Up Inside**.
- The circle in the gutter to the left of the new action method is a *connection indicator*.
- When a connection indicator has a dark gray center, the action method is connected to a UI object.
- When you need to reference a UI object from the associated view controller code file, you need to create an outlet.
- An outlet collection works exactly like a regular outlet except that the outlet property is a collection that can contain many elements rather than a reference to a single UI object.

- A common problem that you will encounter in your app development cycle is lost connections. The resulting symptom is that the object is no longer affected by the code that you write to manipulate it.

- You fix a broken connection in one of two ways.

    1. Select the control with the broken connection in the design surface, and then, in the Connections Inspector, click the **New Referencing Outlet** connection well and drag down to the property outlet in the Code Editor.

    2. Hover your mouse pointer over the empty connection indicator in the Code Editor and then click and drag to the control with the broken connection.

Chapter 10: The Code Editor

As you write iOS apps, you will spend a good portion of your time in the Code Editor. This chapter helps you uncover many of the time-saving features and tips that will make your code writing experience far more productive.

Sections in This Chapter

Working With the Code Editor

If you have already gone through the step-by-step tutorials in *Learn to Code in Swift*, you have learned some of the basics of code editing in Xcode. This chapter dives in deeper to help you to take advantage of all of the code editing tools that Xcode has to offer.

Code Completion

Xcode's code completion can help you write code accurately and quickly. As you enter code in the editor, Xcode displays a popup that provides a list of suggestions for completing the code (Figure 10.1). If Xcode doesn't pop up code completion when you need it, you can press **Escape** to bring it up manually.

To select an item from the code-completion list, either click the item in the list or use up and down arrows to navigate to the item that you want and then press **return** or **tab** to select it.

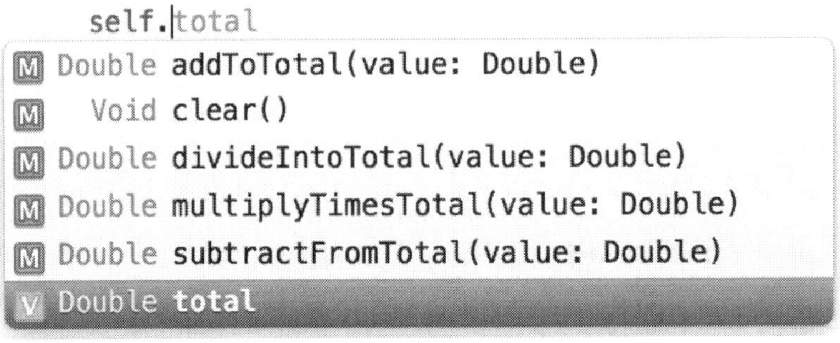

Figure 10.1 The Code Completion popup.

Check out the section Code Completion Preferences in *Chapter 6: The Libraries* for information on how you can change the behavior of Xcode's code completion.

Balancing Delimiters

One of the biggest problems related to writing code for beginning developers is balancing delimiters. In Swift, delimiters are comprised of a beginning (or opening) character and an ending (or closing) character that mark off, or delimit, the beginning and end of a section of code. For example:

- { } – Curly braces mark the beginning and end of a block of code in a method, property, conditional statement, loop, or closure.

- [ ] – Square brackets are used to declare an array type, to specify a subscript to access members in a collection, or to declare a capture list for a closure.

- ( ) – Parentheses mark the beginning and end of a method's parameter list, values in strings, a tuple, or to group items in an expression.

An opening delimiter must always have a matching closing delimiter. It's more difficult to match delimiters when you have a number of nested delimiters. For example, many new developers trip up on matching parentheses in expressions:

```
Int(arc4random_uniform(UInt32(blockPositions.count)))
```

In this example, there are three sets of parentheses to group the parameters in nested method calls.

Xcode provides plenty of help to make sure that you get this right:

- When you type a closing delimiter, Xcode momentarily highlights the matching opening delimiter (Figure 10.2).

```
let randomIndex = Int(arc4random_uniform(UInt32
    (blockPositions.count)))
```

Figure 10.2 Xcode highlights the opening delimiter when you type the closing delimiter.

- Xcode also highlights the opening delimiter if you use the right arrow key to move the cursor past the closing delimiter.

- If you double-click an opening or closing delimiter, Xcode highlights all the text between and including the delimiters (Figure 10.3).

```
let randomIndex = Int(arc4random_uniform(UInt32
    (blockPositions.count)))
```

Figure 10.3 Double-click a delimiter to highlight all of the text contained within.

- A menu option found in **Editor** > **Structure** > **Balance Delimiter** does something similar as double- clicking a delimiter. If you place your cursor within delimited text and then select this menu option, it highlights all the delimited text, including the delimiters. You can also right-click within delimited text to bring up a shortcut menu that invokes the same **Structure** > **Balance Delimiter** feature.

- By default, Xcode automatically inserts a closing curly brace when you type an opening curly brace.

Structuring Your Code

While on the subject of the **Structure** menu, there are other helpful options in this menu that help you to clean up your code:

- **Re-Indent** – Keyboard shortcut: ^|
  Reapplies Xcode's indentation rules to the currently selected code. This comes in handy if you have manually changed the indentation on multiple lines of code and want Xcode to line them back up again.

- **Shift Right** - Command+]
  Moves the selected code to the right. Useful for multiple lines of code.

- **Shift Left** - Command+[
  Moves the selected code to the left. Useful for multiple lines of code.

- **Move Line Up** - Option+ Command+[
  Moves the selected lines of code up one line.

- **Move Line Down** - Option+ Command+]
  Moves the selected lines of code down one line.

- **Comment / Uncomment Selection** – Command+/
  Comments / uncomments the selected lines of code.

Viewing Your Code's Structure With Code Folding

Code folding is an Xcode feature that allows you to "fold up" methods and functions so you see the method declaration but not the associated code. This makes it easy to see all the methods in a code file without having to sift through the associated code in those methods. I find some developers love this option and others don't. If you find yourself in the former category, I'll describe how to fold and unfold your code.

To fold your code, click anywhere in the code editor and then select **Editor** > **Code Folding** > **Fold Methods & Functions** from the Xcode menu. This folds up your methods and displays ellipsis (...) as placeholders for the code (Figure 10.4). This only folds methods in the file currently open in the editor.

```
class ScientificCalculator : Calculator {

    var memory: Double = 0.0

    override func clear() {...}

    func log(value:Double) -> Double {...}

    func sin(value:Double) -> Double {...}

    func cos(value:Double) -> Double {...}

    func tan(value:Double) -> Double {...}
}
```

Figure 10.4 Folded methods.

There are a few ways to unfold your code. If you want to unfold all methods in a file, select **Editor** > **Code Folding** > **Unfold Methods & Functions** from the menu. To unfold a single method, you can double-click the ellipses placeholder for that method. You can also click the small arrow in the code folding ribbon located between the gutter and the Code Editor (Figure 10.5).

```
    override func clear() {...}

    func log(value:Double) -> Double {...}
```

Figure 10.5 Unfolding a method.

This turns the right arrow into a down arrow and shows you the code in that method. To fold the code back up again, just click the down arrow in the code folding ribbon (Figure 10.6).

```
class ScientificCalculator : Calculator {

    var memory: Double = 0.0

    override func clear() {
        super.clear()
        self.memory = 0.0
    }
```

Figure 10.6 Fold a single method.

Xcode's **Editor** > **Code Folding** menu also offers the option to fold comment blocks. This option only folds and unfolds code blocks that begin with the /* delimiter and end with the */ delimiter.

There's another nice feature tucked away at the bottom of the Code Folding menu—**Focus Follows Selection**. This feature is more useful if you are not using code folding. When this feature is on and you click on a method, it highlights that method in white and shades the rest of the code window in gray (Figure 10.7).

```
class ScientificCalculator : Calculator {

    var memory: Double = 0.0

    override func clear() {
        super.clear()
        self.memory = 0.0
    }

    func log(value:Double) -> Double {

        return log(value)
    }
```

Figure 10.7 ***Focus Follows Selection*** *highlights methods that you click on.*

As you can see, it does a good job of highlighting the method that interests you by dimming the code around it. Unlike code folding, this feature doesn't operate on just a single file; it applies to all files you open. If you decide that you don't like this feature, then select **Editor** > **Code Folding** > **Focus Follows Selection** again to toggle it off.

The Xcode Preferences dialog has a few settings that affect the code folding. Under the **Text Editing** section is a **Code folding ribbon** check box that allows you to turn the code folding ribbon off and on (Figure 10.8).

When you turn off the code folding ribbon, you can still fold and unfold code using the **Editor > Code Folding** menu options.

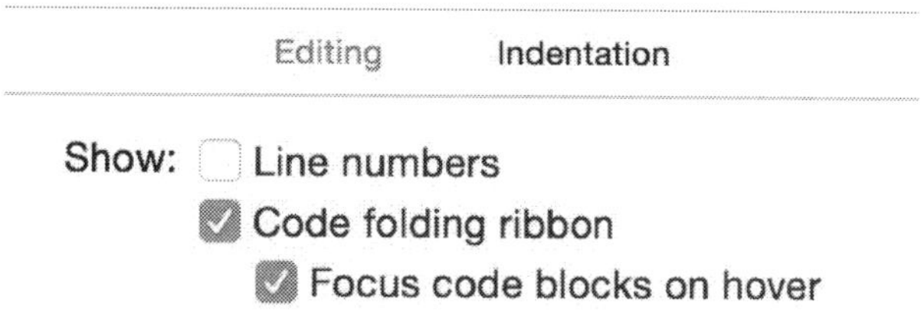

Figure 10.8 Code folding settings in Xcode preferences.

Nested beneath the code folding setting is a **Focus code blocks on hover** setting (Figure 10.8). When this setting is on, you can just hover your mouse pointer over the code folding ribbon to the left of a method to highlight it without having to click on the method.

You can actually have the "focus code blocks" behavior both ways: it turns on when you hover as well as when you click on a method.

Navigating Your Code

You have already learned the ins and outs of selecting your code files in the Project Navigator. This section provides additional information to help you easily move to the code that you want.

Jump Bars

At the top of the Code Editor area is a jump bar (Figure 10.9) that allows you to navigate both within the current code file and to other code files.

Figure 10.9 The Code Editor jump bar.

Each section of the jump bar is a button that you can click to either navigate or jump to another piece of code. The button at the far right lists all members (properties and methods) of the class currently open in the Code Editor (Figure 10.10).

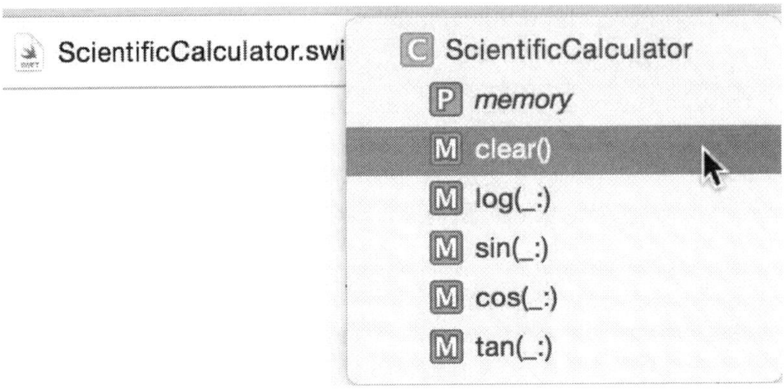

Figure 10.10 Jumping to another class's member.

If you have a class open in the Code Editor, you can click this button and see all properties and methods for the class listed in the order in which they appear in the source code file.

The Code Editor jump bar contains a hierarchical path menu where each button is a different level of the hierarchy. The full path of the currently selected file in Figure 10.9 is represented by the buttons **AdvancedSwiftDemo** (project root) > **AdvancedSwiftDemo** (group) > **ScientificCalculator.swift** (the file itself). If you click the second button from the right (the **AdvancedSwiftDemo** code group), Xcode displays a list of files and subgroups that are in the same Project Navigator group as the current code file (Figure 10.11).

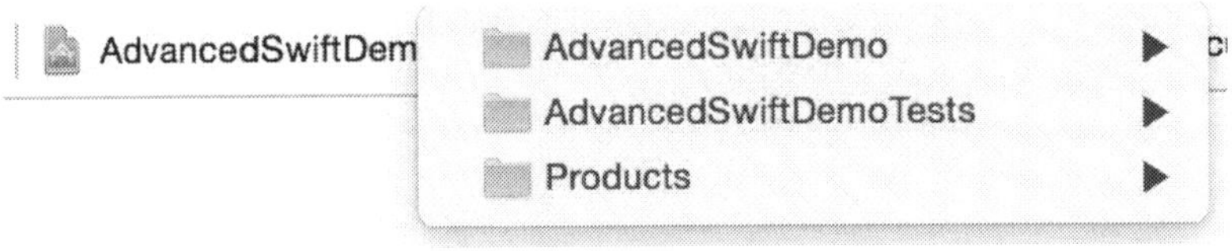

Figure 10.11 Navigating to files in the same group.

As with the Interface Builder jump bar, the Code Editor jump bar also contains a stepper comprised of back and forward arrow buttons (Figure 10.12).

Figure 10.12 The forward and back arrows step through your navigation history.

These buttons allow you to step back and forward through your navigation history, operating similar to back and forward buttons in a web browser.

The Code Editor jump bar also has a "related items" button that allows you to open items related to the code file currently open in the editor (Figure 10.13).

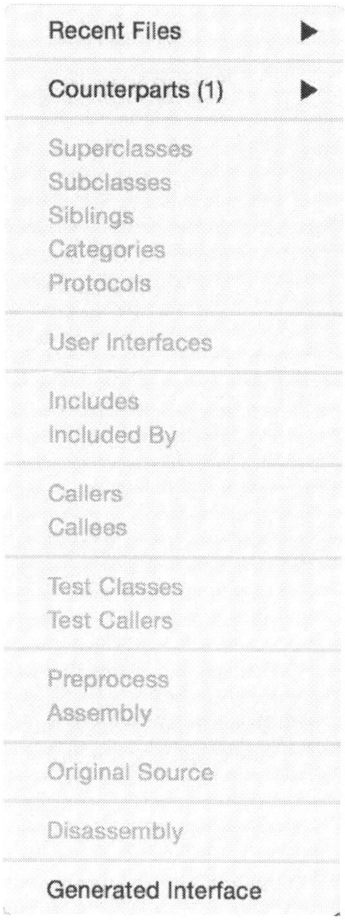

Figure 10.13 The "Related Items" menu.

Here is a description of each menu option. Any menu item that doesn't apply to the file currently open in the editor is grayed out. If you select any file in the submenus, that file is automatically opened in the editor. If you select **Superclasses**, **Subclasses**, **Siblings**, **Categories**, **Protocols**, **Includes**, or **Included By**, the associated class file is loaded—even if it's a Cocoa Touch Framework class:

- **Recent Files** – A list of the files that you have most recently opened in this project. This menu contains the following submenu options:

  - **Clear menu** – Clears the **Recent Files** list.
  - **Number of Recent Files** – Allows you to specify the number of recent files that you want in the list.

- **Counterparts** – A list of files associated with the class that you are currently editing.
- **Superclasses** – A class hierarchy of superclasses that starts with the superclass of the class that you are currently editing.
- **Subclasses** – A list of all of the subclasses of the class that you are currently editing.
- **Siblings** – A list of all classes that are siblings (derived from the same superclass) of the class that you are currently editing.
- **Categories** – A list of all categories that extend the class that you are currently editing.
- **Protocols** – A list of all protocols adopted by the class that you are currently editing.
- **User Interfaces** – A list of all user interfaces associated with the class that you are currently editing. For example, if you are editing a view controller, the associated storyboard is listed.
- **Includes** – A list of all header files imported by the class that you are currently editing.
- **Included By** – A list of all classes that import the header file of the class that you are currently editing.
- **Callers** – When a method is selected in the code file, this displays a list of all methods that call the selected method.
- **Callees** – When a method is selected in the code file, this displays a list of all methods called by the selected method.
- **Test Classes** – A list of all classes that reference the currently selected class file in a unit test.

- **Test Callers** – When a method is selected in the code file, this displays a list of all methods called by the selected method.

- **Preprocess** – An advanced feature that you probably won't use much, the preprocessor evaluates directives (instructions that start with a # sign) in the currently selected code file and converts them to the C language before they are sent to the compiler.

- **Assembly** – An advanced feature you probably won't use much, the assembly output is the instructions in low-level assembly language generated by the compiler from the preprocessed output.

- **Original Source** - It seems this option is for future use. For now it is always disabled.

- **Disassembly** – An advanced feature you probably won't use much and that is only available when you are debugging your app, it shows you the assembly language code for the currently selected file.

- **Generated Interface** - Scans through the currently selected code file and generates a virtual header file that displays its exposed properties and method signatures.

MARK, TODO, and FIXME

Before moving on from the discussion about the Code Editor's jump bar, you should know that Xcode provides three options for organizing your code with the **MARK**, **TODO**, and **FIXME** comment tags.

Swift's **MARK** comment tag is the most commonly used. First, you must physically group related methods together in your source code file. Next, add the following directive in your code file before each group of methods, where **Group Name** is a name you enter describing the type of methods in that group:

```
// MARK: - Group Name
```

For example, you can create a group called **Calculator User Interface** like this:

```
// MARK: - Calculator Core Logic
```

This displays a group in the jump bar member list (Figure 10.14).

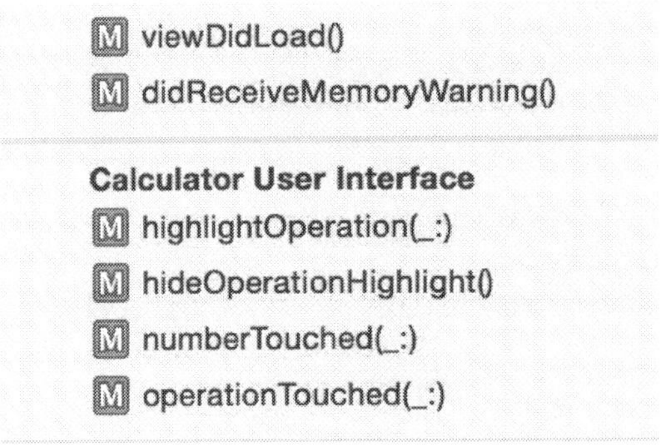

*Figure 10.14 The **Mark** declaration in the code file creates sections in the jump bar member list.*

The **TODO** and **FIXME** comment tags allow you to mark your code that needs further attention. For example, check out these **FIXME** and **TODO** comment tags:

```
class ScientificCalculator : Calculator {
    var memory: Double = 0.0
    // FIXME: Clear all memory properties
    override func clear() {
        super.clear()
        self.memory = 0.0
    }
    // TODO: Implement square root
}
```

This adds the tags to the method drop down box (Figure 10.15). Note that adding a hyphen to the **MARK** tag adds a separator to the method list, but adding a hyphen to **TODO** and **FIXME** does not.

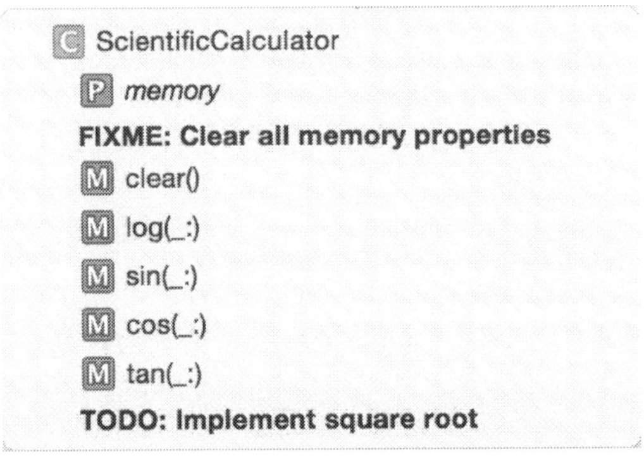

*Figure 10.15 The **FIXME** and **TODO** tags in action.*

Jump to a Symbol's Definition

A navigation technique that I often use is to **Command +Click** a symbol to jump to its definition. This is a quick and easy way to navigate to the code that defines a symbol. For example, as shown in Figure 10.16, if you hold the **Command** key down and hover over a symbol, Xcode displays the symbol as a link that can be selected. (You can also select this option in the shortcut menu when you right-click a symbol.)

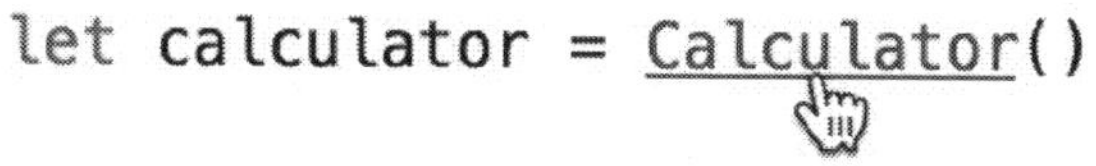

*Figure 10.16 **Command+Click** a symbol to jump to its definition.*

In this example, if you click the **Calculator** link, it opens the **Calculator.swift** code file in the Code Editor. If you want to get back to the code that you originally clicked on, just press the back arrow in the jump bar.

The Navigate Menu

Xcode's **Navigate** menu offers other navigation options. We have already covered the options in the top section of this menu, but here is a list of the other options:

- **Move Focus to Next Area** – Moves the focus from the current editor or area to the next.
- **Move Focus to Previous Area** – Moves the focus from the current editor or area to the previous.
- **Move Focus to Editor...** – Launches the navigation chooser to let you visually select the editor that you want to give focus.
- **Go Forward** – Navigates to the next file/location in the editor (equivalent to the Forward arrow in the jump bar).
- **Go Back** – Navigates to the previous file or location in the editor (equivalent to the back arrow in the jump bar).

- **Jump to Selection** – If the text that you have selected has scrolled off the screen, you can use this option to scroll back to the selected text. This is useful in large code files.

- **Jump to Definition** – Navigates to the symbol's definition as described in the previous section *Jump to a Symbol's Definition*.

- **Jump to Generated Interface** - You can use this option to display the Generated Interface for the currently selected code file.

- **Jump to Next Issue** – If you have multiple compiler warnings or errors (issues), this option navigates to the next issue.

- **Jump to Previous Issue** – If you have multiple compiler warnings or errors, this option navigates to the previous issue.

- **Jump to Instruction Pointer** – When you are debugging your app and have navigated away from the instruction pointer, you can use this option to navigate back to it.

- **Jump to Next Counterpart** – Navigates to the next counterpart of the file currently in the editor (for example, between a class header and its associated implementation files).

- **Jump to Previous Counterpart** – Navigates to the previous counterpart of the file currently in the editor.

- **Jump to Line in "File Name"...** – Pops up a dialog allowing you to enter a line number or symbol that you want to jump to in the currently selected file. Check out the section *Text Editing Preferences* later in this chapter for a discussion of line numbers.

- **Jump to Next Placeholder / Jump to Previous Placeholder** – Placeholders are used in code snippets to hold the place for code that you need to enter (Figure 10.17). This set of menu options allows you to jump to the next/previous placeholder in your code file.

```
class name : super class {
    properties and methods
}
```

Figure 10.17 You can jump to the next or previous placeholder in a code snippet.

Each menu option also has an associated keystroke that you can use if you prefer to keep your hands on the keyboard. Check out the menu in Xcode for each key combination.

Opening Files Quickly

When you work with large projects containing many files, at times it can be difficult to find the file that you need. This is when the Open Quickly feature can help. It allows you to search for a text string in the contents of a file or in the file name.

You can launch the Open Quickly dialog (Figure 10.18) either from the **File > Open Quickly** menu or by typing **Shift+Command+O**.

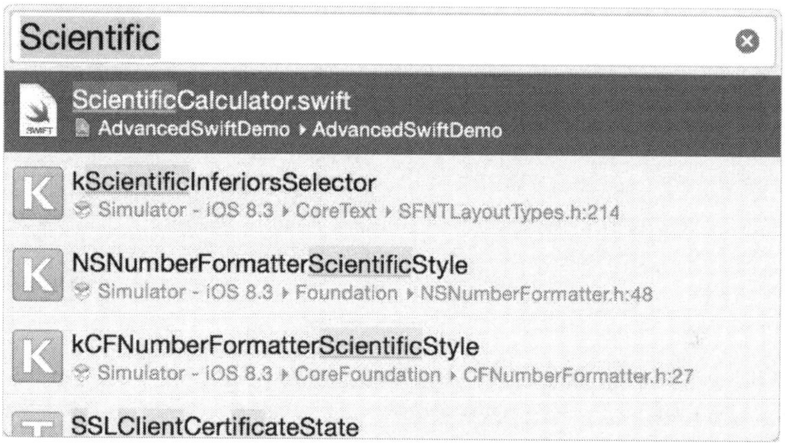

Figure 10.18 The Open Quickly dialog.

The Open Quickly dialog is well named. When you enter the search criteria, it's amazing how quickly it displays results in the list. Listed beneath each item is the folder on your computer where the file is located. Here are some options for opening a file in the list:

- To open the file in the primary editor:
  - Click on it and then press **return**.
  - Double-click an item.
- To open the file in the Assistant Editor:
  - Select an item in the list, and then hold the **Option** key when you

select it and press **return**.

  - **Option+Double-Click** an item.

- To open the navigation chooser that lets you specify where to open the file:
  - Select an item in the list, and then hold the **Option+Shift** keys when you click **Open**.

When searching for file names, Xcode searches for code files, model files, nib files, plist files, and project packages. For symbol-name searches, it only searches source code files.

Fonts and Colors

One of the first things that you notice when opening the Code Editor is that different colors are used for each type of code element. This feature is known as syntax-aware fonts and colors. When code elements are displayed in different colors, it's easier to comprehend at a glance what you're looking at. For example, comments are green by default, so it's easy to find comments (that you have hopefully put in the code) when you need them, and ignore them when you're looking for code.

Syntax coloring also helps you know when something is wrong. For example, if you type the name of a class in a code file and it hasn't changed color when you've finished typing, then you know that either you have mistyped the class name or you need to import the framework for that class.

Before launching the Preferences dialog, it's best to select a code file in the editor because when you change font and color settings, the change is automatically reflected in the code file so you can see the effect of the choices that you make. To view the fonts and colors preferences, select **Xcode > Preferences** from the menu and then select **Fonts & Colors** in the Preferences dialog (Figure 10.19).

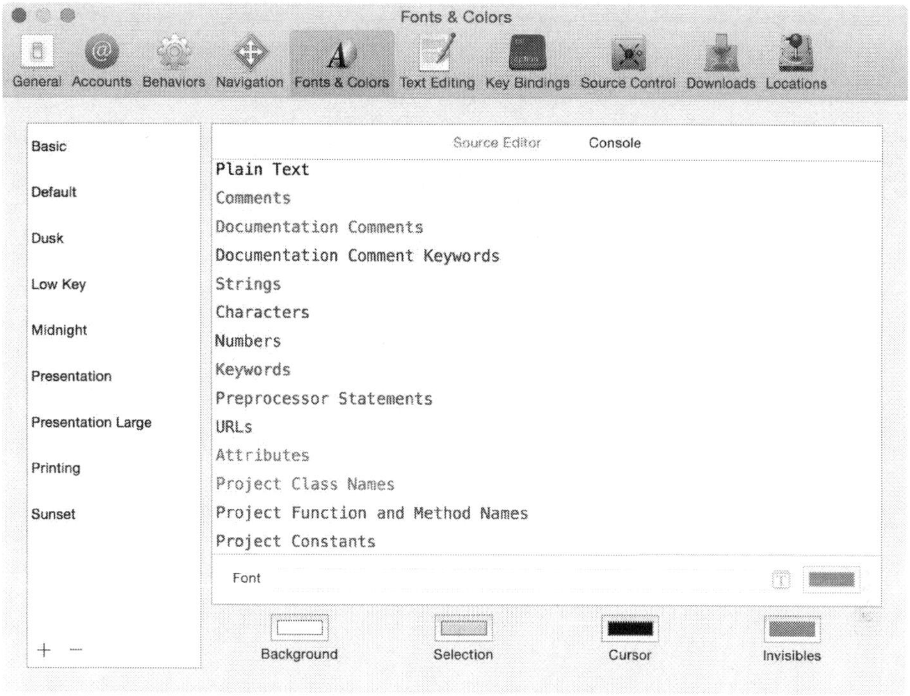

*Figure 10.19 The **Fonts & Colors** settings.*

On the left side of the dialog is the **Theme** list. A theme specifies a group of default fonts and colors that can be applied to your Xcode workspace to suit a variety of tastes. Each theme is just a starting place that you can change to your heart's content.

When you select a theme, a list on the right side of the dialog shows the color in which each code element will be displayed. Notice that at the top of this list you can select whether you want to set fonts and colors for the **Source Editor** (the main Code Editor) or the **Console** (the debug Console window that displays program output). When you select an individual code element from this list, a list box and color picker control are displayed directly below the list (Figure 10.20).

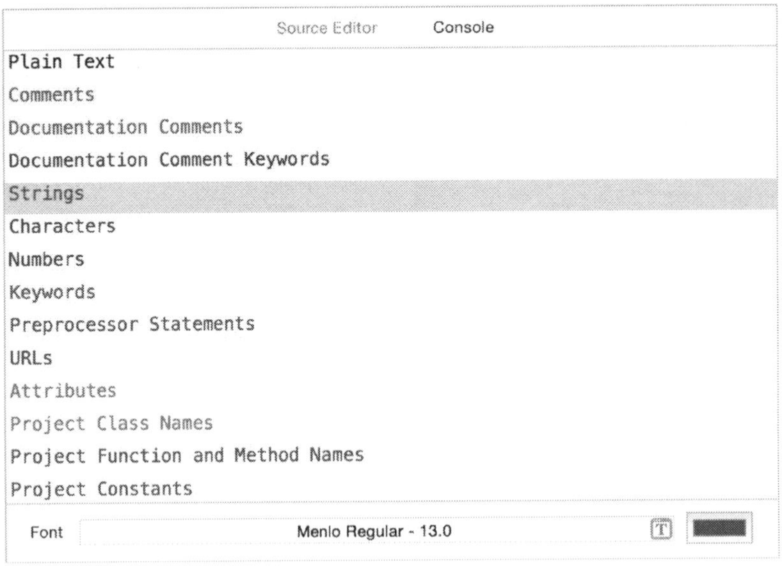

Figure 10.20 Setting the font and color of a code element.

Typically, you want to change all code elements to the same font size. To do this, press **Command+A** to select all fonts. Then, to change the font size, click the **T** inside the small square on the right of the **Font** picker. This displays a dialog from which you can choose the font **Collection**, **Family**, **Typeface**, and **Size** (Figure 10.21).

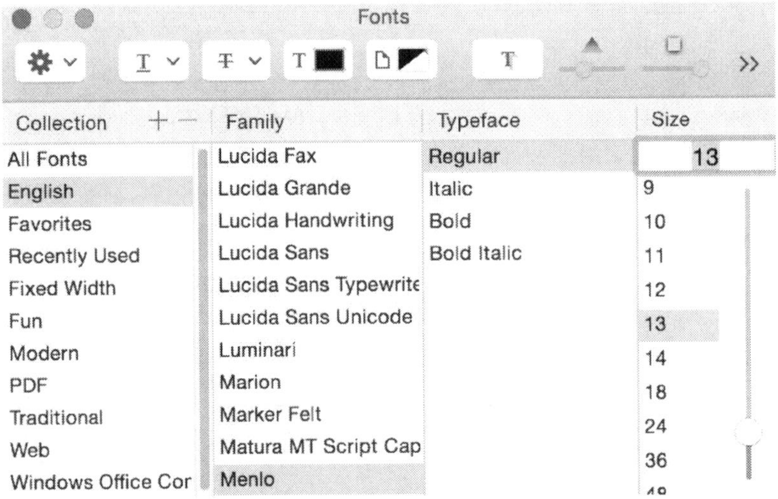

Figure 10.21 Selecting the font.

Although you *can* set the font color from this dialog (the second button from the right at the top), if you have selected all code elements, you don't want to set the font color here. If you do, all code elements will be the same color, which isn't very useful.

After you select new font settings, close the dialog because closing the Preferences dialog won't automatically close it for you.

To change the color of one or more code elements, select those elements in the Settings dialog (Figure 10.19), and then click the color well at the bottom right of the dialog. This launches the color picker dialog (Figure 10.22).

Figure 10.22 The color picker dialog.

Five buttons at the top of the dialog provide different ways to select a color:

- Color wheel
- Color sliders
- Color palettes
- Image palettes

- Crayons (shown in Figure 10.22)

When you've finished selecting a color, close the color picker dialog.

At the bottom of the Fonts & Colors panel are four color wells (Figure 10.19).

- **Background** – Sets the background color of the Code Editor.
- **Selection** – Sets the highlight color when you select an area of code.
- **Cursor** – Sets the color of your cursor in the Code Editor.
- **Invisibles** – "Invisibles" refers to invisible characters such as spaces and tabs. In a perfect world, this setting works in conjunction with the Code Editor's Show Invisibles setting (accessed from the **Editor > Show Invisibles** menu). Selecting this option replaces spaces with a "u" shaped character but doesn't do anything with tabs! This setting is supposed to set the color of the "u" shaped characters, however, setting this color doesn't change a thing!

Text Editing Preferences

Programmers can be *very* particular about how they want their code formatted. Typically, software development shops with multiple developers set up standards for how code should be formatted so the code looks consistent, no matter who writes it, which makes reading another developer's code easier.

In the Xcode Preferences dialog is a **Text Editing** section (Figure 10.23), which allows you to specify a variety of code formatting options and Code Editor behaviors.

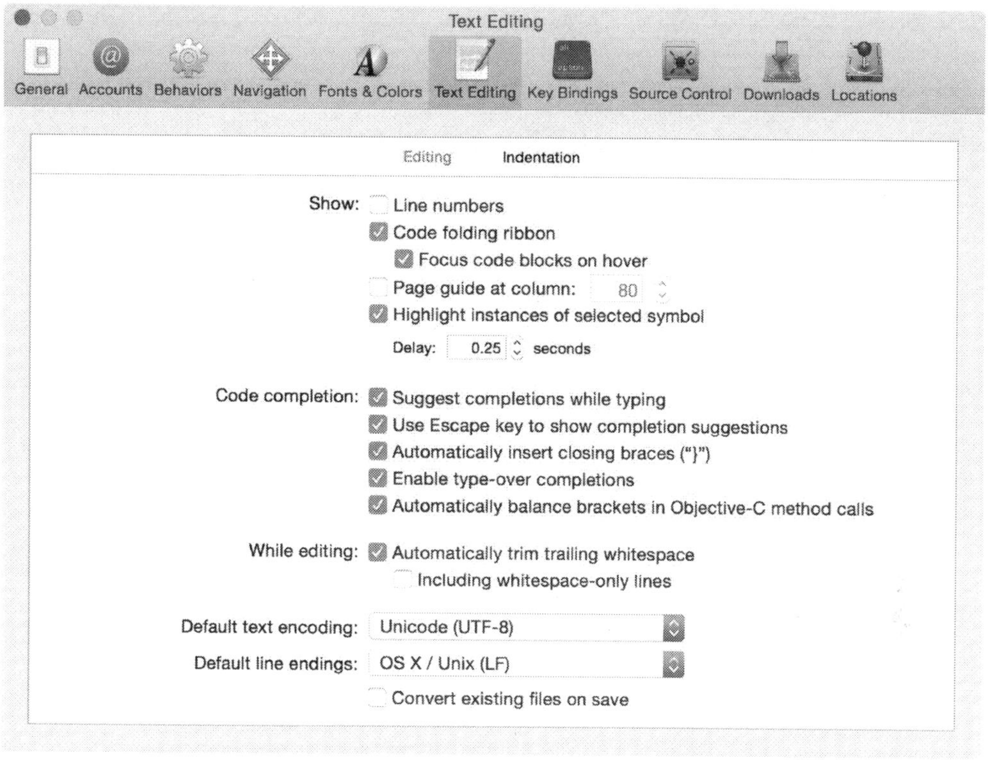

Figure 10.23 ***Text Editing*** *preferences.*

Editing Preferences

The first group of settings is listed under the category **Show**. If the checkbox is selected for a setting, it indicates that you want to show that item. If an item is unselected, it indicates that you do not want to show that item. The **Show** settings are:

- **Line numbers** – When you select this option, Xcode displays line numbers in the gutter to the left of the code window.

- **Code folding ribbon** – This setting toggles the code folding ribbon off and on. This setting and the **Focus code blocks on hover** settings are discussed in the earlier section on Code Folding.

- **Page guide at column** – This setting displays a vertical line at the column position that you specify (Figure 10.24). The width of a column is determined by the em-width of the font that you are using in the Code Editor (the width of the letter "M").

```
@implementation AppDelegate

- (BOOL)application:(UIApplication *)application didFinishLaunchingWithOptions:
    (NSDictionary *)launchOptions
{
    // Override point for customization after application launch.
    return YES;
}

- (void)applicationWillResignActive:(UIApplication *)application
{
    // Sent when the application is about to move from active to inactive state.
        This can occur for certain types of temporary interruptions (such as an
        incoming phone call or SMS message) or when the user quits the application
        and it begins the transition to the background state.
    // Use this method to pause ongoing tasks, disable timers, and throttle down
        OpenGL ES frame rates. Games should use this method to pause the game.
}
```

Figure 10.24 The Page Guide helps you to keep your code lines to a specific width.

If you would like your code to only extend to a particular column, the page guide helps you to know where to shorten a code line and have it wrap to another line.

- **Highlight instances of selected symbol** – If this option is on, when you select a symbol (such as a method name, parameter, or *local variable*) in a code file, Xcode highlights other places in the code that reference that symbol. For example, in Figure 10.25, the value parameter is selected, and the reference to the value parameter in the first line of code has a dotted, u-shaped highlight around it.

```
func multiplyTimesTotal(value:Double) -> Double {

    self.total *= value
    return total
}
```

Figure 10.25 Highlighting instances of the selected symbol.

You don't have to completely highlight the symbol for this feature to work. You can just select it by clicking either anywhere in the name or right before it (but not right after it).

If you hover your mouse pointer over the selected symbol, a small down-arrow is displayed to the right of the symbol. If you click this arrow, three options are displayed in a popup menu:

- **Edit All in Scope** – If you select this option, Xcode highlights all instances of the selected text. You can then edit the text, and all instances will be edited at the same time. You can also select this option from the Xcode menu under **Editor > Edit All in Scope**.

- **Search with Google** – Launches a web browser and performs a Google search on the word.

- **Add to iTunes as a Spoken Track** – If you select this option, the selected text is played in iTunes.

The second group of settings, labeled **Code Completion**, is covered in *Chapter 6: The Libraries* under the section *Code Completion Preferences*.

In the **While editing** section of the **Editing** preferences panel, the **Automatically trim trailing whitespace** setting removes extra spaces or tabs at the end of a line after you press **return**. If the **Including whitespace-only lines** is selected, trailing whitespace is also removed from lines that only contain whitespace.

It isn't likely that you will need to change the last few settings at the bottom of the dialog, but here is a description of each:

- **Default text encoding** – Specifies the character set that the editor uses to display and save new files.

- **Default line endings** – The default line ending style for new files.

- **Convert existing files on save** – When selected, files are converted to use the default line endings style when they are saved. If this setting is off (the default), files are left as is.

Indentation Preferences

If you select the **Indentation** button near the top of the Preferences dialog's Text Editing panel, the settings shown in Figure 10.26 are displayed.

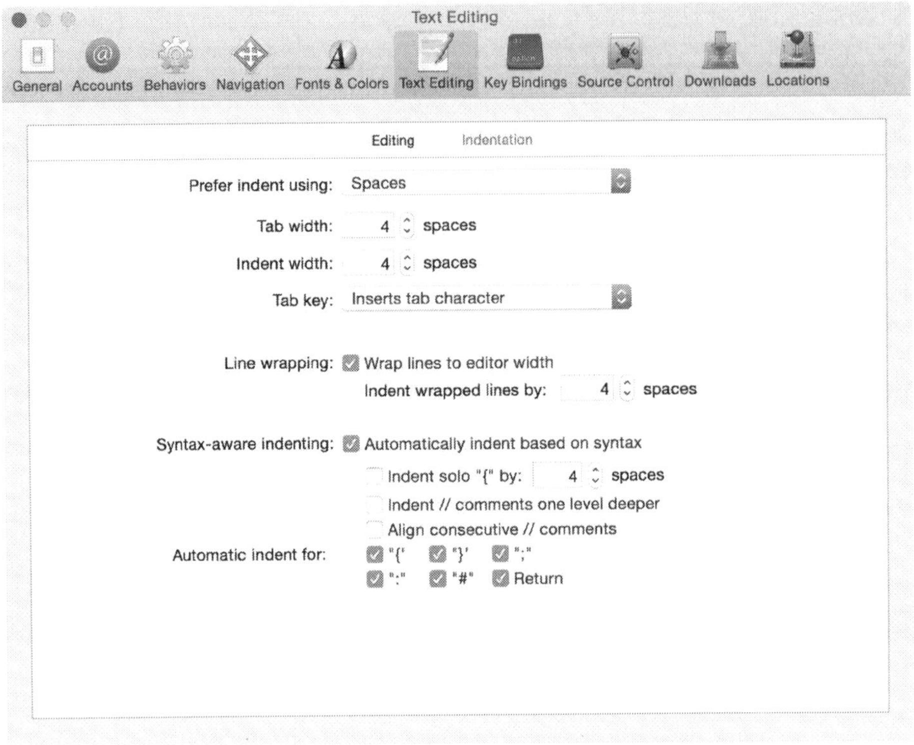

Figure 10.26 Indentation preferences.

Xcode automatically indents code for you in a variety of places—in methods, looping statements, conditional statements, and so on. Indentation makes your code easier to read. Here is a description of Xcode's indentation settings, which allow you to change how indentation is performed:

- **Prefer indent using** – The two choices here are **Spaces** and **Tabs**. Great programmer wars have been fought on whether it's best to use tabs or spaces to indent your code. Ultimately, indentation is listed under Xcode Preferences because it's just that—a preference. If you are working with a team of developers, it's best to use whatever setting the rest of the team is using.

  Personally, I prefer tabs because they are easier to work with. If I use the back arrow to move the cursor to the previous line of code, it requires one keystroke when using tabs. On the other hand, if I back arrow through a spaced indentation, I have to navigate through multiple spaces.

  Another consideration is that different developers have their own preference on how much whitespace that they like to see for indentations.

If you set the indentation to spaces, the amount of indentation whitespace is hard-coded in the file, but if you set the indentation to tabs, developers can set the tab width to whatever they like and Xcode will adjust the whitespace accordingly.

- **Tab width** – The visual width of a tab.

  If **Prefer indent using** is set to **Spaces**, when you press the **Tab** key in your code file, Xcode inserts the number of spaces specified in this setting.

  If **Prefer indent using** is set to **Tabs**, when you press the **Tab** key, Xcode inserts a tab character into the source file and displays the tab with a visual width equivalent to the number of spaces specified in this setting.

- **Indent width** – The number of positions to indent blocks of code.

  If **Prefer indent using** is set to **Spaces**, when Xcode adds an indentation for you, it inserts the physical number of spaces specified in this setting.

  If **Prefer indent using** is set to **Tabs**, when Xcode adds an indentation for you, it inserts a single tab character. However, it displays the indentation with a visual width equivalent to the number of spaces specified in this setting.

- **Tab key** – This setting specifies the behavior of the tab key for indentation. The three options are:
  - **Indents in leading whitespace** – (the default)
  - **Indents always**
  - **Inserts tab character**

- **Line wrapping** – This setting specifies whether to soft- wrap your code. When this is off (the default), long lines of code simply disappear off the right edge of the Code Editor. If you turn this option on, Xcode wraps long lines of code to the next line. The **Indent wrapped lines by** setting specifies how far to indent the soft-wrapped lines.

- **Syntax-aware indenting** – This group of settings allows you to specify Xcode's auto-indentation behavior.
  - **Indent solo "{" by:** – Indents a single left brace.

- **Indent // comments one level deeper** – Adds an extra level of indentation for comments that begin with two forward slashes.
- **Align consecutive // comments** – Tells Xcode to indent consecutive lines of comments at the same indentation level.

- Automatic indent for – Lists a set of characters for which Xcode normally automatically indents. If you want to turn off automatic indentation for any of these characters, just deselect the checkbox.

If your method code is not automatically indented, you should stop and take note. You may be making a mistake common to new developers—placing method code outside curly braces! I emphasize method code because other code such as property declarations should be outside the curly braces of a method and are, therefore, not automatically indented.

Summary

- As you enter code in the editor, Xcode displays a code-completion popup that provides a list of suggestions for completing the code.
- If Xcode doesn't pop up code completion when you need it, you can press **Escape** to bring it up manually.
- At the bottom of the code-completion popup, there is a small area that displays Quick Help for the item that is currently selected.

Balancing Delimiters

- In Swift, delimiters are comprised of a beginning (or opening) character and an ending (or closing) character that mark off, or delimit, the beginning and end of a section of code. Xcode provides plenty of help to make sure that delimiters are properly balanced.

Structuring Your Code

- In Xcode's **Structure** menu, there are helpful options that help you to clean up your code:
    - **Re-Indent**
    - **Shift Left**
    - **Shift Right**
    - **Move Line Up**
    - **Move Line Down**
    - **Comment / Uncomment Selection**

Code Folding

- Code folding is an Xcode feature that allows you to "fold up" methods and functions so you see the method declaration but not the associated code. This makes it easy to see all the methods in a code file without having to sift through the associated code in those methods.

Navigating Code

- At the top of the Code Editor area is a jump bar that allows you to navigate both within the current code file and to other code files.

- Each section of the jump bar is a button you can click either to navigate or jump to another piece of code. The button at the far right lists all members of the class currently open in the Code Editor.

- The Code Editor jump bar contains a hierarchical path menu where each button in the bar is a different level of the hierarchy.

- The Code Editor jump bar also contains a stepper comprised of back and forward arrow buttons that allow you to step back and forward through your navigation history.

- The Code Editor jump bar also has a "related items" button that allows you to open items related to the code file currently open in the editor.

- Xcode provides the ability for you to group items in the jump bar's member list by means of the **MARK**, **TODO**, and **FIXME** comment tags.

- You can **Command+Click** a symbol to jump to its definition. This is a quick and easy way to navigate to the code that defines a symbol.

- The Open Quickly feature allows you to search for a text string in the contents of a file or in the file name.

Preferences

- In Xcode, different colors are used for each type of code element. This feature is known as syntax-aware fonts and colors.

- The Xcode text-editing preferences allow you to specify how you want your code formatted.

Chapter 11: App Architecture

This is one of the most important chapters in the book. It's not information you often find in other iOS books, but it contains critical information that teaches you to create an app that is easy to conceive, design, build, and maintain.

Sections in This Chapter

The Importance of Solid Architecture

Architecture. The word is usually associated with constructing a building. Whether it's as small as a shed or as large as a skyscraper, architecture is important to make sure the design is sound. This is no less true of constructing software. Whether it's a small iOS app or a large business application, a good architecture can make it easier to design, build, and extend your software.

Why should you care about your app's architecture? A poorly-designed app is more difficult to design, create, and maintain. A well-designed app is the gift that keeps on giving. You will save yourself time, energy, and cost by creating an app with a solid architecture.

Although this topic doesn't have anything to do specifically with Xcode, I included this chapter in this book because it's important that you understand the concepts of solid architecture before you learn about data and build your first real app.

Design Patterns to the Rescue

Recently, when I needed to build a horse shed, rather than starting from scratch, I went to the Internet to see what architectural plans other people were sharing. This was my first time building a horse shed, and I knew others had already learned from experience what to do and what not to do. There were specific patterns for building this kind of structure that I wanted to learn rather than make all the mistakes myself.

Fortunately, others have come before you and have built many different types of software applications. What these developers and architects have learned has been distilled into some common design patterns. The great thing about these patterns is they work well regardless of the tools you are using—whether it's Swift and iOS, Java and Android, or C# and Windows Phone. In this chapter, you will learn about some design patterns that Apple has implemented in iOS app development, and you will see how you can easily improve on some of these patterns.

Your App Will Change

Let's be clear about this. Your app will change. Not just once or twice, but many times over—and that's even before you release it to the app store for the first time. After it's released, your app will change even more as others use it, provide feedback and suggest enhancements. You have to be prepared for that because it's a reality of writing apps.

If your app is designed to anticipate change, this process is much easier. If your app is not designed to anticipate change, you are headed for a lot of tedious and unnecessary work. Keep in mind that the majority of your time is not spent in the initial creation of the app— the majority of your time is spent updating and enhancing the app as you roll out subsequent versions. Also, there are changes that come from Apple as they release new devices and add new features to iOS.

If you get a change request and you find that you need to tear apart your app to implement the change, then you didn't do your job as an architect! You want to make sure you have designed your app to anticipate change to make this process as smooth as possible.

Where Do You Put Your Code?

In *Book 1: Diving Into iOS*, you learned there are three main parts of an app:

- User Interface
- Core Logic
- Data

Having these separate parts in mind when creating your app is a great start in creating a solid architecture. When these different parts are too tightly bound together, you create what is known as a "monolithic" architecture that is difficult to change. It creates a situation where you can't change one part of the app without changing the other.

Fortunately, it's not difficult to follow sensible architectural principles. Ultimately, where you put your code has everything to do with how easy it is to write, extend, and maintain your app. Putting your code in logical, predictable places also helps you avoid the game of "where's the code?" that many developers play on a daily basis.

Model-View-Controller

A more formal way to look at the three main parts of an app is by means of the Model-View-Controller design pattern. This design pattern has been around for many years and helps you clearly partition the main parts of your app so it is easier to design, enhance, and maintain.

Because of my background in software architecture, when I first came to the iOS platform back in 2008, I was intrigued to hear that Apple encouraged the use of the Model-View-Controller design pattern in iOS app development.

Here's how the Model-View-Controller (also known as MVC) pattern maps to the main parts of your app:

- Model → Data
- View → User Interface
- Controller → Core Logic

Let's break this down by first looking at a traditional implementation of the MVC pattern, and then we can look at Apple's implementation.

Model

The Model is your application's data and, in iOS, usually

takes the form of ***entities***. An entity represents an object in the real world. For example, if you are creating an app that handles customer orders, you might have a Customer entity, Order entity, and Product entity.

An entity has properties that represent the attributes of a particular real-world object. For example, a Customer entity might have companyName, webAddress, phone, and address properties that hold this information for each customer as shown in Figure 11.1.

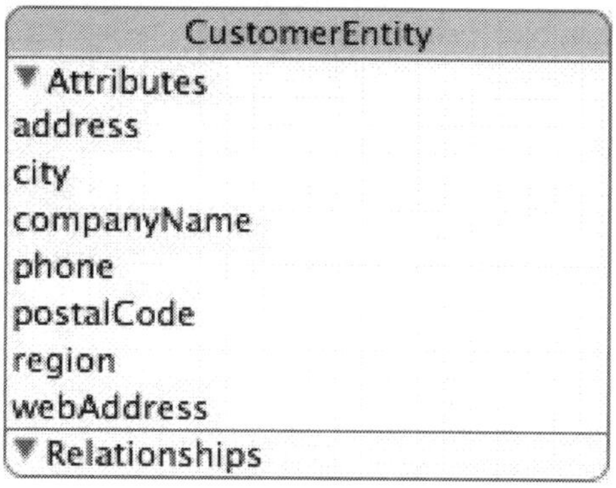

*Figure 11.1 A **CustomerEntity** object.*

You will learn much more about entities in the next chapter on Core Data.

View

The View is the part of the app the user interacts with directly and contains user-interface objects such as buttons, text fields, sliders, and so on. Because of this, Apple refers to each screen full of information in an app as a view.

Controller

The Controller acts as an intermediary between the Model and the View. The Controller is where your core logic goes. Figure 11.2 shows the interaction that occurs between the Model, View, and Controller.

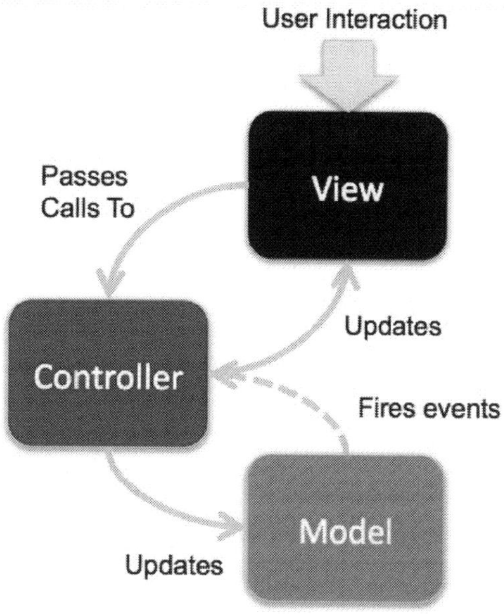

Figure 11.2 Model, View, Controller interaction.

In the MVC pattern, the user interacts with the view— they touch, tap, pinch, or flick a user-interface object. In response, the View passes a call to the Controller, and the Controller does something based on that interaction. For example, the user might change information in a text field and touch a **Save** button, so the controller would take that new information and update a Model entity.

Conversely, sometimes when you save a Model entity, it gets new or default values. For example, if you save a new invoice entity, it may be assigned an invoice number. So, the model can fire an event that tells the controller, "I've got a new invoice number." The controller can then update the view and the new invoice number can be displayed in the user interface.

As already mentioned, the Controller is the place where you should put your app's core logic. For example, in a Calculator app, you could have a Calculator controller object that adds, subtracts, multiplies, and divides (Figure 11.3). If you have a Customer Service app, you could have a Customer controller object that creates new customers, puts customers on credit hold, and so on.

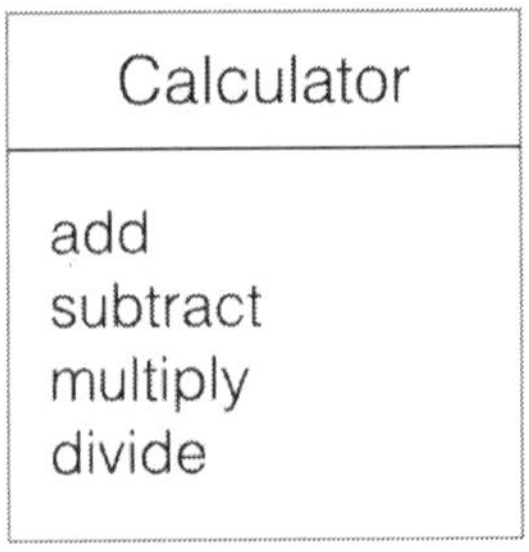

*Figure 11.3 A **Calculator** controller object.*

Separation of Concerns

So, MVC is a great pattern for "separating concerns"— keeping the three parts of your app separate. You want to be able to use your data with any user interface. You want your core logic to be used in multiple places. You want your data and core logic to be independent of your user interface.

In the Model View Controller diagram shown in Figure 11.2, there are communication lines between the Model and the Controller and between the Controller and the View, but you will never see communication between the Model and the View. They never communicate directly with each other. This allows your data and core logic to be used independently of the user interface.

Apple's MVC Implementation

Design patterns are great. However, I have found that, at times, the implementation of a particular pattern may not be true to the pattern's original intent. I was actually surprised at how Apple implemented the MVC pattern because it wasn't a traditional implementation—and this isn't just a matter of semantics or theory. Unfortunately, Apple's implementation of MVC doesn't provide well- defined boundaries between the three main parts of your app—which is the whole purpose of the MVC pattern.

Nothing speaks louder than a real example, so I have created a few sample apps that follow Apple's MVC pattern. By way of comparison, I have also recreated the apps using a better implementation of the MVC pattern.

Calculator Sample App User Interface

The first sample is a Calculator app that looks and acts just like the built-in iOS Calculator app. Follow the steps in this section to get a look at how the user interface of the app has been designed.

1. In Xcode, open the **CalculatorDemo** project in this book's sample code.
2. In the Project Navigator, select the **Main.Storyboard** file. You should see the scene shown in Figure 11.4.

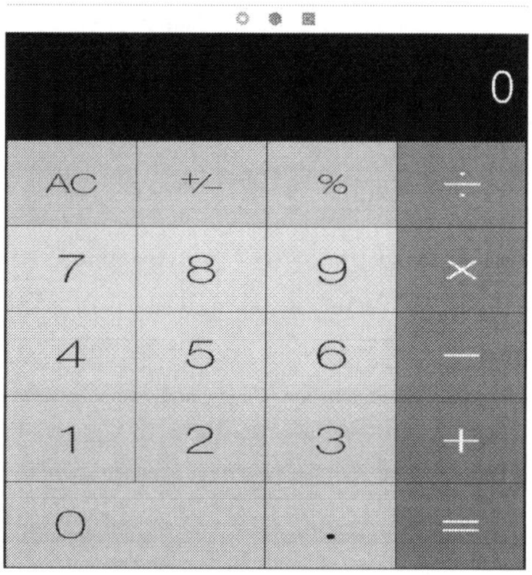

*Figure 11.4 The **CalculatorDemo** project's main scene.*

This looks dangerously like the built-in Calculator app! Let's see what it looks like at run time.

3. Make sure the **Scheme** control at the top left of the Xcode window is set to one of the **iPhone** simulators, and then click the **Run** button. No surprises here. It looks and behaves just like the built-in app.

4. Click any number, and then click an operator such as the multiply sign. Notice a thin dark line appears around the operator just as it does in the built-in Calculator app (Figure 11.5). This indicates the currently selected operation.

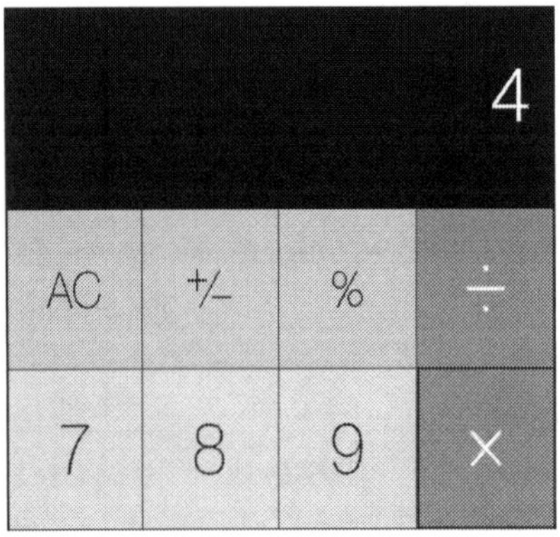

Figure 11.5 The multiply operator is highlighted.

5. Click another number and the equal sign, and you can see the Calculator is fully functioning. You can add, subtract, multiply, divide, and clear the Calculator memory. You can even use common Calculator shortcuts. For example, if you type **1 + =**, and then repeatedly click the = key, the Calculator continually adds one to the previous number.

6. Next, hold down any of the number or operator keys and notice the shading changes slightly to indicate the button has been pressed.

Now let's take a look behind the scenes to see how the Calculator app works.

1. Go back to Xcode and click the **Stop** button. Look in the Project Navigator, and you can see there are just a few files (Figure 11.6).

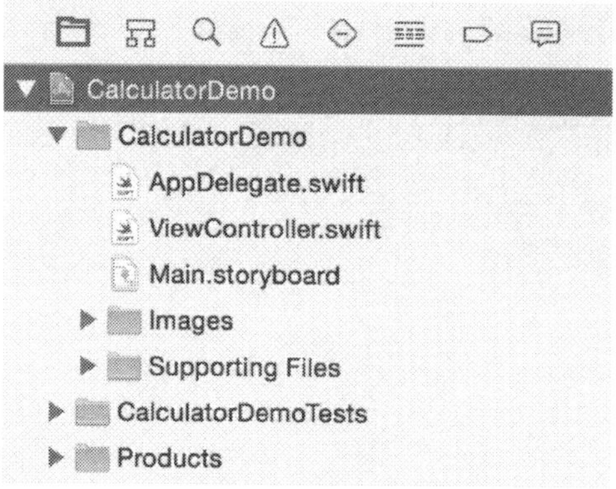

*Figure 11.6 The **CalculatorDemo** project files.*

The **ViewController** class is associated with the scene on the storyboard and contains the user- interface logic and core logic for the Calculator.

2. Click **Main.storyboard** and in the Document Outline window you can see a list of all user-interface objects. There are five image views (with the "img" suffix) and quite a few button objects (Figure 11.7).

Figure 11.7 UI objects in the main storyboard scene.

3. Select **imgCalculatorMain** in the Document Outline pane, and then go to the Attributes Inspector pane (click the third button from the right in the Inspector toolbar). Notice the **Image** attribute is set to **CalculatorBackground.png** (Figure 11.8)

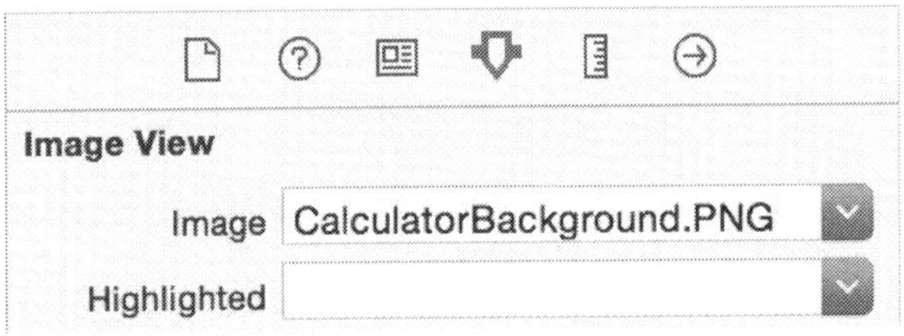

*Figure 11.8 The **CalculatorBackground** image file.*

4. To see what this image looks like when it's not on the view, go to the Project Navigator, expand the **Images** group and select the **CalculatorBackground.png** file. This displays the image in the Interface Builder editor (Figure 11.9).

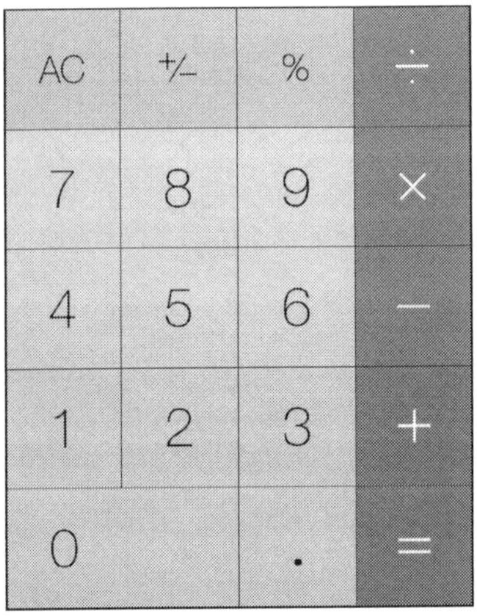

Figure 11.9 The calculator background image.

You may be surprised to see the buttons are not separate images. The calculator background is a single image that includes all the buttons you see at run time! How is the illusion of separate buttons created when you run the app? There is an invisible, rectangular button over each of the buttons.

5. To see this, go back and select the **Main.storyboard** file in the Project Navigator. Click over the number **9** button. As you can see in Figure 11.10,

you have selected an invisible button that is positioned directly over the button.

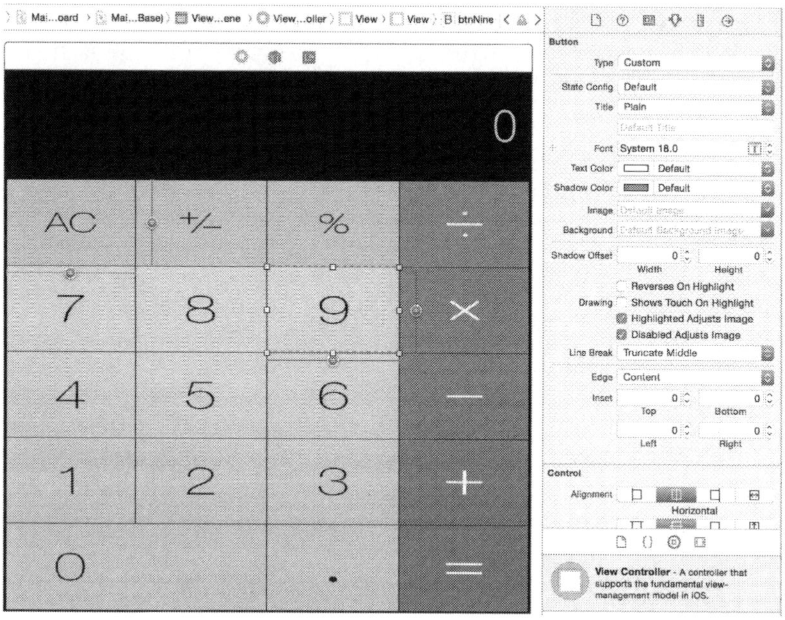

Figure 11.10 The invisible button over the "9" button.

With the invisible button selected, go to the Attributes Inspector. Notice in the header at the top of the Inspector pane that it indicates the object you have selected is a **Button** as shown in Figure 11.10. By default, this button is invisible, allowing the number button on the image below it to show through.

In the Attributes Inspector, the **State Config** list box contains the states the button can be in at run time:

- **Default** – The state of the button when the user is not interacting with it.
- **Highlighted** – The state of the button when the user is holding the button down.
- **Selected** – The state of the button when it is selected.
- **Disabled** – The state of the button when it is disabled.

When you select a state from the **State Config** combo box, it displays the **Title**, **Font**, **Text Color**, **Shadow Color**, **Image**, and **Background** for the selected button state. This allows you to specify different visual effects for each button state.

With the **Default** option selected (Figure 11.10), notice there is no **Image** specified. That's why this button is transparent at run time in its normal state.

6. In the **State Config** list box, select the **Highlighted** state. Notice the **Background** attribute is set to **ButtonHighlighted.PNG** as shown in Figure 11.11.

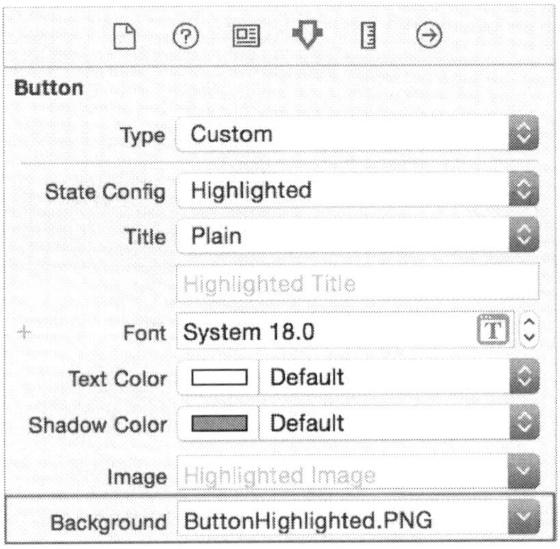

*Figure 11.11 The **Highlighted** button attributes.*

7. To see what this image looks like, go to the Project Navigator, and under the **Support Files** group, select the **ButtonHighlighted.PNG** file. The image is a solid gray square as shown in Figure 11.12.

*Figure 11.12 The **ButtonHighlighted.PNG** file.*

At run time when the user presses their finger on the invisible button, it enters the **Highlighted** state, and this image becomes visible.

8. Now go back to the Project Navigator and select the **Main.storyboard** file again. If it's not selected, reselect the invisible button over the number **9** button. Next, scroll down in the Inspector window until you see the **Alpha** setting (Figure 11.13).

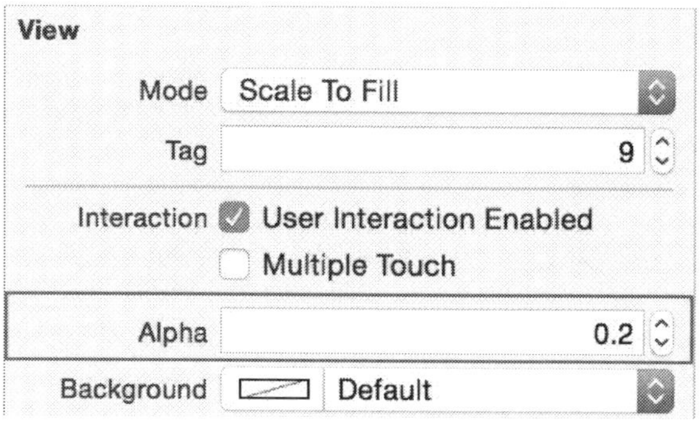

*Figure 11.13 The **Alpha** attribute specifies the transparency of a UI object.*

This setting specifies the transparency of an object. The value of **Alpha** can range between zero and 1. To make the effect more subtle, the **Alpha** value of the button is set to **.2** a shown in Figure 11.13.

9. Also, notice in Figure 11.13 that the **Tag** property of the invisible **9** button is set to **9**. Each of the numeric buttons have their tag number set to the number they represent (the **8** button is set to **8**, and so on). The decimal point button (**.**) has its **Tag** property set to **-1**. You will see in the next section how these tag numbers are used.

10. When the user touches a number button at run time, even though it's invisible, it fires the same events as a visible button.

To see this, with the invisible number button still selected, go to the Connections Inspector by clicking the button on the far right of the Inspector toolbar. As shown in Figure 11.14, there is a connection from the button's **Touch Up Inside** event to the **numberTouched:** action method of the view controller. All number buttons (as well as the decimal point button) are connected to the **numberTouched:** action method.

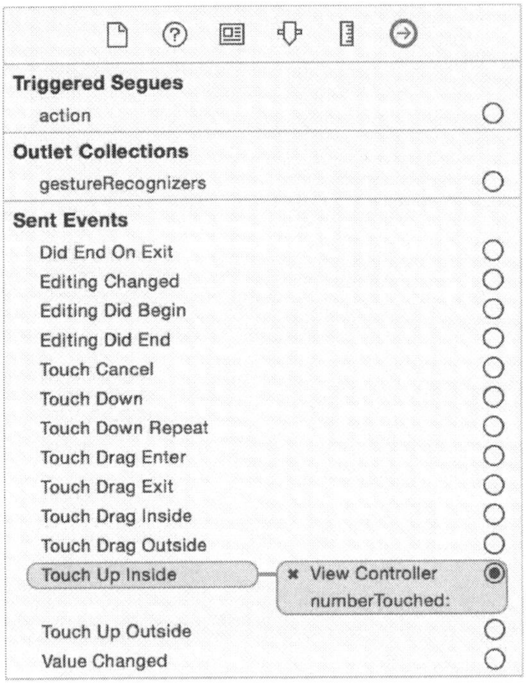

Figure 11.14 Numeric calculator buttons are all connected to the ***numberTouched:*** *action method.*

11. Now let's take a look at the operator buttons. Go back to the scene in the Interface Builder editor, and in the Document Outline pane, select the plus **btnPlus** button, which highlights the plus (+) button covering it.) Now look at the Connections Inspector again. As shown in Figure 11.15, the button's **Touch Up Inside** event is connected to two action methods:

    - **highlightOperation:** – This method adds the highlight around an operation button when it's selected. This connection only exists for the add, subtract, multiply, and divide buttons.

    - **operationTouched:** – This method performs the function associated with the selected key (add, subtract, multiply, divide, and so on).

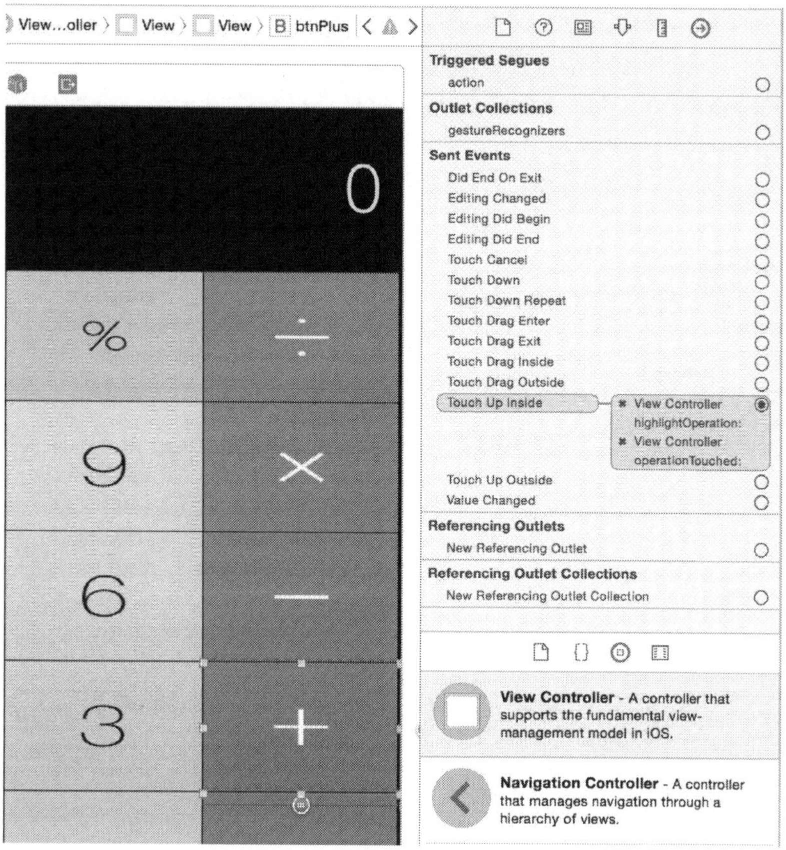

Figure 11.15 Operation button connections.

12. Next, click on the Calculator's numeric display at the top of the view as shown in Figure 11.16.

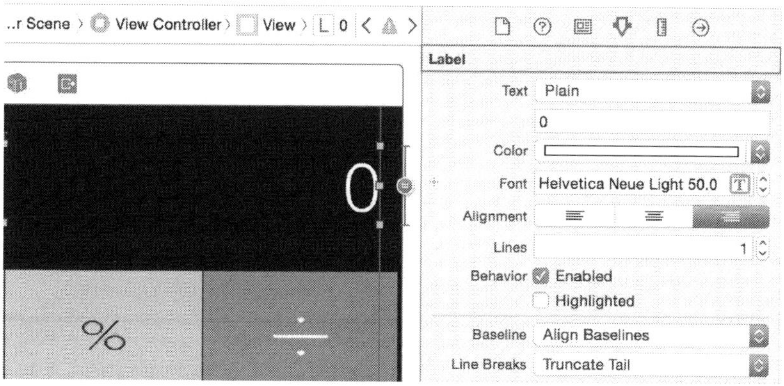

Figure 11.16 The calculator's numeric display is a label.

13. Go to the Attributes Inspector by clicking the fourth button from the left in the Inspector toolbar. As you can see in Figure 11.16, the Calculator's

numeric display is a label whose **Alignment** is set to right justified. By default, the iOS label control doesn't have a margin setting, so to make it look like the label does have a left and right margin, the label does not extend the full width of the view. Its **Background** is set to transparent so the color in the view behind it shows through.

This should give you a basic understanding of how the user interface works in the Calculator sample app.

Calculator Sample App Core Logic

Now let's take a closer look at the view controller code files to see how the core logic code in the view controller interacts with the Calculator user interface.

1. Select the **ViewController.swift** file in the Project Navigator. At the top of the code file is a declaration of an **Operation** enumeration. This enumeration details all operations that can be performed by the **Calculator**:

```
enum Operation: Int {
   case None = 0, Add, Subtract, Multiply,
      Divide, Equals, Clear, MemoryPlus,
      MemoryMinus, MemoryRead, MemoryClear,
      PositiveNegative, Percent
}
```

   An enumeration is a great way to declare a definitive list of operations.

2. Below the **Operation** enum declaration are three property declarations, two of which are Interface Builder outlets. Figure 11.17 shows how the outlet properties connect to the Calculator UI controls.

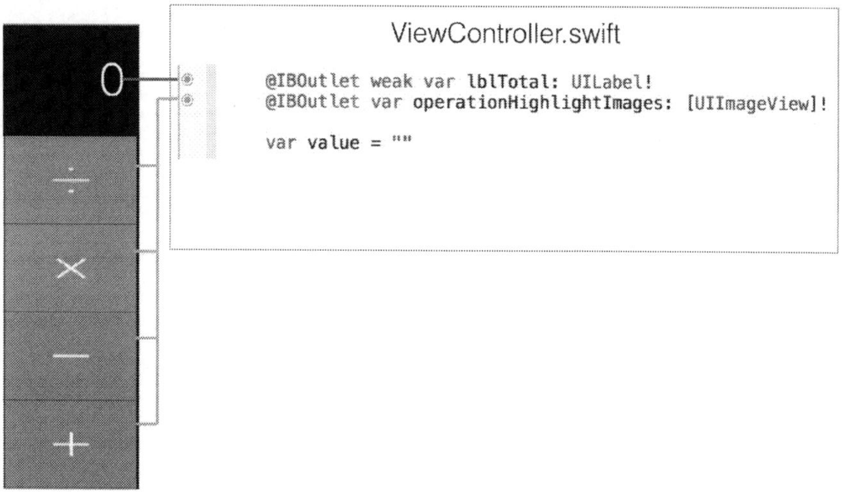

Figure 11.17 Calculator outlet connections.

- **lblTotal** - An IBOutlet property that is connected to the label comprising the Calculator's display.
- **operationHighlightImages** - An IBOutlet collection property that is connected to the highlight images of the add, subtract, multiply, and divide buttons.
- **value** - A regular property that holds the current string value displayed in the Calculator's numeric display label.

3. There are also three action-method declarations in the **ViewController.swift** file. Figure 11.18 shows how these action methods connect to UI controls.

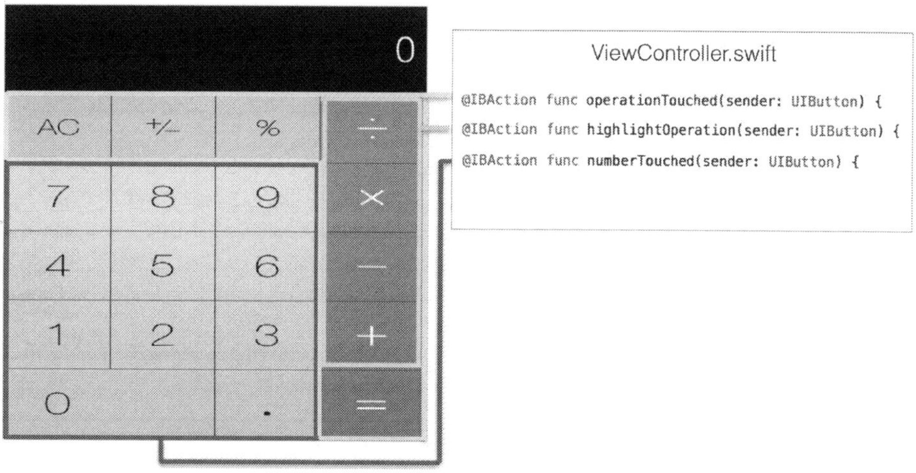

Figure 11.18 Calculator action method connections.

- **operationTouched:** is an action method connected to the **Touch Up Inside** event of all operation buttons.

- **highlightOperation:** is an action method connected to the **Touch Up Inside** event of the add, subtract, multiply, and divide buttons. This method adds the highlight around the selected button and removes it from all other buttons (only one operation can be highlighted at a time).

- **numberTouched:** is an action method connected to the **Touch Up Inside** event of all number buttons, including the decimal point button.

These properties and methods are all user interface specific since they are tied directly to UI controls.

4. Remember, you should keep the user interface separate from the core logic. To help make a division between the user-interface methods and the core logic methods in the view controller, I physically grouped them together. To see this, go to the Project Navigator and select the **ViewController.swift** file. In the jump bar at the top of the Code Editor, click the section on the far right as shown in Figure 11.19.

Figure 11.19 Select the button on the far right.

At the bottom of the popup list, you can see two sections labeled **Calculator User Interface** and **Calculator Core Logic** (Figure 11.20). Notice the three user-interface-specific methods are listed under the **Calculator User Interface** section of the popup.

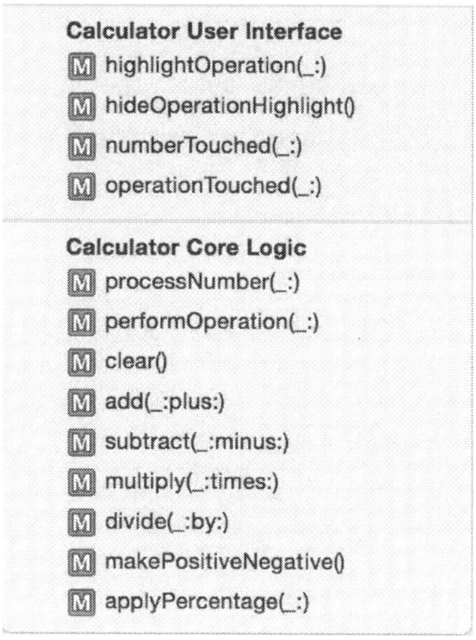

Figure 11.20 Calculator code sections.

These sections exist in the popup because of the // **MARK:** directives in the **ViewController.swift** file (for more information, see *Chapter 10: The Code Editor*). Given the current architecture of this project, creating separate sections in the view controller is about the best you can do to separate user-interface- specific methods from core logic.

5. Figure 11.21 provides a high-level overview of the interaction between the numeric buttons of the Calculator in the user interface and the methods of the **ViewController** class.

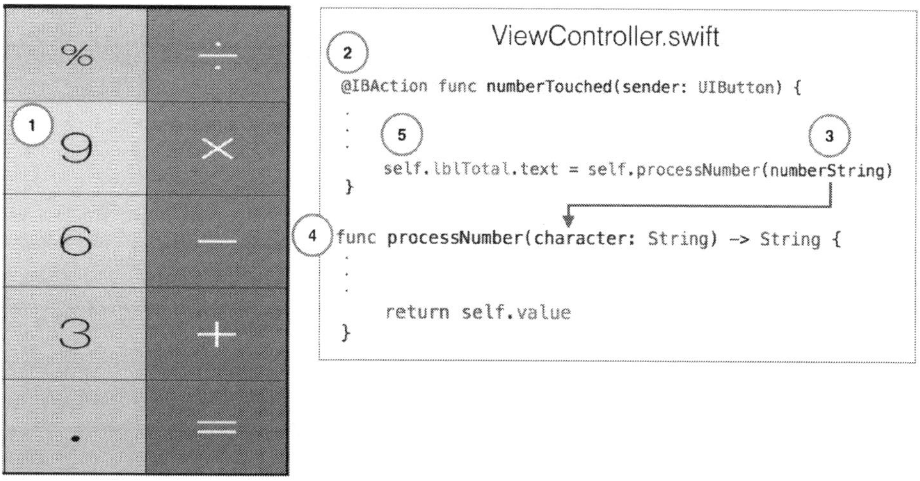

Figure 11.21 Calculator numeric button code interaction.

(1) The user touches a numeric button.

(2) The view controller's **numberTouched:** action method is called, which contains user-interface-specific code.

(3) In the **numberTouched:** method, after executing the user-interface processing, the view controller's **processNumber:** method is called.

(4) The **processNumber:** method executes the Calculator's core logic for handling a new number and returns the new Calculator value.

(5) In the **numberTouched:** method, the return value from the **processNumber:** method is stored in the **text** property of the **lblTotal** label.

6. Now let's take a closer look at these methods. In the jump bar at the top of the Code Editor, click the section on the far right again. From the member popup list, under the **Calculator user interface** section, select the **numberTouched:** method to view it in the Code Editor. You should see this code:

```
@IBAction func numberTouched(sender: UIButton)
{
   var numberString = ""
   var tagNumber = sender.tag
   numberString = (tagNumber == -1) ? "." :
      "\(tagNumber)"
   self.hideOperationHighlight()
   self.lblTotal.text =
      self.processNumber(numberString)
}
```

Remember, this is the method that is immediately called when the user touches a numeric button in the Calculator. Everything that happens in this method is user-interface specific:

- When this method is called, the button passes a reference to itself in the **sender** parameter— buttons are user-interface objects.

- At the top of the method, the tag number is retrieved from the selected button and converted to a string. If the tag number is -1, the string is set to the decimal point. Again, buttons and their tag numbers are part of the user interface.

- Afterward, the **hideOperationHighlight** method is called, which hides any operation key highlight that may be visible on the user interface.

- Next, at the bottom of the method, a call is made to the **processNumber:** method.

7. Figure 11.20 lists the **processNumber:** method under **Calculator Core Logic**. That means the method should contain no user-interface logic—just pure Calculator logic. To see this method, in the Code Editor jump bar, click on the section to the far right again and select the **processNumber:** method from the popup list. Here are this methods key actions:

   - If the last action was an operation, clear the current value.

   - Make sure the user hasn't entered the maximum number of digits.

   - If it's a decimal point, make sure there isn't already a decimal point in the number.

   - Append the new digit or decimal point to the current value.

   - Format the current value to include commas (if any are needed).

   Each of these actions is definitely a part of the Calculator's core logic and is separate from any user-interface considerations.

8. Now let's take a quick look at how the user interface and view controller code interact when an operation is selected by the user as shown in Figure 11.22.

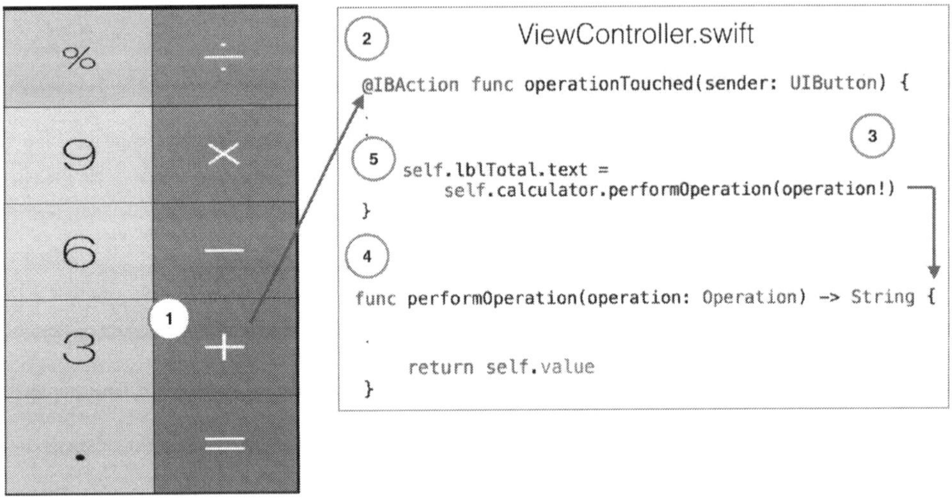

Figure 11.22 Operation button and code interaction.

(1) The user taps an operation button.

(2) The view controller's **operationTouched:** action method is called, which contains user-interface- specific code.

(3) In the **operationTouched:** method, after executing the user-interface processing code, the view controller's **performOperation:** method is called.

(4) The **performOperation:** method executes the Calculator's core logic for performing an operation and return's the Calculator's new value.

(5) In the **operationTouched:** method, the return value from the **performOperation:** method is stored in the **text** property of the **lbTotal** label.

9. Let's take a closer look at these methods. In the jump bar at the top of the Code Editor, click the section on the far right again. From the member popup list, under the **Calculator user interface** section, select the **operationTouched:** method to see this code:

```
@IBAction func operationTouched(sender:
 UIButton) {
 let operation =
      Operation(rawValue: sender.tag)
 self.lblTotal.text =
      self.performOperation(operation!)
}
```

This method is called immediately when the user touches an operation button in the Calculator. Everything that happens in this method is user-interface specific.

- When this method is called, the button passes a reference to itself in the **sender** parameter— buttons are user-interface objects.
- At the top of the method, the tag number is retrieved from the selected button. Buttons and their tag numbers are part of the user interface.
- Next, at the bottom of the method, a call is made to the **performOperation:** method.

10. Figure 11.20 lists the **performOperation:** method under the **Calculator Core Logic** section. Again, that means the method should contain no user-interface logic—just pure Calculator logic.

    To see this method, in the Code Editor jump bar, click on the section to the far right again and select the **performOperation:** method from the popup list. Here are the key actions this method performs:

    - The display value is converted from a string to a double value.
    - If the operation should be performed immediately (such as All Clear, Positive/Negative), the operation is performed.
    - For all other operations, a check is performed to see if there is any previous operation, and if so, that operation is performed.

Again, each action is part of the Calculator's core logic and is separate from any user-interface considerations.

What's Wrong With This Architecture?

The Calculator app works well. It adds, subtracts, multiplies and divides. So what's the problem?

Check out the strong link between the Calculator user interface and the view controller as shown in Figure 11.23. In object-oriented programming terms, this is known as "tight coupling".

The Calculator user interface is inseparably linked to the view controller. There are properties and methods in the view controller the user-interface controls are directly connected to.

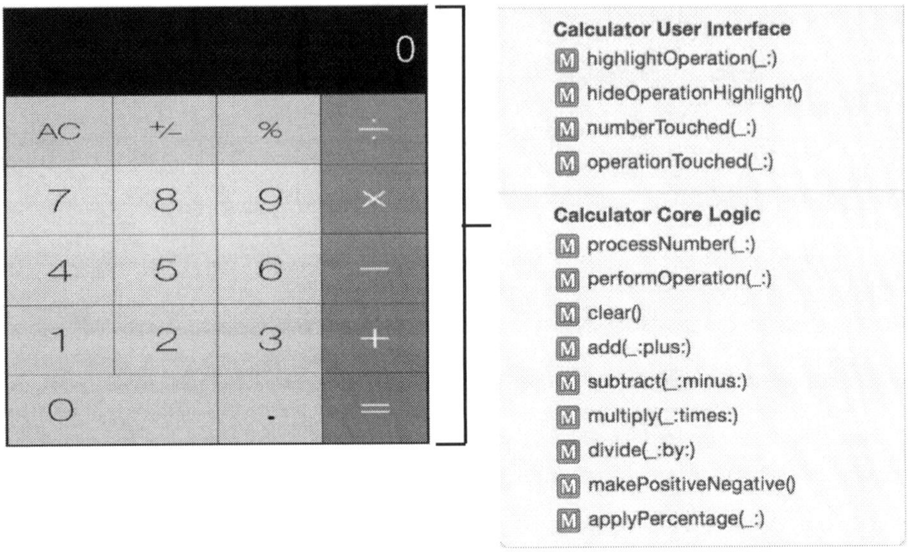

Figure 11.23 Tight coupling between the Calculator UI and core logic.

According to Apple's documentation, this is typical. A view is usually bound to a single view controller. Ultimately, the view controller is a user-interface object. It's not the tight coupling between the view and the view controller that's the problem—that's perfectly fine. The problem is the core logic code that's in the view controller.

Why is this a problem? Because a good app is often a victim of its own success. Let's say you release the Calculator app with its current architecture. If it does well in the App Store, you may consider creating a Scientific Calculator app. Wouldn't it be great to reuse some of the functionality of the Calculator app since the Scientific Calculator does everything the regular Calculator does and more?

Unfortunately, because the Calculator's core logic is buried within the view controller, there isn't a clean way to reuse this logic in another app. It's "stuck in the weeds" of the user interface.

A Better MVC Implementation

So, how do you fix this problem? You need to put the Calculator's core logic in some other place where you can access it from multiple apps or from multiple view controllers in a single app. If you shouldn't put your core logic in a view controller, where should you put it?

Business-Controller Objects

The answer is a *business-controller object* (also known as a *business* or domain object).

A business object provides a neutral place to put your core logic that can be reused from any user interface, including view controllers. As shown in Figure 11.24, you can create a Calculator business object in which you put all the Calculator's core logic methods.

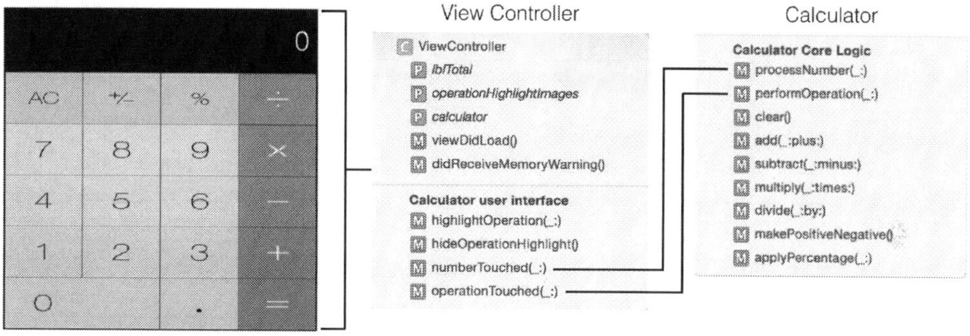

Figure 11.24 Implementing a Calculator business object.

In this figure, the Calculator user interface and View Controller are tightly bound together—and that's OK— they are both user-interface objects. When buttons are tapped on the calculator at run time, action methods in the view controller are called directly.

The only code you should put in the view controller is code that has something to do with the user interface. However, when core logic needs to be performed, the view controller makes a call to an appropriate method in the **Calculator** business object.

With your core logic in the **Calculator** class, you can easily create a **ScientificCalculator** subclass that inherits all the basic functionality of the **Calculator** and extends it by adding additional operations as in Figure 11.25.

Because you have elevated your core logic out of the user interface and into a **Calculator** business object, it makes it far easier to extend by creating a subclass.

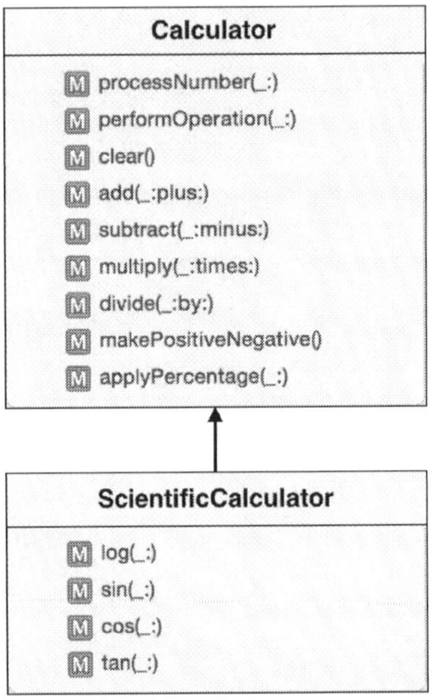

Figure 11.25 You can easily extend the core logic of the Calculator when it resides in its own class.

Other Benefits of Using Business Objects

When you create business objects, you are creating a representation of objects in the real world. In the Calculator app, you are creating a representation of a real-world calculator. In a real estate app, you can create **House**, **Buyer**, **Owner**, and **RealEstateAgent** business classes that represent real-world entities (Figure 11.26).

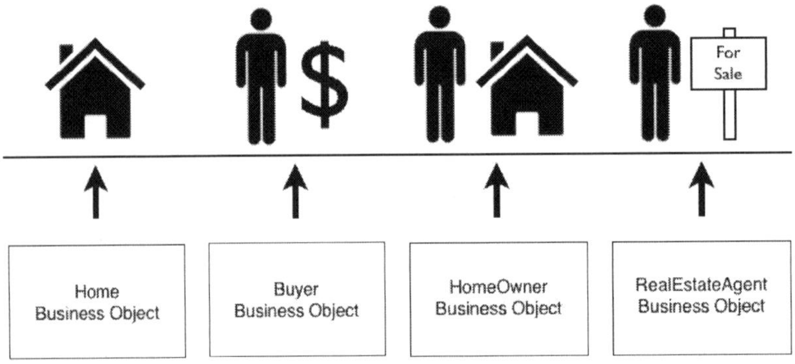

Figure 11.26 Business objects represent real world entities.

Creating business objects helps bridge something called the ***semantic gap***. The semantic gap is the difference between real world entities and how you model, or describe, these objects in your software applications. In many apps, this gap is extremely wide because the developer has not created any business objects. You will find that when you narrow the semantic gap by creating business objects that represent real-world entities, your apps are much easier to conceive, design, build, maintain, and extend.

You model real-world entity attributes by means of properties, and you model their behavior by means of methods. For example, a house has attributes such as address, number of bedrooms, number of baths, price, and so on that can be described, or modeled, as properties. A house also has behavior such as "put on the market," "take off the market," and so on which can be modeled as methods on a business object class.

Another benefit of using business objects is it helps you avoid playing the game of "where's the code?" When your core-logic code is raised out of the weeds of the user interface and into business objects, it's far easier to find the code you want.

For example, all the core-logic code that has something to do with a homeowner is in the **HomeOwner** business object. All the code that has something to do with a real- estate agent is in the **RealEstateAgent** business object, and all the code that has something to do with the user interface is in a view controller. When your code is segregated in this way, it makes it far easier to find the code you need.

In contrast, when your core logic code is tangled up in your user interface, it's much harder to find the code you need. You can see a great example of this in the **CalculatorDemo** project.

1. If it's not already open, in Xcode, open the **CalculatorDemo** project again.

2. In the Navigator panel on the left side of the Xcode window, select the Symbol Navigator by clicking the second button from the left in the Navigator toolbar or by pressing **Command+2**.

   As shown in Figure 11.27, there are only three classes in the project: **AppDelegate**, **ViewController**, and **CalculatorDemoTests**.

3. Expand the **ViewController** node to view all of its members. As you can see, there are many methods in the class: some user interface related and

some containing core logic. This mix of methods can make it difficult to find the code you need.

Figure 11.27 ***CalculatorDemo*** *project classes.*

In the next section, you will compare an improved Calculator sample project in the Symbol Navigator.

And one other thing—using business objects helps you avoid code redundancy. When you don't use business objects, it's easy to create duplicate code because you often forget you have already created a piece of functionality in another view controller. When you are using business objects, it's less likely you will create two methods on the same business object that perform the exact same function.

So, elevate your code, and use business objects.

Now let's see how a **Calculator** business object can help in an improved Calculator sample app.

The Improved Calculator Sample App

To see this proper division of user interface and core logic, let's check out another sample project for this chapter.

1. In Xcode, open the **CalculatorPlusDemo** project located in this book's sample code.

2. Press Xcode's **Run** button. Test the app by performing calculations. As you can see, it works just as the **CalculatorDemo** app. Click Xcode's **Stop** button.

3. In the Project Navigator under the **User Interface** group are the storyboard and view controller user- interface files. Under the **Core Logic** group is the **Calculator.swift** class file Figure 11.28.

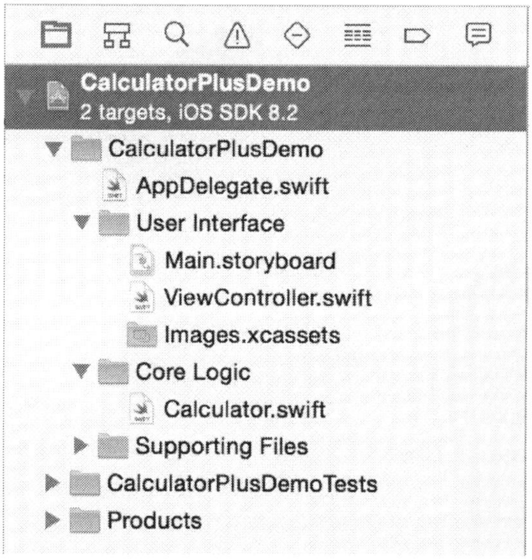

Figure 11.28 ***CalculatorPlusDemo*** *project files.*

4. Select the Symbol Navigator by clicking the second button from the left in the Navigator toolbar or by pressing **Command+2**. Expand the **Calculator** and **ViewController** nodes to see their class members. As shown in Figure 11.29 (the Symbol Navigator is split in two to make it easier to view), there is a clear 6. division of responsibilities between the **Calculator** class and the **ViewController** class.

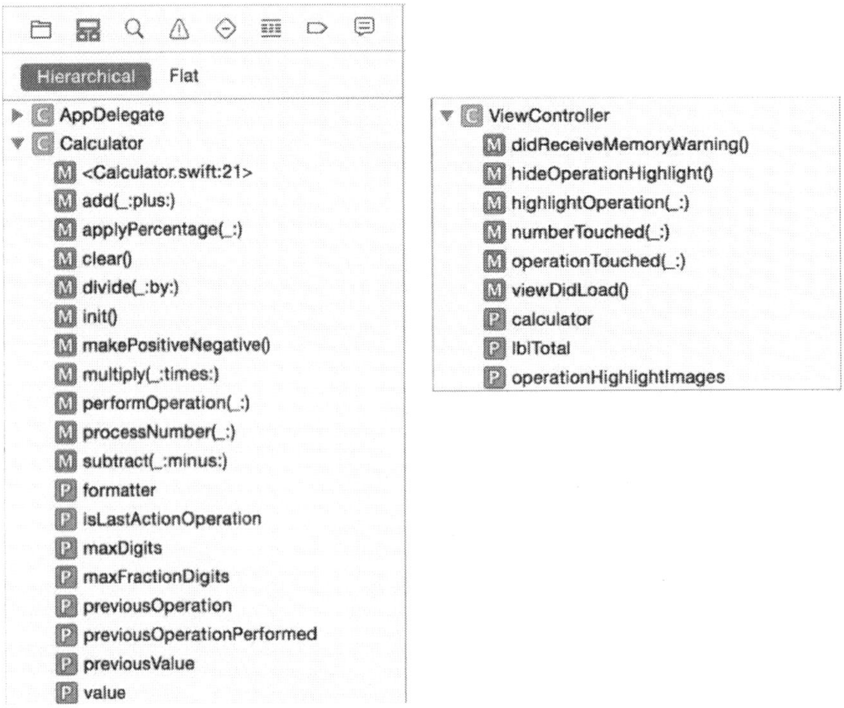

*Figure 11.29 **Calculator** and **ViewController** members.*

5. Let's take a closer look at the source code for these classes. Go back to the Project Navigator by clicking the first button on the left in the Navigator toolbar or by typing **Command+1**. In the Project Navigator, select the **ViewController.swift** file. As we look through the code in this class, remember that a view controller is a user-interface class.

6. The first thing to take note of is that the Operation enumeration that was declared in the view controller in the CalculatorDemo project is missing. This is appropriate because it has nothing to do with the user interface.

   Take a look at the list of properties in the file:

```
@IBOutlet weak var lblTotal: UILabel!
```

```
@IBOutlet var operationHighlightImages:
    [UIImageView]!
var calculator = Calculator()
```

Notice that the **value** property that was in the **CalculatorDemo** project's view controller is missing. Again, this is appropriate, because it has nothing to do with the user interface—it contains the current value of the **Calculator**.

Take note of the new **calculator** property. This property holds a reference to the **Calculator** business object. This allows any method in the view controller to easily access the Calculator object and call its methods.

7. Look below the property declarations to see the public method declarations:

    - **highlightOperation:**
    - **numberTouched:**
    - **operationTouched:**

   These are the same action methods as found in the **CalculatorDemo** project. This is appropriate because these are all user-interface-specific methods that are tied to user-interface controls in the view.

8. Let's contrast the message flow of the improved **CalculatorPlusDemo** app with the **CalculatorDemo** app. Figure 11.30 provides a high-level overview of what happens when a user touches a numeric button in the improved **CalculatorPlusDemo** app.

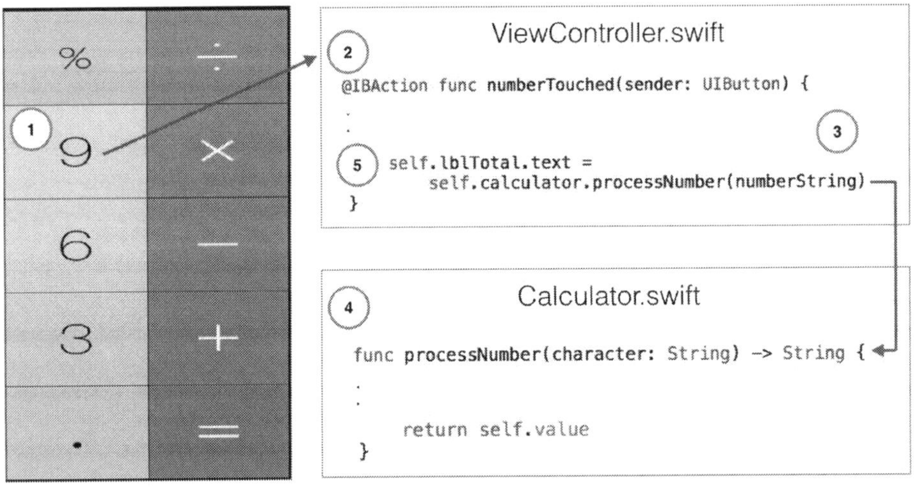

Figure 11.30 Number processing – the improved model.

(1) The user touches a numeric button.

(2) The **numberTouched:** action method in the view controller is called, which contains user- interface-specific code.

(3) After executing the user-interface processing, the view controller calls the Calculator object's **processNumber:** method.

(4) The Calculator object's **processNumber:** method executes the core logic for handling a new number and returns the Calculator's current value.

(5) The view controller takes the value returned from the Calculator's **processNumber:** method and stores it in the **text** property of the **lblTotal** label.

This is very similar to the high-level overview in Figure 11.21 except the **processNumber:** method has been moved from the **ViewController** class to the **Calculator** class.

9. Now let's look at a high-level overview of what happens when the user touches an operation button as shown in Figure 11.31.

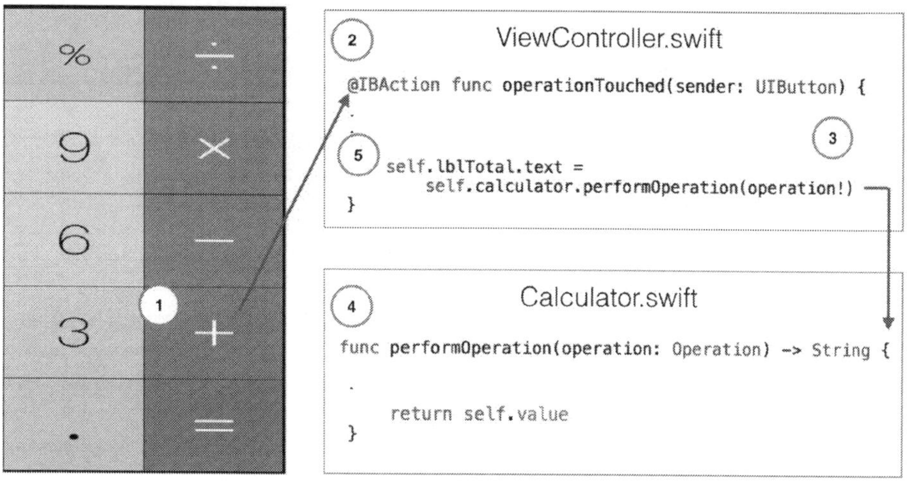

Figure 11.31 Calculator operation button and code interaction–the improved model.

(1) The user touches an operation button.

(2) The **operationTouched:** action method in the view controller is called, which contains user- interface-specific code.

(3) After executing the user-interface processing, the view controller calls the Calculator object's **performOperation:** method.

(4) The Calculator object's **performOperation:** method executes the core-operation logic and returns the Calculator's current value.

(5) The view controller takes the value returned from the Calculator's **performOperation:** method and stores it in the **text** property of the **lblTotal** label.

Again, this is very similar to the high-level overview in Figure 11.22 except the **performOperation:** method has been moved from the **ViewController** class to the **Calculator** class.

Although this simple app has just one business-controller object referenced from a single view controller, more complex apps may reference several business objects. For example, Figure 11.32 shows a view controller that references four different business-controller objects.

You can add properties to the View Controller that reference the business-controller objects just as the **ViewController** class references the Calculator object in the **CalculatorPlusDemo** project.

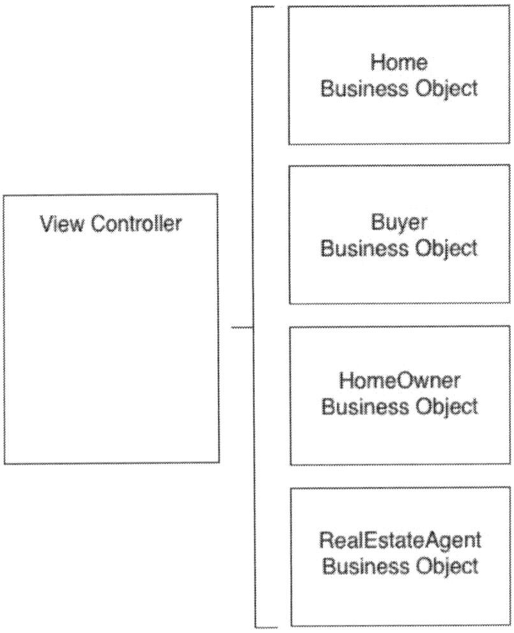

Figure 11.32 A single view controller can reference multiple business objects.

Business Objects are User-Interface Agnostic

It's important to note that business objects knows nothing about the user interface in which they are used. Within the business-object properties and methods there is no reference at all to any user-interface element. This allows you to reuse this business object from any view controller in the app, from a completely different iOS app, or, for that matter, you could even use it in a Mac OS X desktop application!

Business Objects and the MVC Pattern

You have learned the View and View Controller comprise your user interface and together are the "View" in the MVC pattern. You have also learned that your app's core logic should be contained in business objects that represent real-world entities. These business objects are the "Controller" in the MVC pattern.

But what about the Model? Earlier in this chapter you learned that the Model is your app's data and usually takes the form of business entities.

In *Chapter 12: Working With Core Data*, you are going to learn about Core Data, which uses entity objects. Entity objects are half of the business-object picture. They contain attributes that describe real-world entities. Business controllers are the other half of the picture. They model the behavior of a real-world entity as with the **Calculator** and **ScientificCalculator** classes.

Figure 11.33 completes the picture and shows you how each piece fits into the Model-View-Controller design pattern.

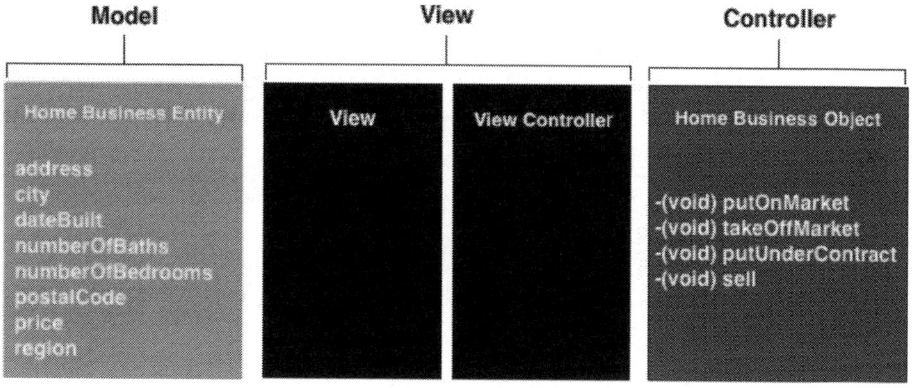

Figure 11.33 The MVC design pattern.

- **Model** – The business entity is the Model in the MVC pattern. The properties of the business entity contain information that comprises the app's data.

- **View** – Both the View and the View Controller are user-interface objects and are the View in MVC. All UI-specific code goes in the view controller.

- **Controller** – The business-object controller is the Controller in the MVC pattern. All core logic goes into the business-object controller.

For each business entity you create for your app, you can create an associated business controller. For example, in Figure 11.34, for every business entity, there s a corresponding business object. The CustomerEntity class has a Customer business object, the ShoppingCartEntity class has a ShoppingCart business object, and so on.

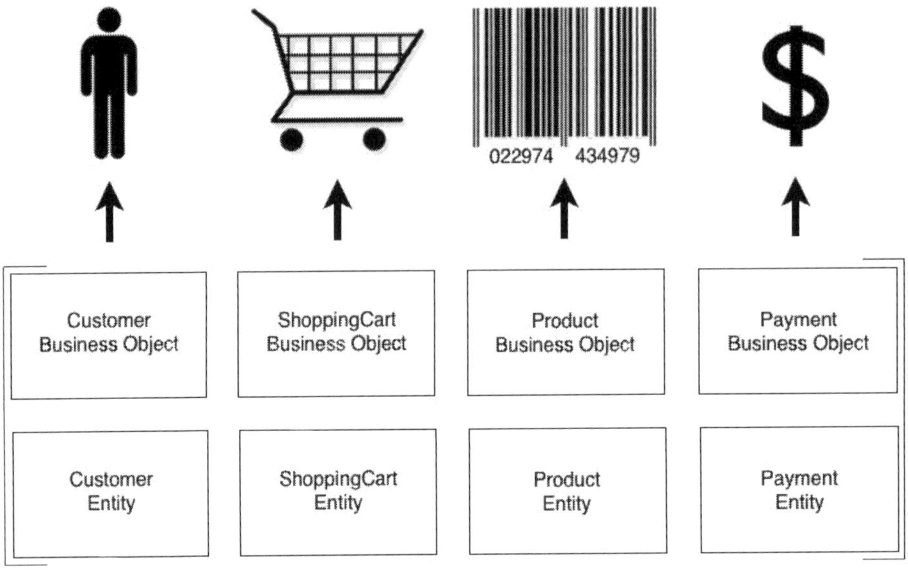

Figure 11.34 For each business entity in your app, you can create a corresponding business controller.

As already mentioned, the entity class models a real- world entity's attributes by means of properties. The associated business-controller object models its behavior by means of methods.

Business controllers can also be used to retrieve and update entity objects. Unfortunately, Apple's default core-data model places the business entity retrieval and update code in the view controller. As you might imagine, this is a bad design because it ties your app's data access to the user interface. Placing your app's data-access logic in the business controller allows you to use your business-controller objects from any user interface. You will learn more about this in *Chapter 12: Working With Core Data.*

Summary

- You will save yourself, time, energy, and cost by creating an app with a solid architecture.
- Design patterns provide common solutions to app design problems.
- The Model-View-Controller, or MVC, design pattern helps you separate the main parts of your app into proper boundaries so it is easier to design, enhance, and maintain.
- In the Model-View-Controller design pattern:
  - **Model** is your app's data and is usually comprised of business entities.
  - **View** is the user interface and is comprised of views and view controllers.
  - **Controller** is your app's core logic and data- access code that resides in business controllers.
- Apple's implementation of MVC in iOS app development tends to create apps that muddy the lines between Model, View, and Controller.
- The View Controller is in reality a user-interface object.
- A strong link between classes is known as "tight coupling" in object-oriented programming terminology.
- Only user-interface-specific code should be placed in the view controller.
- Your app's core logic should be placed in business- controller objects.
- Creating business objects help you bridge the *semantic gap*. The semantic gap is the difference between real-world entities and how you model, or describe, these objects in your software applications.
- You will find that when you narrow the semantic gap by creating business objects that represent real-world entities, your apps are much easier to conceive, design, build, maintain, and extend.

- Another benefit of using business objects is it helps you avoid playing the game of "where's the code?" When your core-logic code is raised out of the weeds of the user interface and into business objects, it's far easier to find the code you want.
- You can add properties to the View Controller that reference business-controller objects.
- A business object knows nothing about the user interface in which it's being used. Within the business-object properties and methods, there is no reference at all to any user-interface element.
- Core Data entity objects are half of the business- object picture. They contain attributes that describe real-world entities. Business controllers are the other half of the business-object picture. They are used to model the behavior of a real-world entity.
- For each business entity you create for your app, you can create an associated business controller.
- Business controllers can also be used to retrieve and update entity objects.

Chapter 12: Working With Core Data

Core Data is the technology that allows you to store and retrieve information on an iOS device. Although it is an advanced technology often difficult to grasp, this chapter helps simplify and encapsulate Core Data so mere mortals can easily use it.

Sections in This Chapter

Core Data is the technology Apple provides to save and retrieve information on an iOS device. It's a great technology, but out of the box, Core Data can be challenging to learn and use.

In this chapter, we'll take a look at Core Data's moving parts, and then we will tame the beast! In the process, we will convert **iDeliverMobile** from a prototype app to a dynamic app using Core Data to display entities retrieved from a database.

Modeling Entities

As mentioned in the previous chapter, your app's data usually takes the form of entities, which are the Model in the Model-View-Controller design pattern. Usually an entity has properties that mirror the attributes of a real- world object.

In iOS apps, you use an entity data model to define the entities used in your app. For example, the entity data model in Figure 12.1 describes a **ShipmentEntity** and **DeliveryStatusEntity** as well as the relationship between these two entities. In this chapter you will learn to design entities using an entity data model and generate Swift classes from these entities.

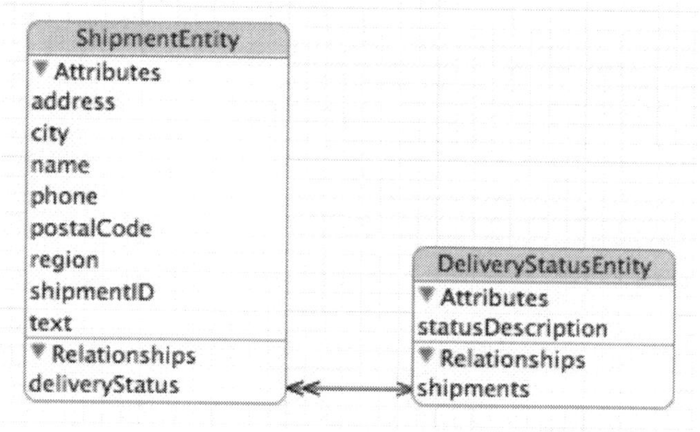

Figure 12.1 An entity data model allows you to visually design your app's entities.

Object-Relational Mapping

Core Data provides ***object-relational mapping*** (ORM) for your iOS apps. This means that Core Data converts your entities into information that can be stored in a database. This allows you to save, retrieve, update, and delete entities without having to learn a database programming language.

The database you use on iOS devices is SQLite, one of the most widely used databases in the world. It's used in Android devices, Microsoft's Windows Phone 8, RIM's Blackberry, and Nokia's Maemo. For more information on SQLite, check out this link: *http://www.sqlite.org/about.html*

Core Data maps each type of entity in your app to its own database table. For example, an **ShipmentEntity** is stored in a table named **ZSHIPMENTENTITY**, and a **CustomerEntity** is stored in a **ZCUSTOMERENTITY** table. Each row in a table represents an individual entity and each entity attribute is represented by a table column.

For example, the **CustomerEntity** object in Figure 12.2 has **name**, **phone**, and **email** properties that contain the following values:

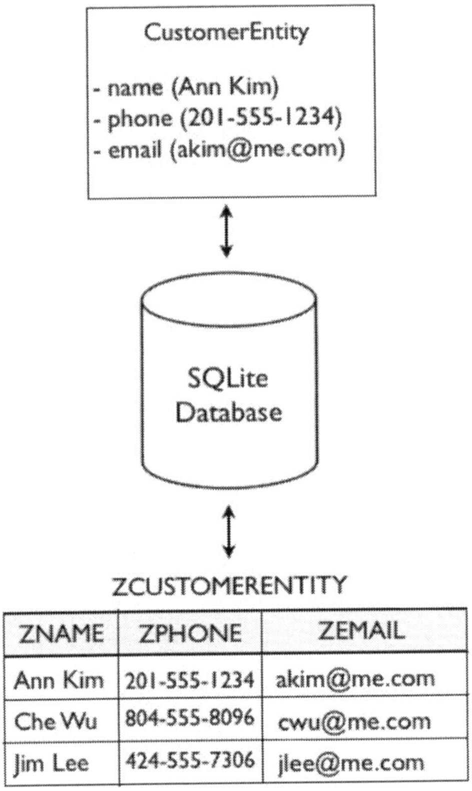

Figure 12.2 Core Data maps entity objects to rows in a database table.

- **name** - Ann Kim
- **phone** - 201-555-1234
- **email** - akim@me.com

When you ask Core Data to save this entity, it stores the entity as a row in the **ZCUSTOMERENTITY** table in the SQLite database. The **name** property value is stored in the **ZNAME** column, the **phone** property value is stored in the **ZPHONE** column, and the **email** property value is stored in the **ZEMAIL** column. The **ZCUSTOMERENTITY** table contains three rows, each representing a unique **CustomerEntity**.

You will get a first hand look at how this mapping works later in this chapter.

Working With the Object Context

NSManagedObjectContext is the primary Core Data class you interact with. You call methods on the object context that retrieve, insert, update, and delete entities. The object context tracks all the entities you retrieve, create and change.

The object context takes an all-or-nothing approach to updating entities. When you send it a **saveEntities** message, it saves all entities that have been created or changed. It doesn't offer the option to save changes to an individual entity.

Behind the scenes, the object context uses a ***persistent store coordinator*** (a **NSPersistentCoordinator** instance), to communicate with the SQLite database. It knows the name and location of the database and uses an instance of the **NSManagedObjectModel** class to find out about all the entities in the data model and their relationships.

Out-of-the-Box Core Data Model

The out-of-the-box Core Data model leaves something to be desired. Figure 12.3 provides an overview of the default model that is generated when creating a new project with the **Use Core Data** option.

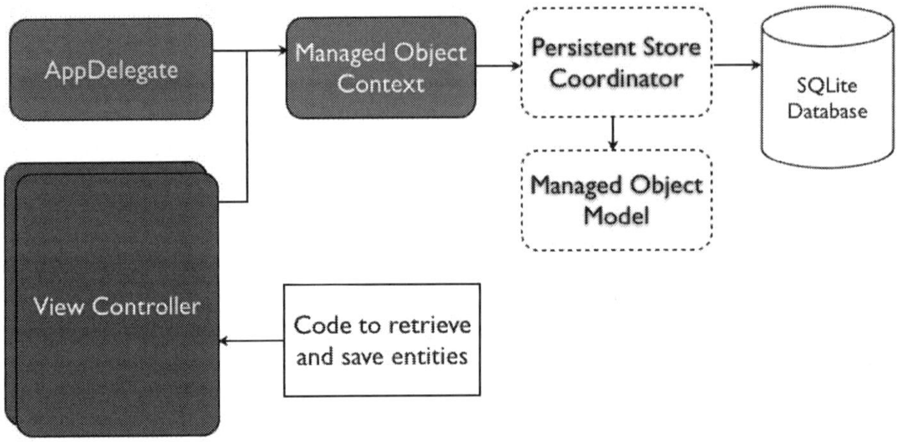

Figure 12.3 The out-of-the-box Core Data Model.

The **AppDelegate** object holds a reference to a **Managed Object Context**. The object context uses a **Persistent Store Coordinator**, which in turn uses a **Managed Object Model** to retrieve and update entities from the SQLite database.

In this default architecture, a single object context attached to the **AppDelegate** is referenced by all view controllers in your app. As each view controller is created, a reference to the **AppDelegate**'s object context is passed to the controller, which it then stores in its own **managedObjectContext** property.

Apple recommends that you put code in your view controllers that sends messages to the object context to create, retrieve, update, and delete entities.

The problem with this approach is that it breaks the rule of separating your app into three distinct sections:

- Data
- User Interface
- Core Logic

or, more formally, into Model, View, and Controller.

As you have learned, the view controller is part of the user interface. The only code that belongs in the view controller is code that has something to do with the user interface. Code that is used to retrieve, manipulate, and update entities does *not* belong in the view controller.

This isn't just ivory tower thinking. Putting your entity manipulation code in the user interface has practical implications that can make it difficult to extend your app in the future. For example, if you enhance your app at a later date to save and retrieve entities to and from the Internet, you're going to have to find all the places that use this Core Data logic and change them.

What you need is a place to put this code that ***encapsulates***, or hides, it from the user interface.

Improved Core Data Model

So where should you put your entity manipulation code? Put it in a business controller class.

Figure 12.4 shows an improved Core Data model where the **Managed Object Context** is attached to a **Business Controller**, and the code to retrieve and save entities is stored in the methods of the **Business Controller**.

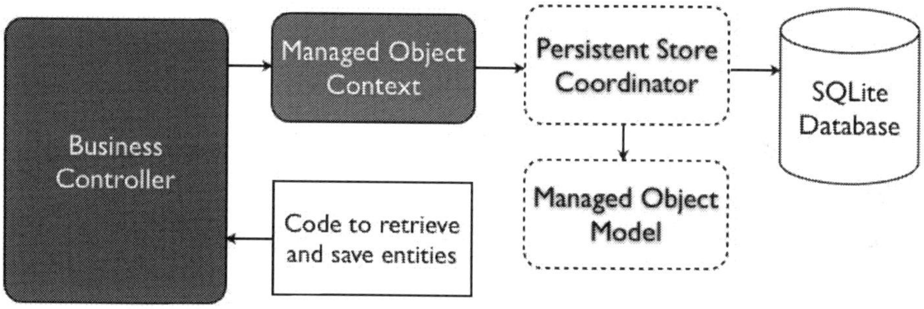

Figure 12.4 An improved Core Data model.

What are the benefits of this approach?

First of all, it encapsulates the entity manipulation code within the business controller. You can now pass messages from within the view controller to the business controller to retrieve and update entities, and the mechanics of how those entities are retrieved and updated are hidden from the user interface. This means you can change where entities are stored at a later date without affecting the user interface.

A good measure of whether you have done your job as an architect is how easy it is to make changes to your app. If you get a change request and realize you are going to have to revamp your entire app to implement that change, you haven't done your job well! In contrast, if changes are isolated to just one or a few areas, you can pat yourself on the back for a job well done.

Another benefit of this model is reusability. When you place your entity retrieval, manipulation, and update code in the methods of a business controller, you can call those same methods from multiple view controllers and even reference them from multiple Xcode projects.

There is another benefit to this architecture that is not readily apparent. Remember, saving data with an object context is an all-or-nothing proposition. When you ask it to save changes, it saves changes to *all* entities in your app. When each business controller has its own object context, it allows finer control over when and how entities get saved to the database. For example, a **Customer** business controller and an **Order** business controller, can each have their own object context. This allows you to retrieve and update **CustomerEntity** objects without affecting **OrderEntity** objects.

However, there are times when you *do* want or need multiple business controllers to share the same object context. As you shall see, this architecture also allows you to do just that.

Adding Core Data to a Project

Since I recommend you don't use Xcode's **Use Core Data** option when creating a new project, how do you add Core Data components to a project? Here are the main steps you need to perform:

1. Add **CoreData.framework** to your project.
2. Add a **Business Layer** group in the Project Navigator.
3. Add an entity data model and **mmBusinessObject** class to the **Business Layer** group.

As promised in *Book 1: Diving Into iOS*, we are going to convert the iDeliverMobile prototype project into a real app. The first step in doing this is to add Core Data to the project:

1. In Xcode, open the **iDeliverMobileCD** project in this book's sample code.

2. In the Project Navigator, select the very first project node (Figure 12.5) to display the Project Editor.

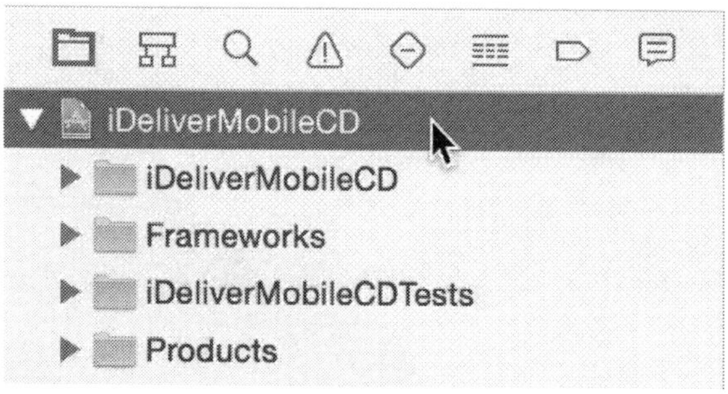

Figure 12.5 Select the first node in the Project Navigator.

3. Select the Project Editor's **General** tab and scroll down to the **Linked Frameworks and Libraries** section. Click the plus (+) button to launch the Choose Frameworks and Libraries dialog.

4. Scroll down, select **CoreData.framework**, and then click the **Add** button (Figure 12.6) to add the framework to the project.

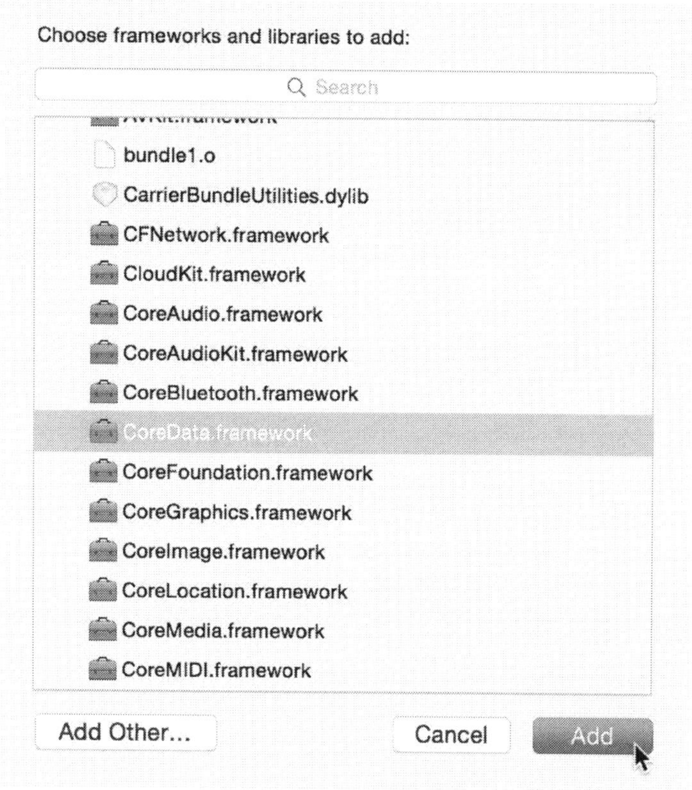

*Figure 12.6 Add **CoreData.framework** to the project.*

5. This adds **CoreData.framework** just below the **Frameworks** group (Figure 12.7).

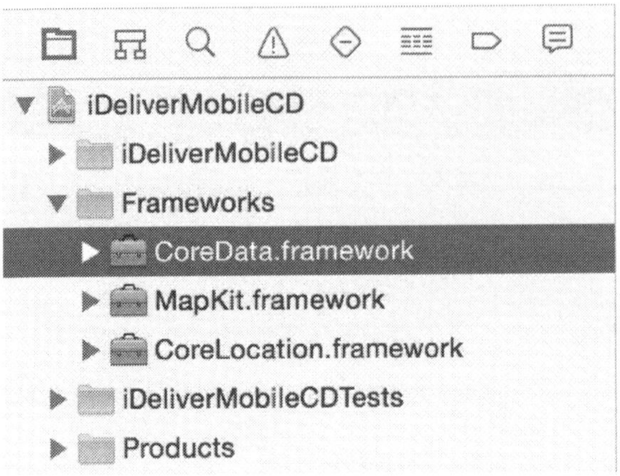

Figure 12.7 The newly added CoreData framework

6. Now let's add a **Business Layer** group to the Project Navigator, which will be used to store our business classes. To do this, right-click the **iDeliverMobileCD** group folder in the Project Navigator, and then select **New Group** from the shortcut menu. This adds a new group to the Project Navigator (Figure 12.8).
7. Next, enter the text **Business Layer** to specify the name of the new group and press **Return**.
8. Finally, let's add an entity data model to the new **Business Layer** group. Right click the **Business Layer** group and select **New File...** from the popup menu.

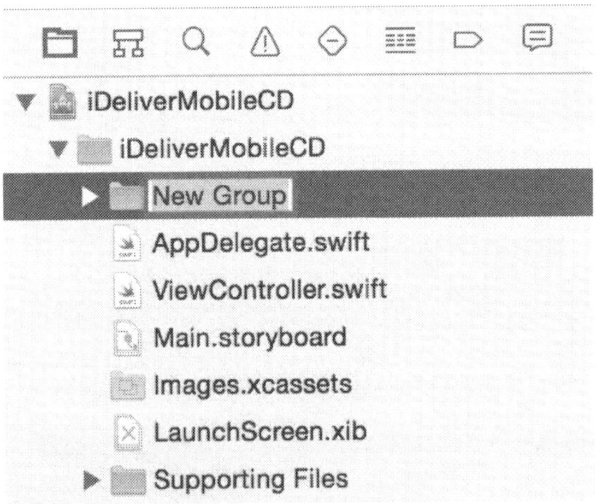

Figure 12.8 Add a new group to the Project Navigator.

9. On the left side of the New File dialog under the **iOS** section, select **Core Data**, and then on the right side of the dialog, select the **Data Model** template as shown in Figure 12.9.

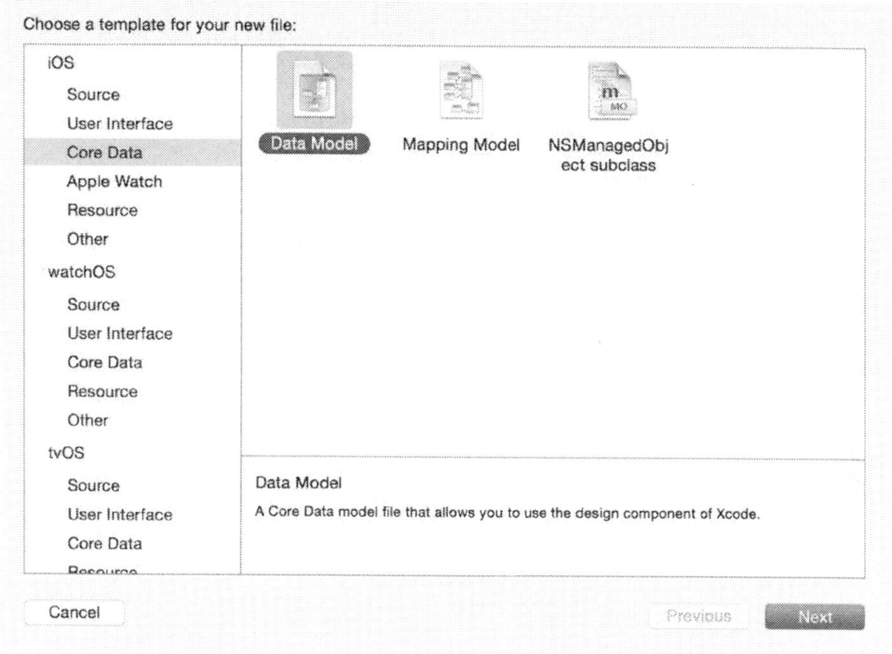

*Figure 12.9 Select the **Data Model** file template.*

10. Click the **Next** button, and change the file name to **iDeliverMobileCD.xcdatamodeld**.

11. Click the **Create** button to add the new entity data model to the project and display it in the Xcode editor region (Figure 12.10).

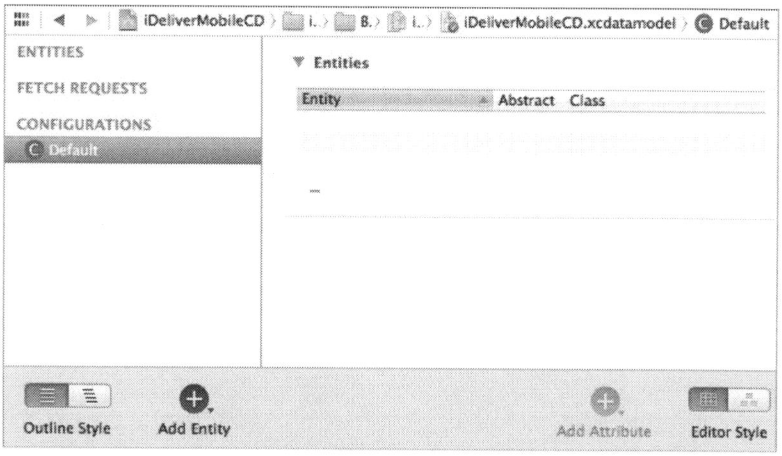

Figure 12.10 The new entity data model

Designing Entities in the Data Model

By default, there are no entities included in the entity data model. In the toolbar at the bottom of the entity data model (Figure 12.10) is an **Add Entity** button that allows you to add new entities to the model. There is also an **Add Attribute** button that allows you to add attributes to the currently selected entity (the button is disabled if no entity is selected).

There is also an **Editor Style** button group that allows you to switch between **Table** and **Graph** styles. After we add some entities, I'll show you the difference between these two viewing styles.

Adding Entities to the Model

In our quest to turn **iDeliverMobileCD** into a working app, we will add a **ShipmentEntity** to the model, which can be used to represent the shipments to be delivered.

A list of shipments is displayed in the **Deliveries** scene of the app as shown in Figure 12.11. Currently, this is a static list created at design time. You are going to change this to a list that is dynamically filled with **ShipmentEnity** objects at run time.

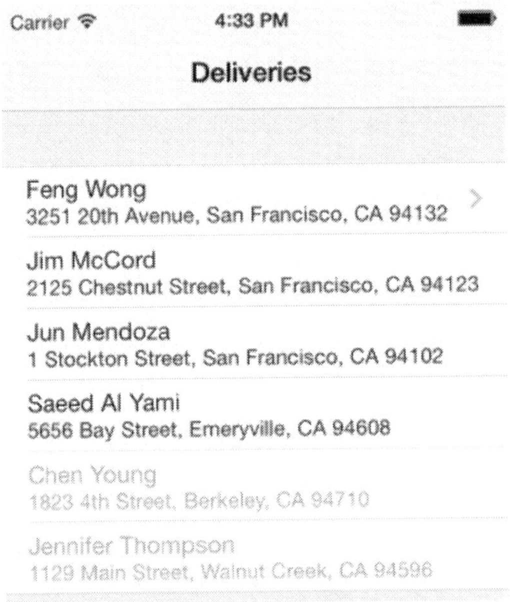

*Figure 12.11 The **Deliveries** scene.*

The first step is creating the **ShipmentEntity**:

1. With the entity data model selected in the Project Navigator and the Entity Data Model Editor open in the design surface, click the **Add Entity** button at the bottom left of the entity data model. This adds a new entity under the **Entities** section in the panel on the left (Figure 12.12).

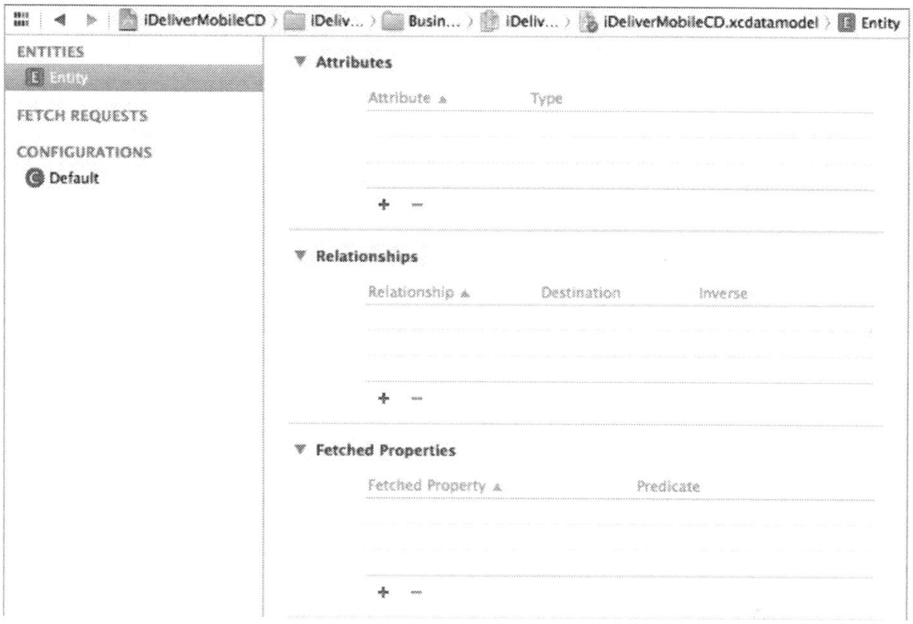

Figure 12.12 Add a new entity to the entity data model.

2. In the panel on the left, double-click the **Entity** name to put it into edit mode and change the name of the entity to **ShipmentEntity** and press **Enter**. You can also change the entity name in the Data Model Inspector, which you can see by clicking the button on the right in the Inspectors toolbar as shown in Figure 12.13.

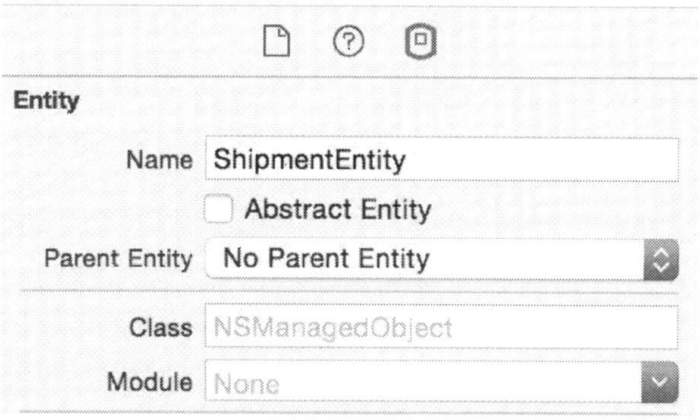

Figure 12.13 The top section of the Data Model Inspector.

3. Now let's add an attribute to the **ShipmentEntity**. Click the **Add Attribute** button at the bottom of the entity data model. This adds an attribute in the **Attributes** section of the entity (Figure 12.14).

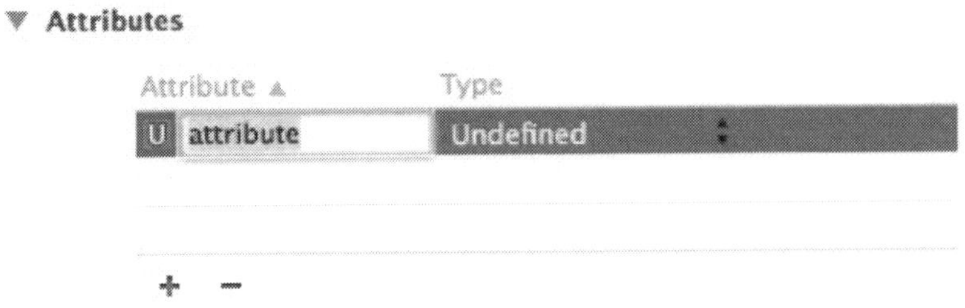

Figure 12.14 The newly added attribute.

Although you can change the name and type of the attribute directly in the model, I find it easier to set this information in the Data Model Inspector as shown in Figure 12.15. As you can see, it contains different settings when an entity's attribute is selected in the Data Model Editor.

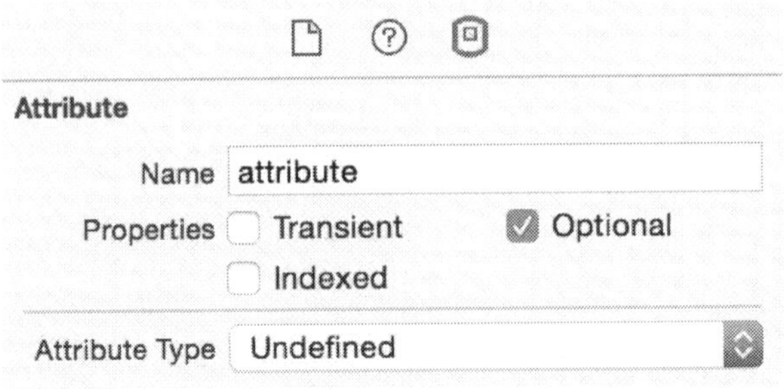

Figure 12.15 The Data Model Inspector for attributes.

Entity Attribute Settings

Let's take a brief detour to explain each of the entity attribute settings:

- **Name** - The name of the entity attribute. This should be ***camel cased*** since Xcode will generate a property name from this attribute.

- **Transient** - When this option is selected, it indicates the attribute value is generated at run time rather than retrieved and stored to the database. For one example of using transient attributes, see this link: *https://developer.apple.com/library/mac/#documentation/Cocoa/Conceptual/CoreData/ Articles/cdNSAttributes.html*

- **Optional** - When this option is selected (it is by default), it indicates the attribute is not required to have a value. For example, in an **Address** entity, you may specify that an **AddressLine2** attribute is optional since most addresses don't have a second address line.

- **Indexed** - Specifies if the corresponding database column is indexed. You should typically select this option for columns on which you need to perform searches. For more information on database indexes, check out this link: *http://en.wikipedia.org/wiki/ Index_(database)*

- **Attribute Type** - Specifies the type of values the attribute holds. The options are:

    - **Undefined** - (default) Unless you mark an attribute as **Transient**, you must choose some other type for the attribute.

    - **Integer 16** - Stores values between -32,768 and 32,767.

    - **Integer 32** - Stores values between -2,147,483,648 and 2,147,483,647.

    - **Integer 64** - Stores values between -9,223,372,036,854,775,808 and 9,223,372,036,854,775,807.

    - **Decimal** - 128-bit fixed-point values (a fixed number of digits after the decimal point). It has more precision and a smaller range than double and float, making it a good choice for financial calculations.

    - **Double** - Stores 64-bit floating-point values (there are no fixed number of digits before or after the decimal point, so the decimal point can float) with 15 digits of precision.

    - **Float** - Stores 32-bit floating-point values with 7 digits of precision.

    - **String** - Stores text values.

    - **Boolean** - Stores YES and NO values.

    - **Date** - Stores dates and timestamps.

    - **Binary Data** - Stores binary data such as images.

- **Transformable** - Works in conjunction with value transformers to create attributes that store a custom type that is not one of the standard types. Check out this link for more information: *https://developer.apple.com/library/mac/#documentation/Cocoa/Conceptual/CoreData/Articles/cdNSAttributes.html.*

If you select one of the numeric attribute types, you see additional **Validation** settings (Figure 12.16). These settings allow you to constrain the value that can be stored in a particular attribute. If a validation rule is broken, an error is displayed when the entity is stored to the database.

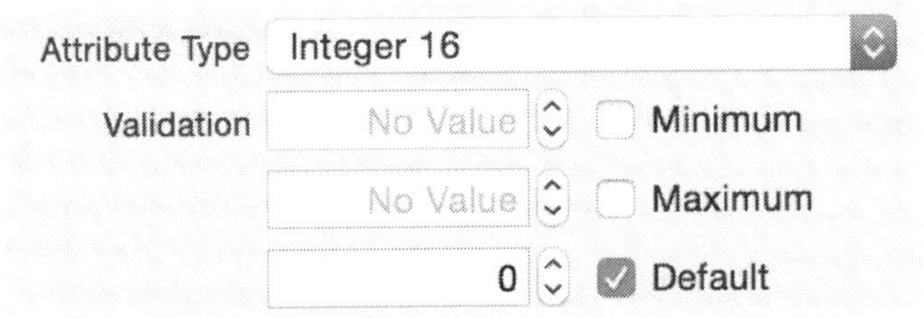

Figure 12.16 Numeric attribute settings.

- **Minimum** - Specifies the minimum value that can be stored in the attribute.

- **Maximum** - Specifies the maximum value that can be stored in the attribute.

- **Default** - Specifies the default value of the attribute when you create a new entity.

If you select the **String** attribute type, you see the additional settings shown in Figure 12.17.

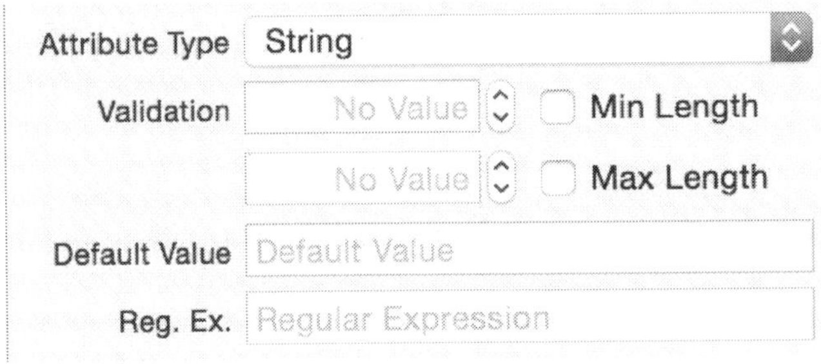

Figure 12.17 String attribute settings.

- **Min Length** - Specifies the minimum length of the string that can be stored in the attribute.

- **Max Length** - Specifies the maximum length of the string that can be stored in the attribute.

- **Default** - Specifies the default value of the attribute when you create a new entity.

- **Reg. Ex.** - Specifies a *regular expression* used to validate the string value. A regular expression provides a way to check the string for specific characters or patterns of characters. For example, you can use a regular expression to validate an email address or URL.

If you select the **Binary Data** attribute type, you see additional **Options** (Figure 12.18).

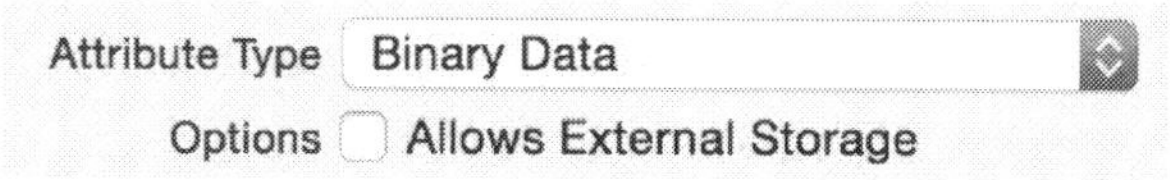

Figure 12.18 Binary Data attribute settings.

- **Allows External Storage** - Selecting this option indicates the binary data can be stored outside of the database. Core Data uses the following rule of thumb for storage based on the size of the binary data:

  - < 100KB - Store directly in the database table.

  - < 1MB - Store in a separate table attached by means of a relationship.

  - > 1MB - Store on disk outside the database, and reference it from Core Data.

Creating ShipmentEntity Attributes

Now that you have an understanding of the various attribute settings, it's time to add attributes to the **ShipmentEntity**.

To remind you of the attributes that need to be added to the **ShipmentEntity**, look at the **Shipment** scene shown in Figure 12.19.

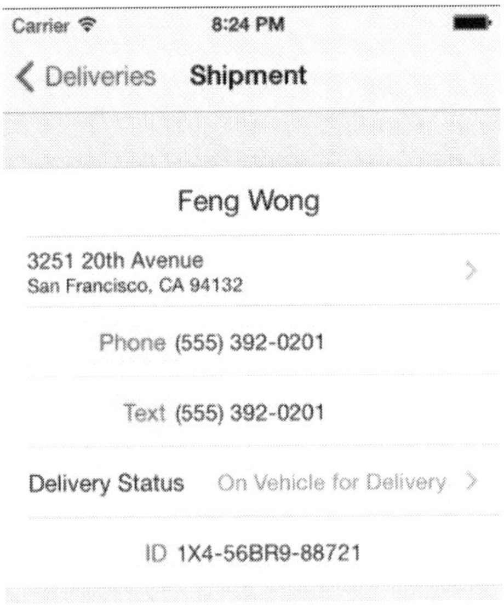

*Figure 12.19 The **Shipment** scene displays a single **ShipmentEntity**.*

The following steps add an attribute to the **ShipmentEntity** for all the information shown in the Shipment scene.

1. In the **iDeliverMobileCD** project, select the **iDeliverMobileCD** entity data model.
2. In the Entity Data Model Editor, make sure the **ShipmentEntity** is selected in the left panel, and select the attribute you added earlier in this chapter (Figure 12.20).

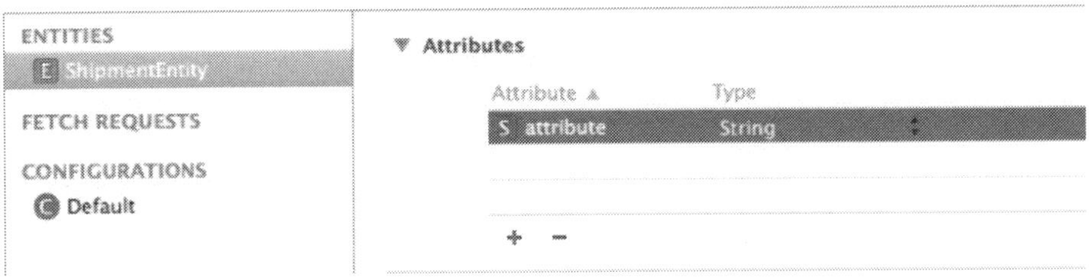

*Figure 12.20 The **ShipmentEntity**'s attribute.*

3. In the Data Model Inspector, set the following attributes as shown in Figure 12.21.

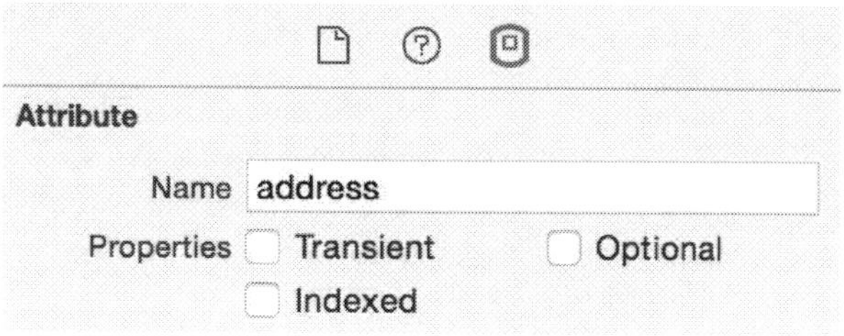

Figure 12.21 The address attribute's settings.

- Set the **Name** to **address** and press **Return**.
- Uncheck the **Optional** check box.
- Set the **Attribute Type** to **String**.

4. Let's add more attributes to **ShipmentEntity**. When you're finished, the entity attributes in the Data Model Editor should look like Figure 12.22.

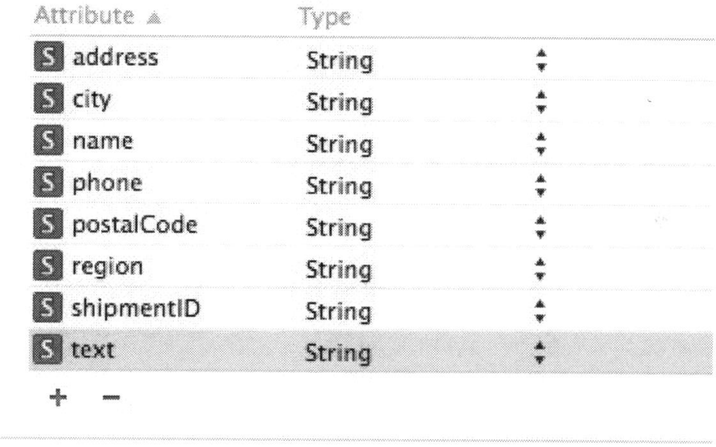

*Figure 12.22 **ShipmentEntity** attributes.*

For each attribute listed below, first click the **Add Attribute** button at the bottom of the Data Model Editor, and then set the specified name. Uncheck the **Optional** check box for each attribute and set the **Attribute Type** to **String**:

- **city**
- **name**
- **phone**

- **postalCode**
- **region**
- **shipmentID**
- **text**

Creating a DeliveryStatusEntity

In Figure 12.19, the second cell from the bottom specifies the **Delivery Status** for the shipment. So why didn't we create a **deliveryStatus** attribute to store the current delivery status? In the next section, we're going to let the Entity Data Model create the attribute for us.

First, we need to create a **DeliveryStatusEntity** for the list of delivery status options in the **Delivery Status** scene (Figure 12.23).

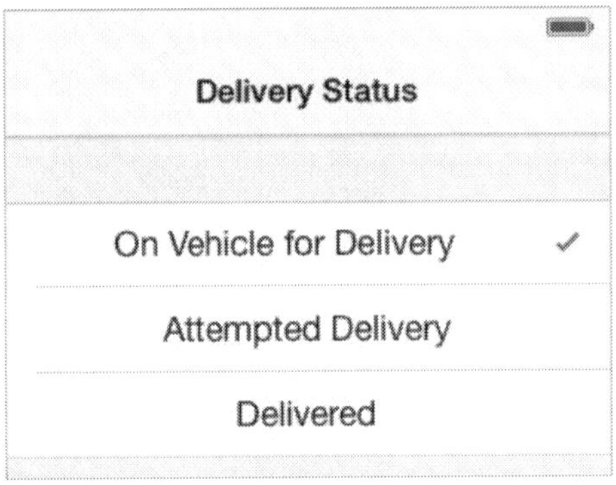

*Figure 12.23 The **Delivery Status** scene.*

1. Select the **iDeliverMobileCD** entity data model in the Project Navigator if it's not already selected.

2. At the bottom of the Data Model Editor, click the **Add Entity** button to add a new entity to the model.

3. In the panel on the left side of the Data Model Editor, change the name of the new entity to **DeliveryStatusEntity** and then press **return**.

4. This entity only has one attribute, so it's very easy to add. With the **DeliveryStatusEntity** still selected, click the **Add Attribute** button.

5. In the Data Model Inspector, set the following attributes. When you're finished, the Data Model Editor should look like Figure 12.24.

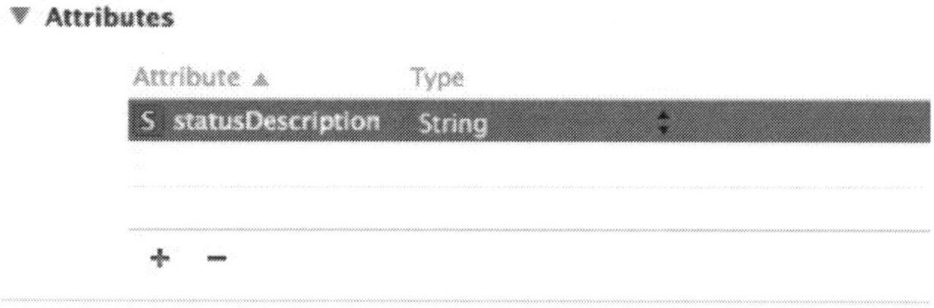

Figure 12.24 ***DeliveryStatusEntity*** *attribute.*

- Set the **Name** to **statusDescription.**
- Uncheck the **Optional** check box.
- Set the **Attribute Type** to **String**.

Data Model Editor Styles

Up to this point, we have done all of our work with the editor set to Table style. Now that there are two entities on the model, it's a good time to view the model in Graph style. To do this, click the right button in the **Editor Style** button group at the bottom of the Data Model Editor. At first, the **DeliveryStatusEntity** is positioned on top of the **ShipmentEntity**. Just click it and drag it to the right. When you do this, you will see the entities displayed as shown in Figure 12.25.

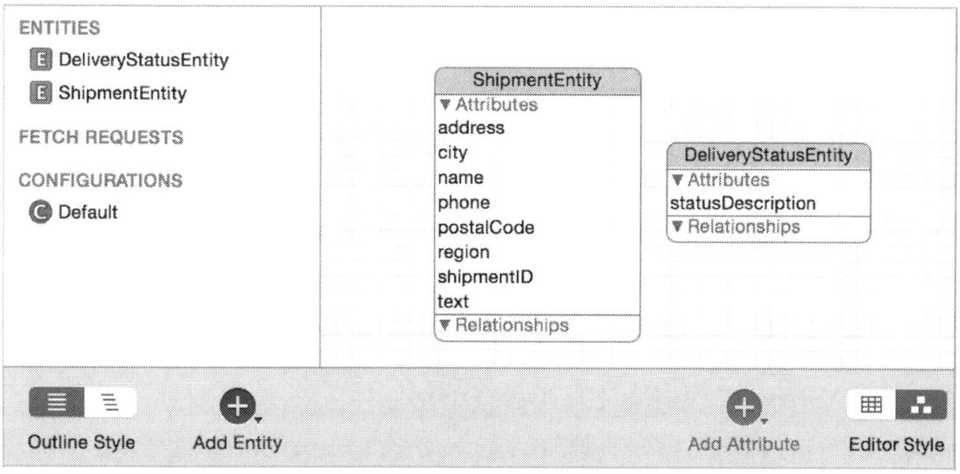

Figure 12.25 The Data Model Editor in Graph style.

You can add entities and attributes in either Table or Graph style, so choose whichever style you prefer to work in.

Personally, I find value in viewing the entities in Graph style because it gives you a more visual depiction of the entities you are creating. It reinforces the concept that you are creating entities that will become objects you can work with in your app.

Entity Relationships

Core Data provides the option to create relationships between entities on your data model.

Relationships can be useful between entities such as the **ShipmentEntity** and **DeliveryStatusEntity**. Creating a relationship in the model between these entities automatically adds a **deliveryStatus** attribute to the **ShipmentEntity**.

Creating relationships also simplifies the code you write when getting and setting the **deliveryStatus** for the **ShipmentEntity**. If you don't use a relationship, you must add a unique ID attribute to the **DeliveryStatusEntity** and save that unique ID in the **ShipmentEntity**'s **deliveryStatus** attribute.

In contrast, when you set up a relationship between these two entities, you simply store a **deliveryStatusEntity** in the **ShipmentEntity**'s **deliveryStatus** property, and the unique ID is automatically handled by Core Data.

It's also useful that entity relationships are usually two- way. For example, in the iDeliverMobileCD app, you can create a relationship from the **ShipmentEntity** to the **DeliveryStatusEntity** and an inverse relationship from the **DeliveryStatusEntity** to the **ShipmentEntity**. The inverse relationship allows you to search for all the **ShipmentEntities** with a specific status.

The Downside of Relationships

There is one major downside to setting relationships in the entity data model. *All entities in a relationship must be retrieved from a single object context if you want to update them later on*!

So, if you retrieve **ShipmentEntity** objects from one object context and **DeliveryStatusEntity** objects from a different object context and then try to save changes to either entity, you will get this run-time error:

"Illegal attempt to establish a relationship between objects in different contexts."

What's the problem with retrieving different types of entities from the same object context?

Remember that the object context saves entities in an all-or-nothing fashion. If the two types of entities are in a close relationship where they are normally saved together, as is the case with **ShipmentEntity** and **DeliveryStatusEntity**, this isn't a problem.

However, if you create relationships between all entities, then all types of entities must be retrieved from the same object context, and you lose the ability to update one type of entity at a time. When you save changes to one type of entity and tell the object context to perform a save, it automatically saves changes to *all* entities.

Given the pros and cons of creating relationships in a data model, I will show you how to create a relationship between **ShipmentEntity** and **DeliveryStatusEntity** and then I'll show you how core data works when you don't create a relationship between entities.

Types of Relationships

There are two main types of relationships in Core Data:

1. To-One
2. To-Many

In a To-One relationship, an entity holds a reference to a single entity of another type. For example, **ShipmentEntity** has a To-One relationship to the **DeliveryStatusEntity** because, in the real world, a shipment can only have one status at a time.

In a To-Many relationship, an entity references multiple entities of another type. For example, **CustomerEntity** has a To-Many relationship with **OrderEntity** because, in the real world, a customer can have many orders.

Creating Relationships

Let's create a relationship between the entities now.

1. In the **iDeliverMobileCD** project, select the **iDeliverMobileCD** entity data model in the Project Navigator, and make sure you are viewing the model in Graph style (it's easier in this style).

2. Hold the **control** key down, then click on the **ShipmentEntity** and drag to the **DeliveryStatusEntity** (Figure 12.26).

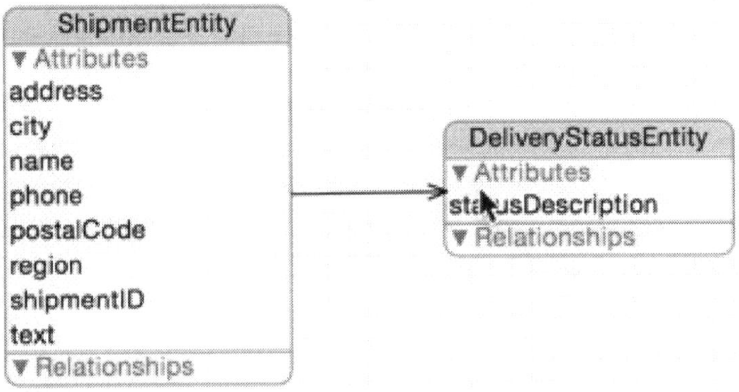

Figure 12.26 Creating a relationship.

3. When you see the arrow between the two entities, let go of the mouse button and Xcode creates a relationship between the two entities (Figure 12.27).

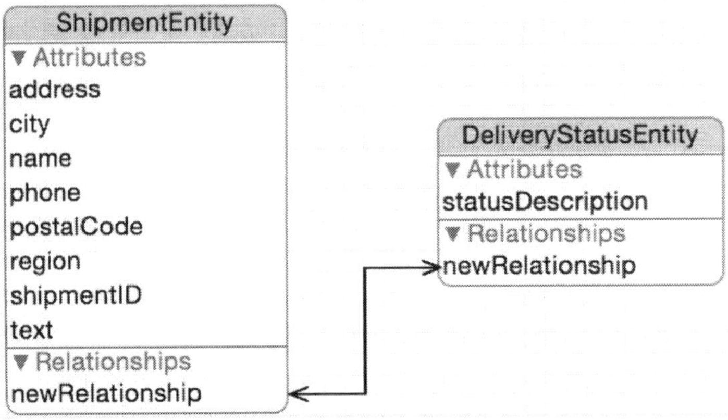

Figure 12.27 The newly created relationship.

Notice there is an arrow at each end of the relationship. This indicates a two-way relationship:

- From **ShipmentEntity** to **DeliveryStatusEntity** and
- From **DeliveryStatusEntity** to **ShipmentEntity**.

There is also a new **Relationships** section at the bottom of each entity that contains an attribute named **newRelationship** (we'll change them to something more meaningful). As you can see, creating a relationship adds a new attribute to the entity that can be used to navigate the relationship.

4. Let's go back to Table mode to continue the relationship setup. To do this, click the left button in the **Editor Style** button group at the bottom of the Data Model Editor and then select **ShipmentEntity** in the pane on the left. You should see the relationship shown in Figure 12.28.

Figure 12.28 The new relationship.

5. Select the relationship and then go to the Data Model Inspector and change the **Name** of the relationship to **deliveryStatus**. When you're finished, the relationship should look like Figure 12.29.

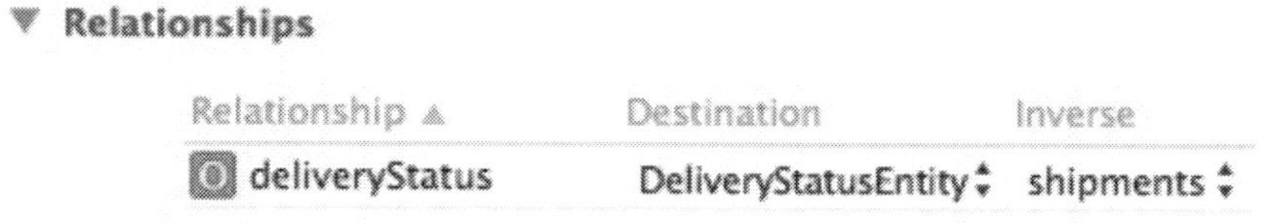

Figure 12.29 The newly renamed relationship.

6. Now select the **DeliveryStatusEntity** in the pane on the left, and then select the relationship. Afterward, go to the Data Model Inspector and change the **Name** of the relationship to **shipments**.

Now that the relationships have meaningful names, it's easier to understand the settings that can be applied to a relationship. Let's take a quick detour to examine these.

Relationship Settings

To examine the **deliveryStatus** relationship, select the **ShipmentEntity** in the pane on the left and then select relationship in the entity data model table. In the Data Model Inspector, you can see the settings shown in Figure 12.30.

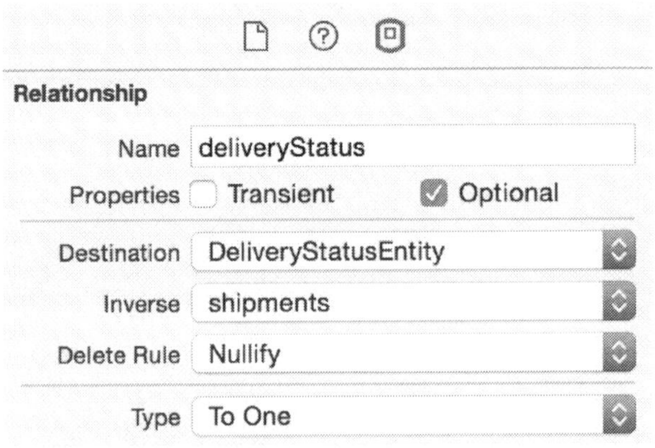

Figure 12.30 Entity relationship settings.

Here is a description of the entity relationship settings:

- **Name** - Specifies the name of the relationship. The name should be descriptive of the relationship so you can immediately understand what it represents. For example, we named the **ShipmentEntity's** relationship **deliveryStatus**. This name precisely indicates that the relationship depicts the delivery status of the shipment.

- **Properties**

    - **Transient** - If this option is selected, the relationship does not get saved to the database. This option is typically left unchecked.

    - **Optional** - Indicates an entity does not have to be present (it can be **nil**) at the other end of the relationship. In the case of the **deliveryStatus** relationship, a **ShipmentEntity** must always have a delivery status, so the relationship isn't optional.

- **Destination** - Specifies the entity at the other end of the relationship (in this case, **DeliveryStatusEntity**). This was set automatically by Xcode when you created the relationship in the data model.

- **Inverse** - Specifies the relation (if any) coming from the destination entity.

- **Type** - You can choose either **To One** or **To Many**.

- **Arranged (Ordered)** - This option is only available for **To Many** relationships. It specifies that the list of entities is kept in the same order as records in the database. You should only choose this option if the order of entities is important, because ordered relationships are significantly less efficient.

- **Count (Minimum, Maximum)** - This option is only available for **To Many** relationships. It indicates the number of entities on the other end of the relationship. In an optional relationship, **Minimum** is always set to **Optional**.

  Although you can specify a specific number of entities on the other side of a To-Many relationship, it's unusual to do so.

- **Delete Rule** - This setting specifies what happens to entities on the other end of the relationship when an entity of this type is deleted. The four options are:

  - **No Action** - The source entity is deleted and no action is taken on entities at the other end of the relationship.

  - **Nullify** - (the default) The source entity is deleted and the entities on the other end of the relationship have their relationship set to **nil**.

  - **Cascade** - The source entity is deleted and the entities on the other end of the relationship are also deleted.

  - **Deny** - If there are any entities on the other end of the relationship, the delete request fails and no entities are deleted on either side of the relationship.

Setting Relationship Attributes

Now that you know more about relationship attributes, let's change a few settings on the two relationships in the entity data model.

1. In the **iDeliverMobileCD** project, select the **iDeliverMobileCD** entity data model in the Project Navigator and make sure you are viewing the model in Table style.

2. Select the **ShipmentEntity** in the left pane and then select the **deliveryStatus** relationship. In the Data Model Inspector, uncheck the **Optional** check box.

3. Next, select the **DeliveryStatusEntity** in the left pane, and then select the **shipments** relationship. You can leave **Optional** selected because there may not be any shipments with a particular delivery status.

4. In the Type attribute, select **To Many** since there can be many shipments with a particular delivery status.

5. Let's see how the relationships look in Graph style. At the bottom of the Data Model Editor, click the right button in the **Editor Style** button group. You will see the entities and relationships in Figure 12.31.

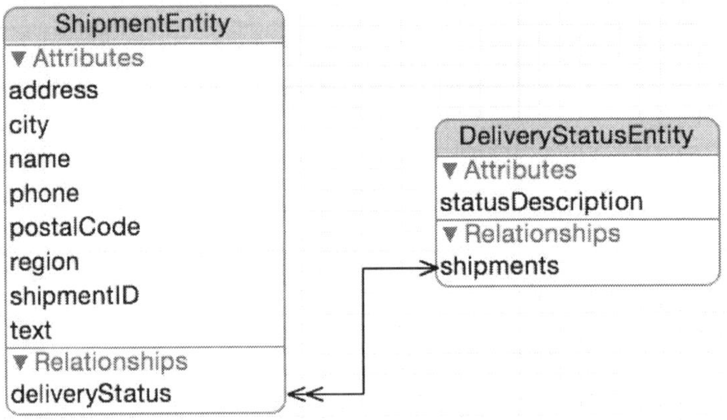

Figure 12.31 The completed relationships.

Notice in the **Relationships** section at the bottom of the **ShipmentEntity**, there is an attribute named **deliveryStatus** that can be used to navigate to the **DeliveryStatusEntity**. Because the arrow pointing to the **DeliveryStatusEntity** has a single-headed arrow, it indicates a To-One relationship.

At the bottom of the **DeliveryStatusEntity** there is an attribute named **shipments** that can be used to find all shipments related to a specific **DeliveryStatusEntity**. For example, you can have it find all **ShipmentEntity** objects that are **Undelivered**. The double-headed arrow pointing to the **ShipmentEntity** indicates a To- Many relationship.

You will get a clearer picture of how these relationships work as we use these entities later in this chapter.

Generating Entity Classes From the Data Model

It's important to note that an entity on a data model is *not* an actual Swift class. You must take an extra step to generate a class from an entity as outlined in the following steps:

1. Select the **iDeliverMobileCD** entity data model in the Project Navigator. You can view the model in either Table or Graph style.

2. From Xcode's **File** menu, select **New** > **File...**, which launches the New File dialog.

3. On the left side of the dialog under **iOS**, select **Core Data**. Then, on the right side of the dialog, select the **NSManagedObject subclass** template.

   It's a requirement that all entities used by Core Data must be a subclass of the **NSManagedObject** class.

4. Click Next, and in the next step of the dialog, make sure the **iDeliverMobileCD** data model's checkbox is selected.

5. Click **Next**, and in the next step of the dialog, select the **ShipmentEntity** and **DeliveryStatusEntity** check boxes (Figure 12.32).

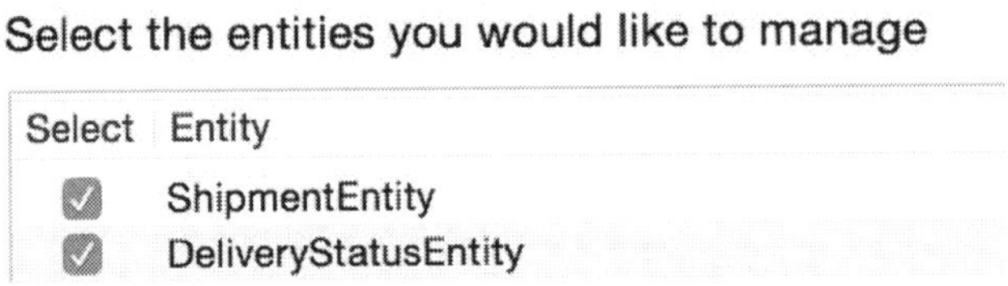

*Figure 12.32 Select **ShipmentEntity** and **DeliveryStatusEntity**.*

6. Click **Next**, and at the bottom of the Save File dialog, *uncheck* the **Use scalar properties for primitive data types** check box (Figure 12.33). When this option is selected, Xcode generates properties for your entities that are *scalar* types (such as float, double, and so on). If this option is not selected, Xcode generates properties of the type **NSNumber** instead.

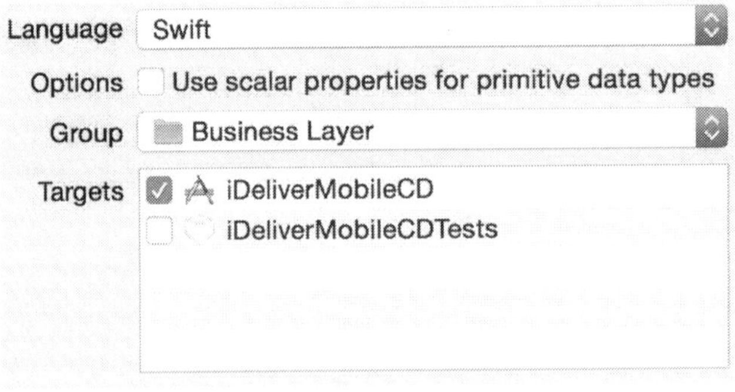

*Figure 12.33 Uncheck **Use scalar properties for primitive data types**.*

I prefer to uncheck this option because some cloud services such as Amazon Web Services can't work with scalar properties.

7. Click **Create** to create a new entity class. Xcode adds **ShipmentEntity and DeliveryStatusEntity** class files to your project (Figure 12.34).

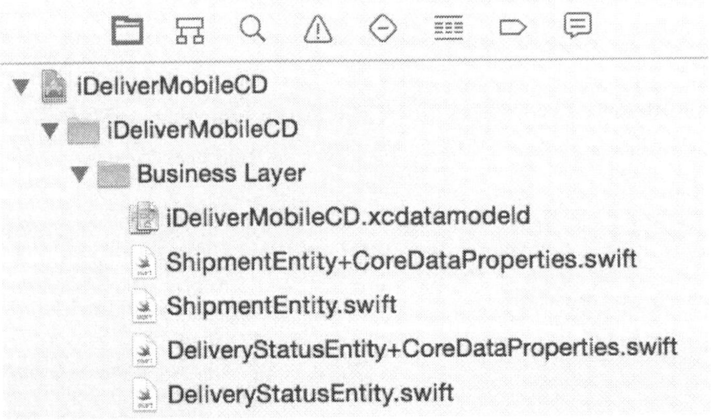

Figure 12.34 The new entity classes.

8. Let's take a closer look at the generated class files. Select the **ShipmentEntity.swift** file in the Project Navigator, and you will see the following code:

```
@objc(ShipmentEntity)
class ShipmentEntity: NSManagedObject {
// Insert code here to add functionality to
}
```

This is the main entity class file. You can add code to this file to extend the entity's functionality. If you make changes to the entity in the data model, and regenerate your entity, this code file will not be overwritten. This provides a safe haven for your custom entity code.

9. Select **ShipmentEntity+CoreDataProperties.swift** in the Project Navigator to see the following code:

```
extension ShipmentEntity {
   @NSManaged var address: String?
   @NSManaged var city: String?
   @NSManaged var name: String?
   @NSManaged var phone: String?
   @NSManaged var postalCode: String?
   @NSManaged var region: String?
   @NSManaged var shipmentID: String?
   @NSManaged var text: String?
   @NSManaged var deliveryStatus:DeliveryStatusEntity?
}
```

A property has been generated for all **ShipmentEntity** attributes including a **deliveryStatus** property that can navigate the relationship to the associated **DeliveryStatusEntity**. Note that if you regenerate your entity, this code file will be overwritten.

Each property is marked as optional even though its corresponding attribute is not Optional in the data model. That's because these properties *can* contain **nil** when an entity is first created. However, this forces you to unwrap the properties each time you access them in your app, which makes coding cumbersome.

10. Based on this, remove the question mark from the end of each property to make them non-optional.

11. Select **DeliveryStatusEntity.swift** in the Project Navigator and you will see the entity class:

```
class DeliveryStatusEntity: NSManagedObject {
// Insert code here to add functionality to
}
```

12. Select **DeliveryStatusEntity+CoreDataProperties.swift** in the Project Navigator and you will see the following code:

```
extension DeliveryStatusEntity {
    @NSManaged var statusDescription: String?
    @NSManaged var shipments: NSSet?
}
```

The new entity class has a **statusDescription** property and a **shipments** relationship property, which references **ShipmentEntity** objects at the other end of the relationship.

13. Delete the question mark from **statusDescription**, but leave it on the optional **shipments** property.

There is one other point to note. After generating an entity class, Xcode automatically sets the entity's **Class** and **Module** settings. As shown in Figure 12.35, the Class is set to the same name as the entity, and the Module is set to Current Product Module. In previous versions of Xcode, you had to set these values manually.

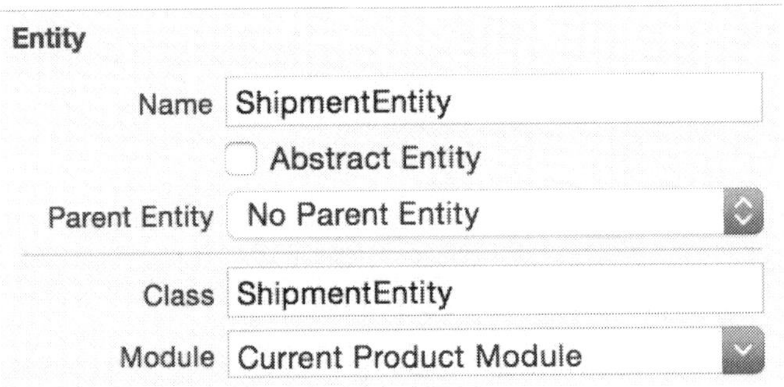

*Figure 12.35 The **Class** and **Module** are automatically set*

Now that you have learned how to design entities and generate Swift classes from those entities, it's time to learn how to manipulate entities in your app.

Manipulating Entities

In the next few sections, I'm going to describe how to work directly with Core Data objects to retrieve, create, update, and delete entities. Afterward, I'll show you how to work with the **mmBusinessObject** class that is provided with this book's sample code. This class encapsulates basic Core Data functionality to make it far easier to work with entity objects.

Retrieving Entities

There are several steps involved in retrieving entities from a data store. Here is a code block that shows a typical example of these steps:

```
// 1. Create the request object
let request = NSFetchRequest()

// 2. Set the entity type to be fetched
let entity =
NSEntityDescription.entityForName("ShipmentEntity"
, inManagedObjectContext: managedObjectContext)
    request.entity = entity

// 3. Set the predicate (optional)
let predicate = NSPredicate(format:
        "region == %@", "a")
request.predicate = predicate

// 4. Set the sort descriptor (optional)
let sortDescriptor = NSSortDescriptor(key:
   "postalCode", ascending: false)

let sortDescriptors = [sortDescriptor]
request.sortDescriptors = sortDescriptors

// 5. Execute the fetch & check for errors
do {
   list = try
   self.managedObjectContext.
```

```
    executeFetchRequest(request) as!
    Array<NSManagedObject>
}
catch let error as NSError {
    print("Fetch failed: \
    (error.localizedDescription)")
}
    return list
}
```

This code is definitely *not* trivial. Don't panic—I'll provide a *much* easier way to retrieve entities in just a bit, but here's an explanation of each step:

1. **Create the request object** - This code creates an instance of **NSFetchRequest**. The request object is configured in the next few steps and then passed to the object context to be executed.

2. **Set the entity type to be fetched** - This code may look complex, but all it does is configure the request object with the type of the entity to be retrieved (in this case, **ShipmentEntity**).

3. **Set the predicate** - This code specifies a filter, or search criteria that returns a subset of entities in the database. In this example, only **ShipmentEntity** objects from a specified **region** are retrieved. This step is optional if you want to retrieve all entities.

4. **Set the sort descriptor** - This code specifies the sort order of entities retrieved from the data store. In this example, entities are sorted by **postalCode**. You can skip this step if you don't need the entities sorted.

5. **Execute the fetch** - This code sends an **executeFetchRequest:** message to the object context, passing the request object. The entities returned from the object context are stored in an **NSMutableArray**.

   Check for errors - If an error occurs at this level, it's usually because you have set something up incorrectly in the database (versus an actual physical database error).

Creating New Entity Objects

Unlike most other classes, you don't create an instance of a Core Data entity by calling its initializer.

To create a new Core Data entity, you must call the **insertNewObjectForEntityForName:inManagedObjectContext**: method of the **NSEntityDescription** class:

```
var newEntity = NSEntityDescription.
 insertNewObjectForEntityForName("ShipmentEntity",
 inManagedObjectContext: managedObjectContext)
 as! NSManagedObject
```

When calling this method, you pass the class of the entity you want to create as well a reference to the object context the new entity is to be associated with.

Deleting Entities

Deleting a Core Data entity is straightforward. All you have to do is send call the **deleteObject**: method on an object context, passing the entity to be deleted:

```
managedObjectContext.deleteObject(entity)
```

Calling the **deleteObject:** method doesn't immediately delete the entity from the data store—it simply marks the entity for deletion. Entities that are marked for deletion are physically removed from the data store the next time the object context saves changes to entities.

Saving Entities

To save all the changes to entities that have been created and retrieved from a particular object context, you call the object context's a **save:** method. For example:

```
if managedObjectContext.hasChanges {
   do {
      try managedObjectContext.save()
   }
   catch let error as NSError {
      saveState = SaveState.Error
```

```
            saveMessage = error.localizedDescription
        }
        saveState = SaveState.SaveComplete
        saveMessage = nil
    }
    else {
        saveState = SaveState.SaveComplete
        saveMessage = nil
    }
```

This code first calls the **hasChanges** method of the object context (no need to save changes if there are no changes to save). Next, it calls the **save:** method of the object context. Again, if you have an error at this level, it's most likely because of a setup issue versus a true physical database error.

Introducing mmBusinessObject

When you first see the code you need to write to retrieve entities in Core Data, it can be a bit daunting. After writing that same code a number of times, you start thinking "there's got to be an easier way." This is where the **mmBusinessObject** class comes in.

The **mmBusinessObject** class, which is included with this book's sample code, doesn't replace Core Data. It simply provides a "wrapper" around the Core Data classes that makes them easier to use and allows you to write less code when you want to create, retrieve, update, and delete entities.

As shown in Figure 12.36, **mmBusinessObject** can be used as the superclass of all the business controller classes in your project. As discussed earlier in this chapter in the section *Improved Core Data Model*, your business controller classes can contain all the code in your app that retrieves and updates entities. For example, all the code that retrieves and updates **ShipmentEntity** objects can be placed in a **Shipment** business controller, the code that retrieves and updates **DeliveryStatusEntity** objects can be placed in the **DeliveryStatus** business controller, and so on.

So let's add **mmBusinessObject** to the **iDeliverMobileCD** project and take a closer look at it.

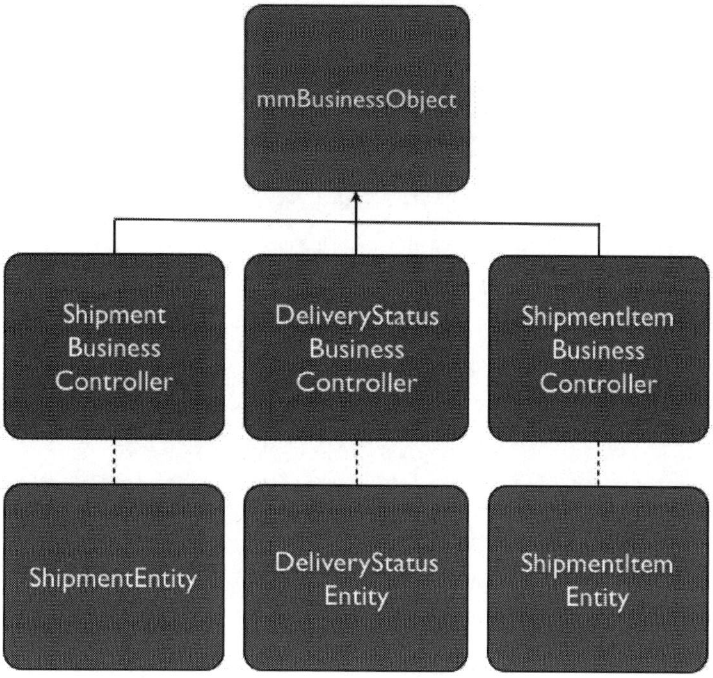

*Figure 12.36 **mmBusinessObject** can be used as the superclass of all your business controller classes.*

mmBusinessObject Properties

1. In the **iDeliverMobileCD** project, right-click the **Business Layer** group and then select **Add Files to "iDeliverMobileCD"...** from the shortcut menu.

2. In the Select File dialog, uncheck **Copy items as needed**, because you only need one copy of **mmBusinessObject** on your development machine.

3. Navigate to the folder where you have stored this book's sample code and expand the **MMiOS** folder. Click the **mmBusinessObject.swift** file to select it.

4. Click the **Add** button to add the file to the Project Navigator.

Let's take a closer look at the **mmBusinessObject** class file. To do this, select the **mmBusinessObject.swift** file in the Project Navigator, and click on the button on the far right side of the jump bar to see a list of properties and methods (Figure 12.37).

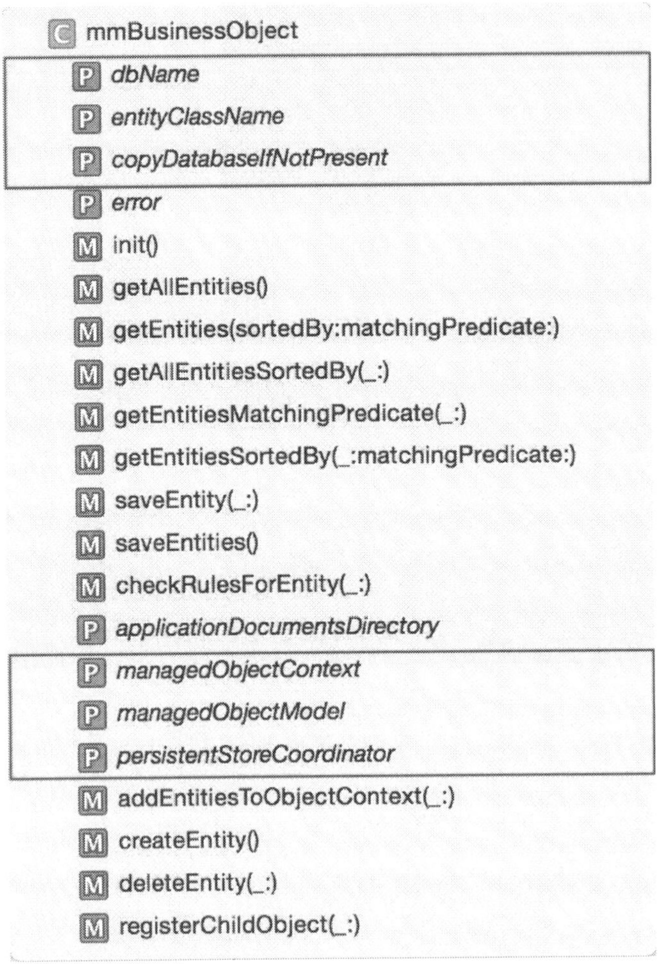

Figure 12.37 ***mmBusinessObject*** *properties and methods.*

As you can see, **mmBusinessObject** has the same three properties you saw earlier on the **AppDelegate** class:

- **managedObjectContext**
- **managedObjectModel**
- **persistentStoreCoordinator**

Since these properties are on the **mmBusinessObject** class, subclasses you create from this class inherit these properties and therefore each have their own object context and associated Core Data objects. This means each business controller can retrieve and update entities without affecting other business controllers.

As you will see in just a bit, there are times when you want business controllers to share the same object context, and this is very easy to do.

The **dbName** property provides a place to specify the name of the database the app is working with. Since most apps typically use just one database, it makes sense to specify the name in one place in your app rather than specifying it in each of your business controllers. The easiest way to do this is to create a class that sits in the hierarchy between **mmBusinessObject** and your app's business controller classes as shown in Figure 12.38, which is what we will do in the next section.

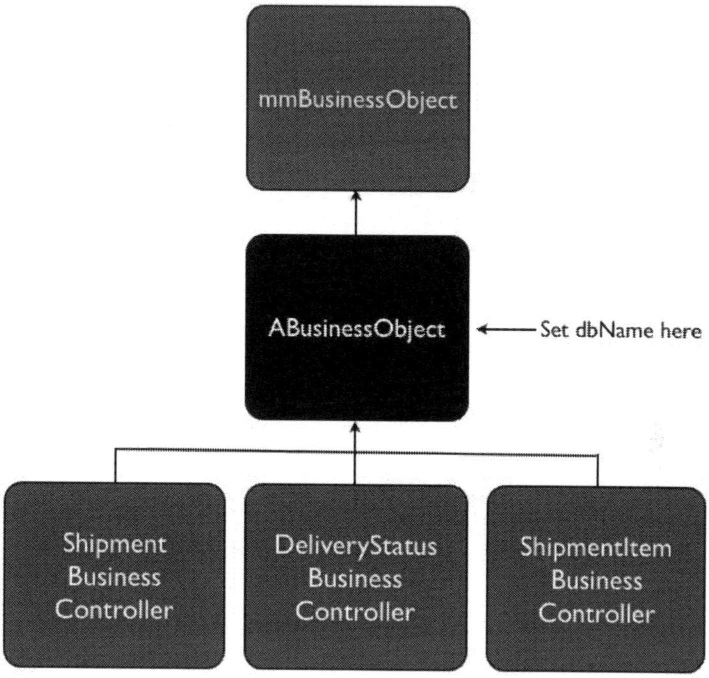

Figure 12.38 The ABusinessObject class is a great place to specify your app's database name.

The **entityClassName** derives the name of the associated entity class from the generic placeholder **T**. That way you don't have to keep specifying the name of the business entity class every time you want to create, retrieve, update, or delete an entity. For detailed information on how Swift's generics are used in the **mmBusinessObject** class, check out *Book 2: Learn to Code in Swift*, under the *Chapter 22: Generics in the Real World.*

The **copyDatabaseIfNotPresent** property specifies whether a database should be created on the user's device the first time the app is run. More on this later!

mmBusinessObject Methods

Figure 12.37 lists a number of methods found in the **mmBusinessObject** class such as:

- createEntity
- deleteEntity:
- getAllEntities
- getEntitiesMatchingPredicate:
- getEntities:sortedBy:matchingPredicate
- saveEntities
- registerChildObject:

You will learn more about these methods as you use them in this chapter and the next. However, if you want to take a quick look at these methods, you will find they simply contain the standard Core Data code you saw earlier in this chapter.

When you use the **mmBusinessObject** class in your project, you are adding this code in one central location, so you don't have to write repetitive Core Data code throughout your app.

This isn't just a good idea for beginning iOS developers. This is a best practice for *all* iOS developers.

The best way for you to understand the concept of business controllers is to use them in a project, so let's do that now. We'll start by creating an application-level **ABusinessObject** business controller class that is a direct subclass of **mmBusinessObject** (Figure 12.38).

Creating an ABusinessObject Class

1. Right-click the **mmBusinessObject.swift** file and then select **New File...** from the shortcut menu. Right-clicking the **mmBusinessObject.swift** file adds the new file directly below this file in the Project Navigator.

2. On the left side of the New File dialog under **iOS**, select **Source**. On the right side of the dialog, select the **Swift File** template (Figure 12.39).

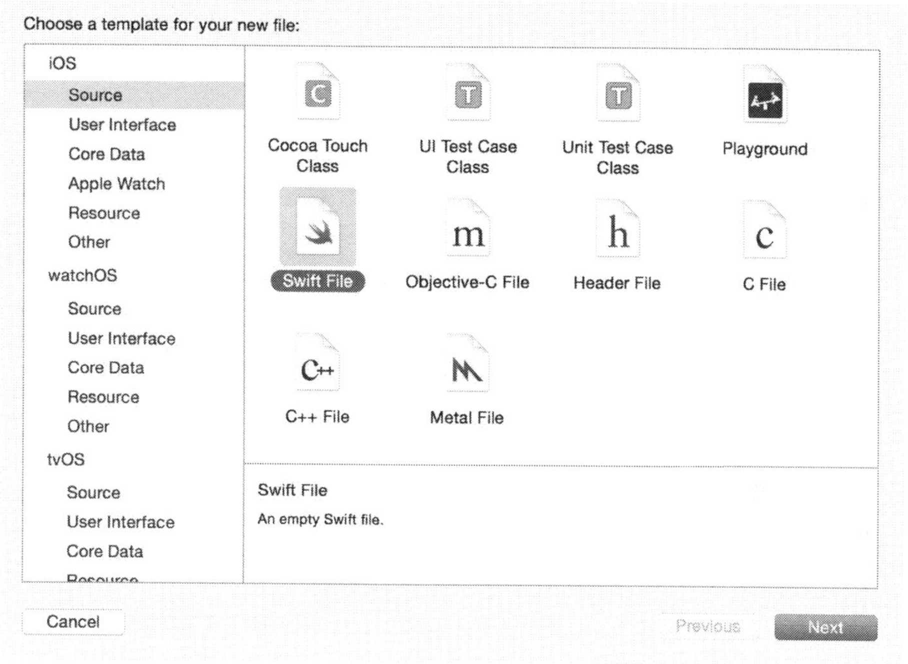

*Figure 12.39 Select the **Swift File** template.*

3. Click the **Next** button to continue. This displays the Save File dialog. In the Save As box, change the name of the file to **ABusinessObject.swift** and then click the **Create** button to add the **ABusinessObject** class file to the project (Figure 12.40).

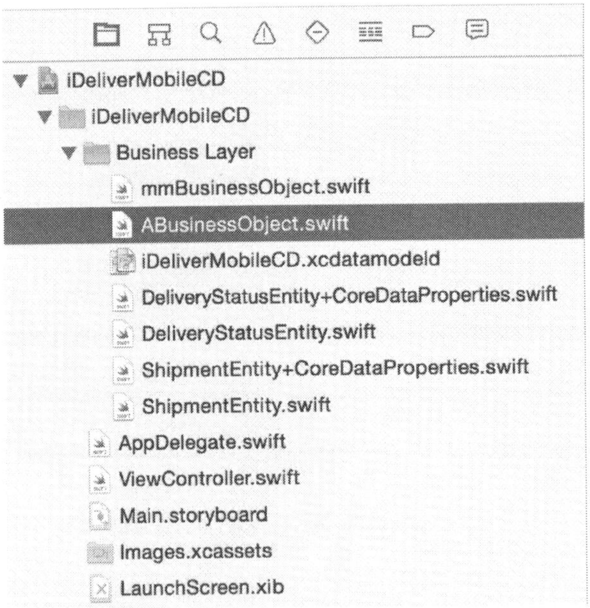

*Figure 12.40 The new **ABusinessObject.swift** file.*

4. Add the following **import** statement and class declaration to the **ABusinessObject.swift** file.

```
import Foundation
import CoreData
class ABusinessObject<T: NSManagedObject>:
 mmBusinessObject<T> {
}
```

This code declares **ABusinessObject** as a subclass of **mmBusinessObject**. The **<T: NSManagedObject>** declaration uses Swift's generics to specify that an class placeholder named **T** that is a subclass of **NSManagedObject** (the superclass of all Core Data entity objects). Basically, this declares all business controller classes can have an associated Core Data entity class.

5. Add the following **init** method to **ABusinessObject**:

```
class ABusinessObject<T: NSManagedObject>:
    mmBusinessObject<T> {

   override init() {
    super.init()
```

```
        self.dbName = "iDeliverMobileCD"
    }
}
```

This code specifies that **iDeliverMobileCD** is the name of the database associated with this app. Since there is just one database for this app, this is the only place you need to specify the database name.

Now we're ready to create some subclasses of the new **ABusinessObject** class.

Creating a Shipment Business Controller

First, let's create a **Shipment** business controller object.

1. In the Project Navigator, right-click the **iDeliverMobileCD** entity data model file (so the new files are added directly below it) and select **New File...** from the popup menu.

2. On the left side of the New File dialog under the **iOS** section, select **Source**. On the right side of the dialog, select the **Swift File** template and then click the **Next** button.

3. In the **Save As** box of the Save dialog, change the name of the class to **Shipment.swift**, and then click **Create** to add the new file to the Project Navigator.

4. Add the following **import** statement and class declaration to the new code file:

```
import Foundation
import CoreData
class Shipment<T:ShipmentEntity>:
 ABusinessObject<T> {
}
```

This code sets **ShipmentEntity** as the default entity class associated with the **Shipment** business controller. This allows you to avoid typing the entity name every time you want to create, retrieve, update, or delete a **ShipmentEntity**.

Creating a DeliveryStatus Business Controller

Now let's create a **DeliveryStatus** business controller.

1. Right-click the **ShipmentEntity.swift** file in the Project Navigator (so the new files are added directly below it) and select **New File...** from the popup menu.

2. On the left side of the New File dialog under the **iOS** section, select **Source**. On the right side of the dialog, select the **Swift** template and then click the **Next** button.

3. In the **Save As** box of the Save dialog, set the name of the class to **DeliveryStatus.swift**, and then click **Create** to add the new file to the Project Navigator.

4. Add the following **import** statement and class declaration to the new code file:

```
import Foundation
import CoreData
class DeliveryStatus<T: DeliveryStatusEntity>:
ABusinessObject<T> {
}
```

This specifies the name of the entity class associated with the business controller as **DeliveryStatusEntity**.

Using Business Controllers With View Controllers

When you place all of your entity manipulation code in business controllers, you create an app design that is easier to conceive, create, and maintain. To use the code within these business controllers, you need to instantiate them from within your app's view controllers and pass messages to them that create, retrieve, update, and delete entities.

Figure 12.41 shows the collaboration between view controllers and business controllers. The grouping of view controllers and business controllers you see in this figure is actually what you are going to set up in the upcoming sections in this chapter. Note that a single view controller can work with multiple business controllers.

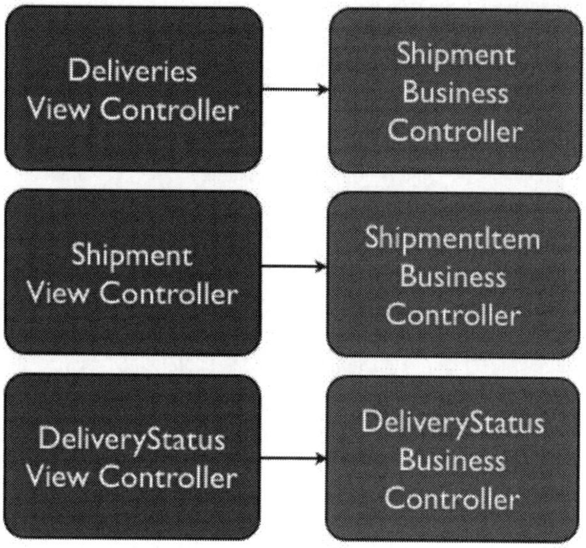

Figure 12.41 View controllers can call on the services of business controllers to manipulate entities.

Setting Up the Deliveries Scene

In this section, we are going to take the prototype app you created in *Book 1: Diving into iOS* and turn it into a real app. We'll start with the Deliveries scene.

1. If it's not already open, in Xcode, open the **iDeliverMobileCD** project.

2. In the Project Navigator, select the **Main.storyboard** file and then scroll the storyboard so you can see the **Deliveries** scene.

3. This scene contains a table view that has six prototype cells which all have the same formatting. We only need one cell that will be used as a prototype for all cells in this table, so let's delete the last five cells in the table view.

   To do this, click the second cell in the table view to select it, hold down the **Shift** key, and click on the third, fourth, fifth, and sixth cells to select them too.

4. With these cells selected, press the **Delete** key to delete these cells and leave the first cell remaining as shown in Figure 12.42.

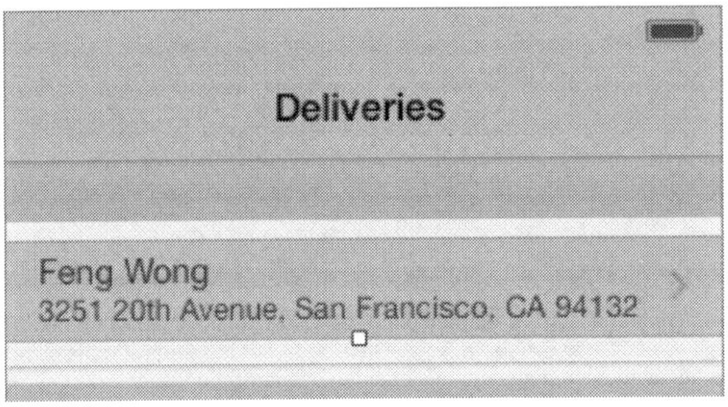

Figure 12.42 Delete all but the first cell.

5. In the **Deliveries** scene, click in the gray area below the table view. Go to the Attributes Inspector (third button from the right in the Inspector toolbar) and change the **Content** attribute from **Static Cells** to **Dynamic Prototypes**. Doing this adds a **Prototype Cells** header label above the table view (Figure 12.43). Header labels are used to describe the contents of a table view, but since the navigation bar already contains the text **Deliveries**, there's no need to use the header label. You can simply ignore the default header label, and it won't appear at run time.

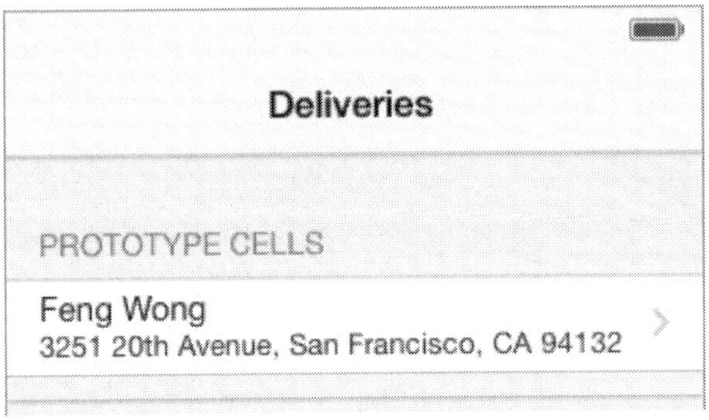

*Figure 12.43 The table view set to **Dynamic Prototypes.***

6. Click on the table view cell to select it, and then go to the Attributes Inspector and change the cell's **Identifier** to **NameAddress** as shown in Figure 12.44.

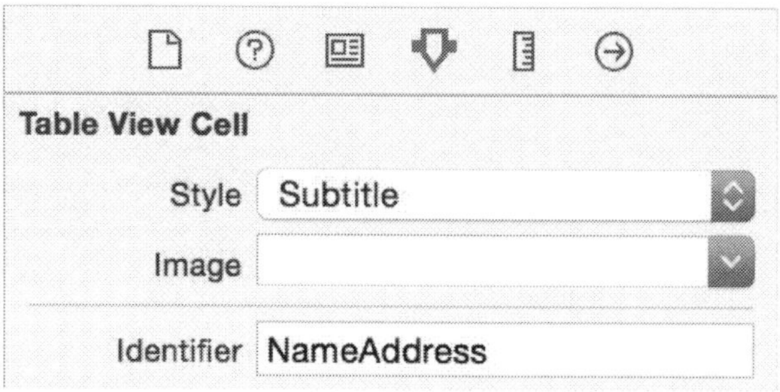

*Figure 12.44 Set the cell's **Identifier** to **NameAddress**.*

This identifier allows you to reference this specific cell from code within your view controller, which we will create next.

Creating a DeliveriesViewController

Now we need to create a table view controller for the Deliveries scene. This table view controller will create an instance of the necessary business controller and fill the table view with delivery entities.

1. Right-click the **Main.storyboard** file in the Project Navigator and select **New File...** from the shortcut menu (this will add the new file under the storyboard file in the Project Navigator).

2. On the left side of the New File dialog under the **iOS** section, select **Source**. On the right side of the dialog, select the **Cocoa Touch Class** template and then click **Next**.

3. In the next step of the dialog, set **Subclass of** to **UITableViewController**, **Class** name to **DeliveriesViewController** and **Language** to **Swift** (Figure 12.45).

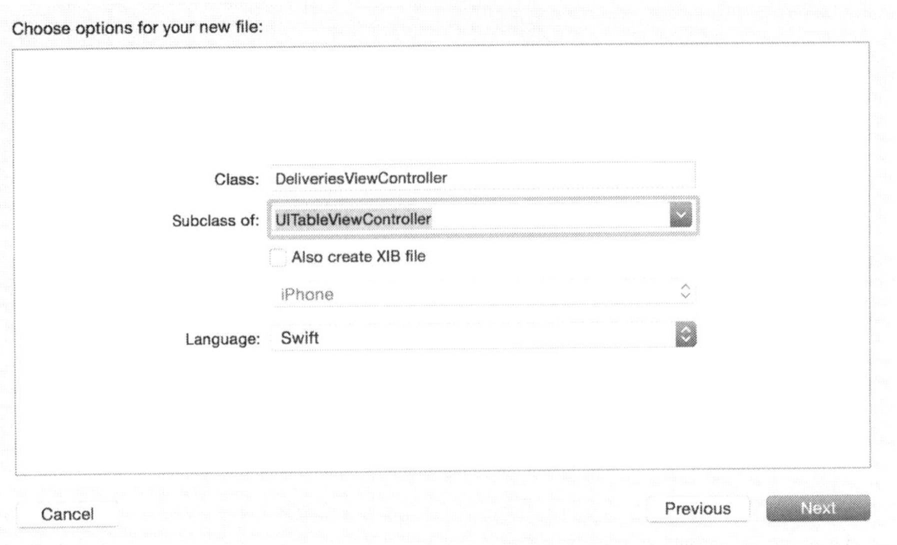

*Figure 12.45 Create **DeliveriesViewController** as a subclass of **UITableViewController**.*

4. Click the **Next** button to display the Save File dialog, and then click **Create** to add the new **DeliveriesViewController** class files to the project (Figure 12.46).

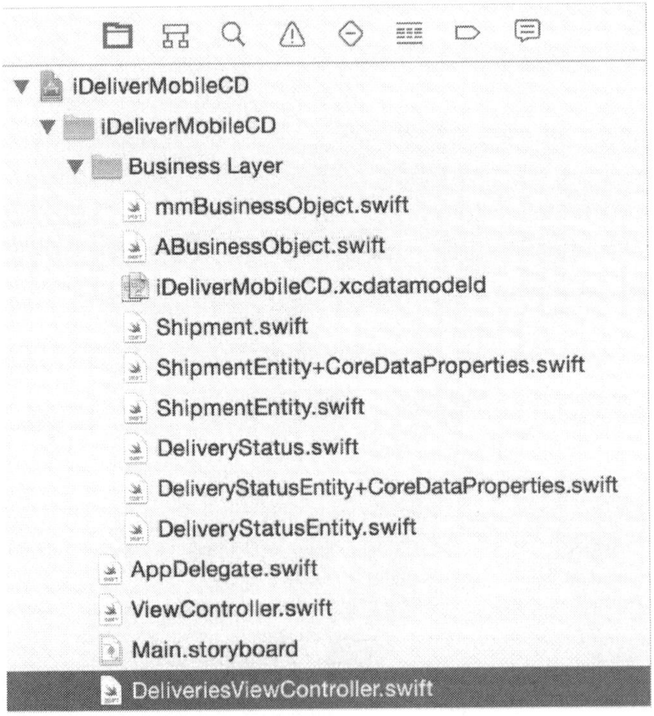

*Figure 12.46 The new **DeliveriesViewController.swift** files.*

5. Whenever you create a new view controller for a particular scene, it's a good idea to immediately go back to that scene and associate it with the scene.

   To do this, go to the Project Navigator, select the **Main.storyboard** file, and then click the status bar at the top of the **Deliveries** scene to select the table view controller. Next, go to the Identity Inspector (the third button from the left in the Inspector toolbar) and change the class to the new **DeliveriesViewController** (Figure 12.47).

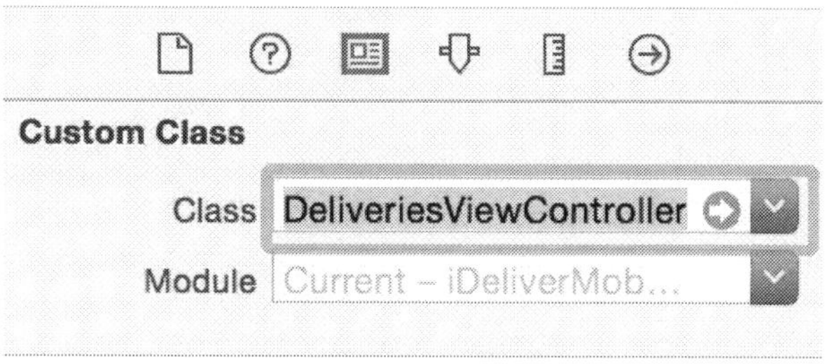

*Figure 12.47 Set the **Class** of the view controller to **DeliveriesViewController**.*

6. Let's go back and set up the **DelivieresViewController** class. Select **DeliveriesViewController.swift** file in the Project Navigator, and add the following property declarations to the file:

```
class DeliveriesViewController:
   UITableViewController {
   var shipment = Shipment()
   var shipmentList = Array<ShipmentEntity>()
```

   The **shipment** property holds a reference to the **Shipment** business controller object, and the **shipmentList** property will be used to hold the **ShipmentEntity** objects returned from the business controller.

7. In the view controller's **viewDidLoad** method, delete all the existing comment lines (the lines in green) and add the following code in its place:

```
override func viewDidLoad() {
    super.viewDidLoad()
   self.shipmentList =
     self.shipment.getAllEntities()
}
```

This code calls the **getAllEntities** method on the shipment business controller, storing the resulting entities into the **shipmentList** array.

8. Scroll down to the **numberOfSectionsInTableView:** method and delete the line that begins with **#warning**.

   Afterward, change the method to return **1**, because there is only one section in this table view:

```
override func numberOfSectionsInTableView
   (tableView: UITableView) -> Int {
     // Return the number of sections.
     return 1
}
```

9. Scroll to the **tableView:numberOfRowsInSection:** method and delete the **#warning** line. Afterward change the **return** statement to the following:

```
override func tableView(tableView:
UITableView, numberOfRowsInSection section:
Int) -> Int {
   // Return the number of rows in the section.
   return shipmentList.count
}
```

   This returns the number of **ShipmentEntity** objects in the **shipmentList** array. This causes the table view to create one row for each entity object in the array.

10. Uncomment the **tableView:cellForRowAtIndexPath:** method by deleting the /* characters before the method and the */ after the method. Next, change the code to the following:

```
override func tableView(tableView:
     UITableView, cellForRowAtIndexPath
      indexPath: NSIndexPath) -> UITableViewCell {
   let cell =
   tableView.dequeueReusableCellWithIdentifier
   ("NameAddress", forIndexPath: indexPath)
```

```
    // Configure the cell...
    let shipmentEntity =
        self.shipmentList[indexPath.row]
    cell.textLabel?.text = shipmentEntity.name
    cell.detailTextLabel?.text =
        "\(shipmentEntity.address),
        \(shipmentEntity.city),
        \(shipmentEntity.region)
        \(shipmentEntity.postalCode)"
    return cell
}
```

This method gets called once for every **ShipmentEntity** in the **shipmentList** array.

The first line of code asks the table view for a cell with the **NameAddress** identifier. The table view returns the prototype cell with that identifier.

Next, this code gets the **ShipmentEntity** in the **shipmentList** with the specified row number. Afterward, the **ShipmentEntity**'s **name** value is stored in the cell's main text label, and its **address**, **city**, **region**, and **postalCode** are combined together and stored in the detail text label.

11. Now that setup of the Deliveries scene is complete, it's time to run the app to see what it looks like at run time. To do this, click Xcode's **Run** button.

You may be surprised to see *there aren't any rows in the table view*! That's because we never created a database and added any records to it. Let's address that issue now.

Examining the SQLite Database

When your app first tries to access a database, if it doesn't exist, Core Data automatically creates an empty database for you. Let's see if this happened when you ran the app in the previous section.

When you run an app in the Simulator, a folder is created on your development computer that contains the compiled app and its related files. To see this folder:

1. Launch the Mac OS X Finder app.

2. In the Finder menu, click **Go**, and then hold down the **Option** key. This adds **Library** to the list of folders as shown in Figure 12.48.

*Figure 12.48 Hold down the **Option** key to add **Library** to the list of folders.*

3. Select the **Library** folder from the menu to display the contents of this folder in Finder.

4. Next, drill down into the **Developer** folder, and then down into the **CoreSimulator** > **Devices** folder. You will see multiple subfolders with unique ID names, one for each version of the iPhone Simulator you have installed on your Mac (Figure 12.49).

*Figure 12.49 The **Devices** folder.*

To get to the actual app files you have to drill down even further. However, the **Devices** folder is a good mid-point when searching for Simulator files, so I recommend dragging this folder to the **Favorites** bar on the left side of the Finder window for easy access.

To make it easy to find your app's Simulator files, I have added a line of code to the mmBusinessObject's **applicationDocumentsDirectory** computed property that displays the location of your app's SQLite database file in Xcode's Console when you run the app in the Simulator.

5. To see this code in action, click Xcode's **Run** button, and then check the Xcode Console (Figure 12.50).

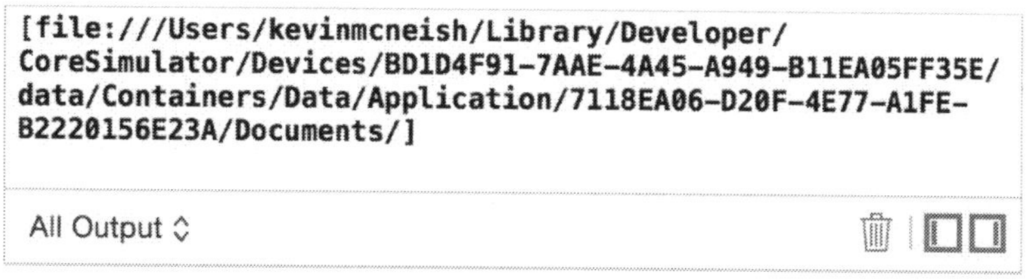

Figure 12.50 Your app's Documents directory is displayed in Xcode's Console.

6. To navigate to this folder, go back to Finder, click on the **Devices** shortcut you created a few steps back and then drill down into the folders listed in the Console until you reach the **Documents** folder where you can see the SQLite files (Figure 12.51). The primary file has a **.sqlite** extension.

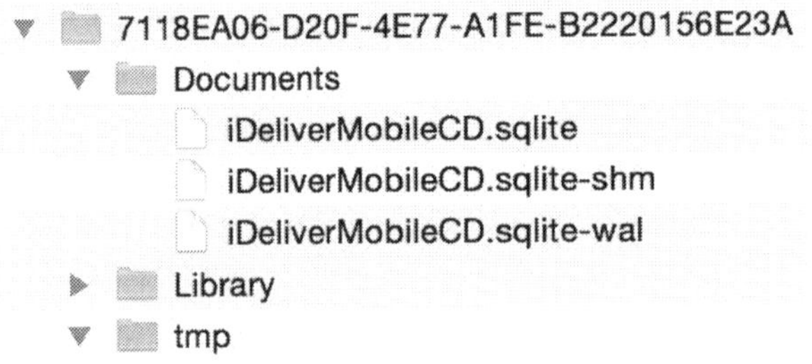

Figure 12.51 The SQLite files.

To examine the contents of the file, you need a special app, which is discussed in the next section.

Firefox and the SQLite Manager

I have found one of the best tools for viewing a SQLite database is the SQLite Manager add-on for the Firefox web browser. I'll show you how to get this tool on your development machine.

1. If you don't already have the Firefox web browser installed on your Mac, go to this link to download and install Firefox:

   http://mozilla.org/firefox

2. Download and install SQLite Manager at this link:

   https://addons.mozilla.org/en-us/firefox/addon/sqlite- manager/

3. Now that you have both Firefox and SQLite Manager installed, launch Firefox (you should be able to find it in your Applications folder on your Mac).

4. In the Firefox **Tools** menu, select **SQLite Manager** to display the SQLite Manager window (Figure 12.52).

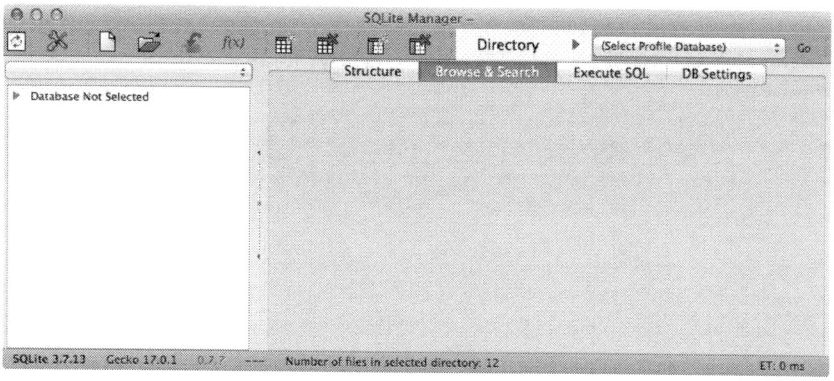

Figure 12.52 The SQLite Manager window.

5. To open the app's SQLite database files, click the **Connect Database** toolbar button at the top of the SQLite Manager window (Figure 12.53).

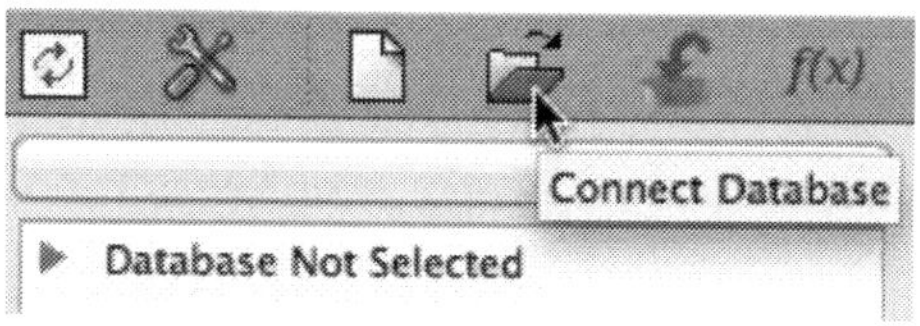

Figure 12.53 Opening a database in SQLite Manager.

6. On the left side of the Select SQLite Database dialog, click the **Devices** folder you added to **Favorites** in the previous section. On the right side of the dialog, drill down into the **Documents** folder that was displayed in the Xcode Console when you ran the app in the Simulator and select the **.sqlite** file (Figure 12.54).

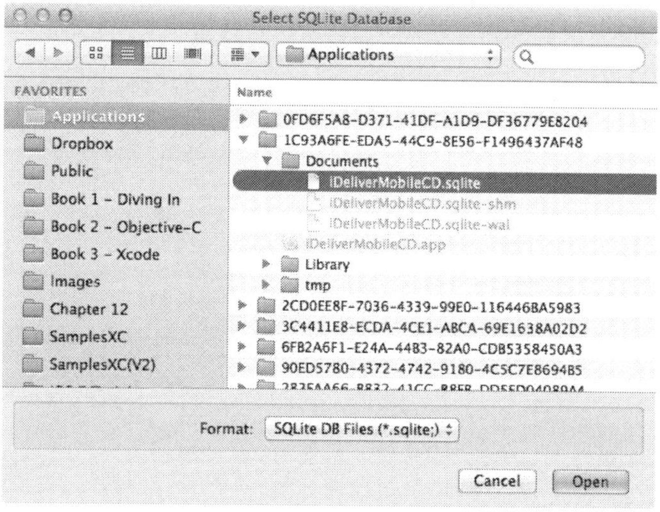

*Figure 12.54 Select the **iDeliverMobileCD.sqlite** file.*

7. Click **Open** to display the SQLite files in the panel on the left (Figure 12.55).

Figure 12.55 ***iDeliverMobileCD*** *database tables.*

You don't need to know all the details about what each table does (one of the main goals of Core Data is to hide these details from you), but it's good to have a basic understanding of the underlying mechanics in case something should go wrong. There are two tables, **ZDELIVERYSTATUSENTITY** and **ZSHIPMENTENTITY** that have the same name as the entities that you added to the entity data model but with a **Z** prefix.

8. Expand the table nodes, and you will see the columns shown in Figure 12.56. **Z_PK** is the primary key (unique identifier) for the entity, **Z_ENT** is the entity ID (every entity of a particular type has the same entity ID), and **Z_OPT** indicates the number of times an entity has been changed (starting with **1** when it is initially added to the database). All the other columns are attributes you added to the entities in the entity data model with a **Z** prefix.

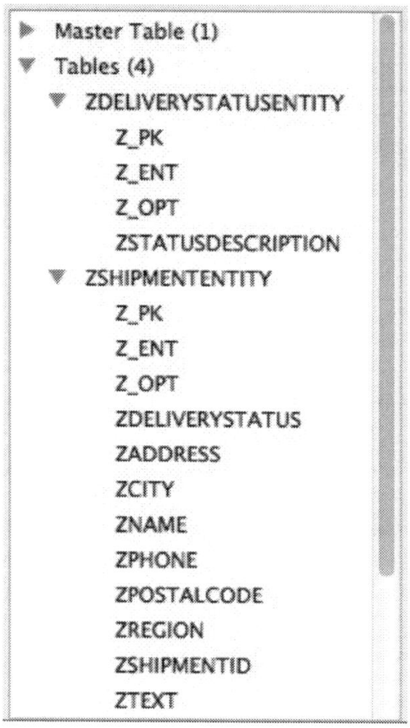

Figure 12.56 ***iDeliverMobileCD*** *table columns.*

9. Let's add records to the database so we have something to view in our app.

   In the panel on the left in the SQLite Manager, select **ZDELIVERYSTATUSENTITY**. Then, on the right side of the panel, make sure the **Browse and Search** tab is selected, and then click the **Add** button. This displays the dialog shown in Figure 12.57.

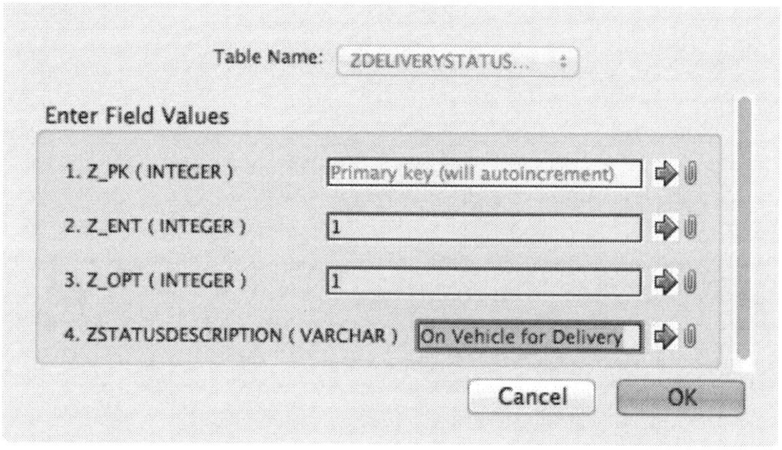

Figure 12.57 Adding a Delivery Status record.

10. Enter **1** in the **Z_ENT** and **Z_OPT** boxes, and in the **ZSTATUSDESCRIPTION** box, enter the text **On Vehicle for Delivery**, and then click the **OK** button. This displays a confirmation dialog (Figure 12.58).

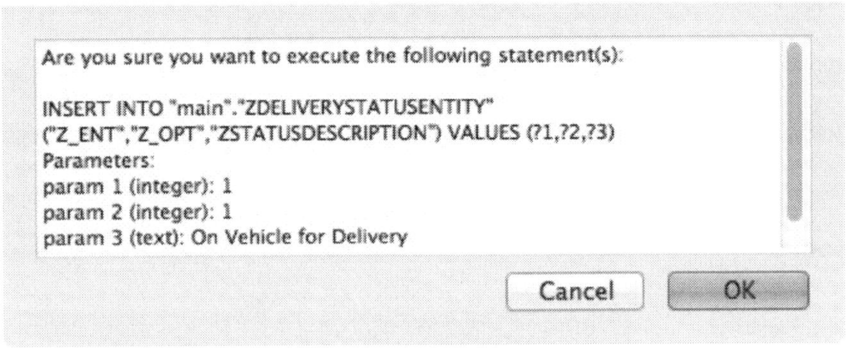

Figure 12.58 The new record confirmation dialog.

11. Click **OK** to add the new record to the database. When you do this, the New Record dialog is redisplayed with a confirmation message at the top. If you press **Cancel**, you will exit the dialog. Otherwise, you can add another new record.

12. To add the next record, press the **Tab** key until the **ZSTATUSDESCRIPTION** box has focus and its contents are highlighted (without changing any other values). Type the text **Attempted Delivery** (which deletes the existing text) and press **OK.** In the confirmation dialog, press **OK** to save the record.

13. Tab to the **ZSTATUSDESCRIPTION** box to add one more record. Enter the text **Delivered** and press **OK**.

    In the confirmation dialog, press **OK** to save the new record. Afterward, press **Cancel** to exit the dialog.

14. Next, lets add a single shipment record to the database. In the panel on the left in the SQLite Manager window, select **ZSHIPMENTENTITY**. Then, on the right side of the dialog, click the **Add** button to display the dialog shown in Figure 12.59.

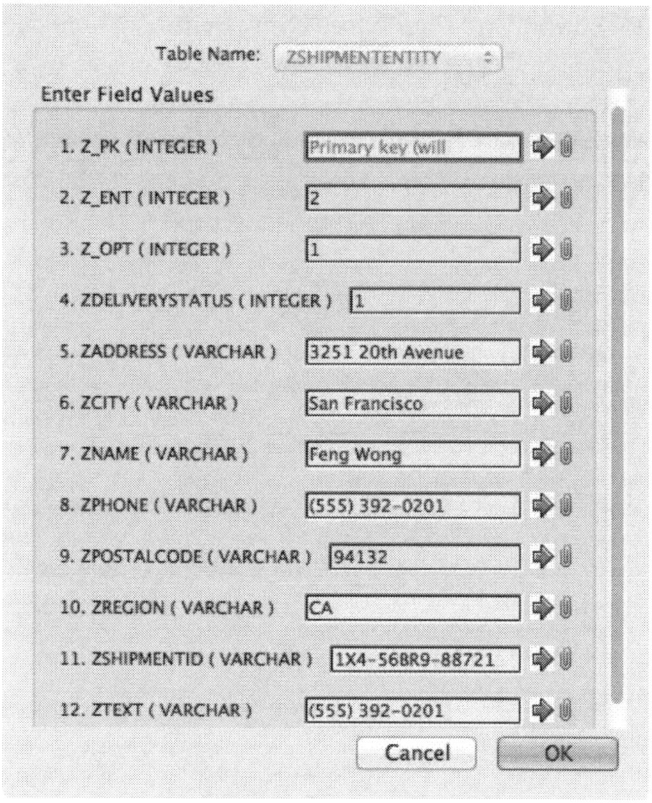

Figure 12.59 Adding a Shipment record.

15. Enter the following values for each column:

- **Z_ENT** - 2
- **Z_OPT** - 1
- **ZDELIVERYSTATUS** - 1
- **ZADDRESS** - 3251 20th Avenue
- **ZCITY** - San Francisco
- **ZNAME** - Feng Wong
- **ZPHONE** - (555) 392-0201
- **ZPOSTALCODE** - 94132
- **ZREGION** - CA
- **ZSHIPMENTID** - 1X4-56BR9-88721
- **ZTEXT** - (555) 392-0201

16. Click the **OK** button, and then in the confirmation dialog, click the **OK** button to save the new record. Afterward, press **Cancel** to exit the dialog.

17. Now that you have records in the database, let's run the app again and see how this data looks at run time. To do this, go back to Xcode and click the **Run** button. You should now see the new record in the **Deliveries** list (Figure 12.60).

Figure 12.60 The new Shipment record at run time.

Now it's time to get some of the other scenes converted from displaying static prototype data to dynamic data retrieved from the database.

Setting Up the Shipment Scene

In this section, you will change the Shipment scene so it displays a **ShipmentEntity** retrieved from the database rather than static prototype data.

1. If it's not already open, in Xcode, open the **iDeliverMobileCD** project. If the app is still running in the Simulator, click Xcode's **Stop** button.

2. In the Project Navigator, select the **Main.storyboard** file and then scroll the storyboard so you can see the **Shipment** scene (Figure 12.61).

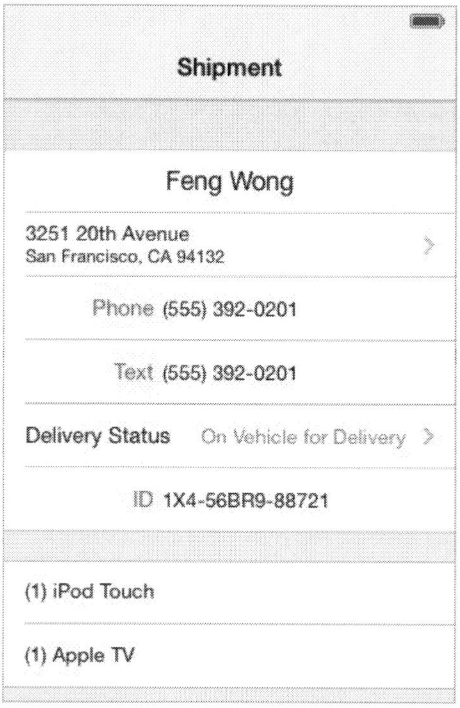

*Figure 12.61 The **Shipment** scene*

When converting a table view containing static data to a table view displaying dynamic data, you need to keep all the cells that have unique formatting and delete the cells with duplicate formatting. All cells in the **Shipment** table view's first section are unique, so we will keep them all.

3. The second table view section has two cells with identical formatting, so we can delete the last cell. To do this, click the second cell in the second section (labeled **(1) Apple TV**) to select it, and then press the **Delete** key to delete it.

4. When converting a prototype table view to live data, you should move all cells to the first table view section so they can be more easily accessed.

   Let's move the first cell in the second section (labeled **(1) iPod Touch**) to the last position in the first section directly below the **ID** cell. To do this, click on the remaining shipment item cell, drag it beneath the last item in the first section as (Figure 12.62), and then release your mouse button.

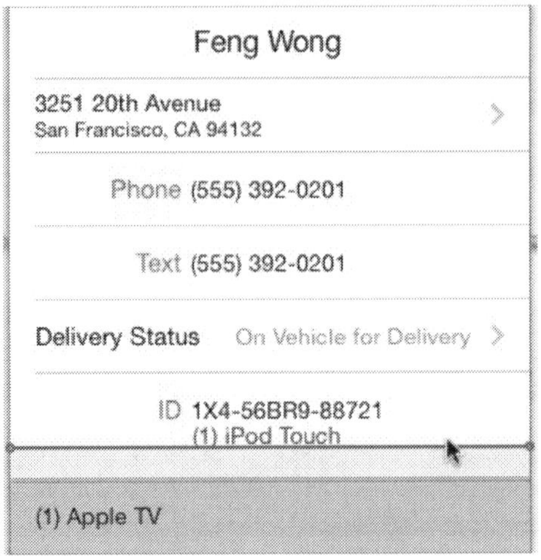

Figure 12.62 Moving the shipment item cell

5. When you're finished, the cell will appear at the bottom of the first section (Figure 12.63).

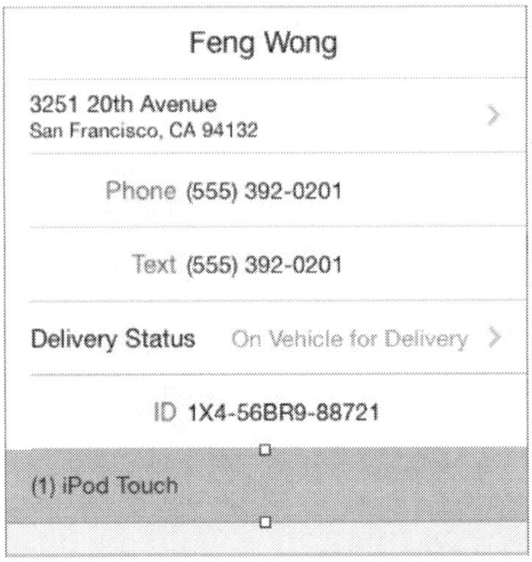

Figure 12.63 The shipment item cell in the first section.

6. Let's change the content type of the table view. Click on the gray area below the table view, go to the Attributes Inspector (third button from the right in the Inspector toolbar), and change the **Content** attribute to **Dynamic Prototypes**.

7. Let's set the reuse identifier for each cell so they can be referenced from the view controller. To change a cell's reuse identifier, click on the cell,

then in the Attributes Inspector an **Identifier**. From top to bottom, set the reuse identifier of the cells as follows:

- NameCell
- AddressCell
- PhoneCell
- TextCell
- DeliveryStatusCell
- ShipmentIDCell
- ShipmentItemCell

Creating a ShipmentViewController

Now let's create a custom view controller class that we can associate with the **Shipment** scene.

1. Right-click the **DeliveriesViewController.swift** file in the Project Navigator and select **New File...** from the shortcut menu.
2. On the left side of the New File dialog under **iOS**, select **Source**. On the right side of the dialog, select the **Cocoa Touch Class** template and then click **Next**.

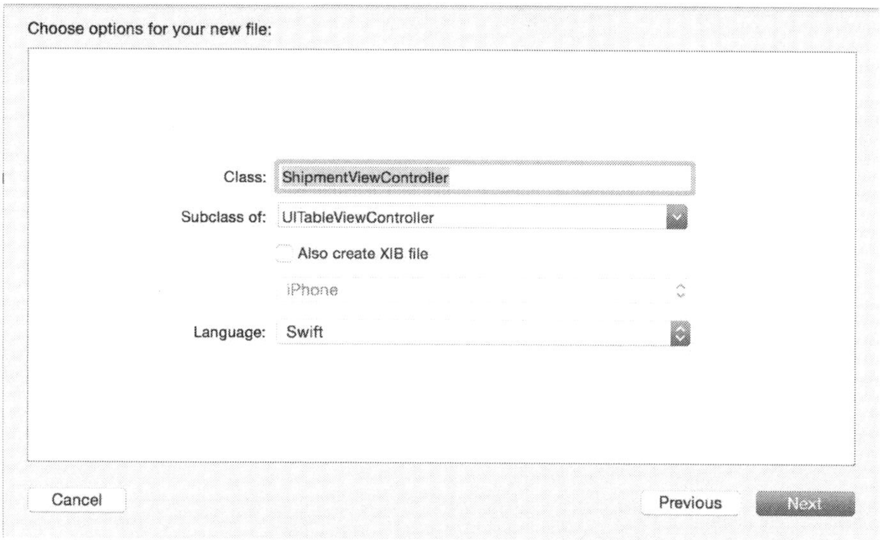

*Figure 12.64 Create the **ShipmentViewController**.*

3. In the next step of the dialog, set the **Subclass of** to **UITableViewController** set the **Class** to **ShipmentViewController**, **Language** to **Swift** (Figure 12.64), and then click **Next**.

4. In the Save File dialog, click the **Create** button to add the new files to the Project Navigator (Figure 12.65).

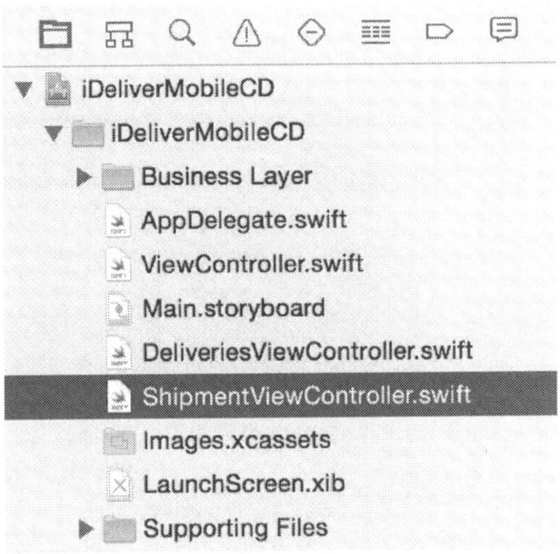

*Figure 12.65 The new **ShipmentViewController.swift** file.*

5. Now let's associate the new view controller with the Shipment scene. To do this, in the Project Navigator, select the **Main.storyboard** file to display the storyboard in the design surface. Click on the dock at the top of the **Shipment** scene to select the table view controller.

6. Go to the Identity Inspector (the third button from the left in the Inspector toolbar) and change the **Class** to **ShipmentViewController** (Figure 12.66).

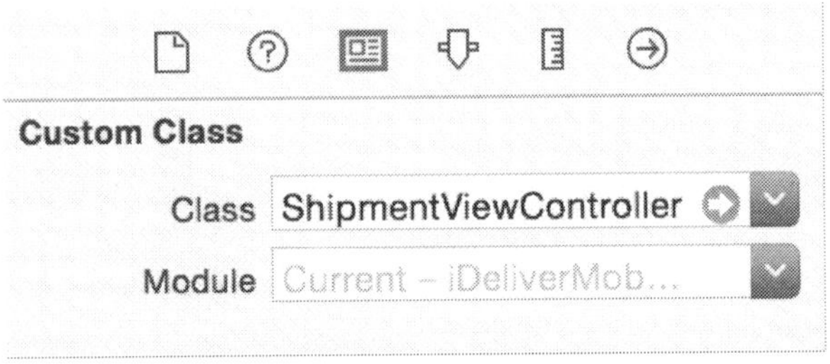

*Figure 12.66 Set the **Class** to **ShipmentViewController**.*

7. Now let's set up the **ShipmentViewController** to display the **ShipmentEntity** object in the Shipment scene's table view.

   Select the **ShipmentViewController.swift** file in the Project Navigator and add the following properties:

```
class ShipmentViewController:
   UITableViewController {
var shipment: Shipment<ShipmentEntity>!
var shipmentEntity: ShipmentEntity!
```

   These properties will be used to hold a reference to the **Shipment** business controller and the currently selected **ShipmentEntity**.

8. Scroll down to the **numberofSectionsInTableView:** method and remove the **#warning** directive. Next, change the **return** statement to return **2**:

```
  override func
   numberOfSectionsInTableView(tableView:
   UITableView) -> Int {
    // Return the number of sections.
    return 2
}
```

   This specifies there are two sections in the table view.

9. In the **tableView:numberOfRowsInSection:** method, remove the **#warning** directive and change the code to the following:

```
override func tableView(tableView:
UITableView, numberOfRowsInSection section:
Int) -> Int {
    // Return the number of rows in the section.
    var rowCount = 0
    if section == 0 {
     rowCount = 6
    }
    return rowCount
}
```

This code returns **6** if the section number is **0** (the first section). We'll worry about the second section later on.

10. Uncomment the **tableView:cellForRowAtIndexPath** method by deleting the /* from the beginning of the method and the */ at the end of the method. Next, add the following code (there are many lines of code because each cell has its own custom configuration):

```
override func tableView(tableView: UITableView,
cellForRowAtIndexPath indexPath: NSIndexPath) ->
UITableViewCell {
    var cell: UITableViewCell!
   if indexPath.section == 0 {
     switch indexPath.row {
     case 0:
        cell = tableView.
           dequeueReusableCellWithIdentifier
           ("NameCell", forIndexPath: indexPath)
        cell.textLabel?.text =
           self.shipmentEntity.name
     case 1:
        cell = tableView.dequeueReusableCellWithIdentifier
      ("AddressCell", forIndexPath: indexPath)
        cell.textLabel?.text =
           self.shipmentEntity.address
        cell.detailTextLabel?.text =
           ("\(self.shipmentEntity.city) ,\
           (self.shipmentEntity.region) \
           (self.shipmentEntity.postalCode)")
     case 2:
        cell = tableView.
        dequeueReusableCellWithIdentifier
           ("PhoneCell", forIndexPath: indexPath)
        cell.detailTextLabel?.text =
           self.shipmentEntity.phone
     case 3:
        cell = tableView.dequeueReusableCellWithIdentifier
          ("TextCell", forIndexPath: indexPath)
        cell.detailTextLabel?.text =
           self.shipmentEntity.text
```

```
        case 4:
            cell = tableView.dequeueReusableCellWithIdentifier
              ("DeliveryStatusCell", forIndexPath: indexPath)
          cell.detailTextLabel?.text =
              self.shipmentEntity.deliveryStatus.
                  valueForKey("statusDescription")
                  as? String
        case 5:
            cell = tableView.dequeueReusableCellWithIdentifier
                ("ShipmentIDCell", forIndexPath: indexPath)
            cell.detailTextLabel?.text =
                self.shipmentEntity.shipmentID
        default:
            break
        }
    }
    return cell
}
```

Before we can see how all of this code works at run time, we need to make a few **Deliveries** scene changes.

Updating the Deliveries Scene

In this section, you are going to create a new segue between the **Deliveries** and **Shipment** scenes. The old segue was connected directly to the first cell in the Deliveries table view, so we need to create a new segue that can be triggered from any cell. We must also add code to the **DeliveriesViewController** to pass the currently selected **ShipmentEntity** to the **ShipmentViewController**.

1. In the Project Navigator, select the **Main.storyboard** file. Next, click the segue between the **Deliveries** and **Shipment** scenes (Figure 12.67) to select it, and then press the **Delete** key to delete it.

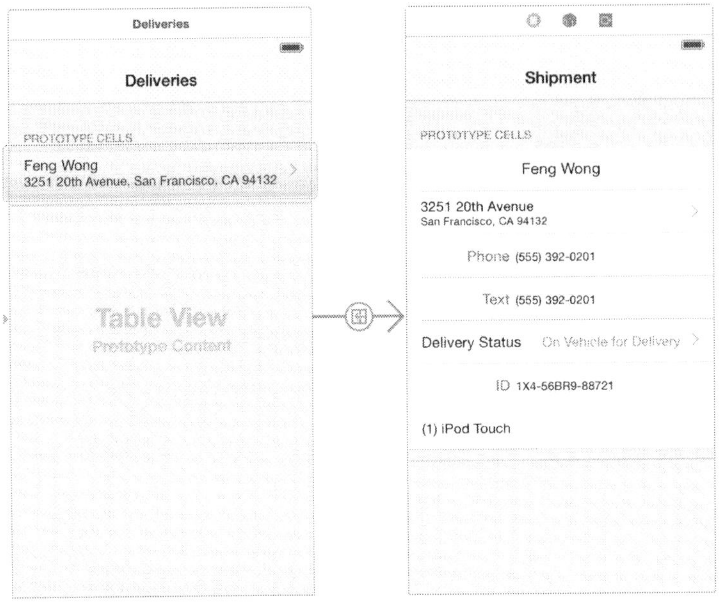

*Figure 12.67 Select the segue between **Deliveries** and **Shipment** scenes.*

2. To create a new segue between the two scenes, first select the **Deliveries** scene. Next, hold the **control** key down, click the view controller icon in the **Deliveries** scene dock, and drag over to the **Shipment** scene (Figure 12.68). Release the mouse button, and when the **Manual Segue** popup appears, select **Push**. This creates a new segue between the two scenes.

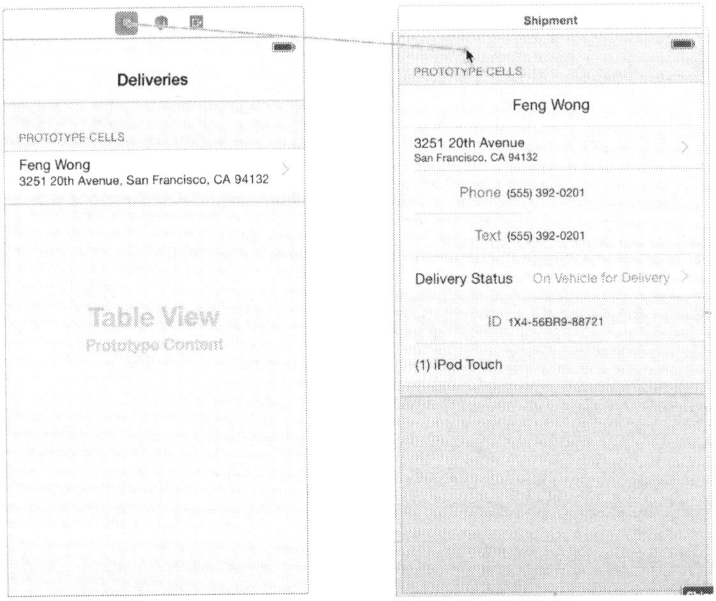

*Figure 12.68 Create a new segue between **Deliveries** and **Shipment** scenes.*

3. Now let's give the segue an identifier so we can reference it from within code in the view controller. To do this, select the segue in the design surface, go to the Attributes Inspector, and set the **Identifier** to **ShipmentSegue** (Figure 12.69).

*Figure 12.69 Set the **Identifier** to **ShipmentSegue**.*

4. Next, select the **DeliveriesViewController.swift** file in the Project Navigator. Scroll to the bottom of the file and delete all the commented methods. Then add the following method before the closing curly brace.

```
override func tableView(tableView: UITableView,
didSelectRowAtIndexPath indexPath: NSIndexPath) {
    self.performSegueWithIdentifier
     ("ShipmentSegue", sender: nil)
  }
}
```

This method is automatically executed when the user taps a row in the **Deliveries** table view at run time. The code in this method initiates the segue to the **Shipment** scene. Notice the reference to the **ShipmentSegue** identifier you set in the previous step.

5. At the bottom of the code file before the closing curly brace, add the following method:

```
override func prepareForSegue(segue:
    UIStoryboardSegue, sender: AnyObject?) {
  if segue.identifier == "ShipmentSegue" {
    // Get the destination view controller
    let tvc = segue.destinationViewController
      as! ShipmentViewController

    // Get the currently selected row
    let indexPath =
```

```
            self.tableView.indexPathForSelectedRow
        // Save the ShipmentEntity for this row
        // on the ShipmentViewController
        tvc.shipmentEntity =
            self.shipmentList[indexPath!.row]
        // Save the Shipment business controller
        // on the ShipmentViewController
        tvc.shipment = self.shipment
      }
   }
}
```

This method is called from the code you added to the **tableView:didSelectRowAtIndexPath:** method in the previous step.

To prepare for the execution of the segue, this code first gets a reference to the destination view controller (**ShipmentViewController**). It then stores the following objects on that view controller:

- The **ShipmentEntity** associated with the row that was selected in the table view.
- A reference to the **Shipment** business controller.

Now let's see how this looks at run time. Click Xcode's **Run** button and, when the app appears in the Simulator, select the delivery in the Deliveries scene, and you should see the **Shipment** scene shown in Figure 12.70. As you might expect, the first section of the table displays the **ShipmentEntity** selected from the previous page. The second section of the table view containing the shipment items doesn't appear because we haven't set that up yet.

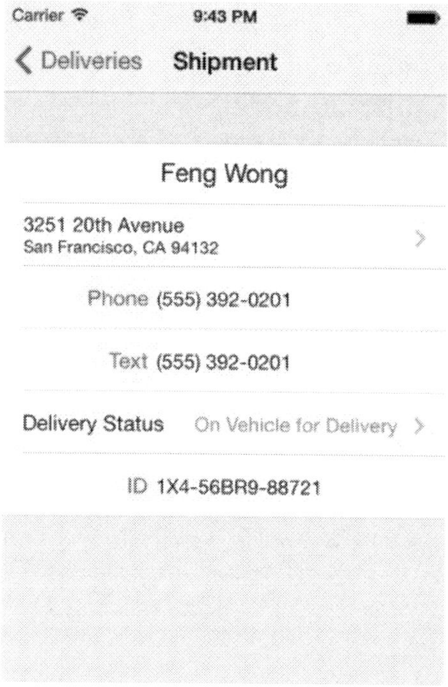

*Figure 12.70 The **Shipment** scene at run time.*

Setting Up the Delivery Status Scene

Now you're ready to change the Delivery Status scene from displaying static prototype data to displaying **DeliveryStatusEntity** objects from the data store.

1. In the Project Navigator, select the **Main.storyboard** file to display the storyboard in the design surface.

2. Scroll the storyboard to the **Delivery Status** scene (Figure 12.71).

Figure 12.71 The Delivery Status scene.

3. Since all the table view cells have the same formatting, we only need to leave one cell remaining. To do this, click on the **Attempted Delivery** cell, hold down the **Shift** key, and then click on the **Delivered** cell to select both of them. With both cells selected, press **Delete** to delete them.

4. Now let's remove the checkmark from the remaining cell. With the first cell still selected, go to the Attributes Inspector and change the **Accessory** attribute to **None**.

5. With the cell still selected, change the cell's **Identifier** attribute to **DeliveryStatusCell**.

6. Next, click in the gray area below the table view, go to the Attribute Inspector, and change the **Content** attribute from **Static Cells** to **Dynamic Prototypes**. When you're finished, the table view should look like Figure 12.72.

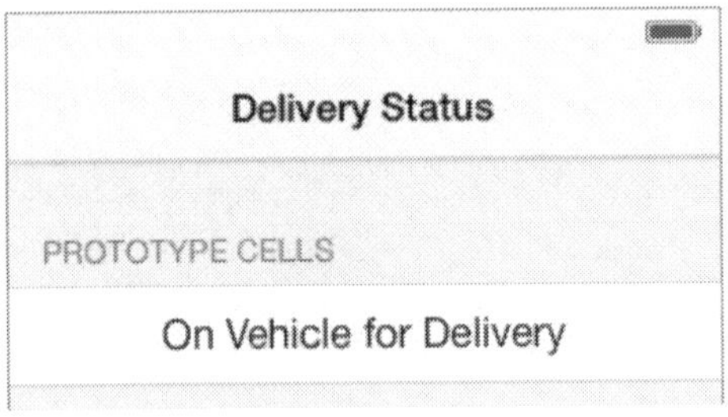

Figure 12.72 The completed ***Delivery Status*** *table view.*

Creating a DeliveryStatusViewController

Now let's create a custom view controller class that we can associate with the Delivery Status scene.

1. Right-click the **ShipmentViewController** group in the Project Navigator and select **New File...** from the shortcut menu.

2. On the left side of the New File dialog under the **iOS** section, select **Source**. On the right side of the dialog, select the **Cocoa Touch class** template and then click **Next**.

3. In the next dialog step set **Subclass of** to **UITableViewController** set the **Class** to **DeliveryStatusViewController** and **Language** to **Swift** (Figure 12.73).

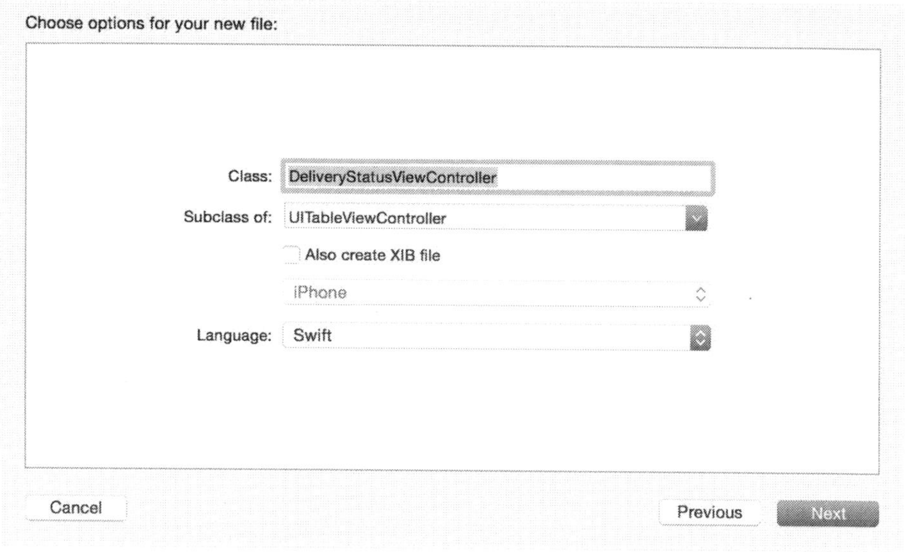

*Figure 12.73 Create a **DeliveryStatusViewController** class.*

4. Click the **Next** button and then click **Create** in the Save File dialog. This adds the new **DeliveryStatusViewController** class file to the Project Navigator (Figure 12.74).

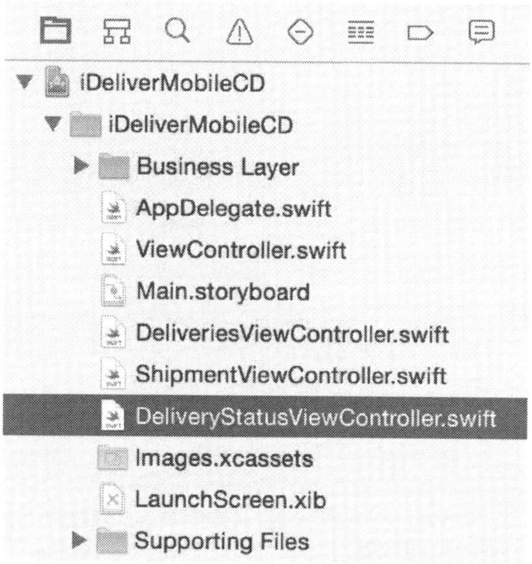

*Figure 12.74 The new **DeliveryStatusViewController** file.*

5. Let's associate the new view controller with the **Delivery Status** scene. To do this, go to the Project Navigator and select the **Main.storyboard** file and click the scene dock at the top of the **Delivery Status** scene to

select the table view controller. Go to the Identity Inspector (the third button from the left in the Inspector toolbar) and change the **Class** to **DeliveryStatusViewController** (Figure 12.75).

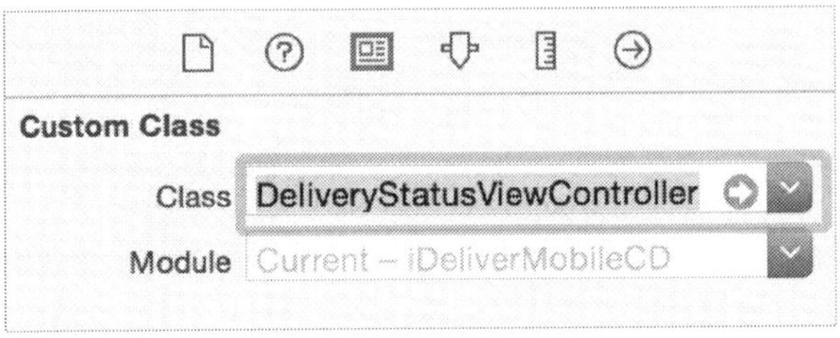

*Figure 12.75 Set the **Class** to **DeliveryStatusViewController**.*

6. Select the new **DeliveryStatusViewController.swift** file in the Project Navigator and add the following property declarations:

```
class DeliveryStatusViewController:
   UITableViewController {

   var shipmentEntity: ShipmentEntity!
   var deliveryStatus = DeliveryStatus()
   var deliveryStatusList =
     Array<DeliveryStatusEntity>()
```

The **shipmentEntity** property will hold a reference to the currently selected **ShipmentEntity** object. The **deliveryStatus** property will hold a reference to the **DeliveryStatus** business controller, and the **deliveryStatusList** array property will hold the list of **DeliveryStatusEntity** objects.

7. In the view controller's **viewDidLoad** method, remove all the existing comments and add the following code in its place:

```
override func viewDidLoad() {
          super.viewDidLoad()
   // Share the shipment entity object context
   self.deliveryStatus.managedObjectContext =
   self.shipmentEntity.managedObjectContext!
   self.deliveryStatusList =
      self.deliveryStatus.getAllEntities()
}
```

The first line of code is of particular interest. It copies the object context from the **shipmentEntity** object to the **DeliveryStatus** object. This causes the **DeliveryStatus** business controller to share the same object context as the **Shipment** business controller as shown in Figure 12.76.

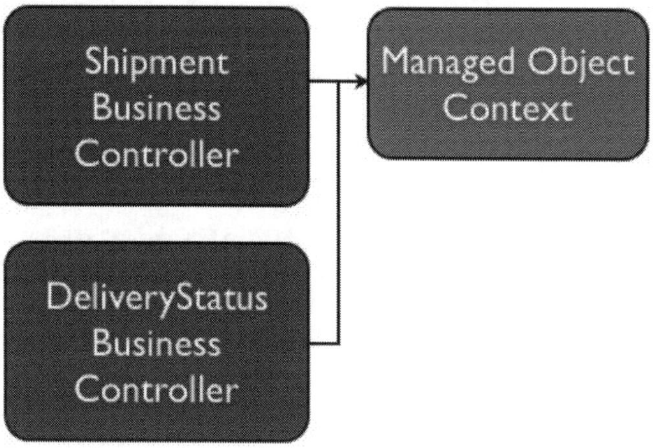

*Figure 12.76 The **Shipment** an **DeliveryStatus** business controllers are sharing a single object context.*

As mentioned earlier in this chapter, Core Data insists that all objects that are related in the entity data model must be associated with the same object context. We were able to get the object context reference off of the **ShipmentEntity** object because all entities retrieved from an object context contain a ***pointer*** to that object context.

The second line of code retrieves **DeliveryStatusEntity** objects from the **DeliveryStatus** business controller and saves them in the **deliveryStatusList** array.

8. Scroll down to the **numberOfSectionsInTableView:** method and delete the **#warning** directive. Afterward, change the method to return

```
override func numberOfSectionsInTableView(
   tableView: UITableView) -> Int {
      // Return the number of sections.
   return 1
}
```

This specifies there is one section in the table view.

9. In the **tableView:numberOfRowsInSection:** method, remove the **#warning** directive. Afterward, change the **return** statement to the following:

```
override func tableView(tableView:
   UITableView, numberOfRowsInSection section:
   Int) -> Int {
      // Return the number of rows in the section.
      return self.deliveryStatusList.count
}
```

10. Uncomment the **tableView:cellForRowAtIndexPath:** method by removing the /* at the beginning of the method and the */ from the end of the method. Afterward, add the following code to the method:

```
override func tableView(tableView: UITableView,
cellForRowAtIndexPath indexPath: NSIndexPath) ->
 UITableViewCell {
let cell = tableView.dequeueReusableCellWithIdentifier
  ("DeliveryStatusCell", forIndexPath:indexPath)

 // Configure the cell...
 let deliveryStatusEntity =
   self.deliveryStatusList[indexPath.row]
 cell.textLabel?.text =
   deliveryStatusEntity.statusDescription

 // Add a check mark if currently selected item
 if deliveryStatusEntity.statusDescription ==
  self.shipmentEntity.deliveryStatus.
   statusDescription {
   cell.accessoryType =
    UITableViewCellAccessoryType.Checkmark
 }
 return cell
}
```

This method is called once for each cell in the table view. It configures the cell from **DeliveryStatusEntity** items in the **deliveryStatusList** array.

The last section of code in the method adds a check mark to the cell if it is the currently selected delivery status.

11. Delete all comments at the bottom of the code file and add this **tableView:didSelectRowAtIndexPath:** method before the closing curly brace:

```
override func tableView(tableView:
    UITableView, didSelectRowAtIndexPath
    indexPath: NSIndexPath) {

    if let oldRow = deliveryStatusList.indexOf
        (self.shipmentEntity.deliveryStatus) {
        // Uncheck the previously checked cell
        let oldIndexPath = NSIndexPath(forRow:
            oldRow, inSection: 0)
        var cell = tableView.
            cellForRowAtIndexPath(oldIndexPath)
        cell?.accessoryType =
            UITableViewCellAccessoryType.None

        // Check the currently selected cell
        cell = tableView.
            cellForRowAtIndexPath(indexPath)
        cell?.accessoryType =
        UITableViewCellAccessoryType.Checkmark

        // Get the new delivery status
        let deliveryStatusEntity =
            deliveryStatusList[indexPath.row]
        self.shipmentEntity.deliveryStatus =
            deliveryStatusEntity
    }
}
}
```

This method is called whenever the user taps a cell in the **DeliveryStatus** scene's table view.

The first section of code unchecks the previously selected cell using these steps:

- The *index* of the previously selected delivery status is retrieved from the **ShipmentEntity** object and stored in the **oldRow** variable.
- An **NSIndexPath** object is created from the combination of the **oldRow** and section **0**.
- The **NSIndexPath** object is used to get the previously selected cell.
- The cell's **accessoryType** is set to **None**, which turns off the check mark.

The second section of code puts a check mark in the currently selected cell.

The third code section gets the **DeliveryStatusEntity** object that corresponds to the selected row and stores it in the **ShipmentEntity** object's **deliveryStatus** property.

Updating the Shipment Scene

Now you are going to change the **Shipment** scene so that it passes information to the **Delivery Status** scene.

1. In the Project Navigator, select the **Main.storyboard** file to display the storyboard in the design surface.
2. Select the segue between the **Shipment** scene and the **Delivery Status** scene (highlighted in red in Figure 12.77). Notice that when you do this, the **Shipment** scene's **Delivery Status** cell gets highlighted. This indicates that tapping this cell fires the segue. This is exactly what you want, so you don't need to create a new segue.

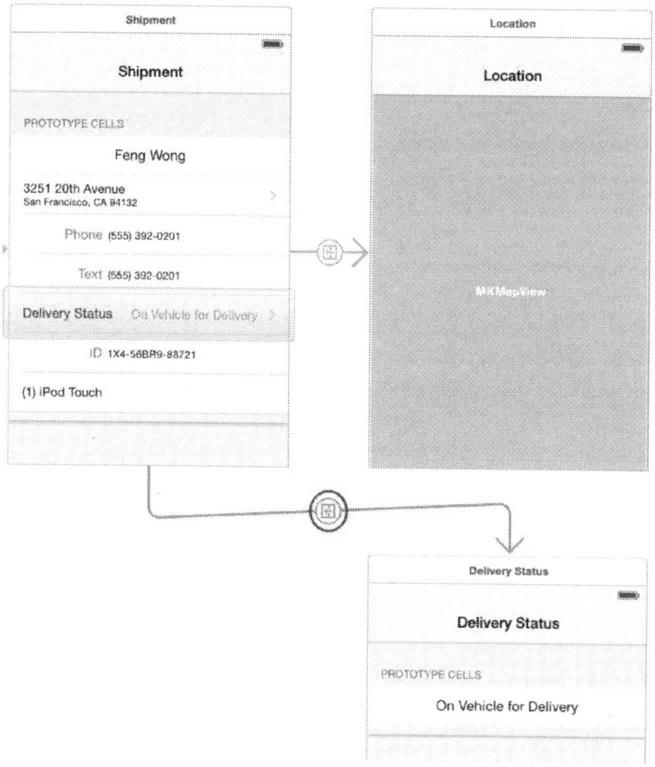

Figure 12.86 Select the Delivery Status segue.

3. With the segue still selected, go to the Attributes Inspector and set its **Identifier** attribute to **DeliveryStatusSegue** so you can reference the segue from code within the view controller.

4. Next, select the **ShipmentViewController.swift** file in the Project Navigator. Scroll to the bottom of the code file, delete all the commented code and add the following method before the closing curly brace:

```
override func prepareForSegue(segue:
  UIStoryboardSegue, sender: AnyObject?) {
    if segue.identifier == "DeliveryStatusSegue" {
      let tvc = segue.destinationViewController
        as! DeliveryStatusViewController
      tvc.shipmentEntity = self.shipmentEntity
    }
  }
}
```

This method is automatically called when any segue is fired from this view controller. Remember, there are two segues attached to this view controller:

- A segue to the Delivery Status scene.
- A segue to the Location scene.

That's why the first line of code in this method checks if the segue identifier is **DeliveryStatusSegue**. It's a best practice to always check the segue identifier, even if there is only one segue attached to the view controller. This helps avoid bugs if you eventually add new segues to the view controller.

If it's the correct segue, the code stores the currently selected **ShipmentEntity** object in the **shipmentEntity** property of the **DeliveryStatusViewController**.

5. Go back to Xcode and click the **Run** button. When the app appears in the Simulator, select the delivery in the **Deliveries** scene, which takes you to the **Shipment** scene. In the **Shipment** scene, select the **Delivery Status** row, and you should see the delivery status items (Figure 12.78).

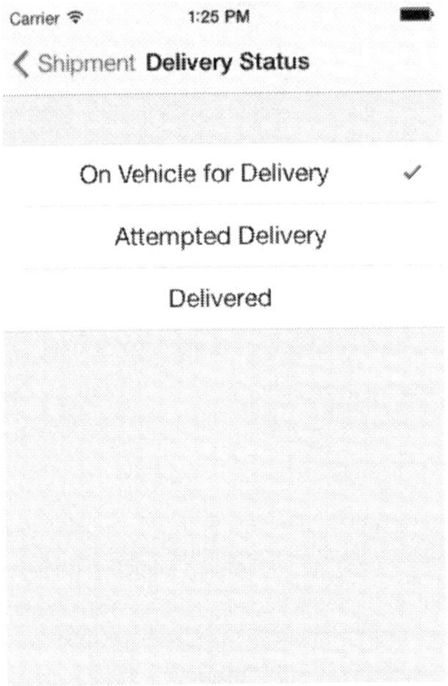

*Figure 12.78 The **Delivery Status** items.*

Select a different delivery status and the check mark disappears from the previously selected item and appears on the newly selected item.

Click the **Shipment** button in the navigation bar at the top of the screen. Notice that the **Delivery Status** cell hasn't changed even though you have selected a new delivery status. That's because we haven't refreshed the **Delivery Status** cell.

To do this, you need to first learn more about table views and passing values between view controllers. This information is covered in the next chapter, and we will fix the update of the **Delivery Status** cell after we cover that information! To manually refresh the cell, you can navigate back to the initial **Deliveries** scene and back again to the **Shipment** scene.

Retrieving Shipment Items

Now it's time to go back to the Shipment scene and retrieve the shipment items associated with a particular shipment.

Retrieving a Subset of Entities

So far, we have retrieved all entities of a particular type. We have retrieved all **ShipmentEntity** objects and all **DeliveryStatusEntity** objects.

However, you often need to return just a subset of entities in a data store. In the next sections, you are going to retrieve a subset of **ShipmentItemEntity** objects. Before you do so, it's important to understand the concepts behind retrieving a subset of entities.

As mentioned earlier in this chapter, in Core Data you can create a ***predicate*** containing filter criteria so only entities that match the specified criteria are retrieved from the database.

You use the **NSPredicate** class to create a filter that specifies the search criteria for entities. A predicate contains a ***condition*** that evaluates to true or false. For example, if you wanted to find all **ShipmentEntity** objects in the city of San Francisco, you can create the following predicate:

```
var predicate =
    NSPredicate(format: "city = 'San Francisco'")
```

If you wanted to find all **ShipmentEntity** objects where the customer's name contains the characters WONG, you can create a predicate like this:

```
var predicate =
    NSPredicate(format: "name CONTAINS 'Wong'")
```

You can also perform comparisons such as:

>	Greater than
<	Less than
>=	Greater than or equal to
<=	Less than or equal to
!=	Not equal to

As well as string-specific comparisons such as:

- **BEGINSWITH** - The string begins with specified characters.
- **CONTAINS** - The string contains specified characters.
- **ENDSWITH** - The string ends with specified characters.
- **LIKE** - You can use a ? to represent a single character in a search or * to represent zero or more characters in a search.

For more information on predicates, check out Apple's *Predicate Programming Guide*.

Creating ShipmentItemEntity and ShipmentItem Classes

Now you're ready to add **ShipmentItemEntity** to the data model. This entity represents the items that belong to a particular shipment.

1. If it's not already open, in Xcode, open the **iDeliverMobileCD** project.
2. Select the **iDeliverMobileCD.xcdatamodeld** file in the Project Navigator to open the entity data model in the design surface.

3. If it's not already in Table mode, switch to Table mode by clicking the left button in the **Editor Style** button group at the bottom of the entity data model.

4. At the bottom of the entity data model, click the **Add Entity** button.

5. In the Data Model Inspector, set the **Name** of the new entity to **ShipmentItemEntity** and also set the **Class** to **ShipmentItemEntity**.

6. Click the **Add Attribute** button at the bottom of the entity data model, and then go to the Data Model Inspector and apply the following settings:

    - **Name** - itemDescription
    - **Optional** - Uncheck this setting.
    - **Attribute Type** - String

    When you're finished, the settings should look like Figure 12.79.

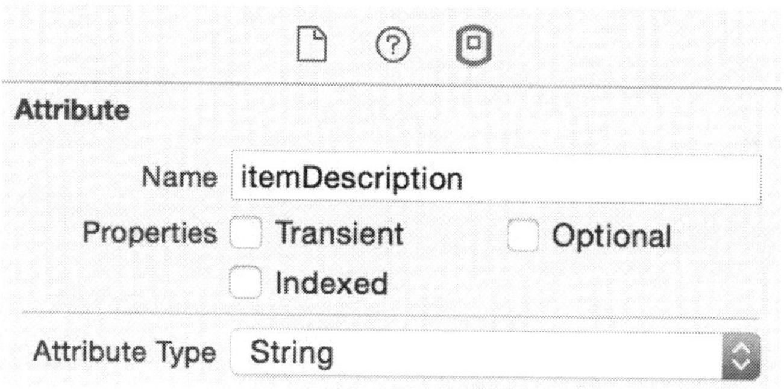

*Figure 12.79 The **itemDescription** attribute settings.*

7. Click the **Add Attribute** button again and add an attribute with the following settings:

    - **Name** - quantity
    - **Optional** - Uncheck this setting.
    - **Attribute Type** - Integer 32
    - **Default** - 1

When you're finished, the settings should look like Figure 12.80.

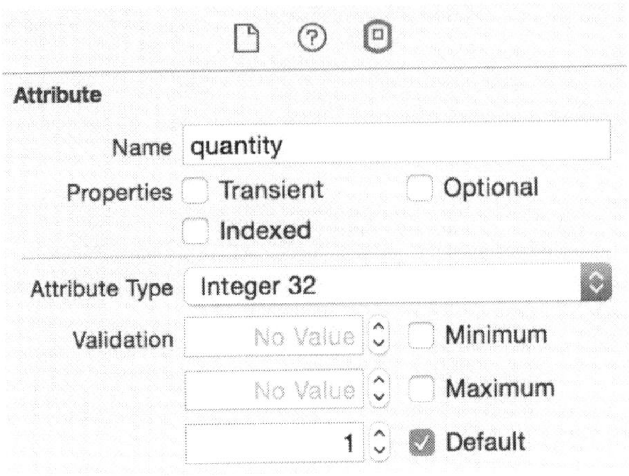

*Figure 12.80 The **quantity** attribute.*

8. Add one more attribute by clicking the **Add Attribute** button. Add an attribute with the following settings:

    - **Name** - shipmentID
    - **Optional** - Uncheck this setting
    - **Attribute Type** - String

    When you're finished, the settings should look like Figure 12.81.

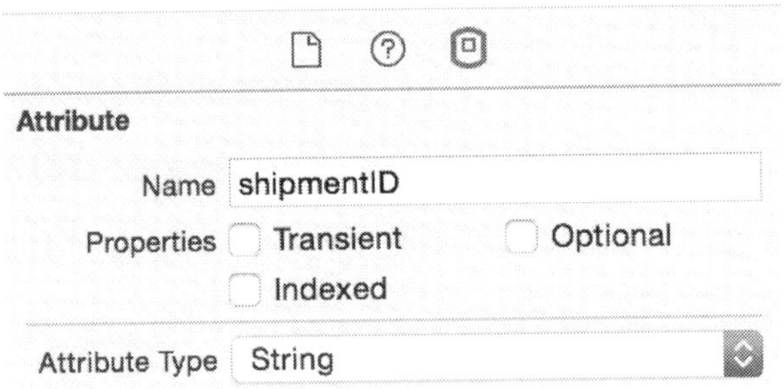

*Figure 12.81 The **shipmentID** attribute.*

Now you're ready to generate a **ShipmentItemEntity** class from the entity on the data model.

1. Select the **DeliveryStatusEntity.swift** file in the Project Navigator so the new file appears below it.

2. Select **File > New > File...** from the Xcode menu.
3. On the left side of the New File dialog, under **iOS**, select **Core Data**, and on the right side of the dialog, select **NSManagedObject subclass**.
4. In the next step of the dialog, select the check box for the **iDeliverMobileCD** data model and click **Next**.
5. In the next step of the dialog, select the check box for **ShipmentItemEntity**, and then click **Next**.
6. In the Save File dialog, unselect the **Use scalar properties for primitive data types** check box.
7. Click the **Create** button to add the new entity class to the Project Navigator.
8. In the **ShipmentItemEntities+CoreDataProperties. swift** file, remove the question marks at the end of each property declaration to make them non-optional

Creating the ShipmentItem Business Controller

Now that you have created the **ShipmentItemEntity** class, it's time to create the associated **ShipmentItem** business controller class.

1. In the Project Navigator, right-click the **DeliveryStatusEntity.swift** file (so the new file is added directly below it) and select **New File...** from the shortcut menu.
2. On the left side of the New File dialog, under **iOS**, select **Source**, and on the right side of the dialog, select the **Swift file** template.
3. Click the **Next** button and in the next step of the dialog in the **Save As** box, set the class name to **ShipmentItem.swift** and then click the **Create** button to add the new class file to the Project Navigator.
4. Add the following **import** statement and class declaration to the new code file:

```
import Foundation
import CoreData
class ShipmentItem<T: ShipmentItemEntity> :
  ABusinessObject <T> {
}
```

This specifies the name of the entity class associated with the business controller as **ShipmentItemEntity**.

5. Since we need to get a subset of **ShipmentItemEntity** objects, let's add a method to the **ShipmentItem** business controller that does that.

   Add the following method to the ShipmentItem class:

```
class ShipmentItem<T: ShipmentItemEntity> :
  ABusinessObject <T> {
    // Get all shipments for the Shipment ID
    func getShipmentItemsForShipmentID(shipmentID:
     String) -> Array<T> {
    let predicate = NSPredicate(format:
      "shipmentID = %@", shipmentID)
    return self.getEntitiesMatchingPredicate(predicate)
    }
}
```

Setting Up ShipmentItems on the Shipment Scene

Now you're ready to add the display of shipment items to the Shipment scene.

1. Select the **ShipmentViewController.swift** file in the Project Navigator and add the following properties to the class file:

```
class ShipmentViewController:
UITableViewController {
 var shipment: Shipment<ShipmentEntity>!
 var shipmentEntity: ShipmentEntity!
var shipmentItem = ShipmentItem()
var shipmentItemList = Array<ShipmentItemEntity>()
```

2. Next, add the following code to the **viewDidLoad** method:

```
override func viewDidLoad() {
 super.viewDidLoad()
self.shipmentItemList =
 self.shipmentItem.getShipmentItemsForShipmentID(
    self.shipmentEntity.shipmentID)
}
```

This code calls the **getShipmentItemsForShipmentID** method on the business controller and stores the entities returned from the data store into the **shipmentItemList** array.

3. Next, go to the **tableView:numberOfRowsInSection:** method and add the following **else if** statement:

```
override func tableView(tableView:
 UITableView, numberOfRowsInSection section:
 Int) -> Int {

   // Return the number of rows in the section.
   var rowCount = 0
   if section == 0 {
      rowCount = 6
   }
   else if section == 1
   {
     rowCount = shipmentItemList.count
   }
   return rowCount
}
```

If the section is equal to 1 (the shipment item section) it returns the number of **ShipmentItemEntity** objects in the **shipmentItemList**.

4. In the **tableView:cellForRowAtIndexPath:** method, add the following **else if** statement to the bottom of the existing **if** statement and above the method's **return** statement:

```
}
else if indexPath.section == 1 {
  let shipItem =
   self.shipmentItemList[indexPath.row]
  cell = tableView. dequeueReusableCellWithIdentifier(
```

```
        "ShipmentItemCell", forIndexPath: indexPath)
        cell.textLabel?.text =
         "(\(shipItem.quantity)) \(shipItem.itemDescription)"
        }
        return cell
    }
```

This code checks if the section number is 1, and if so, gets the shipment item for the specified row and stores its quantity and description in the cell's label.

5. Now you're ready to see what this looks like at run time. In Xcode, click the **Run** button. When the **Deliveries** scene appears, select the delivery, and you should see what is shown in Figure 12.82.

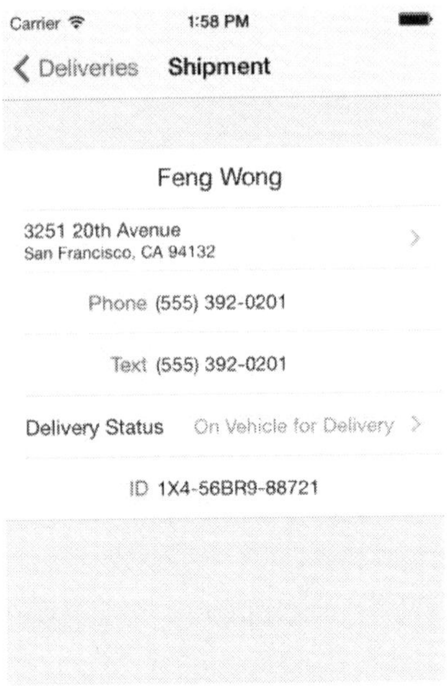

Figure 12.82 No Shipment items appear!

Do you know why no shipment items are displayed? It's because we never added any to the database. Let's fix that now.

Adding ShipmentItem Records to the Database

1. If it's not already launched, run the Firefox web browser Application.

2. In the Firefox menu, select **Tools > SQLite Manager**.

3. The **iDeliverMobileCD** database should be automatically opened. If it isn't, click the **Open** button in the toolbar and open the file manually.

4. On the left side of the SQLite Manager window, you should now see a new **ZSHIPMENTITEMENTITY** table. Expand the table node and you should see the columns shown in Figure 12.83.

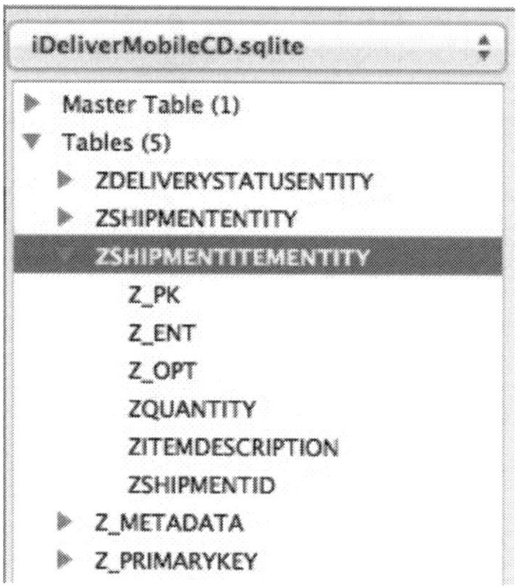

*Figure 12.83 The **ZSHIPMENTITEMENTITY** table.*

5. Let's add two records to this table. Click the **Add** button at the top of the window, and in the dialog, set the following values:

   - **Z_ENT** - 3
   - **Z_OPT** - 1
   - **ZQUANTITY** - 1
   - **ZITEMDESCRIPTION** - iPod Touch
   - **ZSHIPMENTID** - 1X4-56BR9-88721

   Click the **OK** button twice to add the new record.

6. For the second record, all you have to do is change the **ZITEMDESCRIPTION** column, and you get the other boxes set to their current values:

- **ZITEMDESCRIPTION** - Apple TV

Click the **OK** button twice to add the new record.

7. Press the **Cancel** button to close the dialog, and you can see the two new records in the database.

8. Go back to Xcode and click the **Run** button. When the app appears in the Simulator, navigate to the **Shipment** scene, and you should see the two new shipment items (Figure 12.84)!

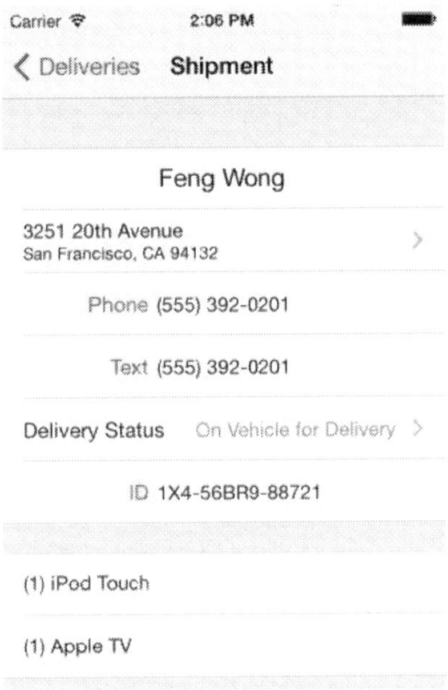

Figure 12.84 Shipment items in the Simulator.

Creating, Deleting, and Saving Entities

Until now, you have only been able to add items to the app using the SQLite Manager. So how do you use a business controller to create and delete entities? This is easy to do as you will see in the next chapter.

To save changes to entities, all you need do is call the **saveEntities** method on a business controller, and all changes to associated entities are saved. It's as easy as that!

However, there are a few things about table views and passing values back from a view controller you need to learn before we add this ability to the **iDeliverMobileCD** app. You will do all this and more in the next chapter!

Migrating Changes to the Data Model

When you run your app for the first time, a SQLite database is automatically created for you when your app tries to access Core Data entities.

However, once the database has been created, if you make a change to the entity data model and then try to run your app again, you will get a Core Data error!

If you don't care about the data in the database (and you don't care about recreating the data), you can get past the error by deleting the SQLite database file. The next time you run the app, Core Data will automatically create a new, empty database for you.

However, what if you want to preserve the data and move it forward to a new database? That's where Core Data's migration comes into play.

I have added special code to the **mmBusinessObject** class file that performs an automatic lightweight migration of your data. Lightweight migration only works for certain types of changes to your data model such as:

- Adding, deleting, or renaming an entity.
- Adding, deleting, or renaming an attribute.
- Changing an attribute from non-optional to optional.
- Changing an attribute from optional to non-optional (as long as you provide a default value).
- Adding, deleting, or renaming a relationship.

For a complete list of everything you can change and still perform a lightweight migration as well as how to migrate more complex changes, check out Apple's Help topic *Core Data Model Versioning and Data Migration* programming guide.

To see the code I have added to initiate lightweight migration, in the Project Navigator, expand the **Business Layer** group and then select the **mmBusinessObject.swift** file. Scroll down to the **persistentStoreCoordinator** method, and you will see the following code:

```
try coordinator.addPersistentStoreWithType
(NSSQLiteStoreType, configuration: nil, URL: url,
options: [NSMigratePersistentStoresAutomaticallyOption:
true,NSInferMappingModelAutomaticallyOption: true])
```

This code sets two options that tell Core Data to do the following when it determines the data model has been changed since the database was first created:

1. Create a new database and migrate the data from the old database to the new database.

2. Try to automatically infer the new mapping by comparing the original version of the data model with a new version of the data model that you create.

This is an important point to note: *After you have created a SQLite database from an entity data model, you must make a new version of that model before making any changes to it!*

Doing this gives Core Data a "before" version of your model it can use to compare to an "after" version and derive a plan for migrating your data.

Automatic Data Migration Step-by-Step

To show you how automatic migration works, let's walk through the steps of a simple change.

1. Select the **iDeliverMobileCD.xcdatamodeld** file in the Project Navigator.

2. Select **Editor > Add Model Version...** from the Xcode menu.

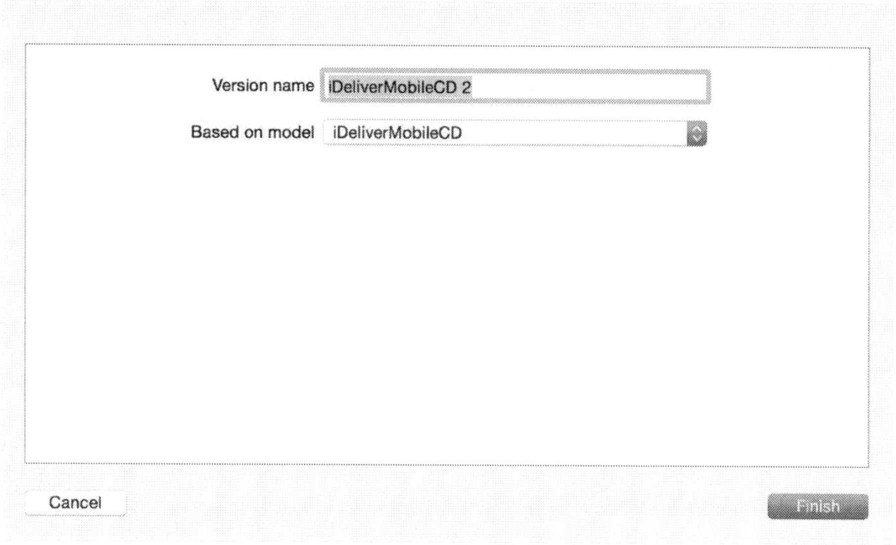

Figure 12.85 Creating a new model version.

3. In the dialog that appears, leave the Version name set to **iDeliverMobileCD 2** and click the **Finish** button (Figure 12.85).

   This adds two sub nodes under the original node, one with the same name as the original node but with a .xcdatamodel extension, and a second node with the name you assigned the new model in the previous step (Figure 12.86).

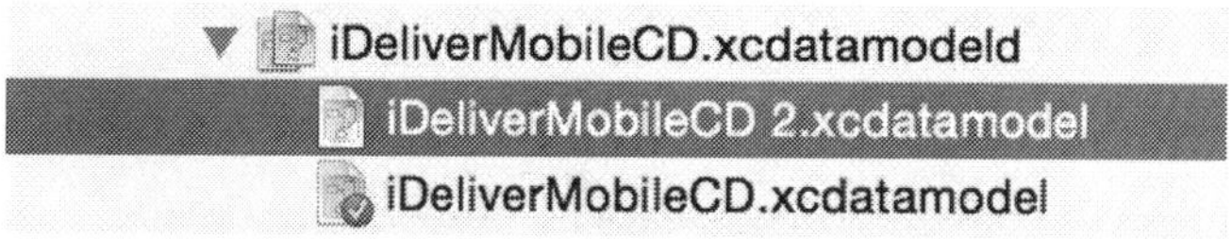

Figure 12.86 The new data model version.

The green check mark next to the original model version indicates it is the "current" version that will be used by the app at run time. Let's make the new model the current version instead. To do this, go to the File Inspector and under the **Model Version** section, change **Current** to **iDeliverMobileCD 2** (Figure 12.87).

Figure 12.87 Set the current model version.

This places the green check mark next to the new model version in the Project Navigator.

Now you're ready to make a change to the entity data model to see how lightweight migration works.

1. Due to a bug in Xcode, you need to make sure you truly have the new model version selected. To do this, select the old model version and then reselect the new model version (the one with the green check mark) in the Project Navigator.

2. In the left side of the Data Model Editor under **Entities**, select the **DeliveryStatusEntity**. Click the plus (+) button to add a new attribute to the entity. Set its name to **order** and its type to **Integer 32** (Figure 12.88). This attribute can be used to specify the display order of the delivery status items within the app.

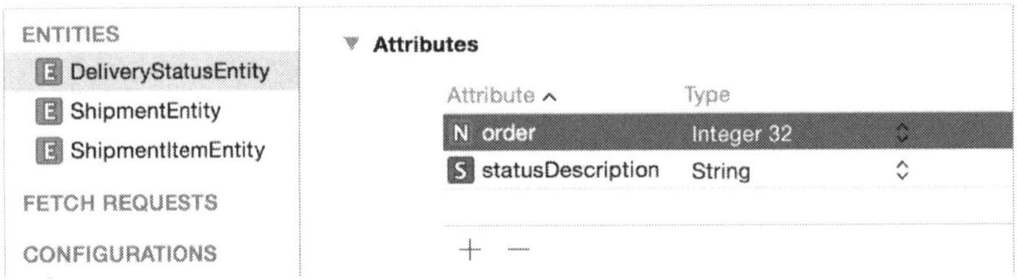

*Figure 12.88 Add a new **order** attribute.*

3. Now go to the Data Model Inspector and uncheck the **Optional** setting, since all delivery status items should have this value set.

That completes the change to the entity data model. Now let's run the app and let Core Data perform an automatic lightweight migration.

1. In Xcode, click the **Run** button. When the app appears in the Simulator, the lightweight migration has been performed!

2. Click Xcode's Stop button.

3. If it's not already open, launch FireFox and then open the SQLite Manager.

4. Open the **iDeliverMobileCD** database. Note that the database location has changed during migration so make sure you check Xcode's Console to determine the correct location.

5. You should see the new **order** column with all items set to zero (Figure 12.89).

Z_PK	Z_ENT	Z_OPT	ZORDER	ZSTATUSDESCRIPT
1	1	1	0	On Vehicle for Delivery
2	1	1	0	Attempted Delivery
3	1	1	0	Delivered

*Figure 12.89 The new **order** column has been added to the **ZDELIVERYSTATUSENTITY** table.*

6. Edit each of the items and set the **ZORDER** column to 1 for the first item, 2 for the second item, and 3 to the last item.

Including a Pre-Populated Database With Your App

Often, you need to include a database with your app that is pre-populated with data. This is extremely easy to do using the **mmBusinessObject** Core Data wrapper class. For an example of how to do this, see *Chapter 13: Managing Lists of Data With Table Views* under the section *Bundling a Pre-Populated Database.*

Summary

- Your app's data usually takes the form of entities, which are the Model in the Model-View-Controller design pattern. An entity represents an object in the real world and has properties that represent the attributes of a real-world object.

- In iOS apps, you use an entity data model (or just "data model" for short) to define the entities used in your app.

- After you have designed your entities, you can then generate Swift entity classes from the entities in the entity data model.

- Core Data provides something called ***object-relational mapping*** (ORM) for your iOS apps. This means that Core Data converts your entity objects into information that can be stored in a relational database (also known as a data "store"). This spares you the burden of learning the intricacies of database programming.

- The database Apple has chosen to use on iOS devices is SQLite. The SQLite database is compact and is one of the most widely deployed databases in the world.
- Core Data maps your entities into rows stored in database tables and your entities' attributes into columns in a table.
- The primary Core Data class you will work with is **NSManagedObjectContext**. You call methods on an instance of the object context to retrieve, insert, update, and delete your app's entities.
- The object context keeps track of all the entities you have retrieved or created as well as any changes you have made to the entities.
- The object context offers an all-or-nothing approach to updating your entities. When you call its **saveEntities** method, it saves all entities that have been changed. It doesn't offer the option to save changes to one or more select entities.
- Apple recommends that you put code in your view controllers that calls methods on the object context to create, retrieve, update, and delete entities. The problem with this approach is that it breaks the rule of separating your app into three distinct sections.
- You should put your entity manipulation code in a business controller class. This provides the following benefits:
    - It encapsulates the entity manipulation code within the business controller, making it easy to extend and reuse.
    - It allows each business controller to have its own object context, providing finer control over when and how entities get saved to the database.
- The main steps for adding Core Data to a project are:
    - Add **CoreData.framework** to your project.

- Add a **Business Layer** group to the project.
- Add an **mmBusinessObject** class and entity data model to the **Business Layer** group.

- You can view the entity data model in either Table or Graph mode.
- Core Data provides the option to create relationships between entities on your data model.
- Creating relationships simplifies the code you need to write when working with entities.
- There are two main types of relationships:

    1. To-One
    2. To-Many

- In a To-One relationship, an entity holds a reference to one other entity of another type.
- In a To-Many relationship, an entity can reference multiple entities of another type.
- Relationships are usually two-way where each relationship has an inverse.
- There is a downside to setting relationships in the entity data model. *All entities in a relationship must be retrieved from a single object context* (if you plan on updating them later on)! This causes you to lose the ability to update one type of entity at a time.
- When using out-of-the-box Core Data, here are the main steps for retrieving entities:

    1. Create the request object.
    2. Set the entity type to be fetched.
    3. Set the predicate.
    4. Set the sort descriptor.
    5. Execute the fetch.
    6. Check for errors.

- To create a new Core Data entity, you call its **insertNewObjectForEntityForName:** method to the **NSEntityDescription** class.

- To delete an entity, you can call the object context's **deleteObject:** method. This marks the entity for deletion. Entities that are marked for deletion are physically removed from the data store the next time the object context is asked to save changes to entities.

- To save all the changes to entities that have been created and retrieved from a particular object context, call the object context's **saveEntities:** method.

- The **mmBusinessObject** class doesn't replace Core Data. It simply provides a "wrapper" around the Core Data classes that makes them easier to use and allows you to write less code when you want to create, retrieve, update, and delete entities.

- **mmBusinessObject** (or an **ABusinessObject** subclass) can be used as the superclass of all the business controller classes in your project.

- Your business controller classes can contain all the code in your app that retrieves and updates entities.

- Business controllers have a **dbName** property where you can specify the name of the app's database. Since most apps use just one database, it makes sense to specify this in a class that sits in the hierarchy between **mmBusinessObject** and your app's business controller classes.

- The methods of a business controller class allow you to create, delete, retrieve, and update entities.

- To use the code within business controllers, you need to instantiate them from within your app's view controllers and call methods on them that create, retrieve, update, and delete entities.

- A single view controller can work with multiple business controllers.

- When your app first tries to access a database, if it doesn't exist, Core Data automatically creates an empty database for you.

- When you run an app in the Simulator, a folder is created for you on your development computer's hard drive that contains the compiled app and its related files, including any database file(s).
- One of the best tools for viewing a SQLite database is the SQLite Manager add-on for Firefox.
- When converting a prototype table view containing static data to a table view displaying dynamic data, you should keep all the cells with unique formatting and delete cells with duplicate formatting.
- When you convert a prototype table view to use live data, you should also move all prototype cells to the first section of the table view so they can be easily retrieved at run time.
- You need to set a reuse identifier for a table view cell if you need to reference the cell from code within a view controller.
- You can specify a *predicate* that contains filter criteria so only entities that match the search criteria are retrieved from the data store.
- If entities are related in the entity data model, business controllers must share the same object context if you need to save changes to the entities. You can copy an object context from one business controller to another.

Step-By-Step Movie 12.1

This movie takes you step-by-step through the process of creating the **ShipmentEntity** and **DeliveryStatusEntity** in the entity data model.

http://www.iosappsfornonprogrammers.com/B3M121.9.html

Step-By-Step Movie 12.2

This movie takes you step-by-step through the process of creating relationships between the **ShipmentEntity** and **DeliveryStatusEntity** in the entity data model.

http://www.iosappsfornonprogrammers.com/B3M122.9.html

Step-By-Step Movie 12.3

This movie takes you step-by-step through the process of generating Swift classes from entities in the data model.

http://www.iosappsfornonprogrammers.com/B3M123.9.html

Step-By-Step Movie 12.4

This movie takes you step-by-step through the process of working with **mmBusinessObject** and creating business controller classes.

http://www.iosappsfornonprogrammers.com/B3M124.9.html

Step-By-Step Movie 12.5

This movie takes you step-by-step through the process of converting the **Deliveries** scene from a prototype to a fully functioning view controller using Core Data.

http://www.iosappsfornonprogrammers.com/B3M125.9.html

Step-By-Step Movie 12.6

This movie takes you step-by-step through the process of converting the **Shipment** scene from a prototype to a fully functioning view controller using Core Data.

http://www.iosappsfornonprogrammers.com/B3M126.9.html

Step-By-Step Movie 12.7

This movie takes you step-by-step through the process of creating a new segue between the **Deliveries** and **Shipment** scenes and passing the currently selected **ShipmentEntity** to the **ShipmentViewController**.

http://www.iosappsfornonprogrammers.com/B3M127.9.html

Step-By-Step Movie 12.8

This movie takes you step-by-step through the process of converting the **Delivery Status** scene from a prototype to a fully functioning view controller using Core Data.

http://www.iosappsfornonprogrammers.com/B3M128.9.html

Step-By-Step Movie 12.9

This movie takes you step-by-step through the process of changing the **Shipment** scene so that it passes information to the **Delivery Status** scene.

http://www.iosappsfornonprogrammers.com/B3M129.9.html

Step-By-Step Movie 12.10

This movie takes you step-by-step through the process of changing the **Shipment** scene so that it displays shipment items using Core Data.

http://www.iosappsfornonprogrammers.com/B3M1210.9.html

Chapter 13: Managing Lists of Data With Table Views

So far in this book series, you have learned just enough about table views to get through some basic exercises. In this chapter, we'll cover some of the basics by way of review, and then you will take a deep dive into the world of managing lists of data with table views!

Sections in This Chapter

1. *Understanding Table Views*
2. *Filling a Table View With Data*
3. *Using Business Controllers*
4. *Custom Table View Controllers*
5. *Configuring Table View Cells*
6. *Passing Data to a View Controller*
7. *Returning Data From a View Controller*

8. *Displaying Images in Table View Rows*
9. *Creating Section Headers and Footers*
10. *Referencing Cells With Enumerations*
11. *Handling Table View User Selection*
12. *Creating Custom Cells*
13. *Creating Indexed Table Views*
14. *Adding a Search Bar to a Table View*
15. *Reordering, Deleting, and Adding Table View Rows*
16. *Summary*

Understanding Table Views

Table views are used to display lists of data in iOS apps. If you have an iOS device of your own, you have used table views frequently since they are found in most of Apple's built-in apps such as Settings (Figure 13.1), iTunes, Photos, Mail, Weather, and Contacts.

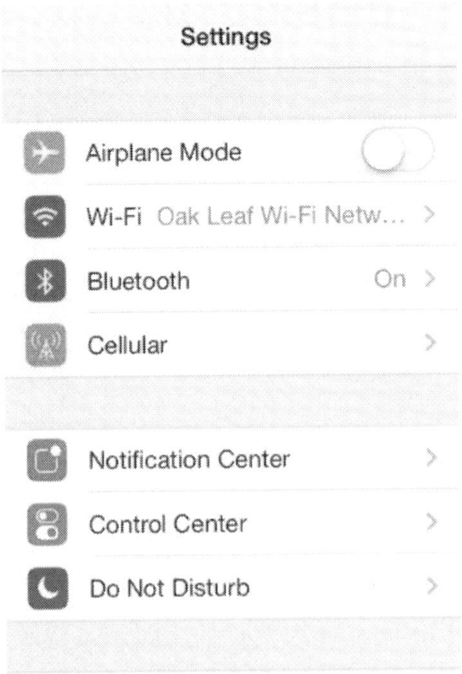

Figure 13.1 The Settings table view

iOS table views are based on the **UITableView** class. They are the View in the Model-View-Controller design pattern. Table views are designed to display large sets of data and are configurable to look any way you want as evidenced by the wide range of table view styles used in the built-in iOS apps.

There are three main table view styles—plain, indexed, and grouped—as shown in Figure 13.2. You will learn more about all three styles later in this chapter.

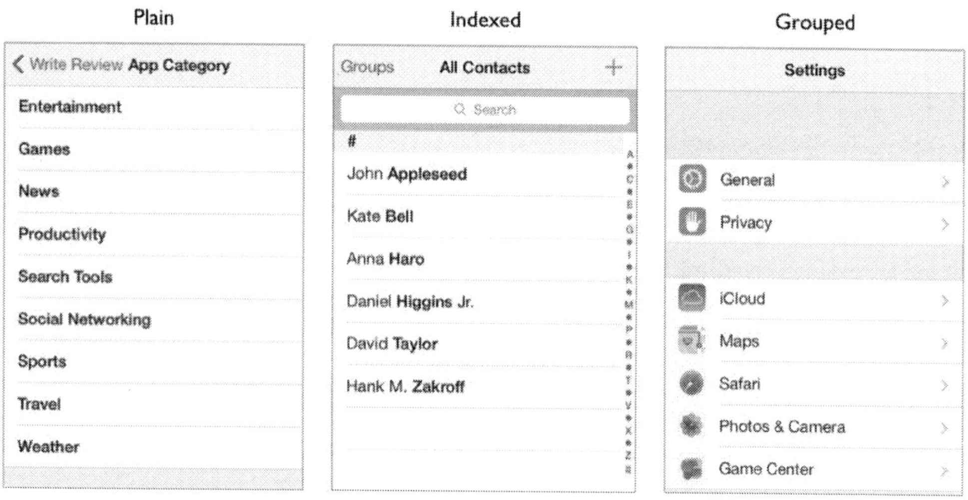

Figure 13.2 Plain, indexed, and grouped table views

Regardless of the table view style used, each item in the table view is a row and a table view can contain an unlimited number of rows. Each row is one column wide and, when using the built-in styles, can contain an image, text, and accessory icon such as the *disclosure indicator* (the grey arrow) shown on the right side of the cells in the **Grouped** image in Figure 13.2. You will learn later in this chapter under the section *Creating Custom Cells* how to create cells that can contain just about anything.

Each division of a table view is a "section". If you have no divisions, you have only one section. For example, in Figure 13.2, the **Plain** table view has just one section, the **Indexed** table view has five sections (**A**, **B**, **H**, **T**, and **Z**), and the **Grouped** table view has two sections.

The iOS table view is extremely fast at run time, even when scrolling through thousands of items. How does it accomplish this? Regardless of the number of items contained in a list, the table view only contains enough cells to display the items visible in the view plus a few additional cells for items that will soon become visible. So, even though you may have thousands of songs on your device, there are only a dozen or so active cells containing song information in the iTunes app's table view at any given time. As cells are scrolled out of view, they are instantly reused to display other content.

Filling a Table View With Data

So how do you fill a table view with data? Some table views are static, so you can create static cells at design time just as you did in the prototype app in

Book 1: Diving Into iOS. However, it's more usual for table views to be dynamically filled at run time as you did in the previous chapter on Core Data.

In iOS apps, table views usually get their data from a data source object—specifically, an object that implements the **UITableViewDataSource** protocol. This object is usually an instance of **UITableViewController**, which implements this protocol and was designed by Apple specifically to work with table views.

Rather than putting code that retrieves entities directly in a view controller, you should put the code in a business controller and then call the business controller methods from the view controller. Ultimately, you still need to be familiar with the standard table view controller methods because you need to know the methods you should place calls to business controllers in.

The **UITableViewDataSource** protocol contains three methods used to fill a table view with data Figure 13.3. It's up to you to create a custom table view controller for your table view and add code in each of these three methods that interacts with a business controller.

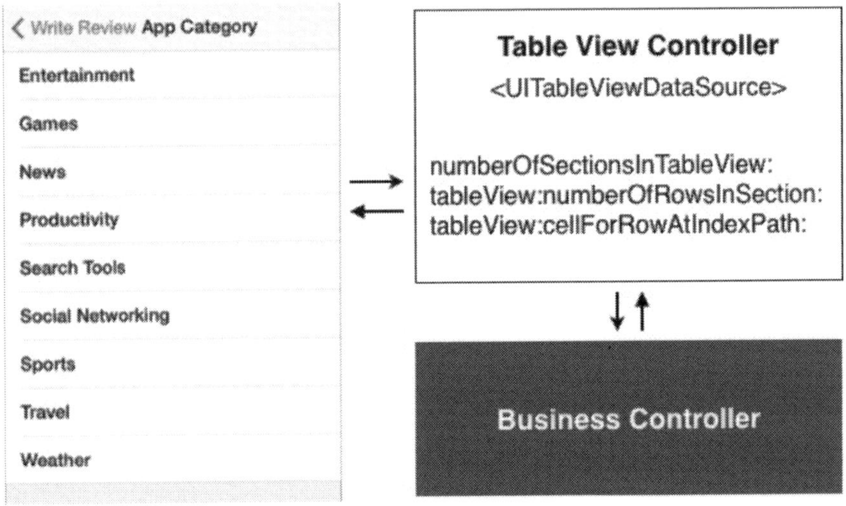

Figure 13.3 A table view makes calls to table view controller methods, which in turn call methods in a business controller.

At run time, before a table view is displayed, it passes method calls to the table view controller in the order shown in Figure 13.4.

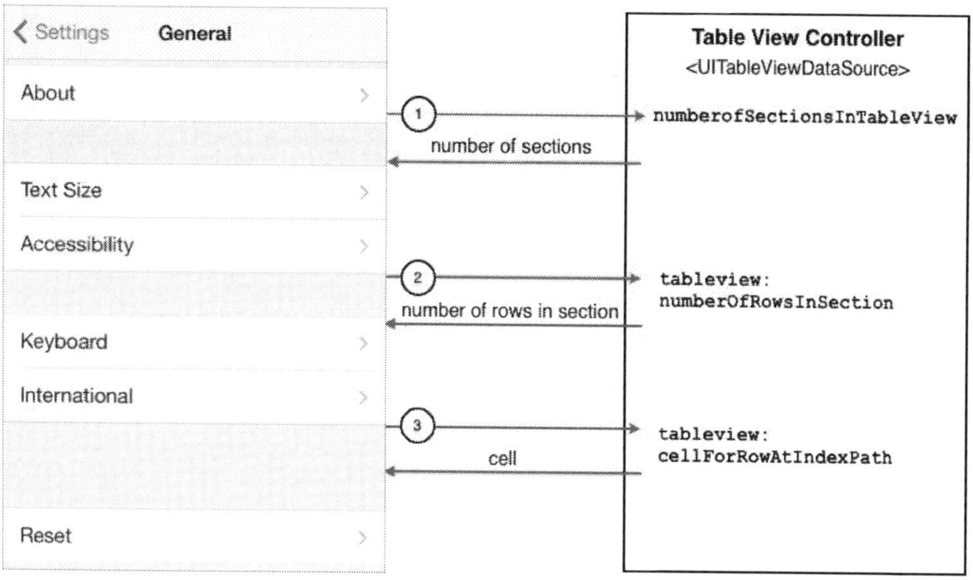

Figure 13.4 The calling sequence of the ***UITableViewDataSource*** *methods.*

Here is an overview of what each method does:

1. **numberOfSectionsInTableView:** is called by the table view first. This method returns the number of sections in the table view. In the example in Figure 13.4, there are four sections in the table view, so this method returns 4. After calling this method, the table view then adds the specified number of sections to itself.

2. **tableView:numberOfRowsInSection:** is called by the table view once for each section. This method returns the number of rows in the specified section. In the example in Figure 13.4, this method is called four times because there are four sections in the table view. Each time the table view calls this method, it passes a section number, starting with zero, one, two, and then three. In this example, the method returns the following row count for each section:

    - 1 for section 0
    - 2 for section 1
    - 2 for section 2
    - 1 for section 3

In the table view in Figure 13.4, the number of rows in each section is fixed. Often, the number of rows is determined dynamically at run time. For example, in the iTunes app, the number of songs in a list is determined by the number of songs stored on your iOS device.

3. **tableView:cellForRowAtIndexPath:** is called by the table view once for each visible (or about to become visible) cell in the table view. This method returns a table view cell object for the specified section and row. In the example shown in Figure 13.4, the method is first called for:

   - Section 0, row 0
   - Section 1, row 0
   - Section 1, row 1
   - Section 2, row 0
   - Section 2, row 1
   - Section 3, row 0

In this way, a table view is dynamically filled with items at run time.

Using Business Controllers

In the previous chapter, you used business-controller objects to retrieve entities to be displayed in table views. Figure 13.5 shows the big picture of how a table view controller uses the services of a business-controller object to fill a table view.

Here are the details for each step:

1. In the table view controller's **viewDidLoad** method, it creates an instance of the **Shipment** business- controller object.

2. The table view controller then calls the **getAllEntities:** method of the **Shipment** business controller and stores the resulting **ShipmentEntity** objects in the **shipmentList** array variable.

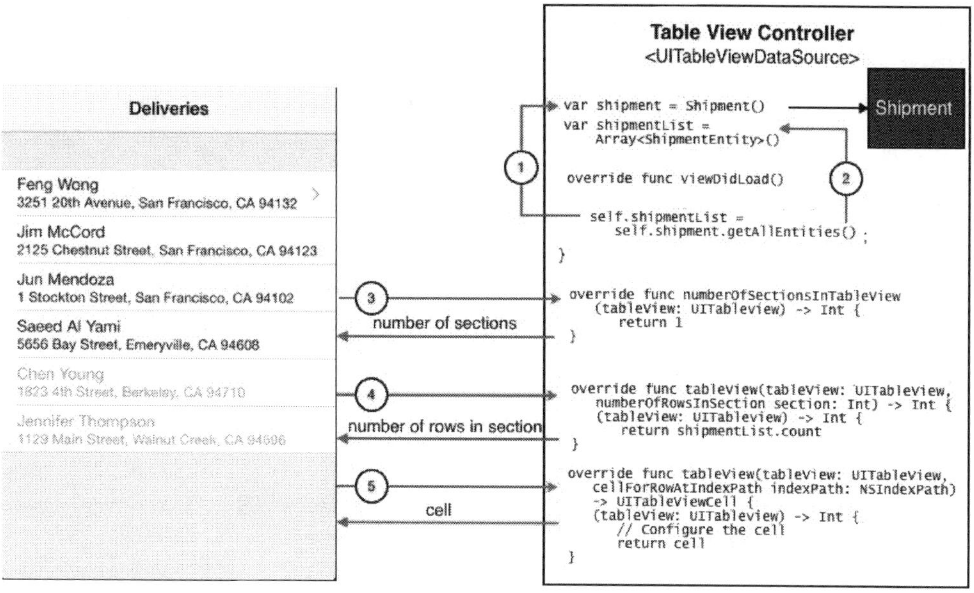

Figure 13.5 Table view controller and business controller collaboration.

3. In its **numberOfSectionsInTableView:** method, the table view controller returns **1** since there is only one section in the table view.

4. In its **tableView:numberOfRowsInSection:** method, the table view controller returns the count of **ShipmentEntity** items stored in the **shipmentList** array variable.

5. In its **tableView:cellForRowAtIndexPath:** method, the table view controller retrieves a **ShipmentEntity** object from the **shipmentList** array by using the specified row number and uses the entity to configure the cell it returns to the table view.

Hopefully, this diagram helps you better understand the interaction between the table view controllers and business controllers you implemented in the **Deliveries**, **Shipment**, and **Delivery Status** scenes in the previous chapter.

Custom Table View Controllers

When you drop a table view controller on a storyboard as you did with the **Deliveries**, **Shipment**, and **Delivery Status** scenes in Book 1, even though you were creating a prototype app, an instance of **UITableViewController** was created to manage the table views—even though the content of the table views was static. However, to provide dynamic content for the table views in these scenes, you must create a custom table view controller class for each scene. Here are the custom view controllers associated with the scenes in Figure 13.6:

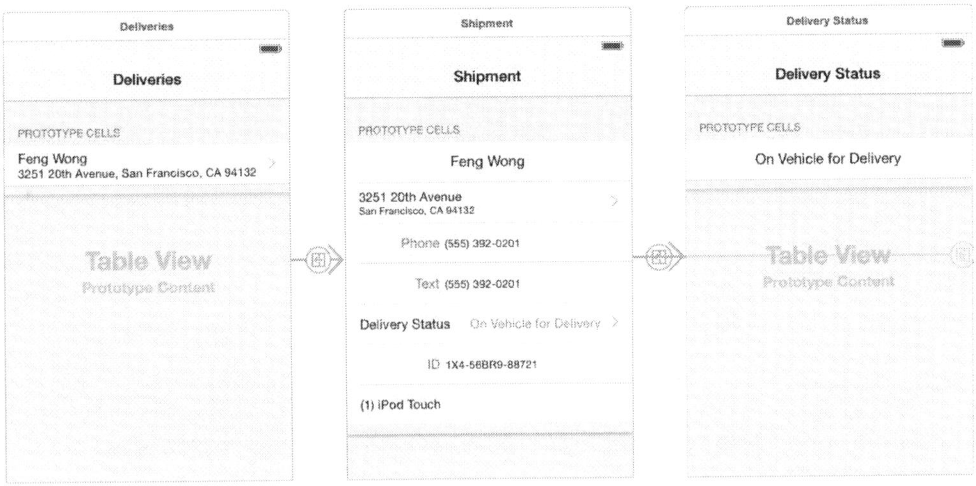

Figure 13.6 Dynamic data requires custom table view controllers.

- **DeliveriesViewController**
- **ShipmentViewController**
- **DeliveryStatusViewController**

Here are the basic steps to create a custom table view controller (don't perform these steps now):

1. Create a new subclass of **UITableViewController** (for example, **DeliveriesViewController**).

2. Go to the storyboard, click on the dock at the top of the scene you want to associate with the new view controller, then go to the Identity Inspector, and change the **Class** of the table view controller to the class you created in the previous step.

   For example, in Figure 13.7, the default **UITableViewController** class is being changed to a custom **DeliveriesViewController** class.

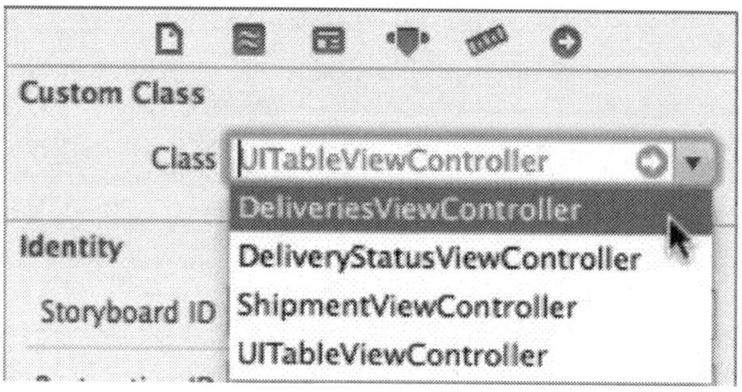

Figure 13.7 Specifying a custom table view controller.

If you find yourself in a position where you have created a custom view controller for a particular scene, but no data shows up in the table view, it may be that you have forgotten this second step.

Configuring Table View Cells

In the previous chapter, you added code to three different table view controllers that configured the cells in the table view. Let's take a closer look at that code to make sure you understand what's going on.

At run time, when a table view is being filled, it calls the **tableView:cellForRowAtIndexPath:** method on its associated table view controller once for each cell in the table view. Basically, the table view is requesting that the table view controller return a fully configured cell object for the specified section and row.

Figure 13.8 provides an overview of the interaction between the table view and table view controller when the **tableView:cellForRowAtIndexPath:** method is executed at run time.

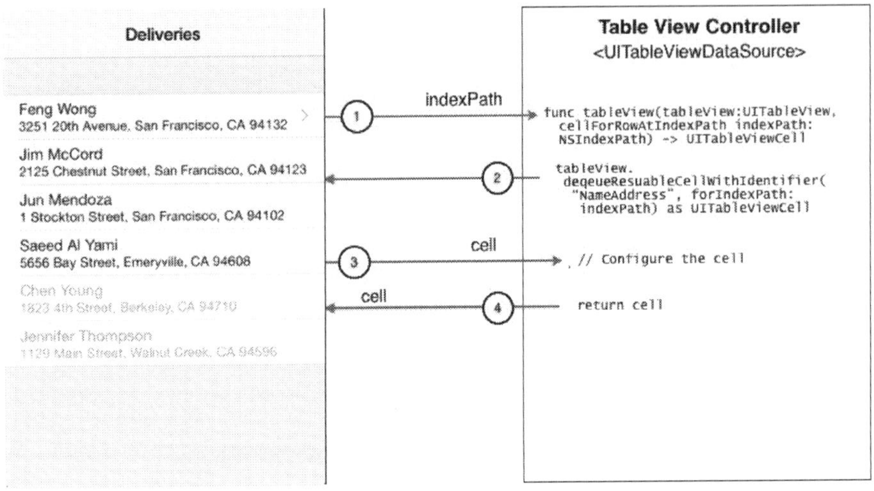

Figure 13.8 Configuring a table view cell at run time.

1. The table view calls the table view controller's **tableView:cellForRowAtIndexPath:** method, passing an **indexPath** object. This **indexPath** object has **section** and **row** properties that indicate the section and row of the cell the table view is requesting from the table view controller.

2. The table view controller calls back to the table view's **dequeueReusableCellWithIdentifer:** method, passing a **Cell Identifier** value.

3. When a user scrolls through a table view, the cells that scroll off screen are added to a queue of cells that can be reused. When the table view's **dequeueReusableCellWithIdentifier:** method is called, the table view checks if there is a reusable cell with the specified identifier in the queue, and if so, it returns the cell. If there are no cells in the queue, it creates a brand new cell of the specified identifier type.

4. Next, the table view controller configures the cell returned from the table view. This usually involves adding code that sets the text of the labels in the cell as well as any accessory indicator.

5. The table view controller returns the configured cell back to the table view, which adds the cell to the list.

Let's take a closer look at the code that you added to the **DeliveriesViewController** for this method in the previous chapter. Here is the first line of code that configures the table view cell:

```
var shipmentEntity = self.shipmentList[indexPath.row]
```

The code gets a **ShipmentEntity** object from the **shipmentList** array using the **indexPath** parameter's **row** property. You need to get a **ShipmentEntity** object so you can get the name and address associated with the shipment and display it in the table view cell.

Now let's look at the next few lines of code:

```
cell.textLabel?.text = shipmentEntity.name
cell.detailTextLabel?.text =
    shipmentEntity.address + ", " +
    shipmentEntity.city + ", " +
    shipmentEntity.region + " " +
    shipmentEntity.postalCode
```

This code sets the **text** property of the cell's main **textLabel** and its secondary **detailTextLabel** as shown in Figure 13.9.

*Figure 13.9 Table view cell **textLabel** and **detailTextLabel**.*

The cell configuration code stores the **ShipmentEntity** object's **name** into the **text** property of the **textLabel**. It then appends the address, city, region, and postal code properties to create the text for the **detailTextLabel**.

There's no need to set the font size and color of the cell because these are picked up from the **ShipmentCell** template that you created as shown in Figure 13.9.

Passing Data to a View Controller

Typically, when navigating between view controllers, the view controller you are navigating *to* (the destination) needs information from the view controller you are navigation *from* (the source).

This usually requires three key steps:

1. Create a property on the destination view controller to hold the data being passed by the source view controller.
2. Configure the segue between the source and destination view controllers.
3. In the source view controller, implement the **prepareForSegue:** method and add code that stores the data to be passed to the destination view controller's property.

For example, in Figure 13.10, the **Shipment** table view controller needs to know which shipment was selected in the **Deliveries** scene, so the **ShipmentEntity** for the selected row is passed from the **DeliveriesViewController** to the **ShipmentViewController**.

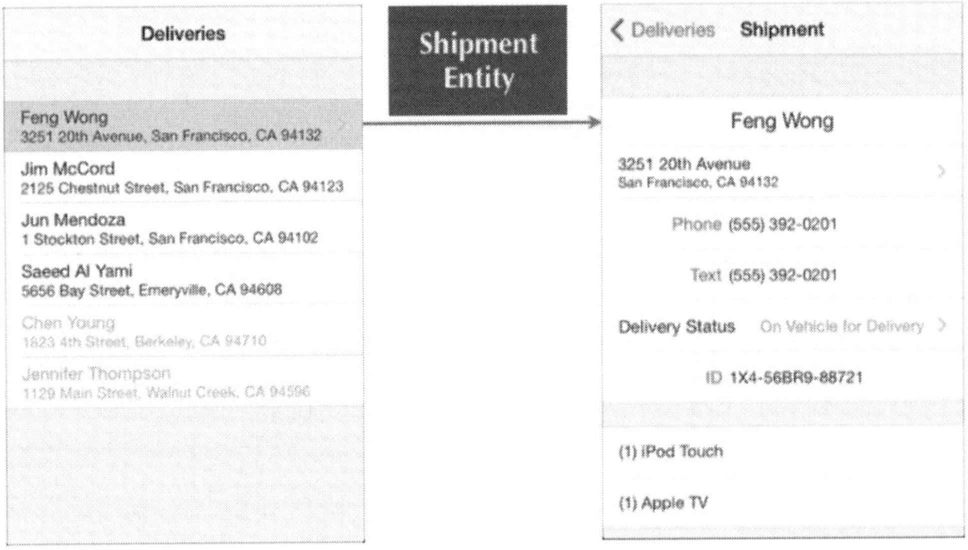

Figure 13.10 Passing an entity between view controllers.

In line with the three steps shown earlier in this section,

a **shipmentEntity** property was first added to the **ShipmentViewController**. This provides a place for the **DeliveriesViewController** to store the selected **ShipmentEntity**.

Second, the segue shown in Figure 13.11 was configured between the two view controllers and was assigned a **ShipmentSegue** identifier.

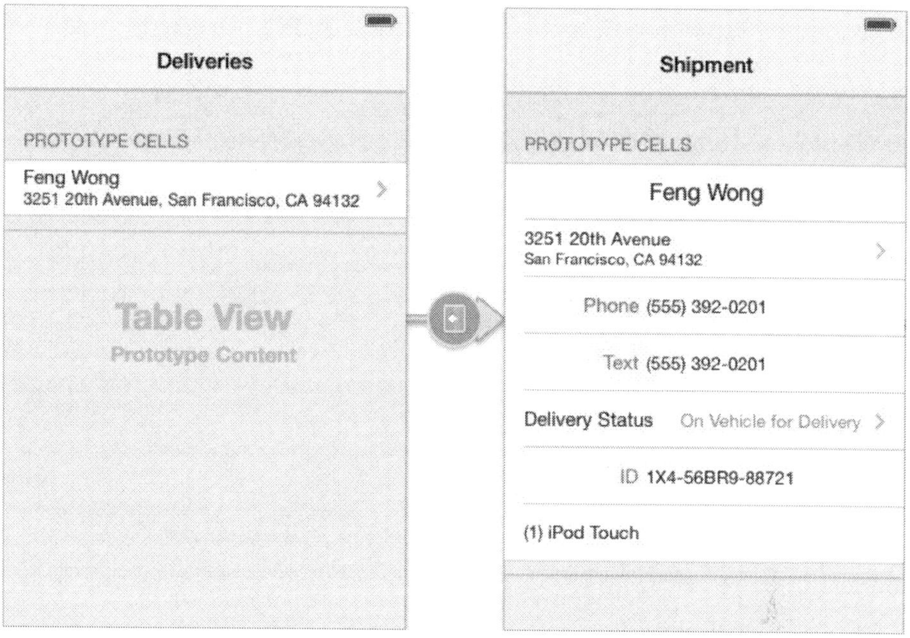

Figure 13.11 The segue between the Deliveries and Shipment scenes.

Third, a **prepareForSegue:** method was added to the **DeliveriesViewController** (I have included only the relevant code):

```
override func prepareForSegue(segue:
UIStoryboardSegue, sender: AnyObject?) {
  if segue.identifier == "ShipmentSegue" {

    // Get the destination view controller
    var tvc = segue.destinationViewController as!
         ShipmentViewController

    // Get the currently selected row
    var indexPath =
         self.tableView.indexPathForSelectedRow()

    // Save the ShipmentEntity for this row
    // on the ShipmentViewController
    tvc.shipmentEntity =
         self.shipmentList[indexPath!.row]
    }
}
```

This code performs the following steps, which are very standard for most methods of this type:

1. Checks the segue identifier to make sure it is the **ShipmentSegue**.
2. Gets a reference to the destination view controller (in this case, **ShipmentViewController**).
3. Gets the index path of the currently selected row.
4. Gets the **ShipmentEntity** associated with the row and stores a reference to the **ShipmentEntity** in the destination view controller's **shipment** property.

You can use this code as a pattern for passing values from a source view controller to a destination view controller.

Returning Data From a View Controller

Although it's more common to pass a value from a source to a destination view controller, you may at times need to pass information from a view controller back to the view controller that originally presented it.

In the previous chapter, the **iDeliverMobileCD** had a small problem where the **Delivery Status** cell was not getting refreshed when the delivery status was changed at run time (Figure 13.12).

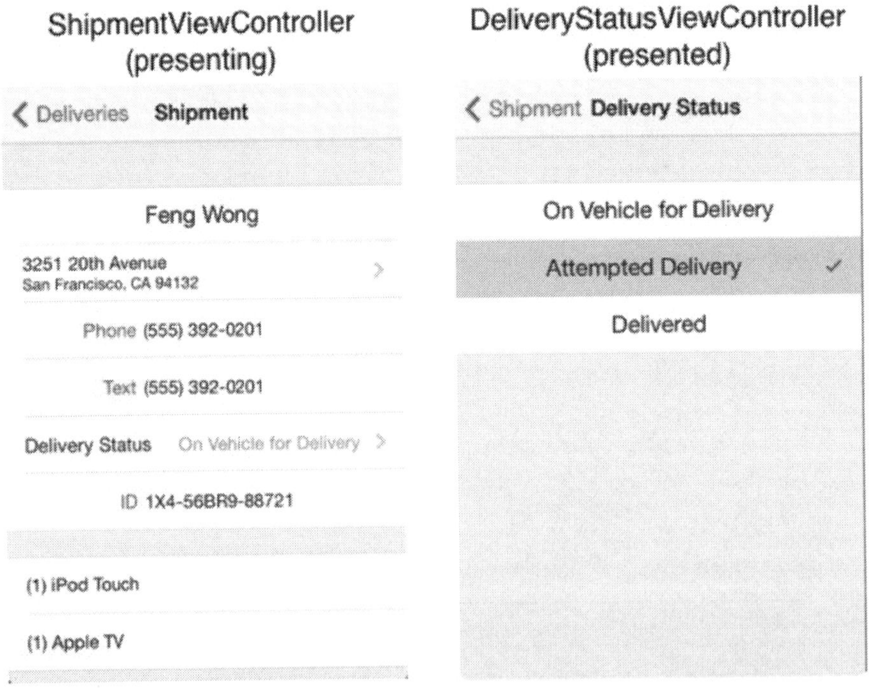

Figure 13.12 The presenting and presented view controllers.

The **DeliveryStatusViewController** (the *presented* view controller) needs to pass back the newly selected **DeliveryStatusEntity** to the **ShipmentViewController** (the *presenting* view controller) so it can refresh the cell. The best way to do this is to create a method on the **ShipmentViewController** that can be called by the **DeliveryStatusViewController**.

Here are the five main steps you need to perform when you need to create a callback method (Figure 13.13):

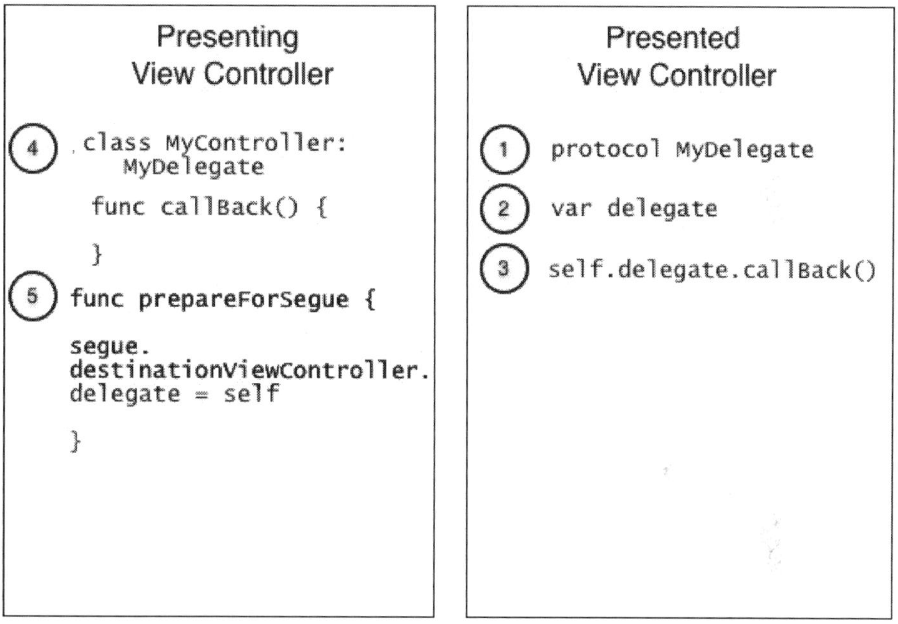

Figure 13.13 Returning data from a view controller.

1. Declare a protocol in the *presented* view controller that specifies a method that can be implemented in the *presenting* view controller. The *presented* view controller calls this method at run time to pass data back to the *presenting* view controller.

2. Declare a **delegate** property on the *presented* view controller that will hold a reference to the *presenting* view controller. The *presented* view controller uses this reference to the *presenting* view controller when it calls the protocol method.

3. Add code to the *presented* view controller that calls the delegate method, passing data to the *presenting* view controller.

4. Implement the delegate protocol method in the *presenting* view controller to do something with the data that was passed back to it.

5. In the *presenting* view controller's **prepareForSegue:** method, have the *presenting* view controller store a reference to itself in the *presented* view controller's **delegate** property.

Refreshing the Delivery Status

Now you're ready to implement these steps to refresh the Delivery Status cell in the **iDeliverMobileCD** project's **Shipment** scene's table view. If it's not already open, in Xcode, open the **iDeliverMobileCD** project found in this book's sample code.

1. **Declare a protocol in the presented view controller.**

   Select the **DeliveryStatusViewController.swift** file in the Project Navigator and add the following protocol declaration to the file:

```
import UIKit
protocol DeliveryStatusDelegate {
    func updateDeliveryStatus(deliveryStatus:
        DeliveryStatusEntity)
}
```

   This protocol declares a method that accepts a **DeliveryStatusEntity** parameter, which the presented view controller can use to pass the entity back to the presenting view controller.

2. **Declare a delegate property in the *presented* view controller.**

   In the **DeliveryStatusViewController.swift** file, add the following **delegate** property declaration:

```
class DeliveryStatusViewController:
   UITableViewController {
   var delegate: DeliveryStatusDelegate?
   var shipmentEntity: ShipmentEntity!
```

   This property can hold a reference to any object that implements the **DeliveryStatusDelegate** protocol.

3. **Add code to the *presented* view controller that calls the delegate method.**

   In **DeliveryStatusViewController.swift**, add the following code to the bottom of the **tableView:didSelectRowAtIndexPath:** method:

```
// Tell delegate to update delivery status
 self.delegate?.updateDeliveryStatus(
  deliveryStatusEntity)
}
```

   You are going to store a reference to the presenting view controller in the **delegate** property, so this code will call the **updateDeliveryStatus:** method on the presenting view controller at run time.

4. **Implement the delegate protocol method in the *presenting* view controller.**

   Select the **ShipmentViewController.swift** file in the Project Navigator and add the following code that adopts the new protocol:

```
class ShipmentViewController: UITableViewController,
DeliveryStatusDelegate {
```

   Now add the following protocol method implementation before the closing parenthesis in the **ShipmentViewController** class:

```
func updateDeliveryStatus(deliveryStatus:
 DeliveryStatusEntity) {
 // Change delivery status and save changes
 self.shipmentEntity.deliveryStatus =
   deliveryStatus
 self.shipment.saveEntities()
 // Update the delivery status cell
 self.tableView.reloadRowsAtIndexPaths(
   [NSIndexPath(forRow: 4, inSection: 0)],
   withRowAnimation:
   UITableViewRowAnimation.None)
  }
}
```

This code takes the **DeliveryStatusEntity** passed back from the **DeliveryStatusViewController** and stores it in the **deliveryStatus** property of the **ShipmentEntity**.

It then calls the **saveEntities** method on the **Shipment** business controller. Afterward, it refreshes the delivery status cell in the table view.

5. **In the *presenting* view controller's prepareForSegue: method, have the *presenting* view controller store a reference to itself in the *presented* view controller's delegate property.**

   In **ShipmentViewController.swift**, add the following code to the bottom of the **prepareForSegue:** method:

```
override func prepareForSegue(segue:
   UIStoryboardSegue, sender: AnyObject?) {

   if segue.identifier == "DeliveryStatusSegue" {
      var tvc = segue.destinationViewController
        as! DeliveryStatusViewController
      tvc.shipmentEntity = self.shipmentEntity
      tvc.delegate = self
   }
}
```

Now that you have implemented these five steps, click Xcode's **Run** button. When the app appears in the Simulator, select the shipment in the first screen, and then select the **Delivery Status** cell in the second screen. Change the delivery status to another setting, press the back button in the navigation bar, and you should see the cell has been refreshed.

Since you also added code to save the **ShipmentEntity** to the data store, the change should persist between Simulator sessions. To see this, go back to Xcode, click the **Stop** button, then press the **Run** button again, and check if the value is still changed.

Displaying Images in Table View Rows

In some cases, displaying images in table view rows can provide a better user experience because it helps your users quickly distinguish the type of items in each row. For example, in Figure 13.12, it would be nice to display an icon in the shipment item rows so the delivery person can easily identify the item being delivered. A different icon for each device family—iPhone, iPod, iPad, and Apple TV—would be best.

Images that are displayed in table view cells should be approximately 40 x 40 pixels or smaller when using the standard table view cell height. If you want high quality images at low cost (or no cost), I highly recommend checking out **http://www.glyphish.com** (I'm not affiliated with the company, just a friendly recommendation).

They have 200 icons for free, and their pro version has 400 icons for $99.

Displaying Static Images

If you want the same image to always be displayed in a particular table view cell, you don't need to write any code. Follow these steps to see how easy it is:

1. If it's not already open, in Xcode, open the **iDeliverMobileCD** project that comes with this book's sample code.

2. In the Project Navigator, select the **Images.xcassets** file, and you will see the Asset Catalog editor (Figure 13.14).

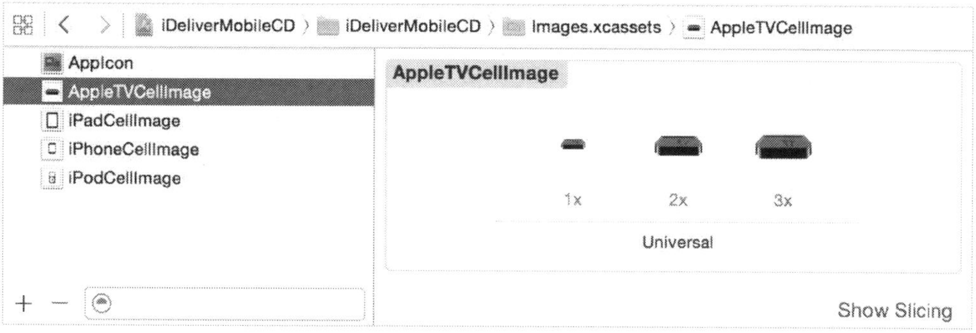

Figure 13.14 App images are stored in an asset catalog.

On the left side of the editor is a list of image sets. If you select an image set in the Project Navigator, the images it contains are displayed on the right.

There is an image set for Apple TV, iPad, iPhone and iPod. To display an image in a table view cell, it must be included in your project—preferably in an image set. You will learn much more about image sets in *Chapter 14: Working with the Project Editor*.

3. In the Project Navigator, select the **Main.storyboard** file to display the storyboard in the design surface.

4. Scroll to the **Shipment** scene, and then select the last cell in the table view, labeled **(1) iPod Touch**.

5. Go to the Attributes Inspector and in the **Image** combo box, select **iPodCellImage** (Figure 13.15).

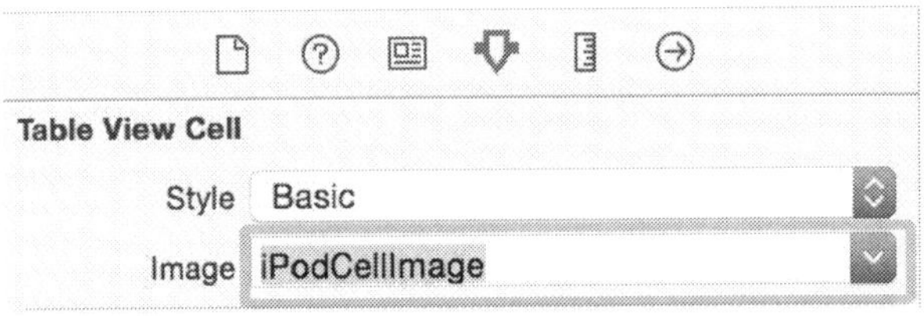

*Figure 13.15 Set the **Image** to **iPodCellImage.***

You should now be able to see the table view cell image in the design surface (Figure 13.16).

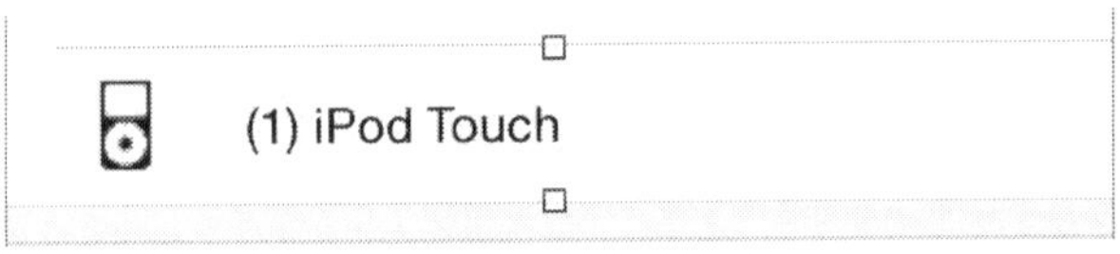

Figure 13.16 The image appears in the table view cell.

6. To see what this looks like at run time, click Xcode's **Run** button, and when the app appears in the Simulator, select the shipment, and you will see the shipment item images shown in Figure 13.17.

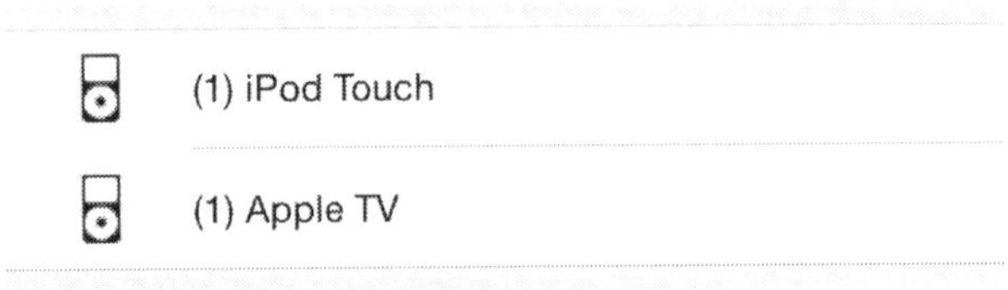

Figure 13.17 Both shipment item cells have the same image.

Displaying Dynamic Images

If you want to dynamically display a different image based on the content of a cell, this is easy to do. It requires a single line of code in the **tableView: cellForRowAtIndexPath:** method.

Here is one example of how this can be done:

1. If it's not already open, in Xcode, open the **iDeliverMobileCD** project that comes with this book's sample code.

2. Select the **ShipmentViewController.swift** file in the Project Navigator and add the following code to the bottom of the **tableView: cellForRowAtIndexPath:** method within the **else if** statement:

```
else if indexPath.section == 1 {
    let shipItem =
     self.shipmentItemList[indexPath.row]

   cell = tableView.dequeueReusableCellWithIdentifier(
    "ShipmentItemCell",forIndexPath:indexPath)

   cell.textLabel?.text =
    "(\(shipItem.quantity))
     \(shipItem.itemDescription)"

   if shipItem.itemDescription. rangeOfString("TV")
      != nil {
       cell.imageView?.image = UIImage(named:
          "AppleTVCellImage")
   }
  }
  return cell
}
```

This code checks if the **itemDescription** property of the **ShipmentItemEntity** contains the text **TV**, and if it does, it sets the image to **AppleTVCellImage.png**. It's as easy as that.

I don't recommend checking the text of an item like this to determine it's type. It's better to add a **deviceFamily** attribute to the **ShipmentItemEntity** and check its value. We just added some "quick and dirty" code so as not to get sidetracked off the main point of displaying images in table view cells.

3. To see how this looks at run time, click Xcode's **Run** button. When the app appears in the Simulator, select the shipment on the first screen, and you should see two different images in the shipment item cells as shown in Figure 13.18.

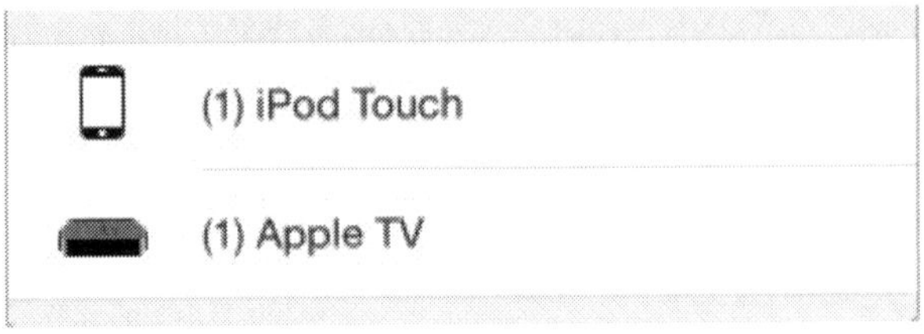

Figure 13.18 Each cell has its own image.

Creating Section Headers and Footers

As you can see in Figure 13.19, table view sections can have both headers and footers. In this example, the first section of the **Sounds** table view has a header that contains a label with the text **Silent**. The second section has a header with the label **Ringers and Alerts**, and a footer with a label that contains information about setting the volume for the ringer and alerts.

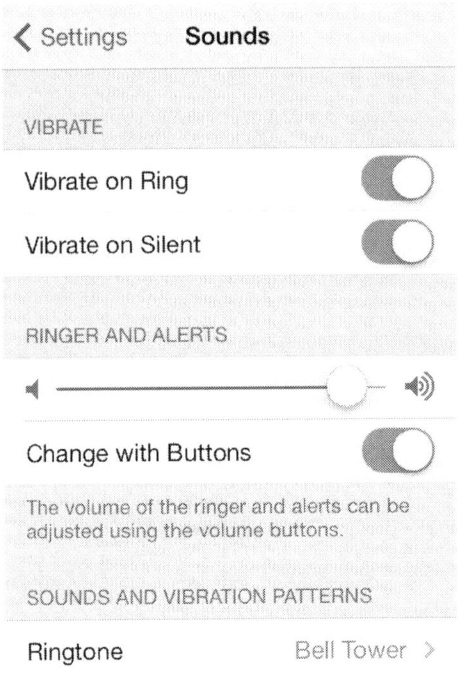

Figure 13.19 Table view section headers and footers.

Headers and Footers for Static Table Views

You can set header and footer text in the Attributes Inspector for table views that have their **Content** set to **Static Cells**. You just select the **Table View Section** in the Document Outline pane and set the **Header** and **Footer** attributes to the text you want displayed (Figure 13.20).

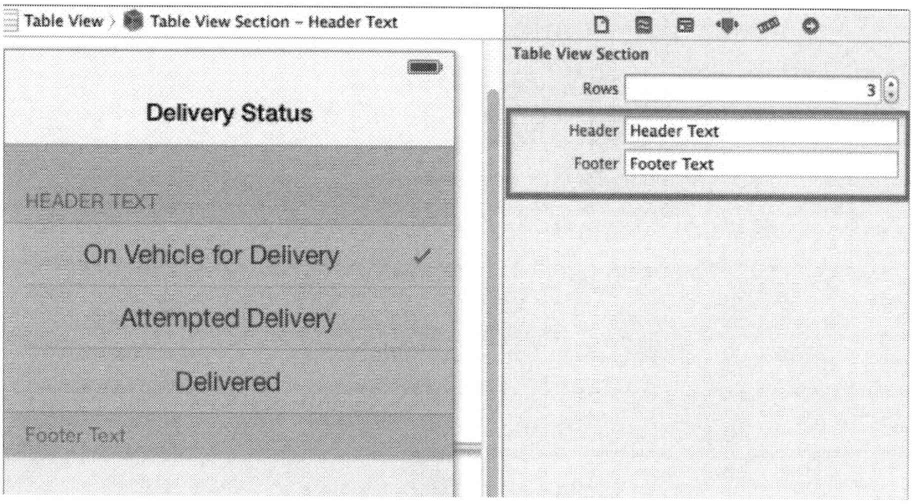

Figure 13.20 You can set header and footer text for static table views in the Attributes Inspector.

If you have changed the background color of the table view to a dark color, the gray header and footer labels don't show up well. You will learn how to change the color of header text in just a bit.

Headers and Footers for Dynamic Table Views

If a table view's **Content** is set to **Dynamic Prototypes**, there is no **Table View Section** in the Document Outline at design time, so you don't have the option of setting header and footer text in this way. However, you *can* set the table view header and footer text in code.

You can use the **tableView:titleForHeaderInSection:** method of a table view controller to set section header text and the **tableView:titleForFooterInSection:** method to set section footer text. These methods can be used to set the text only—not the text color. If you need to set both the text and the color, see the next section, *Custom Headers and Footers.*

Follow these steps to see how header and footer text can easily be created for your dynamic table views:

1. Open the **iDeliverMobileCD** project.

2. Select **ShipmentViewController.swift** in the Project Navigator, and then add the following methods below the **tableView:cellForRowAtIndexPath:** method:

```
override func tableView(tableView: UITableView,
 titleForHeaderInSection section: Int) -> String? {
   switch section {
    case 0:
     return "Customer Information"
    case 1:
     return "Shipment Detail"
    default:
     return nil
   }
}

override func tableView(tableView: UITableView,
 titleForFooterInSection section: Int) -> String? {

   if section == 0 {
    return "Be kind and courteous"
   }
   else {
     return nil
   }
}
```

Each method checks the **section** parameter value and returns the header or footer text for the specified section number. If a particular section doesn't have header or footer text, you can simply return **nil** as shown in this code sample.

3. To see how the headers and footer look at run time, click the **Run** button. When the app appears in the Simulator, select a delivery, and you should see the header and footer text shown in Figure 13.21.

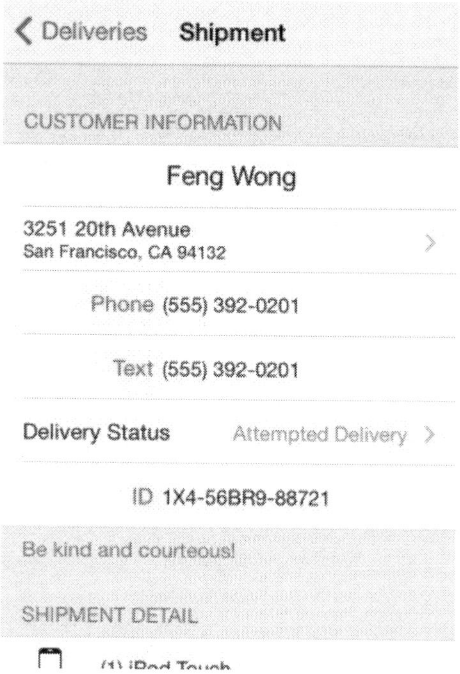

Figure 13.21 Dynamic table view header and footer text.

If you don't like the gray colors of the header and footer labels, how can you change them? This is addressed in the next section.

Custom Headers and Footers

When you want to do more than just set the text of a header or footer, you need to implement one or both of these methods:

- **tableView:viewForHeaderInSection:**
- **tableView:viewForFooterInSection:**

Within these methods, you can create and configure a view containing the user-interface objects you want in the header or footer (usually labels) and return the view from the methods.

You must also implement one or both of these methods that determine the height of the header or footer:

- **tableView:heightForHeaderInSection:**
- **tableView:heightForFooterInSection:**

Custom Headers

Let's create a custom header view for the Shipment table view in the **iDeliverMobileCD** app.

1. If it's not already open, in Xcode, open the **iDeliverMobileCD** project.

2. Select the **ShipmentViewController.swift** code file in the Project Navigator. Locate the **tableView: titleForHeaderInSection:** method you added in the previous section and comment out the entire method (not just the code inside the method). Remember, to select all lines of code, click at the far left of the first line of code, and then drag your mouse down to the closing curly brace. You can then comment out the code by pressing the **Command** + / keys. When you're done, the method should look like this:

```
//    override func tableView(tableView: UITableView,
  titleForHeaderInSection section: Int) -> String? {

//    switch section {
//    case 0:
//       return "Customer Information"
//    case 1:
//       return "Shipment Detail"
//    default:
//       return nil
//     }
//    }
```

3. Now add the following methods directly below the **tableView:cellForRowAtIndexPath:** method:

```
override func tableView(tableView:
    UITableView, viewForHeaderInSection section:
    Int) -> UIView? {

    // Create a view to hold the header label
    let customView = UIView(frame:
      CGRectMake(0.0, 0.0,
      self.view.frame.size.width, 0.0))
    // Create the label object
```

```
        let sectionLabel = UILabel(frame:
        CGRectMake(10, 10,
        self.view.frame.size.width, 21))

        sectionLabel.backgroundColor =
          UIColor.clearColor()
        sectionLabel.textColor =
          UIColor.blackColor()
        sectionLabel.font =
           UIFont.boldSystemFontOfSize(17.0)

        switch section {
          case 0:
           sectionLabel.text =
             NSLocalizedString("Customer Information",
             comment: "")
          case 1:
           sectionLabel.text =
              NSLocalizedString("Shipment Detail",
             comment: "")
          default:
           return nil
        }
        customView.addSubview(sectionLabel)
        return customView
    }
    override func tableView(tableView:
     UITableView, heightForHeaderInSection
     section: Int) -> CGFloat {
        return 40
    }
```

In the first method, the first line of code creates a view named **customView** and initializes it with a frame that has an **x,y** position of **0,0**. This places the new view in the upper-left corner of the header. The frame is given a width that is the same size as the parent view (**self.view.frame.size.width**). This is a good coding practice. The header view will be the full width of the parent view, regardless of the device or orientation your app is running in.

The next section of code creates a label object and configures it. It's initialized with a frame that is also the full width of the view. You must set the **backgroundColor** of the label to **clearColor**, otherwise the background color of the view will not be seen in the empty space of the label. You can change the **textColor** and **font** properties to whatever suits your needs.

The **switch** statement sets the **text** of the section header based on the currently specified section number. Notice this code makes use of the **NSLocalizedString** function, so the text can be easily localized to other languages at a later date. The last few lines of code add the label to the header view and then return the customized header view.

Take a look at the first line of code again. Notice the **height** of the view frame is set to zero. That's because the height of the header is not affected by the height of the header view. That's where the **tableView: heightForHeaderInSection:** method comes in—it specifies the height of the header view. You must implement this method when creating a custom header view. In the code sample, this method returns **40** for all sections. If a section doesn't have a header, just return **nil** for that section.

4. To see how this code works at run time, click the **Run** button, and when the app appears in the Simulator, select a delivery from the **Deliveries** scene. Afterward, you should see the section header labels (Figure 13.22).

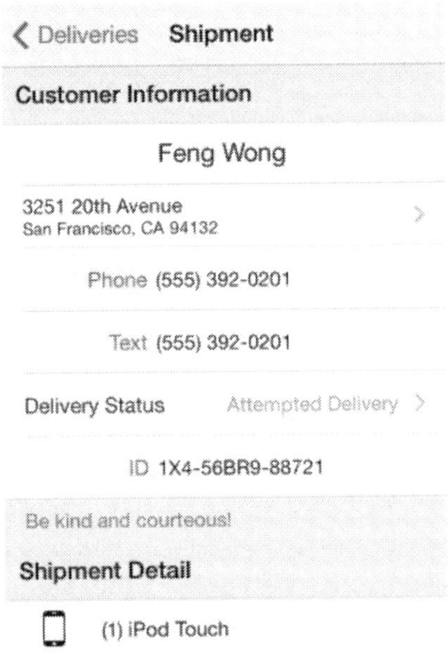

Figure 13.23 Custom header views with black text

Custom Footers

Now let's create a custom view for the footer of the first section with the following steps:

1. In the **ShipmentTableViewController.swift** file, locate the **tableView:titleForFooterInSection:** method and completely comment it out. When you're finished, the method should look like this:

```
//   override func tableView(tableView: UITableView,
titleForFooterInSection section: Int) -> String? {
//         if section == 0 {
//          return "Be kind and courteous"
//         }
//         else {
//            return nil
//      }
//   }
```

2. Add the following methods directly below the methods you added in the previous section:

```
override func tableView(tableView:
    UITableView, viewForFooterInSection
    section: Int) -> UIView? {
    // Create a view to hold the footer label
    let customView = UIView(frame:
      CGRectMake(0.0, 0.0,
         self.view.frame.size.width, 0.0))

    // Create the label object
    let sectionLabel = UILabel(frame:
      CGRectMake(10.0, 10.0,
         self.view.frame.size.width, 21.0))
    sectionLabel.backgroundColor = UIColor.clearColor()
    sectionLabel.textColor = UIColor.blackColor()
    sectionLabel.font = UIFont.systemFontOfSize(15.0)
    sectionLabel.textAlignment = NSTextAlignment.Center
```

```
    if section == 0  {
      sectionLabel.text =
        NSLocalizedString("Be kind and courteous!",
        comment: "")
    } else {
       return nil
    }
    customView.addSubview(sectionLabel)
    return customView
}

override func tableView(tableView:
 UITableView, heightForFooterInSection
 section: Int) -> CGFloat {
    if section == 0 {
       return 35
    }
    else {
       return 0
    }
}
```

This code is similar to the code for the header with a few notable exceptions. First of all, notice the font size of the footer is different from the header. It's not bold, and its size is just 15 points, which is the default font for footers in iOS. Also, notice that **textAlignment** is set to **NSTextAlignmentCenter**, so the text gets centered in the view.

In the **tableView:heightForFooterInSection:** method, the section height is set to 35 for section 0, and since there is no footer in section 1, the height is set to zero (0).

3. Press the **Run** button to see how the footer looks at run time. After the app appears in the Simulator, select a delivery to see a footer like the one shown in Figure 13.23.

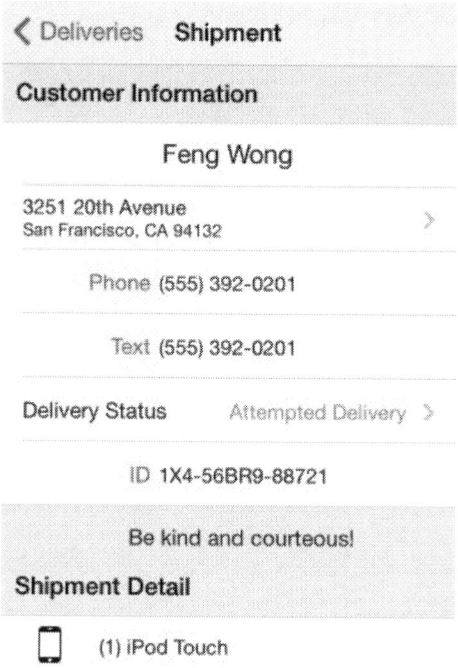

Figure 13.23 The custom footer text centered and black

4. You have learned how to set up a table view footer, but honestly, the footer is somewhat unnecessary in this table view, so let's comment out the code that displays the footer.

   Go back to Xcode, press the **Stop** button, and then, in the **ShipmentTableViewController.swift** file, select the entire **tableView:viewForHeaderInSection:** and **tableView: heightForFooterInSection:** methods (place your cursor at the beginning of the first method, hold the mouse button down, drag to the bottom of the second method, and then release the button). With both methods selected, press **Command** + / to comment out the code.

5. Press the **Run** button to run the app again. Select a delivery, and you should see the footer is no longer displayed below the first section of the table view.

You are not limited to only adding labels to custom header and footer views. You can add any control you like such as an image view, button, or switch.

Also, if you want to add more empty space above a particular section, there is no need to implement the **tableView:viewForHeaderInSection:** method.

Just implement the **heightForHeaderInSection:** method and return the desired size of the header.

Referencing Cells With Enumerations

In the previous chapter, you added code to the **tableView:cellForRowAtIndexPath:** method of the **ShipmentViewController** that checked for a specific cell number (zero through five).

Although this works, there is a better way. Rather than hard-coding cell numbers, you can create an enumeration that provides a human-readable list of cells in a table view.

Doing this not only makes your code easier to read and understand, but, if at a later date you need to add or insert a new cell into a section, it makes your code less susceptible to bugs since you don't have to manually change the numeric value of each affected cell. You can just insert a new value in the enumeration and all the other values change automatically.

Follow these steps to see how this works:

1. If it's not already open, in Xcode, open the **iDeliverMobileCD** project.

2. Select the **ShipmentViewController.swift** code file in the Project Navigator and add the following enumeration declaration:

```
import UIKit
enum ShipmentSection: Int {
    case Name, Address, Phone, Text,
      DeliveryStatus, ID

      static let allValues = [Name, Address,
       Phone, Text, DeliveryStatus, ID]
}
```

   The first item in the enumeration represents the first cell in the section, the second item in the enumeration represents the second item in the section, and so on.

The **allValues** array contains a list of all items in the enumeration and can be used to enumerate through all values as well as get the count of items in the enumeration. The **static** keyword indicates this is a class member rather than an instance member.

3. Now you're ready to update the table view controller methods to use the new enumeration.

   Select the **ShipmentViewController.swift** file in the Project Navigator and scroll to the **tableView: numberOfRowsInSection:** method. Change the code in this method to use **ShipmentSection's allValues** array rather than a hard-coded **6**:

```
override func tableView(tableView:
UITableView, numberOfRowsInSection section:
Int) -> Int {
   // Return the number of rows in the section.
   var rowCount = 0
   if section == 0 {
      rowCount = ShipmentSection.allValues.count
   }
   else if section == 1
   {
    rowCount = shipmentItemList.count
   }
   return rowCount
}
```

4. Now scroll to the **tableView:cellForRowAtIndexPath:** method and change the **switch** statement to use the new enumeration values rather than hard-coded numbers:

```
switch indexPath.row {
case ShipmentSection.Name.rawValue:
   cell = tableView.
      dequeueReusableCellWithIdentifier("NameCell",
      forIndexPath: indexPath)
   cell.textLabel?.text =
     self.shipmentEntity.name

case ShipmentSection.Address.rawValue:
   cell = tableView.
      dequeueReusableCellWithIdentifier("AddressCell",
```

```
        forIndexPath: indexPath)
    cell.textLabel?.text = self.shipmentEntity.address
    cell.detailTextLabel?.text =
        self.shipmentEntity.city + ", " +
        self.shipmentEntity.region + "  " +
        self.shipmentEntity.postalCode

  case ShipmentSection.Phone.rawValue:
        cell = tableView.
           dequeueReusableCellWithIdentifier("PhoneCell",
           forIndexPath: indexPath)
        cell.detailTextLabel?.text =
           self.shipmentEntity.phone

  case ShipmentSection.Text.rawValue:
        cell = tableView.
    dequeueReusableCellWithIdentifier("TextCell",
        forIndexPath: indexPath)
        cell.detailTextLabel?.text =
           self.shipmentEntity.text

  case ShipmentSection.DeliveryStatus.rawValue:
        cell = tableView.
           dequeueReusableCellWithIdentifier(
           "DeliveryStatusCell", forIndexPath: indexPath)
        cell.detailTextLabel?.text =
           self.shipmentEntity.deliveryStatus.
           valueForKey("statusDescription") as? String

  case ShipmentSection.ID.rawValue:
        cell = tableView.
           dequeueReusableCellWithIdentifier(
              "ShipmentIDCell", forIndexPath: indexPath)
        cell.detailTextLabel?.text =
           self.shipmentEntity.shipmentID
     default:
        break
}
```

As you can see, this makes the code far more readable, and resilient to change.

Handling Table View User Selection

Now that you know the basics of configuring lists of information in table views, it's time to learn about handling user selection in a table view.

The **UITableViewDelegate** protocol is designed in part to handle user interaction. As you might guess, the **UITableViewController** class implements this protocol, so any custom table view controllers you create automatically inherit the methods of this protocol. The most common method you use in this protocol is the **tableView:didSelectRowAtIndexPath:** method. This method fires when a user touches a row and then lifts their finger off the row.

Performing Segues

One of the most common uses of the **tableView: didSelectRowAtIndexPath:** method is to perform a segue. In fact, you used this method to do just that in the previous chapter.

If you need all the rows in a table view to trigger the same segue, you can *override* the **tableView: didSelectRowAtIndexPath:** method and add code to perform the segue. For example:

```
override func tableView(tableView: UITableView,
didSelectRowAtIndexPath indexPath: NSIndexPath) {

 self.performSegueWithIdentifier("ShipmentSegue",
    sender: nil)
}
```

Kicking Off a Process

The **tableView:didSelectRowAtIndexPath:** method can also be used to kick off a process when a specific row is selected. This is most often done in table views where the information in a particular row is constant.

For example, in the **iDeliverMobileCD** app's **Shipment** scene, the customer's phone number and text number are always in the same row. You can add code to the **tableView:didSelectRowAtIndexPath:** method of the **ShipmentViewController** to check if either of these rows were selected and, if so, call the telephone number or compose a text. For example (don't add this code right now, it's just for demo purposes):

```
override func tableView(tableView: UITableView,
didSelectRowAtIndexPath indexPath: NSIndexPath) {
  switch indexPath.row {
    case ShipmentSection.Phone.rawValue:
     self.makePhoneCall(self.shipmentEntity.phone)

    case ShipmentSection.Text.rawValue:
     self.composeText(self.shipmentEntity.text)

    default:
       break
  }
}
```

Remember, when checking for a specific row number, it's best to create an enumeration that defines each row then reference members of that enumeration rather than hard-coding the row numbers.

Detail Disclosure Indicators and Detail Disclosure Buttons

There are two different indicators you can use to let the user know that they can see additional information if they tap a table view row:

- Disclosure Indicator
- Detail Disclosure Button

It's important to use these indicators in rows that navigate to another view so users can see that the row will take them to another view when they tap it. In fact, if you don't use these indicators properly, Apple will reject your app.

Apple makes it clear in its documentation that there is a distinct difference between the two types of disclosure indicators you can use in table views. Let's take a look at how Apple uses these in their built-in apps to get a solid grasp of how these indicators should be used.

Disclosure Indicator

As shown in Figure 13.24, the Settings app uses disclosure indicators, which are small gray arrows on the right side of each row. They indicate that tapping anywhere in the row takes you to the next level in the hierarchy.

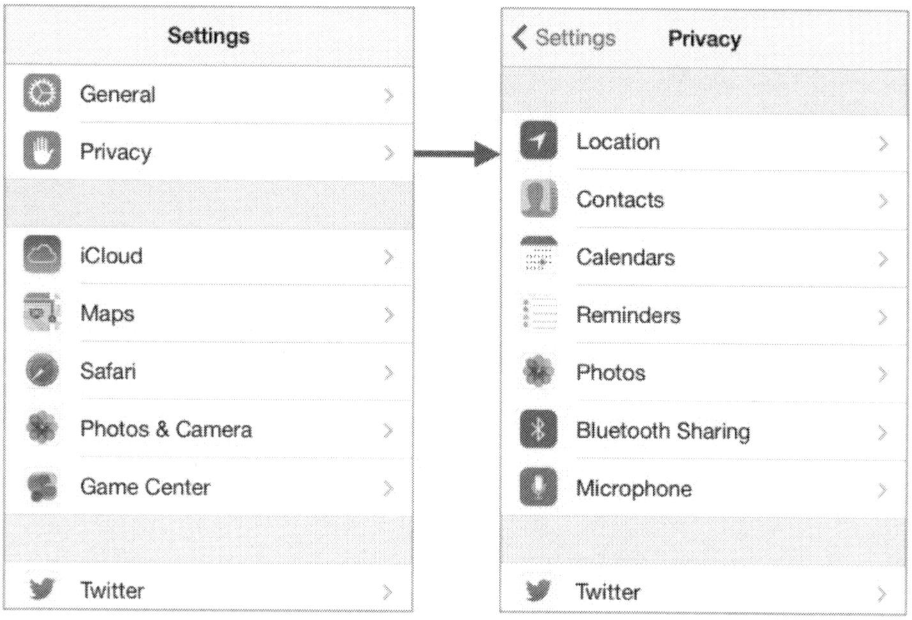

Figure 13.24 The Settings app uses disclosure indicators.

In the views you have worked with so far, the disclosure indicator has been set on the cell at design time. To dynamically display a disclosure indicator for a particular cell, in the **tableView:cellForRowAtIndexPath:** method, set the cell's **accessoryType** as follows:

```
cell.accessoryType =
  UITableViewCellAccessoryType.DisclosureIndicator
```

Remember, if you tie a segue directly to a table view cell, the segue is performed automatically when the user taps the row at run time. If you want a generic segue that is triggered from multiple cells, add code to the table view's **tableView:didSelectRowAtIndexPath:** method to trigger the segue.

Detail Disclosure Buttons

As shown in Figure 13.25, the Phone app uses detail disclosure buttons. On rows that contain detail disclosure buttons, tapping the button itself usually does one thing, and tapping elsewhere in the row does another. For example, in the Phone app, if you tap the detail disclosure button, it displays a view containing details about the contact. If you tap anywhere else in a row, it calls the phone number for that contact.

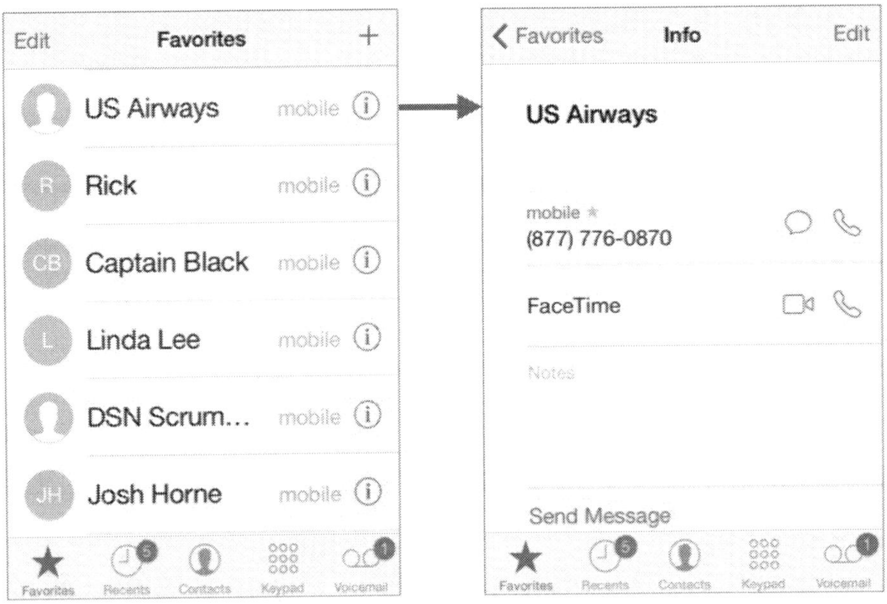

Figure 13.25 The Phone app makes use of detail disclosure indicators.

To dynamically display a disclosure indicator for a particular row, in the **tableView:cellForRowAtIndexPath:** method, set the cell's **accessoryType** as follows:

```
cell.accessoryType =
 UITableViewCellAccessoryType.DetailDisclosureButton
```

Since there are two actions that can be performed in a row that contains a detail disclosure button, there are two methods that handle each type of selection.

tableView:accessoryButtonTappedForRowWithIndexPath: fires if the user taps the detail disclosure button directly. In the Phone app, code in this method might navigate to a view that provides details about the contact:

```
override func tableView(tableView: UITableView,
accessoryButtonTappedForRowWithIndexPath
indexPath: NSIndexPath) {
   self.performSegueWithIdentifier(
  "ShowContactDetail", sender: self)
}
```

The **tableView:didSelectRowAtIndexPath:** method fires if the user taps anywhere else in the row. In the YouTube app, code in this method might play a video:

```
override func tableView(tableView: UITableView,
didSelectRowAtIndexPath indexPath: NSIndexPath) {
  self.playVideo(indexPath.row)
}
```

As a side note, if you connect a segue directly to a cell containing a detail disclosure button, tapping the detail disclosure button does not fire the segue, but tapping anywhere else in the row does. This means you must implement the methods described above if you want the user to tap a row to kick off a process and tap the detail disclosure indicator to navigate to another view.

When NOT to Use Disclosure Indicators

You should always use either a disclosure indicator or a detail disclosure button on a table view cell that navigates to another view—with one exception. If your view contains an indexed list as shown in Figure 13.26, Apple's Human Interface Guidelines dictate that you do not use a disclosure indicator even if selecting a row takes you to another view.

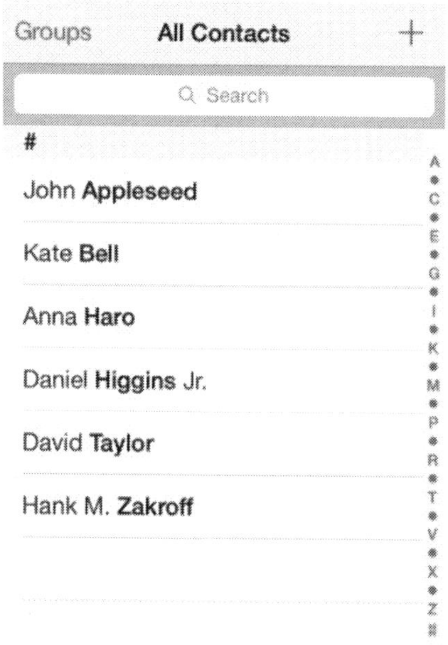

Figure 13.26 Indexed lists should not contain disclosure indicators!

You will learn more about this in the upcoming section *Creating Indexed Table Views.*

Selecting Rows With a Check Mark

As you learned when working with the Delivery Status scene in the **iDeliverMobileCD** app (Figure 13.27), you can let the user select one or more rows and display a check mark next to the selected row(s).

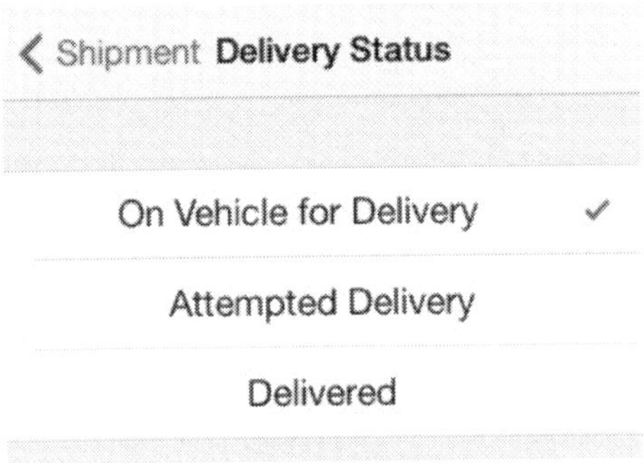

Figure 13.27 A check mark in a table view cell.

Just to be thorough, let's recap the basics of what you must do to implement check marks for selected items in a table view.

1. I In the **tableView:cellForRowAtIndexPath:** method, you need to add code that determines which cell(s) should have a check mark. You can use the following code to add a check mark to a cell:

```
cell.accessoryType =
      UITableViewCellAccessoryType.Checkmark
```

2. If you only want one item to be selected at a time, in the **tableView: didSelectRowAtIndexPath:** method, you need to uncheck the previously selected item and check the newly selected item. For example:

```
// Uncheck the previously checked cell
cell = tableView.cellForRowAtIndexPath(oldIndexPath)
cell.accessoryType = UITableViewCellAccessoryType.None
// Check the currently selected cell
cell = tableView.cellForRowAtIndexPath(indexPath)
cell.accessoryType =
   UITableViewCellAccessoryType.Checkmark
```

The trick is figuring out which row was previously selected. One option is to store the previously selected index path in a property (for example, the **oldIndexPath** property shown above).

Disabling User Interaction

At times, a list of items in a table view is "read-only," meaning the items in the list can be viewed but not selected. In the **iDeliverMobileCD** project, the **Shipment Detail** section of the **Shipment** scene is a great example of this. In the **Customer Information** section of this table view, some rows are meant to be selected, and others are not (such as Customer Name and Shipment ID).

As it stands now, if you tap a row at run time, the background turns gray (Figure 13.28), indicating it is selected, and it doesn't return to white until you tap another row. If you'd like, you can run the app in the Simulator and try this for yourself.

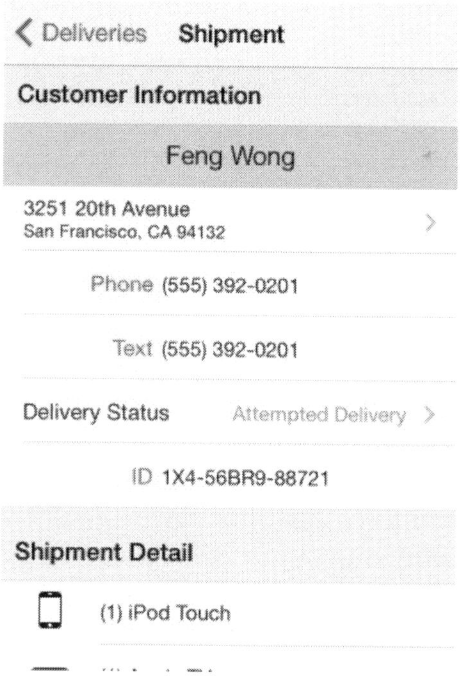

Figure 13.28 By default, "read only" rows turn gray when you tap them.

Fortunately, it's easy to turn off user interaction for a table view cell by changing its **Selection** attribute as outlined in these steps:

1. If it's not already open, in Xcode, open the **iDeliverMobileCD** project.

2. In the Project Navigator, select the **Main.storyboard** file and scroll to the **Shipment** scene.

3. Select the **Name**, **Shipment ID**, and **Delivery Detail** cells as shown in Figure 13.29. To do this, click the first cell, then hold the **Shift** key down ,and click the other cells.

4. Next, go to the Attributes Inspector and change the **Selection** attribute to **None** (Figure 13.29).

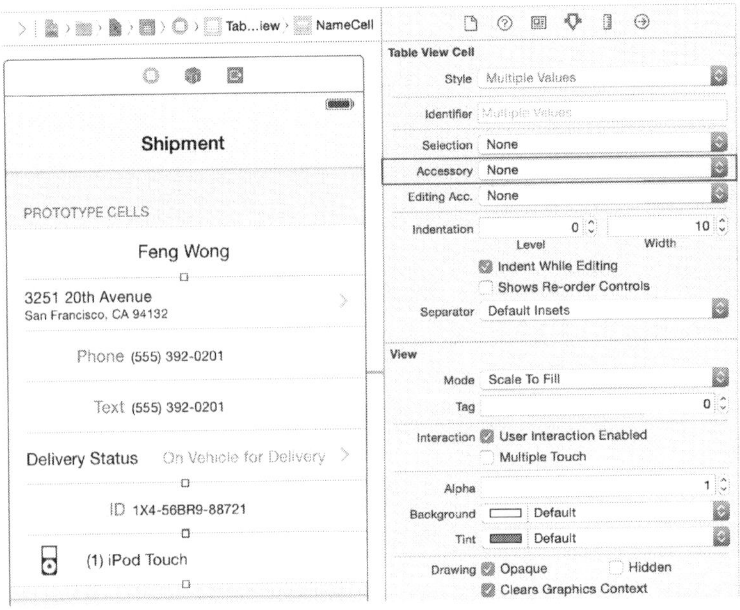

*Figure 13.29 Change a cell's **Selection** attribute to **None** to make it "read-only."*

5. Click Xcode's **Run** button to see how this works at run time.

Now when you select one of these read-only rows, nothing happens—no blue highlight appears on the row.

Creating Custom Cells

At times, you may want to create cells that are different than the standard cell styles. Fortunately, this is very easy to do. The basic steps are:

1. Set the cell **Style** to **Custom**.

2. Drag controls from the Object Library and drop them on the cell.

3. Give each control a unique **Tag** number that you can use to reference them from the table view controller.

4. In the **tableView:cellForRowAtIndexPath:** method of the table view controller, get a reference to the UI controls contained in the cell by calling the cell's **viewWithTag:** method and then configure the cell.

Your first thought might be to create an outlet for the user-interface controls you add to the custom cell, but this will not work. Remember, the custom cell you create is a prototype, or template, for multiple cells in the table view, so there will be many instances of the cell and the user-interface controls it contains, so a single outlet can't be used to reference them. That's why you need to reference the controls using the **tag** number.

To see how this works, let's create a custom cell for the Delivery Status table view in the **iDeliverMobileCD** project. This cell will display an image on the right side of the row rather than the default, which displays images on the left.

1. If it's not already open, in Xcode, open the **iDeliverMobileCD**.

2. In the Project Navigator, select the **Main.storyboard** file and scroll to the **Delivery Status** scene.

3. Click the table view cell to select it, then go to the Attributes Inspector, and change the **Style** to **Custom** (Figure 13.30). When you do this, the default label is removed from the cell.

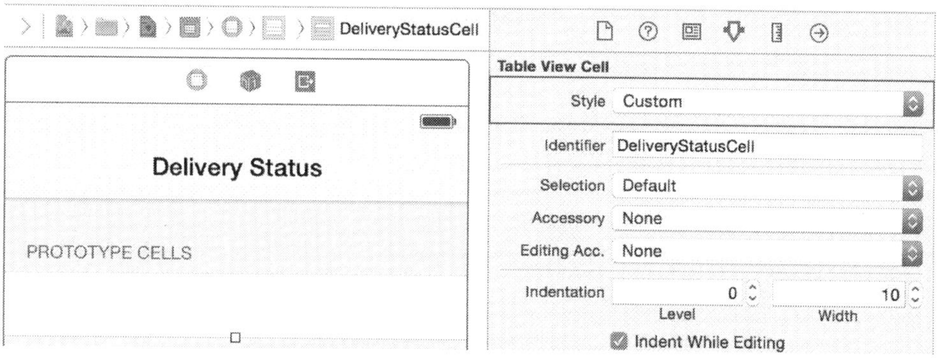

*Figure 13.30 Set the cell's **Style** to **Custom**.*

4. Now that the cell is blank, it's up to you to add your own custom content. First, let's add a label. To do this, click on the **Label** in the Object Library at the bottom-right corner of Xcode (if the Object Library isn't visible, you can select **View > Utilities > Show Object Library** from the Xcode menu), then drag the label onto the left side of the cell until you see the horizontal and vertical guide lines as in Figure 13.31, and then release the mouse button.

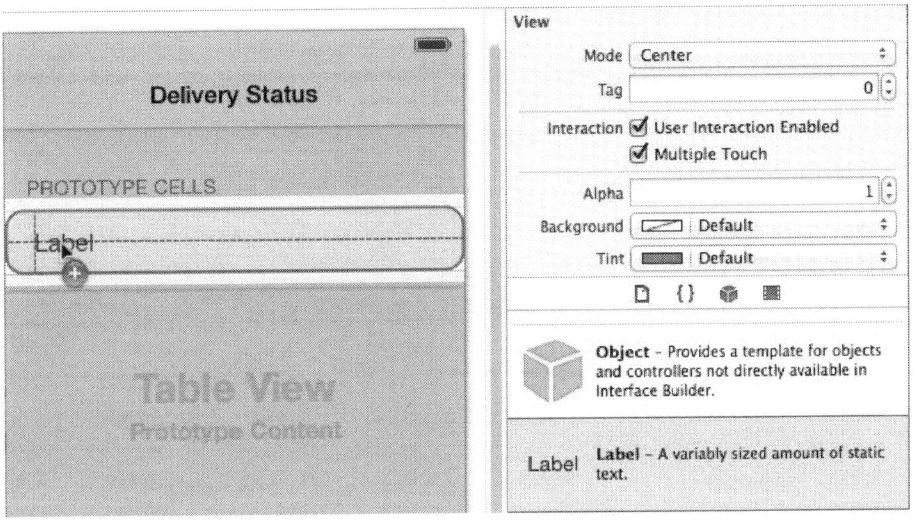

Figure 13.31 Position the label on the left side of the cell until you see the guide lines.

5. Double-click the label to put the text in edit mode, change the text to **Delivery Status** (Figure 13.32), and press the **return** key.

6. Before leaving the Attributes Inspector, change the label's **Tag** attribute to **1** as shown in Figure 13.32. This allows you to refer to the label by tag number from within the table view controller.

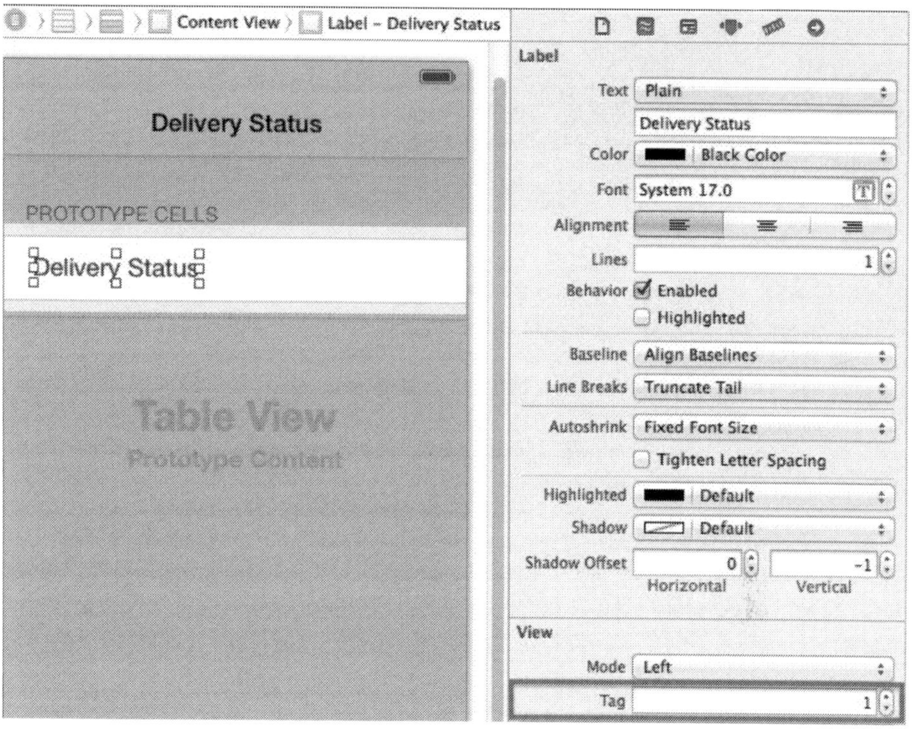

*Figure 13.32 Set the text to **Delivery Status** & the **Tag** to **1**.*

7. Now let's add an image view to the cell. To do this, drag an Image View from the Object Library to the right side of the custom cell until you see the horizontal guide line as shown in Figure 13.33 (the exact horizontal position isn't critical right now), and then release the mouse button.

8. With the image view still selected, go to the Attributes Inspector and set the **Tag** attribute to **2**. Again, this tag number will be used to reference the image view from the table view controller.

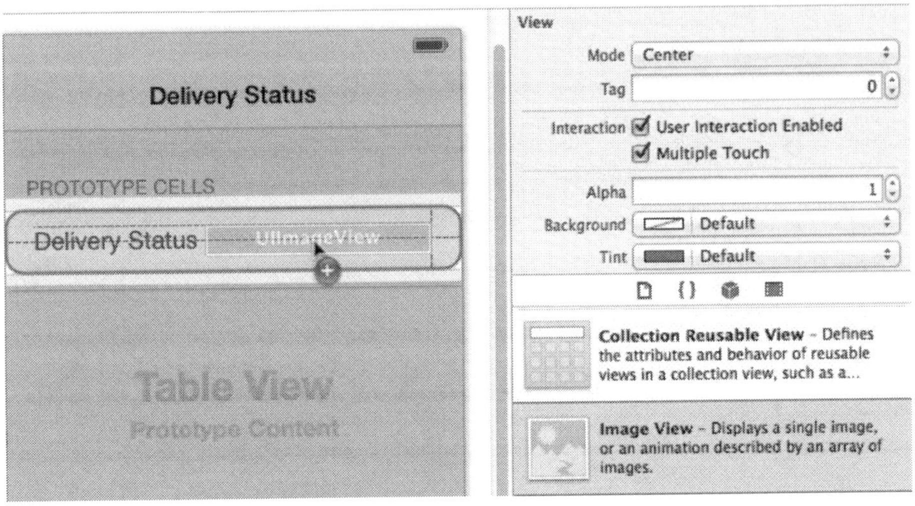

Figure 13.33 Add an image view to the custom cell.

9. With the image view still selected, go to the Size Inspector (second button from the right in the Inspector toolbar) and set both the **Width** and **Height** attributes to **35**. Setting these values will cause the image view to no longer be centered.

10. Click on the image view in the cell and drag it again to position it horizontally near the right edge of the cell as shown in Figure 13.34.

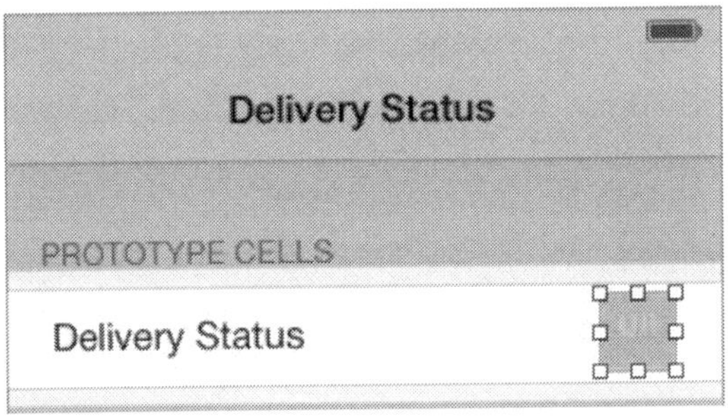

Figure 13.34 Reposition the image view in the cell.

11. Let's make the label larger so it can hold all the text necessary at run time. Drag the resizing handle on the right side of the label until the vertical guide line appears as shown in Figure 13.35.

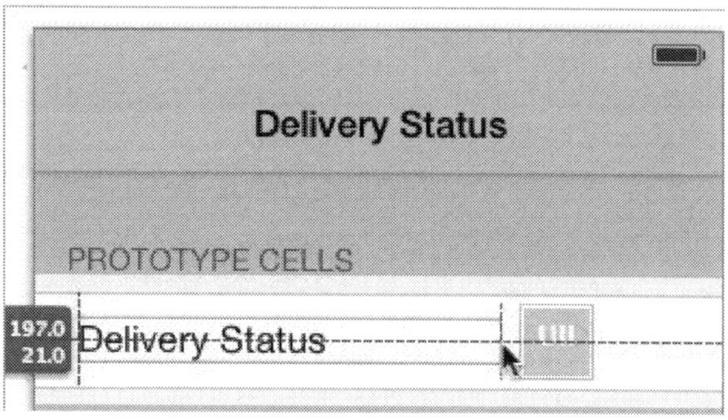

Figure 13.35 Resize the label.

12. To ensure that the image view maintains its position relative to the right side of the cell, click the Auto Layout **Pin** button at the bottom-right corner of the Storyboard editor. Under **Add New Constraints**, select the top, right, and bottom I-bars, and select the **Width** and **Height** check boxes (Figure 13.36). Afterwards, click the **Add 5 Constraints** button

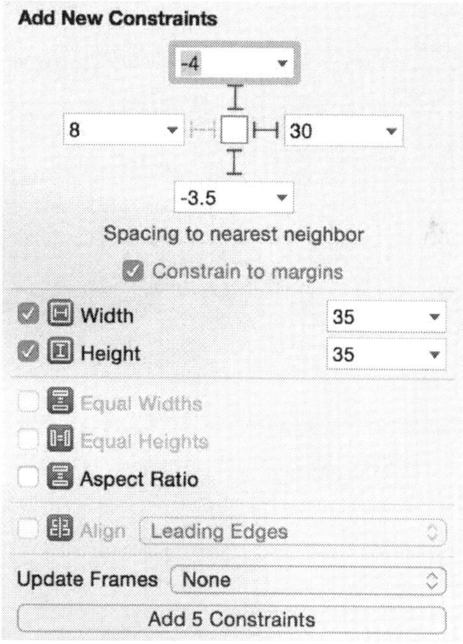

Figure 13.36 Add five constraints

13. Now you're ready to add code that configures the custom cell at run time. In the Project Navigator, select the **DeliveryStatusViewController.swift** file.

14. Scroll to the **tableView:cellForRowAtIndexPath:** method. Currently, this method contains the following code (located midway in the method) that sets the text of the cell:

```
cell.textLabel?.text =
        deliveryStatusEntity.statusDescription
```

15. Delete this line of code (or comment it out if you prefer) and add the following code in its place:

```
let lblStatus = cell.viewWithTag(1) as! UILabel
lblStatus.text =
   deliveryStatusEntity.statusDescription
let imgStatus = cell.viewWithTag(2) as! UIImageView

switch indexPath.row {
case 0:
   imgStatus.image = UIImage(named: "TruckBlack")
case 1:
   imgStatus.image = UIImage(named: "TruckRed")
case 2:
   imgStatus.image = UIImage(named: "TruckGreen")
default:
   break
}
```

This code no longer uses the **textLabel** reference to set the text. That's because this is a custom cell, and it doesn't contain the standard **textLabel**. This code gets a reference to the cell's label by passing a **1** to the cell's **viewWithTag:** method (remember you set the **Tag** of the label to **1**). It then sets the **text** property of the label.

Next, the code gets a reference to the cell's image view control by passing a **2** to the cell's **viewWithTag:** method. It then sets the **image** property of the image view based on the delivery status.

16. To see how this looks at run time, click Xcode's **Run** button. When the app appears in the Simulator, select a delivery in the **Deliveries** scene. Then, in the **Shipment** scene, select the **Delivery Status row**, and you should see the rows shown in Figure 13.37.

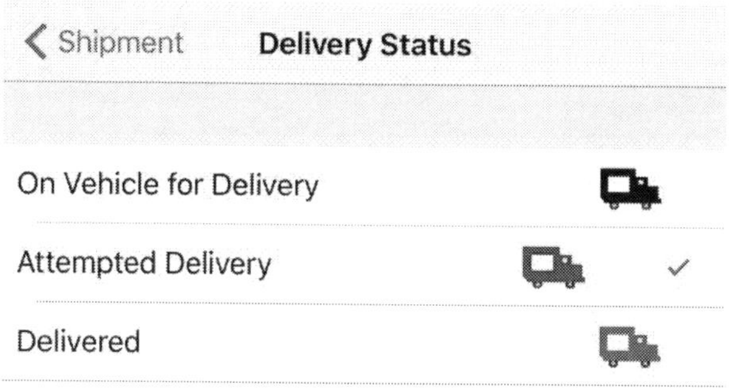

Figure 13.37 The custom cells at run time.

You can create a wide variety of custom cells using the techniques outlined in this section. Just drag and drop the controls you need into the custom cell, set a unique **Tag** number, and configure the cell in the table view controller's **tableView:cellForRowAtIndexPath:** method.

Creating Indexed Table Views

When you have a table view that can potentially contain hundreds or thousands of entries, you should create an index so your users can easily get to the items in the list. For example, the built-in Contacts and Music apps have an alphabetical index located on the right side of the table view that allows users to select a letter of the alphabet to navigate to items in the list that start with that letter.

Understanding How Indexes Work

Figure 13.38 shows an indexed Customers table view. On the right side of the table view is an index containing the letters A through Z. Notice there is also a number sign (#) at the bottom of the index that is used to group items together that begin with a number.

Also note the section headers in Figure 13.38. Customers in the list are grouped by the first letter of their last name. If there are no customer last names that start with a particular leer of the alphabet, there is no group or header shown for that letter.

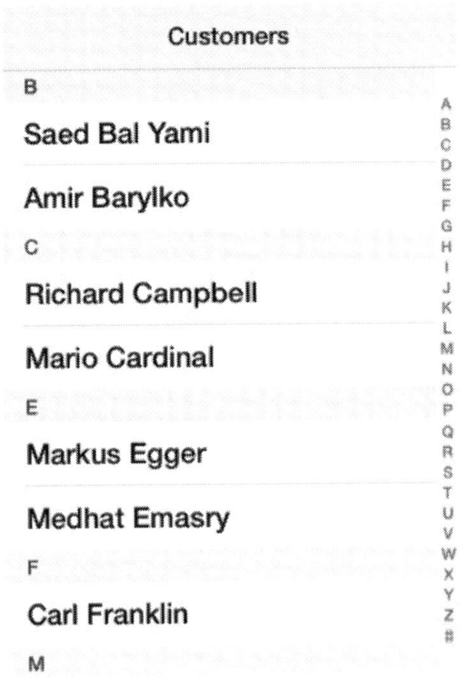

Figure 13.38 An indexed table view.

When the user taps a letter in the index, the table view scrolls to the group associated with that letter. If there is no entry for the selected letter, the table view scrolls to the section that contains the next lowest letter of the alphabet. For example, in Figure 13.38, if the user taps the letter **G** in the index, the table view scrolls to the section for the letter **F**. In the case where there is no lower letter (as with the letter **A** in this example), the table view scrolls to the first section of the table view.

So, how do you add an index to a table view and provide the behavior I just described? There are three main things you need:

1. An array containing all the keys to be listed on the right side.
2. An array containing the "active" keys—keys that have items associated with them.
3. A dictionary with items grouped by each key.

Figure 13.39 shows how a **Customer** business-controller object provides these three collections.

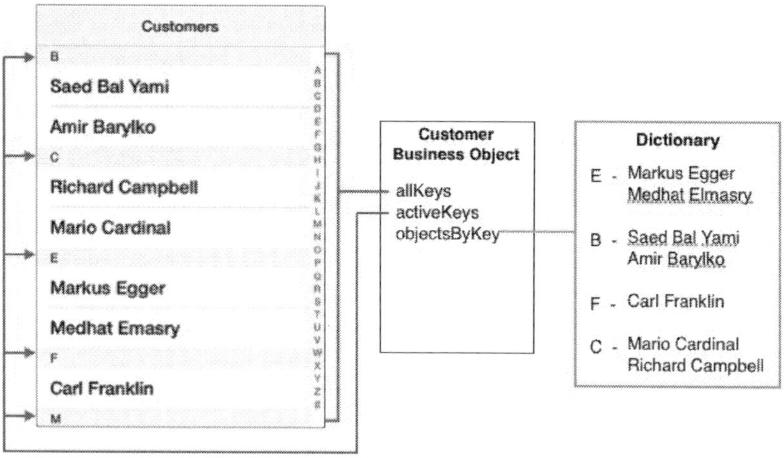

Figure 13.39 Three collections provide the information you need to display a table view index.

With this picture in mind, let's take a closer look at the **Customer** class to see how it provides these three collections. This **Customer** class can be found in the **IndexedTableViewDemo** project that has been provided in this book's sample code.

1. If it's not already open, in Xcode, open the **IndexedTableViewDemo** project that comes with this book's sample code.

2. In the Project Navigator, expand the **Business Layer** group and select the **Customer.swift** file. Near the top of the code file, the **allKeys** array property is declared and initialized:

```
var allKeys =
["A","B","C","D","E","F","G","H","I","J","K","L","M","N",
"O","P","Q","R","S","T","U","V","W","X","Y","Z","#"]
```

   This array contains a list of all keys that will be displayed down the right side of the table view (Figure 13.39).

3. A little further down in the code file is the init method:

```
override init() {
    super.init()
    self.createIndex()
}
```

In the **init**, a call is made to the **createIndex** method. This method generates the other two collections necessary to create the index—the **activeKeys** array and the **objectsByKey** dictionary. Scroll down a little further and we'll take a look at the **createIndex** method.

The first part of the method contains a for loop that loops through the collection of **CustomerEntity** objects:

```
for customer in self.entityList {

   // Get the first letter in the last name
   let index =
      customer.lastName.startIndex.advancedBy(1)
   firstLetter =
      customer.lastName.substringToIndex(index)

   // Check if this is a number
   if let _ =
      self.formatter.numberFromString(firstLetter) {
      // It is, add it to the number list
   arrayOfCustomersWithNumbers.append(customer)
   }
   else {
      // It's not. See if we've come across this
   arrayOfCustomersWithNames =
         dictionary[firstLetter]

      if arrayOfCustomersWithNames == nil {
        // No, create an array to hold items
        arrayOfCustomersWithNames = Array<T>()
      }
      // Add the object to the current array
   arrayOfCustomersWithNames!.append(customer)
   // Store the array in the dictionary
      dictionary[firstLetter] =
        arrayOfCustomersWithNames
      }
}
```

In this loop, the first letter of the **lastName** of the **CustomerEntity** object is examined. All **CustomerEntity** objects whose **lastName** starts with the same letter are added to an array—one array for each unique letter of the alphabet. Arrays are only created for letters of the alphabet that have associated **CustomerEntity** objects. As each new array is created, it's added to a dictionary where the letter of the alphabet is used as the key (Figure 13.39).

Take a look at the next section of code:

```
// Sort first letters into a new array
let keyArray = dictionary.keys.sort()

// Create a copy of the array
self.activeKeys = keyArray
```

This code gets all the keys from the newly created dictionary, sorts them alphabetically, and then stores the result in the **activeKeys** property.

The next section of code handles any names that start with numbers:

```
if arrayOfCustomersWithNumbers.count > 0 {
   dictionary["#"] = arrayOfCustomersWithNumbers
}
```

If any names starting with a number were found, they are added to the dictionary, and the number sign (#) is added to the **activeKeys** array.

At the bottom of the **createIndex** method is code that sorts all items in each array in the dictionary alphabetically:

```
for key in dictionary.keys {
   var array = dictionary[key]
   array?.sort({ $0.lastName < $1.lastName })
   self.objectsByKey[key] = array
}
```

This code uses a closure (as discussed in *Book 4: Learn to Code in Swift* in *Chapter 23: Understanding Closures*) to compare **CustomerEntity** objects and sort them alphabetically. As you can see, the **lastName** and **firstName** properties are appended together before the comparison is run. This ensures customers with the same last name are sorted secondarily by first name.

After each array in the dictionary is sorted, it is added to the **objectsByKey** property, which is the Dictionary used to group the items in the table view by letter of the alphabet.

4. Scroll down further to see the **objectCountForKey:** method:

```
func objectCountForKey(index: Int) -> Int {
   var key = self.activeKeys[index]
   var namesArray = self.objectsByKey[key]
   return namesArray!.count
}
```

   This method makes it easy to determine the number of entity objects for a particular key (in this case, letter of the alphabet). This is a convenience method because it removes the burden of having to enter these three lines of code in the table view controller. Adding this method makes it convenient for someone using this class to easily get the object count.

5. The next method in the **Customer** class is the **objectAtIndexPath:** method:

```
func objectAtIndexPath(indexPath: NSIndexPath)
-> CustomerEntity {
var key = self.activeKeys[indexPath.section]
   var array = self.objectsByKey[key]
   return array![indexPath.row]
}
```

   This is another convenience method that returns a **CustomerEntity** object from the specified index path. The index path section is used to retrieve the key from the array of **activeKeys**. In the next line of code, the key is used to retrieve the array of **CustomerEntity** objects from the **objectsByKey** dictionary. The last line of code uses the index path row to retrieve a specific **CustomerEntity** from the array.

Building a Pre-populated Database

The **IndexedTableViewDemo** project uses Core Data to retrieve **CustomerEntity** objects from the data store. Let's run the app and take a look.

1. If it's not already open, in Xcode, open the **IndexedTableViewDemo** project that comes with this book's sample code.

2. Click Xcode's **Run** button, and, when the app appears in the Simulator, you should see a table view containing a list of customers (Figure 13.40).

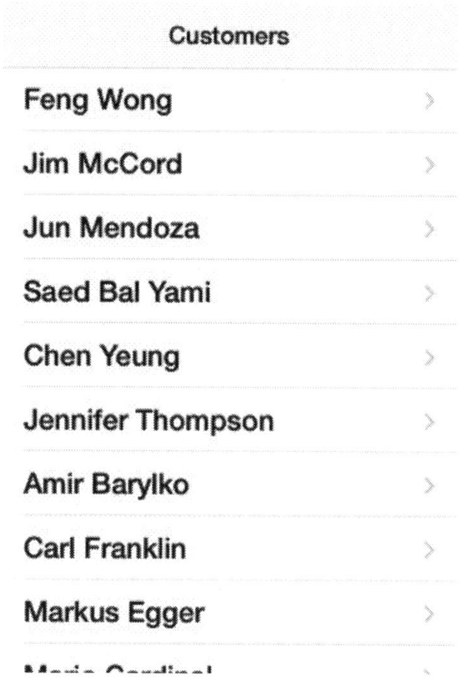

Figure 13.40 The table view contains a list of Customers.

Since this is live data, how did the SQLite database get populated with these customers? Let's find out.

3. Go back to Xcode and press the **Stop** button. Next, go to the Project Navigator and expand the **Business Layer** node. Beneath this node, you can see an **IndexedTableViewDemo.sqlite** database has been included in this project (Figure 13.41).

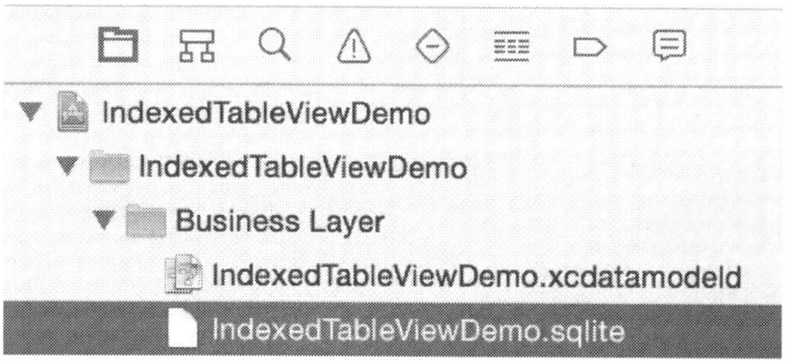

Figure 13.41 A SQLite database is included in the project.

This database contains the customers you see listed in Figure 13.40. However, this is not the database that is used by the app in the Simulator at run time. When the app first starts up, it checks to see if an **IndexedTableViewDemo.sqlite** file already exists in your app's **Documents** folder. If it doesn't exist, a copy is made of the SQLite file in your project and placed in your app's **Documents** folder.

4. To see the code that does all this, in the Project Navigator, select the **mmBusinessObject.swift** file and check out the code located near the top of the **persistentStoreCoordinator** method:

```
if self.copyDatabaseIfNotPresent
{
      let dbcPath = url.path!
      var fileManager =
        NSFileManager.defaultManager()
      // Check if the database already exists
      if !fileManager.fileExistsAtPath(dbcPath)
      {
        // It doesn't. Check if a .sqlite database
           was distributed with this app
        var defaultStorePath =
           NSBundle.mainBundle().pathForResource(
        self.dbName, ofType: "sqlite")
        if defaultStorePath != nil
        {
           // It was, copy the embedded database to
              the app's Documents directory
           do {
              try fileManager.copyItemAtPath(
              defaultStorePath!, toPath: dbcPath)
           }
           catch  {
              //print((error as
                  NSError).localizedDescription)
        }
      }
   }
}
```

The first line checks if the **copyDatabaseIfNotPresent** property is true, and if it is, it gets the app's **Documents** directory. The next section appends the name of the database to get the full path to the database file.

The last section checks if the database already exists and, if it doesn't, copies the SQLite database file from your project folder to the **Documents** folder.

To get this logic to kick in, just set the **copyDatabaseIfNotPresent** property to **YES** in the **init** method of your **ABusinessObject** class which has already been done for you in this project(if this flag is set to **false**, a new, empty database is created instead):

```
override init() {
    super.init()
    self.copyDatabaseIfNotPresent = true
}
```

This is an easy way to pre-populate databases for your own apps.

Building an Indexed Table View

Our goal in this section is to build a **Customers** scene with an indexed table view as shown in Figure 13.38.

1. If it's not already open, in Xcode, open the **IndexedTableViewDemo** project that comes with this book's sample code.

2. In the Project Navigator, select the **Main.Storyboard** file. You will see the **Customers** and **Detail** scenes on the right side of the storyboard (Figure 13.42).

   In the following steps, you will change the **MasterViewController** class files to create an indexed table view in the **Customers** scene. When the user taps on a customer, they will be taken to the **Detail** scene where some simple detail information will be displayed.

*Figure 13.42 The **Customer** and **Detail** scenes.*

3. As already mentioned, you should never use a disclosure indicator in a table view with an indexed list, so let's get rid of it now.

   In the **Customers** scene, select the table view cell, and then go to the Attributes Inspector and change the **Accessory** attribute to **None.**This removes the disclosure indicator from the cell.

4. Select the **MasterViewController.swift** file in the Project Navigator. Check out the properties and methods, and you can see it's already been set up to use the **Customer** business controller to retrieve and display **CustomerEntity** objects in the table view.

5. Scroll down to the **numberOfSectionsInTableView:** method, and change the **return** statement to:

```
override func numberOfSectionsInTableView(tableView:
UITableView) -> Int {
    return self.customer.activeKeys.count
}
```

   Remember, as shown in Figure 13.39, the **activeKeys** property contains a collection of keys (sorted alphabetically) that have items associated with them. So, the number of keys in this collection dictates the number of sections in the table.

6. In the **tableview:numberOfRowsInSection:** method, change the return statement to the following:

```
override func tableView(tableView: UITableView,
numberOfRowsInSection section: Int) -> Int {
  return self.customer.objectCountForKey(section)
}
```

The **objectCountForKey:** method of the **Customer** class makes it easy to get the count of **CustomerEntity** objects for a specified key, which, in this case, is a letter of the alphabet. You could write a few lines of code in the table view controller to derive this information yourself, but it's nice to have the business controller class figure this out for you.

7. In the **tableView:cellForRowAtIndexPath:** method, change the following line of code that retrieves the **CustomerEntity**:

```
override func tableView(tableView: UITableView,
   cellForRowAtIndexPath indexPath: NSIndexPath) ->
   UITableViewCell {
   let cell = tableView.
     dequeueReusableCellWithIdentifier("Cell",
     forIndexPath: indexPath) as! UITableViewCell

   let customerEntity =
        self.customer.objectAtIndexPath(indexPath)

cell.textLabel!.text = customerEntity.fullName
   return cell
}
```

This code makes a call to the **objectAtIndexPath:** method you learned about in the previous section.

8. Add the following method below the **tableView: cellForRowAtIndexPath:** method:

```
override func tableView(tableView: UITableView,
titleForHeaderInSection section: Int) ->
String? {
    return self.customer.activeKeys[section]
}
```

This method provides the titles for the section headers. To see this at work, press the **Run** button and go to the **Customers** scene. The table view should look like Figure 13.43.

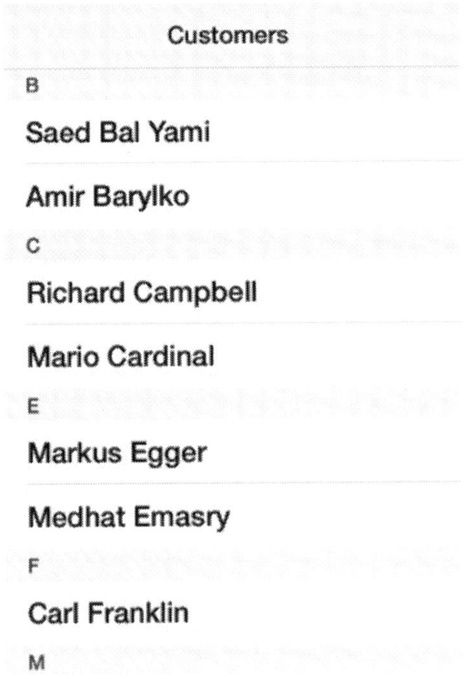

Figure 13.43 The table view with section headers.

9. Go back to Xcode and press the **Stop** button.

10. Next, add the following method directly below the **tableView: titleForHeaderInSection:** method you added in the previous step:

```
override func
sectionIndexTitlesForTableView(tableView:
UITableView) -> [String] {
   return self.customer.allKeys
}
```

This method is part of the **UITableViewDataSource** protocol. It returns an array containing keys to be displayed in the index down the right side of the table view. The **allKeys** property of the **Customer** object contains a list of all possible key values (A-Z and the # sign).

11. To see this code in action, press the **Run** button, and the **Customers** scene and table view should look like Figure 13.44.

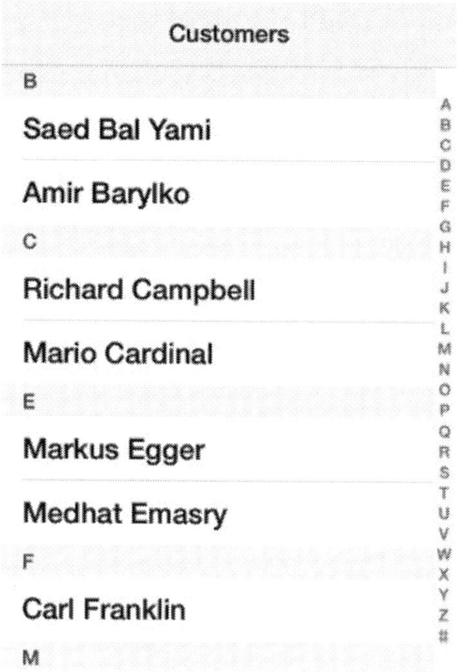

Figure 13.44 The table view with index.

As it stands now, if you tap a letter in the index, it doesn't take you to the corresponding section (although tapping some of the letters scrolls the table view a bit). Let's fix that.

12. Go back to Xcode and press the **Stop** button. Next, add the following method below the **sectionIndexForTitlesForTableView:** method you added in the previous step:

```
override func tableView(tableView: UITableView,
sectionForSectionIndexTitle title: String,
atIndex index: Int) -> Int {
   return self.customer.activeKeyIndexForKey(title)
}
```

This method is also a part of the **UITableViewDataSource** protocol. It tells the table view which section to scroll to when a particular key is selected in the index. If there were always items for every key in the index, it would be easy—tapping the key would go to the associated section. However, since there aren't always items for every key, you need to add logic that determines which section to scroll to when there are no items in the table view for that key.

This method calls the **activeKeyIndexForKey:** method of the **Customer** object, which contains this code:

```
func activeKeyIndexForKey(key: String) -> Int {
   var indexOfSelectedKey: Int
   // See if there are any items in the list
     for the selected key
if let indexOfKey = find(self.activeKeys, key) {
     // There is, return it!
     return indexOfKey
   }
   // There isn't...Get the index of the
   selected key from the full list of keys
indexOfSelectedKey = find(self.allKeys, key)!
// Cycle through the list of keys for items
     in the list
   // Find closest value below the selected key
var indexOfCurrentKey: Int var previousIndex = 0 for
var i = 0; i < self.activeKeys.count; i++ {
     // Get index of the key for items in list
     indexOfCurrentKey = find(self.allKeys,
          self.activeKeys[i])!
     // If the index of the selected key is less
     if indexOfSelectedKey < indexOfCurrentKey {
          break
}
     previousIndex = i
   }
   return previousIndex
}
```

At the top of this method, a check is made to see if there is a section in the table view that matches the specified key. If there is, it's simple—that section number is returned.

If there is no section for the specified key, the code that determines which section to scroll to is executed. The **for** loop at the bottom of the method searches through the set of active keys (representing sections in the table view) and finds the closest section. As mentioned earlier, if there is no entry for the selected key, the table view scrolls to the section that contains the next lowest letter of the alphabet. In the case where there is no lower letter, the table view scrolls to the first section of the table view.

13. To try this out, select **iPhone 4S** in Xcode's Scheme control, and click the **Run** button. When the app appears in the Simulator, select **M** in the index. The table view should scroll to the **M** section of the table view as seen in the image on the left in Figure 13.45.

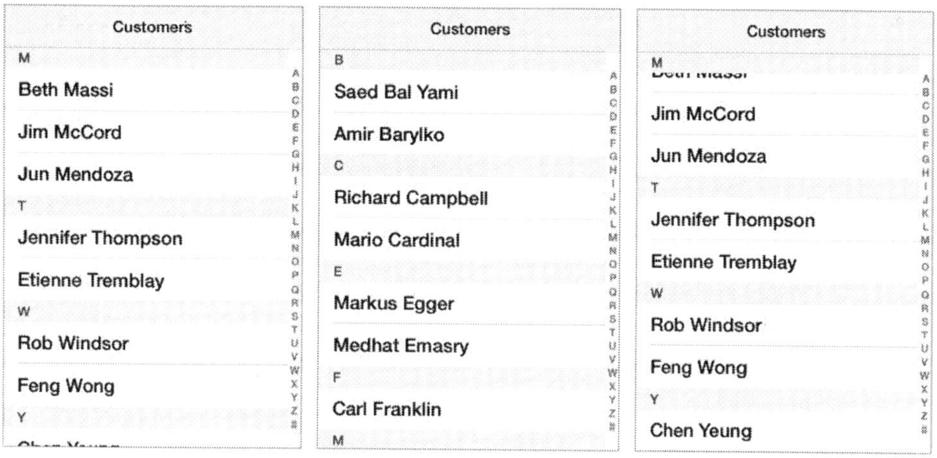

Figure 13.45 Tapping letters in the view scrolls the table view to the corresponding section.

14. Next, select the letter **A**, for which there are no items in the table view. This should scroll the table view to the first section as shown in the center image in Figure 13.45.

15. Finally, select the letter **Z** for which there are also no items in the table view. This should scroll the table view to the last section as shown in the image on the right in Figure 13.45.

That's it—you have a fully functioning index!

Adding a Search Bar to a Table View

In situations where there may be hundreds of items for each key in the index, it's best to add a search bar to the table view so users can more easily find items they are looking for. Some of the built-in apps such as Contacts and Music contain search bars that do just that.

Figure 13.46 shows a search bar in a table view at run time. The image on the left shows the search control "at rest" at the top of the table view.

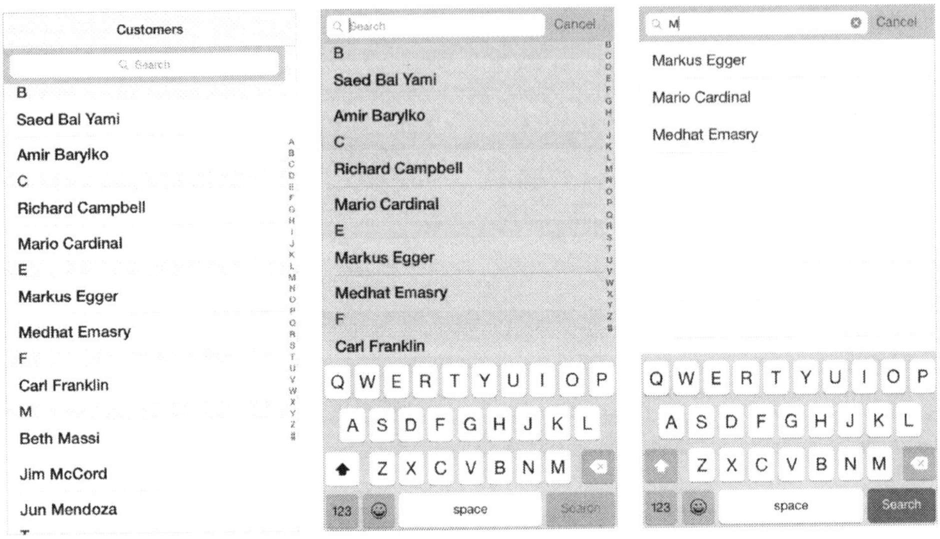

Figure 13.46 The search bar in its various modes.

The image in the center shows what happens when you tap the search control—a dark, translucent view appears over the original table view, and the keyboard pops up.

The image on the right shows what happens when you enter characters in the search bar. Items that match the search string are displayed in the search-results table view. Typically, you select one of the items from the search results list and are taken to a view that shows more detail about the selected item.

Starting in iOS 8, Apple deprecated the traditional **Search Bar** and **Search Display Controller** objects you can find in Xcode's Object Library. There is a newer **Search Controller** you should use instead. However, as of Xcode version 7, you still can't add this search controller in Interface Builder. You must add it in code.

A **Search Controller** has three main parts (Figure 13.47).

1. **A search bar** – The user enters a search string used to filter a list of items in the main table view.
2. **A search controller** – When a user taps the search bar, the controller superimposes the search interface over the main interface.

3. **A search results table view** – The search interface contains a results table view that lists the items matching the search filter.

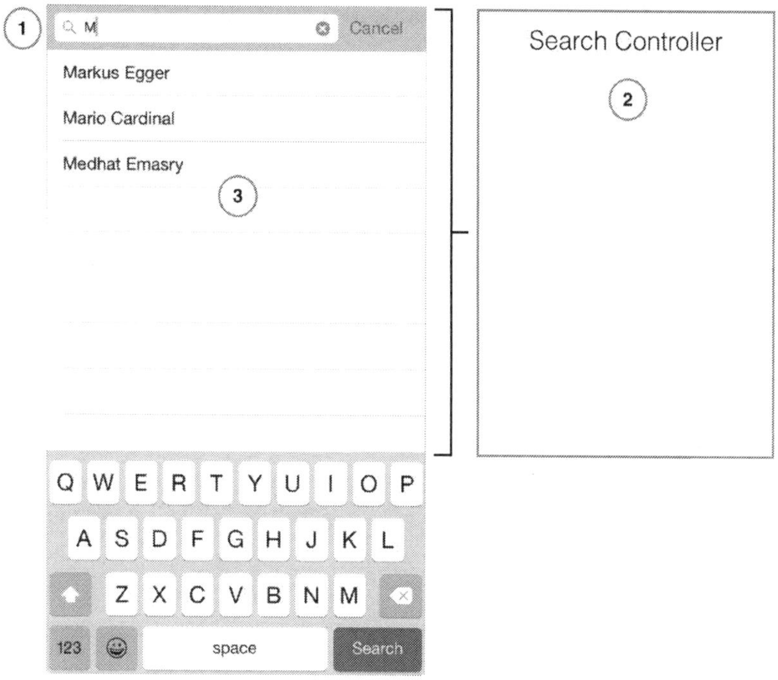

Figure 13.47 A search bar, search-results table view, and search controller.

To learn how the Search Controller works, check out Figure 13.48. There is a **Main View Controller** for the **Main Table View** and a separate **Search Controller** for the **Search Results Table View**.

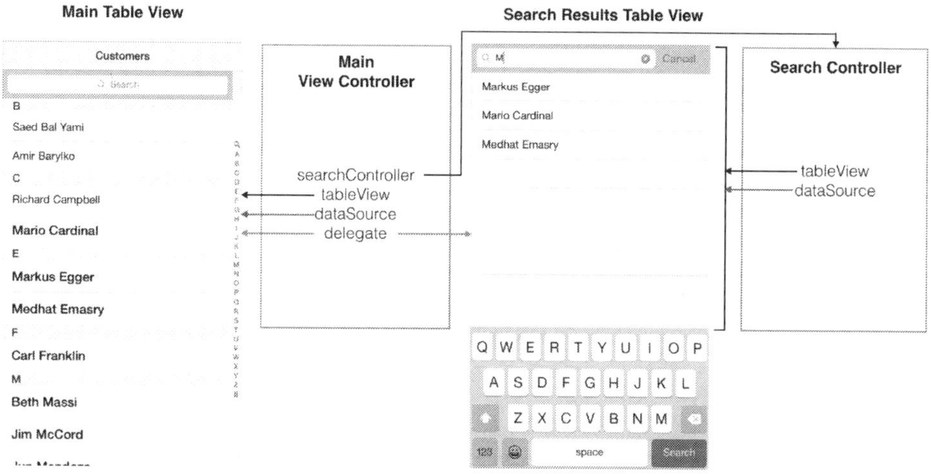

Figure 13.48 High-level overview of ***Search Controller.***

The **Main View Controller** is the data source for the main table view. It is the delegate for both table views, the Search Controller, and the search bar.

The **Search Controller** is the data source for the **Search Results Table View**.

Now that you have an understanding of how the Search Controller work, you're ready to follow these step-by- step instructions for adding search capabilities to the **Customers** scene.

Creating a Search Results Table View Controller

Let's begin by creating a search results table view controller.

1. If it's not already open, in Xcode, open the **IndexedTableViewDemo** project.
2. Let's create a search results table view controller. First, select the **DetailViewController.swift** code file in the Project Navigator, so the new view controller is added below it in the list.
3. Select **File** > **New** > **File...** from Xcode's menu.
4. On the left side of the New File dialog under the iOS section, select **Source**. On the right side of the dialog, select **Cocoa Touch Class**, and click **Next**.
5. In the next step of the New File dialog (Figure 13.49), change **Subclass of** to **UITableViewController**, change **Class** to **SearchResultsTableViewController** and click **Next**.

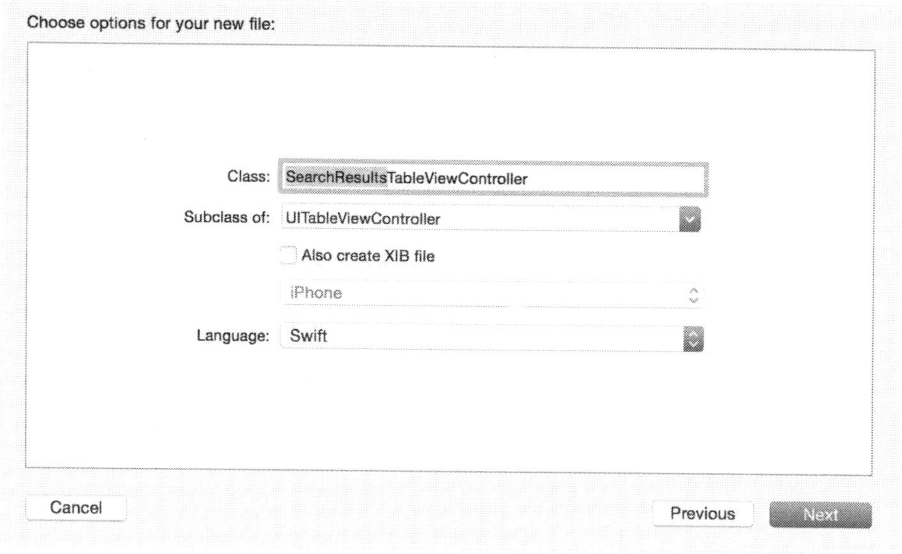

Figure 13.49 Create a SearchResultsTableViewController.

6. In the Save dialog, click **Create**. This adds the new class file to the Project Navigator.

7. Delete the commented methods at the bottom of the code file since you don't need them for this project.

8. At the top of the **SearchResultsTableViewController**, add the following array property:

```
class SearchResultsTableViewController:
   UITableViewController {

var filteredList = Array<CustomerEntity>()
```

The **filteredList** array will be used to store items that match the search string entered by the user and will be the data source for the search-result table view.

9. Change **numberOfSectionsInTableView:** to return 1, since there is only one section in the search results table view and remove the **#warning** comments:

```
override func numberOfSectionsInTableView(tableView:
    UITableView) -> Int {
    return 1
}
```

10. Change the **tableView:numberOfRowsInSection:** method to return the **filteredList** array count and remove the **#warning** comments:

```
override func tableView(tableView: UITableView,
 numberOfRowsInSection section:
   Int) -> Int {
   return self.filteredList.count
}
```

11. Add the following **tableView:cellForRowAtIndexPath:** method before the closing curly brace of the view controller class:

```
override func tableView(tableView:
UITableView, cellForRowAtIndexPath indexPath:
NSIndexPath) -> UITableViewCell {

   let cell = UITableViewCell(style:
      UITableViewCellStyle.Default,
      reuseIdentifier: "Cell")

   let customerEntity = self.filteredList[indexPath.row]
   cell.textLabel?.text = customerEntity.fullName

   return cell
}
```

This code retrieves **CustomerEntity** objects from the **filteredList** array for the search results table view.

Enhancing the MasterViewController

Next, let's make some necessary changes to the **MasterViewController** class.

1. Select the **MasterViewController.swift** file in the Project Navigator, then add the following code that adopts three new protocols:

```
class MasterViewController: UITableViewController
, UISearchBarDelegate,
UISearchControllerDelegate,
UISearchResultsUpdating
{
```

The **MasterViewController** adopts these protocols because it is the delegate for the search controller and the search bar.

2. Add the following highlighted properties to the **MasterViewController**:

```
class MasterViewController:
   UITableViewController, UISearchBarDelegate,
   UISearchControllerDelegate,
   UISearchResultsUpdating {

    var customer = Customer()
    var customerList = Array<CustomerEntity>()
   var searchController: UISearchController!
   var resultsTableViewController =
   SearchResultsTableViewController()
```

The **searchController** property will reference the Search Controller. The **resultsTableViewController** property will reference the search results table view controller.

3. Add the **following** code to the **viewDidLoad** method:

```
override func viewDidLoad() {
    super.viewDidLoad()
    self.customerList = customer.getAllEntities()

// Initialize the search controller
 self.searchController =
   UISearchController(searchResultsController:
   self.resultsTableViewController)
 self.searchController.searchResultsUpdater = self
 self.searchController.searchBar.sizeToFit()
 self.searchController.dimsBackgroundDuringPresentation =
   true
 self.searchController.delegate = self
```

```
    self.searchController.searchBar.delegate = self
    self.resultsTableViewController.tableView.delegate = self

    // Add search bar to the table view header
    self.tableView.tableHeaderView =
       self.searchController.searchBar

    // Ensures the search controller is displayed // within
    bounds of the table view controller
     self.definesPresentationContext = true
}
```

This code creates and initializes a search controller, and adds it to the table view's header. The last line of code is critical. It ensures that the search controller is displayed within the bounds of the table view.

4. Add the following method before the closing curly brace of the **MasterViewController** code file:

```
// MARK: UISearchBarDelegate
func searchBarSearchButtonClicked(searchBar:
 UISearchBar) {
    searchBar.resignFirstResponder()
}
```

   This method is part of the **UISearchBarDelegate** protocol. It's called when the user taps the **Search** button after entering search text and it tells the search bar to resign as first responder.

5. Next, add the following method below the method you added in the previous step:

```
// Mark: UISearchResultsUpdating
func updateSearchResultsForSearchController
(searchController: UISearchController) {
    // update filtered array based on search results
    self.resultsTableViewController.filteredList =
        customer.filterCustomersByName
      (self.searchController.searchBar.text!)
    self. resultsTableViewController.tableView.reloadData()
}
```

This method belongs to the **UISearchResultsUpdating** protocol. It's called when the user changes the text in the search bar. It calls the **Customer** object's **filterCustomerByName** method and stores the results in the **filteredList** array.

6. Now you're ready to test! Click Xcode's **Run** button. When the app appears in the Simulator, you will see the **Customers** scene with the new search bar above the first row in the table view (Figure 13.50). Notice the search box contains the **Search** placeholder and is automatically resized to make room for the index on the right side of the table view. The small magnifying glass you normally see at the top of the index on the right side of the table view is missing. We'll fix that in just a bit.

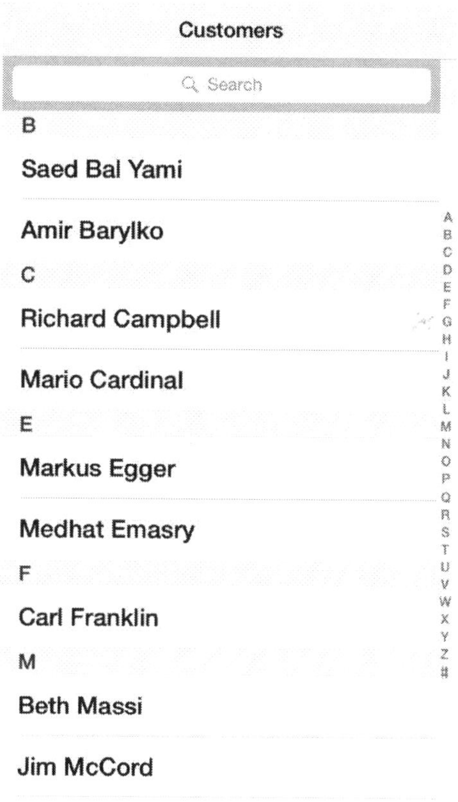

Figure 13.50 The search bar at run time.

Click in the search box and notice the changes shown in Figure 13.51.

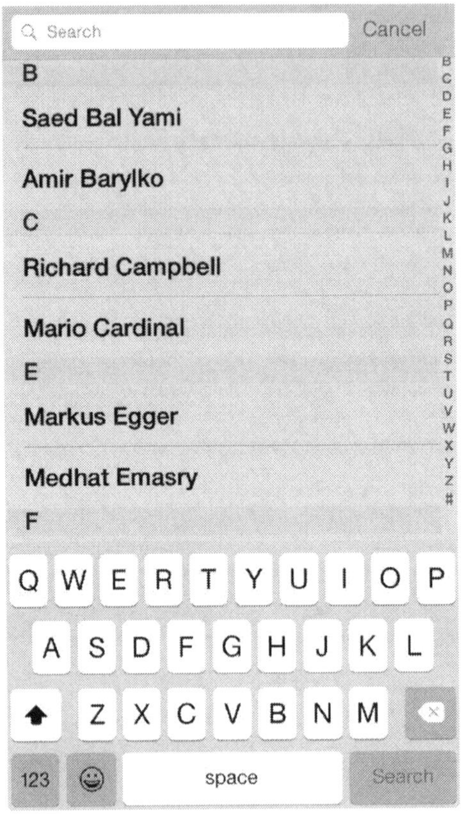

Figure 13.51 Click the search box to display the search view.

- The keyboard is displayed.
- A dark, translucent search view appears on top of the **Customers** table view.
- The navigation bar disappears, providing more room for the search view.
- A **Cancel** button to the right of the search bar.
- If you click the **Cancel** button, the search view closes and the regular table view appears.

7. Enter the letter **M** in the search box. This displays the search-results table view with a filtered list of **Customers** that match the search criteria (Figure 13.52).

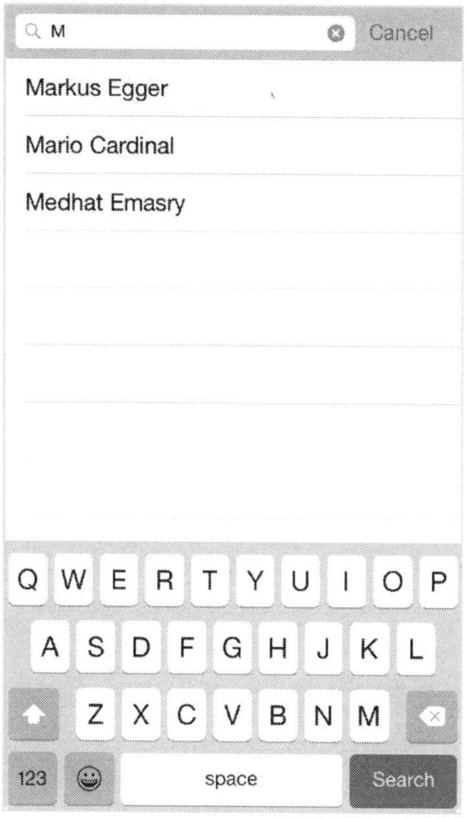

Figure 13.52 The search results table view.

Try typing other characters and see how items are displayed that match the search string.

Adding a Magnifying Glass to the Index

Now it's time to add a magnifying glass to the top of the table view index. When you click the magnifying glass at run time, it should automatically scroll to the top of the Customers table view. There are just a few steps required to set up the magnifying glass:

- Insert the magnifying glass icon into the index in the **sectionIndexTitlesForTableView:** method.
- Change **tableView:sectionForSectionIndexTitle:** to scroll to the top of the view when the magnifying glass is selected.

Let's give it a try.

1. Select **MasterViewController.swift** in the Project Navigator and change the code in the **sectionIndexTitlesForTableView:** method to:

```
override func sectionIndexTitlesForTableView(tableView:
UITableView) -> [AnyObject]! {
    var indexList = self.customer.allKeys
    indexList.insert(UITableViewIndexSearch, atIndex: 0)
return indexList
}
```

   This method creates a new **indexList** from the Customer object's **allKeys** array, and then it inserts the **UITableViewIndexSearch** object (the magnifying glass) at the top of the array.

2. Change the **tableView: sectionForSectionIndexTitle: atIndex:** method to:

```
override func tableView(tableView:
   UITableView, sectionForSectionIndexTitle
   title: String, atIndex index: Int) -> Int {
   if index == 0 {
      // magnifying glass was selected
      tableView.setContentOffset(CGPointZero,
        animated: false)
      return NSNotFound
   }
   else {
       return self.customer.activeKeyIndexForKey(title)
   }
}
```

   This code checks if the magnifying glass icon was tapped by the user (it's the first item in the index, so its index is zero). If it was, the table view's **setContentOffSet:animated:** method is called, passing a **CGPointZero** argument. This tells the table view to scroll to the top because **CGPointZero** represents the location 0,0.

3. Let's see how this looks at run time. Click Xcode's **Run** button and, when the app appears in the Simulator, you should see the magnifying glass icon at the top of the table view index (Figure 13.53).

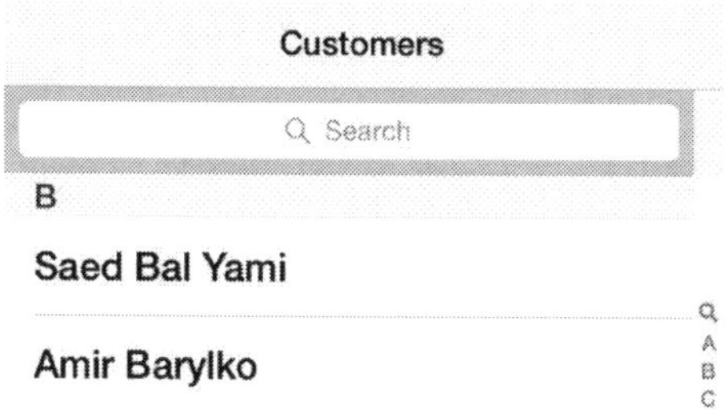

Figure 13.53 The magnifying glass icon appears at the top of the index on the right side of the screen.

4. Scroll to the bottom of the table view, click the magnifying glass icon, and the table view will scroll back the top where you can see the search control.

5. Go back to Xcode and press the **Stop** button.

Selecting Items in a Search Results Table View

Now that you have the search control working, let's learn how to let users to select an item from a search-results table view as shown in Figure 13.54. It's not difficult, but there are a few steps that are not intuitively obvious.

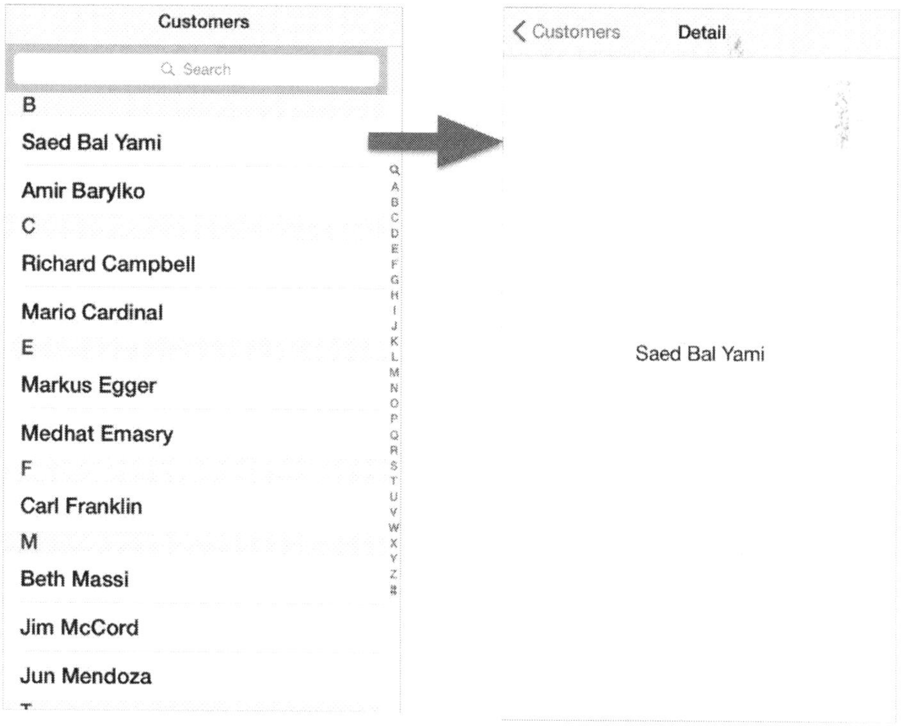

Figure 13.54 Selecting an item in a search-results table view.

In the sample project, when a user selects an item from the search-results table view or from the main table view, you want to perform the same action—navigate to a **Detail** scene that displays information about the selected item.

There are two things to keep in mind when you launch a detail scene:

- There are two table views in the **Customers** scene— the main table view and the search results table view.
- When passing the current **CustomerEntity** object from the **Customers** scene, you need to check which table view is currently active.

Let's give it a try:

1. If it's not already open, in Xcode, open the **IndexedTableViewDemo** project.
2. In the Project Navigator, select the **Main.Storyboard** file to display the storyboard in the design surface.
3. Click on the segue between the **Customers** and **Detail** scene. Notice the table view cell in the **Customers** scene is highlighted (Figure 13.55).

   This means the segue is connected directly to the cell. This worked well when there was only one table view, but now that there are two, you must create a segue that can be used from either table view.

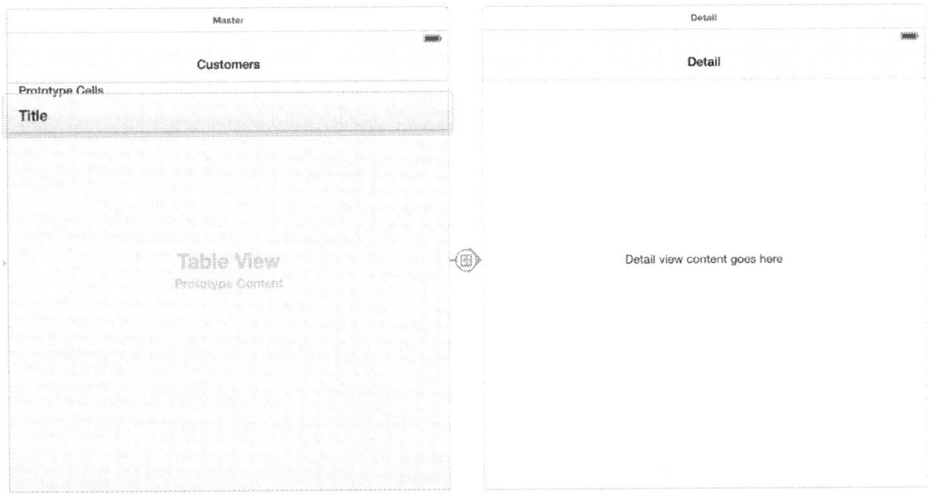

Figure 13.55 The segue is currently connected to the table view cell.

4. With the segue still selected, press the **Delete** key to delete the segue.

5. Next, click scene dock at the top of the **Customers** scene. This displays three icons in the scene dock. The icon on the far left is the view controller icon. This is the view controller from which you need to create the segue. To do this, hold the **Control** key down, click the icon on the far left in the **Customers** scene dock, and then drag your mouse over to the **Detail** scene. When the scene becomes highlighted (Figure 13.56), release your mouse button.

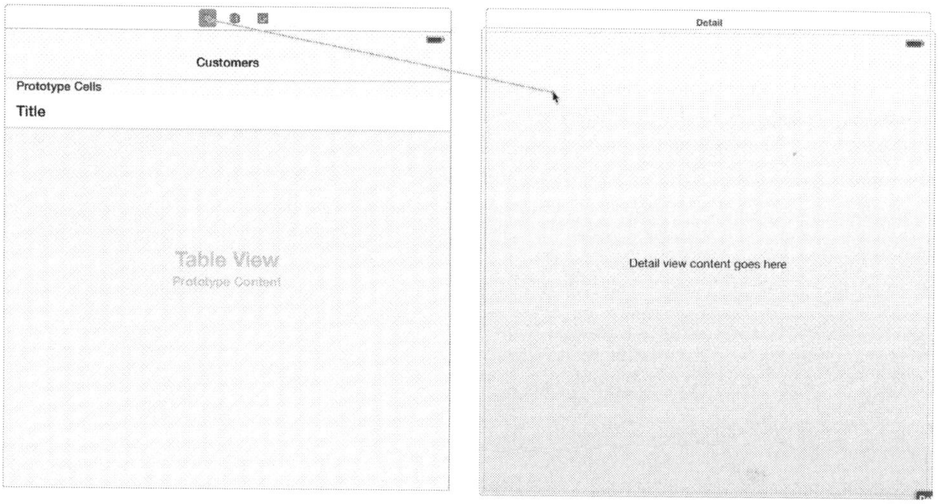

*Figure 13.56 Create a new segue from the **Customers** table view controller to the **Detail** scene.*

6. When the **Manual Segue** popup appears, select **Show** to create a new segue. Click on the segue to select it and notice that the entire **Customers** scene is highlighted (Figure 13.57). This indicates the segue is not tied to a particular cell. This is exactly the type of segue you need in this situation.

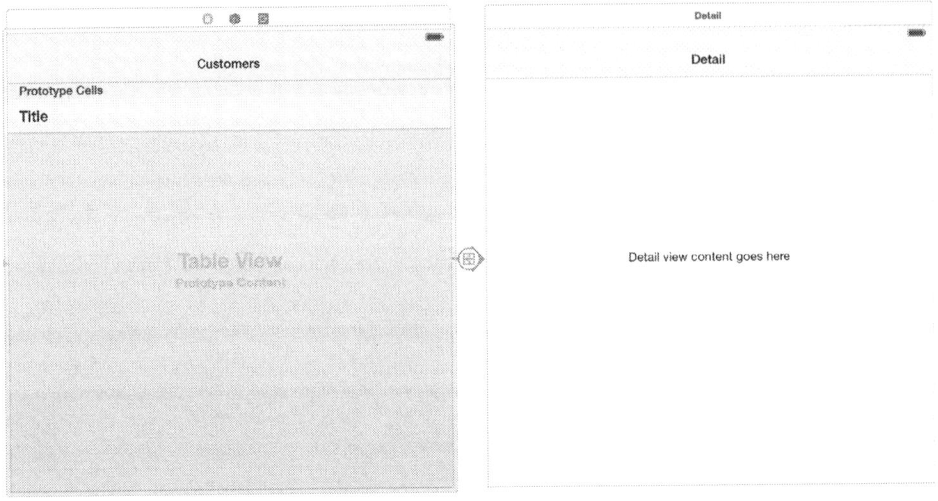

*Figure 13.57 Selecting the new segue highlights the entire **Customers** scene.*

7. With the segue still selected, go to the Attributes Inspector (third button from the right in the Inspector toolbar) and set the **Identifier** attribute to **DetailSegue** (Figure 13.58).

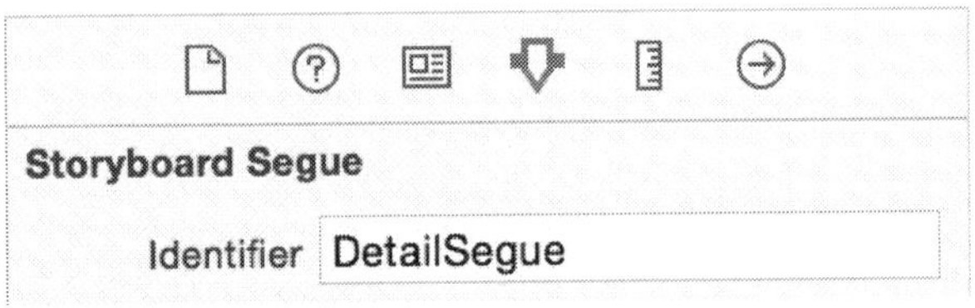

*Figure 13.58 Set the segue **Identifier** to **DetailSegue**.*

8. Now you need to add a method that triggers the segue when the user taps a table view row at run time. Select the **MasterViewController.swift** file in the Project Navigator and add the following method above the **prepareForSegue:sender**: method:

```
override func tableView(tableView:
UITableView, didSelectRowAtIndexPath
indexPath: NSIndexPath) {
 self.performSegueWithIdentifier("DetailSegue",
   sender: nil)
}
```

9. Next, we need to change the **MasterViewController**'s **prepareForSegue:** method to pass the appropriate **CustomerEntity** to the **Detail** scene as follows:

```
override func prepareForSegue(segue:
   UIStoryboardSegue, sender: AnyObject?) {
  if segue.identifier == "DetailSegue" {
     var customerEntity: CustomerEntity

     if self.searchController.searchBar.isFirstResponder(){
         let indexPath =
           self.resultsTableViewController.
              tableView.indexPathForSelectedRow!
       customerEntity =
          self.resultsTableViewController.
          filteredList[indexPath.row]
     }
     else {
         let indexPath =
         self.tableView.indexPathForSelectedRow
       customerEntity =
          self.customer.objectAtIndexPath(indexPath!)
     }
     let dvc = segue.destinationViewController
           as! DetailViewController
     dvc.customerEntity = customerEntity
  }
}
```

After checking if it is the **DetailSegue** that is getting fired, this code checks if the search bar is the first responder, meaning, it currently has focus. If it does, then the search results table view is active. In that case, the code gets the currently selected row in the search results table view and gets the corresponding **CustomerEntity** from the **filteredList**.

If the main table view has focus, the **else** statement gets its currently selected row and then gets the corresponding **CustomerEntity** by calling the **Customer** object's **objectAtIndexPath** method.

Afterward, the associated **CustomerEntity** object is stored in the **customerEntity** property of the **DetailViewController**.

10. Now you're ready to test the search capabilities of the app. Click the **Run** button in Xcode, and when the app appears in the Simulator, click the search bar. Type in one or more characters to filter the results and then select a customer from the search results list. The **Detail** scene should display that customer's name (Figure 13.59).

*Figure 13.59 The **Detail** view shows the customer's name.*

11. Next, you can test the selection of an item from the main **Customers** table view. To do this, press the **Customers** button to get back to the Customers view, and then click **Cancel** to close the search view. Now you can pick any customer from the main table view, and the app will navigate to the **Detail** view and display the selected customer's name in the label.

That covers most of what you need to know to add search capabilities to your table views. If you have table views with the potential for thousands of items, your users will thank you for adding the ability to search and select items.

Reordering, Deleting, and Adding Table View Rows

As shown in Figure 13.60, table views have two modes:

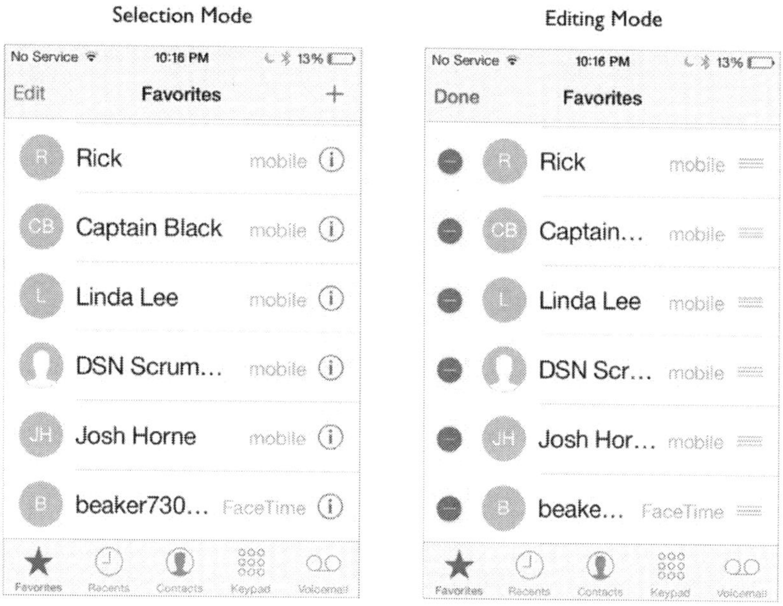

Figure 13.60 Table view Selection and Editing modes.

1. Selection (normal) mode

2. Editing mode

All the table views you have worked with so far have always been in selection mode. In this mode, users can view, scroll, and tap the rows but can't change anything about them.

When a table view is in editing mode, it typically displays deletion controls on the left that allow users to delete rows from the table view as well as reordering controls on the right that allow users to move rows to a different position.

Putting a Table View Into Editing Mode

A table view goes into editing mode when its **setEditing:animated:** method is called. This method call usually comes from an action method associated with an **Edit** button as shown in the top left of the image in Figure 13.61. If the first argument in the **setEditing:animated:** method call is **true**, the table view goes into edit mode. If it's **false**, the table view goes into selection mode.

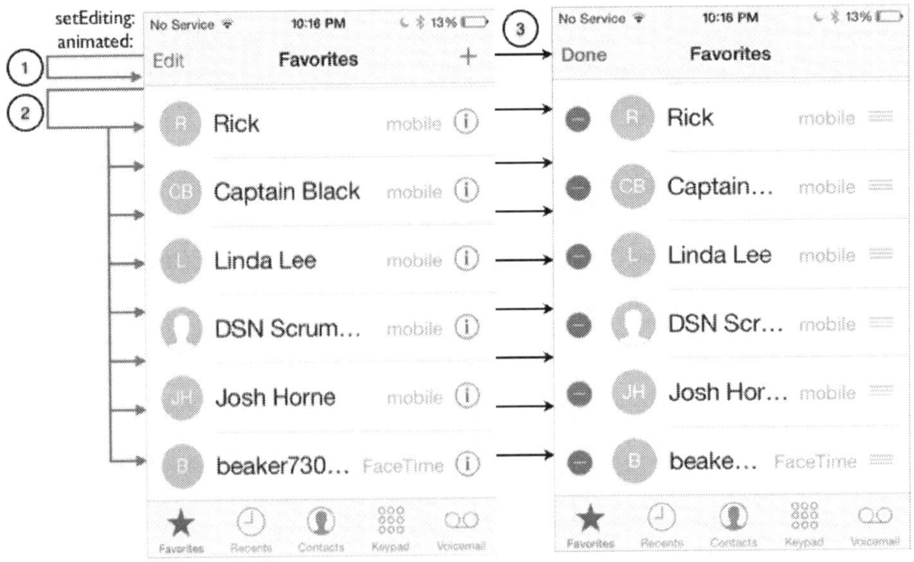

Figure 13.61 A ***setEditing:animated:*** *message is sent to the table view and then to each cell.*

Figure 13.61 shows the order of events that occur when the table view is in selection mode and the user presses the **Edit** button:

1. When the user taps the **Edit** button, it calls the **setEditing:animated:** method on the table view with **YES** as the first argument.

2. The table view then calls the **setEditing:animated:** method on each of its cells.

3. The **Edit** button changes to **Delete** and the cells display a deletion control on the left and a reordering control on the right.

When the user taps the **Done** button, the same methods called, except **false** is passed as the first argument in the **setEditing:animated:** method, and the table view and its cells go back to selection mode.

It's easy to add an edit button on either the left or right side of a navigation bar. All it takes is one line of code in the **viewDidLoad** method of a table view controller. For example, the following code adds an **Edit** button to the right side of the navigation toolbar:

```
override func viewDidLoad() {
  super.viewDidLoad()
  self.navigationItem.rightBarButtonItem =
    self.editButtonItem()
}
```

This code adds a button to the left side of the navigation toolbar:

```
override func viewDidLoad() {
  super.viewDidLoad()
  self.navigationItem.leftBarButtonItem =
    self.editButtonItem()
}
```

The **rightBarButtonItem** and **leftBarButtonItem** are properties of the **UINavigationItem** class that make it easy to create standard or custom buttons in a navigation bar (their cousins, **rightBarButtonItems** and **leftBarButtonItems** allow you to specify multiple buttons on the right or left of the navigation bar).

The **editButtonItem** property is inherited from the **UIViewController** class and has built-in functionality that automatically toggles the title of the button between **Edit** and **Done**. It also automatically calls the **setEditing: animated:** method of the table view controller when it's tapped by the user.

Examining the ToDoList Project

You're going to use the ToDoList app that comes with this book's sample code to learn about editing table views. Let's first take a look at the app's architecture.

1. In Xcode, open the **ToDoListDemo** project.

2. Let's see what the app looks like before you make any changes. Click the **Run** button in Xcode, and when the app appears in the Simulator, you should see a list of items in a **To Do list** (Figure 13.62).

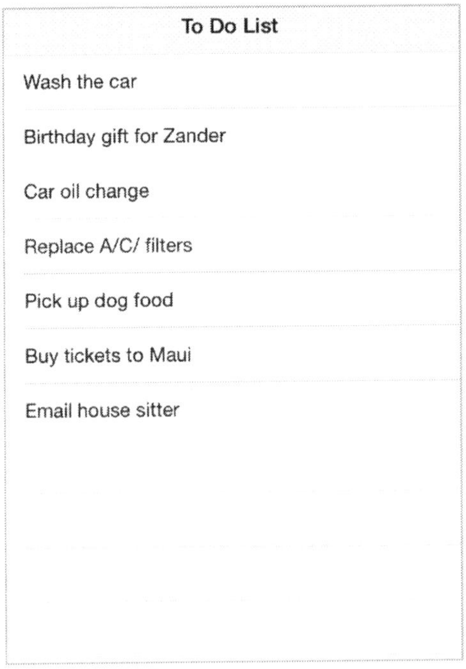

*Figure 13.62 The **ToDoListDemo** project at run time.*

3. Go back to Xcode and press the **Stop** button and let's take a look at how this app works.

4. Select the **ToDo.swift** business class code file in the Project Navigator. Notice the **entityList** property near the top of the code file:

```
class ToDo<T: ToDoEntity>: ABusinessObject<T> {
    var entityList: Array<T>!
```

This property is maintains an internal list of **ToDoEntity** objects. This is an alternative to keeping an external list in a view controller property.

When the **getAllEntitiesByDisplayOrder** method is called on an instance of the **ToDo** class, the results are stored into the **entityList** property:

```
func getAllEntitiesByDisplayOrder() -> Array<T>
{
   let sortDescriptor = NSSortDescriptor(key:
      "displayOrder", ascending: true)
   self.entityList =
      self.getAllEntitiesSortedBy(sortDescriptor)
```

Other methods in the **ToDo** class add, delete and reorder entities in this list.

5. Next, select the **ToDoTableViewController.swift** file in the Project Navigator. Notice the first line of code in the **viewDidLoad** method:

```
override func viewDidLoad() {
   super.viewDidLoad()
   self.toDo.getAllEntitiesByDisplayOrder()
```

This code doesn't need to save the entities returned from the **getAllEntitiesByDisplayOrder** method, because the **ToDo** object maintains its own internal list of entities in its **entityList** property.

The **ToDo** object's **entityList** property is also used as a data source for the table view, as you can see in methods such as **tableView:numberOfRowsInSection:**

```
override func tableView(tableView: UITableView,
   numberOfRowsInSection section: Int) -> Int {

      // Return the number of rows in the section
      return self.toDo.entityList.count
}
```

Enhancing the ToDoList Project

Let's add editing functionality to the **ToDoList** project.

1. Add the following code that adds a button to the left side of the navigation toolbar to **viewDidLoad**:

```
override func viewDidLoad() {
   super.viewDidLoad()
   self.toDo.getAllEntitiesByDisplayOrder()
   self.navigationItem.leftBarButtonItem =
      self.editButtonItem()
}
```

2. Press Xcode's **Run** button, and when the app appears in the Simulator, you can see the **Edit** button in the navigation toolbar (Figure 13.63).

3. Click the **Edit** button, and, as shown in the center image in Figure 13.63, the button changes to **Done**, and red delete icons appear on the left side of the rows. Notice there are no reordering controls on the right side of the table view yet.

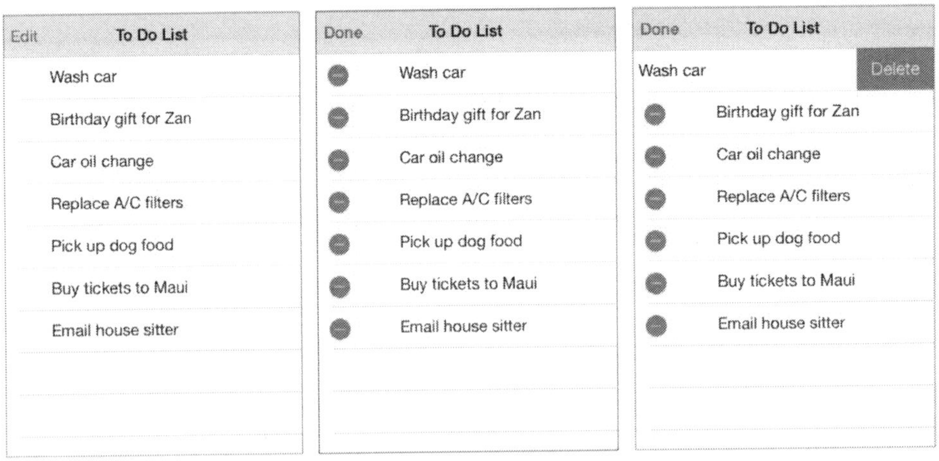

Figure 13.63 Table view editing modes.

4. Click one of the delete icons. Notice it rotates to the left, and a **Delete** button appears on the right side of the row as shown in the image on the right in Figure 13.63. Notice how far left the row's text is shifted. That's why I created a custom cell for the table view and indented the label 50 points so the text doesn't shift off the screen when the delete icon is selected.

5. Right now, the **Delete** button doesn't do anything, but if you click the **Done** button, the table view ends edit mode and goes back to selection mode. It does this because the **Done** button calls the **setEditing: animated:** message on the table view.

6. Go back to Xcode and press the **Stop** button.

As you can see, you get some great functionality by adding just one line of code.

Reordering Rows in a Table View

As already mentioned, the reordering controls did not appear on the right side of the view. How do you get these controls to appear?

All you need to do is implement the **tableView: moveRowAtIndexPath:** method in the table view controller. You don't even have to put any code in the method to make the reordering controls appear (although you do need code to save row order changes).

Before doing this, let's take a high-level look at how reordering works as shown in Figure 13.64.

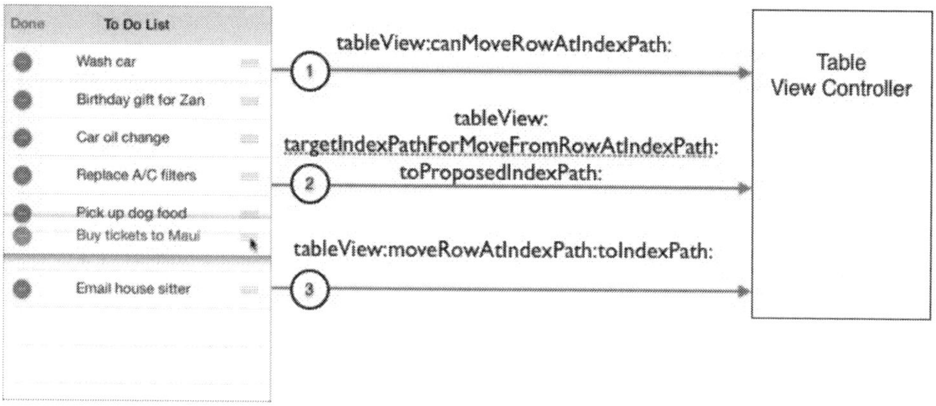

Figure 13.64 Table view and controller reordering messages.

1. When the taps the **Edit** button, the table view calls the **tableView: canMoveRowAtIndexPath:** method on the table view controller once for each visible row in the table view. If this method returns **true** for a cell, that cell displays a reordering control. If the method returns **false**, no reordering control appears.

   If you don't implement the method or return **true** from the method, all cells in the table view will have a reordering control. If you return **false**, none of the cells in the table view will have a reordering control.

2. When the user hovers a row over a new destination, the table view calls the **tableView: targetIndexPathForMoveFromRowAtIndexPath: toProposedIndexPath:** method on the table view controller. If you don't want a row moved to a particular index path, you can add code to this method that returns a different index path. In most table views, you don't need to implement this method at all because users are allowed to move rows to any other location.

3. When the user drops a row into a new position, the table view calls the table view controller's

tableView:moveRowAtIndexPath:toIndexPath: method. This method provides a place where you can put code to change the data source and save the new position of the row.

You *must* implement this method for the reordering controls to even appear in the table view. That's why you didn't see any reordering controls when you ran the app and pressed the **Edit** button (Figure 13.63)— this method hasn't been implemented yet.

Displaying the Reordering Controls

Let's start by adding an empty implementation of the **tableView: moveRowAtIndexPath:toIndexPath** method.

1. Select the **ToDoTableViewController.swift** file in the Project Navigator and add the following empty method before the closing curly brace of the class:

```
override func tableView(tableView:
 UITableView, moveRowAtIndexPath
 sourceIndexPath: NSIndexPath, toIndexPath
 destinationIndexPath: NSIndexPath) {
}
```

Press the **Run** button. When the app appears in the Simulator, click the **Edit** button, and you will see reordering controls (Figure 13.65).

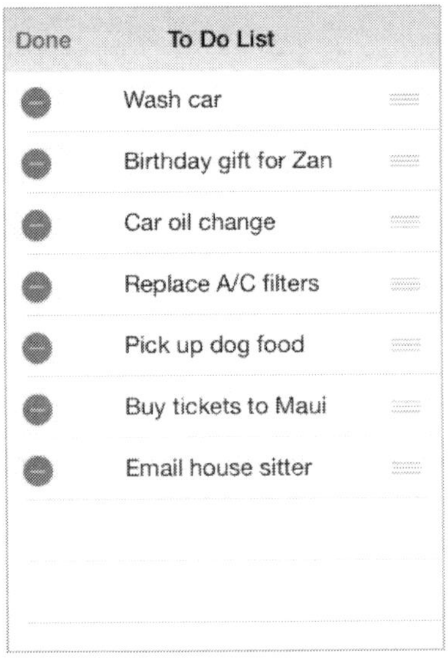

Figure 13.65 The reordering controls.

Click on one of the reordering controls, hold the mouse key down, and drag the row to a new position as shown in Figure 13.66. As you move the row to a new position, the other rows slide up or down to show where the destination of the moved row would be if you dropped it in that location.

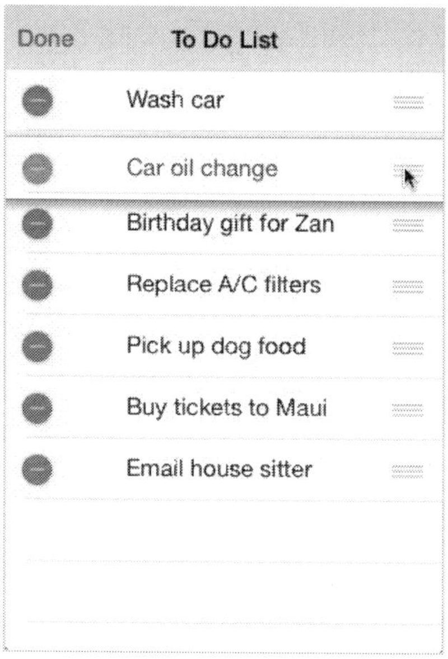

Figure 13.66 The reordering controls allow you to drag and drop rows to other index locations.

2. Now I'd like to demonstrate that, as the app stands now, any reordering change you make is only temporary. Go back to Xcode, click the **Stop** button, and then press the **Run** button again. As you can see, the rows are back in their original order.

3. Go back to Xcode, and then click the **Stop** button.

Saving Changes to Item Order

To get the reordering change to persist when you close the app and restart it, you need to implement the **tableView:moveRowAtIndex:toIndexPath:** method. In this method, you need to make a corresponding change to the order of items in the table view's data source.

1. Select the **ToDoTableViewController.swift** file in the Project Navigator, and add the following code to the empty **tableView: moveRowAtIndex:toIndexPath:** method you added earlier:

```
override func tableView(tableView:
   UITableView, moveRowAtIndexPath
   sourceIndexPath: NSIndexPath, toIndexPath
   destinationIndexPath: NSIndexPath) {
  self.toDo.moveObjectAtIndexPath (sourceIndexPath,
  destinationIndexPath: destinationIndexPath)
}
```

When the user moves a row into a new location, this method is called by the table view, which passes the original index path of the row (**sourceIndexPath**) and the new index path (**destinationIndexPath**).

The code you just added makes a call to the **ToDo** business controller's **moveObjectAtIndexPath: toIndexPath:** method, passing the source and destination index path. Let's take a look.

2. In the Project Navigator, select the **ToDo.swift** implementation file and scroll down to the **moveObjectAtIndexPath:toIndexPath:** method, which contains the following code:

```
func moveObjectAtIndexPath(sourceIndexPath:
NSIndexPath, destinationIndexPath: NSIndexPath) {

   let from = sourceIndexPath.row
   let to = destinationIndexPath.row

   if from == to {
      return
   }

   // Get the entity, remove it from its old
   // position and add it in its new position
   let toDoEntity = self.entityList[from]
   self.entityList.removeAtIndex(from)
   self.entityList.insert(toDoEntity, atIndex: to)

   // Set the new order of the object
   var lower = 0.0
   var upper = 0.0

   // Check for an item before it
```

```
    if to > 0 {
       lower =
         Double(self.entityList[to-1].displayOrder)
    }
    else {
       lower =
        Double(self.entityList[1].displayOrder) - 2.0
    }

    // Check for an item after it
    if to < self.entityList.count - 1 {
       upper =
        Double(self.entityList[to + 1].displayOrder)
    }
    else {
       upper =
        Double(self.entityList[to - 1].displayOrder) +
        2.0
    }

    // Add the upper and lower, divide by two
    // to derive the new order
    let newOrder = (lower + upper) / 2.0
    toDoEntity.displayOrder = newOrder
}
```

This code first gets the source and destination row numbers from the index paths and stores them in **from** and **to** variables, making the rest of the code far more readable.

Next, the entity is removed from its old position in the array into its new position.

The last section of code calculates the new **displayOrder** value of the entity. The **displayOrder** property of the **ToDoEntity** is of type **Double**. This makes it much easier to specify the new order when an item is moved because the **displayOrder** doesn't have to be a whole number. This is an old programming trick where you take the **displayOrder** of the item before and the item after in the list, add them together, and divide by two to derive the newly moved **ToDoEntity**'s **displayOrder**.

This code reorders the entity but doesn't save changes. We will take care of that in the next step.

3. Select the **ToDoTableViewController.swift** file in the Project Navigator and insert the following method below the **viewDidLoad** method.

```
override func setEditing(editing: Bool,
animated: Bool) {
  super.setEditing(editing, animated: animated)
  if !editing {
     self.toDo.saveEntities()
  }
}
```

This code checks if the editing parameter is **false** (indicating the table view is leaving edit mode), and if so, it calls the **ToDo** object's **saveEntities** method, which saves the changes to the database for any entities that have been moved.

4. Let's see how this code works. Press Xcode's **Run** button, then, when the app appears, click the **Edit** button, move one or more of the rows, and then click the **Done** button.

   Next, go back to Xcode and press the **Stop** button. To see if the changes have been saved, press the **Run** button again. You should see items in the **To Do List** displayed in the new order!

The code that changes the order of items in the data source shouldn't be placed in the table view controller. It belongs with the data source, which, in this case, is the **ToDo** business controller, making it self-contained. This allows you to use the **ToDo** business controller in another view without having to write the same reordering code twice. Wherever the **ToDo** object goes, the reordering code goes with it!

Preventing Rows From Being Reordered

You can prevent rows from being reordered by implementing the **tableView:canMoveRowAtIndexPath:** method and returning **false** for row(s) you do not want to allow the user to reorder. Let's give it a try:

1. Open the **ToDoListDemo** project in Xcode.

2. Select the **ToDoTableViewController.swift** file in the Project Navigator and add the following method below the **tableView:cellForRowAtIndexPath:** method:

```
override func tableView(tableView: UITableView,
canMoveRowAtIndexPath indexPath: NSIndexPath) ->
Bool {
    return indexPath.row != 0
}
```

This code returns **false** if the row is zero and returns **true** for every other row.

3. To see how this code works, click Xcode's **Run** button, and when the app appears in the Simulator, click the **Edit** button. You will see all rows but row zero have a reordering control (Figure 13.67).

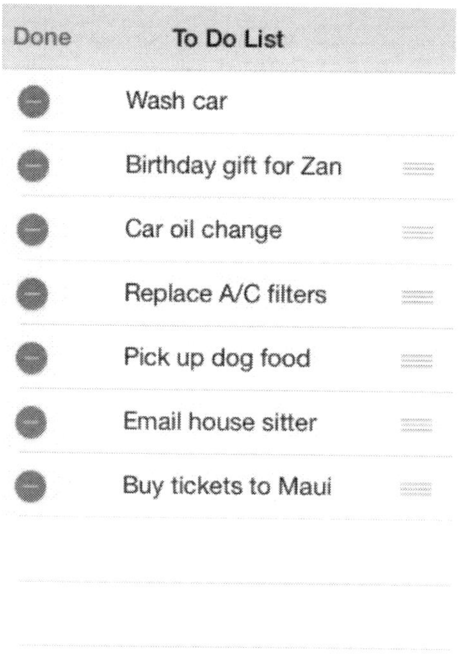

Figure 13.67 Row zero doesn't have a reordering control.

4. Go back to Xcode and click the **Stop** button. Afterward, completely comment out the **tableView: canMoveRowAtIndexPath:** method you created in Step 2 since we no longer need it.

Deleting Rows From a Table View

Now that you understand the basics of how editing in a table view works, it's easy to learn how to delete rows from a table view.

Figure 13.68 provides an overview of the method calls that are passed between the table view and table view controller when deleting a row.

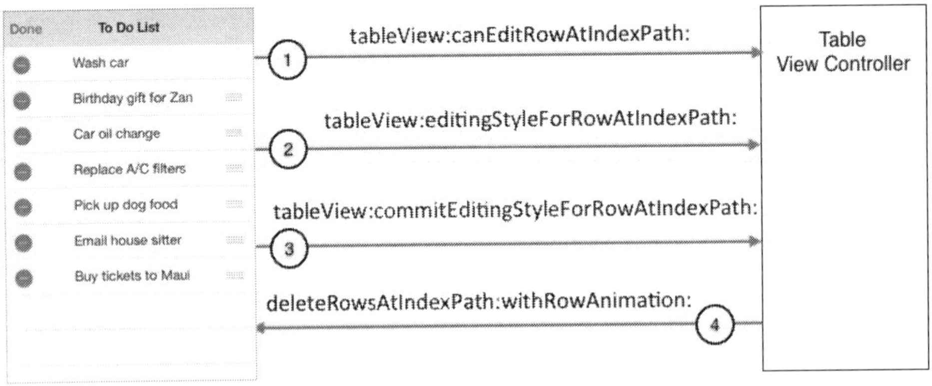

Figure 13.68 Method calls between the table view and table view controller when deleting a row.

1. When a table view goes into edit mode, it calls the **tableView:canEditRowAtIndexPath:** method on the table view controller (if the table view controller implements it) for each row. Normally, you don't need to implement this method because you want the user to be able to delete any table view row.

   If you don't implement the method at all, or simply return **true** from the method, all rows in the table view will have a deletion control. If you return **false** from the method, none of the rows will have a deletion control—you may want to do this if you want to allow users to reorder items, but not delete them. You can also check the **indexPath** argument and return **false** for some rows and **true** for others.

2. The table view calls the **tableView:editingStyleForRowAtIndexPath:** method of the table view controller (if it implements it), which returns the editing style of the row. The options are:

   - **UITableViewCellEditingStyle.None** – Displays no editing control.

- **UITableViewCellEditingStyle.Delete** – Displays a deletion control, which is a red circle containing a minus sign (Figure 13.67).
- **UITableViewCellEditingStyle.Insert** – Displays an insertion control, which is a green circle containing a plus sign.

You don't normally need to implement this method because if you don't, a deletion control is displayed for each row in the table view, which is usually what you want. If you implement this method, you can return one of the styles listed above for all rows, or you can return different values for different rows. Displaying an insertion control is uncommon, so we provide an alternate method for adding new items to a table view later in this chapter.

3. When the user taps a deletion control, a **Delete** button is displayed on the row. If the user taps the **Delete** button, the table view calls the **tableView: commitEditingStyle:forRowAtIndexPath** method on the table view controller.

4. In this method, the table view controller calls **deleteRowsAtIndexPath:withRowAnimation:** on the table view, which deletes the row from the data source.

Now that you have a high-level overview of the method calls that pass between the table view and table view controller when deleting a row, follow these steps to implement deletion in the **ToDoList** app:

1. Open the **ToDoListDemo** project in Xcode.

2. Select **ToDoTableViewController.swift** in the Project Navigator and add the following method below the **tableView:cellForRowAtIndexPath:** method:

```
override func tableView(tableView: UITableView,
commitEditingStyle editingStyle:
UITableViewCellEditingStyle, forRowAtIndexPath
indexPath: NSIndexPath) {
 if editingStyle ==
    UITableViewCellEditingStyle.Delete {
    self.toDo.deleteEntity
      (self.toDo.entityList[indexPath.row])
```

```
        self.toDo.entityList.removeAtIndex (indexPath.row)
        self.tableView. deleteRowsAtIndexPaths([indexPath],
          withRowAnimation:
          UITableViewRowAnimation.Automatic)
      }
   }
```

This code first calls the **deleteEntity:** method on the **toDo** business controller, which marks the entity for deletion, however, doing this doesn't remove it from the **toDo.entityList** array.

The second line of code removes the entity from the **entityList** array. This is important since this array is the data source for the table view.

Next, the code calls the **deleteRowsAtIndexPath:** method on the table view, which removes the row from the table view. The **UITableViewRowAnimation.**

Automatic setting chooses an appropriate animation style for you based on the location from where the row was removed.

3. To see how this works at run time, press Xcode's **Run** button, and when the app appears in the Simulator, press the **Edit** button. Click on the deletion control in one of the rows, and then click the **Delete** button on the right to delete the item as shown in the image on the left in Figure 13.69. This removes the row from the table view and shifts all rows below it up to fill in the empty space.

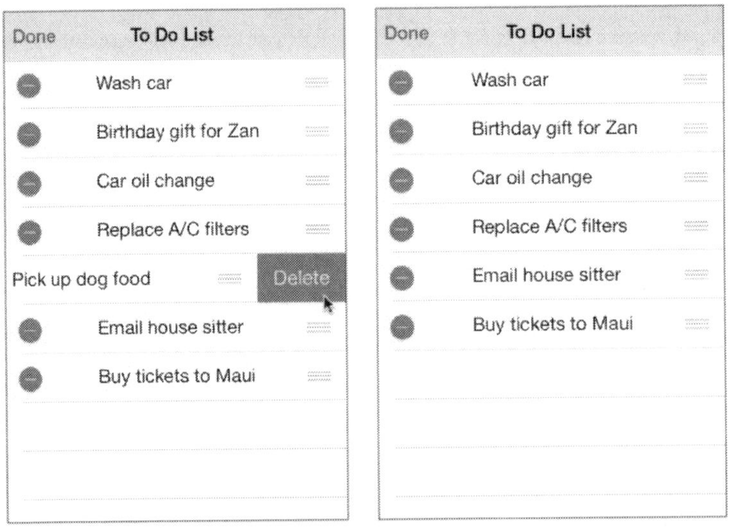

*Figure 13.69 Press the **Delete** button to remove a table view row.*

4. Click the **Done** button to exit editing mode in the table view. Remember, when you do this, the table view controller's **setEditing:animated:** is invoked, and the **saveEntities** method is called on the **ToDo** business controller object, which writes the changed **ToDoEntities** back to the database.

5. To prove that the row deletion has been persisted, go back to Xcode, click the **Stop** button, and then click the **Run** button. When the app appears in the Simulator, you should have one less row as shown in the image on the right in Figure 13.69.

Preventing Rows From Being Deleted

As mentioned in the previous section, you can prevent a row from being deleted by implementing the **tableView: canEditRowAtIndexPath:** method in your view controller and returning **false** for the given row.

To see how this works, follow these steps to prevent the user from deleting the first row:

1. Select the **ToDoTableViewController.swift** file in the Project Navigator and add the following method below the **tableView: cellForRowAtIndexPath:** method:

```
override func tableView(tableView:
UITableView, canEditRowAtIndexPath indexPath:
NSIndexPath) -> Bool {
    return indexPath.row != 0
}
```

2. To see how this looks at run time, click Xcode's **Run** button and, when the app appears in the Simulator, click the **Edit** button. As shown in Figure 13.70, a deletion control does not appear in the first row.

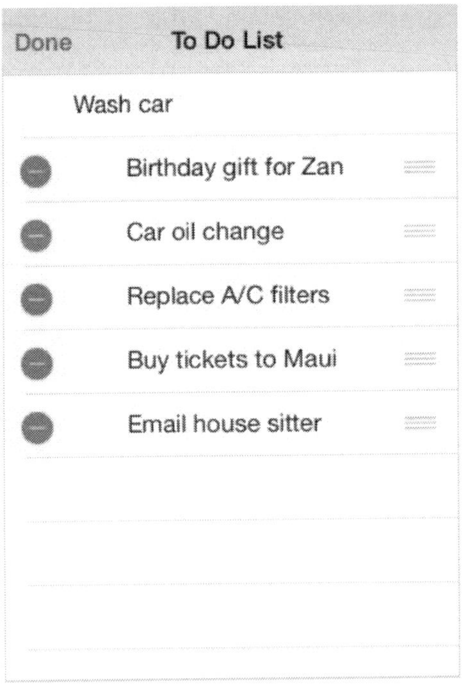

Figure 13.70 No deletion icon in the first row.

Adding Rows to a Table View

As mentioned in the previous section, when a table view goes into editing mode, you can either display a deletion or insertion control on the left side of the rows. However, it's unusual to display an insertion control to add a new row. In fact, if you read Apple's documentation on table views, they take a different approach for adding new rows to a table view by placing a plus (**+**) button in the navigation toolbar. This is the approach we will take in this section.

As shown on the right side of Figure 13.71, you are going to create a **New Item** view and associated view controller that together allow the user to enter the text of a new **To Do** item. When they click the **Done** button, the **New Item** view controller passes back the new item, and the **To Do List** table view controller adds the item to the list.

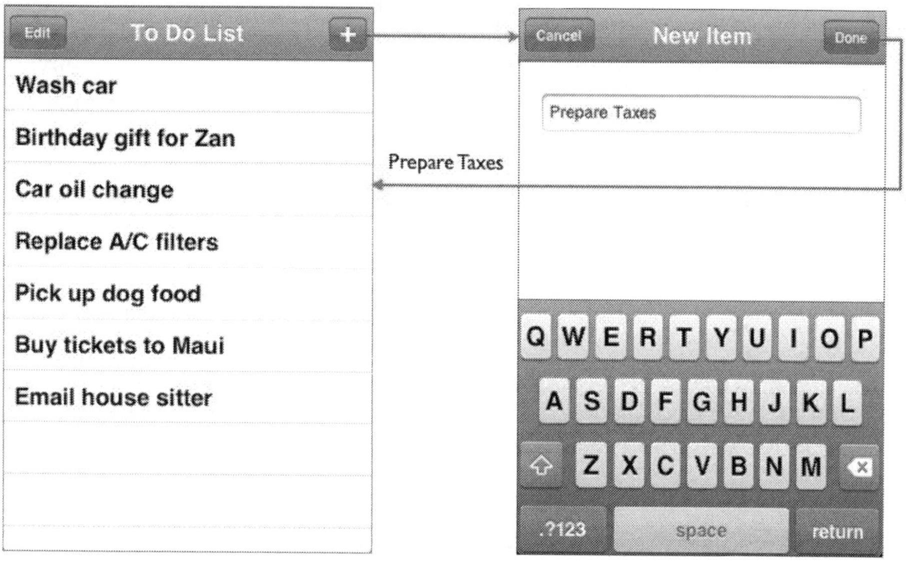

*Figure 13.71 The **New Item** view controller passes the new item back to the **To Do List** table view controller.*

Creating the New Item User Interface

Follow these steps to create the user interface for the **New Item** view.

1. Open the **ToDoListDemo** project in Xcode.

2. In the Project Navigator, select **Main.Storyboard**. Drag a **Navigation Controller** from the Object Library to the right of the **To Do List** scene (Figure 13.72). When you add a navigation controller to a storyboard, it automatically adds an associated table view controller, which is just what we need.

   We are adding a navigation controller rather than just a table view controller because we are going to create a modal segue between the **To Do List** and **Add Item** scenes. Modal scenes do not automatically inherit a navigation bar from the source scene so the easiest way to add a navigation bar to the Add Item scene is to give it its own navigation controller.

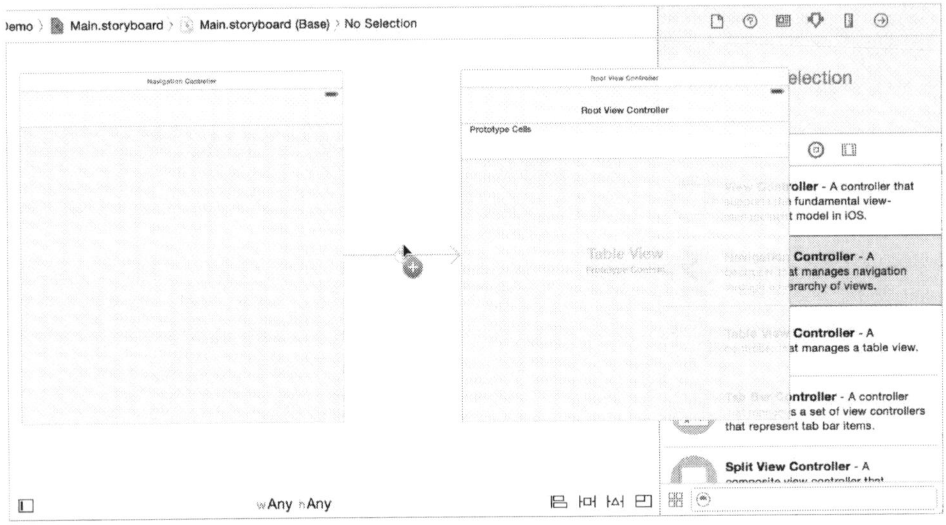

Figure 13.72 Add a navigation controller to the storyboard.

3. Now we need a way to launch the New Item scene from the **To Do List** scene. Drag a **Bar Button Item** from the Object Library to the right side of the **To Do List** navigation bar until you see the blue rounded rectangle appear, and then release your mouse button to drop it (Figure 13.73).

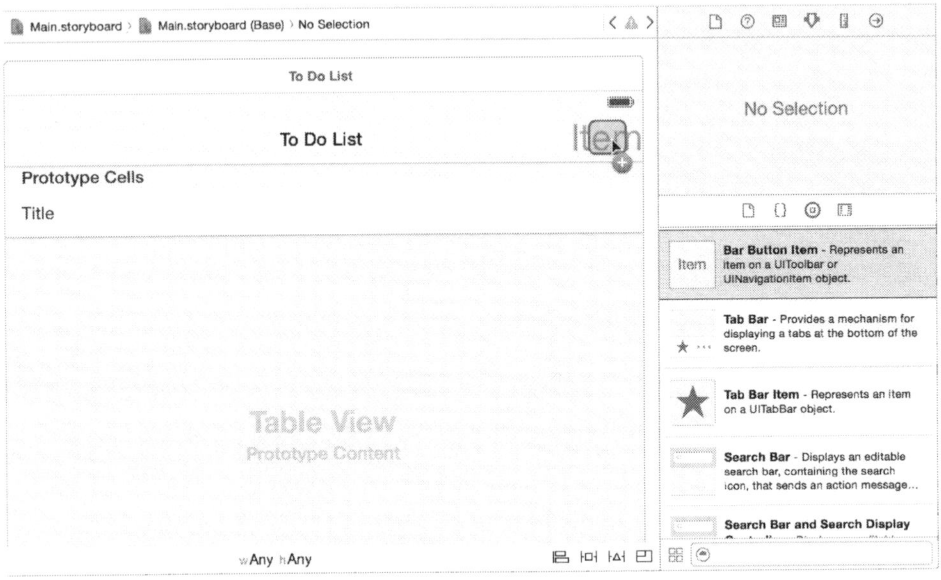

*Figure 13.73 Add a **Bar Button Item** to the To Do List scene's navigation bar.*

4. Next, go to the Attributes Inspector and change thc **Systen Item** to **Add**. This changes the button to a plus (+) sign (Figure 13.74).

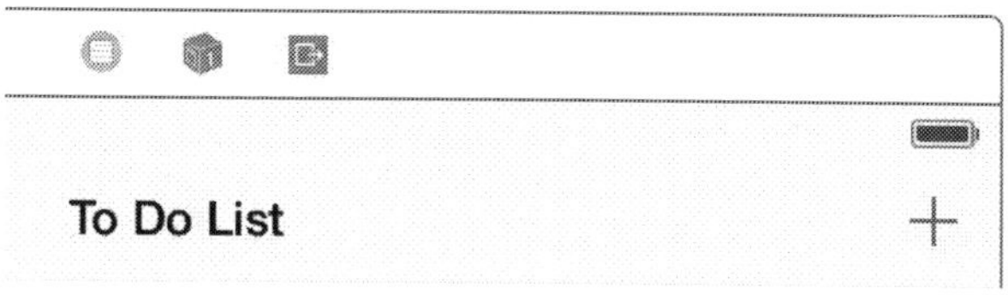

*Figure 13.74 Set the button's **Identifier** to **Add**.*

5. Now let's create a segue between the **To Do List** scene and the new navigation controller. Hold the **Control** key down, click on the Add (+) button, and drag your mouse to the new navigation controller until it turns blue (Figure 13.75).

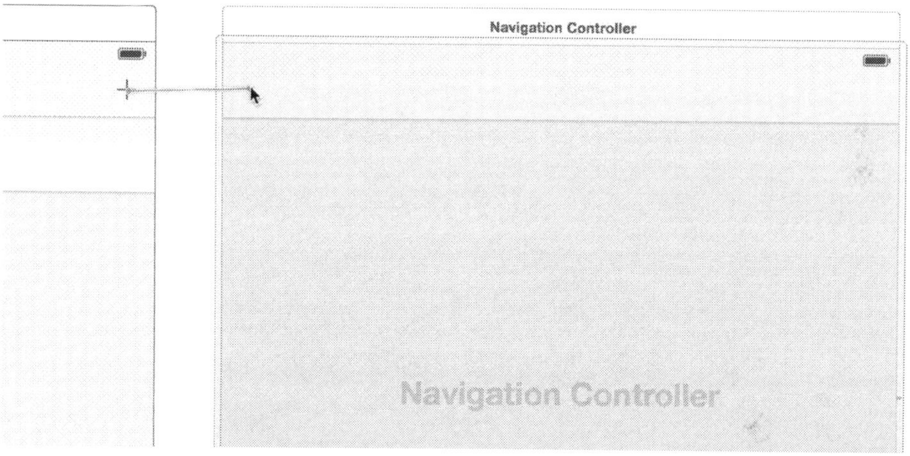

Figure 13.75 Create a segue to the navigation controller.

6. Release the mouse button to display the segue popup, and in the popup, select the **Present Modally** option.

7. Next, double-click the navigation bar of the new table view scene labeled **Root View Controller** to put it in edit mode. Change the title to **New Item** (Figure 13.76), then press **return** to exit edit mode.

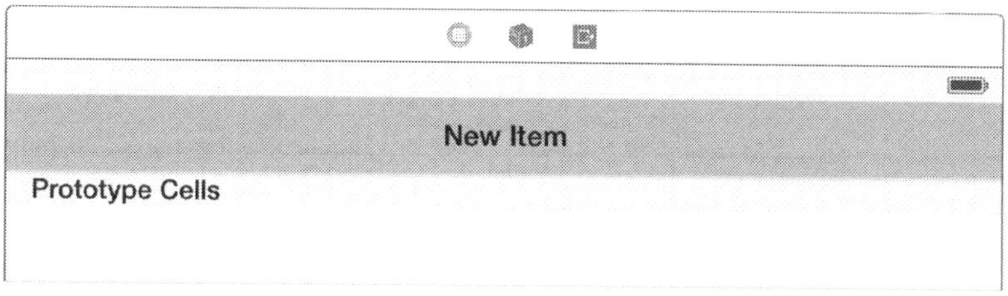

*Figure 13.76 Change the title to **New Item**.*

Now let's add **Cancel** and **Done** buttons to the New Item scene's navigation bar.

8. Drag a **Bar Button Item** from the Object Library and drop it on the left side of the **New Item** scene's navigation bar.

   In the Attributes Inspector, change the new button's **Systen Item** to **Cancel**.

9. Drag a **Bar Button Item** from the Object Library and drop it on the right side of the **New Item** scene's navigation bar.

   In the Attributes Inspector, change the new button's **System Item** to **Done**. When you're finished the buttons should look like Figure 13.77.

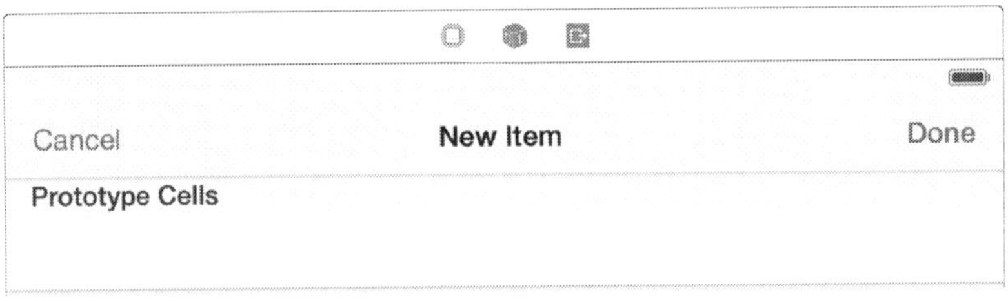

*Figure 13.77 The new **Cancel** and **Done** buttons.*

10. Let's create a custom table view controller for the **New Item** table view controller scene. Right-click the **ToDoTableViewController.swift** file in the Project Navigator (this adds the new file directly below this file). From the popup menu, select **New File...** option.

11. On the left side of the New File dialog under **iOS**, select **Source**. On the right side of the dialog, select **Cocoa Touch Class** and click **Next**.

12. In the next step, set **Subclass Of** to **UITableViewController** and set **Class** to **NewItemTableViewController** (Figure 13.78). Make sure **Language** is set to **Swift**, and click **Next**.

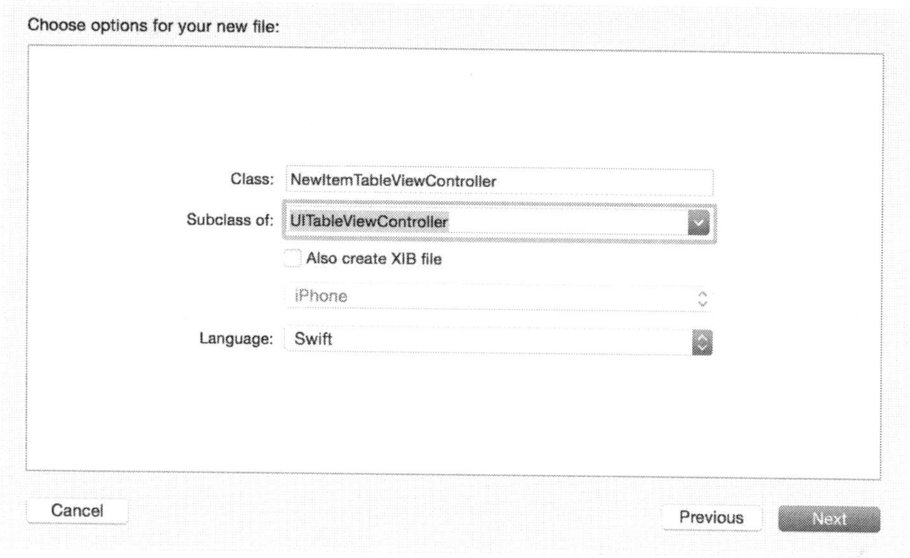

Figure 13.78 Create a new table view controller.

13. In the Save dialog, click **Create** to add the new table view controller to the project. When you're finished, you can see the **NewItemTableViewController.swift** file in the Project Navigator.

14. Now you need to associate the new table view controller with the **New Item** scene.

    Click **Main.storyboard** in the Project Navigator and then click the scene dock at the top of the **New Item** scene. Next, go to the Identity Inspector by clicking the third button from the left in the Inspector toolbar, and set the **Class** to **NewItemTableViewController** (Figure 13.79).

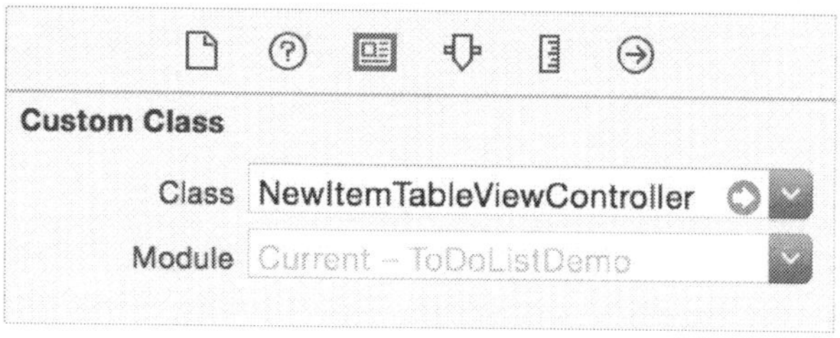

*Figure 13.79 Set the Class to **NewItemTableViewController**.*

Working with Unwind Segues

Earlier in this chapter under the section *Returning Data From a View Controller*, you learned how to use a protocol to pass data back from a destination to a source view controller. In this example, you will learn how to use *unwind segues* to do the same thing. An unwind segue navigates from a destination view controller back to a source destination view controller.

As shown in Figure 13.80, there are three main parts of an unwind segue:

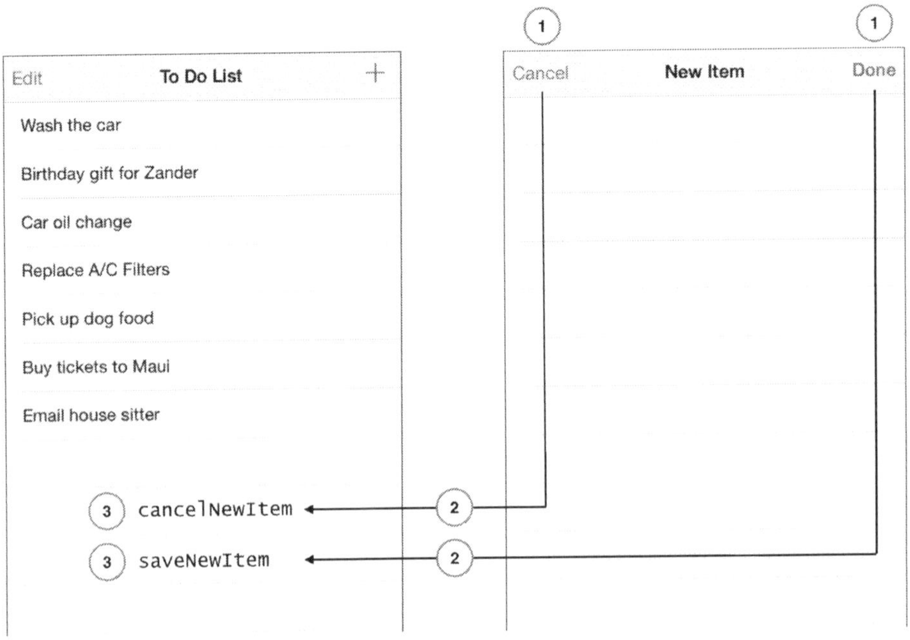

Figure 13.80 Unwind segue overview.

1. An object that fires the segue
2. The unwind segue itself
3. A method called on the source view controller by the unwind segue.

Let's create unwind methods in the **To Do List** view controller and unwind segues to connect to them from the **New Item** scene.

1. Select **ToDoTableViewController.swift** in the Project Navigator. Add the following methods before the closing curly brace of the class:

```
@IBAction func
 cancelNewItem(segue:UIStoryboardSegue) {
}
@IBAction func
 saveNewItem(segue:UIStoryboardSegue) {
 }
}
```

These methods will be called when the user taps the **Cancel** and **Done** buttons in the **New Item** scene.

2. Let's create an unwind segue for the Cancel button. Select the **Main.storyboard** file in the Project Navigator. In the **New Item** scene, **Control+Click** the **Cancel** button and drag over to the Exit icon on the far right in the scene dock (Figure 13.81).

Figure 13.81 Create a Cancel unwind seque.

3. Release your mouse button and select the **cancelNewItem:** from the Action Segue popup (Figure 13.82).

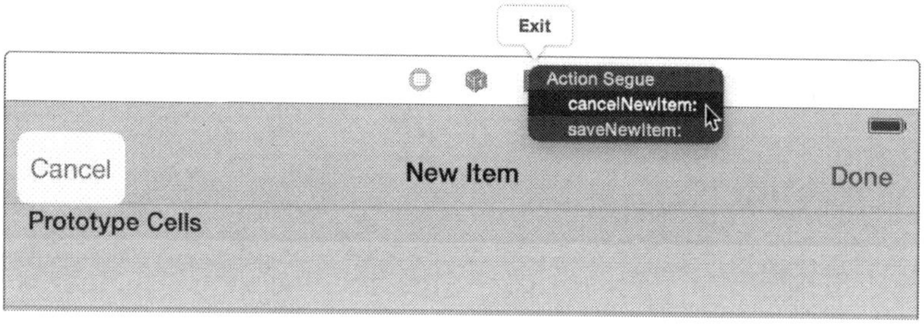

*Figure 13.82 Select the **cancelNewItem:** method.*

Typically, when you are connecting user interface controls to methods in a code file, those methods are found in the scene's associated view controller. This is different because you are connecting the buttons to methods in the **To Do List** scene's view controller.

To determine which methods should be displayed in the Figure 13.83 popup when creating an unwind segue, Xcode works backwards.

- Xcode looks at the segue connecting the **To Do List** and **New Item** scenes and determines that **To Do List** is the source scene.

- Next, it detects that **ToDoTableViewController** is the view controller class associated with the **To Do List** scene.

- Xcode then finds all **IBAction** methods in the view controller that accept a single segue parameter and includes these in the popup list.

4. Follow the same steps to connect the **New Item** scene's **Done** button to the **saveNewItem:** method in the **ToDoTableViewController**.

5. Look in the Document Outline and you will see the two new unwind segues listed there (Figure 13.83).

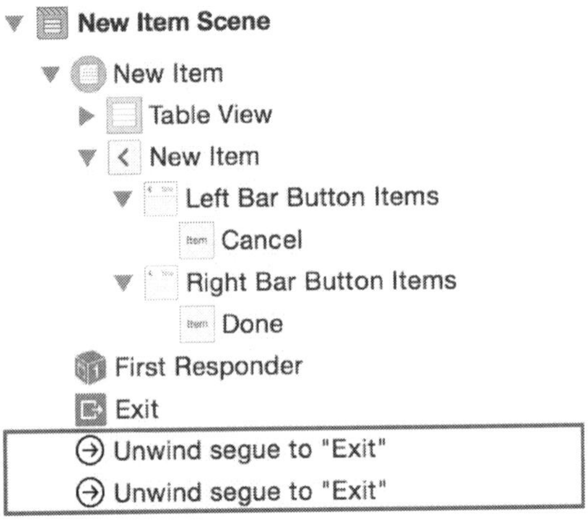

Figure 13.83 Unwind segues in the Document Outline.

Click on the last unwind segue in the list, then go to the Attributes Inspector. The **Action** setting indicates this unwind segue is connected to the **saveNewItem:** method. We need to reference this segue from code, so set its **Identifier** to **UnwindSaveNewItem** (Figure 13.84).

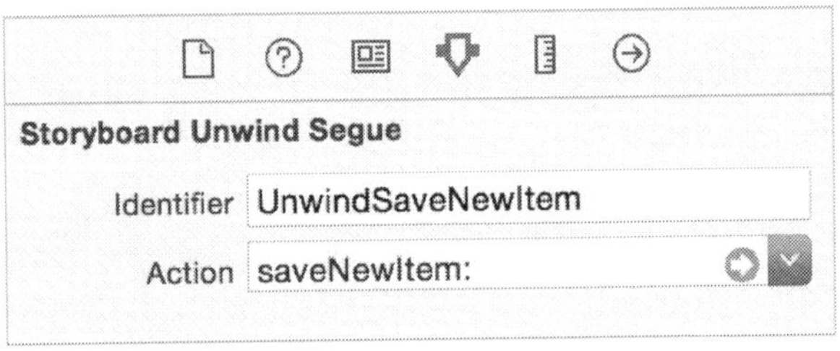

*Figure 13.84 Set the unwind segue's **Identifier**.*

Setting Up the New Item Scene

In this section, you will add the ability to enter new items in the **New Item** scene. In most of Apple's built-in apps, users enter new data in text fields hosted inside of table view cells. This is exactly what we're going to do in the **New Item** scene.

1. In the **New Item** scene, click in the gray area labeled **Table View Prototype Content** to select the scene's table view.

2. In the Attributes Inspector, change the **Content** attribute to **Static Cells** and the **Style** to **Grouped** (Figure 13.85).

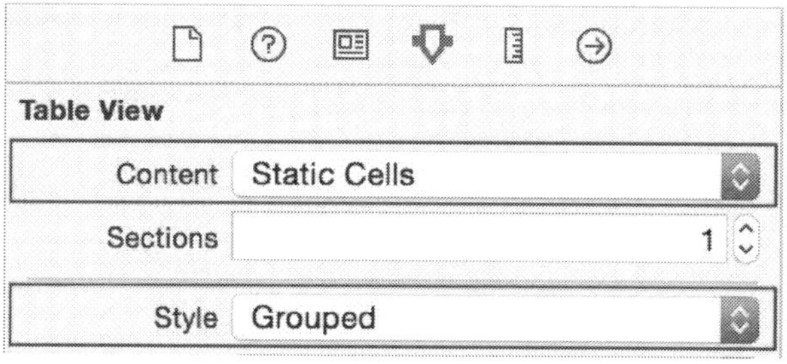

*Figure 13.85 Set the **Content** and **Style** attributes.*

3. There are now three cells in the table view (Figure 13.86), but we only need one. Click on the center cell to select it, hold the **Shift** key down and then click on the bottom cell to select it. Press the **Delete** key to leave a single remaining cell.

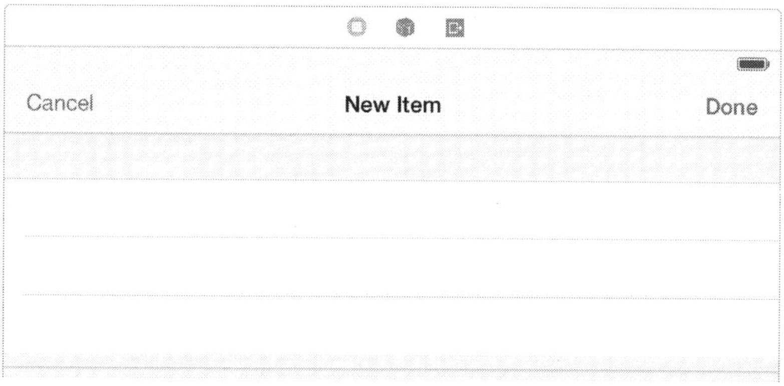

Figure 13.86 Three cells in the table view.

4. In the Document Outline, select the table view's **Table View Section**, then go to the Attributes Inspector and set the **Header** attribute to **Item**

Description. Xcode capitalizes this text and displays it in the header area above the table view section (Figure 13.87).

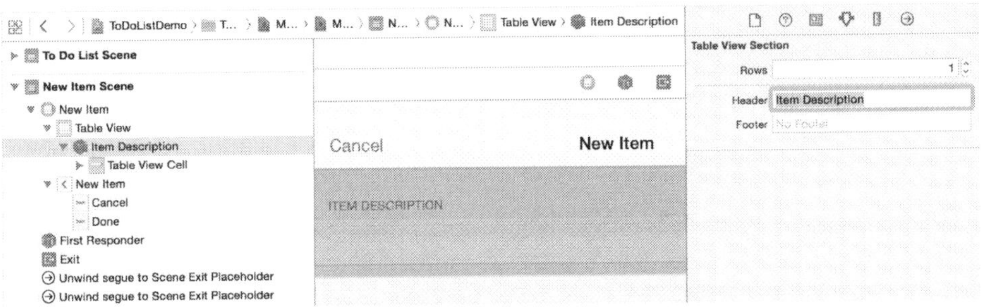

Figure 13.87 Set the table view's header text.

5. Now let's add a text field to the table view cell. Drag a **Text Field** from the Object Library and position it on the left center of the cell until the horizontal and vertical guide lines appear (Figure 13.88).

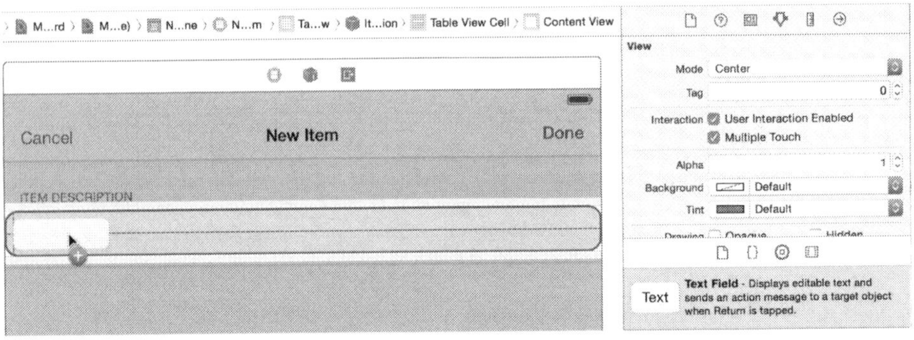

Figure 13.88 Add a text field to the cell.

6. Click on the resizing handle on the right side of the text field, drag it to the right edge of the cell until you see the vertical guide line appear (Figure 13.89).

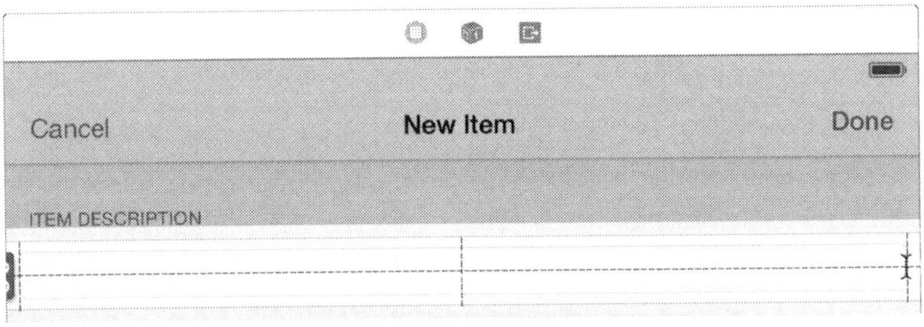

Figure 13.89 Resize the text field.

7. With the text field still selected, go to the Attributes Inspector and set the **Font** attribute to **Body** and the **Placeholder** to **Enter item description** (Figure 13.90).

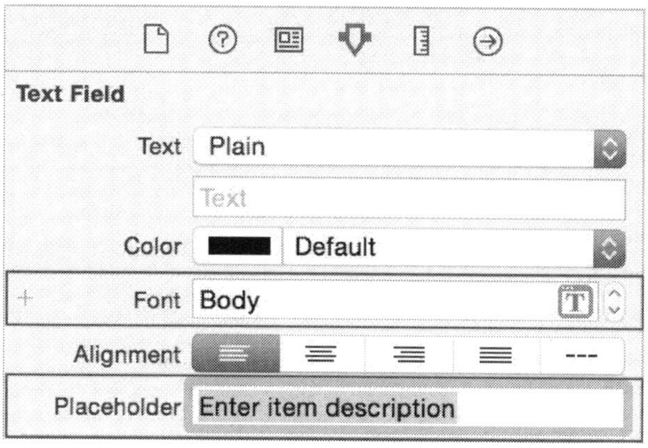

Figure 13.90 Set the text field attributes.

8. At run time, if the user taps the cell in the narrow area surrounding the text field, we don't want the cell to appear selected (gray by default). To fix this, in the Document Outline, select the **Table View Cell**, then go to the Attributes Inspector and set the **Selection** attribute to **None**.

9. Now let's add an outlet we can use to reference the text field from the New Item view controller.

10. Display the Assistant Editor by clicking the center button in the Editor button group at the top right side of the Xcode toolbar. This should display the **NewItemTableViewController.swift** file in the Assistant Editor. If it doesn't, click the **Manual** button at the top of the Assistant Editor window and select **Automatic > NewItemTableViewController.swift** from the popup menu.

11. **Control+Click** the text field and drag your mouse down into the code file just above the **viewDidLoad** method until the **Insert Outlet, Action, or Outlet Collection** popup appears (Figure 13.91).

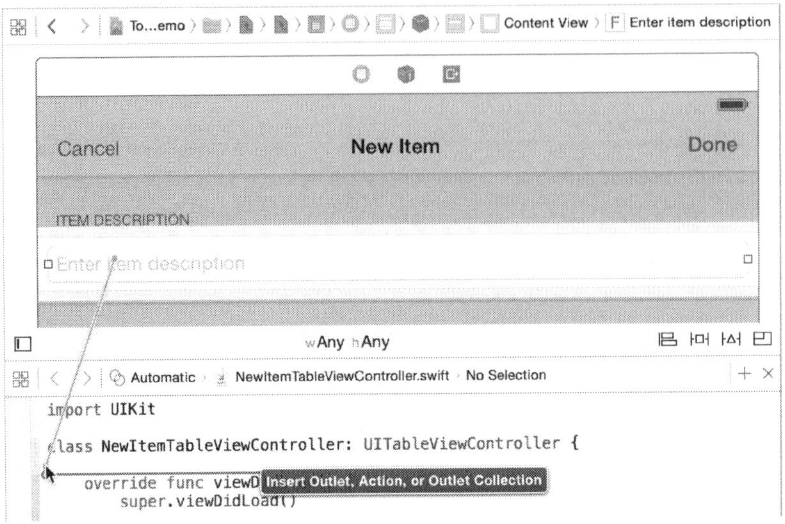

Figure 13.91 Create an outlet for the text field.

12. In the Create Connection popup, set the **Name** to **txtDescription** and click **Connect**. This adds a new outlet to the view controller code file (Figure 13.92).

```
class NewItemTableViewController: UITableViewController {

    @IBOutlet weak var txtDescription: UITextField!

    override func viewDidLoad() {
        super.viewDidLoad()
```

*Figure 13.92 The new **txtDescription** outlet property.*

13. Since the table view contains only a static cell, there is no need for the data source methods that were added to **NewItemTableViewController.swift** when it was first created. If you were to run the project now, these methods prevent the static cell from being displayed, so let's delete them.

    First, turn off the Assistant Editor by clicking the Standard Editor button (the button on the left) in the Editor button group in the Xcode toolbar. Next, select the **NewItemTableViewController.swift** file in the Project Navigator.

    Starting with the comment line // **MARK: Table View Data Source**, delete all the comments and code down to, but not including the closing curly brace.

14. Let's make another change in this view controller that will enhance the user experience. This view only has one input control. Rather than forcing the user to tap the text field to enter a new item, let's put focus on the text field automatically. Your users will thank you for saving them unnecessary steps!

    Select the **NewItemTableViewController.swift** file in the Project Navigator. Scroll to the **viewDidLoad** method and add the following code (you can delete the existing comments for this method too):

```
override func viewDidLoad() {
   super.viewDidLoad()
   self.txtDescription.becomeFirstResponder()
}
```

Passing the New Item Back

Now it's time to add code to the **New Item** scene's table view controller that passes the newly added item back to the **To Do List** scene.

1. In the **NewItemTableViewController.swift** code file, add the following property:

```
class NewItemTableViewController:
  UITableViewController {

@IBOutlet weak var txtDescription: UITextField!
var newItemDescription: String!
```

   This property provides a convenient place for the **To Do List** scene's view controller to grab the description of the new item.

2. Add the following method below the **viewDidLoad** method in the **NewItemTableViewController.swift** code file:

```
override func prepareForSegue(segue:
UIStoryboardSegue, sender: AnyObject?) {
 if segue.identifier == "UnwindSaveNewItem" {
    self.newItemDescription =
     self.txtDescription.text
 }
}
```

This method is automatically called when the **Cancel** or **Done** button's unwind segue is executed. The first line of code checks if the segue is for the **Done** button (you set this segue's identifier in the previous section). If it is, it takes the value from the text field's text property and stores it in the **newItemDescription** property.

Why not just let the **To Do List** view controller grab the text value from the text field directly? Because that would break encapsulation—the To Do List scene would know too much about the inner workings of the New Item scene. It's best to place the new item description in a neutral property.

3. For your last step, you need to add code to the T**o Do List** scene's view controller that grabs the text of the new item and creates a new **ToDoListEntity** object from it.

   Select the **ToDoTableViewController.swift** code file in the Project Navigator, and add the following code to the **saveNewItem** method. Remember, this is the method that is connected to the **Done** button's unwind segue:

```
@IBAction func saveNewItem(segue:UIStoryboardSegue) {
    let tvc = segue.sourceViewController as!
      NewItemTableViewController
    self.toDo.addItemToList(tvc.newItemDescription)

    let indexPath = NSIndexPath(forRow:
      (self.toDo.entityList.count - 1), inSection: 0)

    self.tableView.insertRowsAtIndexPaths
      ([indexPath], withRowAnimation:
      UITableViewRowAnimation.Automatic)

    self.tableView.scrollToRowAtIndexPath
     (indexPath, atScrollPosition:
     UITableViewScrollPosition.Bottom, animated: true)
}
```

   The first line of code casts the general **segue.sourceViewController** to the specific **NewItemTableViewController**.

Next, it gets the value of the **newItemDescription** property and passes it to the **ToList** object's **addItemToList** method, which creates a new entity with the specified description.

The rest of the code inserts a new row into the To Do List scene's table view and scrolls to the new item.

Testing the App

Now let's see how passing a value from one controller to another works at run time.

1. Press the Xcode **Run** button to run the app. When the app appears in the Simulator, click the Add (+) button to add a new item.

2. In the **New Item** scene, type **Clean garage** (or any other text you want) into the text field, and then click the **Done** button.

   This closes the **New Item** view, and you can see your new item in the **To Do List** (Figure 13.93).

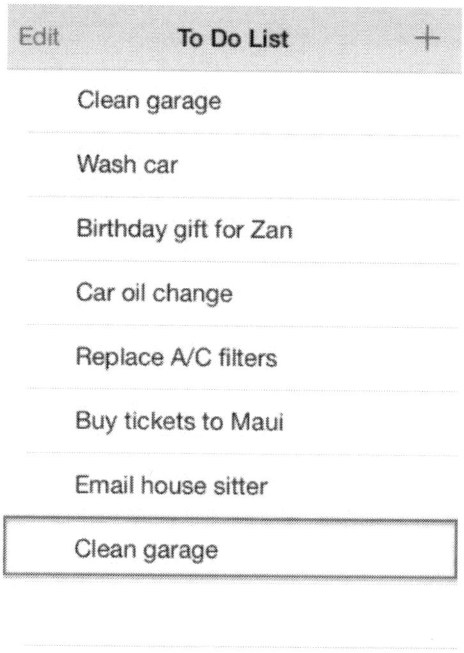

*Figure 13.93 The new item is added to the **To Do List**.*

Now you know how to use best practices and multiple ways to add items to a table view and return values from one view controller to another!

Summary

Here are important points to remember about managing lists of data in your iOS apps.

Understanding Table Views

- iOS table views are based on the **UITableView** class. They are the View in the Model-View-Controller design pattern.

- Table views are designed to display large sets of data and are configurable to look any way you want as evidenced by the wide range of looks for table views used in the built-in iOS apps.

- There are three main table view styles—plain, indexed, and grouped.

- Regardless of the table view style used, each item in the table view is a row, and a table view can contain an unlimited number of rows. Each row is one column wide and, when using the built-in styles, can contain an image, text, and an accessory icon such as a disclosure indicator.

- Each division of a table view is a "section". If you have no divisions, you have only one section.

- Regardless of the number of items contained in a list, the table view only contains enough cells to display the items visible in the view plus a few additional cells for items that will soon become visible.

Filling a Table View With Data

- In iOS apps, dynamically filled table views get their data from a data source object—specifically, an object that implements the **UITableViewDataSource** protocol. This object is a table view controller, which implements this protocol and was designed by Apple specifically to work with table views.

- The **UITableViewDataSource** protocol contains three key methods that are used to fill a table view with data. It's up to you to create a custom table view controller for your table view and to add code in each of these three methods that interacts with a business controller. The three methods are:

  - **numberOfSectionsInTableView:** returns the number of sections in the table view.
  - **tableView:numberOfRowsInSection:** is called by the table view once for each section. This method returns the number of rows in the specified section.
  - **tableView:cellForRowAtIndexPath:** is called by the table view once for each visible (or about to become visible) cell in the table view. This method returns a table view cell object for the specified section and row.

- To provide dynamic content for a table view, you must create an associated custom table view controller class.

- At run time when a table view is being filled, it calls the **tableView:cellForRowAtIndexPath:** method on its associated table view controller once for each cell in the table view. The table view request that the table view controller return a fully configured cell object for the specified section and row.

- You can set a cell's **Identifier** attribute at design time, and then, at run time, you pass this identifier to **dequeueReusableCellWithIdentifier:** which uses the cell with the specified identifier as a template for the cells it creates.

- Passing data to a presented view controller usually requires three key steps:

  1. Create a property on the destination view controller to hold the data being passed by the source view controller.
  2. Configure the segue between the source and destination view controllers.
  3. In the source view controller, implement the **prepareForSegue:** method and add code that stores the data to be passed to the destination view controller's property.

Custom Table View Controllers

- When you drop a table view controller on a storyboard, an instance of **UITableViewController** is created to manage the table views.

- To provide dynamic content for a table view, you must create a custom table view controller class.

- Here are the basic steps to create a custom table view controller (don't perform these steps now):

    1. Create a new subclass of **UITableViewController**.

    2. Go to the storyboard, click on the dock at the top of the scene you want to associate with the new view controller, then go to the Identity Inspector, and change the **Class** of the table view controller to the class you created in the previous step.

Configuring Table View Cells

- At run time, when a table view is being filled, it calls the **tableView:cellForRowAtIndexPath:** method on its associated table view controller once for each cell in the table view. The table view requests that the table view controller return a fully configured cell object for the specified section and row.

- Here is an overview of the interaction between a table view and table view controller at run time.

    1. The table view calls the table view controller's **tableView: cellForRowAtIndexPath:** method, passing an **indexPath** object. This **indexPath** object has **section** and **row** properties that indicate the section and row of the cell the table view is requesting from the table view controller.

    2. The table view controller calls back to the table view's **dequeueReusableCellWithIdentifer:** method, passing a **Cell Identifier** value.

       When a user scrolls through a table view, the cells that scroll off screen are added to a queue of cells that can be reused. When the table view's

dequeueReusableCellWithIdentifier: method is called, the table view checks if there is a reusable cell with the specified identifier in the queue, and if so, it returns the cell. If there are no cells in the queue, it creates a brand new cell of the specified identifier type.

3. The table view controller configures the cell returned from the table view. This usually involves code that sets the text of the labels in the cell as well as any accessory indicator.

4. The table view controller returns the configured cell back to the table view, which adds the cell to the list.

Passing Data To a View Controller

- Typically, when navigating between view controllers, the view controller you are navigating *to* (the destination) needs information from the view controller you are navigation *from* (the source).

This usually requires three key steps:

1. Create a property on the destination view controller to hold the data being passed by the source view controller.

2. Configure the segue between the source and destination view controllers.

3. In the source view controller, implement the **prepareForSegue:** method and add code that stores the data to be passed to the destination view controller's property.

Returning Data From a View Controller

- When returning data from a presented view controller to the presenting view controller using delegation, there are five main steps to perform:

    1. Declare a protocol in the *presented* view controller that specifies a method that can be implemented in the *presenting* view controller. The *presented* view controller will call this method at run time to pass data back to the *presenting* view controller.

    2. Declare a **delegate** property on the *presented* view controller that will hold a reference to the *presenting* view controller. The *presented* view

controller will use this reference to the *presenting* view controller when it calls the protocol method.

3. Add code to the *presented* view controller that calls the delegate method, passing data to the *presenting* view controller.

4. Implement the **delegate** protocol method in the *presenting* view controller to do something with the data that was passed back to it.

5. In the *presenting* view controller's **prepareForSegue:** method, have the *presenting* view controller store a reference to itself in the *presented* view controller's **delegate** property.

Displaying Images in Table View Rows

- Images that are displayed in table view cells should be approximately 40 x 40 points or smaller.

- If you want the same image to always be displayed in a particular table view cell, you can just set the cell's **Image** attribute to an image that is included with your project.

- Dynamically specifying an image for a table view cell requires just one line of code in the **tableView: cellForRowAtIndexPath:** method:

```
cell.imageView.image = [UIImage
imageNamed:@"AppleTVCellImage.png"];
```

Creating Section Headers and Footers

- You can set header and footer text in the Attributes Inspector for table views that have their **Content** set to **Static Cells**. Just set the **Header** and **Footer** attributes to the text you want displayed at run time.

- If a table view's **Content** is set to **Dynamic Prototypes**, you can use the **tableView: titleForHeaderInSection:** method of a table view controller to set section-header text and the **tableView: titleForFooterInSection:** method to set section-footer text.

- When you want to do more than just set the text of a header or footer (i.e. change the font size or color), you need to implement one or both of these methods:

- **tableView:viewForHeaderInSection:**
- **tableView:viewForFooterInSection:**

Within these methods, you create and configure a view containing the user-interface objects you want in the header or footer (usually labels) and return the view from the methods.

You must also implement one or both of these methods that determine the height of the header or footer:

- **tableView:heightForHeaderInSection:**
- **tableView:heightForFooterInSection:**

Referencing Cells with Enumerations

- Rather than hard-coding cell numbers, you can create an enumeration that provides a human- readable list of the cells in the table view.

Handling Table View User Interaction

- The **UITableViewDelegate** protocol is designed in part to handle user interaction. The **UITableViewController** class implements this protocol, so any custom table view controllers you create automatically inherit the methods of this protocol. The most commonly used method in this protocol is the **tableView:didSelectRowAtIndexPath:** method. This method fires when a user touches a row and then lifts his or her finger off the row.

- There are two different indicators you can use to let the user know that they can see additional information if they tap a table view row:

  - Disclosure Indicator
  - Detail Disclosure Button

  It's important to use these indicators in rows that navigate to another view so users can see up front that the row will take them to another view when they tap it. If you don't use these indicators properly, Apple will reject your app.

- Disclosure indicators are simple gray arrows that indicate tapping anywhere in the table view row takes you to the next level in the hierarchy.

- On rows that contain detail disclosure buttons, tapping the button itself does one thing, and tapping elsewhere in the row does another.

- If your view contains an indexed list, Apple's Human Interface Guidelines dictate that you do not use a disclosure indicator even if selecting a row takes you to another view.

- To use check marks to indicate selected rows, you must do the following:

  - In the **tableView:cellForRowAtIndexPath:** method, you need to add code that determines when the cells are initially being added to the table view and which cell(s) should have a check mark. When you determine that a cell should have a check mark, you can use the following code to set one in the cell:

    ```
    cell.accessoryType =
       UITableViewCellAccessoryType.Checkmark
    ```

  - If you only want one item to be selected at a time, in the **tableView: didSelectRowAtIndexPath:** method, you need to uncheck the previously selected item and check the newly selected item.

  - To turn off user interaction for a table view cell, set its **Selection** attribute to **None**.

Creating Custom Cells

- Here are the basic steps for creating a custom cell:

  1. Set the cell **Style** to **Custom**.

  2. Drag controls from the Object Library and drop them on the cell.

  3. Give each control a unique **Tag** number, which you can use to reference them from the table view controller.

  4. In the **tableView:cellForRowAtIndexPath:** method, get a reference to the UI controls contained in the cell by calling the cell's **viewWithTag:** method, and then configure the cell.

Creating Indexed Table Views

- When you have a table view that can potentially contain hundreds or thousands of entries, you should create an index so your users can easily get to the items in the list.
- When the user taps a letter in a table view index, the table view scrolls to the group associated with that letter. If there is no entry for the selected letter, the table view scrolls to the section that contains the next lowest letter of the alphabet.
- There are three main things you need for a table view index:
    1. An array containing all the keys to be listed on the right side.
    2. An array containing the "active" keys—keys that have items associated with them.
    3. A dictionary with items grouped by each key.

Bundling a Pre-populated Database

- When the app first starts up and tries to access data, the **mmBusinessObject** class checks to see if a SQLite database file already exists in your app's **Documents** folder (it won't after the app is first installed on a device).
- If the business object's **copyDatabaseIfNotPresent** flag is set to **true** (this is usually set in your project's **ABusinessObject** class), the business object checks if you have bundled a copy of the database with your app. If so, a copy is made of the SQLite file in your project and placed in your app's **Documents** folder. If this flag is set to **false**, a new, empty database is created instead.

Adding a Search Bar to a Table View

- In situations where there may be hundreds of items for each key in an index, it's best to add a search bar to the table view so users can more easily find items they are looking for.
- Starting in iOS 8, Apple deprecated the traditional Search Bar and Search Display Controller objects listed in Xcode's Object Library. There is a

newer Search Controller you should use instead. However, as of Xcode version 7.1, you still can't add this search controller in Interface Builder. You must add it in code.

- A **Search Bar and Search Display Controller** is comprised of three main elements.

  1. **A search bar** – The user enters a search string used to filter a list of items in the main table view.

  2. **A search display controller** – When a user taps the search bar, the controller superimposes the search interface over the main interface.

  3. **A search-results table view** – The search interface contains a results table view that lists the items matching the search filter

- In a Search Controller is a **Main View Controller** for the **Main Table View** and a separate **Search Controller** for the **Search Results Table View**.

- The **Main View Controller** is the data source for the main table view. It is the delegate for both table views, the Search Controller, and the search bar.

- The **Search Controller** is the data source for the **Search Results Table View**.

- Whether a user selects an item from the search- results table view or from the main table view, you want to perform the same action—go to a **Detail** scene that displays details about the selected item.

Adding a Magnifying Glass to an Index

- To add a magnifying glass to a table view index:

  - Insert the magnifying glass icon into the index in the **sectionIndexTitlesForTableView:** method.

  - Change **tableView:sectionForSectionIndexTitle:** to scroll to the top of the view when the magnifying glass is selected.

Editing Table View Rows

- Table views have two modes:

    1. Selection (normal) mode - Users can view, scroll, and tap the rows but can't change anything about them.

    2. Editing mode - Typically displays deletion controls on the left that allow users to delete rows from the table view as well as reordering controls on the right that allow users to move rows to a different position.

- A table view goes into editing mode when its **setEditing:animated:** method is called, which is usually done by an action method associated with an **Edit** button. If the first argument in the **setEditing: animated:** method call is set to **YES**, the table view goes into edit mode. If it's set to **NO**, the table view goes into selection mode.

- To get the reordering change to persist when you close the app and restart it, you need to implement the **tableView:moveRowAtIndex:toIndexPath:** method. Within this method, you need to make a corresponding change to the order of items in the table view's data source, which should typically be a business controller.

- You can prevent one or more rows from being reordered by implementing the **tableView: canMoveRowAtIndexPath:** method and returning **NO** for the row(s) you do not want to allow the user to reorder.

- You can prevent one or more rows from being deleted by implementing the **tableView: canEditRowAtIndexPath:** method in your view controller and returning **NO** for the row(s) you do not want to allow the user to delete.

- It's unusual to display an insertion control to add a new row to a table view. Apple recommends placing an **Add** button in the navigation toolbar and launching a modal dialog from which new items can be added to the table view

Working with Unwind Segues

- An unwind segue navigates from a destination view controller back to a source destination view controller.
- There are three main parts of an unwind segue:
  1. An object that fires the segue
  2. The unwind segue itself
  3. A method called on the source view controller by the unwind segue
- Typically, when you are connecting user interface controls to methods in a code file, those methods are found in the scene's associated view controller. This is different when creating an unwind segue because you are connecting to methods in the source scene's view controller.

  To determine which methods should be displayed in when creating an unwind segue, Xcode works backwards.
  - Xcode looks at the segue connecting the **To Do List** and **New Item** scenes and determines that **To Do List** is the source scene.
  - Next, it detects that **ToDoTableViewController** is the view controller class associated with the **To Do List** scene.
  - Xcode then finds all **IBAction** methods in the view controller that accept a single segue parameter and includes these in the popup list.

Chapter 14: Working With the Project Editor

The Project Editor allows you to edit a variety of settings that determine how your project should be built. In this chapter, you will learn important concepts such as products, targets, and schemes that will help you take full advantage of Xcode for creating advanced builds for your iOS apps.

Sections in This Chapter

1. *Understanding Products and Targets*
2. *Project Editor in Depth*
3. *The General Pane*
4. *The Capabilities Pane*
5. *The Info Pane*
6. *The Build Settings Pane*
7. *The Build Phases Pane*

8. *The Build Rules Pane*

9. *Project Version and Build Number*

10. *Summary*

The Project Editor allows you to specify important settings that affect your entire project.

To view the Project Editor (Figure 14.1), select the first node in the Project Navigator. If you don't see the panel on the left that contains the Project and Targets, click the small, rectangular arrow button highlighted in red.

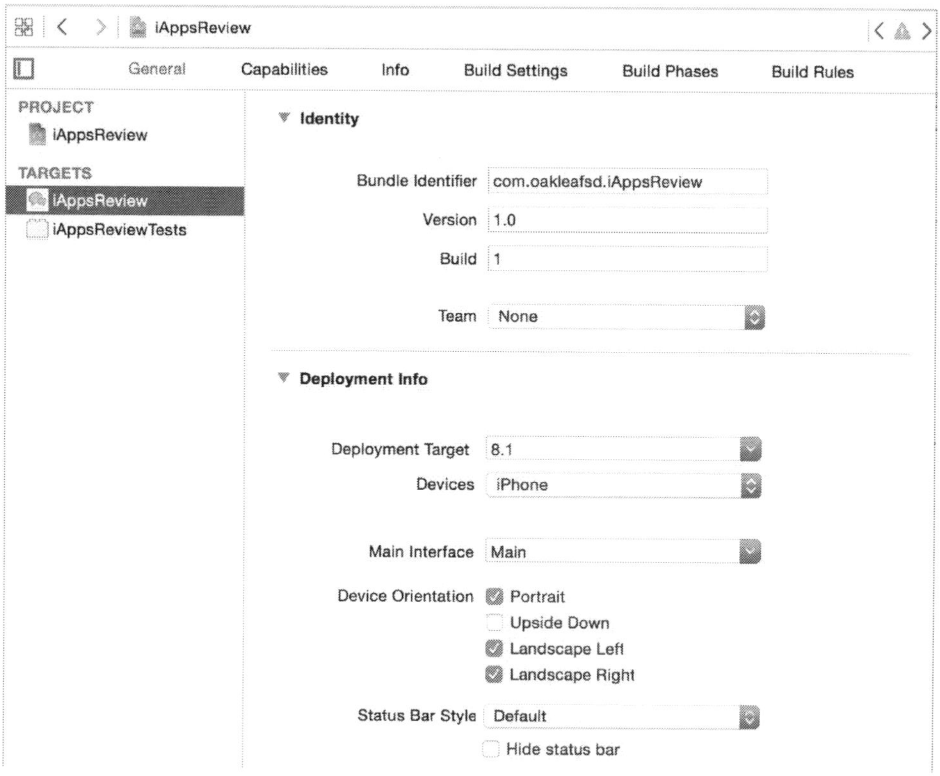

Figure 14.1 The Project Editor

Before diving into the details of the Project Editor, you should first understand some basic concepts, including products and targets.

Understanding Products and Targets

When you are working with an Xcode project, your final goal is to create a product—an iOS app. In the Project Navigator, a group named **Products** contains your .app file (Figure 14.2).

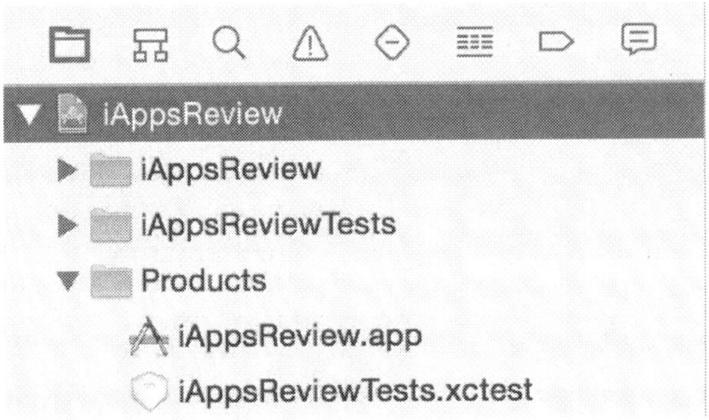

*Figure 14.2 You can find your .app file in the Project Navigator's **Products** group.*

This file is also known as the *application bundle* because it contains your application's executable and any resources such as UI files, images, and settings files that you have bundled with it.

A product is built from a *target*. A target specifies a single product to be built. It contains a set of instructions in the form of build settings and build phases that tell Xcode how to create a product from a set of files in a project or workspace. By default, a project has one or more targets—one for the main project and one or more for unit tests. You can create additional targets, but each target produces a single product (Figure 14.3).

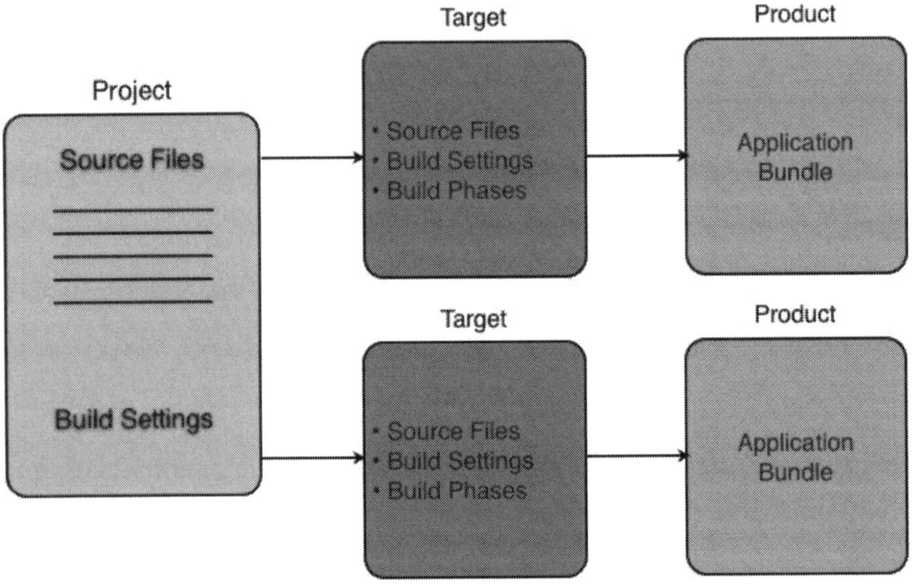

Figure 14.3 A project can have multiple targets that each produce its own product.

You can see these three different elements—Project, Product, and Target—in Xcode as shown in Figure 14.4 (color-coded to match the shapes in Figure 14.3).

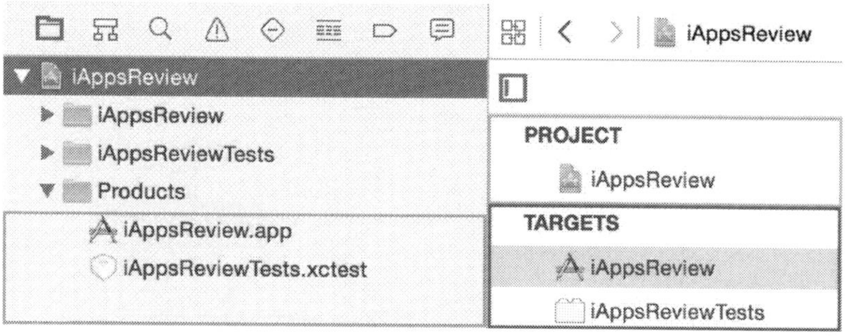

Figure 14.4 The Project, Target, and Product

To see this view of a project, just click on the first item in the Project Navigator to bring up the Project Editor. In the list on the left side of the Project Editor, you can see **Project** and **Targets**. To see the product, expand the **Products** group in the Project Navigator.

Project Editor in Depth

Now that you understand some of the basics regarding projects, products, and targets, let's take a closer look at the Project Editor. If you select a target under the **Targets** section on the left side of the Project Editor, you will see that it displays six panes in the Project Editor:

- General
- Capabilities
- Resource Tags
- Info
- Build Settings
- Build Phases
- Build Rules

The following sections cover each of these Project Editor panes in detail.

The General Pane

The **General** pane contains most of the settings that you normally change for a target. You rarely need to change a setting in one of the other panes. In fact, the **General** pane takes the most important settings from the other panes and presents them in a single place.

Identity

The section labeled **Identity** contains the settings shown in Figure 14.5.

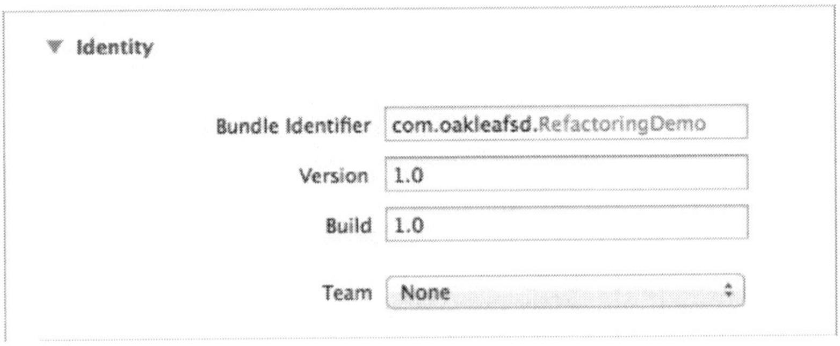

*Figure 14.5 **Identity** settings*

- **Bundle Identifier** – Your app's unique identifier. By default, this is a combination of the company identifier and the product name that you specified when you first created the project. If you don't like the default bundle identifier Xcode generated for you when you first created your project, you can change it here.

- **Version** – The version number of your app (see the last section in this chapter for more information).

- **Build** – The build number for your app (see the last section in this chapter for more information).

- **Team** – Each Xcode project is associated with a team, even if you are a one-person team. When you specify the team, Xcode may try to create a team provisioning file if you have an iOS device connected or previously registered a device. A team provisioning file allows an app to be signed and run by all team members on all their devices.

Deployment Info

Here is a description of each setting in the **Deployment Info** section (Figure 14.6):

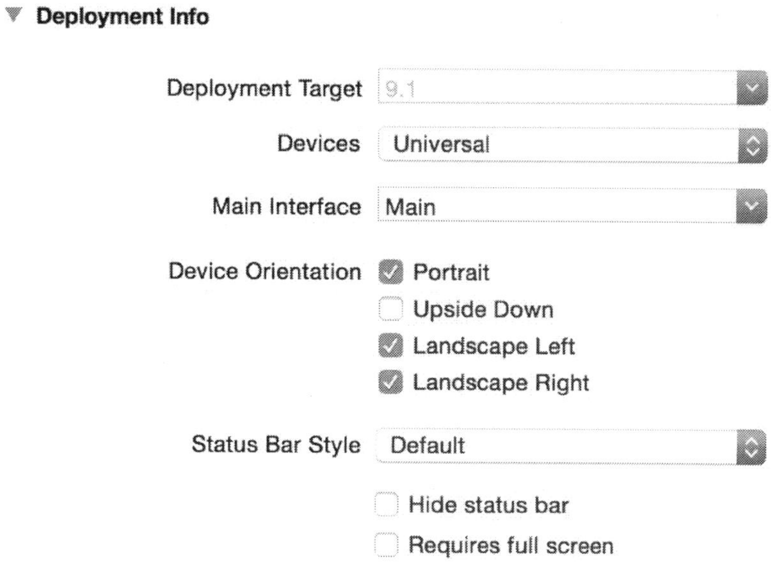

Figure 14.6 ***Deployment Info*** *settings*

- **Deployment Target** – Specifies the minimum iOS version your app supports. Your app runs on this minimum iOS version and all newer versions.

- **Devices** – Specifies if the app runs on **iPhone** (only), **iPad** (only), or **Universal** (both iPhone and iPad). This setting defaults to whatever you specified when you first created your project, but you can change the setting here.

For the next set of settings, if you have specified Universal for your Devices, you will see iPhone and iPad buttons you can click to toggle between settings for each. If you have specified iPhone only or iPad only, then you won't see these buttons.

- **Main Interface** – If you are using storyboards in your app, this setting specifies the main storyboard when the app first runs. You can have more than one storyboard in your app. For example, when creating a universal app, you typically have one storyboard for the iPhone and one for the iPad.

- **Device Orientations** – This setting allows you to specify at the app level which orientations your app supports. Selecting a check box indicates a supported orientation. If all of the view controllers in your app support the same orientation, you can set the supported orientations here and be done.

  However, if there are view controllers in your app that don't support a particular orientation, you can override the settings at the view controller level in the controller's **supportedInterfaceOrientations** method.

  At runtime, iOS intersects the app's supported orientations with the view controller's supported orientations to determine whether to rotate. This means you can't support an orientation at the view controller level that is not supported at the app level. So, for example, if you specify at the app level that you don't support landscape-left orientation, you can't say you support it at the view controller level.

- **Status Bar Style** – This setting lets you specify the appearance of your app's status bar (the bar at the top of the screen that contains the battery icon).

  - The options for this setting are **Default** and **Light**.

- **Hide status bar** – Specifies if the status bar is hidden when your app first launches.

- **Require full screen** – If selected, it specifies that you do not want your app to be presented in iOS 9's new slide-over or split-view configurations for multi-tasking.

App Icons and Launch Images

This section specifies the source for your app icons—the icon that appears for your app in the iOS Home screen, and optionally in the iOS Spotlight search results and Settings app. By default, a new iOS project stores its app icons in an asset catalog, whereas older projects store them as discrete files in the project.

This section also lets you specify launch image and a launch screens for your app. This is important because Apple requires at least one launch image for your iOS app. When your app is first launched, this image is temporarily displayed to give the user immediate feedback while your app is initializing.

Embedded Binaries

This section allows you to embed binaries in your .app file. For example, when you create a watchOS app, the watch extension is embedded in the associated iOS app.

Linked Frameworks and Libraries

This section allows your app to frameworks and libraries (Figure 14.7). Xcode automatically adds the most critical Cocoa Touch Framework libraries to your project when you first create it. Unlike embedded binaries, linked frameworks are not included in your .app file. They exist in a common folder on the device and are referenced from within your app.

Figure 14.7 Linked Frameworks and Libraries

The Capabilities Pane

The Capabilities pane (Figure 14.8) allows you to specify whether your app has privileges to access special capabilities or features such as iCloud, Game Center, Passbook, Apple Pay, Maps, and so on. Just flip the switch to enable Apple services, and Xcode manages your teams, certificates, and entitlements for you.

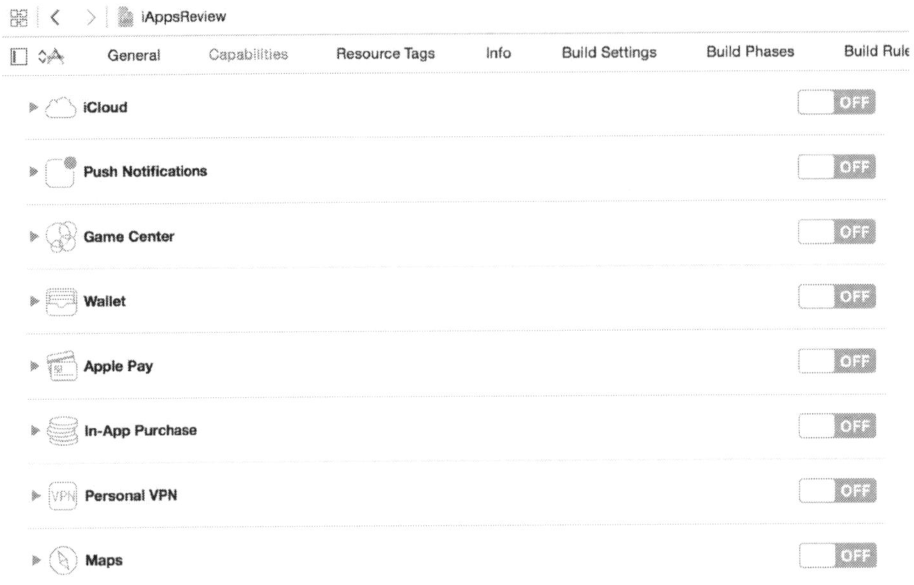

*Figure 14.8 The Project Editor's **Capabilites** pane*

For example, if you flip the **Maps** switch **ON**, you will see the set of check boxes shown in Figure 14.9, which allow you to specify that your app can accept transit routing requests for users traveling by **Airplane, Bike**, **Bus**, and so on. Also, notice under the **Steps** section that Xcode automatically added **Mapkit.framework** to your project when you turned on this switch.

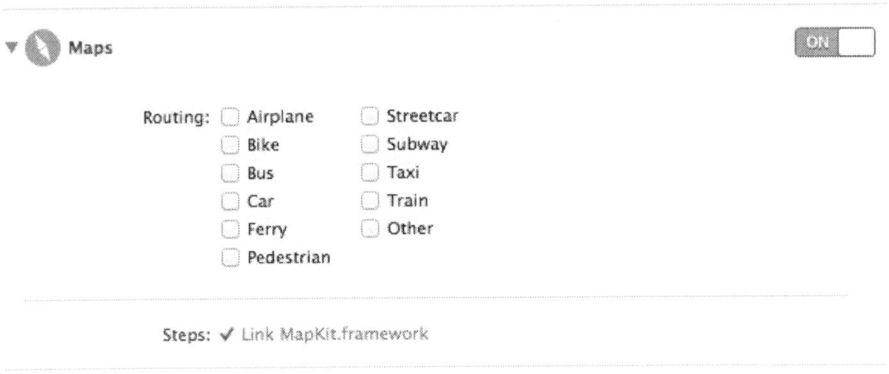

Figure 14.9 Maps capability settings

Resource Tags

The Resource Tags pane allows you to identify and manage sets of on-demand resources for your app. For more information about on-demand resources, check out Apple's *On Demand Resources Essentials* guide.

The Info Pane

The Info pane (Figure 14.10) contains important settings, and some of them are also on the **General** pane.

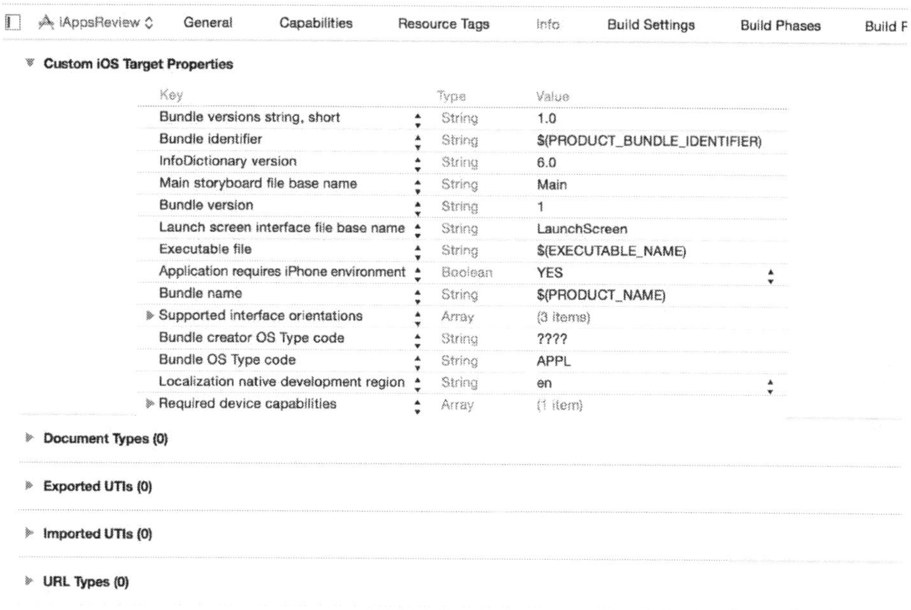

*Figure 14.10 The Project Editor's **Info** pane*

Here are a few important settings:

- **Bundle display name** – The name displayed under the icon for your app on the iOS Home Screen. If your project name is not the same as the name that you want for your app, you can change it here.

- **Document Types** – Allows you to specify the types of files that your app reads and writes (if any).

- **Exported UTIs** and **Imported UTIs** (Uniform Type Identifiers) – Allows you to specify a proprietary file format that you want others to access (exported) or that you want to be able to read (imported).

- **URL Types** – Allows you to create a custom URL (uniform resource locator) scheme that allows other apps to communicate with your app. You will learn more about communicating with other apps later in this book series.

The Build Settings Pane

The **Build Settings** pane is shown in Figure 14.11. By default, targets inherit their build settings from the project. If you want to override a particular setting at the target level, this is the place to do it.

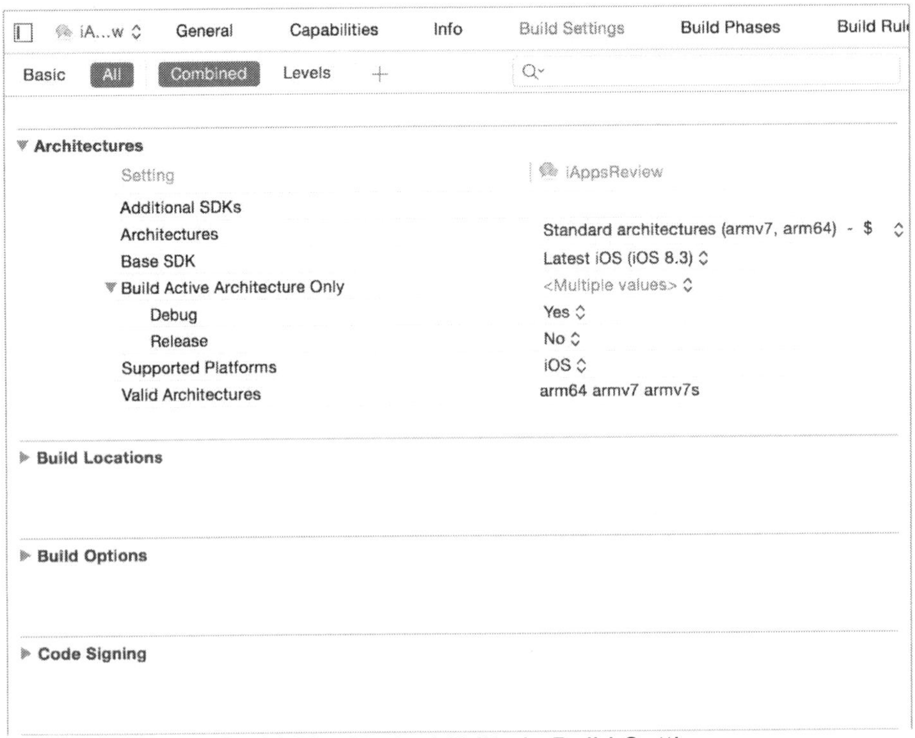

Figure 14.11 The Project Editor's Build Settings pane

There are many settings on this pane. In fact, at the top of the **Build Settings** pane is a toolbar containing options that allow you to filter the list of settings. On the left side of the toolbar are two buttons, **Basic** and **All**. The **All** button (selected by default) displays all available settings. If you select the **Basic** button, only the most commonly used settings are displayed. On the right side of the toolbar is a search box where you can enter a search string so only the settings containing that text will be displayed in the list.

Another set of buttons in the toolbar is labeled **Combined** and **Levels**. When the **Combined** option is selected (the default as shown in Figure 14.11), the current value of the build setting is displayed. If you select the **Levels** button, four columns appear:

1. Resolved
2. The name of the target
3. The name of the project
4. iOS Default

These columns let you see the level at which a setting has been applied. The level at which the build setting is set is highlighted in green. The actual value of the build setting is listed in the **Resolved** column. If a setting has been changed from the default, it's shown in bold.

The Build Phases Pane

The **Build Phases** pane contains several sections. Each section represents a different phase in the build process listed in order of execution (Figure 14.12). The build process executes either when you press **Command+B** in Xcode or when you press the **Run** button.

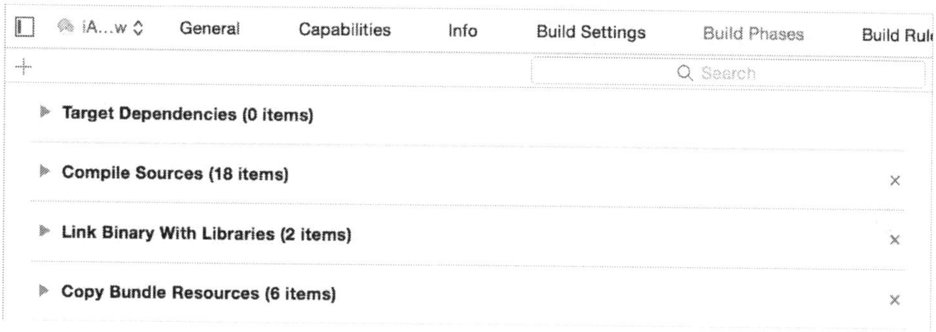

*Figure 14.12 The Project Editor **Build Phases** pane*

This pane is a great place to see all the items in the project that are included in the selected target. Here is a description of each section:

- **Target Dependencies** – If you have more than one target in your project, this section allows you to specify that one target depends on another. This tells Xcode to build the target that is depended on first.
- **Compile Sources** – This lists all the source code files in the project that are compiled when you build the project.

When you add a new code file to the project, Xcode automatically adds it to the list of compile sources. If you don't want to compile a particular file but just want to include it with your app, you can drag the file from the **Compile Sources** section to the **Copy Bundle Resources** section.

- **Link Binary With Libraries** – This section, also shown in the **General** pane, lists all the libraries that you have included with your project.

- **Copy Bundle Resources** – This section contains a list of files that are not source code but need to be included in your application bundle. This includes UI files such as storyboards, settings files, and images.

The Build Rules Pane

Xcode has a set of built-in rules that it uses to process files of different types. The **Build Rules** pane (Figure 14.13) allows you to see a list of default rules and to customize a rule to suit your needs.

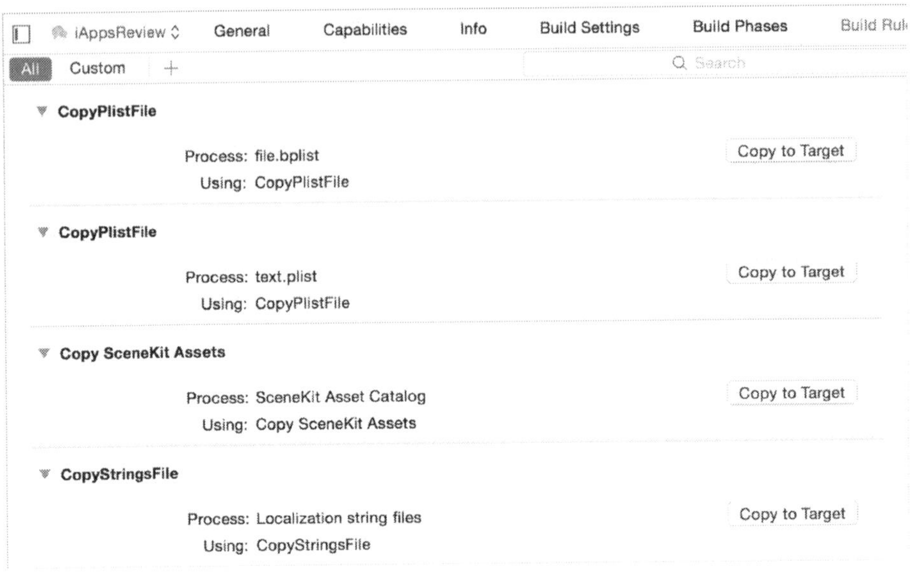

*Figure 14.13 The Project Editor **Build Rules** pane*

If you select the **All** button in the toolbar at the top left of the **Build Rules** pane, you can see all the default build rules. If you select the **Target** button, any rules that you have specified for the target (there are no target-specific rules by default) will be listed. If you want to customize a built-in build rule, just click the **Copy to Target** button and fill in the build-rule template. You can also add a new build rule to the target by clicking the **Add Build Rule** button at the bottom of the Project Editor.

Project Version and Build Number

Now that you have a basic understanding of the different panes in the Project Editor, let's take a closer look at the **Version** and **Build** settings and how you can use build phases to automatically increment your project build number.

A typical pattern for a product version number is a three- part number:

```
MajorVersion.MinorVersion.Revision
```

- Major version – Significant jump in functionality
- Minor version – Minor features or major bug fixes
- Revision – Minor bug fixes

Sometimes a fourth unpublished number indicates the software build number, which often denotes the number of project builds that it took to get to a particular version. This build number doesn't automatically change in Xcode, but you can add a script to run each time that you build the project to automatically increment the build number. To do this:

1. In the Project Navigator, select the top project node to load the Project Editor.
2. On the left side of the Project Editor under **Targets**, select the project target.
3. Select the **General** pane, and in the **Identity** section, set **Build** to the number zero (**0**) (Figure 14.14).

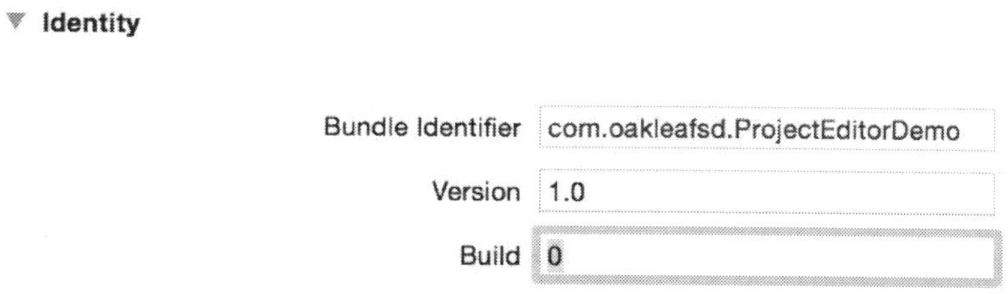

*Figure 14.14 Set **Build** to zero (**0**).*

4. Select the **Build Phases** pane.

5. Click the plus button (+) at the top-left corner of the editor and select **New Run Script Phase** from the popup menu. This adds a new build phase labeled **Run Script** to the **Build Phases** pane.

6. Drag and drop the new **Run Script** phase directly above the **Copy Bundle Resources** phase (Figure 14.15). This causes the script to be run before the **Copy Bundle Resources** phase.

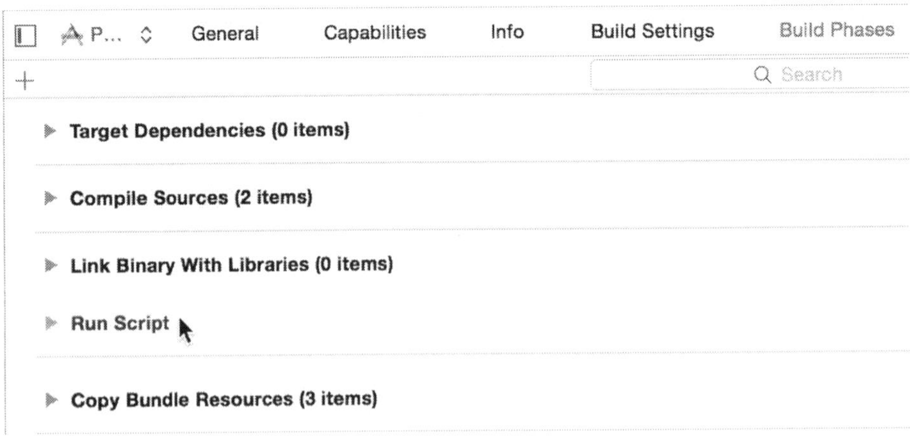

*Figure 14.15 Drag and drop the **Run Script** phase above the **Copy Bundle Resources** phase.*

7. Expand the **Run Script** build phase by clicking on the arrow on the left of the **Run Script** bar.

8. Add the following script code to the box just below the **Shell** text field:

```
buildNumber=$(/usr/libexec/PlistBuddy -c
"Print CFBundleVersion" "${PROJECT_DIR}/${INFOPLIST_FILE}")
buildNumber=$(($buildNumber + 1))
/usr/libexec/PlistBuddy –c "Set:CFBundleVersion
$buildNumber" "${PROJECT_DIR}/${INFOPLIST_FILE}"
```

When you're done, the **Run Script** code should look like Figure 14.16.

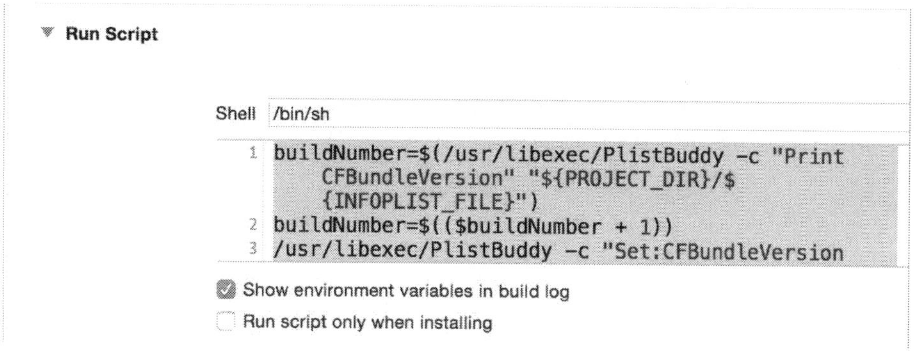

Figure 14.16 The final script code

That's all you need to do to implement the script.

9. To see this script at work, select the **General** pane so you can see the **Build** setting.

10. Press **Command+B** to build the project. Afterward, the **Build** setting should be set to 1 as shown in Figure 14.17.

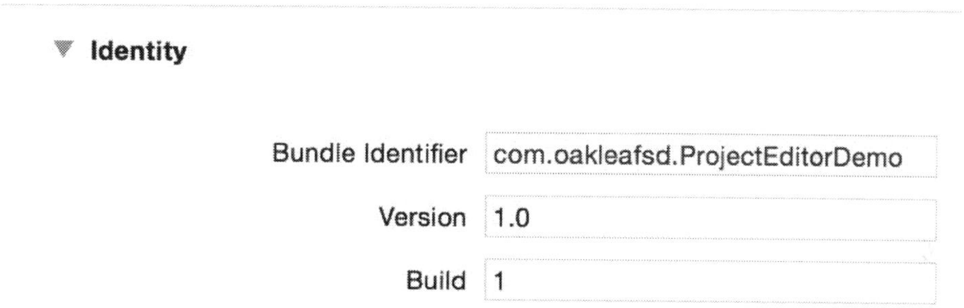

*Figure 14.17 The **Build** setting is automatically incremented.*

That's it—now your build number automatically increments whenever you build your project!

Summary

- When you are working with an Xcode project, your final goal is to create a product—an iOS app.

- Your .app file is also known as an *application bundle* because it contains your application's executable and any resources such as UI files, images, and settings files that you have bundled with it.

- A product is built from a *target*. A target specifies a single product to be built. It contains a set of instructions in the form of build settings and build phases that tell Xcode how to create a product from a set of files in a project or workspace.

- An Xcode project has one or more targets: one for the app and one or more for unit tests. You can create additional targets, but each target produces a single product.

- The Project Editor's **General** pane contains most of the settings that you normally change for a target. It takes the most important settings from the other panes and presents them in a single place.

- The *bundle identifier* is your app's unique identifier. By default, this is a combination of the company identifier and the product name that you specified when you first created the project. If you don't like the default bundle identifier Xcode generated for you when you first created your project, you can change it in the **General** pane of the Project Editor.

- The **Capabilities** pane allows you to specify whether your app has privileges to access special capabilities or features such as iCloud, Game Center, Passbook, Maps, and so on.

- Your app's **Bundle Display Name** is the name displayed under the icon for your app on the iOS Home Screen. You can change this setting in the **Info** pane of the Project Editor.

- By default, targets inherit their build settings from the project. If you want to override a particular setting at the target level, you can do this in the **Build Settings** pane of the Project Editor.

- The **Build Phases** pane contains several sections that each represent a different phase in the build process listed in order of execution. The build process executes either when you press **Command+B** in Xcode or when you press the **Run** button.

- Xcode has a set of built-in rules that it uses to process files of different types. The **Build Rules** pane allows you to see a list of default rules and to customize a rule to suit your needs.

Chapter 15: Mastering Dynamic Type

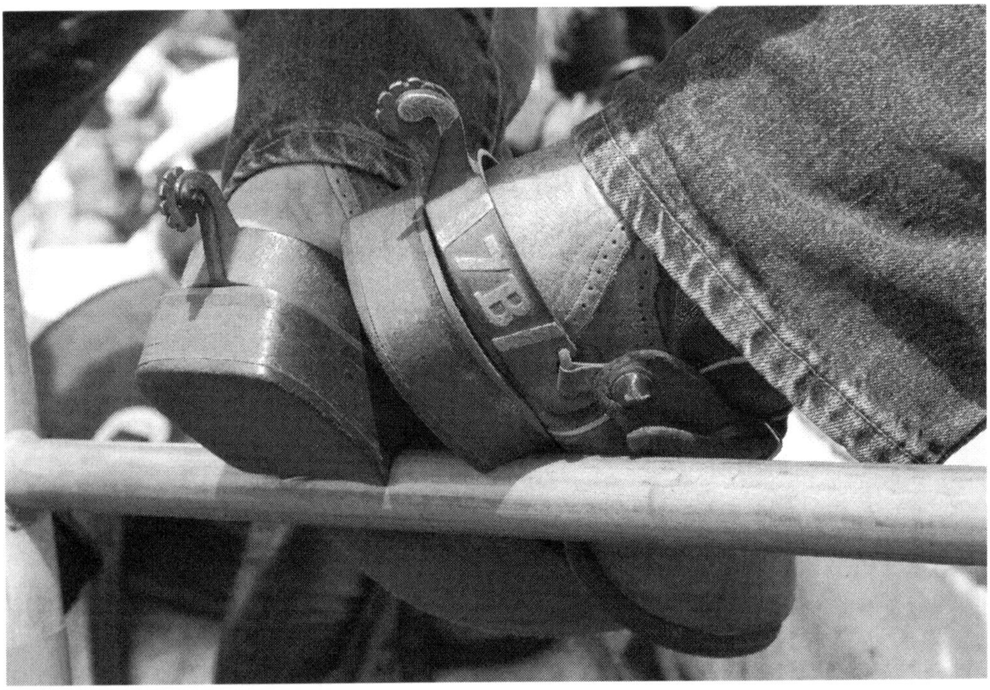

Apple has announced they expect third party apps to support Dynamic Type. However, if you have tried to implement it in your apps, you know there are some unexpected land mines along the way. In this chapter you will learn how Dynamic Type works under the hood and how to get it working properly in a variety of scenarios.

Sections in This Chapter

1. *What is Dynamic Type?*
2. *Running the Sample App*
3. *Working with Text Styles*
4. *Dynamic Type and Prototype Cells*
5. *Line Wrapping Label Text*
6. *Dynamic Row Heights*

7. *Using Auto Layout With Dynamic Type*

8. *Dynamic Type Changes & Custom Cells*

9. *An Improved Dynamic Type Solution*

10. *Dynamic Type and Static Text*

11. *Dynamic Type and Static Table View Cells*

12. *Dynamic Type and Special Controls*

13. *Summary*

What is Dynamic Type?

Apple's Dynamic Type technology allows users to specify their preferred font size (for apps that support Dynamic Type) in the Settings app.

This makes it easy for visually impaired users to increase the size of the text or, on the other end of the spectrum, those with sharp vision to decrease the font size to fit more information on each screen.

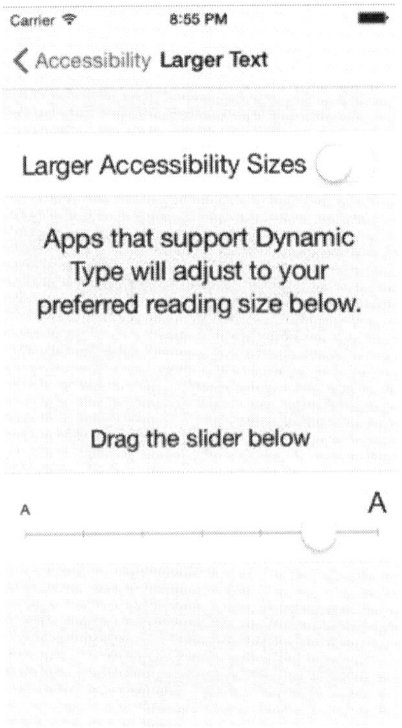

*Figure 15.1 The **Larger Text** accessibility settings.*

To change the Dynamic Type setting, in the Settings app, select **General** > **Accessibility** > **Larger Text**, which displays the Accessibility screen (Figure 15.1). You can move the slider to the left to decrease the font size or to the right to increase it. To get even larger font sizes, you can turn on the **Larger Accessibility Sizes** option at the top of the screen.

The left side of Figure 15.2 shows the smallest font size in the Contacts app. The right side shows the largest non- accessibility font setting.

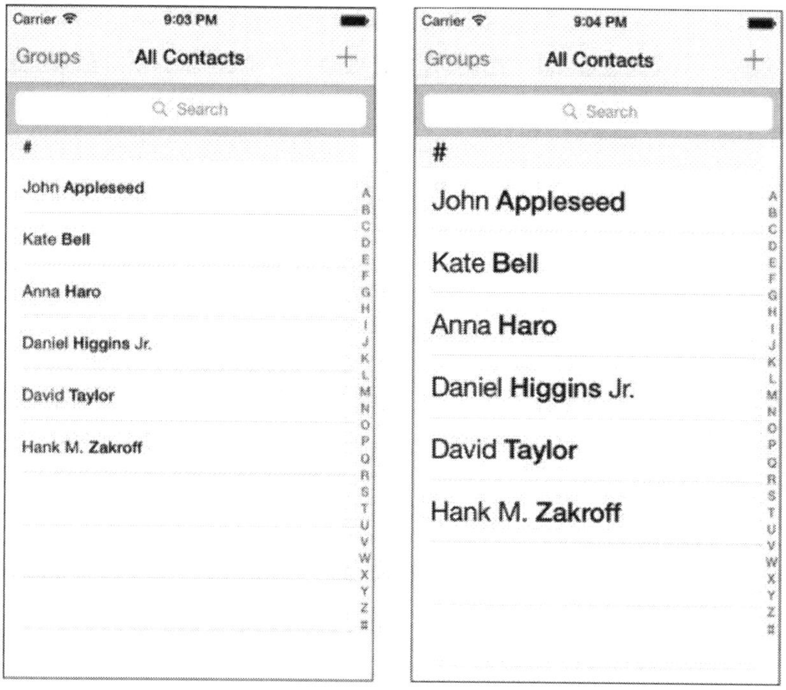

Figure 15.2 Small and large font sizes in the Contacts app.

Here are some of the built-in apps that currently support Dynamic Type:

- Messages
- Calendar
- Maps
- Notes
- Health
- Reminders
- Contacts
- Weather

Since these built-in apps support Dynamic Type, users are beginning to expect the apps you create to support it as well. Let's dive in and see what it takes.

Running the Sample App

Let's begin by checking out an existing project.

1. In Xcode, open the **IDeliverMobleDynamicType** project that is part of this book's samples.
2. Before running the app, in the menu, select **Xcode** > **Open Developer Tool** > **iOS Simulator**.
3. In the Simulator's menu, select **Hardware** > **Device** > **iPhone 5s**.
4. Next, launch the Settings app and navigate to **General** > **Accessibility** > **Larger Text**. Drag the slider all the way to the right to select the largest text.
5. Go back to Xcode, and in the Scheme control at the top left of the Xcode screen, select **iPhone 5s** from the list of devices.
6. Click Xcode's **Run** button. When the app appears in the Simulator, you can see that the font is still small. Obviously we need to make a change to support Dynamic Type.
7. Go back to Xcode and click the **Stop** button.

Working with Text Styles

Currently, all the user interface controls in the sample app have hard-coded font names and sizes. To support Dynamic Type, you need to change these hard-coded fonts to *text styles.*

Text styles are similar to styles in a word processing app. They allow you to specify the relative size and weight of the font used for each text element in your app. Figure 15.3 contains a list of the font styles to choose from.

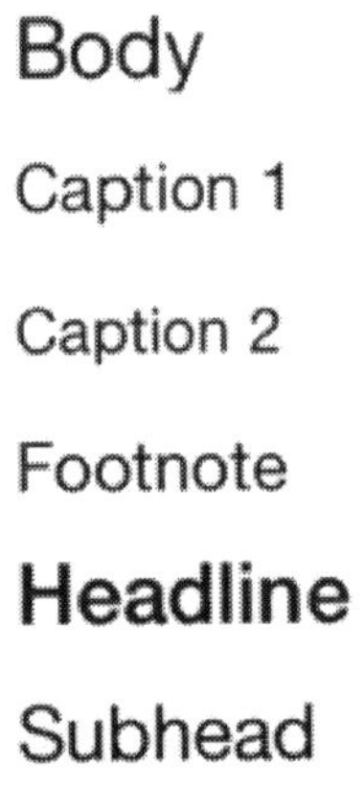

Figure 15.3 The Dynamic Type text styles.

Let's give some of these styles a try.

1. In the Project Navigator, select the **Main.storyboard** file.

2. In the **Deliveries** scene, select the **Feng Wong** label, then go to the Attributes Inspector and change the **Font** to **Headline** (Figure 15.4).

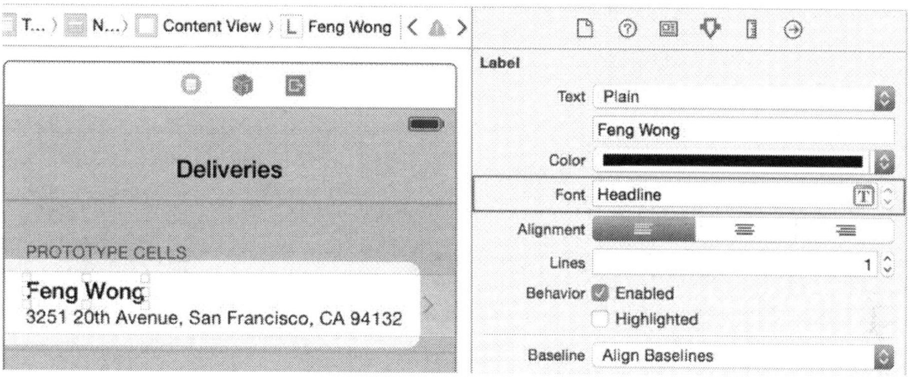

*Figure 15.4 Set the **Font** to **Headline.***

3. Select the address label and set its **Font** to **Subhead**.

4. To see the full effect of the Dynamic Type change, set the address label's **Autoshrink** setting to **Fixed Font Size** (Figure 15.5). This causes the address label text to be cut off, but we'll fix that later.

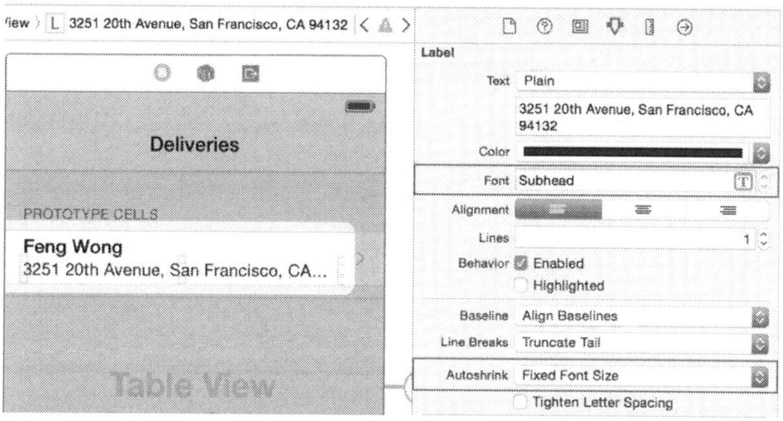

*Figure 15.5 Set the address label's **Font** to **Subhead** and **Autoshrink** to **Fixed Font Size.***

5. Click Xcode's **Run** button. When the app appears in the Simulator, the font size has increased to match the new setting (Figure 15.6).

Figure 15.6 Dynamic Type at work!

Also, notice the row height has increased slightly to accommodate the larger font size.

What happens if the user changes the font size in Settings while the app is running? Let's find out.

1. If the **iDeliverMobileDynamicType** app is not currently running, click the **Run** button in Xcode.
2. When the app appears in the Simulator, press the **Shift+Command+H** keys to go to the Home screen.
3. Launch the Settings app and navigate to the **General** > **Accessibility** > **Larger Text** screen. Drag the slider to the far left to decrease the text size.
4. Press **Shift+Command+H** to go back to the Home screen and launch the **iDeliverMobileDynamicType** app again. Notice the labels' fonts have changed to match the new smaller font setting (Figure 15.7).

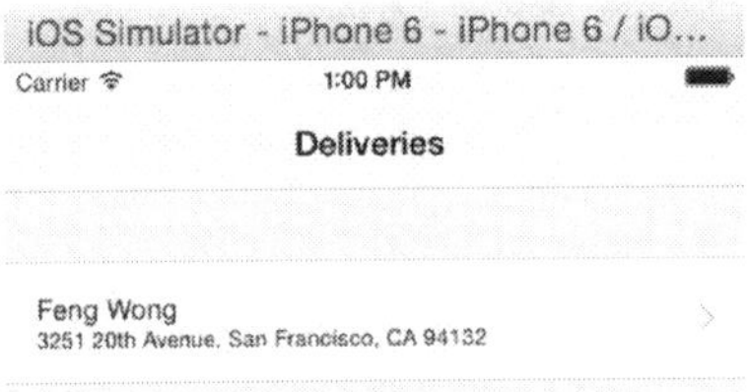

Figure 15.7 The fonts change dynamically.

5. Go back to Xcode and click the **Stop** button.

Dynamic Type and Prototype Cells

The ability to automatically respond to changes in Dynamic Type size is unique to table views with:

1. Table view **Content** set to **Dynamic Prototype**
2. Cells using one of the built-in styles.

As you can see in Figure 15.5, the table view in the sample app is using prototype cells.

If you select the table view cell in the **Deliveries** scene and go to the Attributes Inspector, you can see the **Style** is set to **Subtitle** (Figure 15.8).

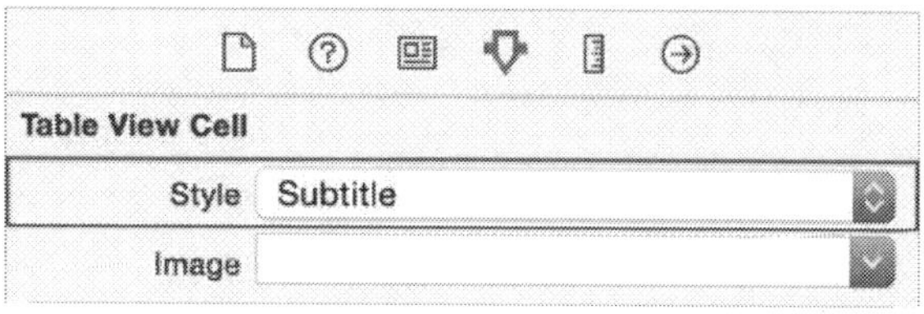

*Figure 15.8 The **Style** is set to **Subtitle.***

As you will learn, table views with static and custom cells behave differently.

Line-Wrapping Label Text

In some of the built-in iOS apps, Apple allows text to be truncated when the user increases the font size. You can see this in the email address of the Contacts app shown in Figure 15.9.

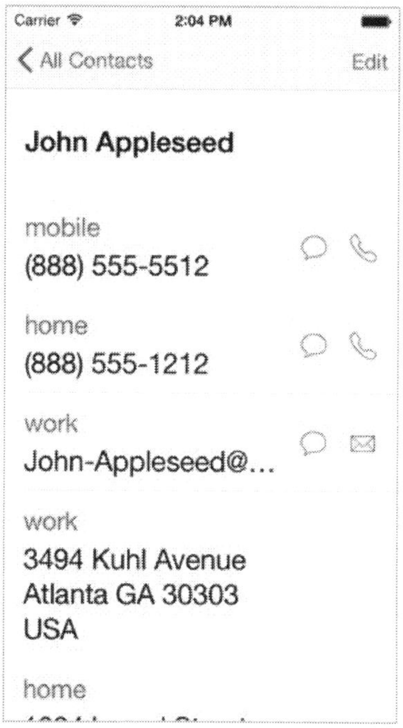

Figure 15.9 The email address is truncated.

You can truncate text in your own apps, or you can have the text wrap to the next line. Let's see how wrapping the text works.

In the **Deliveries** scene, select the detail text label then go to the Attributes Inspector and set the number of lines to zero (**0**). This causes the address text to wrap to the next line (Figure 15.10).

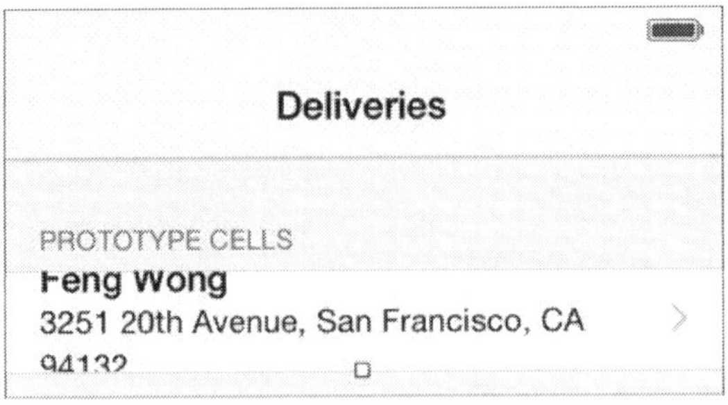

Figure 15.10 The label's text exceeds the row's height.

Unfortunately, iOS is no longer able to properly determine the height of the row. This brings us to a bigger discussion of dynamic row heights.

Dynamic Row Heights

When implementing Dynamic Type in a table view, its row height must be dynamic to accommodate changes in font size. Apple provides three strategies to achieve this:

1. Set the table view's **rowHeight** property.
2. Implement the **tableView:heightForRowAtIndexPath:** delegate method.
3. Self-sizing cells.

Using the **rowHeight** Property

Even though your table view row heights need to be dynamic, you can still use the classic table view **rowHeight** property. Whenever the font size changes (you will learn how to be notified of this later in this chapter), you can recalculate a new height and store it in the table view's **rowHeight** property.

The advantage of using the **rowHeight** property is speed. It provides the best scrolling performance because no calculations need to be performed on the fly while the user is scrolling.

The downside is that you have to perform your own calculations to determine the proper height for rows. In addition, all rows must be the same height.

In newer iOS versions, the default height of a table view is **UITableViewAutomaticDimension** (a constant that equates to -1). If you want to use the **rowHeight** property, you need to set its initial value in the Attributes Inspector or in your view controller's **viewDidLoad**.

Implementing **heightForRowAtIndexPath**

You can use the **tableView:heightForRowAtIndexPath:** view controller method to individually calculate the height of each row.

There is one big disadvantage to this approach. The height of all rows is request up front, even before the rows have been created. If you have tens of thousands of rows, this can be a real performance drag.

Self-Sizing Table View Cells

To use self-sizing table view cells, rather than setting the **rowHeight** property, you either set the table view's **estimatedRowHeight** property or implement the **tableView:estimatedHeightForRowAtIndexPath** delegate method.

Here are the basic steps performed by the runtime to create a self-sizing cell:

1. Before a row comes on screen, it's sized using the **estimatedRowHeight** property or delegate method.
2. When the row is scrolled onto the screen, the cell is created.
3. The cell is asked how big it should be.
4. If the height is different from the estimated height, it's used to adjust the content size of the table view cell.
5. The cell is displayed on screen.

In step 3, there are two ways a cell can communicate the height it needs to be:

1. Auto Layout
2. Manual sizing code

The table view calls **systemLayoutSizeFittingSize** on your cell. This method knows if you have implemented constraints on your cell, and if so, the Auto Layout engine specifies the cell size.

If you haven't implemented Auto Layout constraints, the table view calls the **sizeThatFits** method on your cell. You can return a cell height from this method based on your own calculations—the cell width is already calculated for you.

Using Auto Layout With Dynamic Type

Let's use Auto Layout in our sample project to see how it works with Dynamic Type. We first need to make sure Auto Layout is turned on for the project's storyboard.

1. Click on the white background of the storyboard to select it.

2. Next, go to the File Inspector by selecting the button on the far left in the Inspector toolbar. Under the **Interface Builder Document** section, make sure **Use Auto Layout** is selected (Figure 15.11).

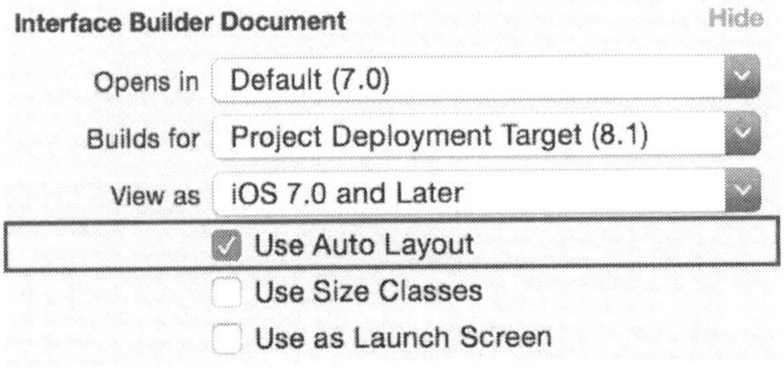

*Figure 15.11 Select **Use Auto Layout.***

3. Now we need to change the **Deliveries** scene's table view cell to use a custom style. To do this, click on the table view cell to select it, go to the Attributes Inspector and change the **Style** to **Custom**. This removes both labels from the cell.

4. Let's change the design-time height of the cell to make it easier to lay out in Interface Builder. Click in the gray area below the table view to select it. Next, go to the Size Inspector by clicking the second button from the right in the Inspector toolbar. Set the **Row Height** to **60**.

5. Next, drag a label from the Object Library and position it in the cell so you can see the horizontal and vertical guide lines shown in Figure 15.12.

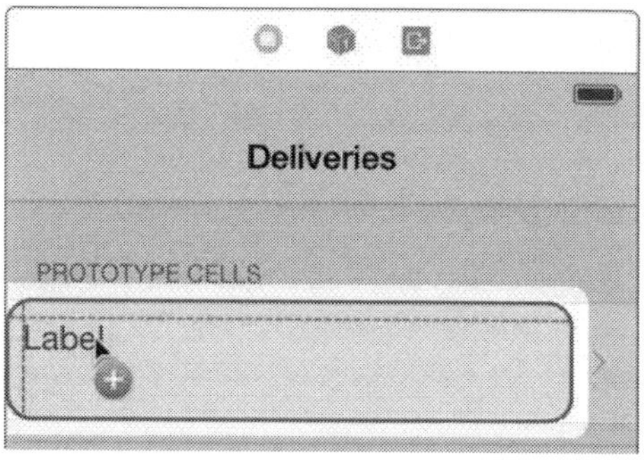

Figure 15.12 Add a label to the cell.

6. Grab the resizing handle on the right side of the label and drag it to the right side of the cell until the vertical guideline shown in Figure 15.13 appears.

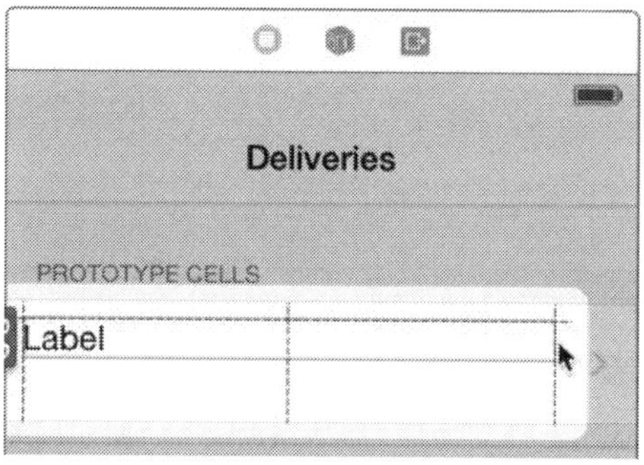

Figure 15.13 Resize the label's width.

7. With the label still selected, in the Attributes Inspector set **Font** to **Headline** and **Tag** to **1.**

8. Drag a second label from the Object Library and position it below the first label so you see the guide lines (Figure 15.14).

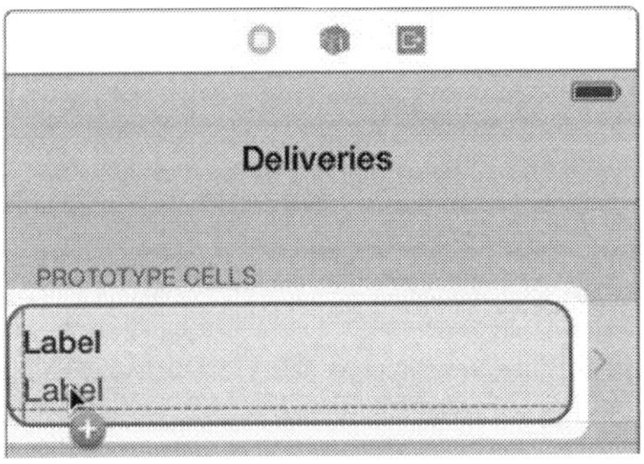

Figure 15.14 Add a second label to the cell.

9. Grab the resizing handle on the right side of the label and drag it to the right side of the cell until the vertical guidelines appear, just as with the first label.

10. With the label still selected, in the Attributes Inspector set **Font** to **Subhead**, **Lines** to **0** and **Tag** to **2**. Setting **Lines** to **0** causes the label to wrap to the next line when displaying long text strings.

11. Click on the Headline label at the top of the cell to select it in the design surface.

12. At the bottom right of the Interface Builder editor, click the Pin button (Figure 15.15). In the popup dialog, uncheck the **Constrain to margins** check box, and then click on each of the four red I-bars at the top of the dialog. This pins the label's top, bottom, left and right sides to their nearest neighbors. Next, select the **Height** check box, and then click the **Add 5 Constraints** button at the bottom of the dialog.

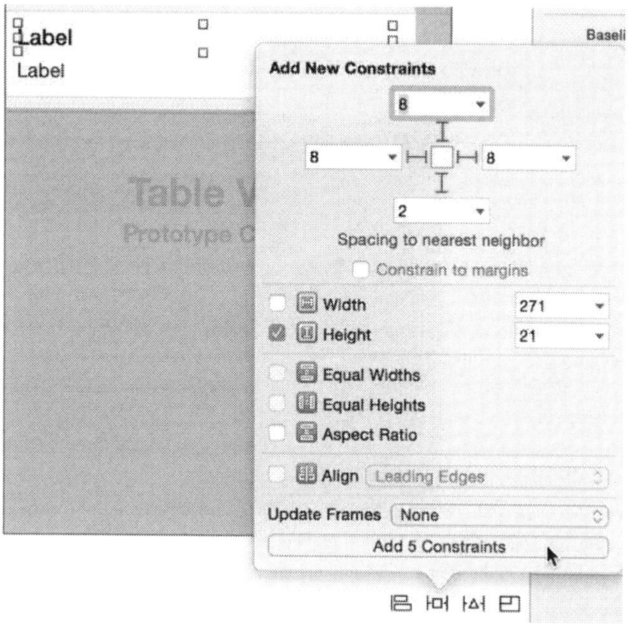

Figure 15.15 Add constraints to the top label.

13. Select the Subhead label at the bottom of the cell and click the Pin button again to display the Constraints popup dialog.

14. You need to select the same constraints as you did with the Headline label: Uncheck the **Constraints to margin** check box, select all four I-bars at the top of the dialog, select the **Height** check box, and then click the **Add 5 constraints** button at the bottom of the dialog.

15. With the lower Subhead label still selected, go to the Size Inspector by clicking the second button from the right in the Inspector toolbar.

    Click the **Height** constraint's **Edit** button (Figure 15.16) and change the operator to greater than or equal to (≥). This allows the height of the button to grow to accommodate multiple lines of text.

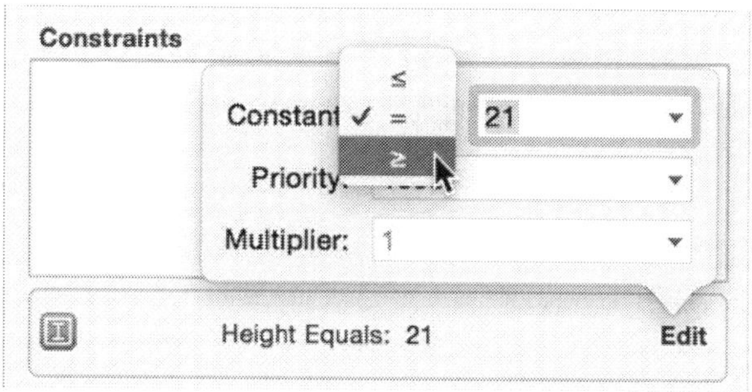

*Figure 15.16 Change the **Height** constraint's operator to (≥).*

16. Now you need to do the same for the Heading label. Click the Heading label in the design surface to select it. In the Size Inspector, click the **Height** constraint's **Edit** button and change the operator to great than or equal to (≥).

17. Now you need to change the code in the table view controller to work with the new custom labels.

    Select **DeliveriesViewController.swift** in the Project Navigator. In the **tableView:cellForRowAtIndexPath** method, change the code that configures the cell to the following:

```
    // Configure the cell...
    var shipmentEntity =
        self.shipmentList[indexPath.row]
    let nameLabel = cell.viewWithTag(1) as! UILabel
    nameLabel.text = shipmentEntity.name

    let addressLabel = cell.viewWithTag(2) as! UILabel
    addressLabel.text =
        shipmentEntity.address + ", " +
        shipmentEntity.city + ", " +
        shipmentEntity.region + " " +
        shipmentEntity.postalCode
    addressLabel.preferredMaxLayoutWidth =
        addressLabel.bounds.size.width
    return cell
}
```

    This code uses the **viewWithTag** method to get a reference to the new labels using the **Tag** numbers you set for each. The last line of highlighted code is necessary to get around a "feature" that sometimes prevents labels from wrapping text to the next line properly. Setting a label's **preferredMaxLayoutWidth** property to the label's current width does the trick.

18. Scroll to the top of the **DeliveriesViewController.swift** file and add the following code to the bottom of the **viewDidLoad** method:

```
override func viewDidLoad() {
   super.viewDidLoad()
   self.shipmentList =
      self.shipment.getAllEntities()
   self.tableView.estimatedRowHeight = 60
   self.tableView.rowHeight = UITableViewAutomaticDimension
}
```

Setting the table view's **estimatedRowHeight** property specifies the approximate height of the cell. Setting the **rowHeight** property of the table view to **UITableViewAutomaticDimension** tells iOS that you want it to automatically resize the cells for you. Let's give it a try!

19. Go the Simulator, launch the Settings app and set the text size to the largest setting. Next, click Xcode's **Run** button. When the app appears in the Simulator the address wraps to the next line (Figure 15.17)!

Figure 15.17 The address wraps to the next line!

Dynamic Type Changes & Custom Calls

Currently, when the **Deliveries** scene first loads, the labels in the table view take on the font size the user has specified in the Settings app. Previously, when the cell was set to the built-in Subtitle style, if the user changed the font size while the app was running, the font size of the labels changed dynamically. Unfortunately, this is not the case when using a custom cell style. Let's try it.

1. If the **iDeliverMobileDynamicType** app is not currently running, click the Run button in Xcode.

2. When the app appears in the Simulator, press the **Shift+Command+H** keys to go to the Simulator's Home screen.

3. Launch the Settings app and set the text size to the smallest setting.

4. Press **Shift+Command+H** to go back to the Home screen and launch the **iDeliverMobileDynamicType** app again. As you can see, the label's font size hasn't changed. Go back to Xcode and click the **Stop** button and we'll address this issue.

To get labels (or any other text-based control) in a custom cell to dynamically change font size in response to changing the font size in the Settings app, you must:

1. Register with **NSNotificationCenter** for the **UIContentSizeCategoryDidChangeNotification** in your view controller's **init** or **viewDidLoad** method.

2. In the code that responds to the font change notification, store the label's style setting back into its font property. For example:

```
nameLabel.font =
  UIFont.preferredFontForTextStyle(UIFontTextStyleHeadline)
```

3. Unregister for notifications in the view controller's **deinit** method.

Let's try this with the Deliveries scene.

1. In the **DeliveriesViewController.swift** file, add the following code to the bottom of **viewDidLoad**:

```
NSNotificationCenter.defaultCenter().addObserver
  (self, selector: "handleDynamicTypeChange:",
   name: UIContentSizeCategoryDidChangeNotification,
   object: nil)
}
```

   This code asks the Notification Center to call the **handleDynamicTypeChange** method when the user changes the Dynamic Type setting.

2. Add the following handler method below the **viewDidLoad** method:

```
func handleDynamicTypeChange(notification:
    NSNotification) {
```

```
        self.tableView.reloadData()
    }
```

This handler method reloads the table view's data.

3. Now add the following code to the bottom of the **tableView:cellForRowAtIndexPath** method:

```
        nameLabel.font = UIFont.preferredFontForTextStyle
            (UIFontTextStyleHeadline)
        addressLabel.font = UIFont.preferredFontForTextStyle
            (UIFontTextStyleSubheadline)
      return cell
    }
```

This code resets the label's font style.

4. Finally, add the following **deinit** method below the **viewDidLoad** method:

```
    deinit {
        NSNotificationCenter.defaultCenter().
            removeObserver(self)
    }
```

5. Let's try this code to see how it works at run time. Click Xcode's **Run** button. When the app appears in the Simulator, you should see the small text from when you previously changed font size. Press the **Shift+Command+H** keys to go to the Simulator's Home screen.

6. Go back to the settings app and set the text to the largest size.

7. Press **Shift+Command+H** to go back to the Home screen and launch the **iDeliverMobileDynamicType** app again. As you can see, the label's font size has increased without having to restart the app!

8. Go back to Xcode and click the **Stop** button.

What's Bad About This Model

Here are a few things that make this model undesirable:

- You have to set the font for all controls twice. Once in the Attributes Inspector and a second time in code.
- When working with static table view cells, you must create outlets for all text-based controls, even if you don't need them for any other purpose.
- You have to add this same code to all view controllers in your app.

In situations where you must add redundant code in multiple places in your app, it's time to create a universal solution you can reuse in all your projects.

I've created a set of classes you can add to any project that makes it easy to implement Dynamic Type handling in your app. Before giving it a try, let's get rid of the code you added in the previous section.

1. Delete the following code from the **viewDidLoad** method:

```
    NSNotificationCenter.defaultCenter().
    addObserver(self, selector: "handleDynamicTypeChange:",
    name: UIContentSizeCategoryDidChangeNotification,
    object: nil)
}
```

2. Delete the following handler method below the **viewDidLoad** method:

```
func handleDynamicTypeChange(notification:
    NSNotification) {
    self.tableView.reloadData()
}
```

3. Delete the following code from the bottom of the **tableView:cellForRowAtIndexPath:** method:

```
nameLabel.font = UIFont.preferredFontForTextStyle
    (UIFontTextStyleHeadline)
addressLabel.font = UIFont.preferredFontForTextStyle
    (UIFontTextStyleSubheadline)
return cell
}
```

4. Remove the **deinit** method located below the **viewDidLoad** method:

```
deinit {
    NSNotificationCenter.defaultCenter().
      removeObserver(self)
}
```

An Improved Dynamic Type Solution

Now let's try a better solution.

1. Right-click the **Main.storyboard** file in the Project Navigator and select **Add Files to iDeliverMobileCD...** from the shortcut menu.

2. In the dialog, uncheck **Copy items if needed**.

3. Navigate to the folder where you have downloaded this book's sample code. Drill into the **MMiOS** folder, select the **mmDynamicTypeExtensions.swift** file and click **Add**.

   We'll take a closer look at this code later, but let's first see how the code works at design and run time.

4. Select the **Main.storyboard** file in the Project Navigator. In the **Deliveries** scene, select the Heading label at the top of the cell.

5. Go to the Attributes Inspector. Notice there is a new **Type Observer** attribute (Figure 15.18).

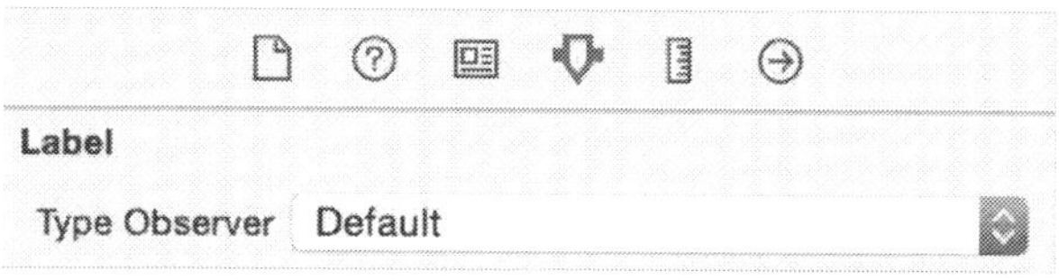

*Figure 15.18 The new **Type Observer** attribute.*

   The code you just included in the project added this **Type Observer** property to the label.

6. Change the **Type Observer** setting to **On**.

7. Select the Subhead label at the bottom of the cell. In the Attributes Inspector, set the **Type Observer** attribute to **On**.

8. That's it! Let's give it a try. Click Xcode's **Run** button. When the app appears in the Simulator, you should see the large text from when you previously changed font size. Press the **Shift+Command+H** keys to go to the Simulator's Home screen.
9. Go to the Settings app and set the font to the smallest size.
10. Press **Shift+Command+H** to go to the Home screen and run the **iDeliverMobileDynamicType** app again. As you can see, the label's font size has changed!
11. Go back to Xcode and click the **Stop** button.

Dynamic Type Handling

Let's take a closer look at the code that makes this work.

1. Select the **mmDynamicTypeExtensions.swift** file in the Project Navigator.
2. At the top of the file is a protocol that declares a single **typeObserver** property of type **Bool**. You set this property **On** for table view labels:

```
protocol DynamicTypeChangeHandler {
    var typeObserver: Bool {get set}
}
```

3. Just below the protocol declaration is an extension of the **UILabel** class:

```
extension UILabel : DynamicTypeChangeHandler {
   @IBInspectable var typeObserver: Bool {
   get {
      return DynamicTypeManager.sharedInstance.
         isControlRegistered(self)
   }
   set {
      DynamicTypeManager.sharedInstance.
        registerControl(self, fontKeyPath: "font")
  }
 }
}
```

The extension adopts the **DynamicTypeChangeHandler** protocol and implements the **typeObserver** property.

The **@IBInspectable** attribute is what makes the property appear in the Attribute Inspector. The property setter makes a call to a Dynamic Type Manager's **registerControl** method.

4. Scroll a little further down in the code file and you can see the **DynamicTypeManager** is declared as a Singleton:

```
  // Dynamic Type Manager (Singleton)
   private let dynamicTypeManager =
      DynamicTypeManager()
   class DynamicTypeManager {
    // Reference to the shared instance
    class var sharedInstance: DynamicTypeManager {
      return dynamicTypeManager
}
```

The Singleton design pattern restricts the number of instances of a class to one. When an instance is requested, one is created if it doesn't already exist. If an instance exists, it returns a reference to that object.

Figure 15.19 contains a sequence diagram that depicts the architecture I have created for handling Dynamic Type changes. Here are the main steps:

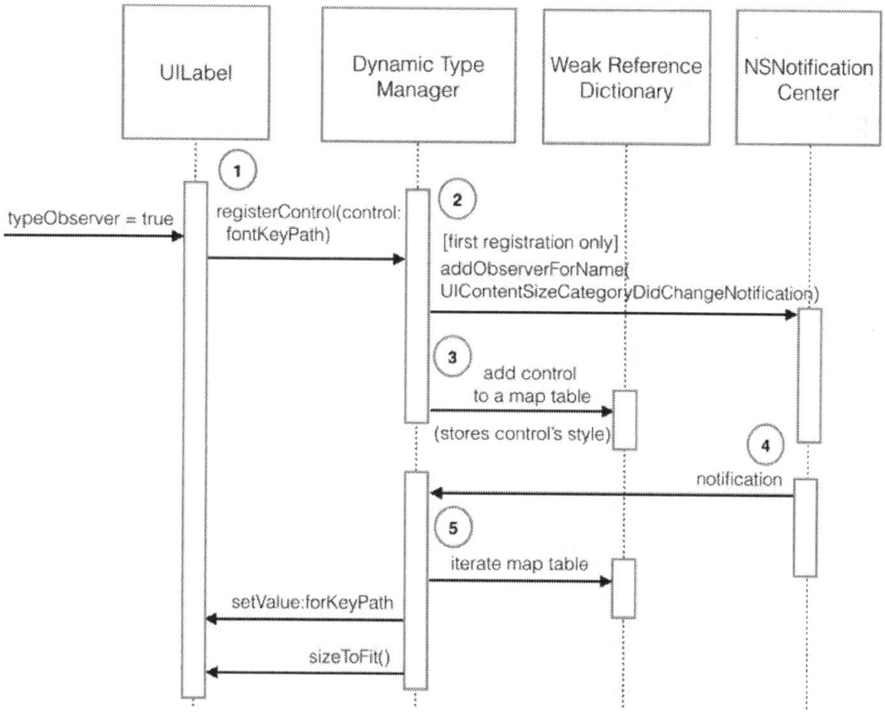

Figure 15.19 Dynamic Table handling sequence diagram.

1. User interface controls register themselves with the Dynamic Type Manager when their **typeObserver** property is set to **true** (**On** in the Attribute Inspector), passing a path to their **font** property.

2. When the first control registers itself, an instance of the Dynamic Type Manager is created, and registers itself with the **NSNotificationCenter** for Dynamic Type changes.

3. A reference to the control and its font style is stored in an **NSMapTable**. A map table is a special kind of dictionary that holds weak references to objects, so entries are removed automatically when either the key or the value is deallocated. This is a perfect fit for this scenario where we don't want to hold strong references to user interface controls. When the UI controls are released (for example, when the user navigates to a different scene and the view controller is deallocated), the control references are automatically removed from the **NSMapTable** (Thanks to the folks at Big Nerd Ranch for this tip!)

4. When the user changes the font size in the Settings app, **NSNotificationCenter** alerts the Dynamic Type Manager.

5. The Dynamic Type Manager iterates through the list of user interface controls in the map table. For each control, it sets the font style and calls the control's **sizeToFit** method.

What is there to like about this architecture?

- It uses extensions rather than subclasses. This allows you to use the out-of-the-box **UIKit** controls.

- When you add the **mmDynamicTypeExtensions.swift** code file to your project, it "just works".

- There is no need to create outlets for UI controls. You simply set a property in the Attribute Inspector.

- This architecture is loosely coupled. The UI controls provide information about themselves to the Dynamic Type Manager. This means you can register your own custom controls (or new controls that Apple releases in the future) without changing the Dynamic Type Manager.

- Since you don't need to use this feature for prototype table view cells that are set to one of the default styles, this "opt in" model, lets you choose which controls you want to register with the Dynamic Type Manager.

Dynamic Type and Static Text

Let's check out how Dynamic Type works with static table view cells.

1. In the **iDeliverMobileDynamicType** project, select the **Main.storyboard** file and scroll over to the **Deliveries** scene (Figure 15.20).

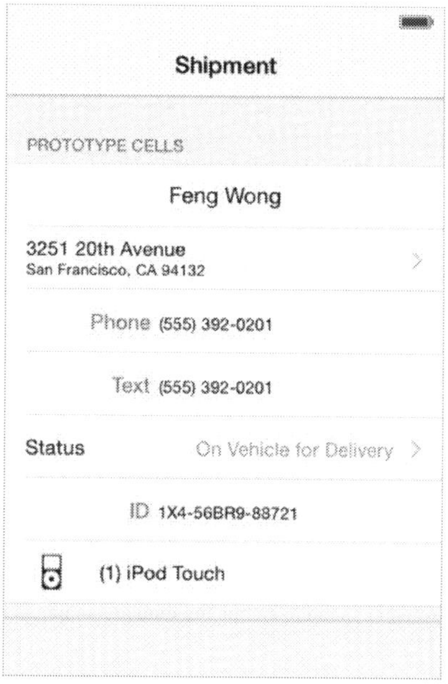

Figure 15.20 The Shipment Scene

2. The table view in this scene contains dynamic prototype cells, just as the Deliveries scene. The main difference is the **Shipment** scene contains both dynamic and static text. The blue text (**Phone**, **Text**, and **ID**) is static as well as the **Status** text. This means the text doesn't change as you examine different shipments. The rest of the text in the table view is dynamic, changing for each shipment.

3. To get the labels on this scene to adapt to Dynamic Type, select each label in the design surface, then go to the Attributes Inspector and change the **Font** to one of the iOS text styles. Here are some recommendations:

- **Name** - Headline
- **Address Line 1** - Body
- **Address Line 2** - Subhead
- **Phone labels** - Body
- **Text labels** - Body
- **Status labels** - Body
- **ID labels** - Body
- **iPod Touch label** - Body

4. In the **ShipmentViewController.swift** file, add the following code to the bottom of the **viewDidLoad** method:

```
override func viewDidLoad() {
   super.viewDidLoad()
   self.shipmentItemList =
      self.shipmentItem. getShipmentItemsForShipmentID
     (self.shipmentEntity.shipmentID)
   self.tableView.estimatedRowHeight = 45
   self.tableView.rowHeight =
      UITableViewAutomaticDimension
}
```

   Remember, this code tells the table view to use self- sizing cells.

5. Let's see how this works at run time. Click Xcode's **Run** button, and when the app appears in the Simulator, select the shipment in the **Deliveries** scene to navigate to the **Shipment** scene. You should see the small type that was last specified in the Settings app.

6. Now let's see if the app responds to a Dynamic Type change while the app is running. Go to the Settings app and select the largest font size. Afterward, go back to the **iDeliverMobileDynamicType** app.

As shown in Figure 15.21, all the static text is missing! This is an iOS bug, and unfortunately, it still isn't fixed in the latest version of Xcode. I'm hoping

Apple will fix it, but for now you can get around the issue without resorting to creating custom cells. You just need to add code to the **tableView: cellForRowAtIndexPath:** method that resets the static text.

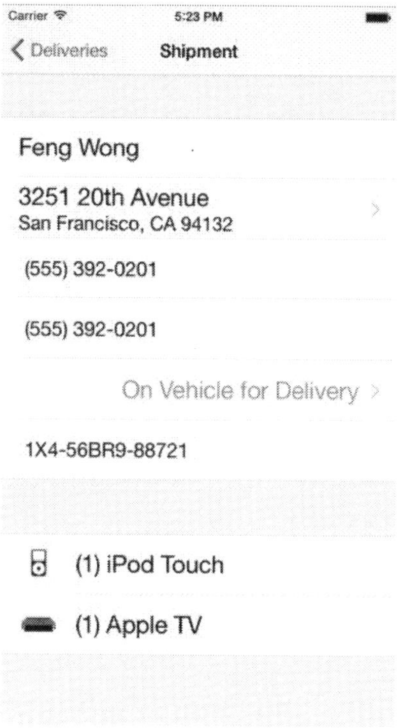

Figure 15.21 All static text is missing!

One other problem is that the name text in the first cell is no longer centered. We can also work around this problem by adding code to the same method.

1. In the **tableView:cellForRowAtIndexPath:** method of the **ShipmentViewController.swift** file, add the following highlighted code:

```
if indexPath.section == 0 {
  switch indexPath.row {
     case ShipmentSection.Name.rawValue:
        cell =
         tableView.dequeueReusableCellWithIdentifier
         ("NameCell", forIndexPath: indexPath)
        cell.textLabel?.text =
          self.shipmentEntity.name
        cell.textLabel?.textAlignment =
```

```
        NSTextAlignment.Center

    case ShipmentSection.Address.rawValue:
          cell = tableView.
            dequeueReusableCellWithIdentifier
            ("AddressCell", forIndexPath: indexPath)
          cell.textLabel?.text =
              self.shipmentEntity.address
          cell.detailTextLabel?.text =
             self.shipmentEntity.city + ", " +
             self.shipmentEntity.region + " " +
             self.shipmentEntity.postalCode

    case ShipmentSection.Phone.rawValue:
       cell = tableView.
        dequeueReusableCellWithIdentifier("PhoneCell",
        forIndexPath: indexPath) as! UITableViewCell
       cell.detailTextLabel?.text =
          self.shipmentEntity.phone
       cell.textLabel?.text = NSLocalizedString
          ("Phone",comment: "Phone number")

    case ShipmentSection.Text.rawValue:
       cell = tableView.
          dequeueReusableCellWithIdentifier("TextCell",
          forIndexPath: indexPath)
       cell.detailTextLabel?.text =
          self.shipmentEntity.text
       cell.textLabel?.text = NSLocalizedString
          ("Text",comment: "Text message number")

    case ShipmentSection.DeliveryStatus.rawValue:
         cell = tableView.
        dequeueReusableCellWithIdentifier
          ("DeliveryStatusCell", forIndexPath: indexPath)
        cell.detailTextLabel?.text =
          self.shipmentEntity.deliveryStatus.
          valueForKey("statusDescription") as? String
        cell.textLabel?.text = NSLocalizedString
          ("Status", comment: "Delivery Status")

    case ShipmentSection.ID.rawValue:
```

```
        cell = tableView.
           dequeueReusableCellWithIdentifier
          ("ShipmentIDCell", forIndexPath: indexPath)
        cell.detailTextLabel?.text =
          self.shipmentEntity.shipmentID
        cell.textLabel?.text = NSLocalizedString
           ("ID",comment: "Identification Number")
    default:
        break
        }
    }
```

2. Click Xcode's **Run** button and when the app appears in the Simulator, navigate to the **Shipment** scene.

3. Go to the Settings app and set the Dynamic Type font size to the smallest setting. Then go back to the **iDeliverMobileDynamicType** app and you should see the static text is back (Figure 15.22)! This works because the table view's **reloadData** method is automatically called when a Dynamic Type change is made.

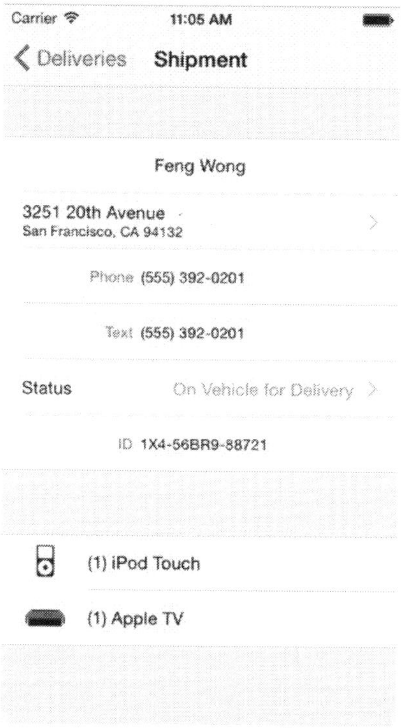

Figure 15.22 The static text is back!

Dynamic Type & Static Table View Cells

As you might guess, static table view cells do not adapt well to changes in Dynamic Type. Let's take a look at a static table view in the sample app.

1. In the **iDeliverMobileCD** project, select the Main.storyboard file in the Project Navigator and scroll to the Map Options scene (Figure 15.23).

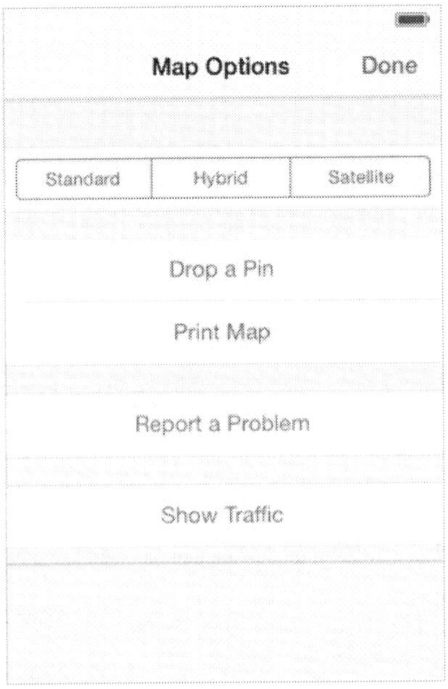

Figure 15.23 The Map Options scene.

2. Select the gray area below the **Show Traffic** button to select the table view, then go to the Attributes Inspector. Notice the **Content** is set to **Static Cells**.

3. We'll discuss the segmented control in the next section, but go ahead and change the **Font** of all labels in the other rows from a fixed font to **Body** so they will adapt to Dynamic Type changes.

4. Click Xcode's **Run** button. When the app appears in the Simulator, navigate to the **Shipment** screen and select the address to navigate to the **Location** scene. At the bottom right of the **Location** scene, tap the information button (Figure 15.24).

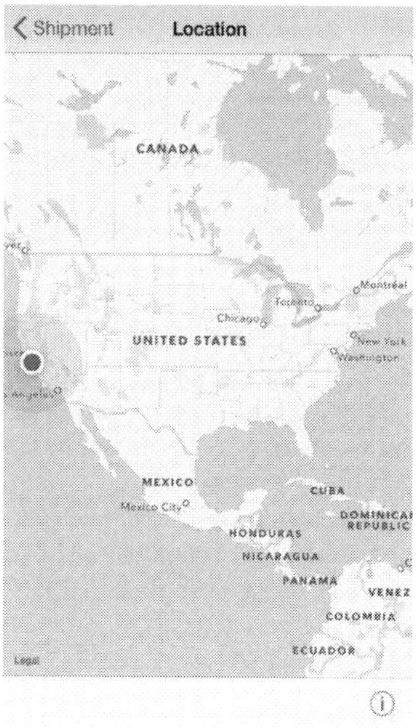

*Figure 15.24 Tap the **Location** scene's Information button.*

This displays the **Map Options** scene. Go to the **Settings** app and set the font to the largest size. Go back to the **iDeliverMobileCD** app and you can see that all the text has disappeared, except for the segmented control in the first row (Figure 15.25).

Figure 15.25 All the text in the rows is missing!

Based on what we have seen with static text in dynamic prototype rows, this isn't completely unexpected, but again, is an iOS bug.

You have two choices to get around this issue:

1. Change the table view **Content** setting to **Dynamic Prototypes** and implement the table view delegate methods in **MapOptionsTableViewController.swift**.

2. Change the **Style** of the table view cells from **Basic** to **Custom**, then add a single label to each cell.

We'll leave this as an exercise for the end of this chapter.

Dynamic Type and Special Controls

Not all controls have a simple **font** property like the label and text controls. A great example of this is the segmented control (Figure 15.26).

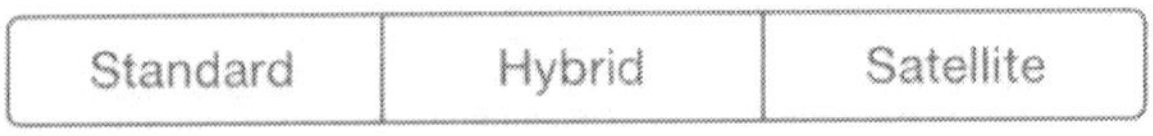

Figure 15.26 The segmented control.

To set the font on a segmented control, you need to call its **setTitleTextAttributes** method, passing a dictionary of text attributes.

To accommodate these more complex controls, the Data Manager class has a **registerControl:font:withClosure:** method that allows a control to pass a closure which can be used to execute the necessary code for setting the font dynamically.

The **mmDynamicTypeExtensions** class has an extension of the **UISegmentedControl** class that calls this method:

```
extension UISegmentedControl: DynamicTypeChangeHandler {

@IBInspectable varMa DynamicType: Bool {

   get {
      return DynamicTypeManager.sharedInstance.
         isControlRegistered(self)
   }
```

```
    set {

    var attributes = self.titleTextAttributesForState
       (UIControlState.Normal)

    DynamicTypeManager.
       sharedInstance.registerControl(self, font:
       attributes[NSFontAttributeName] as! UIFont) {
       (fontStyle) -> () in

       let attributes = [NSFontAttributeName:
          UIFont.preferredFontForTextStyle(fontStyle)]

        self.setTitleTextAttributes(attributes,
          forState: UIControlState.Normal)
        }
      }
   }
}
```

Since you can't set the font of the segmented control in the Attributes Inspector, you need to add code to the **viewDidLoad** method of the view controller that contains the segmented control that sets its font to the desired style and sets the **DynamicType** property to **true**. For example:

```
var attributes = [NSFontAttributeName:
    UIFont.preferredFontForTextStyle
    (UIFontTextStyleBody)]

self.segmentedControl.setTitleTextAttributes
 (attributes, forState: UIControlState.Normal)

self.segmentedControl.DynamicType = true
```

If you have custom controls that have similar needs for setting fonts, you can create your own extension that uses this method.

Problems with UISegmentedControl

In the current version of iOS, **UISegmentedControl** changes the font size of the text within each segment in response to Dynamic Type changes. However, the *size* of the control does not change accordingly.

I'm hoping Apple fixes this soon, but in the interim, there are a few relatively easy workarounds you can use.

1. Set the segmented control's font to one of the smaller font styles such as **UIFontTextStyleSubheadline**.

2. If you have the segmented control in a container such as a table view cell, add a hidden label to the cell and use it to adjust the cell size in response to Dynamic Type changes. This allows the segmented control size to grow proportionately.

Summary

- Dynamic Type allows users to specify their preferred font size (for apps that support Dynamic Type) in the Settings app.
- Text styles are similar to styles in a word processing app. They allow you to specify the relative size and weight of the font used for each text element in your app.
- To support Dynamic Type, you need to change hard- coded fonts in your app to *text styles*.
- The ability to automatically respond to changes in Dynamic Type size is unique to table views with:

    1. Table view Content set to Dynamic Prototype
    2. Cells using one of the built-in styles.

- Setting a label's **Lines** attribute to zero (**0**) causes the text to wrap to the next line.

Dynamic Row Heights

- When implementing Dynamic Type in a table view, its row height must be dynamic to accommodate changes in font size. Apple provides three strategies to achieve this:

    1. Set the table view's **rowHeight** property. The advantage of using the **rowHeight** property is speed. It provides the best scrolling performance because no calculations need to be performed on the fly while the user is scrolling.

       The downside is that you have to perform your own calculations to determine row height, and all rows must be the same height.

    2. Use the **tableView:heightForRowAtIndexPath:** delegate method. There is one big disadvantage to this approach. The height of all rows is requested up front, even before the rows have been created. If you have tens of thousands of rows, this can be a real performance drag.

3. Self-sizing cells. Rather than setting the **rowHeight** property, you either set the table view's **estimatedRowHeight** property or use the **tableView:estimatedHeightForRowAtIndexPath** delegate method.

- There are two ways a cell can communicate the height it needs to be:

  1. Auto Layout

  2. Manual sizing code

  If you have implemented constraints on your cell, the Auto Layout engine specifies the cell height.

  If you haven't implemented Auto Layout constraints, the table view calls the **sizeThatFits** method on your cell. You can return a cell height from this method based on your own calculations—the cell width is already calculated for you.

- To have iOS automatically resize table view cells for you, add code to the **viewDidLoad** method that sets the table view's estimatedRowHeight and rowHeight properties. For example:

```
override func viewDidLoad() {
   super.viewDidLoad()
   self.tableView.estimatedRowHeight = 60
   self.tableView.rowHeight =
      UITableViewAutomaticDimension
}
```

Dynamic Type Change and Custom Cells

- Here are a few things that make the out-of-the box model for handling Dynamic Type change undesirable:

  - You have to set the font for all controls twice. Once in the Attributes Inspector and a second time in code.

  - When working with static table view cells, you must create outlets for all text-based controls, even if you don't need them for any other purpose.

  - You have to add this same code to all view controllers in your app.

- Here are the benefits of using the Dynamic Type Manager found in this book's sample code:

  - It uses extensions rather than subclasses, which allows you to use out-of-the-box **UIKit** controls.

  - When you add the **mmDynamicTypeExtensions** code file to your project, it "just works".

  - There is no need to create outlets for UI controls. You simply set a property in the Attribute Inspector.

  - This architecture is loosely coupled. The UI controls provide information about themselves to the Dynamic Type Manager. This means you can register your own custom controls (or new controls that Apple releases in the future) without changing the Dynamic Type Manager.

  - Since you don't need to use this feature for prototype table view cells that are set to one of the default styles, this "opt in" model, lets you choose which controls you want to register with the Dynamic Type Manager.

Dynamic Type and Static Text

- iOS currently has a problem handling Dynamic Type changes on static text, causing the text to disappear and/or lose its formatting. You have two choices to get around this issue:

  1. Change the table view **Content** setting to **Dynamic Prototypes** and implement the table view delegate methods in the view controller.

  2. Create custom cells that handle changes through Auto Layout.

UISegmentedControl

- In the current version of iOS, **UISegmentedControl** changes the font size of the text within each segment in response to Dynamic Type changes. However, the *size* of the control does not change accordingly.

  There are a few relatively easy workarounds:

1. Set the segmented control's font to one of the smaller font styles such as **UIFontTextStyleSubheadline**.

2. If you have the segmented control in a container such as a table view cell, add a hidden label to the cell and use it to adjust the cell size in response to Dynamic Type changes. This allows the segmented control size to grow proportionately.

Chapter 16: Adopting In-App Purchases

One of the best ways to monetize your app is to offer in-app purchases (IAP). This chapter provides all the information you need to provide a great in-app purchase experience for your users and provides an In-App Purchase Manager class to make the whole process easier.

Sections in This Chapter

8. *User Story: Purchasing Products*
9. *Purchasing Products—Behind the Scenes*
10. *Processing Transactions*
11. *Validating Receipts*
12. *User Story: Restoring In-App Purchases*
13. *Summary*

Types of In-App Purchases

In-app purchases must fall into one of the following categories defined by Apple:

- **Consumables** - Purchases that are used up over a period of time such as supplies in a game.

- **Non-consumables** - Purchases that only need to be bought once and do not expire, such as extra levels in a game, color themes, books and magazine issues.

- **Auto-Renewable Subscriptions** - Purchases that allow the user to access content for a set duration of time, such as delivery of magazine issues, subscriptions to audio or video feeds, and dating services.

- **Free Subscriptions** - An extension of Auto-Renewable subscriptions that permit free subscription content to be delivered to Newsstand-enabled apps.

- **Non-Renewing Subscriptions** - Allows the sale of services for a limited time, such as a one month subscription to an online database.

For more information on these categories, check out Apple's *Getting Started with In-App Purchases on iOS and OS X.*

Providing In-App Purchase Content

There are three ways you can provide in-app purchase content to your users:

1. Bundle the content in your app and make it available to the user after it has been purchased.

2. Host the content on your own servers and download it when it is purchased by the user.

3. Host the content on Apple's servers and download it when it is purchased by the user. Apple offers this service for free!

In this chapter you will see an example of the first option —bundling the content in an app.

In-App Purchase User Stories

A user story is an agile software development tool that captures a software feature from an end-user's perspective. Here are the three main user stories you need to consider when adding in-app purchases to your iOS apps:

- Users can view products that can be purchased.
- Users can purchase products.
- Users can restore purchases.

In this chapter you will see how to implement each of these user stories in a real-world iOS app.

User Story: Viewing Products That Can Be Purchased

Apple provides all of the behind-the-scenes "plumbing" classes you need to implement a store in your app by means of the **StoreKit** framework. However, you need to design your own user interface where users can view and select items to be purchased.

The **TicTacToe** project included in this book's sample code contains a store user interface that allows the user to view, purchase, and restore in-app purchases. The app includes several free color themes the user can choose to change the color of the Tic-Tac-Toe board and the X's and O's. It also offers additional color themes the user can purchase. This game doesn't have a Tic-Tac-Toe engine, but simply lets two people play each other.

Let's take a quick look at the project.

1. Open the **TicTacToe** sample project in Xcode.
2. Expand the **Frameworks** node in the Project Navigator to see **StoreKit.framework** is included in the project (Figure 16.1).

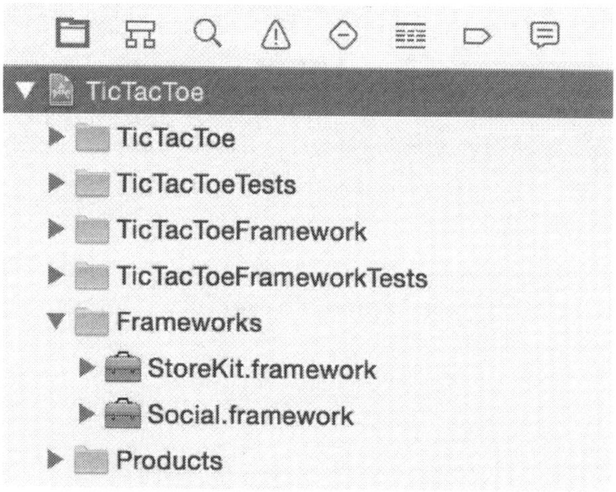

*Figure 16.1 The **StoreKit** framework*

3. In the Project Navigator, there are two main projects other than the unit tests projects—**TicTacToe** and **TicTacToeFramework**. The **TicTacToe** project contains the user interface classes for the app. Select **Main. storyboard** and you can see the various scenes that comprise the app including the two scenes in Figure 16.2 that are used to display items the user can purchase.

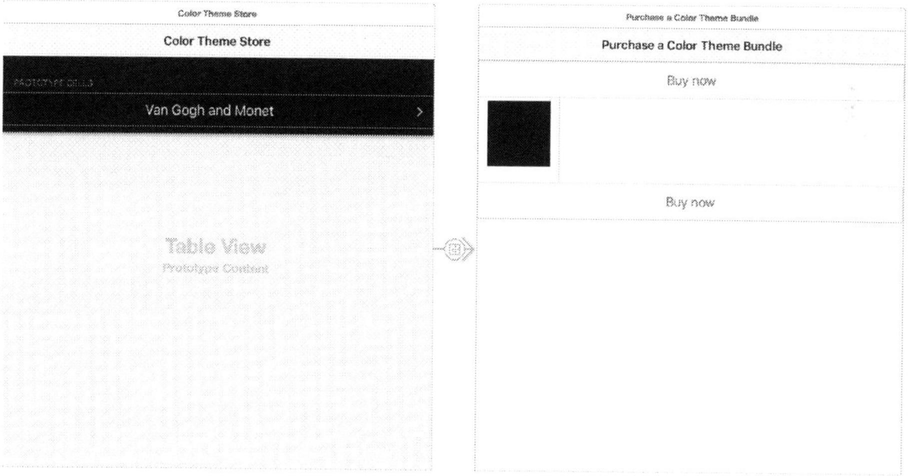

*Figure 16.2 **The TicTacToe** app store scences*

4. The **TicTacToeFramework** project contains all the core logic business classes for the app. The main class to note in this project is **InAppPurchaseManager**. I have created this class to make it easier to integrate in-app purchase functionality in your iOS apps.

After you learn about the in-app purchase setup steps, you will run the sample app so you can see the store user interface at run time.

Setting Up Your App

Apple provides a testing environment, called the *sandbox*, that allows you to test in-app purchases without incurring any charges. There are several steps you need to take to set up your app environment:

1. Create a store user interface in your app.
2. Specify a unique app ID.
3. Generate a provisioning file.
4. Submit your app metadata in iTunes Connect.
5. Add one or more products for in-app purchase.
6. Create a sandbox tester account.
7. Set the list of product IDs in your app.

To help walk you through these steps, we are going to use the **TicTacToe** project included with this book's sample code. *Note that you must have a paid iOS developer account in order to follow these steps!*

Specifying a Unique App ID

Follow these steps to specify a unique app id.

1. Open the **TicTacToe** project in Xcode.
2. Select the first node in the Project Navigator to display the Project Editor.
3. In the panel on the left in the Project Editor, under Targets, select **TicTacToe**. In the panel on the right, make sure the **General** tab is selected and you should see the **Bundle Identifier** is set to **com.MyCompany.TicTacToe** (Figure 16.3). Change the **MyCompany** portion of the bundle ID to your company name (or some other unique name).

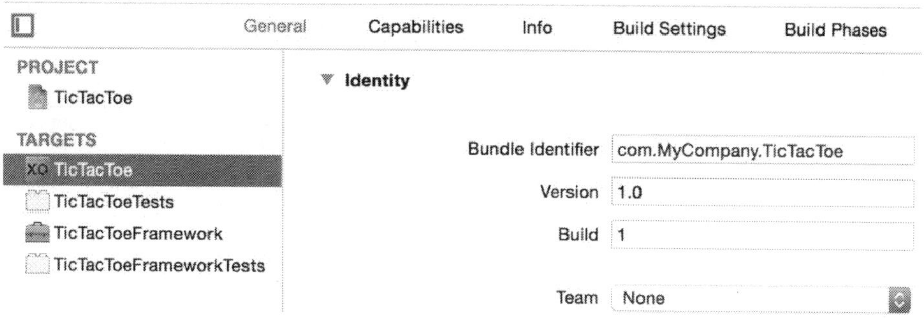

*Figure 16.3 Set the **Bundle Identifier.***

4. Select the **TicTacToeFramework** target and change the **MyCompany** portion of the Bundle Identifier to the same value you set in the previous step.

Generate a Provisioning File

1. Reselect the **TicTacToe** target. In the **Team** combo box, select the development team you want to use to generate provisioning files for the project.

2. You should see a **No matching provisioning files found** warning. Click the **Fix Issue** button (Figure 16.4). A **Fixing Code Signing Issues** dialog should pop up for a few seconds and then the warning should go away.

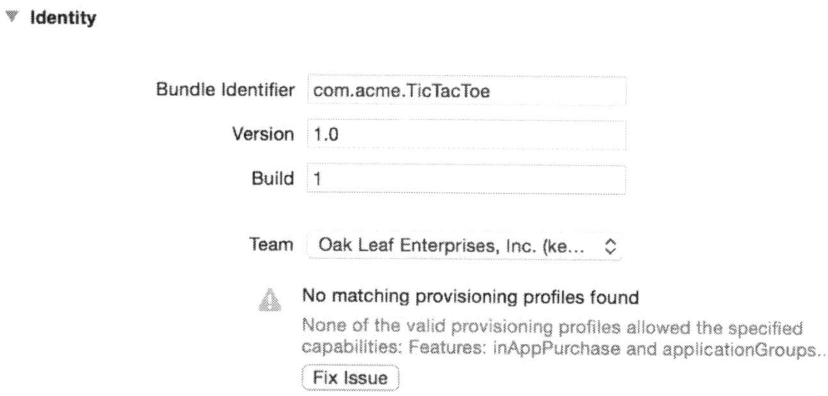

*Figure 16.4 Click the **Fix Issue** button.*

3. Select the **Capabilities** tab in the Project Editor. Notice the **In-App Purchase** capability is set to **On** (Figure 16.5). If you any provisioning errors with an associated **Fix Issue** button, let Xcode fix the issue.

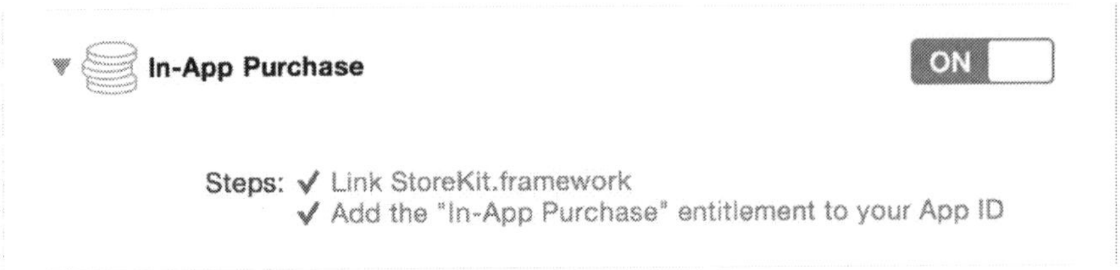

*Figure 16.5 The **In-App Purchase** capability is turned on.*

4. To see your app settings in the iOS Dev Center, in your web browser, navigate to this link:

   https://developer.apple.com/account/overview.action.

   Under iOS Apps, select **Identifiers**.

5. In the panel on the left under **Identifiers**, select **App IDs** and you should see your app ID in the panel on the right. Click on the app ID and you should that **In- App Purchase** is enabled.

Add the App to the App Store

Now you're ready to add the app to the App Store.

1. Log into iTunes Connect at https://itunesconnect.apple.com.

2. Select the **My Apps** option, click the plus (+) button in the **My Apps** page and select **New iOS App**.

3. In the New iOS App dialog (Figure 16.6), enter the following information:

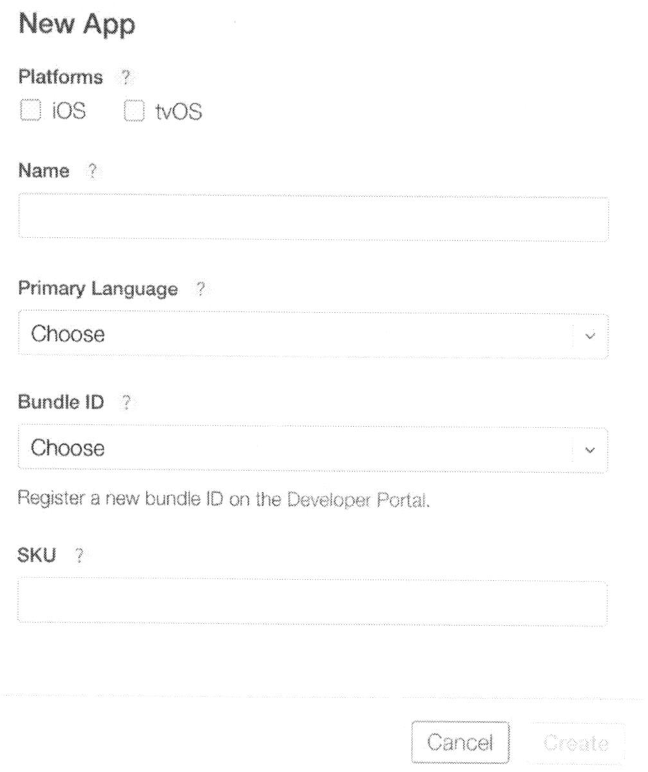

Figure 16.6 The New iOS App dialog

- **Platforms:** *iOS*
- **Name:** *My Company Tic Tac Toe* (replace *My Company* with your own company name)
- **Primary Language:** *English*
- **Bundle ID:** Select your bundle id from the list
- **SKU:** This can be any unique number, but I recommend using the bundle ID you have specified for the app.

4. Click the **Create** button to add the app.

Stay in iTunes Connect to complete the steps outlined in the next section.

Adding In-App Purchases

Now you need to add an in-app purchase for the app.

1. Click the **Features** link at the top of the page. This takes you to the In-App Purchases page where you will see an empty page since you have not yet added any In-App purchases.

2. Click the **Plus (+)** button.

3. In the **Select Type** page, select **Non-Consumable**.

4. Under **In-App Purchase Summary** (Figure 16.7), enter the following information:

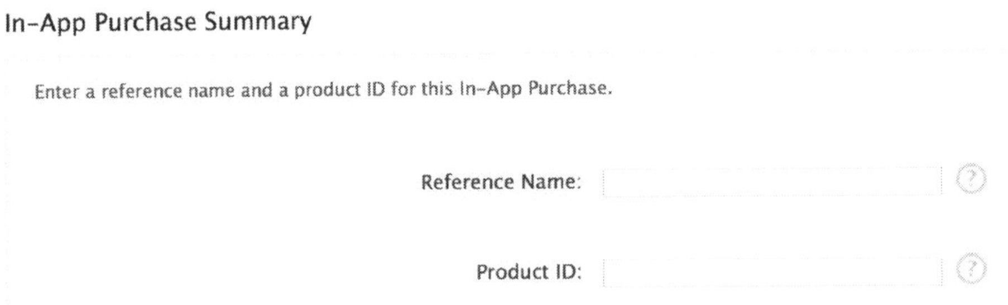

Figure 16.7 The In-App Purchase Summary

   - **Reference Name**: *Tic-Tac-Toe Artists Color Theme*

   - **Product ID:** *com.MyCompany.ArtistsTheme* (replace **MyCompany** with the company you have specified in the bundle ID).

5. Under **Pricing and Availability** (Figure 16.8), make sure **Cleared for Sale** is set to **Yes**, and set the **Price Tier** to **Tier 1**.

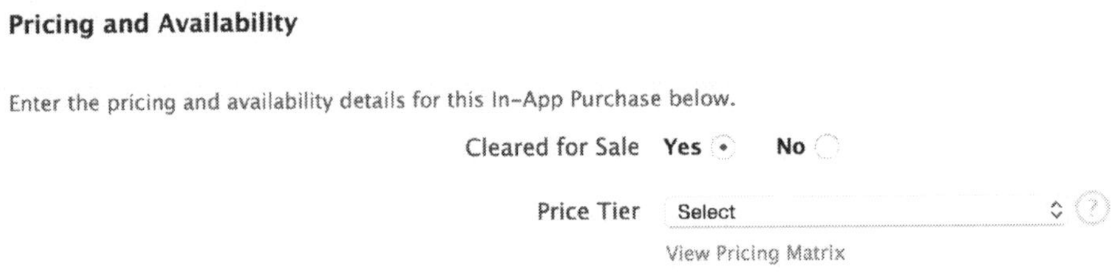

Figure 16.8 Pricing and Availability

6. Scroll down to the **In-App Purchase Details** section (Figure 16.9) and under **Language**, click the **Add Language** button.

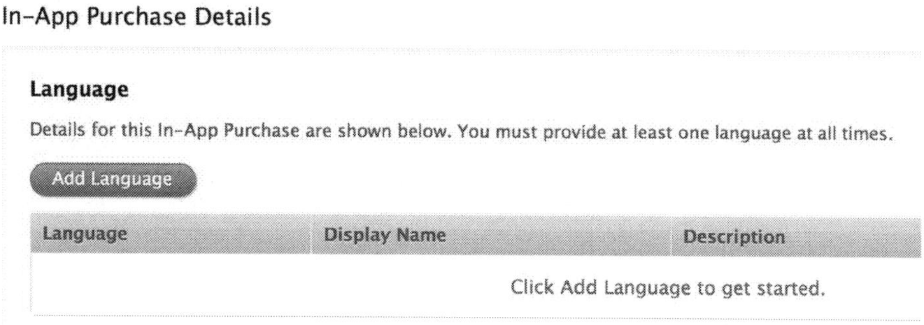

Figure 16.9 In-App Purchase Details

7. In the Add Language dialog (Figure 16.10), set the following values:

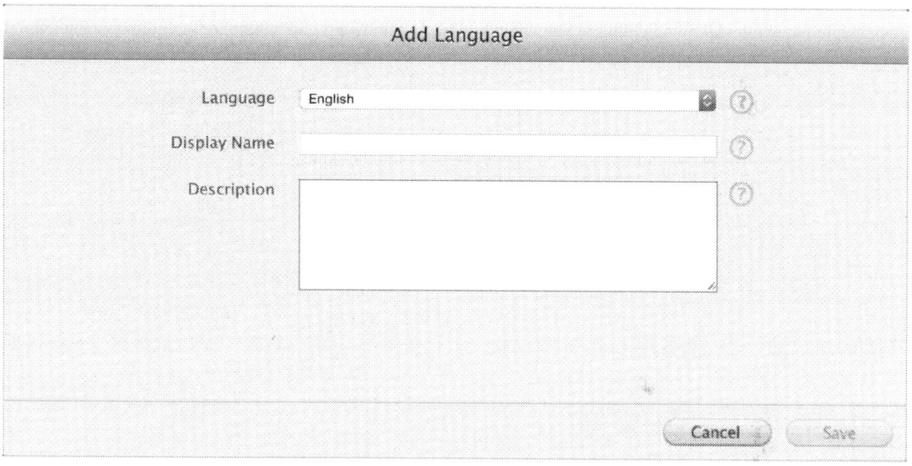

Figure 16.10 The Add Language dialog

- **Language**: *English*
- **Display Name**: *Van Gogh & Monet Colors*
- **Description**: *Adds 19 color themes to the game.*

8. Click the **Save** button.

9. Under the section **Screenshot for Review** (Figure 16.11), click the **Choose File** button. Navigate to the folder where you have stored this book's sample code and under the **TicTacToe** subfolder, select the **ArtistsTheme.png** file and click **Choose**.

Figure 16.11 Screenshot for Review

10. To save the in-app purchase, click the **Save** button. This takes you back to the In-App Purchases page.

11. Click the **App Store** link at the top of the screen, and then click the **1.0 Prepare for Submission** link (Figure 16.12). Scroll down to the **In-App Purchases** section and click the plus (+) button.

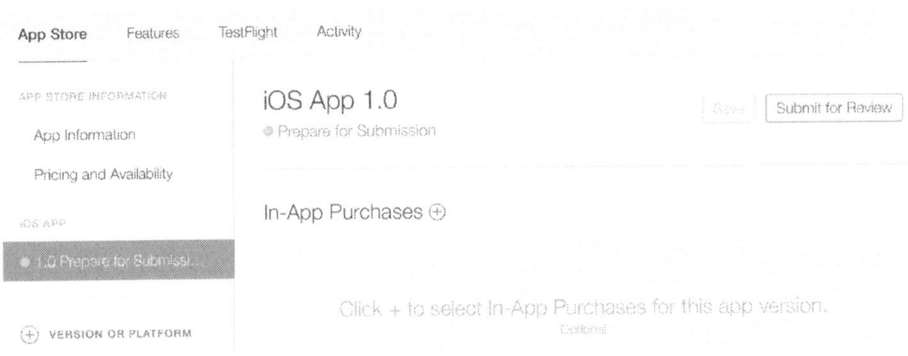

Figure 16.12 The In-App Purchases section

12. In the **Add In-App Purchases** dialog (Figure 16.13), select the check box to the left of the in-app purchase you just created and click the **Done** button.

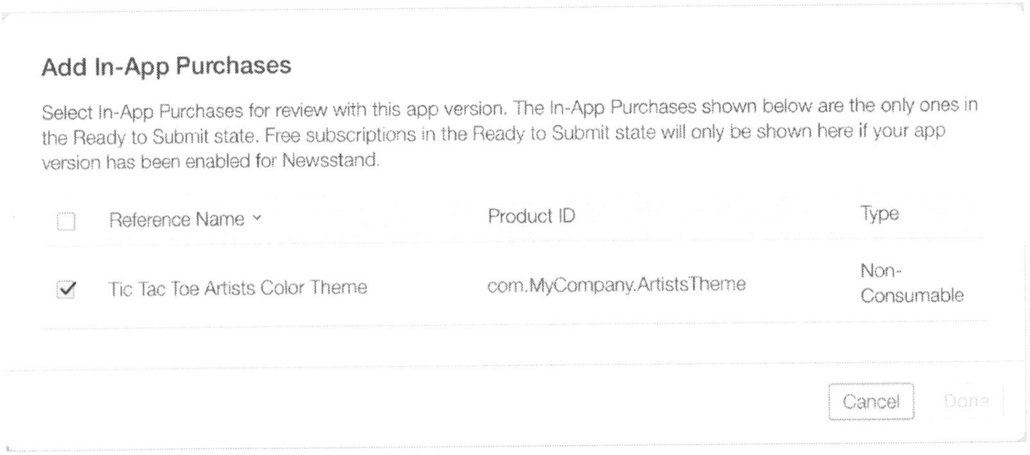

Figure 16.13 Add In-App Purchases

You now have an app registered with iTunes Connect that contains a single in-app purchase product.

Creating a Sandbox Tester Account

To create a test user account, you must have iTunes Connect **Admin** or **Technical** permissions.

Since you can't edit sandbox tester accounts once they have been created, Apple recommends that you plan ahead and make a spreadsheet containing your test user account information. Here is the information you need to enter for each tester:

- First Name
- Last Name
- Email address (this address can't be associated with any existing Apple account)
- Password
- Secret question and answer
- Date of birth
- Store territory

To create a new sandbox tester:

1. Sign in to iTunes Connect: https://itunesconnect.apple.com.
2. Click **Users and Roles**.
3. At the top of the **Users and Roles** page (Figure 16.14), click **Sandbox Testers**. If you don't see this option, it means you don't have the necessary permissions.

Figure 16.14 Users and Roles

4. Click the plus (+) button to add a new sandbox tester (Figure 16.15).

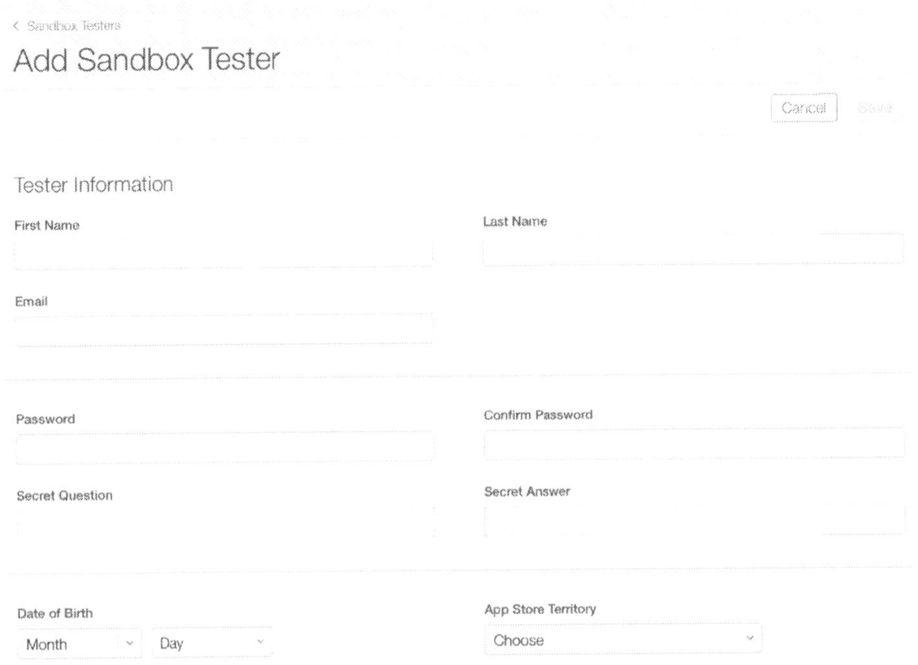

Figure 16.15 Add a new sandbox tester.

5. Enter information for the tester and click **Save**.

Setting the Product ID's In the App

You can have your app retrieve a list of product IDs from your server or you can read them from a file in your app bundle. The Tic-Tac-Toe app stores product identifiers in a SQLite database using Core Data. We need to update these product IDs to match the bundle identifier you have specified.

1. Launch the FireFox browser (if you haven't installed the FireFox browser and SQLite Manager tool, check out the instructions in *Chapter 12: Working with Core Data* under the section Firefox and the SQLite Manager) and then launch the SQLite Manager tool by selecting **Tools | SQLite Manager** from the Firefox menu.

2. Click the **Connect Database** toolbar button (the folder with the arrow) at the top of the SQLite window. Navigate to the folder where the Tic-Tac-Toe project is stored, expand the **TicTacToe** subfolder, select the

TicTacToe.sqlite file and click the **Open** button.

3. In the panel on the left side of the SQLite window, select the **ZTHEMEBUNDLEENTITY** table.

4. On the right side of the window, double-click the second item in the list to display the data editor (Figure 16.16). Change the **ZTHEMEBUNDLEID** field to the product identifier you specified for the in-app purchase you created (change **MyCompany** to your company name). Click **OK** to save changes.

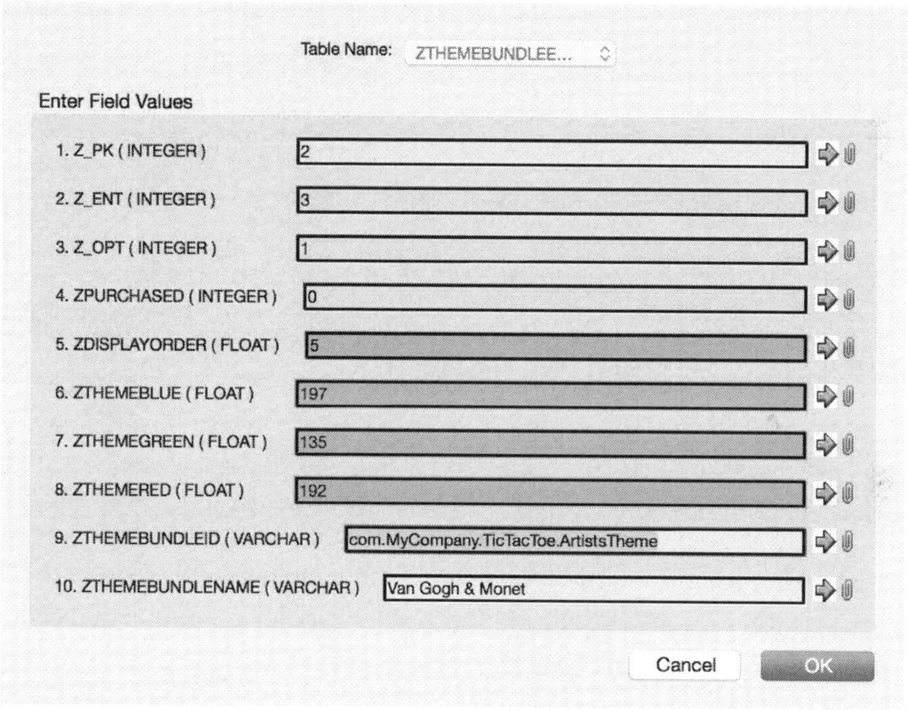

Figure 16.16 The SQLite Manager data editor

5. In the panel on the left side of the SQLite window, select the **ZTHEMEENTITY** table.

6. At the top-right of the window, click the **Execute SQL** button. In the **Enter SQL** box, enter the following command, changing the *first* occurrence of **com.MyCompany.TicTacToe.ArtistsTheme** to the in-app purchase product identifier you specified:

```
UPDATE ZTHEMEENTITY SET ZTHEMEBUNDLEID =
```

```
'com.MyCompany.TicTacToe.ArtistsTheme'
WHERE ZTHEMEBUNDLEID =
'com.MyCompany.TicTacToe.ArtistsTheme'
```

For example, the name of the company has been changed to **acme** in Figure 16.17.

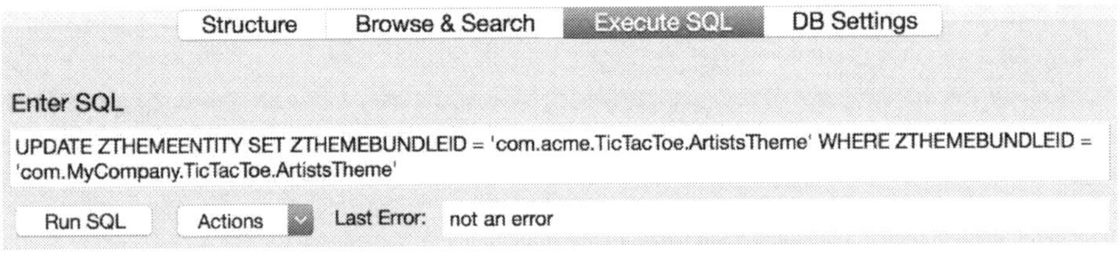

Figure 16.17 Enter the SQL command

7. Click the **Run SQL** button. This SQL code replaces all occurrences of MyCompany for ArtistsTheme in the **ZTHEMEENTITY** table with your custom identifier.

8. Close the SQLite Manager app to save changes to the database.

Displaying In-App Purchases

Now you're ready to run the sample **Tic-Tac-Toe** app to see how displaying in-app purchases works at run time. Afterwards, we'll take a close look at the code that makes it happen.

1. If you have already run the sample app before changing the SQLite database, remove the sample app from your iOS device so it installs with a new copy of the database.

2. Connect your iOS device to your development machine.

3. Now you need to sign in as the sandbox user. On your iOS device, go to the Settings app and select **iTunes & App Store**. Tap your Apple ID and then tap **Sign Out**. Now sign back in using the credentials you set up for your in-app purchase sandbox user.

4. In the Scheme control at the top left of the Xcode window, select your iOS device from the list of devices.

5. Click Xcode's **Run** button. When the app appears in the device, you will

see a Tic-Tac-Toe board. By default, the Tic-Tac-Toe app displays a blue playing board, with blue X's and white O's (Figure 16.18).

Figure 16.18 The default Tic-Tac-Toe color scheme

6. Tap the **Settings** button (the gear) at the top-right side of the scene. You will see the three options shown in Figure 16.19.

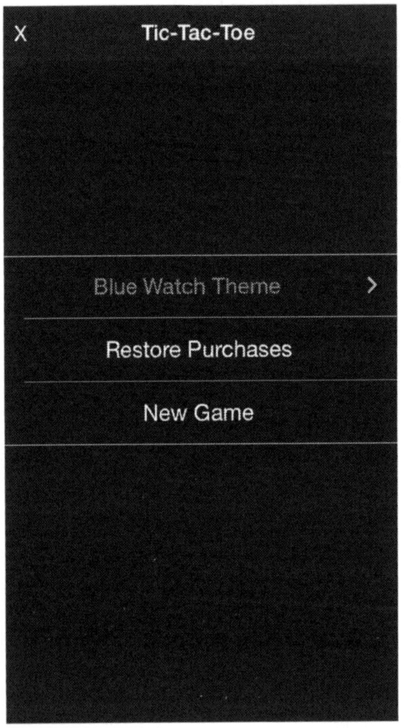

Figure 16.19 The Tic-Tac-Toe Settings Scene

Click the **Blue Watch Theme** option. This displays the **Select a Color Theme** scene (Figure 16.20) where the user can select from several free color themes.

Figure 16.20 The Tic-Tac-Toe Color Theme scene

7. Tap the **More Color Themes...** button. This takes you to the Color Theme Store scene where you should see the **Van Gogh and Monet Color Themes** in-app purchase you have set up on iTunes Connect. In a real app, you would create many color themes the user can choose from.

   Note: If you don't see the in-app purchase item, check out debugging steps in the next section.

8. Tap the **Van Gogh and Monet Color Themes** item. This takes you to a screen where you can see the themes that are part of this set (Figure 16.21).

Figure 16.21 Van Gogh and Monet color themes

9. Click Xcode's **Stop** button.

The Tic-Tac-Toe app demonstrates best practices for presenting in-app purchases to the user. Rather than popping up irritating dialogs that prompt the user to make a purchase, the content is part of the natural flow of the app.

When the user changes the color theme, they see free themes as well as a prompt that allows them to explore additional themes they can purchase.

For more information, I highly recommend Apple's WWDC video *Designing a Great In-App Purchase Experience*: https://developer.apple.com/videos/wwdc/2014/#218.

Debugging Invalid Product Identifiers

If you didn't see the in-app purchase in the previous section, there are several things you can check. I discovered this handy list online from the folks @gamedonia (http://blog.gamedonia.com/solve-invalid-product-ids#3).

- Have you enabled In-App Purchases for your App ID?
- Have you selected **Cleared for Sale** for your in-app purchase in iTunes Connect?
- Does your project's .plist Bundle ID match your App ID?
- Have you generated and installed a new provisioning profile for the new App ID?
- Have you configured your project to code sign using this new provisioning file?
- Are you using the full product ID when making an SKProductRequest?
- Have you waited several hours since adding your product to iTunes Connect?
- Have you tried deleting the app from your device and reinstalling?
- Is your device jailbroken? If so, you need to revert the jailbreak for IAP to work.
- Are you logged out from your real iTunes account?
- Are you on an iOS device (viewing purchases works in the Simulator, but purchasing and restoring purchases does not)?
- Have you tried restarting the device?

Displaying In-App Purchases— Behind the Scenes

Before displaying a list of products, your app must first send a list of product identifiers to the App Store to be validated. You do this to ensure the user will be able to make the purchase when it's time.

The App Store responds by sending back two lists:

- A list of valid products
- A list of invalid product identifiers

After receiving the response from the App Store, you should only display the list of valid products. Figure 16.22 shows a high-level overview of this process.

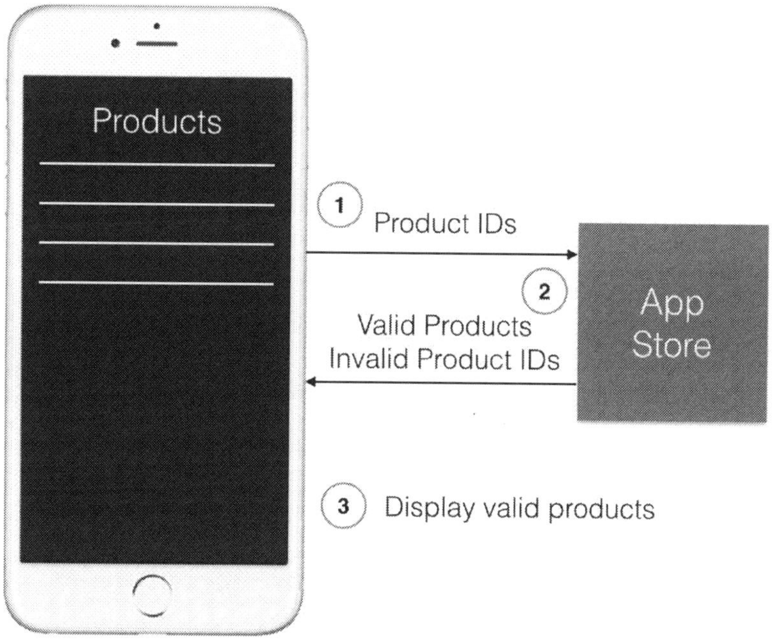

Figure 16.22 Displaying in-app purchases

There is another other reason you retrieve a list of valid products from the App Store before displaying them to the user. When the App Store returns a list of valid products, it includes the price of each product in the user's local currency as well as a product name and description in the user's language. You use this data to display a locale-specific list of products to the user.

Now let's take a more detailed look at the process of displaying in-app purchases to the user. Figure 16.23 contains a sequence diagram that shows the object interactions that occur within the app to display the list of in-app purchases to the user.

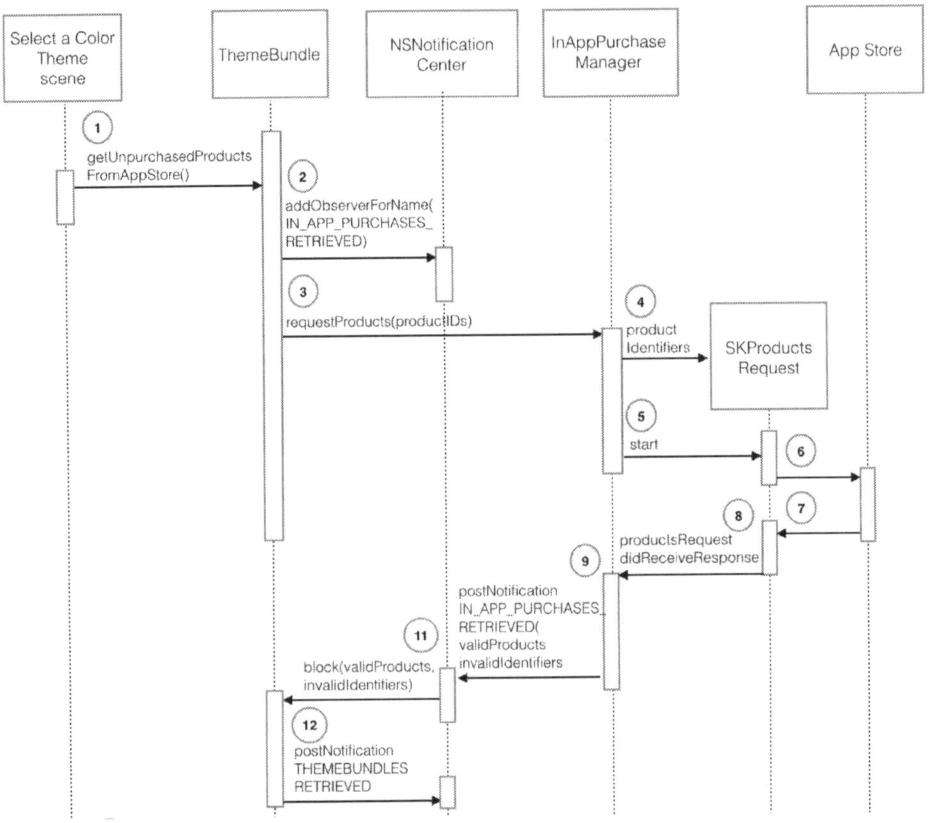

Figure 16.23 Displaying un-purchased products

Here's the breakdown:

1. The **ColorThemeCollectionViewController** calls the **getUnpurchasedProductsFromAppStore** method on the **ThemeBundle** object.

2. The **ThemeBundle** object registers for notification of the **IN_APP_PURCHASES_RETRIEVED.**

3. The **ThemeBundle** object next calls **requestProducts** on the **InAppPurchaseManager**, passing a list of product identifiers that it stores locally in Core Data.

4. The **InAppPurchaseManager** creates an **SKProductsRequests** object, passing the product identifiers in the constructor.

5. The **InAppPurchaseManager** calls **start** on the **SKProductsRequest** object.

6. The **SKProductsRequest** object sends a request to the **App Store** to validate the product identifiers

7. The **App Store** passes back a list of invalid product identifiers and a list of valid products to the **SKProductsRequest** object.

8. The **SKProductsRequest** object passes the list of invalid product identifiers and valid products in its call to the **productsRequest:didReceiveResponse** method on the **InAppPurchaseManager** object.

9. The **InAppPurchaseManager** posts the **IN_APP_PURCHASES_RETRIEVED** notification.

10. **NSNotificationCenter** executes the block that was registered by the **ThemeBundle** object, passing the list of valid products and invalid product identifiers to the block.

11. The code in the **ThemeBundle** object's block processes the valid products and invalid product identifiers, producing an array of **ThemeBundleEntity** objects that have been validated by the App Store.

12. It then posts the **THEMEBUNDLES_RETRIEVED** notification. At this point, if there are any observers of this notification, they can receive the list of approved products and display them to the user.

Figure 16.24 outlines how the display of color themes takes place in the Tic-Tac-Toe app.

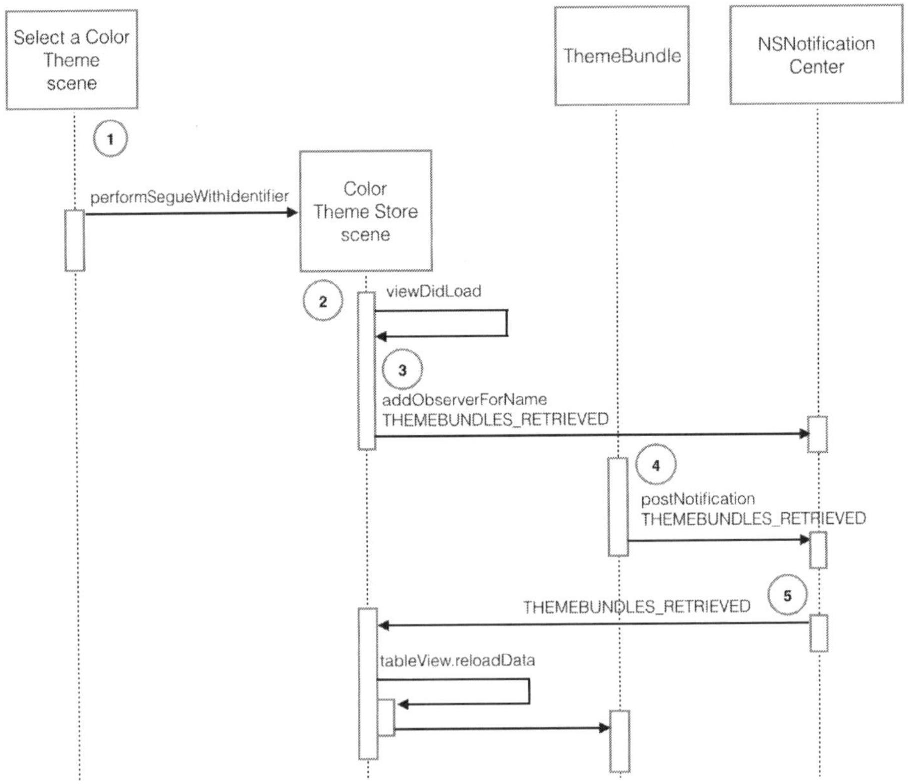

Figure 16.24 Displaying approved products.

1. The **Select a Color Theme** scene launches the **Color Theme Store** scene. Remember, the **Select a Color Theme** scene initiates the request for un-purchased products in its **viewDidLoad** method. This gives the app time to retrieve the products before the user navigates to the **Select a Color Theme** scene.

2. The **Color Theme Store** scene's view controller's **viewDidLoad** method automatically executes. If the **ThemeBundle** object has finished retrieving products, the **Color Theme Store** view controller's table view uses the **ThemeBundle** object as its data source, and automatically displays the approved products.

3. If the **ThemeBundle** object hasn't finished retrieving products, the **Color Theme Store** view controller registers for the **THEMEBUNDLES_RETRIEVED** notification.

4. When the **ThemeBundle** object retrieves approved products, it posts the **THEMEBUNDLES_RETRIEVED** notification.

5. The **Color Theme Store** view controller receives the **THEMEBUNDLES_RETRIEVED** notification and calls **reloadData** on its table view, which loads and displays the approved products.

User Story: Purchasing Products

Let's run the sample app to see how the user can make an in-app purchase.

1. Connect your iOS device to your development machine and run the **TicTacToe** app from Xcode on your device.

2. Tap the Settings button in the navigation bar, and tap **More Color Themes...** in the **Select a Color Theme** scene.

3. In the **Color Theme Store** scene, tap **Van Gogh and Monet Color Themes**.

4. At the top of the scene, tap **Buy now: $0.99** (*you will not actually be charged*; your localized price is displayed here). If this is the first time the sandbox Apple ID has been used to make a simulated purchase, you will be prompted to review your account information. Otherwise, this displays the confirmation dialog (Figure 16.25).

Figure 16.25 The purchase confirmation dialog

5. Tap the **Buy** button. In the background, you can see the activity indicator spinning. After several seconds you should see the **Thank You** dialog (Figure 16.26). Tap **OK** to close the dialog.

Figure 16.26 The purchase was successful!

Purchasing Products— Behind the Scenes

There is a lot going on behind the scenes when a user makes an in-app purchase. Let's take a look at the code that gets the whole process started.

Select **AppDelegate.swift** in the Project Navigator. Notice the following code at the bottom of **application:didFinishLaunchingWithOptions:**

```
// Begin observing StoreKit transactions
InAppPurchaseManager.sharedInstance.observeTransactions()
```

This code executes when your app is first launched. It registers the **InAppPurchaseManager** as an observer for StoreKit transactions so it is notified when transaction comes in from the App Store.

Figure 16.27 contains a sequence diagram that shows the object interactions that occur within the app during the actual purchase. Here's the breakdown:

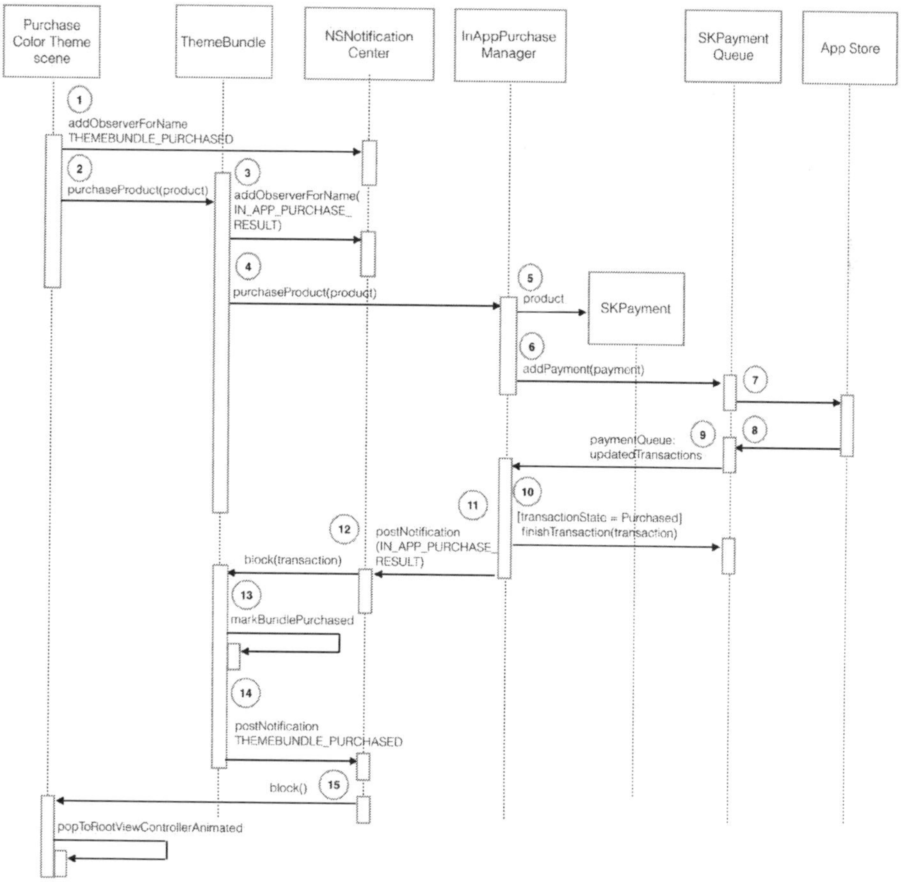

Figure 16.27 Purchasing a product

1. The **Purchase Color Theme** view controller registers for the **THEMEBUNDLE_PURCHASED** notification.

2. The view controller next makes a call to the **ThemeBundle** object's **purchaseProduct** method, passing the product to be purchased.

3. The **ThemeBundle** object registers for the **IN_APP_PURCHASE_RESULT** notification.

4. The ThemeBundle object calls the **purchaseProduct** method on the **InAppPurchaseManager**, passing the product to be purchased.

5. The **InAppPurchaseManager** creates an **SKPayment** object, passing a reference to the product to be purchased.

6. The **InAppPurchaseManager** calls the **addPayment** method of **SKPaymentQueue**, passing the **SKPayment** object.

7. The **SKPaymentQueue** object calls out to the **App Store** to make the payment.

8. The **App Store** responds to the **SKPaymentQueue** request.

9. The **SKPaymentQueue** calls the **paymentQueue:updatedTransactions:** method of the **InAppPurchaseManager**, passing one or more transaction objects.

10. If a transaction object's state is **Purchased**, the **InAppPurchaseManager** calls **finishTransaction** on **SKPaymentQueue**. This lets the App Store know that the transaction has been handled.

11. The **InAppPurchaseManager** posts the **IN_APP_PURCHASE_RESULT** notification.

12. This calls the block on the **ThemeBundle** object (which has registered for this notification) passing the transaction.

13. The **ThemeBundle** calls its **markBundlePurchased** method, marking the color theme bundle as purchased.

14. The **ThemeBundle** object posts the **THEMEBUNDLE_PURCHASED** notification.

15. This calls the block on the **Purchase Color Theme** view controller (which registered for this notification). The view controller then calls **popToRootViewControllerAnimated** on itself.

Processing Transactions

The sequence diagram in Figure 16.27 shows what happens when an in-app purchase transaction is successful. Let's take a closer look at the code associated with step 10 of the diagram to find out more about how transactions are processed.

Select the **InAppPurchaseManager.swift** file in the Project Navigator, and scroll down to the **paymentQueue:updatedTransactions:** method. This method is part of the **SKPaymentTransactionObserver** protocol and is called automatically whenever there is a new transaction to be processed:

```
public func paymentQueue(queue: SKPaymentQueue!,
updatedTransactions transactions: [AnyObject]!) {

   for transaction in transactions as!
   [SKPaymentTransaction]! {

      switch transaction.transactionState {

      case .Purchasing:
      // Purchase is in progress
      break

      case .Purchased:
      // Purchase has completed
     queue.finishTransaction(transaction)
      let receiptURL =
         NSBundle.mainBundle().appStoreReceiptURL
      let receipt =
         NSData(contentsOfURL: receiptURL!)
      // TODO: Validate the receipt
```

```
        // Post a purchase notification
    self.postPurchaseSucceededNotification(
        transaction)

        case .Deferred:
        // Waiting for parental consent. Let them
        // continue to use the app
        break

        case .Failed:
        // Purchase failed
        queue.finishTransaction(transaction)
    self.postPurchaseFailedNotification
        (transaction)

        case .Restored:
        // Restored transaction
        queue.finishTransaction(transaction)
        self.postPurchaseRestoreSucceededNotification
        (transaction)
        }
    }
}
```

As indicated by the switch statement in this code, a transaction can have one of the following states:

- **Purchasing** - The purchase is in progress
- **Purchased** - The purchase has successfully completed
- **Deferred** - The purchase is awaiting parental consent. You should continue to let them use the app.
- **Failed** - The purchase did not succeed.
- **Restored** - The user is restoring a previous purchase.

In each case, a call is always made to **finishTransaction** message is sent to the queue object. This removes the transaction from the queue and tells StoreKit you have completed processing the transaction. If you don't call

finishTransaction, the transaction stays in the queue and the **paymentQueue:updatedTransactions:** method is called each time your app is launched until the transaction is marked as finished.

Validating Receipts

Notice in the code in the previous section, there is a TODO reminder to **Validate the Receipt.** This is an additional step you need to take that the **InAppPurchaseManager** does not perform for you. It's important to take this step because there are those who have successfully hacked Apple in-app purchase process in the past to get free in-app purchases, and there are those who will do the same in the future. The validation of the receipt guarantees that the purchase information you received in your app is truly from Apple.

There are three main ways you can validate receipts:

1. Create logic internal to your app that validates the receipt on the device.
2. Make a call from your app on the device to Apple's servers to perform validation.
3. Make a call from your app to your own server, which in turn makes a call to Apple's servers to perform validation.

For the most secure validation, Apple recommends you use option 3. However, they don't supply the code for you to do this. Why not? If they publish specific code, then hackers will find a way around that code. So instead, Apple offers some suggestions and points you in the right direction.

For more information, I highly recommend checking out Apple's WWDC video: Optimizing In-App Purchases:

https://developer.apple.com/videos/wwdc/2014/#303.

User Story: Restoring In-App Purchases

If you are selling non-consumable, auto-renewable subscriptions, or non-renewing subscription products, Apple requires that you provide a UI that allows the purchases to be restored. If you don't, your app will be rejected by Apple.

You must allow users to restore these purchases because Apple requires that you make these purchases available on all iOS devices owned by the user. In addition, if the user deletes your app and reinstalls it, they need to be able to restore their purchases. It's up to you to decide whether you want the user to restore one purchase at a time, or all purchases at once.

Let's see how the user can restore in-app purchases in the **TicTacToe** app.

1. Open the **TicTacToe** app in Xcode and connect your iOS device to your development machine.
2. If you haven't already purchased an item in the TicTacToe app, do so now by following the instructions in the Purchasing Products section earlier in this chapter.
3. Delete the **TicTacToe** app from your iOS device.
4. Make sure Xcode's Scheme control is set to run on your iOS device and click the **Run** button.
5. When the app appears on your device, tap the Settings button in the navigation bar. This displays the Settings scene with an option to **Restore Purchases** (Figure 16.19).
6. Tap **Restore Purchases** and an action sheet appears asking if you want to restore your purchases. Tap **Restore**.
7. After several seconds you will see a **Restore Successful** dialog. Click **OK** to close it.
8. You are automatically taken to the **Select a Color Theme** scene where you can see the newly restored color theme in the list.

Restoring Purchases—Behind the Scenes

Let's take a behind-the-scenes look at the process of restoring purchases as illustrated in the sequence diagram shown in Figure 16.28.

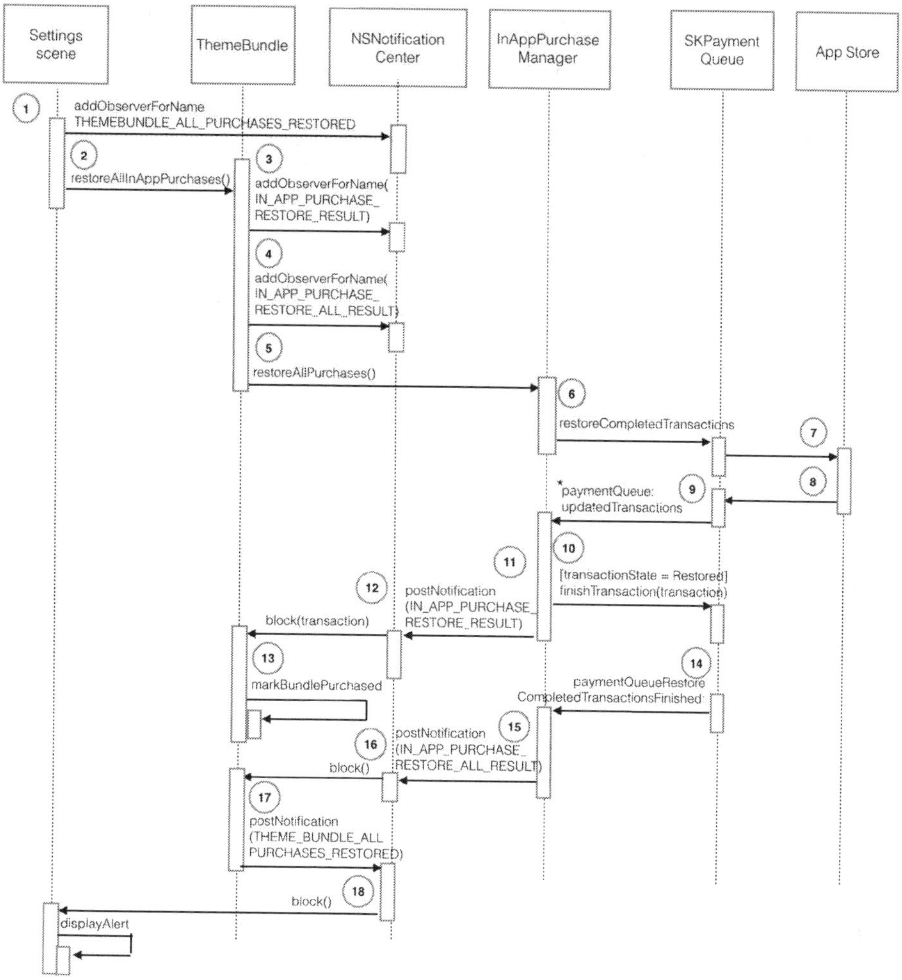

Figure 16.28 Restore Purchases sequence diagram

1. When the user taps the **Restore Purchases** button in the **Settings** scene, the view controller registers for the **THEMEBUNDLE_ALL_PURCHASES_RESTORED** notification. This notification is posted after all in-app purchases have been restored.

2. The view controller calls **restoreAllInAppPurchases** on the **ThemeBundle** object.

3. The **ThemeBundle** object registers for the **IN_APP_PURCHASE_RESTORE_RESULT** notification, which gets posted when a single purchase is restored.

4. The **ThemeBundle** object also registers for the

IN_APP_PURCHASE_RESTORE_ALL_RESULT notification, which gets posted only after all purchases are restored.

5. The **ThemeBundle** object calls restoreAllPurchases on the **InAppPurchaseManager**.
6. The **InAppPurchaseManager** calls **restoreCompletedTransactions** on the **SKPaymentQueue** object.
7. The **SKPaymentQueue** interacts with the App Store to request the set of transactions to be restored.
8. The App Store sends the list of transactions to the **SKPaymentQueue**.
9. The **SKPaymentQueue** calls paymentQueue**: updatedTransactions:** once for each transaction to be restored (as indicated by the asterisk in the sequence diagram).
10. The **InAppPurchaseManager** calls **finishTransaction** on the **SKPaymentQueue**, which tells StoreKit the app has completed processing on the transaction.
11. The **InAppPurchaseManager** posts the **IN_APP_PURCHASE_RESTORE_RESULT** notification, indicating a single transaction has been restored.
12. This executes the block on the **ThemeBundle** object.
13. The block marks the color theme bundle as purchased.
14. When all in-app purchases have been restored, the **SKPaymentQueue** object calls **paymentQueueRestoreCompletedTransactionsFinished** on the **InAppPurchaseManager**.
15. The **InAppPurchaseManager** posts the **IN_APP_PURCHASE_RESTORE_ALL_RESULT** notification.
16. This executes the block on the **ThemeBundle** object.

17. The **ThemeBundle** object posts the **THEME_BUNDLE_ALL_PURCHASES_RESTORED** notification.

18. This executes the block on the **Settings** view controller, which displays an alert that purchases have been restored. If there were no in-app purchases to be restored, the alert informs the user.

Summary

Here are important points to remember about in-app purchases.

Types of In-App Purchases

In-app purchases must fall into one of the following categories defined by Apple:

- **Consumables** - Purchases that are used up over a period of time such as supplies in a game.
- **Non-consumables** - Purchases that only need to be bought once and do not expire, such as extra levels in a game, color themes, books and magazine issues.
- **Auto-Renewable Subscriptions** - Purchases that allow the user to access content for a set duration of time, such as delivery of magazine issues, subscriptions to audio or video feeds, and dating services.
- **Free Subscriptions** - An extension of Auto-Renewable subscriptions that permit free subscription content to be delivered to Newsstand-enabled apps.
- **Non-Renewing Subscriptions** - Allows the sale of services for a limited time, such as a one month subscription to an online database.

Providing In-App Purchase Content

There are three ways you can provide in-app purchase content to your users:

1. Bundle the content in your app and make it available to the user after it has been purchased.
2. Host the content on your own servers and download it when it is purchased by the user.
3. Host the content on Apple's servers and download it when it is purchased by the user. Apple offers this service for free!

In-App Purchase User Stories

Here are the three main user stories you need to consider when adding in-app purchases to your iOS apps:

- Users can view products that can be purchased.
- Users can purchase products.
- Users can restore purchases.

User Story: Viewing Products

Apple provides all of the behind-the-scenes "plumbing" classes you need to implement a store in your app by means of the **StoreKit** framework. However, you need to design your own user interface where users can view and select items to be purchased.

Setting Up Your App

Apple provides a testing environment, called the *sandbox*, that allows you to test in-app purchases without incurring any charges. There are several steps you need to take to set up your app environment:

1. Create a store user interface in your app.
2. Specify a unique app ID.
3. Generate a provisioning file.
4. Submit your app metadata in iTunes Connect.
5. Add one or more products for in-app purchase.
6. Create a sandbox tester account.
7. Set the list of product IDs in your app.

Displaying In-App Purchases

The Tic-Tac-Toe app demonstrates best practices for presenting in-app purchases to the user. Rather than popping up irritating dialogs that prompt the user to make a purchase, the content is part of the natural flow of the app. When the user changes the color theme, they see free themes as well as a prompt that allows them to explore additional themes they can purchase.

Validating Receipts

There are three main ways you can validate receipts:

1. Create logic internal to your app that validates the receipt on the device.

2. Make a call from your app on the device to Apple's servers to perform validation.

3. Make a call from your app to your own server, which in turn makes a call to Apple's servers to perform validation.

User Story: Restoring In-App Purchases

- If you are selling non-consumable, auto-renewable subscriptions, or non-renewing subscription products, Apple requires that you provide a UI that allows the purchases to be restored. If you don't, your app will be rejected by Apple.

- You must allow users to restore these purchases because Apple requires that you make these purchases available on all iOS devices owned by the user. In addition, if the user deletes your app and reinstalls it, they need to be able to restore their purchases.

- It's up to you to decide whether you want the user to restore one purchase at a time, or all purchases at once.

Conclusion

With a much greater understanding for Xcode, app architecture, Core Data, and Table Views, where do you go from here?

Where Do You Go From Here?

Now that you have finished Book 3 in this series, you have learned how to create a prototype app (Book 1), the ins and outs of Swift (Book 2), and in Book 3 you have learned how to:

- Take full advantage of Xcode's many tools and features.
- Use the many UI controls in your iOS apps.
- Lay out your user interface using springs and struts or the new Auto Layout.
- Create a solid app architecture.
- Use Core Data to store, retrieve, and manipulate business entities.
- Manage lists of data with table views.
- Use Dynamic Type.
- Adopt In-App Purchases

But there is still so much to learn! The iOS tool set is broad and deep, and it continues to gain new features with each iOS version release.

Some of the topics that will be covered later in this series include:

- Storing and retrieving data on on the web using web services and iCloud.
- Getting user location and working with Apple Maps technology.
- Interacting with other apps.
- Working with media such as images and video.
- Making your app multi-lingual.
- Making your app accessible to visually-impaired users.
- Getting your app ready for the app store.

As time goes by, we will continue to release new books as well as update our existing books to the newest technologies (one of the great features of eBooks!)

Ask Questions on Our Forum!

To get answers to your questions and engage with others like yourself, check out our forum:

http://iOSAppsForNonProgrammers.com/forum

Books in This Series by Kevin McNeish

1. Book 1: Diving Into iOS
2. Book 2: Learn to Code In Swift
3. Book 3: Mastering Xcode 7 and Swift

Rate and Recommend This Book

If you have enjoyed this book and think it's worth telling others about, please leave your comments and rating for this book and tell your friends. Thanks!

About the Author

So, I was supposed to be a hardware guy.

While I was in college, majoring in electronic engineering, I worked at a small company as I paid my way through school. Brian, the head of the software department, would tell me on a regular basis, "You know, I think you're a software guy!"

Hardware guys typically do *not* want to be software guys, so I just ignored it as good-natured harassment. Then, one day, I decided to get him off my back by giving it a try.

As they say, the rest is history. I fell in love with writing software, and the honeymoon is definitely not over!

I learned that writing software is a *very* creative process. In just a matter of hours, I could conceive an idea, create a software design, and have it up and running on a computer.

The first software I wrote was a tutorial program that helped new computer users understand how a computer works (this was not long after the birth of the PC). I came up with the idea after watching new computer users give up on themselves before they started.

Since then, I've devoted my teaching career to making difficult concepts easy to understand. So when Apple released the iPhone and a platform for building apps, I immediately started teaching classes to empower others to join this software revolution and share in the fun. Maybe you'll find you're a software "guy" too. — Kevin

Questions and Comments for the Author

Email me at kevin@iOSAppsForNonProgrammers.com.

Glossary

Accessor methods

Accessor methods are the combination of the getter and setter methods used to retrieve and store values for a property, usually getting and setting the value to an associated instance variable.

Action

In the Target-Action design pattern, the action is the method to be invoked.

Activity Viewer

The Activity Viewer is an area at the top center of the Xcode window that displays status messages, project build warnings and errors and the progress of tasks currently executing.

Animation

An animation is a smooth transition from one user-interface state to another. For example, when the user taps a button, one view slides out and another view slides in during an animation.

App

An app is a relatively small software application designed to perform one or more related tasks. In the context of this book, an App is specifically a software application that runs on an iPhone, iPod Touch, or iPad.

Application bundle

An application bundle is the .app file that bundles an app's executable code, images, media, and miscellaneous resources together.

Argument

An argument is an additional piece of data that is passed to an object in a message call.

You often see the words *argument* and *parameter* used interchangeably, but there is a subtle difference. An *argument* is a piece of data that you pass to a method. A *parameter* is a part of the method declaration that dictates the argument(s) to be passed to the method. In short, arguments appear in message calls, parameters appear in method declarations.

Attribute

Attributes describe the characteristics of an object. Xcode's Attributes Inspector allows you to view and change the attributes of user-interface objects.

For every object *attribute* you see in Xcode's Attribute Inspector, there is a corresponding *property* in the class definition.

An object's attributes are defined as properties in the class blueprint from which the object was created. Each attribute has a default value, which is also specified in the class. After an object has been created, you can change the values of its attributes. You can change an attribute on one object without affecting any other objects.

In this context, attributes and properties are similar. In Xcode, an object has attributes; in Swift, the class on which an object is based has properties.

Breakpoint

A breakpoint is a debugging feature in Xcode that allows you to temporarily pause an app and examine the value of variables, properties, and so on.

Bundle identifier

The bundle identifier is Apple's way of uniquely identifying your App. By default, it is comprised of your company identifier and product name joined together.

Business Object

Business objects contain the core business logic of your App. They often represent real-world entities such as a customer, invoice, product, or payment.

Call stack

The call stack is a "breadcrumb trail" of how execution arrived at the current line of code (this line of code called that line of code, which called this other line of code, and so on). Your App's call stack is displayed at run time in the Debug Navigator.

Camel case

Camel case is a term used to describe the capitalization style of symbols such as method and parameter names. A camel-cased name always begins with a lowercase letter, and then the first letter of each word in a compound word is uppercased (like a camel's head and its humps). For example, the method names **areYouOld** and **amIOld** are both camel cased.

Class

A **class** is like a blueprint for an object. You create objects from a class.

Cocoa Touch Framework

The Cocoa Touch Framework is a set of many smaller frameworks (which contain sets of classes) each focusing on a set of core functionality that provides access to important features and services such as multi-touch gestures, user-interface controllers, saving and retrieving data, maps, the camera, and the compass.

Code Completion

Code Completion is Xcode's way of helping you write code. Based on the characters you type, it provides its best guess as to what you need to complete a code statement.

Collection

A collection is a grouping of one or more related objects. Cocoa Touch Framework collection classes such as **NSArray**, **NSDictionary**, and **NSSet** allow you to group multiple items together into a single collection.

Comment

A comment is text that is added to a code file to provide an explanation of the functionality of a particular section of code. Comments are not code and are, therefore, not executed.

Compiler

A compiler is a software program that interprets, or converts, the Swift code that you write into machine code, which an iOS device can actually execute.

Concatenate

The act of joining two character strings together end to end.

Condition

A condition is an expression that is checked to determine if it is true or false. For example, in the following **if** statement, the condition in parentheses is checked, and if (**age** > **100**) evaluates to **true**, the **NSLog** statement is executed.

```
if (age > 100) {
   NSLog(@"You are old!");
}
```

Connection indicator

A connection indicator is a circle in the gutter to the left of an action method. When the connection indicator has a dark gray center, the action method is connected to a UI object.

Constraint

A constraint describes rules for the layout of user-interface objects. For example, you can create a constraint that specifies the width of an element or the spacing between multiple elements.

Core logic

The core logic is the code in an app required to perform actions when a user-interface object is touched or any other processing takes place automatically. Whenever an app "does something," it requires code to execute a set of instructions.

Data

Data is the information and preferences maintained by an app. This can be as simple as storing the user's zip code or as complex as storing large amounts of data such as thousands of pictures and songs.

Disclosure indicator

A disclosure indicator is an arrow on the right side of a table view cell that indicates to the user that touching the row displays a screen with additional information.

Encapsulation

Encapsulation is an object-oriented programming term that refers to hiding unnecessary information within a class. When you design your classes, you don't want to expose more information to the outside world than is necessary.

Entity

An entity represents an object in the real world. For example, if you are creating an app that handles customer orders, you might have a Customer entity, Order entity, and Product entity.

Enumeration

An enumeration is a group of related constants. Enumerations and their member names are Pascal cased and typically begin with a suffix that describes what type that they are. For example, in the **UITextBorderStyle** enumeration, each member of the enumeration begins with the prefix "UITextBorderStyle":

- UITextBorderStyleBezel
- UITextBorderStyleLine
- UITextBorderStyleNone
- UITextBorderStyleRoundedRect

Event

In the same way that objects have properties and methods, they can also have a set of events. In this context, an event is an action that occurs in a control and is usually initiated by the user.

Format specifier

A format specifier is a special set of characters within a string that begins with a percent sign (%) and is followed by one or more characters that specify how to format the argument that follows, which is inserted into the string.

For example, in the following statement:

```
NSLog(@"Sum: %f", sum);
```

The **f** in the format specifier tells **NSLog** that the second argument is a **double**, or float number, which is converted and then inserted into the string.

Frame

A frame is a rectangle that specifies a user-interface object's position on the user interface (in x and y coordinates) as well as its width and height.

Function

A function is a lot like a method; it groups together one or more lines of code that perform a specific task. However, unlike a method, a function is not attached to an object or a class; it's stand-alone, or "free floating."

Getter

A getter is one of the two methods associated with a property. It *gets* the value of the property, usually from an associated instance variable.

Group

In the Project Navigator, a group is a means for organizing related files together. When you create a new project, several groups are already added to your project.

Groups do not directly correspond to folders on your Mac's hard drive! They are simply a logical grouping of related items.

Header file

See Class header file

Implementation file

See Class implementation file

Index

When used in the context of a Swift collection, an index is a number that references an item by its position in the collection.

Instance

An object created from a class is referred to as an instance of the class.

Instantiate

The term instantiate refers to the act of creating an instance of a class. The process of instantiation creates an object from a class definition.

Interface Builder

The Interface Builder Editor is located in the center area of the Xcode window and allows you to lay out the user interface of your app.

iOS

On an iOS device, iOS is the operating system. It is the software provided by Apple that manages the device hardware and provides the core functionality for all apps running on the device.

Local variable

Variables declared within a method are known as local variables because they can only be accessed locally from within the method in which they are declared.

Localize

The term localize is used in iOS and other software platforms to describe the process of translating and adapting your app to different cultures, countries, regions, or groups of people.

Message

A message is the name of the method and associated arguments sent to an object to be executed.

Message call

A message call is the act of sending a message to an object.

Method

The behavior of an object, or the actions that it can perform, are defined in the class blueprint as methods. A method is comprised of one or more (usually more) lines of code grouped together to perform a specific task.

Method signature

A method signature is the name of the method and the number of and type of its parameters, not including the return type.

Modal

A modal segue works a little differently than the push segue. Creating a modal segue does not add a navigation bar to the top of the destination view. In iOS, a modal window is usually a "dead end." The user transitions to a modal scene and back again, but the modal scene doesn't take you to another new scene.

Object

Software objects are similar to real-world objects. They have both attributes and behavior. Apps have user-interface objects such as text fields, sliders, web views, and labels as well as business objects that contain the app's core logic and represent real-world entities such as a Customer, Address, Album, Song, and Calculator.

In Swift, you create objects at run time from classes, which act like blueprints.

Object-relational mapping

Core Data provides something called object-relational mapping (ORM) for your iOS apps. This means that Core Data converts your entity objects into information that can be stored in a relational database (also known as a data store). This spares you the burden of learning the intricacies of database programming. You can save, retrieve, update, and delete entities without learning a database programming language.

Outlet

An outlet is a special property that holds a reference to a UI object.

Override

You can override a method inherited from a superclass by creating a method with the same signature in the subclass. Overriding allows you to extend an inherited method or completely change its implementation.

Parameter

A parameter is a part of the method declaration that dictates the argument(s) to be passed to the method. For example, the following method has a parameter of type **double** that is named **value**:

```
(double) addToTotal:(double)value;
```

You often see the words *argument* and *parameter* used interchangeably, but there is a subtle difference. An *argument* is a piece of data that you pass to a method. A *parameter* is a part of the method declaration that dictates the argument(s) to be passed to the method. In short, arguments appear in message calls, and parameters appear in method declarations.

Persistent store coordinator

In Core Data, the object context uses a persistent store coordinator object (an instance of the **NSPersistentCoordinator** class), which it uses to communicate with the SQLite database. The persistent store coordinator knows the name and location of the database. It uses a managed object model (an instance of **NSManagedObjectModel**) that knows about all the entities in the entity data model and their relationships.

Pointer

A pointer is a reference to an object's location in memory. A pointer is like a book index that points to a specific page where information can be found.

Polymorphism

Polymorphism is one of the core principles of object-oriented programming. This term refers to the ability of a class to take many different forms. Polymorphism allows you to declare a variable of a particular type and then store a reference to an object of that type or *any of its subclasses* in that variable.

For example, you can declare a variable of type **UIControl** and then store a reference to any class that is a subclass of **UIControl**:

```
UIControl* control;
control = [[UITextField alloc] init];
control = [[UIButton alloc] init];
control = [[UISwitch alloc] init];
```

Polymorphism allows you to write more generic code that works with families of objects rather than writing code for a specific class.

Predicate

In Core Data, a predicate contains filter criteria so that only entities that match the search criteria are retrieved from the database.

Prefix header file

When you create a new project in Xcode, a prefix header file (with a .pch extension) is automatically added to your project.

When you build your project, the compiler automatically adds the content of the prefix header file to every source code file in your project. This is a powerful tool that makes it easy to add **import** statements in one place so that you don't have to add them manually to each and every source code file in your project.

Programmatically

When you perform an action in code, it is considered to be done programmatically, or in the program's code.

For example, if you add a user-interface control to a view by writing code (rather than dragging and dropping it on a view at design time), you are doing it programmatically.

Property

A property is the part of a class definition that describes a class's attributes or characteristics. A property defined in a class corresponds to an object attribute in Xcode, which can be viewed using the Attributes Inspector.

Protocol

A protocol is an advanced feature of Swift that allows you to define a standard set of behavior that other classes can implement.

For example, the **UIPickerViewDataSource** protocol declares methods required by an object that wants to act as a data source for the picker view, and the **UIPickerViewDelegate** protocol declares methods required by an object that wants to act as a delegate for the picker view.

Protocols are equivalent to interfaces in languages such as Java and C#.

Refactoring

Refactoring refers to safely and efficiently altering your app's code without changing its behavior or introducing errors. Typically, you refactor your code to reduce its complexity, to make it more maintainable, or to restructure it so it can more easily be extended with new features.

Regular expression

A regular expression provides a way to check the string for specific characters or patterns of characters. For example, you can use a regular expression to validate an email address or URL.

Run time

Run time is when an app is running in the Simulator or on an iOS device.

Scalar values

Scalar refers to primitive data types that contain only a single value such as Booleans, integers, and doubles.

Scene

Each iPhone screen on the storyboard is known as a scene.

Scene dock

The dark rectangular area below the scene is known as the scene dock. It contains an icon on the left that represents the first responder (the object with which the user is currently interacting). The icon on the right represents the view controller associated with the view.

SDK

The acronym SDK stands for *software development kit*. In iOS, an SDK is a collection of frameworks created by Apple that represent a specific version of the iOS operating system.

Segue

A segue is a visual object in a storyboard that defines transitions between different scenes. A segue allows you to specify the UI control that fires the transition, the type of transition (sliding, curling, dissolving), and the scene that is moved into place as the new current view.

Semantic gap

The semantic gap is the difference between real-world entities and how you model, or describe, these objects in your software applications. In many apps, this gap is extremely wide because the developer has not created any business objects. You will find that when you narrow the semantic gap by creating business objects that represent real-world entities, your apps are much easier to conceive, design, build, maintain, and extend.

Setter

A setter is one of the two methods associated with a property. It *sets* the value of the property, usually by storing it to an associated instance variable.

Storyboard

A storyboard is a design surface on which you can create a visual representation of your app's user interface. It allows you to lay out your app's user interface and navigation in a graphical, user-friendly way.

Subclass

In an inheritance relationship, a subclass is a class that is derived from another class (its superclass). It is sometimes referred to as a "child class." In Swift, a class can have zero, one, or many subclasses.

Superclass

In an inheritance relationship, the superclass is a class from which other classes are derived. It is sometimes referred to as a "parent class." In Swift, a class can only have one superclass.

Table view

A table view is a user-interface control used to display lists of data in iOS Apps. Each item in the table view is a row and a table view can contain an unlimited number of rows.

Table view cell

A table view cell is a user-interface control contained within a table view that you set up at design time. At run time, table view rows are created from table view cell definitions.

Table view controller

A table view controller is responsible for displaying an associated table view at run time, filling the table view with data, and responding to the user interacting with the table view.

Table view row

A table view row is a single item listed in a table view at run time. A row is one column wide and can contain an image, text, and accessory icon such as the disclosure indicator. At run time, a table view row is created from a table view cell that you configure at design time.

Table view section

Each division of a table view is a section. If you have no divisions, you have only one section.

Target

A target specifies a single product to be built. It contains a set of instructions in the form of build settings and build phases that tell Xcode how to create a product from a set of files in a project or workspace.

UI

UI is an acronym for User Interface.

URL

URLs (*uniform resource locators)* are character strings that reference an Internet resource or a local file on the device. Typically, a URL is a web address that points to a resource such as a website, HTML page, image, or video (e.g. **http://www.apple.com)**.

Variable

A variable is a place in memory where you can store and retrieve information. It's called a variable because you can change the information that you store in it. You can store one piece of information in a variable but then, later on, store another piece of information in the same variable.

View

A view contains one screen of information on an iOS device. More generally, all user-interface controls are derived from the **UIView** class and can also be referred to as views.

View Controller

Every view in an iOS App has a view controller that works behind the scenes in conjunction with the view.

It has properties that (among other things):

- Indicate if the user can edit items in the view,
- Report the orientation of the user interface (portrait or landscape), and
- Allow you to access user-interface elements.

It has methods that:

- Allow you to navigate to other views,
- Specify the interface orientations that the view supports, and
- Indicate when the associated view is loaded and unloaded from the screen.

View controller objects are based on the Cocoa Touch Framework's **UIViewController** class or one of its subclasses.

Workspace

A workspace is an Xcode container that can contain multiple projects.

Made in United States
Orlando, FL
04 November 2026

90202360R00404